CICS/VS Command Level with ANS Cobol Examples

DAVID C. WEST

CICS/VS Command Level
with
ANS Cobol Examples

Pacifico A. Lim

VAN NOSTRAND REINHOLD DATA PROCESSING SERIES

VNR VAN NOSTRAND REINHOLD COMPANY
NEW YORK CINCINNATI TORONTO LONDON MELBOURNE

Copyright © 1982 by Van Nostrand Reinhold Company Inc.

Library of Congress Catalog Card Number: 81-21899
ISBN: 0-442-22607-1

Manufactured in the United States of America

Published by Van Nostrand Reinhold Company Inc.
135 West 50th Street, New York, N.Y. 10020

Van Nostrand Reinhold Publishing
1410 Birchmount Road
Scarborough, Ontario MIP 2E7, Canada

Van Nostrand Reinhold Australia Pty. Ltd.
17 Queen Street
Mitcham, Victoria 3132, Australia

Van Nostrand Reinhold Company Limited
Molly Millars Lane
Wokingham, Berkshire, England

15 14 13 12 11 10 9 8 7 6 5 4 3 2 1

Library of Congress Cataloging in Publication Data

Lim, Pacifico A.
    CICS/VS command level with ANS COBOL examples.

    (Van Nostrand Reinhold data processing series)
    Includes index.
    1. CICS/VS (Computer system) 2. COBOL (Compu-
ter program language) I. Title. II. Title:
C.I.C.S./V.S. command level with A.N.S. C.O.B.O.L.
examples. III. Series.
HF5548.4.C53L55   001.64'25   81-21899
ISBN 0-442-22607-1   AACR2

To my brothers,
Alvi, Boy, and Bing
and
my sister, Gloria

Series Introduction

Good examples help to make things clear. When discussing capable but extensive software packages, such as IBM's CICS (*C*ustomer *I*nformation *C*ontrol *S*ystem), then good examples of CICS usage can make the difference between confusion and understanding. In *CICS/VS Command Level with ANS Cobol Examples,* Mr. Lim provides many practical examples of actual CICS application programs to illustrate important points about the use of CICS.

In the first part of the book, CICS features and commands are explained in an organized manner, with attention given to cross-references and interactions. There is also a chapter devoted to debugging CICS programs, an important matter. The importance of local conventions and standard practices, and why some things should be handled in particular ways, is shown. Furthermore, the significance of the systems programmer's supporting role is clearly demonstrated.

For any reader with a knowledge of Cobol, *CICS/VS Command Level with ANS Cobol Examples* is a readable, useful guide to CICS, and is illustrated with realistic examples.

— Ned Chapin, Ph.D.
Series Editor

THE VAN NOSTRAND REINHOLD DATA PROCESSING SERIES

Edited by Ned Chapin, Ph.D.

Logical Data Base Design
    Robert M. Curtice and Paul E. Jones, Jr.

Decision Tables in Software Engineering
    Richard B. Hurley

CICS/VS Command Level with ANS Cobol Examples
    Pacifico A. Lim

Preface

The development of on-line applications has been with us for quite some time. Management has long realized that there is a need to have certain information available at a moment's notice. Knowing the status of a purchase order, for instance, or the availability of a certain item in inventory helps tremendously in the running of a company.

Such applications often require the use of *c*athode *r*ay *t*ube (CRT) terminals* where the user initiates programs to access on-line files. These terminals may be active concurrently and may access the same files simultaneously. Unfortunately, compilers do not allow the application programmer to control multiple terminals accessing on-line files. If he (or she) were to write an on-line application, he would have the problem of writing routines to control terminals and files. This is like requiring the batch-oriented programmer to write access-method routines for his program.

However, to help users, the hardware manufacturers as well as independent software companies have developed packages to free the application programmer from these problems. Such packages are known as teleprocessing monitors, and one of them is IBM's *C*ustomer *I*nformation *C*ontrol *S*ystem (CICS). It is quite popular, has many useful features, and is written to work with IBM's various virtual-storage (VS) operating systems.

The programmer may think of CICS/VS as an extension of the programming language since he codes the request for on-line services (display data on a terminal, read an on-line file, etc.) right in his program, interspersing them with other statements of the language. He may also think of CICS/VS as an extension of the operating system because it interfaces between the application program and the operating system, using telecommunication and data-access methods available in the latter.

---

*Also known as video terminals.

CICS/VS first became available in the macro level, where the statements for CICS/VS services were in the form of Assembler macros. In addition, the programmer was required to know some CICS/VS internals. Although a teleprocessing monitor was already a big help, the use of Assembler-type macros was a little bit foreign to high-level application programmers. The introduction of the command-level feature solved this problem. It replaced the macros with commands that were more similar in format to statements that high-level application programmers were used to. In addition, it was no longer necessary to know CICS/VS internals.

CICS/VS is very easy to use, and the experienced programmer can grasp its basic features in a few days. In fact, it is much easier for an experienced programmer to learn CICS/VS than for a novice to learn ANS Cobol. The programmer learning CICS/VS can think of the terminal as the input reader that he reads data from as well as the output printer that he prints data on.

CICS/VS Command Level with ANS Cobol Examples will not present the complete features of CICS/VS. Rather, it will present a coding style based on the author's experience and will cover the most useful and common features that the application programmer will need. Most of the features mentioned will be shown in actual program examples. The reader who is interested in features not mentioned should read the IBM-supplied *CICS/VS Application Programmer's Reference Manual* (Form SC33-0077-1).

This book is written primarily for ANS Cobol application programmers who are interested in or will be involved in writing CICS/VS application programs. They will benefit most from the overall presentation and the program examples. Furthermore, non-Cobol application programmers may also benefit from the discussion of CICS/VS techniques. In fact, the commands are basically identical no matter what the language is.

The programs in this book have been tested using an IBM 4341 under DOS/VSE. However, they should execute properly in other operating systems, and IBM hardware that is supported by CICS/VS.

Contents

1

On-Line Systems

BATCH PROCESSING

The first business computer systems were slow and had primitive input/output devices: card readers, line printers, and slow-speed tape drives. These limitations required users to adopt a processing technique that enabled them to run many different applications on the computer system. This technique is known as batch processing. In batch processing, data corresponding to a processing period (e.g., a day, week, or month, etc.) are verified for accuracy through one or more edit runs and are then used to update a master file (usually on magnetic tape) containing records that are sequenced in ascending order according to a key. Once the update is finished, the reports required can then be prepared. Data that belong to the current period, but were not entered, are then entered on the next processing period.

The five most important characteristics of batch processing are:

1. The data needed to update a master file are batched together before the file is updated.

2. It takes some time to prepare the data before final processing.

3. The output usually consists of printed reports (most likely prepared at the computer center).

4. The master file can be used by only one program at any given time. Other programs have to wait for the file to be released.

5. Each step required in the application is scheduled and is started by the computer operator loading the appropriate program.

Figure 1.1 shows a typical batch application.

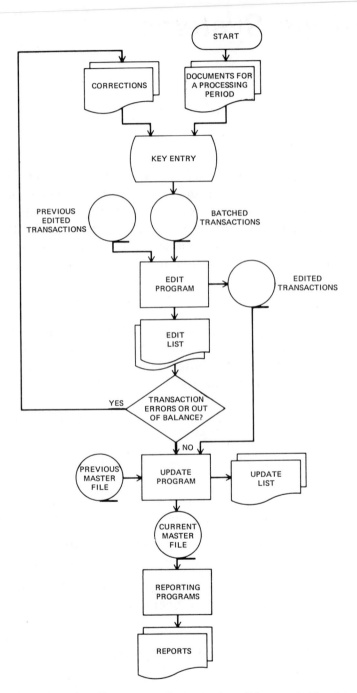

Fig. 1.1. Batch processing. From start to the preparation of the reports takes days or weeks depending on how many edit runs are made to complete the data for a processing period.

ON-LINE PROCESSING

While batch processing can readily be used in applications where only periodic reports are required, for instance, annual Departmental Operating Statement or some Payroll applications, it is rather limited for applications like Purchase Order, Inventory, etc., where it is important to get information at a moment's notice.

This required an on-line system whose growth in the commercial sector was helped spurred by three hardware developments. The development of direct access storage devices (of which the magnetic disk is the most popular medium) made it possible to store and access data randomly in fractions of a second, unlike magnetic tapes, whose records have to be read in sequence. Furthermore, faster and faster central processing unit (CPU) speed resulted from better hardware, especially the extensive use of integrated circuits. This fostered the development of multiprogramming, that is, many applications could share CPU time and in effect run simultaneously. While this was not absolutely necessary for on-line applications, it nevertheless helped many commercial installations acquire on-line facilities with minimal additional hardware because they could use the very same CPU they were using for batch applications. Finally, the development of low-cost CRT terminals made feasible the attachment of many such devices to the computer system, allowing many user personnel to run on-line applications simultaneously.

The five most important characteristics of on-line processing are:

1. Data needed to update a master file do not have to be batched and may be used as soon as it is available.

2. Updating is done in a matter of seconds.

3. The output for the user is generally displayed on CRT terminals at the user site.

4. Multiple actions may be done on the file. While some terminals are updating it, others may do inquiry (display information) from it.

5. The user himself usually starts programs for applications right from the terminal any time and without scheduling them with the computer operators.

On-line systems also have the following characteristics: security procedures for files and programs so unauthorized personnel cannot access them through terminals that may be in many locations; adequate computer response* (generally in terms of seconds); and the capability to generate data (called journals) that is to be used later on as an audit trail of transactions entered or for file recovery. A typical on-line application (File Update) is shown in Figure 1.2.

BENEFITS

Some benefits of on-line processing can be deduced from what we have discussed. The master file is up to date, unlike in batch processing where the master file is only accurate as of the last processing period. Also, data is entered by the user himself, and any question about the data can be easily resolved. In batch processing, documents are translated into machine-readable form generally by data-entry operators who may not be able to resolve questions about the data. Finally, the user may use the computer any time without having to schedule his requirements with computer operators.

The availability of on-line facilities also has several advantages. On-line program development packages can be used, thus increasing programmer productivity. Other packages can give the installation the ability to test programs on-line, which also increases programmer productivity. Still other packages can be used in applications or for computer performance measurements. Lastly, data-entry requirements that are of low volume or have unpredictable schedules can be "off-loaded," freeing the data-entry department to concentrate on large-volume, regularly scheduled input.

TELEPROCESSING MONITORS

The three hardware developments discussed previously were not enough to give commercial installations the ability to develop on-line applications easily. The systems that resulted were more sophis-

---

*Response time is the time it takes for a computer to display the result of a processing step and wait for further operator action after a program is initiated (which is generally done by hitting a key like ENTER).

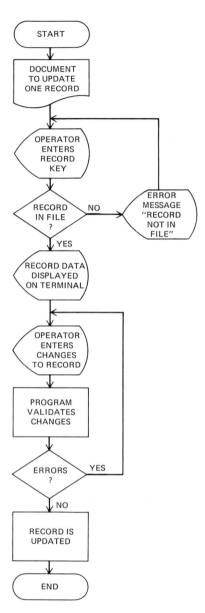

Fig. 1.2. On-line file update. From start to end takes from several seconds to several minutes depending on the amount of changes entered and whether or not the program detects errors during validation.

ticated and, consequently, more complex than preceding systems. Thus, the new systems required additional functions before the user could run on-line applications. Some of the more important functions are: transmitting data from terminals to computer memory and vice versa; controlling many concurrently running programs attached to terminals that share the same computer memory and access the same on-line files so that each may be serviced according to some priority: keeping user application programs independent of the physical characteristics of telecommunication devices so that even if the devices are changed, the user does not have to rewrite his programs; and giving the user the ability to develop on-line applications using the very same programming language he is using to write batch applications.

Packages known as teleprocessing monitors solved these problems. They were the last link in the chain of developments that brought on-line capabilities to many commercial installations, freeing the application programmer to concentrate on actual applications. To the programmer, these teleprocessing monitors are extensions of the programming language because requests for on-line services (display data on a terminal, read an on-line file, etc.) are coded right in the application program, which are then provided to the program through the monitor. As a result, on-line programs are in many ways similar to batch programs.

One such teleprocessing monitor is IBM's Customer Information Control System (CICS), which works with IBM's various virtual storage (VS) operating systems. The command-level feature of CICS/VS allows the programmer to code requests for on-line services in statements similar in format to those in the high-level language he is used to.

2
CICS/VS

INTRODUCTION

*C*ustomer *I*nformation *C*ontrol *S*ystem/*V*irtual *S*torage (CICS/VS) is a powerful teleprocessing monitor that provides the support neces- sary for writing on-line programs. With the command-level feature, the requests for on-line services (display data on a terminal, read an on-line file, etc.) are coded as simple, easy-to-use commands in the user's application program (ANS Cobol, PL/I, Assembler, or RPG II). CICS/VS interfaces between the application program and the oper- ating system, utilizing telecommunication and data-access methods available in the latter. The relationship between the three can be shown in Figure 2.1.

FEATURES

The usual characteristics of on-line systems are present in CICS/VS. For instance, it is terminal-oriented, provides security procedures for files and programs, can have fast response time, and provides adequate backup and journal (audit trail) generation procedures. The other features are:

1. *Transaction driven.* A transaction identifier entered by the operator or generated by another program* determines the program that will first execute. The application that corres- ponds to the program can thus be selected by the operator.

2. *Multitasking.* A task is created for a program being used at a given terminal.** CICS/VS controls many such tasks, run- ning concurrently in a single partition, through a technique

---

*This is by far the most common way of initiating programs. Other methods will be ex- plained later on.
**Four terminals using different programs constitutes four tasks. The same four terminals using the same program also constitutes four tasks.

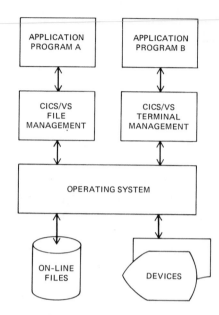

Fig. 2.1. CICS/VS interfaces between application programs and the operating system.

called task switching. In task switching, a task is suspended (generally on a command that causes a wait) and the next highest-priority task that is waiting takes control. CICS/VS provides service to the suspended task, depending on the command, and it is then placed in the queue of waiting tasks according to its priority number.

3. *Multithreading.* Several terminals requiring the same program will use only one copy of the program, thus saving main storage. This feature is possible because multitasking allows each task requiring the same program to use part of the same copy of the program when that task is active.

4. *Quasi-reentrant.* Multithreading requires that application programs be serially reusable. Therefore, a task must restore any data or instruction it altered before it is suspended so the next task that uses the same program does not use a "modified" version. With the command-level feature, ANS Cobol programs are automatically quasi-reentrant since all tasks have their own copy of the WORKING-STORAGE section and the

only part of the program that is common to all is the PRO-CEDURE DIVISION. Even the ALTER* statement does not modify the PROCEDURE DIVISION code but just changes values in the Task Group Table (TGT) to control execution, and the TGT is unique for each task.

5. *Priority processing.* Priority ratings can be assigned by the user to each operator, terminal, or transaction identifier (hence program). These ratings are used by CICS/VS to provide the fastest response time to certain operators, terminals, and applications.

COMPONENTS

The CICS/VS nucleus consists of modules that support multitasking, multithreading, priority processing, file security, etc. These are modules that oversee the execution of multiple tasks in a single partition, and application programmers are not really concerned with them. There are, however, other modules that provide services to satisfy commands coded in the application program. These modules are called control programs.

In one example of a control program, a command to read data from a terminal (RECEIVE MAP) invokes Basic Mapping Support which in turn invokes Program Control to determine the format of the data, and Storage Control to secure main storage for the data. CICS/VS automatically provides the necessary control programs to satisfy the requirements of a single command. The control programs that execute in a task are as follows:

When A Task Is Started

1. *Terminal Control.* Upon entry of a transaction identifier, Terminal Control, which monitors terminal operations and uses standard telecommunication access methods available in the operating system, requests Storage Control to create a

---

*Proponents of structured programming avoid the use of ALTER. It is being deleted from the language in the Cobol-80 standard.

terminal input/output area, then reads the input into this area. Terminal Control then passes control to Task Control.

2. *Task Control.* Task Control creates a task for the transaction, then checks whether the transaction identifier is valid and present in the Program Control Table (PCT). If the transaction identifier is invalid, an error message is sent to the terminal and the task is terminated. Otherwise, it requests Storage Control to secure a Task Control Area and a Transaction Work Area (if the application requires it). Task Control assigns a priority number to the task, then places it in the queue of waiting tasks. Control then passes to Program Control.

3. *Program Control.* When a program is to execute for the first time in a task, Task Control requests Program Control to take the program from virtual storage and load it into main storage if it is not already in the latter. It also intercepts program abends so that if the program terminates, the whole CICS/VS partition does not terminate.

A Task Executing In Multitasking

1. *Task Control.* Whenever the CICS partition is free, Task Control dispatches the highest-priority task in the wait queue and then transfers control to the corresponding application program. It suspends tasks on commands that cause waits and then places those tasks in the queue according to their priority numbers. It also terminates tasks.

2. *The Application Program.* The application program gets control generally until such time that a command that causes a wait is executed. The task corresponding to the application program is then suspended.

3. *Basic Mapping Support.* The application program requests Basic Mapping Support (BMS) to read data from a terminal or to display data on a terminal. BMS uses Terminal Control facilities for data transmission, Program Control to determine

the format of the data read or displayed, and Storage Control to secure main storage for the data.

4. *File Control.* The application program requests File Control to retrieve records from files, write records into files, etc. File Control requests Storage Control to secure main storage for records to be read, and uses data-access methods available in the operating system.

5. *Temporary Storage Control.* The application program requests Temporary Storage Control to save in main storage or virtual storage information that will be used later on by another task (the same or another program).

6. *Journal Control.* The application program requests Journal Control to write into special-purpose sequential files information that may be used offline as an audit trail or to reconstruct files.

7. *Trace Control.* The program requests Trace Control to provide a trace of the commands as a debugging aid.

8. *Dump Control.* The application program requests Dump Control to write all transaction-related storage areas into a dump file to be printed out later on by a dump utility program. The printout is also used as a debugging aid.

9. *Interval Control.* The application program requests Interval Control to start a task at some future time or at a certain time of day.

10. *Storage Control.* The application program requests Storage Control to acquire main storage for any data required in the program. On input commands, the corresponding control programs automatically request Storage Control to secure Main Storage for the data that will be read if the area is defined in the LINKAGE section.

Suppose we have a program that reads in data from a terminal and temporary storage, processes the data, then displays it on the same terminal. The flow of control is shown in Figure 2.2.

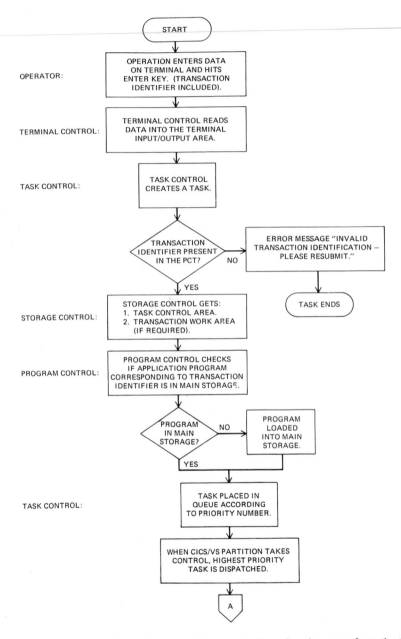

Fig. 2.2. One example of flow of control within a task. Note that the events from the time the task is first dispatched to the time the task is terminated are not done in one contiguous time. The task is suspended and redispatched several times, generally on commands that cause a wait.

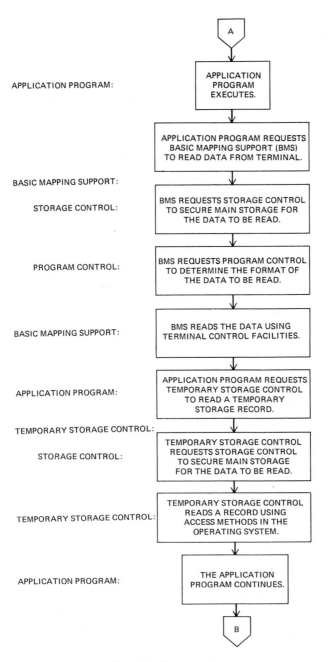

APPLICATION PROGRAM: — APPLICATION PROGRAM EXECUTES.

APPLICATION PROGRAM REQUESTS BASIC MAPPING SUPPORT (BMS) TO READ DATA FROM TERMINAL.

BASIC MAPPING SUPPORT:

STORAGE CONTROL: — BMS REQUESTS STORAGE CONTROL TO SECURE MAIN STORAGE FOR THE DATA TO BE READ.

PROGRAM CONTROL: — BMS REQUESTS PROGRAM CONTROL TO DETERMINE THE FORMAT OF THE DATA TO BE READ.

BASIC MAPPING SUPPORT: — BMS READS THE DATA USING TERMINAL CONTROL FACILITIES.

APPLICATION PROGRAM: — APPLICATION PROGRAM REQUESTS TEMPORARY STORAGE CONTROL TO READ A TEMPORARY STORAGE RECORD.

TEMPORARY STORAGE CONTROL:

STORAGE CONTROL: — TEMPORARY STORAGE CONTROL REQUESTS STORAGE CONTROL TO SECURE MAIN STORAGE FOR THE DATA TO BE READ.

TEMPORARY STORAGE CONTROL: — TEMPORARY STORAGE CONTROL READS A RECORD USING ACCESS METHODS IN THE OPERATING SYSTEM.

APPLICATION PROGRAM: — THE APPLICATION PROGRAM CONTINUES.

Fig. 2.2. (Continued)

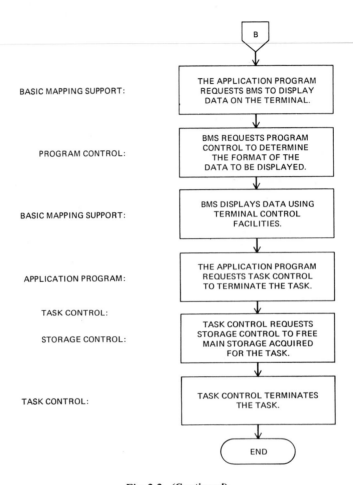

Fig. 2.2. (Continued)

TASK INITIATION

A session constitutes the whole set of activities performed by the operator and the program from the time the operator starts an application until he leaves the terminal or starts another application. In the pseudoconversational mode of processing (see page 79), each session will be implemented through the initiation and termination of many tasks. There are six ways of initiating tasks in CICS/VS:

1. *Transaction identifier entered by the operator.* This is the most common way of starting a session.

2. *Temporary transaction identifier.* The last program that executed at the same terminal, before the task is terminated, specifies the transaction identifier to be used on the next task initiation. This is the method used to continue a session in the pseudoconversational mode of processing.

3. *Interval Control transaction identifier.* The Interval Control command START TRANSID specifies the transaction identifer that will be used for a new task, the time the task will be initiated, and, optionally, a terminal identification if the task is associated with a terminal.

4. *Automatic task initiation.* If the systems programmer specifies a nonzero trigger level for a particular transient data intrapartition destination in the Destination Control Table at systems generation, a task is automatically initiated when the number of entries in the queue (destination) reaches the specified level. Control is passed to an application program that processes the data in the queue.

5. *Permanent transaction identifier.* For terminals that cannot start a task through a transaction identifier because of hardware characteristics, a permanent transaction identifier may be defined for the terminal in the Terminal Control Table.* The application program that corresponds to the permanent transaction identifier will then select the specific application program that will actually process the transaction.

6. *3270 Attention identifier.* For 3270-type terminals, each of the programmer attention (PA) keys, program function (PF) keys, the selector light pen, the cursor select key, or an operator identification badge can be defined in the PCT to initiate specific programs. Thus by hitting the appropriate PA or PF keys, selecting a detectable field with the selector light pen or the cursor select key, or using an operator identification badge,

---

*This is maintained by the systems programmer.

the appropriate program is initiated without a transaction identifier.

PREPARING APPLICATION PROGRAMS

Application programs written in CICS/VS are prepared in the following way:

1. The format of the data to be entered or displayed on the terminal will be translated into a map program that will be assembled offline independently of the application program. However, this map program must be completed and the maps generated before the application program is used.

2. The application program is coded with commands for CICS/VS services interspersed with regular Cobol statements in the PROCEDURE DIVISION.

3. The program is passed through a command-language translator (a preprocessor). This creates an output source similar to the original program except that each command is translated into one or more MOVE statements and a CALL statement* to the Execute Interface program, which in turn makes a CALL to the appropriate CICS/VS control programs. The operands in the command are translated into arguments of the CALL statement.

4. The output is then compiled through a regular ANS Cobol compiler and link-edited in the usual way.

5. Each transaction identifier used in the application program must have an entry in the Program Control Table. This is usually maintained by the systems programmer and the entry takes effect the next time CICS/VS is initialized (usually at the beginning of the day).

6. Each application program and map set (see page 32) must have an entry in the Processing Program Table (PPT) that is

---

*This is the case for ANS Cobol.

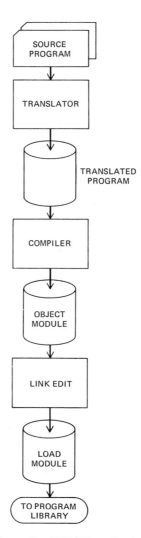

Fig. 2.3. Generating CICS/VS application programs.

also maintained by the systems programmer. Program Control uses the PPT to load the appropriate application program or map set when required.

7. Each on-line file must have an entry in the File Control Table, which is also maintained by the systems programmer, so it can be used in application programs.

8. CICS/VS, when initialized (usually at the beginning of the day), loads production programs into virtual storage. Therefore, programs and map sets created or modified after CICS/VS initialization will not be immediately usable unless the programmer uses the CICS/VS service:

CSMT NEW, PGRMID = phase name

where the phase name is that of the application program or the map set. He should then get the answer:

PROGRAM phase name
IS NOW A NEW COPY

The preparation of application programs is shown in Figure 2.3.

The programmer has the option of keeping part of the original source program in its translated version and then including that for compilation and link editing.

We said before that commands are translated into one or more MOVE statements and a CALL statement. For instance, given the command:

```
EXEC CICS
        RECEIVE MAP     ('ORCHM02')
                MAPSET  ('ORCHS02')
                SET     (MAP2-POINTER)
END-EXEC.
```

Fig. 2.4. Example of a command.

The translated code is shown in Figure 2.5.

```
*      EXEC CICS
*          RECEIVE MAP      ('ORCHMO2')
*                  MAPSET ('ORCHSO2')
*                  SET      (MAP2-POINTER)
*      END-EXEC.
       MOVE 'ORCHMO2' TO DFHEIV1 MOVE 'ORCHSO2' TO DFHEIV2 MOVE '
-         '          ' TO DFHEIVO CALL 'DFHEI1' USING DFHEIVO
       DFHEIV1 MAP2-POINTER DFHEIV98 DFHEIV2.
```

Fig. 2.5. The command of Fig. 2.4 as translated.

You will observe that the original command has been translated into notes (with asterisks in column 7), and that 3 MOVE and one CALL statements have been generated.

3

Screen Layout

INTRODUCTION

The user enters data on and reads data from terminals. The terminal screen layout is designed for ease of use, clarity of information display, and ready use of features available in the terminals being used. This book will deal only with the 3270-type CRT terminal, which is the most popular terminal used with CICS/VS. This terminal has special features like highlighting of fields (some of the displayed information is made to appear much brighter), special keys that allow the programmer to control the program logic, etc.

COMPONENTS OF A LAYOUT

A screen is usually divided into three parts, the title area, the application data area, and the operator message area.

The title area occupies the top one or two lines of the screen and should contain a title that identifies the application to the operator. For example, "PURCHASE ORDER — FILE INQUIRY" for a file inquiry of the Purchase Order master file; or "PURCHASE ORDER — FILE UPDATE" for the update to the purchase order master file. It may also contain a page number, if multiple pages are used.

The application data area is the main body of the screen. It contains relevant information from files, entered by the operator, or generated in the program. Four types of fields are found in this area: field identifiers, the data, STOPPER fields, and SKIP fields.

The field identifiers are constants that identify the data that comes after it or below it in the display. For instance, a field identifier with value "DATE" means that the data following it or below it is a date; a field identifier with value "NAME" means that the data following it or below it is a name. STOPPER and SKIP fields are one-byte fields specified by the programmer to automatically control the cursor as the operator enters data on the screen.

The operator message area, which is the bottom portion of the screen, is where the messages that help the operator are displayed by the program.

EXAMPLE

Figure 3.1 is the screen layout for a file inquiry program.

FIELD CHARACTERISTICS

Fields on the screen will have different characteristics depending on their use. We will present the usual characteristics of fields as they are generally defined.

Fields In The Title Area

Fields in the title area should have the following characteristics:

1. Brightness. They will be much brighter than the surrounding display to stand out.

2. Autoskip. They cannot be modified by the operator because the cursor will automatically skip the fields during normal operation. If he manipulates the cursor positioning keys of the terminal to position the cursor on this field and then attempts to change it, the keyboard will lock.

3. Initial value. They will have an initial value that is the literal constant comprising the title or part of the title. Usually the program does not modify this field, but may do so (for instance, a page number as part of the title).

Field Identifiers

The field identifiers should have the following characteristics:

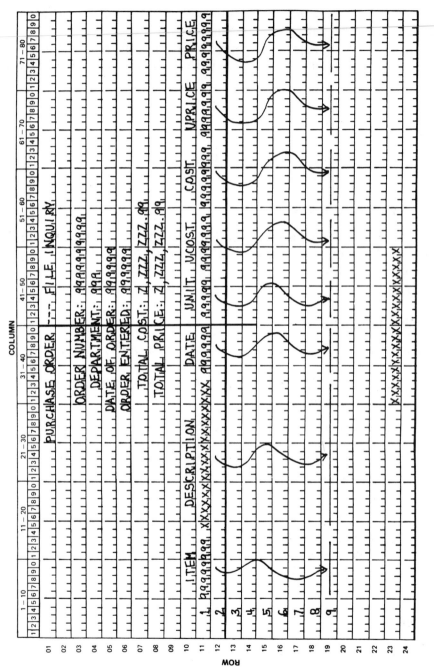

Fig. 3.1. File Inquiry Screen Layout. Note that Xs represent alphanumeric characters while 9s represent numeric digits.

1. Normal. They will be of normal intensity in contrast to the data fields they identify, which will be brighter.

2. Autoskip. Same as in the Title Area section.

3. Initial value. This is the literal constant comprising the identifier, as in "DATE" or "NAME".

Data Fields

The data fields should have the following characteristics:

1. Brightness. They will be much brighter than the field identifiers to stand out.

2. a. Autoskip. This is defined for data fields that should not be entered or changed by the operator, for instance, data in inquiry, browse applications, or any data that will show on the terminal but should not be touched by the operator.
   b. Unprotected. This is defined for data fields that can be entered or changed by the operator. This will be defined further as either alphabetic or numeric.

3. Initial value. Generally, there will be no initial value since what will show on the terminal is either what was entered by the operator, generated in the program, or came from files. However, in certain fields to be entered by the operator, the programmer may want to define an initial value that may be used as a guide, for instance, MMDDYY in a date field to be entered by the operator so he knows that the format is 2 digits for the month, 2 digits for the day, and 2 digits for the year. The operator will actually type over this initial value when he enters the data.

Operator Messages

The operator messages should have the following characteristics:

1. Brightness. Same as in the Data Fields section.

2. Autoskip. Same as in the Data Fields section.

3. Initial value. Generally, there will be no initial value since the messages are generated by the program interactively. However, the programmer may want to display a message whenever a particular screen layout is displayed. For instance, in a data-entry application with multiple screen layouts, the programmer may want to display a prompting message to the operator when one screen comes up, for instance, "ENTER SALES DATA" when the sales data screen comes up.

STOPPER AND SKIP FIELDS

As the operator enters data on the terminal, the cursor is controlled automatically for unprotected and autoskip fields, or the operator uses cursor positioning keys to manually move it between fields. However to control the cursor following an unprotected field, special one-byte STOPPER or SKIP fields are used. The rules are:

1. If there is any unused space (screen position) between an unprotected field and the next field (regardless whether this next field is unprotected or autoskip), then the cursor will stop on this unused position once the unprotected field is completed. Since we do not want this to happen (we want the cursor to skip automatically to the next unprotected field), we prevent this through one-byte fields that effectively control the cursor.

2. If the operator always enters a fixed number of characters on a field (for instance, a social security number), we will use a one-byte autoskip field so the cursor will automatically skip to the next unprotected field (the cursor will wrap around to the very first unprotected field if there are no more unprotected fields). This one-byte field is known as a SKIP field.

3. If the operator always enters a variable number of characters on a field (for instance, a name), we will use a one-byte protected field so that the keyboard will lock if the operator attempts to enter more characters than the maximum allo-

cated to the field. This one-byte field is known as a STOPPER field. Note that this is the only time a field should be defined as protected, since autoskip (which by definition is also protected) is the more useful characteristic.

4. Regardless whether we use a SKIP or STOPPER field, the cursor will go to the next unprotected field (and thus skip even the STOPPER field) if the operator hits the SKIP key before the field is completed.

Let us show how STOPPER and SKIP fields are used after unprotected fields. As an example, we enter two fields on the terminal, name (variable length, 30 characters maximum), and social security number. The name field will be followed by a STOPPER field while the social security number will be followed by a SKIP field. The data area portion of the screen layout is shown in Figure 3.2.

When the screen is first displayed, only the two field identifiers will appear and the cursor will initially be at position A so the operator may enter the name. If he attempts to enter more than 30 characters, the keyboard will lock at position B (STOPPER field). If he enters 30 characters or less and then uses the SKIP key, the cursor will be positioned at C.

After entering the social security number, the SKIP field D will move the cursor automatically to A.

FIELD JUSTIFICATION

Each field that is transmitted from the terminal to the application program and vice versa will have three entries in the program: a binary halfword that contains the length of the data entered by the operator, a one-byte alphanumeric field for the attributes (characteristics) of the field, and the field itself. These entries are diagrammed in Figure 3.3.

If the field is defined as numeric, then the keyboard will be in numeric shift (but may be overridden by the operator by pressing the alphabetic shift key). Any data entered will be transmitted to the application program padded with zeroes on the left, and the length will be set to the actual number of characters entered. For

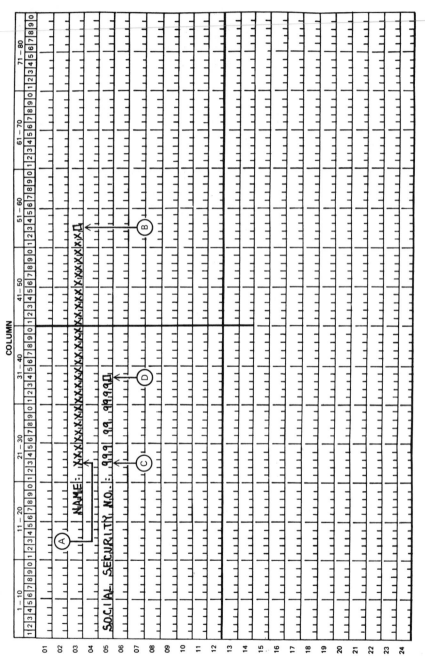

Fig. 3.2. SKIP and STOPPER fields.

Fig. 3.3. Entries corresponding to a field.

instance, if for a 6-byte numeric field the operator enters 167, the length will be 3 (the number of characters entered), and the data transmitted will be 000167.

If the field is defined as alphabetic, then the keyboard will be in alphabetic shift (but may be overridden if the operator presses the numeric shift key) and any data entered will be transmitted to the application program padded with spaces on the right, and the length will be set to the actual number of characters entered. For instance, if for an 8-byte alphabetic field the operator enters BAKER, the length will be 5 and the data transmitted will be BAKERƀƀƀ, where a ƀ is a space.

The program may actually check the length field to see if anything was entered, or it can go to the actual field itself. How to choose which one to use (or both) will be discussed on page 178.

4

Creating Maps

INTRODUCTION

Each screen layout is translated into one physical map and one symbolic description map. The physical map is a program by itself (a phase), and is used by BMS to convert data read from or displayed on terminals into the format required by the application program.

The symbolic description map is the set of source statements used by the application program to symbolically refer to data read from or displayed on terminals. In Cobol, it is the set of data-name definitions (data names, PICTURE clause, USAGE clause, etc.) that define the fields that will contain the data. To make the symbolic description map independent of the application program (the physical map is already so), it is best that it be catalogued into the appropriate source statement library, then copied into the application program when it is compiled. The programmer may use the Cobol COPY clause or the appropriate feature if the installation uses program development packages (like LIBRARIAN/on-line or PANVALET/on-line).

MAP PROGRAM

The physical and symbolic description maps are generated by a map program that is coded with BMS macros (Assembler format) and is assembled offline (independently of the application program). The idea is to have only one map program for each screen layout that contains all operands necessary to generate both maps so that only one source program needs to be maintained. This program is then assembled twice. First, it is assembled to get the physical map. Then, with a temporary change to the TYPE operand in the first macro, it is again assembled to get the symbolic description map. The operands that are only used to generate the symbolic description map will be ignored when the physical map is being generated and vice versa.

The sequence of steps followed in the creation of maps is shown in Figure 4.1.

There are two options to choose from in creating map programs. First, the programmer may conveniently use an available CICS/VS program where he formats the screen according to what it will look like to the operator. This will then be translated by the program into the map program. Usually, however, there will be some minor modifications to the macros before it can be used.

Second, the programmer may code the program himself. This is not really difficult to do since there are only three macros that will be used. In fact, even if he chooses the first option, he should know how the macros are used since, as we mentioned before, he may have to modify the generated map program before it is used. Also, a minor change to a screen layout does not necessitate the production of a new map program; the programmer may just change a few macros and the modified map program may be used.

BASIC MAPPING SUPPORT (BMS)

Basic Mapping Support is a CICS/VS control program that gives the application programmer the ability to code map programs without

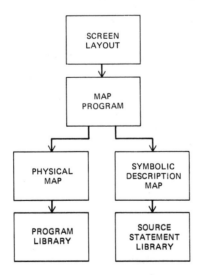

Fig. 4.1. Generating maps.

consideration as to what physical device will actually be used as a terminal, to generate the maps independently of the application program, and to read data from or display data on a terminal using simple commands in the PROCEDURE DIVISION. Specifically, BMS has the following functions:

1. It allows the programmer to define operands in the map program without having to know the physical requirements of the actual terminals to be used.

2. It uses Program Control to load the appropriate physical map into main storage when required.

3. On a command to read data from a terminal, it uses Storage Control to secure main storage for the symbolic description map.

4. It uses Terminal Control facilities to transmit data from or to a terminal.

5. On a command to read data from a terminal, it strips formatting information from the transmitted stream so that only relevant data is placed in the main storage corresponding to the symbolic description map. On a command to display data on a terminal, it inserts terminal formatting information into the data being transmitted.

6. It provides the application program with some degree of data independence. The maps are assembled offline and generated before the application program is used. Then, on a change to the screen layout, the application program may not have to be modified; it may or may not even have to be recompiled and relinked.

Device Independence

The capacity to write map programs without having to know the physical requirements of the terminal means that even if the terminal is changed to a different model later on, the map program, in general, does not have to be modified. Exceptions are certain operands in macros that are unique to a specific device or type of device. In either case, the application program does not have to be modified or recompiled and relinked.

Data Independence

BMS gives the programmer some degree of data independence in addition to device independence. If the screen layout is changed, requiring that the physical map be regenerated, the symbolic description map may or may not have to be modified. If the symbolic description map is not modified, then the application program is not modified. If it is modified, then the application program may still not have to be modified, depending on certain factors. The rules for the modifications are as follows:

1. If the screen layout is changed, the map program is correspondingly modified and the physical map is regenerated.

2. Since only fields coded with labels (see page 36) have corresponding entries in the symbolic description map, if the change to the map program adds a new field with a label, deletes a field with a label, rearranges fields, or changes the length or shift (numeric to alphabetic or vice versa) of a field with a label, then and only then will the symbolic description map have to be modified. In many cases it is simpler to just modify the existing symbolic description map rather than regenerate it from the modified map program.

3. If the symbolic description map is modified, then the application program has to be recompiled and relinked to reflect the modifications. Whether it is modified before the compilation depends on the type of modification done to the symbolic description map.

4. If a field with a label is added to the map program, then the programmer will probably add statements in the PROCEDURE DIVISION to process the new field (otherwise why is it added in the first place?).

5. If a field with a label is deleted, then the programmer will have to remove or modify statements that refer to the field since it will no longer be in the symbolic description map.

6. If the length of a field with a label is changed, the programmer may or may not have to modify the program to take account of the change in length. If the application program issues the GETMAIN command for the symbolic description map, then the LENGTH operand of the command will have to be changed.

7. If the shift of a field with a label is changed, then the statements that process that field may have to be changed.

MACROS

BMS macros are coded in the same style as the more common Assembler macros. There are three of them, and the rules for coding are:

1. The label is from one to seven characters long with the first character being alphabetic. This will start in column 1.

2. The op code is separated from the label by at least one space. However, we start coding it in column 10 for the sake of readability. It is always six columns long.

3. The operands start in column 17 and are separated by commas. If there is a need for a second line, the last operand must be followed by a comma, and column 72 must have a continuation character (any nonblank character will do but an 'X' or '*' are generally used). The continuation line then starts in column 16 of the next line.

4. The END statement is coded as the last statement to delimit the program. This is coded in columns 10 to 12.

First Macro

The first macro has the following functions:

1. defines a map set which consists of one or more maps;

2. specifies whether the program will generate physical maps or symbolic description maps;

3. specifies whether the maps will be used as input, output, or both;

4. may specify whether the data format is field or block.

The macro is coded in the following manner:

1. Label. This is the name of the map set and will be used in the command in the PROCEDURE DIVISION that reads data (RECEIVE MAP) from or displays data (SEND MAP) on a terminal. This is identical to the phase name when the map program is compiled to get the physical map.

2. Op code. This is DFHMSD.

3. Operands.

   a. TYPE = $\left\{\begin{array}{l}\text{MAP} \\ \text{DSECT}\end{array}\right\}$

   Use MAP to generate the physical map, and DSECT to generate the symbolic description map. My suggestion is to use MAP as the permanent operand because in a modification of the screen layout, the physical map is always regenerated but the symbolic description map may or may not have to be. To generate the symbolic description map, TYPE is temporarily changed to DSECT and later on restored to MAP.

   b. MODE = $\left\{\begin{array}{l}\text{IN} \\ OUT \\ \text{INOUT}\end{array}\right\}$ *OUT* is the default

   Use IN if the map is used solely to read data from a terminal; OUT if used solely to display data on a terminal; INOUT if used for both. Most maps are defined as INOUT. They can then be used as either input or output in the program.

   c. CTRL=FREEKB

   This operand is normally used so that the keyboard is unlocked after the map is displayed. The operator may then use the keyboard to enter data on the screen. Alternately, this operand may be omitted if the FREEKB operand is specified in the SEND MAP command.

d. LANG= $\begin{Bmatrix} ASM \\ COBOL \\ PL1 \end{Bmatrix}$ *ASM* is the default

This operand specifies the programming language in whose format the symbolic description map is generated. In this book, we will use Cobol.

e. TIOAPFX=YES

This operand will generate a 12-byte filler prefix for the symbolic description map. When using the command-level feature (as in this book), this operand is always used.

f. DATA= $\begin{Bmatrix} FIELD \\ \\ BLOCK \end{Bmatrix}$ *FIELD* is the default

In this book, we omit this operand so it takes on the default. We will then define the fields in the mapset.

g. TERM=terminal type   3270 is the default.
   In this book, we omit this operand so it takes on the default.

Second Macro

The second macro has these functions:

1. defines a map within a map set;

2. defines the position of the map on the page (the actual screen);

3. specifies the size of the map;

4. may specify whether the data format is field or block.

The macro is coded in the following manner:

1. Label. This is the name of the map and will be used in the command in the PROCEDURE DIVISION that reads data

(RECEIVE MAP) from or displays data (SEND MAP) on a terminal.

2. Op code. This is DFHMDI.

3. Operands.
    a. SIZE=(lines, columns)
       This defines the size of the map and cannot be greater than the size of the screen being used (the page size).

    b. LINE=n
       On the screen, n specifies the line number where the map starts and can be from 1 to 240; the default is 1 and most maps start at line 1.

    c. COLUMN=n
       The column number is also specified by n and tells where the map starts. It can be from 1 to 240; the default is again 1 and most maps start at column 1.

    d. $DATA = \begin{Bmatrix} FIELD \\ BLOCK \end{Bmatrix}$ *FIELD* is the default

       In this book, we omit this operand so it takes on the default. We will then define the fields in the map.

Third Macro

The third macro has the following functions:

1. defines a field within a map;

2. specifies the position of the field;

3. specifies the length of the field;

4. may specify the attributes (characteristics) of the field.

5. may also specify default values, whether the field is part of a group, etc.

The macro is coded in the following manner:

1. Label. Labels are specified for fields that will have entries generated for them when the symbolic description map is generated. Therefore, only fields that will be used in statements in the PROCEDURE DIVISION should really have labels. Coding labels for other fields will just make the symbolic description map larger (consequently requiring a larger main storage allocation) without achieving anything. In fact, data transmission time would be longer. We specify labels for fields entered by the operator (and used in the program), fields used for messages displayed by the program for the operator, fields displayed on the screen from files (as in inquiry applications), etc.

2. Op code. Use DFHMDF.

3. Operands.

    a. $POS = \begin{Bmatrix} \text{line, column} \\ \text{n } (0\text{--}1919) \end{Bmatrix}$

    This specifies the position of the field's attribute byte, which is one position before the actual start of the field. For example, in Fig. 3.1 the position of the title is given by $POS=(01,25)$, or $POS=24$. You will notice that the title itself really starts in line 1, column 26 (position 25). This position is determined relative to the start of the map (line and column operands in the previous macro). Since most maps start in line 1 and column 1, this position is generally with respect to line 1 and column 1 of the actual screen page and is thus easier to interpret.

    Position can be specified with line and column coordinates as in (01,25), or as a number with the first position being 0. Thus $POS=(01,25)$ is identical to $POS=24$. If we use numbers, the position specification will wrap around to the next line. Therefore, in a screen with a column size of 80, line 1, column 80 is identical to position 79 and line 2, column 1 identical to position 80.

b. LENGTH=n

The maximum length of the field is given by n. It does not include the attribute byte. For instance, the title of Fig. 3.1 has length equal to 31.

c. ATTR=(attribute$_1$, attribute$_2$, attribute$_3$, . . . attribute$_n$) must be specified for a map defined with mode OUT or INOUT.

1. attribute$_1$ = $\left\{ \begin{array}{l} \text{ASKIP} \\ \text{PROT} \\ \text{UNPROT} \end{array} \right\}$

   a. ASKIP. The field is autoskip and thus cannot be modified by the operator. It will automatically be skipped by the cursor.

   b. PROT. The field is protected and thus cannot be modified by the operator, but will not be skipped automatically by the cursor. It is used only for STOPPER fields.

   c. UNPROT. The operator may modify the field, and the cursor will at one time fall under this field during normal operation.

      If the whole ATTR operand is omitted, ASKIP is the default; if the ATTR operand is specified, but attribute$_1$ is omitted, UNPROT is the default.

2. attribute$_2$ =NUM

   This specifies that the terminal keyboard is in numeric shift and is really only significant for unprotected fields.* If not specified, the keyboard will be in alphabetic shift for an unprotected field. Many CICS/VS programmers do not bother specifying UNPROT if NUM is also specified since in this case UNPROT is the default.

3. attribute$_3$ = $\left\{ \begin{array}{l} \text{BRT} \\ \textit{NORM} \\ \text{DRK} \end{array} \right\}$ *NORM* is the default

---

*For autoskip or protected fields, the actual value will be what is either specified in the map program (INITIAL = "value") or what is generated in the application program.

      a. BRT. This makes the field brighter than normal displays.

      b. NORM. The field will appear with normal intensity.

      c. DRK. The field will not show on the screen; however, it can still be accessed by the program if the macro has a label. This attribute is useful for information that is used by the program but should not show on the screen; for instance, a password entered.

      Note that NORM is the default, regardless whether ATTR is coded or not.

4. attribute$_4$ =FSET

Each field defined with a label (having an entry in the symbolic description map) will have a corresponding modified data tag monitored by CICS/VS. Only those fields with modified data tag ON will be transmitted into the application program when the map is read. This optimizes transmission time since other data will not be transmitted unnecessarily. If the operator entered or changed an unprotected field, then the modified data tag for the field will be set ON. If the programmer also wants data from an autoskip or protected field (the data may come from a file) to be transmitted to the application program, then FSET (field set) must be specified. This forces the modified data tag of the field to be set ON if the field has a value other than hexadecimal zeroes (BMS will not cause hexadecimal zeroes to be transmitted). Fields with modified data tags OFF will not be transmitted to the application program even if they appear on the terminal screen.

5. attribute$_5$ =IC

The insert cursor (IC) attribute specifies the field under which the cursor will be positioned when the physical map is displayed on the screen. This is useful for maps defined with mode IN or INOUT so that the cursor is automatically positioned on the first field that the operator usually enters or modifies. The program may interactively override this during a series of terminal inputs and outputs for a map with mode INOUT so that the cursor will always be under the first field that the operator is supposed to enter or change. This is done through the symbolic cursor positioning technique (page 124).

d. INITIAL='literal constant'
This operand specifies the literal value of the field on a command to display the physical map. If the field is defined with a label and the symbolic description map is included in the display, the value in the symbolic description map will override the initial value if the former is not hexadecimal zeroes.

e. PICIN='Cobol PICTURE specification'
For fields defined with labels, this defines the PICTURE specification of the field in the generated symbolic description map if the map is defined with mode IN or INOUT. PICIN is specified only for numeric fields* since the default is alphanumeric (PICTURE X's).

f. PICOUT= 'Cobol PICTURE specification'
This is used just like the PICIN operand, but for a map defined with mode OUT or INOUT.

g. GRPNAME=name
GRPNAME identifies this line and succeeding lines defined with the same GRPNAME value as elementary items of the group. There will be only one length field and one attribute byte generated in the symbolic description map for the group. Only the first field in a group must have the ATTR operands; also, the POS operand for fields after the first in a group must point to where the attribute byte would be if there was one.

---

*This includes autoskip fields that are used in statements as numeric.

   h. OCCURS=n

This operand is mutually exclusive with GRPNAME and specifies that this field is repeated a number of times.

The DFHMSD macro is used again as the last macro in the program and the entry is simple:

DFHMSD TYPE=FINAL

MAP PROGRAM EXAMPLE

Let us now show a complete map program for Figure 3.1. Note the use of the PRINT NOGEN macro to eliminate the printing of the generated macro expansion in Figure 4.2.

Note the following;

1. PRINT NOGEN at statement 1 is optional but is used so that the expansion of the macros do not print out in the listing.

2. The DUMMY field at statement 40 at the beginning of the map is explained on page 173).

3. The END statement at statement 1225 is used to indicate the end of the Assembler program.

MAPS IN A MAPSET

The programmer may specify as many maps as he wants in a map set. The underlying principle is that when any map is used in a command, CICS/VS will load the entire map set that contains the map into main storage if it is not yet there. Thus, maps that may not be required in that task will also be loaded if specified as part of the map set and may waste main storage. Therefore, unless maps are used in the same task (perhaps in overlapping displays), generally only one map is specified in a map set.

To specify several maps in a mapset, the macros are coded as shown in Figure 4.3.

```
STMT    SOURCE STATEMENT                         DOS/VS ASSEMBLER REL 34.0 14.03 80-07-27

    1               PRINT NOGEN                                                      00000020
    2 ORIQSO1       DFHMSD TYPE=MAP,MODE=INOUT,CTRL=FREEKB,LANG=COBOL,TIOAPFX=YES    00000030
   12 ORIQMO1       DFHMDI SIZE=(24,80)                                              00000040
   40 DUMMY         DFHMDF POS=(01,01),LENGTH=01,ATTRB=(ASKIP,DRK,FSET),          X00000050
                    INITIAL='1'                                                      00000060
   52               DFHMDF POS=(01,25),LENGTH=31,ATTRB=(ASKIP,BRT),               X00000070
                    INITIAL='PURCHASE ORDER --- FILE INQUIRY'                        00000080
   64               DFHMDF POS=(03,30),LENGTH=13,ATTRB=ASKIP,                      X00000090
                    INITIAL='ORDER NUMBER '                                          00000100
   76 ORDER         DFHMDF POS=(03,44),LENGTH=10,ATTRB=(NUM,BRT,IC)                  00000110
   87               DFHMDF POS=(03,55),LENGTH=01,ATTRB=PROT                          00000120
   98               DFHMDF POS=(04,32),LENGTH=11,ATTRB=ASKIP,INITIAL='DEPARTMENT '   00000130
  110 DEPT          DFHMDF POS=(04,44),LENGTH=03,ATTRB=(ASKIP,BRT)                   00000140
  121               DFHMDF POS=(05,29),LENGTH=14,ATTRB=ASKIP,                      X00000150
                    INITIAL='DATE OF ORDER '                                         00000160
  133 DATEOR        DFHMDF POS=(05,44),LENGTH=06,ATTRB=(ASKIP,BRT)                   00000170
  144               DFHMDF POS=(06,29),LENGTH=14,ATTRB=ASKIP,                      X00000180
                    INITIAL='ORDER ENTERED '                                         00000190
  156 DATEENT       DFHMDF POS=(06,44),LENGTH=06,ATTRB=(ASKIP,BRT)                   00000200
  167               DFHMDF POS=(07,32),LENGTH=11,ATTRB=ASKIP,INITIAL='TOTAL COST '  00000210
  179 TOTCOST       DFHMDF POS=(07,44),LENGTH=12,ATTRB=(ASKIP,BRT),               X00000220
                    PICOUT='Z,ZZZ,ZZZ.99'                                            00000230
  190               DFHMDF POS=(08,31),LENGTH=12,ATTRB=ASKIP,                      X00000240
                    INITIAL='TOTAL PRICE '                                           00000250
  202 TOTPRCE       DFHMDF POS=(08,44),LENGTH=12,ATTRB=(ASKIP,BRT),               X00000260
                    PICOUT='Z,ZZZ,ZZZ.99'                                            00000270
  213               DFHMDF POS=(10,07),LENGTH=04,ATTRB=ASKIP,INITIAL='ITEM'         00000280
  225               DFHMDF POS=(10,17),LENGTH=11,ATTRB=ASKIP,INITIAL='DESCRIPTION'  00000290
  237               DFHMDF POS=(10,35),LENGTH=04,ATTRB=ASKIP,INITIAL='DATE'         00000300
  249               DFHMDF POS=(10,42),LENGTH=04,ATTRB=ASKIP,INITIAL='UNIT'         00000310
  261               DFHMDF POS=(10,48),LENGTH=05,ATTRB=ASKIP,INITIAL='UCOST'        00000320
  273               DFHMDF POS=(10,57),LENGTH=04,ATTRB=ASKIP,INITIAL='COST'         00000330
  285               DFHMDF POS=(10,65),LENGTH=06,ATTRB=ASKIP,INITIAL='UPRICE'       00000340
  297               DFHMDF POS=(10,74),LENGTH=05,ATTRB=ASKIP,INITIAL='PRICE'        00000350
  309 LINE1         DFHMDF POS=(11,03),LENGTH=01,ATTRB=ASKIP                         00000360
  320 ITEM1         DFHMDF POS=(11,05),LENGTH=08,ATTRB=(ASKIP,BRT),               X00000370
                    PICIN='99999999',PICOUT='99999999'                               00000380
  331 DESC1         DFHMDF POS=(11,14),LENGTH=19,ATTRB=(ASKIP,BRT)                   00000390
  342 LNDATE1       DFHMDF POS=(11,34),LENGTH=06,ATTRB=(ASKIP,BRT)                   00000400
  353 UNIT1         DFHMDF POS=(11,41),LENGTH=05,ATTRB=(ASKIP,BRT),               X00000410
                    PICIN='99999',PICOUT='99999'                                     00000420
  364 UCOST1        DFHMDF POS=(11,47),LENGTH=07,ATTRB=(ASKIP,BRT),               X00000430
                    PICIN='9999999',PICOUT='9999999'                                 00000440
  375 COST1         DFHMDF POS=(11,55),LENGTH=08,ATTRB=(ASKIP,BRT),               X00000450
                    PICIN='99999999',PICOUT='99999999'                               00000460
  386 UPRICE1       DFHMDF POS=(11,64),LENGTH=07,ATTRB=(ASKIP,BRT),               X00000470
                    PICIN='9999999',PICOUT='9999999'                                 00000480
  397 PRICE1        DFHMDF POS=(11,72),LENGTH=08,ATTRB=(ASKIP,BRT),               X00000490
                    PICIN='99999999',PICOUT='99999999'                               00000500
  408 LINE2         DFHMDF POS=(12,03),LENGTH=01,ATTRB=ASKIP                         00000510
  419 ITEM2         DFHMDF POS=(12,05),LENGTH=08,ATTRB=(ASKIP,BRT),               X00000520
```

Fig. 4.2. Example of a map program.

```
STMT     SOURCE STATEMENT                                  DOS/VS ASSEMBLER REL 34.0 14.03 80-07-27
              PICIN='99999999',PICOUT='99999999'                          00000530
430 DESC2     DFHMDF POS=(12,14),LENGTH=19,ATTRB=(ASKIP,BRT)              00000540
441 LNDATE2   DFHMDF POS=(12,34),LENGTH=06,ATTRB=(ASKIP,BRT)             00000550
452 UNIT2     DFHMDF POS=(12,41),LENGTH=05,ATTRB=(ASKIP,BRT),           X00000560
              PICIN='99999',PICOUT='99999'                                00000570
463 UCOST2    DFHMDF POS=(12,47),LENGTH=07,ATTRB=(ASKIP,BRT),           X00000580
              PICIN='9999999',PICOUT='9999999'                            00000590
474 COST2     DFHMDF POS=(12,55),LENGTH=08,ATTRB=(ASKIP,BRT),           X00000600
              PICIN='99999999',PICOUT='99999999'                          00000610
485 UPRICE2   DFHMDF POS=(12,64),LENGTH=07,ATTRB=(ASKIP,BRT),           X00000620
              PICIN='9999999',PICOUT='9999999'                            00000630
496 PRICE2    DFHMDF POS=(12,72),LENGTH=08,ATTRB=(ASKIP,BRT),           X00000640
              PICIN='99999999',PICOUT='99999999'                          00000650
507 LINE3     DFHMDF POS=(13,03),LENGTH=01,ATTRB=ASKIP                    00000660
518 ITEM3     DFHMDF POS=(13,05),LENGTH=08,ATTRB=(ASKIP,BRT),           X00000670
              PICIN='99999999',PICOUT='99999999'                          00000680
529 DESC3     DFHMDF POS=(13,14),LENGTH=19,ATTRB=(ASKIP,BRT)              00000690
540 LNDATE3   DFHMDF POS=(13,34),LENGTH=06,ATTRB=(ASKIP,BRT)             00000700
551 UNIT3     DFHMDF POS=(13,41),LENGTH=05,ATTRB=(ASKIP,BRT),           X00000710
              PICIN='99999',PICOUT='99999'                                00000720
562 UCOST3    DFHMDF POS=(13,47),LENGTH=07,ATTRB=(ASKIP,BRT),           X00000730
              PICIN='9999999',PICOUT='9999999'                            00000740
573 COST3     DFHMDF POS=(13,55),LENGTH=08,ATTRB=(ASKIP,BRT),           X00000750
              PICIN='99999999',PICOUT='99999999'                          00000760
584 UPRICE3   DFHMDF POS=(13,64),LENGTH=07,ATTRB=(ASKIP,BRT),           X00000770
              PICIN='9999999',PICOUT='9999999'                            00000780
595 PRICE3    DFHMDF POS=(13,72),LENGTH=08,ATTRB=(ASKIP,BRT),           X00000790
              PICIN='99999999',PICOUT='99999999'                          00000800
606 LINE4     DFHMDF POS=(14,03),LENGTH=01,ATTRB=ASKIP                    00000810
617 ITEM4     DFHMDF POS=(14,05),LENGTH=08,ATTRB=(ASKIP,BRT),           X00000820
              PICIN='99999999',PICOUT='99999999'                          00000830
628 DESC4     DFHMDF POS=(14,14),LENGTH=19,ATTRB=(ASKIP,BRT)              00000840
639 LNDATE4   DFHMDF POS=(14,34),LENGTH=06,ATTRB=(ASKIP,BRT)             00000850
650 UNIT4     DFHMDF POS=(14,41),LENGTH=05,ATTRB=(ASKIP,BRT),           X00000860
              PICIN='99999',PICOUT='99999'                                00000870
661 UCOST4    DFHMDF POS=(14,47),LENGTH=07,ATTRB=(ASKIP,BRT),           X00000880
              PICIN='9999999',PICOUT='9999999'                            00000890
672 COST4     DFHMDF POS=(14,55),LENGTH=08,ATTRB=(ASKIP,BRT),           X00000900
              PICIN='99999999',PICOUT='99999999'                          00000910
683 UPRICE4   DFHMDF POS=(14,64),LENGTH=07,ATTRB=(ASKIP,BRT),           X00000920
              PICIN='9999999',PICOUT='9999999'                            00000930
694 PRICE4    DFHMDF POS=(14,72),LENGTH=08,ATTRB=(ASKIP,BRT),           X00000940
              PICIN='99999999',PICOUT='99999999'                          00000950
705 LINE5     DFHMDF POS=(15,03),LENGTH=01,ATTRB=ASKIP                    00000960
716 ITEM5     DFHMDF POS=(15,05),LENGTH=08,ATTRB=(ASKIP,BRT),           X00000970
              PICIN='99999999',PICOUT='99999999'                          00000980
727 DESC5     DFHMDF POS=(15,14),LENGTH=19,ATTRB=(ASKIP,BRT)              00000990
738 LNDATE5   DFHMDF POS=(15,34),LENGTH=06,ATTRB=(ASKIP,BRT)             00001000
749 UNIT5     DFHMDF POS=(15,41),LENGTH=05,ATTRB=(ASKIP,BRT),           X00001010
              PICIN='99999',PICOUT='99999'                                00001020
760 UCOST5    DFHMDF POS=(15,47),LENGTH=07,ATTRB=(ASKIP,BRT),           X00001030
```

Fig. 4.2. (Continued)

```
STMT    SOURCE STATEMENT                          DOS/VS ASSEMBLER REL 34.0 14.03 80-07-27
                    PICIN='9999999',PICOUT='9999999'                          00001040
771 COST5      DFHMDF POS=(15,55),LENGTH=08,ATTRB=(ASKIP,BRT),             X00001050
                    PICIN='99999999',PICOUT='99999999'                        00001060
782 UPRICE5    DFHMDF POS=(15,64),LENGTH=07,ATTRB=(ASKIP,BRT),             X00001070
                    PICIN='9999999',PICOUT='9999999'                          00001080
793 PRICE5     DFHMDF POS=(15,72),LENGTH=08,ATTRB=(ASKIP,BRT),             X00001090
                    PICIN='99999999',PICOUT='99999999'                        00001100
804 LINE6      DFHMDF POS=(16,03),LENGTH=01,ATTRB=ASKIP                       00001110
815 ITEM6      DFHMDF POS=(16,05),LENGTH=08,ATTRB=(ASKIP,BRT),             X00001120
                    PICIN='99999999',PICOUT='99999999'                        00001130
826 DESC6      DFHMDF POS=(16,14),LENGTH=19,ATTRB=(ASKIP,BRT)                 00001140
837 LNDATE6    DFHMDF POS=(16,34),LENGTH=06,ATTRB=(ASKIP,BRT)                 00001150
848 UNIT6      DFHMDF POS=(16,41),LENGTH=05,ATTRB=(ASKIP,BRT),             X00001160
                    PICIN='99999',PICOUT='99999'                              00001170
859 UCOST6     DFHMDF POS=(16,47),LENGTH=07,ATTRB=(ASKIP,BRT),             X00001180
                    PICIN='9999999',PICOUT='9999999'                          00001190
870 COST6      DFHMDF POS=(16,55),LENGTH=08,ATTRB=(ASKIP,BRT),             X00001200
                    PICIN='99999999',PICOUT='99999999'                        00001210
881 UPRICE6    DFHMDF POS=(16,64),LENGTH=07,ATTRB=(ASKIP,BRT),             X0C001220
                    PICIN='9999999',PICOUT='9999999'                          00001230
892 PRICE6     DFHMDF POS=(16,72),LENGTH=08,ATTRB=(ASKIP,BRT),             X00001240
                    PICIN='99999999',PICOUT='99999999'                        00001250
903 LINE7      DFHMDF POS=(17,03),LENGTH=01,ATTRB=ASKIP                       00001260
914 ITEM7      DFHMDF POS=(17,05),LENGTH=08,ATTRB=(ASKIP,BRT),             X00001270
                    PICIN='99999999',PICOUT='99999999'                        00001280
925 DESC7      DFHMDF POS=(17,14),LENGTH=19,ATTRB=(ASKIP,BRT)                 00001290
936 LNDATE7    DFHMDF POS=(17,34),LENGTH=06,ATTRB=(ASKIP,BRT)                 00001300
947 UNIT7      DFHMDF POS=(17,41),LENGTH=05,ATTRB=(ASKIP,BRT),             X00001310
                    PICIN='99999',PICOUT='99999'                              00001320
958 UCOST7     DFHMDF POS=(17,47),LENGTH=07,ATTRB=(ASKIP,BRT),             X00001330
                    PICIN='9999999',PICOUT='9999999'                          00001340
969 COST7      DFHMDF POS=(17,55),LENGTH=08,ATTRB=(ASKIP,BRT),             X00001350
                    PICIN='99999999',PICOUT='99999999'                        00001360
980 UPRICE7    DFHMDF POS=(17,64),LENGTH=07,ATTRB=(ASKIP,BRT),             X00001370
                    PICIN='9999999',PICOUT='9999999'                          00001380
991 PRICE7     DFHMDF POS=(17,72),LENGTH=08,ATTRB=(ASKIP,BRT),             X00001390
                    PICIN='99999999',PICOUT='99999999'                        00001400
1002 LINE8     DFHMDF POS=(18,03),LENGTH=01,ATTRB=ASKIP                       00001410
1013 ITEM8     DFHMDF POS=(18,05),LENGTH=08,ATTRB=(ASKIP,BRT),            X00001420
                    PICIN='99999999',PICOUT='99999999'                        00001430
1024 DESC8     DFHMDF POS=(18,14),LENGTH=19,ATTRB=(ASKIP,BRT)                 00001440
1035 LNDATE8   DFHMDF POS=(18,34),LENGTH=06,ATTRB=(ASKIP,BRT)                 00001450
1046 UNIT8     DFHMDF POS=(18,41),LENGTH=05,ATTRB=(ASKIP,BRT),            X00001460
                    PICIN='99999',PICOUT='99999'                              00001470
1057 UCOST8    DFHMDF POS=(18,47),LENGTH=07,ATTRB=(ASKIP,BRT),            X00001480
                    PICIN='9999999',PICOUT='9999999'                          00001490
1068 COST8     DFHMDF POS=(18,55),LENGTH=08,ATTRB=(ASKIP,BRT),            X00001500
                    PICIN='99999999',PICOUT='99999999'                        00001510
1079 UPRICE8   DFHMDF POS=(18,64),LENGTH=07,ATTRB=(ASKIP,BRT),            X00001520
                    PICIN='9999999',PICOUT='9999999'                          00001530
1090 PRICE8    DFHMDF POS=(18,72),LENGTH=08,ATTRB=(ASKIP,BRT),            X00001540
```

Fig. 4.2. (Continued)

```
STMT    SOURCE STATEMENT                          DOS/VS ASSEMBLER REL 34.0 14.03 80-07-27
                     PICIN='99999999',PICOUT='99999999'                              00001550
1101 LINE9    DFHMDF POS=(19,03),LENGTH=01,ATTRB=ASKIP                               00001560
1112 ITEM9    DFHMDF POS=(19,05),LENGTH=08,ATTRB=(ASKIP,BRT),                       X00001570
                     PICIN='99999999',PICOUT='99999999'                              00001580
1123 DESC9    DFHMDF POS=(19,14),LENGTH=19,ATTRB=(ASKIP,BRT)                         00001590
1134 LNDATE9  DFHMDF POS=(19,34),LENGTH=06,ATTRB=(ASKIP,BRT)                         00001600
1145 UNIT9    DFHMDF POS=(19,41),LENGTH=05,ATTRB=(ASKIP,BRT),                       X00001610
                     PICIN='99999',PICOUT='99999'                                    00001620
1156 UCOST9   DFHMDF POS=(19,47),LENGTH=07,ATTRB=(ASKIP,BRT),                       X00001630
                     PICIN='9999999',PICOUT='9999999'                                00001640
1167 COST9    DFHMDF POS=(19,55),LENGTH=08,ATTRB=(ASKIP,BRT),                       X00001650
                     PICIN='99999999',PICOUT='99999999'                              00001660
1178 UPRICE9  DFHMDF POS=(19,64),LENGTH=07,ATTRB=(ASKIP,BRT),                       X00001670
                     PICIN='9999999',PICOUT='9999999'                                00001680
1189 PRICE9   DFHMDF POS=(19,72),LENGTH=08,ATTRB=(ASKIP,BRT),                       X00001690
                     PICIN='99999999',PICOUT='99999999'                              00001700
1200 ERROR    DFHMDF POS=(23,30),LENGTH=20,ATTRB=(ASKIP,BRT)                         00001710
1211          DFHMSD TYPE=FINAL                                                      00001720
1225          END                                                                    00001730
```

Fig. 4.2. (Continued)

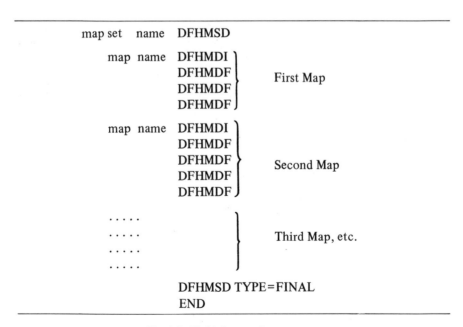

Fig. 4.3. Multiple maps in a mapset.

5

Program Components

INTRODUCTION

The application program basically looks like any batch Cobol program but with some minor differences. First, the INPUT-OUTPUT section of the ENVIRONMENT DIVISION is no longer coded since each file can be accessed using the identification of the file in the File Control Table. Second, the FILE section of the DATA DIVISION is no longer coded and the file record descriptions are instead placed in the LINKAGE section.* Third, requests for CICS/VS services (display data on a terminal, read an on-line file, etc.) are coded as commands and are interspersed with regular Cobol statements in the PROCEDURE DIVISION. The first two differences inform us that the FILE CONTROL select statements and the FILE section File Descriptions (FD) entries are no longer coded.

THE IDENTIFICATION AND ENVIRONMENT DIVISIONS

These two divisions may actually be coded with three entries. The required lines are:

```
              IDENTIFICATION DIVISION.
              PROGRAM-ID.    program-id.
              ENVIRONMENT DIVISION.
```

The programmer may wish to add other paragraphs in these two divisions, for instance, SOURCE-COMPUTER, etc. Also, it is a very good idea to put comment cards (asterisks in column 7) after the ENVIRONMENT DIVISION header, explaining what the program

---

*These entries, as well as other entries coded in the LINKAGE section, may actually be placed in the WORKING-STORAGE section. We, however, prefer to use the LINKAGE section since this makes the program smaller, thus saving main storage.

does. We should then EJECT before the DATA DIVISION header. An example is given in Figure 5.1.

You will note that SKIP statements are used to improve the presentation of the program.

THE WORKING-STORAGE SECTION

The WORKING-STORAGE section is the first section coded in the DATA DIVISION and should be used only for the following data:

1. If the program sends a communication area to another program, then the field to be sent is defined as the first level-01 entry. For a reason explained on page 89, programs in this book will use this communication area.

2. The next level-01 entry will contain the following level-05 entries:
   a. A 23-byte data area with the label "JOB-NORMAL-END-MESSAGE" and with the value "JOB NORMALLY TERMINATED." This will be displayed on the terminal when the operator decides to terminate the job.

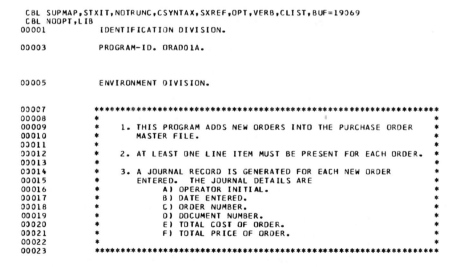

```
CBL SUPMAP,STXIT,NOTRUNC,CSYNTAX,SXREF,OPT,VERB,CLIST,BUF=19069
CBL NOOPT,LIB
00001          IDENTIFICATION DIVISION.

00003          PROGRAM-ID. ORADO1A.


00005          ENVIRONMENT DIVISION.


00007          ************************************************************
00008          *                                                         *
00009          *    1. THIS PROGRAM ADDS NEW ORDERS INTO THE PURCHASE ORDER *
00010          *       MASTER FILE.                                      *
00011          *                                                         *
00012          *    2. AT LEAST ONE LINE ITEM MUST BE PRESENT FOR EACH ORDER. *
00013          *                                                         *
00014          *    3. A JOURNAL RECORD IS GENERATED FOR EACH NEW ORDER  *
00015          *       ENTERED.   THE JOURNAL DETAILS ARE                *
00016          *          A) OPERATOR INITIAL.                           *
00017          *          B) DATE ENTERED.                               *
00018          *          C) ORDER NUMBER.                               *
00019          *          D) DOCUMENT NUMBER.                            *
00020          *          E) TOTAL COST OF ORDER.                        *
00021          *          F) TOTAL PRICE OF ORDER.                       *
00022          *                                                         *
00023          ************************************************************
```

Fig. 5.1. IDENTIFICATION and ENVIRONMENT divisions.

b. A data area with the label "JOB-ABORTED-MESSAGE," which will be displayed if a job is to be aborted and consists of two level-10 entries:
1. A 15-byte filler with the value "JOB ABORTED − ;"
2. A data area with the label "MAJOR-ERROR-MSG" that will contain the message corresponding to the error that caused the job to be aborted. The length will be the maximum error message length.

c. A data area with the label "OLD-EIB-AREA," which will contain certain information from the Execute Interface Block when the DUMP command is issued on an error that aborts the job. This field will be used for debugging and will be discussed further on page 523. It will contain three level-10 entries:
1. a 7-byte filler with the value "OLD EIB;"
2. a 2-byte data area with the label "OLD-EIBFN" and PIC XX;
3. a 6-byte data area with the label "OLD-EIBRCODE" and PIC X (6).

d. Other fields that contain fixed data. For instance, table data hard coded in the program or loaded from a file, or factors* that may change within the lifetime of the program (especially if used in more than one statement in the program).

The style used in 2.b. saves main storage since the literal, "JOB ABORTED − ," is made common to all messages sent to the terminal to signify an abnormal job termination. To be consistent, the normal termination message in 2.a. is also coded in the WORKING-STORAGE section. The actual error messages appended to "JOB ABORTED − " are from the appropriate paragraph in the ABNORMAL-TERMINA-TION section** that handles the particular error.

My suggestion is that only these data be directly coded in the WORKING-STORAGE section. All other data needed in the program

---

*We generally prefer to code constants, including factors, as part of the statement for the sake of efficiency. However, if a factor may change within the lifetime of the program, we should code it as a data name in working storage for easier maintainability.
**See page 99.

will be stated either as constants in statements or coded in the LINK-AGE section.

An example of this part of the WORKING-STORAGE section is shown in Figure 5.2.

There are, however, two entries that the program may copy from a source statement library. These are the standard attention identifier list (DFHAID), used to determine the terminal key the operator used to initiate a terminal or BMS operation, and the standard attribute list (DFHBMSCA), which is used to provide for or modify the attributes of fields displayed on terminals.

The programmer should copy DFHAID into the WORKING-STORAGE section if the program uses keys other than "ENTER" to control the program logic. For instance, in a browse application, the program may use PF1 to browse forward and PF2 to browse

```
   2        ORIQ01A        12.55.39        08/02/80

00014         DATA DIVISION.


00016         WORKING-STORAGE SECTION.


00018         01  COMMUNICATION-AREA.

00020             05  COMMAREA-PROCESS-SW     PIC X.


00022         01  AREA1.

00024             05  JOB-NORMAL-END-MESSAGE  PIC X(23) VALUE
00025                 'JOB NORMALLY TERMINATED'.

00027             05  JOB-ABORTED-MESSAGE.
00028                 10  FILLER              PIC X(15) VALUE 'JOB ABORTED --'.
00029                 10  MAJOR-ERROR-MSG     PIC X(16).


00031             05  HEXADECIMAL-ZEROES      PIC 9999 COMP VALUE ZEROES.


00033             05  FILLER REDEFINES HEXADECIMAL-ZEROES.
00034                 10  FILLER              PIC X.
00035                 10  HEX-ZEROES          PIC X.


00037             05  OLD-EIB-AREA.
00038                 10  FILLER              PIC X(7) VALUE 'OLD EIB'.
00039                 10  OLD-EIBFN           PIC XX.
00040                 10  OLD-EIBRCODE        PIC X(6).
```

Fig. 5.2. Programmer-coded Entries in working storage.

backwards. At the start of the PROCEDURE DIVISION, the value of the EIBAID field of the Execute Interface Block is checked against the DFHAID entries. The use of this list is shown on page 95.

The programmer should also copy a standard attribute list into the program if there is a need to provide for or modify the attributes of a field to be transmitted to a terminal (map defined with mode OUT or INOUT). For instance, a field defined as unprotected, allowing the operator to enter a value on it, may be changed to autoskip so that it can no longer be changed. This may be done in an update application — the operator enters a record number; when it is determined to be valid, the screen comes back with the attribute of the record number changed to autoskip so that the operator can no longer change it when he enters the fields used in the update. The use of this list is shown on page 123.

There is also an entry which is automatically generated by the command-language translator. This is DFHEIVAR, which is used in the CALL statements generated from the commands.

An example of this part of working storage is given in Figure 5.3.

The programmer should understand that whenever a program first executes in a task, all fields in working storage will revert to their original values. Thus, data to be saved across tasks can not be coded in working storage (they are generally coded in Temporary Storage).

THE LINKAGE SECTION

The LINKAGE section is the next section coded in the DATA DIVISION. It contains descriptions of the entries that will be allocated main storage when required by the program. The main storage areas thus acquired are not really part of the object program. To keep the program small, most data used in the program should be described in the LINKAGE section.

There is one entry that is automatically generated by the command-language translator. This is the Execute Interface Block, containing information like transaction identifier, terminal identification, results of a command, etc. This block is updated by CICS/VS every time a command is executed, and the information may be used by the application program. A one-byte DFHCOMMAREA field is also generated, if not coded, by the programmer.

The entries coded by the programmer are for main storage areas that will be required by the CICS/VS service requested by the command. For instance, if a program uses several screen layouts, there has to be a symbolic description map for each layout; there must be a file record description for each file record used; the transaction work area, temporary storage area, and common work area must be defined if used. The details of these descriptions will be discussed in the next chapter.

THE PROCEDURE DIVISION

Commands for CICS/VS services are interspersed with other Cobol statements in the PROCEDURE DIVISION. The choice of such commands and their options and the overall coding style are very critical since it is of utmost importance that the resulting program be as efficient as possible. While the programmer has more leeway in

```
        3          ORDLO1A          13.28.44          08/02/80

00042                01   DFHAID COPY DFHAID.
00043 C              01      DFHAID.
00044 C                 02   DFHNULL    PIC  X   VALUE IS ' '.
00045 C                 02   DFHENTER   PIC  X   VALUE IS QUOTE.
00046 C                 02   DFHCLEAR   PIC  X   VALUE IS ' '.
00047 C                 02   DFHPEN     PIC  X   VALUE IS '='.
00048 C                 02   DFHOPID    PIC  X   VALUE IS 'W'.
00049 C                 02   DFHPA1     PIC  X   VALUE IS '%'.
00050 C                 02   DFHPA2     PIC  X   VALUE IS ' '.
00051 C                 02   DFHPA3     PIC  X   VALUE IS ','.
00052 C                 02   DFHPF1     PIC  X   VALUE IS '1'.
00053 C                 02   DFHPF2     PIC  X   VALUE IS '2'.
00054 C                 02   DFHPF3     PIC  X   VALUE IS '3'.
00055 C                 02   DFHPF4     PIC  X   VALUE IS '4'.
00056 C                 02   DFHPF5     PIC  X   VALUE IS '5'.
00057 C                 02   DFHPF6     PIC  X   VALUE IS '6'.
00058 C                 02   DFHPF7     PIC  X   VALUE IS '7'.
00059 C                 02   DFHPF8     PIC  X   VALUE IS '8'.
00060 C                 02   DFHPF9     PIC  X   VALUE IS '9'.
00061 C                 02   DFHPF10    PIC  X   VALUE IS ' '.
00062 C                 02   DFHPF11    PIC  X   VALUE IS '#'.
00063 C                 02   DFHPF12    PIC  X   VALUE IS 'a'.
00064 C                 02   DFHPF13    PIC  X   VALUE IS 'A'.
00065 C                 02   DFHPF14    PIC  X   VALUE IS 'B'.
00066 C                 02   DFHPF15    PIC  X   VALUE IS 'C'.
00067 C                 02   DFHPF16    PIC  X   VALUE IS 'D'.
00068 C                 02   DFHPF17    PIC  X   VALUE IS 'E'.
00069 C                 02   DFHPF18    PIC  X   VALUE IS 'F'.
00070 C                 02   DFHPF19    PIC  X   VALUE IS 'G'.
00071 C                 02   DFHPF20    PIC  X   VALUE IS 'H'.
00072 C                 02   DFHPF21    PIC  X   VALUE IS 'I'.
00073 C                 02   DFHPF22    PIC  X   VALUE IS ' '.
00074 C                 02   DFHPF23    PIC  X   VALUE IS '.'.
00075 C                 02   DFHPF24    PIC  X   VALUE IS 'a'.
```

Fig. 5.3. Copied or System-generated Entries in working storage.

4   ORDLO1A   13.28.44   08/02/80

```
00077        *     THIS COPY IS A LIST OF ALL VALID 3270 ATTRIBUTE COMBINATIONS
00078        *     TAKEN FROM 3270 REFERENCE SUMMARY, PAGE 9.


00080        01  ALL-VALID-ATTRIBUTES.
00081            05  ATTR-UNPROT                        PIC X VALUE ' '.
00082            05  ATTR-UNPROT-FSET                   PIC X VALUE 'A'.
00083            05  ATTR-UNPROT-PEN                    PIC X VALUE 'D'.
00084            05  ATTR-UNPROT-PEN-FSET              PIC X VALUE 'E'.
00085            05  ATTR-UNPROT-BRT-PEN                PIC X VALUE 'H'.
00086            05  ATTR-UNPROT-BRT-PEN-FSET          PIC X VALUE 'I'.
00087            05  ATTR-UNPROT-DRK                    PIC X VALUE 'α'.
00088            05  ATTR-UNPROT-DRK-FSET              PIC X VALUE '('.
00089            05  ATTR-UNPROT-NUM                    PIC X VALUE '&'.
00090            05  ATTR-UNPROT-NUM-FSET              PIC X VALUE 'J'.
00091            05  ATTR-UNPROT-NUM-PEN                PIC X VALUE 'M'.
00092            05  ATTR-UNPROT-NUM-PEN-FSET          PIC X VALUE 'N'.
00093            05  ATTR-UNPROT-NUM-BRT-PEN            PIC X VALUE 'Q'.
00094            05  ATTR-UNPROT-NUM-BRT-PEN-FSET      PIC X VALUE 'R'.
00095            05  ATTR-UNPROT-NUM-DRK                PIC X VALUE '*'.
00096            05  ATTR-UNPROT-NUM-DRK-FSET          PIC X VALUE ')'.
00097            05  ATTR-PROT                          PIC X VALUE '-'.
00098            05  ATTR-PROT-FSET                     PIC X VALUE '/'.
00099            05  ATTR-PROT-PEN                      PIC X VALUE 'U'.
00100            05  ATTR-PROT-PEN-FSET                PIC X VALUE 'V'.
00101            05  ATTR-PROT-BRT-PEN                  PIC X VALUE 'Y'.
00102            05  ATTR-PROT-BRT-PEN-FSET            PIC X VALUE 'Z'.
00103            05  ATTR-PROT-DRK                      PIC X VALUE '%'.
00104            05  ATTR-PROT-DRK-FSET                PIC X VALUE ' '.
00105            05  ATTR-PROT-ASKIP                    PIC X VALUE '0'.
00106            05  ATTR-PROT-ASKIP-FSET              PIC X VALUE '1'.
00107            05  ATTR-PROT-ASKIP-PEN                PIC X VALUE '4'.
00108            05  ATTR-PROT-ASKIP-PEN-FSET          PIC X VALUE '5'.
00109            05  ATTR-PROT-ASKIP-BRT-PEN            PIC X VALUE '8'.
00110            05  ATTR-PROT-ASKIP-BRT-PEN-FSET      PIC X VALUE '9'.
00111            05  ATTR-PROT-ASKIP-DRK                PIC X VALUE 'a'.
00112            05  ATTR-PROT-ASKIP-DRK-FSET          PIC X VALUE QUOTE.
```

Fig. 5.3. (Continued)

5   ORDLO1A   13.28.44   08/02/80

```
00114         01  DFHEIVAR COPY DFHEIVAR.
00115 C       01  DFHEIVAR.
00116 C           02  DFHEIV0   PICTURE X(26).
00117 C           02  DFHEIV1   PICTURE X(8).
00118 C           02  DFHEIV2   PICTURE X(8).
00119 C           02  DFHEIV3   PICTURE X(8).
00120 C           02  DFHEIV4   PICTURE X(6).
00121 C           02  DFHEIV5   PICTURE X(4).
00122 C           02  DFHEIV6   PICTURE X(4).
00123 C           02  DFHEIV7   PICTURE X(2).
00124 C           02  DFHEIV8   PICTURE X(2).
00125 C           02  DFHEIV9   PICTURE X(1).
00126 C           02  DFHEIV10 PICTURE S9(7) USAGE COMPUTATIONAL-3.
00127 C           02  DFHEIV11 PICTURE S9(4) USAGE COMPUTATIONAL.
00128 C           02  DFHEIV12 PICTURE S9(4) USAGE COMPUTATIONAL.
00129 C           02  DFHEIV13 PICTURE S9(4) USAGE COMPUTATIONAL.
00130 C           02  DFHEIV14 PICTURE S9(4) USAGE COMPUTATIONAL.
00131 C           02  DFHEIV15 PICTURE S9(4) USAGE COMPUTATIONAL.
00132 C           02  DFHEIV16 PICTURE S9(9) USAGE COMPUTATIONAL.
00133 C           02  DFHEIV17 PICTURE X(4).
00134 C           02  DFHEIV18 PICTURE X(4).
00135 C           02  DFHEIV19 PICTURE X(4).
00136 C           02  DFHEIV97 PICTURE S9(7) USAGE COMPUTATIONAL-3 VALUE ZERO.
00137 C           02  DFHEIV98 PICTURE S9(4) USAGE COMPUTATIONAL VALUE ZERO.
00138 C           02  DFHEIV99 PICTURE X(1)  VALUE SPACE.
```

Fig. 5.3. (Continued)

sacrificing efficiency for the sake of maintainability in batch programs, CICS/VS programs must provide the fastest response time to the operator, and the best way of assuring this is to make the program as efficient as possible.

The actual details in the coding of this division will be shown in Chapter 7.

GENERAL EFFICIENCY TECHNIQUES

Program efficiency is much more critical in an on-line program than in a batch program, and CICS/VS programs should be written to optimize response time.

CICS/VS executes in a virtual-storage environment, and the basic goal of the programmer is to code his program to minimize page faults, which occur when a reference is made to instructions or data that do not currently reside in real storage. When this happens, the page in virtual storage that contains the required instructions or data must be paged into real storage. The more paging occurs, the lower the overall system performance.

Efficiency techniques that are inherent in ANS Cobol will not be discussed because they are best studied in a manual or book that deals mainly with ANS Cobol. There are three areas of consideration in writing on-line application programs that run in a virtual-storage environment.

Locality of Reference

The application program should consistently reference, for relatively long periods of time, instructions and data within a relatively small number of pages compared to the total number of pages in the program. This is implemented in the following techniques:

1. The program should execute in a straight line as much as possible, with no branch logic reference beyond a small range of address space (making it short range). However, routines that are executed only rarely, including error-handling routines, should be separated from the main program code. This is explained further on page 81.

2. Subroutines should be placed as near to the caller (PERFORM statement) as possible. This is explained further on page 83.

3. If possible, try to use XCTL instead of LINK to transfer control to another program.

4. Initialize data as close as possible to its first use. This increases the chance that the page the data resides in will still be in main storage when it is first referenced.

5. Define data in the order it is referenced. Refer to elements within arrays in the order they are stored.

6. Avoid GETMAIN commands if possible.

7. For ANS Cobol programs, avoid using the EXAMINE statement or variable move operations because they expand into subroutine executions.

Working Set

The working set is the number and combination of program pages needed during a given period. The application programmer should make this as small as possible by using the following techniques:

1. Programs should be coded in modules (Cobol sections), which are grouped according to their frequency and/or anticipated time of reference. This is explained further on page 82.

2. Do not tie up main storage awaiting a reply from the terminal operator. This can be avoided by using the pseudoconversational mode of processing.

3. Use the locate-mode input/output feature of file control commands rather than move-mode.

4. Specify constants directly rather than as data variables in working storage.

5. Where possible, avoid using LINK commands because they generate requests for main storage.

Validity of Reference

The program should be able to directly determine the correct page where the wanted data resides. This is implemented in the following techniques:

1. Avoid long searches for data.

2. Use data structures that can be addressed directly, such as arrays, rather than structures that must be searched, such as chains.

3. Avoid indirect addressing and any method that simulates indirect addressing.

ANS COBOL TRANSLATOR OPTIONS

The translator options are specified in the CBL card to control options in the command-language translator. For OS/VS, options may also be specified in the EXEC job control statement that invokes the translator. If both methods are used, the last specification for each option takes precedence. The options are:

1. DEBUG/*NODEBUG*. This specifies whether or not the translator is to pass the translator line number to CICS/VS to be displayed by the Execution Diagnostic Facility (EDF).* The default is NODEBUG.

2. FE. The bit pattern corresponding to the first argument of the CALL statement that is generated by the translator is printed in hexadecimal notation. The bit pattern has the encoded message that the Execute Interface program uses to determine which functions (on-line service) are required and which options are specified. With this option, all diagnostic messages are listed regardless of the FLAG option.

3. FLAGI/*FLAGW*/FLAGE. This specifies the diagnostics the translator will list. FLAGI allows all severity levels to print;

---

*This is the interactive application program debugging feature and will not be explained in the book.

FLAGW allows severity levels W, C, E, and D to print; FLAGE allows severity levels C, E, and D to print. The default is FLAGW.

4. *LIST*/NOLIST (DOS/VS only). LIST will produce a listing of the ANS Cobol input to the translator. The default is LIST.

5. NOSPIE. This prevents the translator from trapping unrecoverable errors; instead, a dump is produced.

6. NUM/*NONUM*. This specifies whether or not the translator is to use the line numbers appearing in columns 1 through 6 of the card, in the diagnostic messages and cross-reference listing. If NUM is not specified, the translator uses its own line numbers. NONUM is the default.

7. OPT/NOOPT. This specifies whether or not the translator is to generate SERVICE RELOAD statements to address the Execute Interface Block and the DFHCOMMAREA. The default is OPT for OS/VS and NOOPT for DOS/VS. The same value for this option must be specified for the translator and the compiler.

8. QUOTE/*APOST*. QUOTE specifies to the translator that double quotation marks (") should be accepted as the character to delineate literals; APOST specifies that the apostrophe character (') be used instead. The default is APOST and the same value for this option must be specified for the translator and the compiler.

9. *SEQ*/NOSEQ. This specifies whether or not the translator is to check for the sequence of source statements. If SEQ is specified and a statement is not in sequence, it is flagged. The default is SEQ.

10. *SOURCE*/NOSOURCE. This specifies whether or not the translator will produce a listing of the source program. The default is SOURCE.

11. *SPACE1*/SPACE2/SPACE3. This specifies the spacing to be used in the output listing: SPACE1 will produce single spacing; SPACE2 double spacing; SPACE3 triple spacing. The default is SPACE1.

12. XREF/*NOXREF.* This specifies whether or not the translator will produce a cross-reference list of all CICS/VS commands in the input. The default is NOXREF.

ANS COBOL LIMITATIONS

ANS Cobol programs written to execute in CICS/VS cannot use the following features:

1. ENVIRONMENT DIVISION and DATA DIVISION entries normally associated with data management;

2. FILE SECTION of the DATA DIVISION;

3. These special features: ACCEPT, DISPLAY, EXHIBIT, REPORT WRITER, SEGMENTATION, SORT, TRACE, and UNSTRING. For OS/VS, any feature that requires an OS/VS GETMAIN;

4. Options that require the use of Operating System services: COUNT, FLOW, STATE, STXIT, or SYMDMP for DOS/VS; COUNT, ENDJOB, FLOW, DYNAM, STATE, SYMDUMP, SYST, or TEST for OS/VS;

5. ANS COBOL statements: READ, WRITE, OPEN, and CLOSE;

6. The optimization feature option of the DOS ANS Cobol V3 compiler;

7. The link-editing of separate ANS Cobol routines.

The Linkage Section

INTRODUCTION

As mentioned before, the commands for CICS/VS services are translated into MOVE statements and a CALL statement* to the Executive Interface program. The Executive Interface program then "calls" the CICS/VS control programs that provide the service. To conserve main storage, which is shared by many tasks, the information transmitted by these services should not be sent to permanently assigned storage locations (that is, to working storage) but to main storage acquired for them only when they require it. These main storage locations are therefore not part of the program; the format of the data corresponding to them is defined in the LINKAGE section. In a single execution of the program, only part of the LINKAGE section will require main storage, and those that do will not require it at the same time. For instance, to display data, the programmer may code as shown in Figure 6.1.

MAP1-AREA is the 01 entry that is the symbolic description map defined in the LINKAGE section that defines the displayed data. It is advisable to issue an EJECT statement before this section.

THE EXECUTE INTERFACE BLOCK

Actually, the Execute Interface Block is automatically generated by the command-language translator and is placed as the first entry of the LINKAGE section. The programmer may access this block to get information like the terminal identification of the terminal being used, the transaction identifier that initiated the task, the date the

---

*This is the case for ANS Cobol. In PL/I, each command is replaced by a single CALL statement. In Assembler, each command is replaced by the DFHEICAL macro, which expands (during Assembly) into a system-standard sequence.

```
01010                         EXEC CICS
01011                              SEND MAP    ('GRCHM01')
01012                                   MAPSET ('ORCHS01')
01013                                   FROM   (MAP1-AREA)
01014                                   DATAONLY
01015                         END-EXEC.
```

Fig. 6.1. Command To Display Data On A Terminal. Note that MAP1-AREA is an entry in the LINKAGE section.

task was initiated, the results of the last command executed, etc. For instance, he may use the terminal identification and transaction identifier as the key of a temporary storage record. The date can be used when generating journal records; and the results of the last executed command can be used for debugging.

CICS/VS automatically updates certain fields of this block when the task is initiated and after each command is executed. The Execute Interface Block is shown in Figure 6.2.

```
00139           LINKAGE SECTION.
00140           01   DFHEIBLK COPY DFHEIBLK.
00141 C         *      EIBLK EXEC INTERFACE BLOCK
00142 C         01   DFHEIBLK.
00143 C         *      EIBTIME      TIME IN 0HHMMSS FORMAT
00144 C                02 EIBTIME   PICTURE S9(7) USAGE COMPUTATIONAL-3.
00145 C         *      EIBDATE      DATE IN 00YYDDD FORMAT
00146 C                02 EIBDATE   PICTURE S9(7) USAGE COMPUTATIONAL-3.
00147 C         *      EIBTRNID     TRANSACTION IDENTIFIER
00148 C                02 EIBTRNID  PICTURE X(4).
00149 C         *      EIBTASKN     TASK NUMBER
00150 C                02 EIBTASKN  PICTURE S9(7) USAGE COMPUTATIONAL-3.
00151 C         *      EIBTRMID     TERMINAL IDENTIFIER
00152 C                02 EIBTRMID  PICTURE X(4).
00153 C         *      DFHEIGDI     RESERVED
00154 C                02 DFHEIGDI  PICTURE S9(4) USAGE COMPUTATIONAL.
00155 C         *      EIBCPOSN     CURSOR POSITION
00156 C                02 EIBCPOSN  PICTURE S9(4) USAGE COMPUTATIONAL.
00157 C         *      EIBCALEN     COMMAREA LENGTH
00158 C                02 EIBCALEN  PICTURE S9(4) USAGE COMPUTATIONAL.
00159 C         *      EIBAID       ATTENTION IDENTIFIER
00160 C                02 EIBAID    PICTURE X(1).
00161 C         *      EIBFN        FUNCTION CODE
00162 C                02 EIBFN     PICTURE X(2).
00163 C         *      EIBRCODE     RESPONSE CODE
00164 C                02 EIBRCODE  PICTURE X(6).
00165 C         *      EIBDS        DATASET NAME
00166 C                02 EIBDS     PICTURE X(8).


    6           ORDL01A         13.28.44         08/02/80


00167 C         *      EIBREQID     REQUEST IDENTIFIER
00168 C                02 EIBREQID  PICTURE X(8).
```

Fig. 6.2. The Execute Interface Block.

The following are the fields of the Execute Interface Block:

1. EIBTIME. This contains the time the task was initiated and is updated when the task is initiated. It may also be updated by the programmer with the ASKTIME command.

2. EIBDATE. This contains the date the task was initiated and is updated when the task is initiated. It may also be updated by the programmer with the ASKTIME command.

3. EIBTRNID. This contains the transaction identifier and is updated when the task is initiated.

4. EIBTASKN. This contains the task number assigned to the task by CICS/VS and is the same number that appears in trace-table entries generated while the task is in control.

5. EIBTRMID. This field contains the symbolic terminal identifier of the terminal or the logical unit associated with the task. It is updated when the task is initiated.

6. EIBPOSN. This contains the cursor address (position) associated with the last terminal control or BMS input operation from a display device such as the 3270.

7. EIBCALEN. This contains the length of the communication area passed to the application program from the previous application program. If no communication area was passed, this field contains zeroes. This field is updated when the program first executes within a task.

8. EIBAID. This contains the attention identifier code associated with the last terminal control or BMS input operation from a display device such as the 3270. This field may be compared against the standard attention identifier list (DFHAID) to check which key the operator used to initiate the terminal control or BMS input operation.

9. EIBFN. This contains a code that identifies the last CICS/VS command issued by the task. This field is updated when the service(s) corresponding to the command has been completed, whether or not an error occured. This field

can be used for debugging programs that have been aborted and any time a dump is requested.

10. EIBRCODE. This contains the CICS/VS response code returned after the service(s) corresponding to the command has been completed. Almost all of the information in this field may be used in the HANDLE CONDITION command. This field can also be used in debugging when a program is aborted and any time a dump is requested.

11. EIBDS. This contains the symbolic identifier of the last file used in a File Control command.

12. EIBREQID. This contains the request identifier assigned by CICS/VS to certain Interval Control commands; it is not used if a request identifier is specified in the command.

DFHCOMMAREA

We mentioned before that the communication area sent by a program is coded in the WORKING-STORAGE section. This communication area, as received by the program invoked (XCTL or LINK command) or the first program that executes on the next task associated with the same terminal (RETURN), is the first programmer-defined entry in the LINKAGE section.

This is the DFHCOMMAREA field and we will use the first byte of the field as a switch to control the pseudoconversational mode of processing. A one-byte DFHCOMMAREA field is actually generated by the command-language translator if not defined by the programmer.

An example of this field is shown in Figure 6.3.

You will note that we are using condition-names for the switch; also, SKIP statements are used to improve the readability of the program.

THE LINKAGE POINTERS

The linkage pointers, known as base locators for linkage (BLL), are the next entries coded by the programmer, and their function is to

```
00059               LINKAGE SECTION.
00060               01  DFHCOMMAREA.
00061                   SKIP1
00062                   05  PROCESS-SW              PIC X.
00063                       88  INITIAL-ENTRY-TIME          VALUE '0'.
00064                       88  ORDER-VALIDATION-TIME       VALUE '1'.
```

Fig. 6.3. The DFHCOMMAREA entry.

point to succeeding 01-level entries. Each pointer is a binary fullword and appears in the same sequence as the 01-level entry it points to. Therefore, if the program has two symbolic description maps, an order master file, a Transaction Work Area, and a Temporary Storage area, the LINKAGE section will be as shown in Figure 6.4.

The correspondence between the linkage pointers and the 01-level entries are shown by the arrows. Note also that there is a FILLER fullword in front of the linkage pointers and this is used by CICS/VS to provide addressability to the linkage pointers.

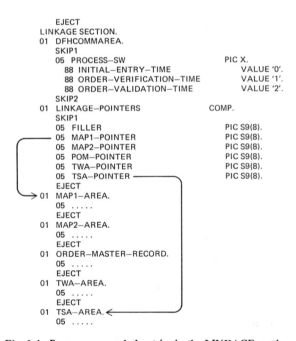

```
          EJECT
          LINKAGE SECTION.
          01  DFHCOMMAREA.
              SKIP1
              05  PROCESS-SW                    PIC X.
                  88 INITIAL-ENTRY-TIME              VALUE '0'.
                  88 ORDER-VERIFICATION-TIME         VALUE '1'.
                  88 ORDER-VALIDATION-TIME           VALUE '2'.
              SKIP2
          01  LINKAGE-POINTERS                  COMP.
              SKIP1
              05  FILLER                        PIC S9(8).
              05  MAP1-POINTER                  PIC S9(8).
              05  MAP2-POINTER                  PIC S9(8).
              05  POM-POINTER                   PIC S9(8).
              05  TWA-POINTER                   PIC S9(8).
              05  TSA-POINTER                   PIC S9(8).
              EJECT
          01  MAP1-AREA.
              05  .....
              EJECT
          01  MAP2-AREA.
              05  .....
              EJECT
          01  ORDER-MASTER-RECORD.
              05  .....
              EJECT
          01  TWA-AREA.
              05  .....
              EJECT
          01  TSA-AREA.
              05  .....
```

Fig. 6.4. Programmer-coded entries in the LINKAGE section.

These pointers are specified in input commands, for instance, to read data from a terminal, a file, Temporary Storage, Transient Storage, etc. For instance, to read in data from a terminal that has the first screen layout, the programmer may code:

```
EXEC CICS
        RECEIVE MAP      ('ORCHM01')
                 MAPSET ('ORCHS01')
                 SET      (MAP1-POINTER)
        END-EXEC.
```

When this command is executed, CICS/VS will, among other things, secure main storage for the area corresponding to MAP1–POINTER (MAP1–AREA in Fig. 6.4) and establish addressability to the area so it can be used in the application program. This method of using pointers to gain access to the corresponding main storage in an input command is known as the locate-mode method and will be the one used in this book.

To improve the readability of this section, I would suggest that in addition to the EJECT statement at the beginning of the section, the programmer should code a SKIP2 statement before the linkage pointers and an EJECT statement before each 01-level entry that corresponds to the pointers. See Figure 6.4.

Actually, this one-to-one correspondence between the linkage pointers and the areas they point to is true only if all of the areas are not greater than 4096 bytes. For an area greater than 4096 bytes, additional pointers have to be specified for each additional 4096 bytes or less. For instance, if the order master record has more than 4096 bytes but less than 8192 bytes, the LINKAGE section in Figure 6.4 would have been coded as shown in Figure 6.5.

Two linkage pointers now correspond to one area. Also, since the command actually establishes addressability only to the first 4096 bytes of the area, the programmer has to establish addressability to areas beyond 4096 bytes. This is done by adding 4096 to the first extra pointer, 8192 to the next extra pointer, and so on, right after the input command. For Figure 6.5, we establish addressability to the whole ORDER–MASTER–RECORD by:

```
EXEC CICS
      RECEIVE MAP       ('ORCHM01')
      MAPSET            ('ORCHS01')
      SET               (MAP1-POINTER)
END-EXEC.
ADD 4096 POM-POINTER1  GIVING POM-POINTER 2.
```

THE SYMBOLIC DESCRIPTION MAPS

The symbolic description maps define the fields that correspond to data read from or displayed on terminals. To standardize the sequence of 01 entries, and since most CICS/VS activities are centered on terminal data processing (and thus maps), I suggest that the symbolic description maps be coded right after the linkage pointers.

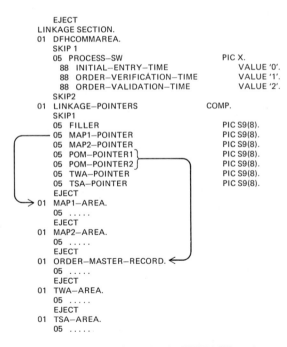

```
      EJECT
LINKAGE SECTION.
01  DFHCOMMAREA.
    SKIP 1
    05  PROCESS-SW                      PIC X.
        88  INITIAL-ENTRY-TIME              VALUE '0'.
        88  ORDER-VERIFICATION-TIME         VALUE '1'.
        88  ORDER-VALIDATION-TIME           VALUE '2'.
    SKIP2
01  LINKAGE-POINTERS                   COMP.
    SKIP1
    05  FILLER                          PIC S9(8).
    05  MAP1-POINTER                    PIC S9(8).
    05  MAP2-POINTER                    PIC S9(8).
    05  POM-POINTER1                    PIC S9(8).
    05  POM-POINTER2                    PIC S9(8).
    05  TWA-POINTER                     PIC S9(8).
    05  TSA-POINTER                     PIC S9(8).
    EJECT
01  MAP1-AREA.
    05  . . . . .
    EJECT
01  MAP2-AREA.
    05  . . . . .
    EJECT
01  ORDER-MASTER-RECORD.
    05  . . . . .
    EJECT
01  TWA-AREA.
    05  . . . . .
    EJECT
01  TSA-AREA.
    05  . . . . .
```

Fig. 6.5. Multiple pointers in the LINKAGE section.

A problem occurs when symbolic description maps are generated. Although correct and acceptable, they are not in the format that structured programs are supposed to be written. For instance, the generated symbolic description map for Fig. 3.1 is shown in Figure 6.6.

You will notice that this is not the best way to code data descriptions in Cobol. You cannot readily determine from the data names what the data contains because the names are not self-documenting. Also, the keyword 'PIC' is best coded near column 40 to align the picture specifications. Therefore, to improve the descriptions, I advise that the programmer modify them as shown in Fig. 6.7.

You will now notice that this is an improved version of Fig. 6.6 and the lines are easier to interpret.

If your installation has on-line program development facilities (you probably do since you already have on-line facilities anyway), then the changes can be made very easily. Otherwise, you may have to make a new set of descriptions based on the generated symbolic description map, the screen layout, or the map program.

The guide for modifying or creating a symbolic description map is as follows:

1. Only fields defined with labels in the map program will have entries in the symbolic description map.

2. The first entry in the symbolic description map is a 12-byte FILLER that is used by CICS/VS. This is generated by the TIOAPFX=YES operand in the first macro.

3. Each macro that generates entries will have three entries generated. These are:
   a. A binary halfword length field. I suggest that the data name used be identical to that of the data field but with an '-L' suffix.
   b. A one-byte attribute field. I suggest that the data name used be identical to that of the data field but with an '-A' suffix.
   c. The data field itself, which will contain the data read from or displayed on the terminal.

```
01   URIQMO1I.
     02  FILLER PIC X(12).
     02  DUMMYL     COMP  PIC  S9(4).
     02  DUMMYF     PICTURE X.
     02  FILLER REDEFINES DUMMYF.
         03  DUMMYA     PICTURE X.
     02  DUMMYI  PIC X(1).
     02  ORDERL     COMP  PIC  S9(4).
     02  ORDERF     PICTURE X.
     C2  FILLER REDEFINES ORDERF.
         03  ORDERA     PICTURE X.
     02  ORDERI  PIC X(10).
     02  DEPTL      COMP  PIC  S9(4).
     02  DEPTF      PICTURE X.
     02  FILLER REDEFINES DEPTF.
         03  DEPTA      PICTURE X.
     02  DEPTI  PIC X(3).
     02  DATEORL    COMP  PIC  S9(4).
     02  DATEORF    PICTURE X.
     02  FILLER REDEFINES DATEORF.
         03  DATEORA    PICTURE X.
     C2  DATEORI  PIC X(6).
     02  DATEENTL   COMP  PIC  S9(4).
     C2  DATEENTF   PICTURE X.
     02  FILLER REDEFINES DATEENTF.
         03  DATEENTA   PICTURE X.
     02  DATEENTI  PIC X(6).
     C2  TOTCOSTL   COMP  PIC  S9(4).
     02  TOTCOSTF   PICTURE X.
     02  FILLER REDEFINES TOTCOSTF.
         03  TOTCOSTA   PICTURE X.
     C2  TOTCOSTI  PIC X(12).
     02  TOTPRCEL   COMP  PIC  S9(4).
     02  TOTPRCEF   PICTURE X.
     02  FILLER REDEFINES TOTPRCEF.
         03  TOTPRCEA   PICTURE X.
     02  TOTPRCEI  PIC X(12).
     02  LINE1L     COMP  PIC  S9(4).
     02  LINE1F     PICTURE X.
     02  FILLER REDEFINES LINE1F.
         03  LINE1A     PICTURE X.
     02  LINE1I  PIC X(1).
     02  ITEM1L     COMP  PIC  S9(4).
     02  ITEM1F     PICTURE X.
     02  FILLER REDEFINES ITEM1F.
         03  ITEM1A     PICTURE X.
     C2  ITEM1I  PIC 99999999.
     02  DESC1L     COMP  PIC  S9(4).
     02  DESC1F     PICTURE X.
     C2  FILLER REDEFINES DESC1F.
         03  DESC1A     PICTURE X.
     02  DESC1I  PIC X(19).
     C2  LNDATE1L   COMP  PIC  S9(4).
     02  LNDATE1F   PICTURE X.
     02  FILLER REDEFINES LNDATE1F.
         03  LNDATE1A    PICTURE X.
```

Fig. 6.6. The Symbolic Description Map As Generated From The Map Program. Compare This To Fig. 6.7.

```
02  LNDATE1I  PIC X(6).
02  UNIT1L    COMP PIC  S9(4).
02  UNIT1F    PICTURE X.
02  FILLER REDEFINES UNIT1F.
   03  UNIT1A    PICTURE X.
02  UNIT1I  PIC 99999.
02  UCOST1L    COMP PIC  S9(4).
02  UCOST1F    PICTURE X.
02  FILLER REDEFINES UCOST1F.
   03  UCOST1A    PICTURE X.
02  UCOST1I  PIC 9999999.
02  COST1L    COMP PIC  S9(4).
02  COST1F    PICTURE X.
02  FILLER REDEFINES COST1F.
   03  COST1A    PICTURE X.
02  COST1I  PIC 99999999.
02  UPRICE1L    COMP PIC  S9(4).
02  UPRICE1F    PICTURE X.
02  FILLER REDEFINES UPRICE1F.
   03  UPRICE1A    PICTURE X.
02  UPRICE1I  PIC 9999999.
02  PRICE1L    COMP PIC  S9(4).
02  PRICE1F    PICTURE X.
02  FILLER REDEFINES PRICE1F.
   03  PRICE1A    PICTURE X.
02  PRICE1I  PIC 99999999.
02  LINE2L    COMP PIC  S9(4).
02  LINE2F    PICTURE X.
02  FILLER REDEFINES LINE2F.
   03  LINE2A    PICTURE X.
02  LINE2I  PIC X(1).
02  ITEM2L    COMP PIC  S9(4).
02  ITEM2F    PICTURE X.
02  FILLER REDEFINES ITEM2F.
   03  ITEM2A    PICTURE X.
02  ITEM2I  PIC 99999999.
02  DESC2L    COMP PIC  S9(4).
02  DESC2F    PICTURE X.
02  FILLER REDEFINES DESC2F.
   03  DESC2A    PICTURE X.
02  DESC2I  PIC X(19).
02  LNDATE2L    COMP PIC  S9(4).
02  LNDATE2F    PICTURE X.
02  FILLER REDEFINES LNDATE2F.
   03  LNDATE2A    PICTURE X.
02  LNDATE2I  PIC X(6).
02  UNIT2L    COMP PIC  S9(4).
02  UNIT2F    PICTURE X.
02  FILLER REDEFINES UNIT2F.
   03  UNIT2A    PICTURE X.
02  UNIT2I  PIC 99999.
02  UCOST2L    COMP PIC  S9(4).
02  UCOST2F    PICTURE X.
02  FILLER REDEFINES UCOST2F.
   03  UCOST2A    PICTURE X.
02  UCOST2I  PIC 9999999.
```

Fig. 6.6. (Continued)

```
02  COST2L    COMP  PIC  S9(4).
02  COST2F    PICTURE X.
02  FILLER REDEFINES COST2F.
   03  COST2A    PICTURE X.
02  COST2I  PIC 99999999.
02  UPRICE2L    COMP  PIC  S9(4).
02  UPRICE2F    PICTURE X.
02  FILLER REDEFINES UPRICE2F.
   03  UPRICE2A    PICTURE X.
02  UPRICE2I  PIC 9999999.
02  PRICE2L    COMP  PIC  S9(4).
02  PRICE2F    PICTURE X.
02  FILLER REDEFINES PRICE2F.
   03  PRICE2A    PICTURE X.
02  PRICE2I  PIC 99999999.
02  LINE3L    COMP  PIC  S9(4).
02  LINE3F    PICTURE X.
02  FILLER REDEFINES LINE3F.
   03  LINE3A    PICTURE X.
02  LINE3I  PIC X(1).
02  ITEM3L    COMP  PIC  S9(4).
02  ITEM3F    PICTURE X.
02  FILLER REDEFINES ITEM3F.
   03  ITEM3A    PICTURE X.
02  ITEM3I  PIC 99999999.
02  DESC3L    COMP  PIC  S9(4).
02  DESC3F    PICTURE X.
02  FILLER REDEFINES DESC3F.
   03  DESC3A    PICTURE X.
02  DESC3I  PIC X(19).
02  LNDATE3L    COMP  PIC  S9(4).
02  LNDATE3F    PICTURE X.
02  FILLER REDEFINES LNDATE3F.
   03  LNDATE3A    PICTURE X.
02  LNDATE3I  PIC X(6).
02  UNIT3L    COMP  PIC  S9(4).
02  UNIT3F    PICTURE X.
02  FILLER REDEFINES UNIT3F.
   03  UNIT3A    PICTURE X.
02  UNIT3I  PIC 99999.
02  UCOST3L    COMP  PIC  S9(4).
02  UCOST3F    PICTURE X.
02  FILLER REDEFINES UCOST3F.
   03  UCOST3A    PICTURE X.
02  UCOST3I  PIC 9999999.
02  COST3L    COMP  PIC  S9(4).
02  COST3F    PICTURE X.
02  FILLER REDEFINES COST3F.
   03  COST3A    PICTURE X.
02  COST3I  PIC 99999999.
02  UPRICE3L    COMP  PIC  S9(4).
02  UPRICE3F    PICTURE X.
02  FILLER REDEFINES UPRICE3F.
   03  UPRICE3A    PICTURE X.
02  UPRICE3I  PIC 9999999.
02  PRICE3L    COMP  PIC  S9(4).
```

Fig. 6.6. (Continued)

```
02  PRICE3F     PICTURE X.
02  FILLER REDEFINES PRICE3F.
 03  PRICE3A     PICTURE X.
02  PRICE3I  PIC 99999999.
02  LINE4L     COMP PIC  S9(4).
02  LINE4F     PICTURE X.
02  FILLER REDEFINES LINE4F.
 03  LINE4A     PICTURE X.
02  LINE4I  PIC X(1).
02  ITEM4L     COMP PIC  S9(4).
02  ITEM4F     PICTURE X.
02  FILLER REDEFINES ITEM4F.
 03  ITEM4A     PICTURE X.
02  ITEM4I  PIC 99999999.
02  DESC4L     COMP PIC  S9(4).
02  DESC4F     PICTURE X.
02  FILLER REDEFINES DESC4F.
 03  DESC4A     PICTURE X.
02  DESC4I  PIC X(19).
02  LNDATE4L     COMP PIC  S9(4).
02  LNDATE4F     PICTURE X.
02  FILLER REDEFINES LNDATE4F.
 03  LNDATE4A     PICTURE X.
02  LNDATE4I  PIC X(6).
02  UNIT4L     COMP PIC  S9(4).
02  UNIT4F     PICTURE X.
02  FILLER REDEFINES UNIT4F.
 03  UNIT4A     PICTURE X.
02  UNIT4I  PIC 99999.
02  UCOST4L     COMP PIC  S9(4).
02  UCOST4F     PICTURE X.
02  FILLER REDEFINES UCOST4F.
 03  UCOST4A     PICTURE X.
02  UCOST4I  PIC 9999999.
02  COST4L     COMP PIC  S9(4).
02  COST4F     PICTURE X.
02  FILLER REDEFINES COST4F.
 03  COST4A     PICTURE X.
02  COST4I  PIC 99999999.
02  UPRICE4L     COMP PIC  S9(4).
02  UPRICE4F     PICTURE X.
02  FILLER REDEFINES UPRICE4F.
 03  UPRICE4A     PICTURE X.
02  UPRICE4I  PIC 9999999.
02  PRICE4L     COMP PIC  S9(4).
02  PRICE4F     PICTURE X.
02  FILLER REDEFINES PRICE4F.
 03  PPICE4A     PICTURE X.
02  PRICE4I  PIC 99999999.
02  LINE5L     COMP PIC  S9(4).
02  LINE5F     PICTURE X.
02  FILLER REDEFINES LINE5F.
 03  LINE5A     PICTURE X.
02  LINE5I  PIC X(1).
02  ITEM5L     COMP PIC  S9(4).
02  ITEM5F     PICTURE X.
```

Fig. 6.6. (Continued)

```
02  FILLER REDEFINES ITEM5F.
 03  ITEM5A     PICTURE X.
02  ITEM5I PIC 99999999.
02  DESC5L     COMP PIC  S9(4).
02  DESC5F     PICTURE X.
02  FILLER REDEFINES DESC5F.
 03  DESC5A     PICTURE X.
02  DESC5I PIC X(19).
02  LNDATE5L     COMP  PIC  S9(4).
02  LNDATE5F     PICTURE X.
02  FILLER REDEFINES LNDATE5F.
 03  LNDATE5A     PICTURE X.
02  LNDATE5I PIC X(6).
02  UNIT5L     COMP PIC  S9(4).
02  UNIT5F     PICTURE X.
02  FILLER REDEFINES UNIT5F.
 03  UNIT5A     PICTURE X.
02  UNIT5I PIC 99999.
02  UCOST5L     COMP PIC  S9(4).
02  UCOST5F     PICTURE X.
02  FILLER REDEFINES UCOST5F.
 03  UCOST5A     PICTURE X.
02  UCOST5I  PIC 9999999.
02  COST5L     COMP PIC  S9(4).
02  COST5F     PICTURE X.
02  FILLER REDEFINES COST5F.
 03  COST5A     PICTURE X.
02  COST5I PIC 99999999.
02  UPRICE5L     COMP PIC  S9(4).
02  UPRICE5F     PICTURE X.
02  FILLER REDEFINES UPRICE5F.
 03  UPRICE5A     PICTURE X.
02  UPRICE5I PIC 9999999.
02  PRICE5L     COMP PIC  S9(4).
02  PRICE5F     PICTURE X.
02  FILLER REDEFINES PRICE5F.
 03  PRICE5A     PICTURE X.
02  PRICE5I PIC 99999999.
02  LINE6L     COMP PIC  S9(4).
02  LINE6F     PICTURE X.
02  FILLER REDEFINES LINE6F.
 03  LINE6A     PICTURE X.
02  LINE6I PIC X(1).
02  ITEM6L     COMP PIC  S9(4).
02  ITEM6F     PICTURE X.
02  FILLER REDEFINES ITEM6F.
 03  ITEM6A     PICTURE X.
02  ITEM6I PIC 99999999.
02  DESC6L     COMP PIC  S9(4).
02  DESC6F     PICTURE X.
02  FILLER REDEFINES DESC6F.
 03  DESC6A     PICTURE X.
02  DESC6I PIC X(19).
02  LNDATE6L     COMP PIC  S9(4).
02  LNDATE6F     PICTURE X.
02  FILLER REDEFINES LNDATE6F.
```

Fig. 6.6. (Continued)

```
    03   LNDATE6A      PICTURE X.
   02   LNDATE6I   PIC X(6).
   02   UNIT6L     COMP   PIC   S9(4).
   02   UNIT6F     PICTURE  X.
   02   FILLER  REDEFINES  UNIT6F.
    03   UNIT6A      PICTURE  X.
   02   UNIT6I   PIC  99999.
   02   UCOST6L      COMP   PIC   S9(4).
   02   UCOST6F      PICTURE  X.
   02   FILLER  REDEFINES  UCOST6F.
    03   UCOST6A      PICTURE  X.
   02   UCOST6I   PIC  9999999.
   02   COST6L     COMP   PIC   S9(4).
   02   COST6F     PICTURE  X.
   02   FILLER  REDEFINES  COST6F.
    03   COST6A      PICTURE  X.
   02   COST6I   PIC  99999999.
   02   UPRICE6L      COMP   PIC   S9(4).
   02   UPRICE6F      PICTURE  X.
   02   FILLER  REDEFINES  UPRICE6F.
    03   UPRICE6A      PICTURE  X.
   02   UPRICE6I   PIC  9999999.
   02   PRICE6L     COMP   PIC   S9(4).
   02   PRICE6F     PICTURE  X.
   02   FILLER  REDEFINES  PRICE6F.
    03   PRICE6A      PICTURE  X.
   02   PRICE6I   PIC  99999999.
   02   LINE7L     COMP   PIC   S9(4).
   02   LINE7F     PICTURE  X.
   02   FILLER  REDEFINES  LINE7F.
    03   LINE7A      PICTURE  X.
   02   LINE7I   PIC  X(1).
   02   ITEM7L     COMP   PIC   S9(4).
   02   ITEM7F     PICTURE  X.
   02   FILLER  REDEFINES  ITEM7F.
    03   ITEM7A      PICTURE  X.
   02   ITEM7I   PIC  99999999.
   02   DESC7L     COMP   PIC   S9(4).
   02   DESC7F     PICTURE  X.
   02   FILLER  REDEFINES  DESC7F.
    03   DESC7A      PICTURE  X.
   02   DESC7I   PIC  X(19).
   02   LNDATE7L      COMP   PIC   S9(4).
   02   LNDATE7F      PICTURE  X.
   02   FILLER  REDEFINES  LNDATE7F.
    03   LNDATE7A      PICTURE  X.
   02   LNDATE7I   PIC  X(6).
   02   UNIT7L     COMP   PIC   S9(4).
   02   UNIT7F     PICTURE  X.
   02   FILLER  REDEFINES  UNIT7F.
    03   UNIT7A      PICTURE  X.
   02   UNIT7I   PIC  99999.
   02   UCOST7L      COMP   PIC   S9(4).
   02   UCOST7F      PICTURE  X.
   02   FILLER  REDEFINES  UCOST7F.
    03   UCOST7A      PICTURE  X.
```

Fig. 6.6. (Continued)

```
02  UCOST7I   PIC 9999999.
02  COST7L    COMP  PIC  S9(4).
02  COST7F    PICTURE X.
02  FILLER REDEFINES COST7F.
   03  COST7A    PICTURE X.
02  COST7I   PIC 99999999.
02  UPRICE7L     COMP  PIC  S9(4).
02  UPRICE7F     PICTURE X.
02  FILLER REDEFINES UPRICE7F.
   03  UPRICE7A     PICTURE X.
02  UPRICE7I  PIC 9999999.
02  PRICE7L   COMP  PIC  S9(4).
02  PRICE7F   PICTURE X.
02  FILLER REDEFINES PRICE7F.
   03  PRICE7A    PICTURE X.
02  PRICE7I  PIC 99999999.
02  LINE8L    COMP  PIC  S9(4).
02  LINE8F    PICTURE X.
02  FILLER REDEFINES LINE8F.
   03  LINE8A    PICTURE X.
02  LINE8I  PIC X(1).
02  ITEM8L    COMP  PIC  S9(4).
02  ITEM8F    PICTURE X.
02  FILLER REDEFINES ITEM8F.
   03  ITEM8A    PICTURE X.
02  ITEM8I   PIC 99999999.
02  DESC8L    COMP  PIC  S9(4).
02  DESC8F    PICTURE X.
02  FILLER REDEFINES DESC8F.
   03  DESC8A    PICTURE X.
02  DESC8I  PIC X(19).
02  LNDATE8L     COMP  PIC  S9(4).
02  LNDATE8F     PICTURE X.
02  FILLER REDEFINES LNDATE8F.
   03  LNDATE8A     PICTURE X.
02  LNDATE8I  PIC X(6).
02  UNIT8L    COMP  PIC  S9(4).
02  UNIT8F    PICTURE X.
02  FILLER REDEFINES UNIT8F.
   03  UNIT8A    PICTURE X.
02  UNIT8I  PIC 99999.
02  UCOST8L    COMP  PIC  S9(4).
02  UCOST8F    PICTURE X.
02  FILLER REDEFINES UCOST8F.
   03  UCOST8A    PICTURE X.
02  UCOST8I  PIC 9999999.
02  COST8L    COMP  PIC  S9(4).
02  COST8F    PICTURE X.
02  FILLER REDEFINES COST8F.
   03  COST8A    PICTURE X.
02  COST8I  PIC 99999999.
02  UPRICE8L     COMP  PIC  S9(4).
02  UPRICE8F     PICTURE X.
02  FILLER REDEFINES UPRICE8F.
   03  UPRICE8A     PICTURE X.
02  UPRICE8I  PIC 9999999.
```

Fig. 6.6. (Continued)

```
02   PRICE8L      COMP  PIC   S9(4).
02   PRICE8F      PICTURE  X.
02   FILLER REDEFINES PRICE8F.
   03   PRICE8A      PICTURE  X.
02   PRICE8I   PIC 99999999.
02   LINE9L       COMP  PIC   S9(4).
02   LINE9F       PICTURE  X.
02   FILLER REDEFINES LINE9F.
   03   LINE9A       PICTURE  X.
02   LINE9I   PIC  X(1).
02   ITEM9L       COMP  PIC   S9(4).
02   ITEM9F       PICTURE  X.
02   FILLER REDEFINES ITEM9F.
   03   ITEM9A       PICTURE  X.
02   ITEM9I   PIC 99999999.
02   DESC9L       COMP  PIC   S9(4).
C2   DESC9F       PICTURE  X.
02   FILLER REDEFINES DESC9F.
   03   DESC9A       PICTURE  X.
C2   DESC9I   PIC  X(19).
02   LNDATE9L      COMP  PIC   S9(4).
02   LNDATE9F      PICTURE  X.
02   FILLER REDEFINES LNDATE9F.
   03   LNDATE9A      PICTURE  X.
02   LNDATE9I   PIC  X(6).
02   UNIT9L       COMP  PIC   S9(4).
02   UNIT9F       PICTURE  X.
C2   FILLER REDEFINES UNIT9F.
   03   UNIT9A       PICTURE  X.
02   UNIT9I   PIC 99999.
C2   UCOST9L      COMP  PIC   S9(4).
02   UCOST9F      PICTURE  X.
02   FILLER REDEFINES UCOST9F.
   03   UCOST9A      PICTURE  X.
C2   UCOST9I   PIC 9999999.
02   COST9L       COMP  PIC   S9(4).
C2   COST9F       PICTURE  X.
C2   FILLER REDEFINES COST9F.
   03   COST9A       PICTURE  X.
02   COST9I   PIC 99999999.
02   UPRICE9L     COMP  PIC   S9(4).
02   UPRICE9F     PICTURE  X.
02   FILLER REDEFINES UPRICE9F.
   03   UPRICE9A      PICTURE  X.
C2   UPRICE9I   PIC 9999999.
02   PRICE9L      COMP  PIC   S9(4).
02   PRICE9F      PICTURE  X.
02   FILLER REDEFINES PRICE9F.
   03   PRICE9A      PICTURE  X.
02   PRICE9I   PIC 99999999.
02   ERRORL       COMP  PIC   S9(4).
02   ERRORF       PICTURE  X.
02   FILLER REDEFINES ERRORF.
   03   ERRORA       PICTURE  X.
02   ERRORI   PIC  X(20).
01   ORIQM01O REDEFINES ORIQM01I.
```

Fig. 6.6. (Continued)

```
02   FILLER PIC X(12).
02   FILLER PICTURE X(3).
02   DUMMYO  PIC X(1).
02   FILLER PICTURE X(3).
02   ORDERO  PIC X(10).
02   FILLER PICTURE X(3).
02   DEPTO   PIC X(3).
02   FILLER PICTURE X(3).
02   DATEORO  PIC X(6).
02   FILLER PICTURE X(3).
02   DATEENTO  PIC X(6).
02   FILLER PICTURE X(3).
02   TOTCOSTO  PIC Z,ZZZ,ZZZ.99.
02   FILLER PICTURE X(3).
02   TOTPRCEO  PIC Z,ZZZ,ZZZ.99.
02   FILLER PICTURE X(3).
02   LINE10  PIC X(1).
02   FILLER PICTURE X(3).
02   ITEM10  PIC 99999999.
02   FILLER PICTURE X(3).
02   DESC10  PIC X(19).
02   FILLER PICTURE X(3).
02   LNDATE10  PIC X(6).
02   FILLER PICTURE X(3).
02   UNIT10  PIC 99999.
02   FILLER PICTURE X(3).
02   UCOST10  PIC 9999999.
02   FILLER PICTURE X(3).
02   COST10  PIC 99999999.
02   FILLER PICTURE X(3).
02   UPRICE10  PIC 9999999.
02   FILLER PICTURE X(3).
02   PRICE10  PIC 99999999.
02   FILLER PICTURE X(3).
02   LINE20  PIC X(1).
02   FILLER PICTURE X(3).
02   ITEM20  PIC 99999999.
02   FILLER PICTURE X(3).
02   DESC20  PIC X(19).
02   FILLER PICTURE X(3).
02   LNDATE20  PIC X(6).
02   FILLER PICTURE X(3).
02   UNIT20  PIC 99999.
02   FILLER PICTURE X(3).
02   UCOST20  PIC 9999999.
02   FILLER PICTURE X(3).
02   COST20  PIC 99999999.
02   FILLER PICTURE X(3).
02   UPRICE20  PIC 9999999.
02   FILLER PICTURE X(3).
02   PRICE20  PIC 99999999.
02   FILLER PICTURE X(3).
02   LINE30  PIC X(1).
02   FILLER PICTURE X(3).
02   ITEM30  PIC 99999999.
02   FILLER PICTURE X(3).
```

Fig. 6.6. (Continued)

```
02   DESC30   PIC X(19).
02   FILLER PICTURE X(3).
02   LNDATE30   PIC X(6).
02   FILLER PICTURE X(3).
02   UNIT30   PIC 99999.
02   FILLER PICTURE X(3).
02   UCOST30   PIC 9999999.
02   FILLER PICTURE X(3).
02   COST30   PIC 99999999.
02   FILLER PICTURE X(3).
02   UPRICE30   PIC 9999999.
02   FILLER PICTURE X(3).
02   PRICE30   PIC 99999999.
02   FILLER PICTURE X(3).
02   LINE40   PIC X(1).
02   FILLER PICTURE X(3).
02   ITEM40   PIC 99999999.
02   FILLER PICTURE X(3).
02   DESC40   PIC X(19).
02   FILLER PICTURE X(3).
02   LNDATE40   PIC X(6).
02   FILLER PICTURE X(3).
02   UNIT40   PIC 99999.
02   FILLER PICTURE X(3).
02   UCOST40   PIC 9999999.
02   FILLER PICTURE X(3).
02   COST40   PIC 99999999.
02   FILLER PICTURE X(3).
02   UPRICE40   PIC 9999999.
02   FILLER PICTURE X(3).
02   PRICE40   PIC 99999999.
02   FILLER PICTURE X(3).
02   LINE50   PIC X(1).
02   FILLER PICTURE X(3).
02   ITEM50   PIC 99999999.
02   FILLER PICTURE X(3).
02   DESC50   PIC X(19).
02   FILLER PICTURE X(3).
02   LNDATE50   PIC X(6).
02   FILLER PICTURE X(3).
02   UNIT50   PIC 99999.
02   FILLER PICTURE X(3).
02   UCOST50   PIC 9999999.
02   FILLER PICTURE X(3).
02   COST50   PIC 99999999.
02   FILLER PICTURE X(3).
02   UPRICE50   PIC 9999999.
02   FILLER PICTURE X(3).
02   PRICE50   PIC 99999999.
02   FILLER PICTURE X(3).
02   LINE60   PIC X(1).
02   FILLER PICTURE X(3).
02   ITEM60   PIC 99999999.
02   FILLER PICTURE X(3).
02   DESC60   PIC X(19).
02   FILLER PICTURE X(3).
```

Fig. 6.6. (Continued)

```
02   LNDATE60   PIC X(6).
02   FILLER PICTURE X(3).
02   UNIT60   PIC 99999.
02   FILLER PICTURE X(3).
02   UCOST60   PIC 9999999.
02   FILLER PICTURE X(3).
02   COST60   PIC 99999999.
02   FILLER PICTURE X(3).
02   UPRICE60   PIC 9999999.
02   FILLER PICTURE X(3).
02   PRICE60   PIC 99999999.
02   FILLER PICTURE X(3).
02   LINE70   PIC X(1).
02   FILLER PICTURE X(3).
02   ITEM70   PIC 99999999.
02   FILLER PICTURE X(3).
02   DESC70   PIC X(19).
02   FILLER PICTURE X(3).
02   LNDATE70   PIC X(6).
02   FILLER PICTURE X(3).
02   UNIT70   PIC 99999.
02   FILLER PICTURE X(3).
02   UCOST70   PIC 9999999.
02   FILLER PICTURE X(3).
02   COST70   PIC 99999999.
02   FILLER PICTURE X(3).
02   UPRICE70   PIC 9999999.
02   FILLER PICTURE X(3).
02   PRICE70   PIC 99999999.
02   FILLER PICTURE X(3).
02   LINE80   PIC X(1).
02   FILLER PICTURE X(3).
02   ITEM80   PIC 99999999.
02   FILLER PICTURE X(3).
02   DESC80   PIC X(19).
02   FILLER PICTURE X(3).
02   LNDATE80   PIC X(6).
02   FILLER PICTURE X(3).
02   UNIT80   PIC 99999.
02   FILLER PICTURE X(3).
02   UCOST80   PIC 9999999.
02   FILLER PICTURE X(3).
02   COST80   PIC 99999999.
02   FILLER PICTURE X(3).
02   UPRICE80   PIC 9999999.
02   FILLER PICTURE X(3).
02   PRICE80   PIC 99999999.
02   FILLER PICTURE X(3).
02   LINE90   PIC X(1).
02   FILLER PICTURE X(3).
02   ITEM90   PIC 99999999.
02   FILLER PICTURE X(3).
02   DESC90   PIC X(19).
02   FILLER PICTURE X(3).
02   LNDATE90   PIC X(6).
02   FILLER PICTURE X(3).
```

Fig. 6.6. (Continued)

```
00109          ***************************************************************
00110          *                                                             *
00111          *               DISPLAY MAP DESCRIPTION                       *
00112          *                                                             *
00113          ***************************************************************


00115          01   MAP1-AREA.
00116               05   FILLER                        PIC X(12).
00117               05   MAP1-DUMMY-L                  PIC S9999 COMP.
00118               05   MAP1-DUMMY-A                  PIC X.
00119               05   MAP1-DUMMY                    PIC X.
00120               05   MAP1-ORDER-NUMBER-L           PIC S9999 COMP.
00121               05   MAP1-ORDER-NUMBER-A           PIC X.
00122               05   MAP1-ORDER-NUMBER             PIC X(10).
00123               05   MAP1-DEPARTMENT-L             PIC S9999 COMP.
00124               05   MAP1-DEPARTMENT-A             PIC X.
00125               05   MAP1-DEPARTMENT               PIC XXX.
00126               05   MAP1-ORDER-DATE-L             PIC S9999 COMP.
00127               05   MAP1-ORDER-DATE-A             PIC X.
00128               05   MAP1-ORDER-DATE.
00129                    10   MAP1-ORDER-DATE-MONTH    PIC XX.
00130                    10   MAP1-ORDER-DATE-DAY      PIC XX.
00131                    10   MAP1-ORDER-DATE-YEAR     PIC XX.
00132               05   MAP1-ORDER-DATE-ENTERED-L     PIC S9999 COMP.
00133               05   MAP1-ORDER-DATE-ENTERED-A     PIC X.
00134               05   MAP1-ORDER-DATE-ENTERED       PIC X(6).
00135               05   MAP1-TOTAL-COST-L             PIC S9999 COMP.
00136               05   MAP1-TOTAL-COST-A             PIC X.
00137               05   MAP1-TOTAL-COST               PIC Z,ZZZ,ZZZ.99.
00138               05   MAP1-TOTAL-PRICE-L            PIC S9999 COMP.
00139               05   MAP1-TOTAL-PRICE-A            PIC X.
00140               05   MAP1-TOTAL-PRICE              PIC Z,ZZZ,ZZZ.99.
00141               05   MAP1-LINE-ITEM                OCCURS 9
00142                                                  INDEXED BY MAP1-LINE-I.
00143                    10   MAP1-LINE-NUMBER-L       PIC S9999 COMP.
00144                    10   MAP1-LINE-NUMBER-A       PIC X.
00145                    10   MAP1-LINE-NUMBER         PIC 9.
00146                    10   MAP1-ITEM-NUMBER-L       PIC S9999 COMP.
00147                    10   MAP1-ITEM-NUMBER-A       PIC X.
00148                    10   MAP1-ITEM-NUMBER         PIC 9(8).
00149                    10   MAP1-ITEM-DESCRIPTION-L  PIC S9999 COMP.
00150                    10   MAP1-ITEM-DESCRIPTION-A  PIC X.
00151                    10   MAP1-ITEM-DESCRIPTION    PIC X(19).
00152                    10   MAP1-ITEM-DATE-L         PIC S9999 COMP.
00153                    10   MAP1-ITEM-DATE-A         PIC X.
00154                    10   MAP1-ITEM-DATE           PIC X(6).
00155                    10   MAP1-UNIT-L              PIC S9999 COMP.
00156                    10   MAP1-UNIT-A              PIC X.
00157                    10   MAP1-UNIT                PIC 9(5).
00158                    10   MAP1-UNIT-COST-L         PIC S9999 COMP.
00159                    10   MAP1-UNIT-COST-A         PIC X.
```

Fig. 6.7. The Symbolic Description Map of Fig. 6.6 As Modified By Programmer.

```
00160          10   MAP1-UNIT-COST          PIC 9(7).
00161          10   MAP1-COST-L             PIC S9999 COMP.
00162          10   MAP1-COST-A             PIC X.
00163          10   MAP1-COST               PIC 9(8).
00164          10   MAP1-UNIT-PRICE-L       PIC S9999 COMP.
00165          10   MAP1-UNIT-PRICE-A       PIC X.
00166          10   MAP1-UNIT-PRICE         PIC 9(7).
00167          10   MAP1-PRICE-L            PIC S9999 COMP.
00168          10   MAP1-PRICE-A            PIC X.
00169          10   MAP1-PRICE              PIC 9(8).
00170       05      MAP1-ERROR-L            PIC S9999 COMP.
00171       05      MAP1-ERROR-A            PIC X.
00172       05      MAP1-ERROR              PIC X(20).
```

Fig. 6.7. (Continued)

THE FILE DESCRIPTIONS

The file-record descriptions (including those for journal records) are actually coded just like those in batch processing. These descriptions are best placed in the source statement library so that they may be copied into the program at compilation time.

THE TRANSACTION WORK AREA

The Transaction Work Area is part of the Task Control Area. It is used for work areas (counters, switches, temporary areas) that are used within the task but that do not have to be saved during the series of terminal inputs and outputs in pseudoconversational mode of processing. The programmer should understand that the values of the fields in this area must be set within the task because all values are set to binary zeroes when this area is acquired at the time the task is initiated.

With the command-level feature, the CICS/VS programmer can code his work areas in the WORKING-STORAGE section* rather than in the Transaction Work Area. This is because each task gets its own copy of the WORKING-STORAGE section while a Transaction Work Area is secured at the start of a task and is also unique for a task. However, since the Transaction Work Area is part of the Task

---

*For macro-level programmers, the WORKING-STORAGE section is common to many tasks using the same program so data that has been changed will have to be restored before the task is suspended to maintain quasi-reentrancy. Programmers can avoid this by using the Transaction Work Area, leaving working storage for fixed data.

Control Area, which is already used by CICS/VS, it is inherently more efficient to put data here since it belongs to a block that is already being used rather than in working storage, which is in a different block.

OTHER AREAS

The Temporary Storage Area, Common Work Area, Transient Data Area, and Terminal Control Table User Area are also defined in the LINKAGE section. The programmer may also define additional areas here, especially if the areas are seldom used in the application program so that main storage will be used for them only when they require it.

7

The Procedure Division

INTRODUCTION

The most important consideration in coding the PROCEDURE DIVISION for an on-line program that executes in a virtual-storage environment is how to write it in the most efficient way possible. The heavy use of efficiency techniques, while making the source code less "structured," does not, however, make it less understandable since CICS/VS programs are by nature modular. On each execution of the program in pseudoconversational mode, only one section of the program is used and its logic is straightforward, for instance, read in data entered by the operator, validate it, then use it to update a file.

We showed before the general efficiency techniques needed to accomplish this goal. Some of those techniques will be explained more fully here. Before we do so, let us mention one efficiency technique that is important because of multitasking. This is the SUSPEND command and is explained on page 163.

PSEUDOCONVERSATIONAL MODE

One efficiency technique is the freeing of system resources (especially main storage) while awaiting a reply from a terminal user. This is implemented through the pseudoconversational mode of processing. The task is terminated just before the operator enters data on the terminal so all resources taken by the task will be released.* This is accomplished in the following steps:

At The Beginning of The Session

1. The operator enters a transaction identifier that corresponds to the application program he needs.

---

*The programmer may save necessary data in temporary storage.

2. He hits the ENTER key or any PF key.

3. A task is initiated and the transaction identifier is validated by Task Control in the Program Control Table and if valid, Program Control will load the corresponding application program from virtual storage into main storage if it is not yet there.

4. The task is placed in the wait queue. At some point, it will gain control to execute the initial routines (load in a table, get temporary storage if required, etc.).

5. The program displays on the terminal the first map to be used by the operator.

6. The program issues the command to terminate the task. The command will include a temporary transaction identifier, which will be the next one used in the same terminal. Also included is a communication area switch* that will determine the section of the program that will execute the next time.

At this point, the task is terminated and the operator enters data on the terminal, the format controlled by the map specified in the command in step 5.

At Other Times During The Session

1. The operator finishes entering data on the terminal.

2. He hits the ENTER key or any PF or PA keys.

3. A task is initiated and the transaction identifier sent by the previous task on the same terminal is validated by Task Control in the Program Control Table. If valid, Program Control will load the corresponding program into main storage if it is not yet there. The program to be used is usually the same as the one that sent the transaction identifier. On the ENTER key or any PF key, Terminal Control reads the data into the Terminal Input/Output Area (TIOA).

---

*This is my technique. See page 86 for variations.

4. The task is placed in the wait queue. At some point, it will gain control to execute the appropriate section as determined by the value of the communication area switch sent by the previous task on the same terminal.

5. The section issues the command to read the data from the TIOA into the area defined by the symbolic description map.

6. The program processes the data.

7. The program displays the next map to be used by the operator.

8. The program issues the command to terminate the task. This command will likewise include a transaction identifier and a communication area switch.

STRAIGHT LINE CODING

Writing a program so that there is as much straight-line coding as possible with no branch logic reference beyond a small range of address space (thus short-range) is another major efficiency technique. We implement this in CICS/VS application programs in two ways: first, by making the overall logic modular; second, by coding each section to make the logic execute in as much of a straight-line as possible.

Overall Program Design

The best way to modularize the overall program logic is to have the Main Line of the program control other sections in the program, each section being a specific initiation of the program to implement the pseudoconversational mode of processing. The diagram for this is shown in Figure 7.1.

When the task is initiated, control goes to the MAIN-LINE section, which will then select the next section to be executed. Each of these sections have the following general characteristics:

1. A section is coded to implement one particular initiation of the task in the pseudoconversational mode of processing. For

instance, the section may validate data from a terminal and use it to update a file, or display the record to be updated, etc.

2. Each section is self-contained and will not execute routines in other sections, which minimizes paging. There may be some duplication of code, but this is necessary for optimum response time in a virtual-storage environment.

3. Exceptions are code to be executed on an exceptional condition that will terminate the session, as for instance, an I/O error when reading a file, etc. These routines are placed in the ABNORMAL-TERMINATION section, which is the last section of the program.

4. Routines for exceptional conditions that will not terminate the session, for instance, a record not in the file in an inquiry or update application, should be coded at the end of the section to keep the most commonly used code in as much of a straight line as possible.

5. At the end of the section, the command to terminate the task is coded and a communication area switch is set to determine which section is to be used next.

6. The sections controlled by the MAIN-LINE section are arranged according to frequency of use, the most commonly used section coded ahead of the others.

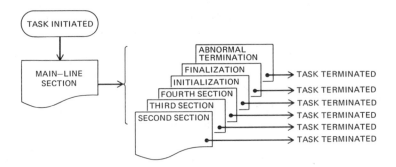

Fig. 7.1. Overall Program Structure.

7. The third to the last section is the INITIALIZATION section, which is executed only once in a session and contains the initial routines to be executed when the session is started.

8. The second to the last section is the FINALIZATION section, which is also executed only once in a session and contains housekeeping routines to be executed when the operator decides to terminate the session.

9. The last section is the ABNORMAL-TERMINATION section, which contains the routines to be executed on various errors, including CICS/VS command exceptional conditions that will abort the session.

General Design Of A Section

In writing the section, the code can be easily kept in a straight line most of the time. Since the logic of a particular section is generally straightforward, all the programmer has to do is code the statements and CICS/VS commands as they are required. Exceptions occur when there is a need for a logic branch. The following suggestions are offered:

1. Code statements and CICS/VS commands one after the other as they are needed without doing a logic branch unless it is required to implement an iteration logic or unless the code will seldom be executed.

2. To implement an iteration, I suggest the use of PERFORMs. However, the performed paragraph (or paragraphs) should be placed as close as possible to the PERFORM statement. The PERFORM statement itself is followed by a GO TO statement that branches around the paragraph. This way, paging is kept to a minimum. The PERFORM statement should never be used to execute a paragraph that is not executed repeatedly. The code should instead by coded in-line.

3. A set of code that is seldom executed should be placed out of the way, generally at the end of the section.

4. Code corresponding to CICS/VS command exceptional conditions that will not terminate the session should also be placed out of the way at the end of the section.

To implement an iteration using PERFORMs or to implement a code that is seldom used, we offer the set of codes in Figure 7.2 as an example:

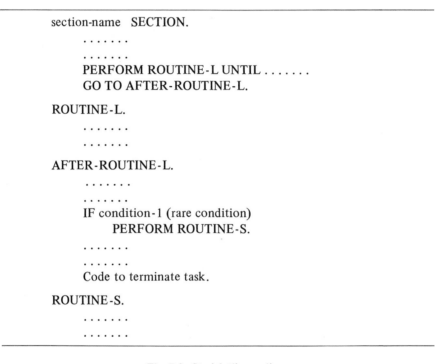

```
section-name  SECTION.
        . . . . . . .
        . . . . . . .
        PERFORM ROUTINE-L UNTIL . . . . . . .
        GO TO AFTER-ROUTINE-L.

ROUTINE-L.
        . . . . . . .
        . . . . . . .

AFTER-ROUTINE-L.
        . . . . . . .
        . . . . . . .
        IF condition-1 (rare condition)
            PERFORM ROUTINE-S.
        . . . . . . .
        . . . . . . .
        Code to terminate task.

ROUTINE-S.
        . . . . . . .
        . . . . . . .
```

Fig. 7.2. Straight-line coding.

CICS/VS COMMANDS

CICS/VS commands are coded with two delimiters so the command-language translator can distinguish them from regular ANS Cobol statements. These are the "EXECUTE CICS" or "EXEC CICS" delimiter before the command, and "END-EXEC" after the command. For instance, the ADDRESS command is coded as:

```
EXEC  CICS
        ADDRESS
                TWA   (TWA-POINTER)
                CWA   (CWA-POINTER)
        END-EXEC.
```

However, in this book the delimiters will not be shown, unless the command is used as part of a program code.

8

The Main-Line Section

INTRODUCTION

We mentioned in the previous chapter that the MAIN-LINE section controls the execution of the whole program. It selects the section to be executed during a single execution of a program in pseudoconversational mode of processing.

SELECTION OF SECTIONS

There are five alternatives in the selection of sections.

Transaction Identifier

Each section may return a different transaction identifier to be used for the next execution of the program. Part of the MAIN-LINE section would then be coded as:

```
if transaction identifier 1
    go to section 1
else if transaction identifier 2
    go to section 2
else if transaction identifier 3
    go to section 3
. . . . .
. . . . .
```

The main problem with this code is that each program is associated with many transaction identifiers, causing the Program Control Table to become large, necessitating a larger space for entries. Also, the search in the PCT to validate the transaction identifier will take longer. However, a transaction identifier other than the one that initiated the current task may be used if another program is to be executed next.

You will note that we execute the appropriate section by means of GO TOs. Although a PERFORM will work just as well, I prefer to use GO TOs here because control will not return to the MAIN-LINE section until the next initiation of the task. The sections following the MAIN-LINE section should be arranged in order of frequency of use, with the most frequently used sections being coded first.

Temporary Storage Switch

In the temporary storage switch method, all sections return the very same transaction identifier, but each sets a different value to the switch that is then used to select the next section to execute. Part of the MAIN-LINE section would then be coded as:

```
read temporary storage.
if switch equal to 1
    go to section 1
else if switch equal to 2
    go to section 2
else if switch equal to 3
    go to section 3
. . . . .
. . . . .
```

The problem here is that not all applications require temporary storage, and we really would not want to use it for a single switch. The use of temporary storage incurs some overhead because we have to read the temporary storage record at the start of every task and re-write it before the end of the task.

Map Switch

In this method, a switch, which is also set to different values by each section, is used as part of a map. The switch is in one of the unused positions of the screen. It is defined as autoskip, so it cannot be modified by the operator, dark, so it cannot be seen, and FSET, so it can be transmitted back to the application program. This field may then be used in place of the DUMMY field, which is defined at the start of the map to prevent MAPFAIL errors. Part of the MAIN-LINE section would then be coded as:

```
read map information.
if switch equal to 1
    go to section 1
else if switch equal to 2
    go to section 2
else if switch equal to 3
    go to section 3
. . . . .
. . . . .
```

The problem with this method is that it can be used only if the application program uses only one map since the map has to be read before the switch is tested and the command that reads the map identifies the specific map required.

Terminal Control Table User Area

The Terminal Control Table User Area may be used to pass data from one task to another if such tasks use the same terminal. Part of the MAIN-LINE section would then be coded as:

```
provide addressability to TCTUA.
if switch equal to 1
    go to section 1
else if switch equal to 2
    go to section 2
else if switch equal to 3
    go to section 3
. . . . .
. . . . .
```

This area is defined in the LINKAGE section and addressability to it established with the ADDRESS command at the beginning of the MAIN-LINE section.

Communication Area Switch

This method does not have the limitations of the first three and is very easy to use. It is the method used in this book. The communication area switch is transmitted by a previous program and can be immediately tested at the start of the MAIN-LINE section of the current program. The EIBCALEN field of the Execute Interface Block will contain the length of the field communicated, and the field itself is the DFHCOMMAREA field in the LINKAGE section. Part of the MAIN-LINE section would then be coded as:

```
if eibcalen not equal to zeroes
    if switch equal to 1
        go to section 1
    else if switch equal to 2
        go to section 2
    else if switch equal to 3
        go to section 3
. . . . .
. . . . .
```

COMMUNICATION AREA SWITCH

The use of the communication area switch to control the pseudoconversational mode of processing is based on the following techniques:

1. The area communicated by the current program is defined in the WORKING-STORAGE section as the COMMUNICATION-AREA entry. The switch may or may not be the only item of this entry. The program will set the value of this switch and then specify it in the command that terminates the task (RETURN).

2. The first program to execute when the task is next initiated on the same terminal will receive this area in the DFHCOMMAREA field. The EIBCALEN field of the Execute Interface Block will specify the length of the field communicated.

For a program that is directly executed when a task is initiated (not through a XCTL or LINK command), the EIBCALEN field will be zeroes the very first time it is used in a session and will thus be used to execute the INITIALIZATION section. At other times, it will have a value other than zeroes and the DFHCOMMAREA field will have a value. Part of the MAIN-LINE section would then be coded as:

```
          if eibcalen not equal to zeroes
             if switch equal to 1
                 go to section 1
             else if switch equal to 2
                 go to section 2
             else if switch equal to 3
                 go to section 3
             . . . . .
             . . . . .
             else go to process-switch-error.
          if eibcalen equal to zeroes
             go to initialization section.
```

The sections executed may be coded as:

```
section 1.
     . . . . . . .
     . . . . . . .
     set the switch to 2.
     terminate the task (RETURN).

section 2.
     . . . . . . .
     . . . . . . .
     set the switch to 3.
     terminate the task (RETURN).

section 3.
     . . . . . . .
     . . . . . . .
     set the switch to 1.
     terminate the task (RETURN).
```

initialization section.

. . . .

. . . .

    set the switch to 1.

    terminate the task (RETURN).

You will note that when the program is first executed in a session, the INITIALIZATION section is executed, which sets the communication area switch to 1 and then terminates the task. Upon initiation of the next task for the same terminal, the EIBCALEN field will not be zeroes and the switch will cause Section 1 to be executed.

Section 1 in turn sets the communication area switch to 2, which will cause Section 2 to be executed the next time around, which sets the switch to 3 to cause Section 3 to be executed after it. Section 3 sets the switch to 1 so Section 1 is executed the next time around, and so forth.

Thus, the switch controls the pseudoconversational mode of processing. The PROCESS-SWITCH-ERROR paragraph is coded at the ABNORMAL-TERMINATION section just in case of an invalid switch value.

If the very same program used in the pseudoconversational mode of processing is first used in a session by using an XCTL command, with a communication area included (I suggest a value of 0), the EIBCALEN field will always have a value greater than zero. This is typical in applications where the user requires all operators to sign on by using a master sign-on program that will then select, through an XCTL command, the specific application program that will continue the session. In this case, if EIBCALEN is equal to zeroes, there is a sign-on violation. Part of the MAIN-LINE section would then be coded as:

```
if eibcalen not equal to zeroes
    if switch equal to 1
        go to section1
    else if switch equal to 2
        go to section2
    else if switch equal to 3
        go to section3

        . . . . .
```

```
. . . . .
else if switch equal to 0
    go to initialization
else go to process-switch-error.

if eibcalen equal to zeroes
    go to sign-on-violation.
```

Note that on a communication area switch value of zero, the INITIALIZATION section is executed. Also, if EIBCALEN is zero, this is a sign-on violation that will terminate the session.

THE ADDRESS COMMAND

As we mentioned before, CICS/VS automatically acquires main storage if needed by certain services (all of which are input commands). For instance, when the program issues a command to read data from a terminal, CICS/VS gets main storage for the corresponding symbolic description map if the latter is defined in the LINKAGE section. This helps optimize response time because main storage, which is limited, is not used until needed.

There are, however, three storage areas that are acquired for the program before it executes in a task. These are the Transaction Work Area (TWA), the Common Work Area (CWA), and the Terminal Control Table User Area (TCTUA). The program gains access to them through the ADDRESS command, which specifies their pointers. The format is:

```
address
    twa     (twa-pointer)
    cwa     (cwa-pointer)
    tctua   (tctua-pointer)
```

If the program uses any of these storage areas, this command should be coded at the beginning of the MAIN-LINE section. For instance, if a Transaction Work Area is used, part of the MAIN-LINE section would be coded as:

EXEC CICS
   ADDRESS TWA (TWA-POINTER)
END-EXEC.

routine to select sections.

THE HANDLE AID COMMAND

The HANDLE AID command,* which should be coded at the start of the MAIN-LINE section, specifies up to 12 terminal keys (or other attention identifiers) and the corresponding routines that the program unconditionally asynchronously executes (a GO TO is effectively done) when certain special keys are used by the operator. It may be standardized, for instance, for the CLEAR key to terminate the session for all applications in the installation. The program should also specify the actions to be done when the PA keys are used since they result in a MAPFAIL error if used with the command to read in data from a terminal. These PA keys may be effectively used, for instance, to bypass the current input during a data-entry or file-update application if the operator cannot resolve an error that prevents the completion of the current input. The format of the command is:

```
handle aid
      key1  (routine1)
      key2  (routine2)
      . . . . . . .
      . . . . . . .
```

The attention identifiers that can be used are the CLEAR key, the ENTER key, the PA keys (PA1 to PA3), the PF keys (PF1 to PF24), ANYKEY (any PA or PF key, or the CLEAR key), OPERID (the operator identification card reader), and LIGHTPEN (a light pen attention). If the programmer wants to terminate the session when the CLEAR key is used and bypass the current input if the PA keys are used, part of the MAIN-LINE section may be coded as:

---

*The HANDLE AID command is actually a terminal input command but is discussed here instead of Chapter 11 since it is coded in this section.

address command (if any).

```
EXEC CICS
    HANDLE AID
        CLEAR  (FINALIZATION)
        PA1    (BYPASS-INPUT)
        PA2    (BYPASS-INPUT)
        PA3    (BYPASS-INPUT)
END–EXEC.
```

routine to select sections.

THE HANDLE CONDITION COMMAND

The HANDLE CONDITION command is coded at the MAIN-LINE section and at other sections to specify the routines that asynchronously execute when exceptional conditions occur during the execution of CICS/VS commands; for instance, MAPFAIL, when reading in terminal map data, NOTFND when attempting to read a file, and so on. The default for most of these conditions is for CICS/VS to terminate the task with a dump printout. Since we do not want a dump printout to result when some of these conditions occur, we should specify the routines for them. The format of the command is:

```
handle condition
    error1  (routine1)
    error2  (routine2)
    . . . . . . .
    . . . . . . .
```

I suggest that two conditions be coded in a HANDLE CONDITION command in the MAIN-LINE section. The first is MAPFAIL, which will abnormally terminate the session on a map failure error, and I suggest their use here for programs that deal with maps (the large majority do). The second condition is ERROR, which is the catchall condition that will also abnormally terminate the session on various CICS/VS exceptional conditions (generally major ones) not specified in a HANDLE CONDITION command. A part of the MAIN-LINE section would then be coded as:

address command (if any).

handle aid command.

```
EXEC CICS
      HANDLE CONDITION
            MAPFAIL  (MAPFAIL-ERROR)
            ERROR    (MAJOR-ERROR)
END-EXEC.
```

routine to select sections.

Within a task, a specific condition will remain in effect and thus will always point to a specific routine. When that condition is again specified, the new specification will supersede the old one. If the condition is specified without a corresponding routine, that condition will take on the default and will not be covered by the ERROR catch-all condition.

USING THE EIBAID FIELDS

While the HANDLE AID command is used for unconditionally executing routines corresponding to certain attention identifiers, a method of conditionally doing this is also needed. For instance, while the ENTER key is the most common key used by the operator to initiate a task, the PF keys are often used in certain applications where the operator is given the option to flip back and forth between pages. However, we generally want the operator to have the option only on certain conditions.

For example, in a File Inquiry application where the data to be displayed can not fit into one page of the screen, the programmer has to go to a second page for the rest of the data. In this case, the PF1 key may be used to display the second page, if we are currently in the first page, and the PF2 key may be used to redisplay the first page, if we are currently in the second page.

At the MAIN-LINE section, we can determine which key the operator used to initiate the task by comparing the EIBAID (attention identifier) field of the Execute Interface Block with certain DFHAID fields. A part of the MAIN-LINE section would then be coded as:

address command (if any).

handle aid command.

handle condition command.

```
if eibcalen not equal to zeroes
    if switch equal to 1
        go to section1
    else if switch equal to 2
        go to section2
    . . . . . . .
    . . . . . . .
    else if switch equal to m (on first page)
            if record key has been changed
                go to validate-record-key
            else if eibaid equal to dfhpf1
                    go to display-page2
            else go to wrong-key-used
    else if switch equal to n (on second page)
            if record key has been changed
                go to validate-record-key
            else if eibaid equal to dfhpf2
                    go to display-page1
            else go to wrong-key-used
    . . . . . . .
    . . . . . . .
    else go to process-switch-error.
```

When the previous task has displayed the first page of the data (switch equal to m) and the task has been reinitiated, we check if the record key on the screen has been changed by the operator. If so, we immediately go to the section that validates the new record key regardless of which attention identifier was used. However, if the record key has not been changed, and if the operator used the PF1 key, we display the second page. Otherwise, the wrong attention identifier was used. A similar technique is used for displaying the first page while at the second page.

We cannot specify the PF1 and PF2 keys in the HANDLE AID command because we want them to be effective only on certain conditions.

EXAMPLE

A complete MAIN-LINE section from a File Add application is shown in Figure 8.1.

You see the ADDRESS, HANDLE AID, and HANDLE CONDITION commands. When EIBCALEN is not equal to zero, we either go to the ORDER-VALIDATION section, the INITIALIZATION section, or the PROCESS-SWITCH-ERROR paragraph in the ABNORMAL-TERMINATION section, depending on the value of the communication area switch.

You may have deduced that this program was first executed in a session by the XCTL command from another program. If this were started directly by the operator, then we would go to the SIGN-ON-VIOLATION paragraph of the ABNORMAL-TERMINATION section to abort the session.

```
00318              EJECT
00319          PROCEDURE DIVISION.
00320              SKIP2
00321      **********************************************************************
00322      *                                                                    *
00323       MAIN-LINE SECTION.                                                  *
00324      *                                                                    *
00325      **********************************************************************
00326              SKIP2
00327              EXEC CICS
00328                  ADDRESS TWA (TWA-POINTER)
00329              END-EXEC.
00330              EXEC CICS
00331                  HANDLE AID
00332                      CLEAR (FINALIZATION)
00333                      PA1 (BYPASS-INPUT)
00334                      PA2 (BYPASS-INPUT)
00335                      PA3 (BYPASS-INPUT)
00336              END-EXEC.
00337              EXEC CICS
00338                  HANDLE CONDITION
00339                      MAPFAIL (MAPFAIL-ERROR)
00340                      ERROR   (MAJOR-ERROR)
00341              END-EXEC.
00342              IF EIBCALEN NOT EQUAL TO ZEROES
00343                  IF ORDER-VALIDATION-TIME
00344                      GO TO ORDER-VALIDATION
00345                  ELSE IF INITIAL-ENTRY-TIME
00346                      GO TO INITIALIZATION
00347                  ELSE GO TO PROCESS-SWITCH-ERROR.
00348              SKIP1
00349              IF EIBCALEN EQUAL TO ZEROES
00350                  GO TO SIGN-ON-VIOLATION.
```

Fig. 8.1. The MAIN-LINE section.

The Housekeeping Sections

INTRODUCTION

There are three sections that are coded at the end of the program because they are either executed only once in a session or are only executed on certain errors. They are therefore best kept out of the way of the other sections that are used often.

THE INITIALIZATION SECTION

The routines to be executed when a program is first used in a session are coded in the INITIALIZATION section. This secures, if required, temporary storage for the application, displays the first map required by the operator, then sets the correct values to the communication area switch and terminates the task. To avoid the reexecution of part of this section during the session (thus reducing the possibility of paging), other sections needing to display the first map must do so themselves. An example of this section is shown in Figure 9.1.

The SEND MAP command will display the first map required, the switch is set to '1', and then the RETURN command terminates the task.

THE FINALIZATION SECTION

The routines to be executed when the operator decides to terminate a session are coded in the FINALIZATION section. To standardize the choice of the terminal key that signifies the end of a session, I suggest that applications use the CLEAR key since this actually requires an additional key to be depressed at the same time (the alternate key) and avoids accidental use.

This section displays an unformatted message to the operator, signifying the end of a session, deletes temporary storage taken by the

```
 11        ORDLO1A          13.02.04        08/02/80

00315      ************************************************************************
00316      *                                                                      *
00317       INITIALIZATION SECTION.
00318      *                                                                      *
00319      ************************************************************************

00321      *     EXEC CICS
00322      *         SEND MAP    ('ORDLMO1')
00323      *             MAPSET ('ORDLSO1')
00324      *             MAPONLY
00325      *             ERASE
00326      *     END-EXEC.
00327            MOVE 'ORDLMO1' TO DFHEIV1 MOVE 'ORDLSO1' TO DFHEIV2 MOVE 'QD
00328      -    '& D     ESD  -' TO DFHEIVO CALL 'DFHEI1' USING DFHEIVO
00329            DFHEIV1 DFHEIV99 DFHEIV98 DFHEIV2.
00330
00331
00332
00333            MOVE '1' TO COMMAREA-PROCESS-SW.

00335      *     EXEC CICS
00336      *         RETURN TRANSID  ('ORDL')
00337      *             COMMAREA (COMMUNICATION-AREA)
00338      *             LENGTH    (1)
00339      *     END-EXEC.
00340            MOVE 'ORDL' TO DFHEIV5 MOVE 1 TO DFHEIV11 MOVE '+H- D  & '
00341            TO DFHEIVO CALL 'DFHEI1' USING DFHEIVO DFHEIV5
00342            COMMUNICATION-AREA DFHEIV11.
00343
00344
```

Fig. 9.1. The INITIALIZATION section.

application (unless there is a reason to save it), then terminates the task. An example of this is shown in Figure 9.2.

The SEND command displays the unformatted message "JOB NORMALLY TERMINATED" on top of the screen, the HANDLE CONDITION command specifies the routine to be executed in case the temporary storage queue to be deleted does not exist, the DELETEQ TS command deletes the temporary storage queue, and the RETURN command terminates the task. If the RETURN command does not specify a transaction identifier (as in the case of the other sections) and if the task is at the highest logical level, then a task can no longer be reinitiated by simply using an attention identifier and the operator can no longer continue the session.

THE ABNORMAL TERMINATION SECTION

Routines that are to be executed asynchronously when errors or CICS/ VS command exceptional conditions occur, which will abnormally

```
01039      **************************************************************
01040      *                                                            *
01041       FINALIZATION SECTION.
01042      *                                                            *
01043      **************************************************************


01045       PREPARE-TERMINATION-MESSAGE.
01046           MOVE JOB-NORMAL-END-MESSAGE TO TWA-OPERATOR-MESSAGE.


01048       JOB-TERMINATED.

01050      *   EXEC CICS
01051      *       SEND FROM   (TWA-OPERATOR-MESSAGE)
01052      *             LENGTH (31)
01053      *             ERASE
01054      *   END-EXEC.
01055           MOVE 31 TO DFHEIV11 MOVE 'DDO D   A      ' TO DFHEIVO CALL '
01056       -   'DFHEI1' USING DFHEIVO DFHEIV99 DFHEIV98 TWA-OPERATOR-MESSAGE
01057           DFHEIV11.
01058
01059
01060      *   EXEC CICS
01061      *       HANDLE CONDITION
01062      *           QIDERR (END-OF-JOB)
01063      *   END-EXEC.
01064           MOVE 'BD   D%              ' TO DFHEIVO CALL 'DFHEI1' USING
01065           DFHEIVO GO TO END-OF-JOB DEPENDING ON DFHEIGDI.
01066
01067
01068           MOVE EIBTRMID  TO  TSA-TERM-ID.
01069           MOVE EIBTRNID  TO  TSA-TRANS-ID.

01071      *   EXEC CICS
01072      *       DELETEQ TS
01073      *           QUEUE (TSA-QUEUE-ID)
01074      *   END-EXEC.
01075           MOVE ' F  D / ' TO DFHEIVO CALL 'DFHEI1' USING DFHEIVO
01076           TSA-QUEUE-ID.
01077
01078


01080       END-OF-JOB.

01082      *   EXEC CICS
01083      *       RETURN
01084      *   END-EXEC.
01085           MOVE '+H  D  & ' TO DFHEIVO CALL 'DFHEI1' USING DFHEIVO.
01086
01087
```

Fig. 9.2. The FINALIZATION section.

terminate the session, are coded as part of the ABNORMAL-TER-
MINATION section. The programmer may code as many routines as
he wants in this section. The most common routines are:

1. FILE-NOT-OPEN. This is used for the NOTOPEN exceptional
   condition for applications using files.

2. MAPFAIL-ERROR. A routine used for the MAPFAIL exceptional condition if no data is sent to the application program

from the Terminal Input/Output Area on the RECEIVE MAP command.

3. PROCESS-SWITCH-ERROR. This is employed if the value of the communication area switch that controls pseudoconversational mode of processing is not within the correct range of values.

4. SIGN-ON-VIOLATION. This is used if an application that is supposed to be started only by an XCTL command (as for instance from a sign-on program) is instead directly executed (generally through a transaction identifier).

5. MAJOR-ERROR. This is used for the catchall ERROR exceptional condition for CICS/VS command exceptional condition not covered by a specific HANDLE CONDITION command.

An example of the ABNORMAL-TERMINATION section is shown in Figure 9.3.

Note that I am using an XCTL command to execute a program that displays an installation standard message on a NOTOPEN error. The routines for a MAPFAIL error, a process switch error, and a sign-on violation will display the appropriate message to the operator, then terminate the session.

The routine for the catchall ERROR condition will likewise display a message to the operator, then terminate the session. In addition, I suggest the use of the DUMP command to produce a dump for debugging purposes.

```
    13        ORDLO1A        13.02.04        08/02/80

00375       ****************************************************************
00376       *                                                             *
00377          ABNORMAL-TERMINATION SECTION.
00378       *                                                             *
00379       ****************************************************************

00381          FILE-NOT-OPEN.

00383       *    EXEC CICS
00384       *        XCTL PROGRAM ('TEL2OPEN')
00385       *    END-EXEC.
00386             MOVE 'TEL2OPEN' TO DFHEIV3 MOVE '+D  D  B ' TO DFHEIVO CALL
00387             'DFHEI1' USING DFHEIVO DFHEIV3.
00388
00389          MAPFAIL-ERROR.
00390             MOVE 'MAP FAILURE' TO MAJOR-ERROR-MSG.
00391             GO TO PREPARE-ABORT-MESSAGE.

00393          PROCESS-SWITCH-ERROR.
00394             MOVE 'PROCESS ERROR' TO MAJOR-ERROR-MSG.
00395             GO TO PREPARE-ABORT-MESSAGE.

00397          SIGN-ON-VIOLATION.
00398             MOVE 'SIGNON VIOLATION' TO MAJOR-ERROR-MSG.
00399             GO TO PREPARE-ABORT-MESSAGE.

00401          MAJOR-ERROR.
00402             MOVE  EIBFN      TO  OLD-EIBFN.
00403             MOVE  EIBRCODE   TO  OLD-EIBRCODE.

00405       *    EXEC CICS
00406       *        DUMP DUMPCODE ('ERRS')
00407       *    END-EXEC.
00408             MOVE 'ERRS' TO DFHEIV5 MOVE '*B  D  = ' TO DFHEIVO CALL 'DFH
00409       -     'EI1' USING DFHEIVO DFHEIV5.
00410
00411             MOVE 'MAJOR ERROR' TO MAJOR-ERROR-MSG.
00412             GO TO PREPARE-ABORT-MESSAGE.

00414          PREPARE-ABORT-MESSAGE.
00415             MOVE JOB-ABORTED-MESSAGE TO TWA-OPERATOR-MESSAGE.
00416             GO TO JOB-TERMINATED.
```

Fig. 9.3. The ABNORMAL-TERMINATION section.

10

Processing Sections

INTRODUCTION

Sections that will be executed one after the other during a session are called processing sections, and they will be coded after the MAIN-LINE section. Their position in the program depends on their frequency of use, the most used sections being coded ahead of the others. Each section is self-contained and will not execute routines beyond that section. This reduces the possibility of paging. There may thus be some redundancy of code among the sections.

An exhaustive discussion on sections is beyond the scope of this book. Rather, this chapter will discuss some typical sections that may be required in various on-line applications.

THE RECORD-KEY-VERIFICATION SECTION

In a File Update or File Inquiry application, the record key entered by the operator must be verified to see if it corresponds to a valid record. If File Control can locate the corresponding record, the data will then be displayed; otherwise, an error message like "RECORD NOT FOUND" is displayed. As a minimum, this section does the following functions:

1. HANDLE CONDITION command for NOTOPEN and NOTFND. NOTOPEN will abnormally terminate the session while NOTFND will display the "RECORD NOT FOUND" message to the operator. In a File Inquiry using an alternate key, DUPKEY must also be specified.

2. RECEIVE MAP command to read the record key entered by the operator.

3. READ DATASET command to read the file.

4. If the record is in the file:
    a. SEND MAP command to display the record information.
    b. Set the communication area switch for the next section (for instance, in an update application, the section that validates the changes to be entered).
    c. RETURN command to terminate the task.

5. If the record is not in the file:
    a. SEND MAP command to display the "RECORD NOT FOUND" message.
    b. Set the communication area switch for the same section to give the operator the option to correct the record key or enter a new one.
    c. RETURN command to terminate the task.

An example of the RECORD-KEY-VERIFICATION section is given in Figure 10.1.

Note that if the record was in the file, we set the communication area switch to '2' (line 366), thus executing the section to validate changes entered by the operator. On the other hand, if the record was not in the file, we set the switch to '1' (line 382) to reexecute the same section and verify the corrected record key or a new record key that would have been entered by the operator.

DATA-VALIDATION SECTION

In a File Update or File Add Application, the DATA-VALIDATION section is the one most used by the operator. Since there is much more data entered in the DATA-VALIDATION section than in the RECORD-KEY-VERIFICATION section, there are also more chances to enter errors in it. There will be instances when the operator will have to correct entered data, in which case this section will be reexecuted several times for a single record. For this reason, it is generally coded as the first section after the MAIN-LINE section. As a minimum, this section does the following:

```
   10        ORIQ01A          16.10.10       12/27/80

00308       **********************************************************************
00309       *                                                                    *
00310        ORDER-VERIFICATION SECTION.
00311       *                                                                    *
00312       **********************************************************************


00314       *     EXEC CICS
00315       *         HANDLE CONDITION
00316       *             NOTOPEN (FILE-NOT-OPEN)
00317       *             NOTEND  (RECORD-NOT-FOUND)
00318       *     END-EXEC.
00319             MOVE '                        ' TO DFHEIVO CALL 'DFHEI1' USING
00320             DFHEIVO GO TO FILE-NOT-OPEN RECORD-NOT-FOUND DEPENDING ON
00321             DFHEIGDI.
00322
00323
00324       *     EXEC CICS
00325       *         RECEIVE MAP   ('ORCHM01')
00326       *                 MAPSET ('ORCHS01')
00327       *                 SET    (MAP1-POINTER)
00328       *     END-EXEC.
00329             MOVE 'ORCHM01' TO DFHEIV1 MOVE 'ORCHS01' TO DFHEIV2 MOVE '
00330       -     '                  ' TO DFHEIVO CALL 'DFHEI1' USING DFHEIVO
00331             DFHEIV1 MAP1-POINTER DFHEIV98 DFHEIV2.
00332
00333
00334             IF MAP1-ORDER-NUMBER NOT NUMERIC
00335                 GO TO INVALID-ORDER-RTN.

00337             MOVE MAP1-ORDER-NUMBER TO TWA-ORDER-RECORD-KEY.

00339       *     EXEC CICS
00340       *         READ DATASET ('ORTEST')
00341       *              SET     (POM-POINTER)
00342       *              RIDFLD  (TWA-ORDER-RECORD-KEY)
00343       *     END-EXEC.
00344             MOVE 'ORTEST' TO DFHEIV3 MOVE '              ' TO DFHEIVO CALL 'D
00345       -     'FHEI1' USING DFHEIVO DFHEIV3 POM-POINTER DFHEIV98
00346             TWA-ORDER-RECORD-KEY.
00347
00348


00350       *         HERE MOVE RECORD FIELDS INTO THE SYMBOLIC DESC. MAP.


00352        DISPLAY-ORDER.

00354       *     EXEC CICS
00355       *         SEND MAP    ('ORCHM01')
00356       *              MAPSET ('ORCHS01')
00357       *              FROM   (MAP1-AREA)
00358       *              ERASE
```

Fig. 10.1. The RECORD-KEY-VERIFICATION section.

```
   11           ORIQ01A        16.10.10        12/27/80

00359       *     END-EXEC.
00360             MOVE 'ORCHM01' TO DFHEIV1 MOVE 'ORCHS01' TO DFHEIV2 MOVE '
00361       -     '      S      ' TO DFHEIVO CALL 'DFHEI1' USING DFHEIVO
00362             DFHEIV1 MAP1-AREA DFHEIV98 DFHEIV2.
00363
00364
00365
00366             MOVE '2' TO COMMAREA-PROCESS-SW.


00368       RETURN-AT-RECORD-KEY-VERIFY.

00370       *     EXEC CICS
00371       *          RETURN TRANSID (EIBTRNID)
00372       *                 COMMAREA (COMMUNICATION-AREA)
00373       *                 LENGTH   (1)
00374       *     END-EXEC.
00375             MOVE 1 TO DFHEIV11 MOVE '            ' TO DFHEIVO CALL 'DFHEI1'
00376             USING DFHEIVO EIBTRNID COMMUNICATION-AREA DFHEIV11.
00377
00378
00379
00380       RECORD-NOT-FOUND.

00382             MOVE '1'  TO  COMMAREA-PROCESS-SW.
00383             MOVE 'RECORD NOT FOUND' TO MAP1-ERROR.
00384             GO TO DISPLAY-INVALID-ORDER-MESSAGE.


00386       DISPLAY-INVALID-ORDER-MESSAGE.

00388       *     EXEC CICS
00389       *          SEND MAP   ('ORCHM01')
00390       *               MAPSET ('ORCHS01')
00391       *               FROM   (MAP1-AREA)
00392       *               ERASE
00393       *     END-EXEC.
00394             MOVE 'ORCHM01' TO DFHEIV1 MOVE 'ORCHS01' TO DFHEIV2 MOVE '
00395       -     '      S      ' TO DFHEIVO CALL 'DFHEI1' USING DFHEIVO
00396             DFHEIV1 MAP1-AREA DFHEIV98 DFHEIV2.
00397
00398
00399
00400             GO TO RETURN-AT-RECORD-KEY-VERIFY.


00402       INVALID-ORDER-RTN.

00404             MOVE '1'  TO  COMMAREA-PROCESS-SW.
00405             MOVE 'INVALID ORDER NUMBER' TO MAP1-ERROR.
00406             GO TO DISPLAY-INVALID-ORDER-MESSAGE.
```

Fig. 10.1 (Continued)

File Update Application

1. RECEIVE MAP command to read the data entered by the operator.

2. Edits data.

3. If there are no errors:
   a. HANDLE CONDITION command for NOTOPEN and NOTFND.* NOTOPEN will abnormally terminate the session while NOTFND will display the "RECORD NOT FOUND" message to the operator.
   b. READ DATASET command with UPDATE option to make the record available for update.
   c. Moves the changes to the file record defined in the LINKAGE section.
   d. REWRITE DATASET command to update the record.
   e. SEND MAP command to display the next map required by the operator.
   f. Sets the communication area switch for the next section (the RECORD-KEY-VERIFICATION section).
   g. RETURN command to terminate the task.

4. If there are errors:
   a. SEND MAP command to display the error messages.
   b. Sets the communication area switch to reexecute the DATA-VALIDATION section, to edit the corrections to be entered by the operator.
   c. RETURN command to terminate the task.

An example of this section is shown in Figure 10.2.

---

*The NOTOPEN and NOTFND options are specified because somebody could easily close the file or delete the record between the READ in the RECORD-KEY-VERIFICATION section and the incoming READ.

```
       13           ORCHO1A          16.20.58        12/27/80


00437      ****************************************************************
00438      *                                                              *
00439      DATA-VALIDATION SECTION.
00440      *                                                              *
00441      ****************************************************************


00443      *      EXEC CICS
00444      *          RECEIVE MAP    ('ORCHMO2')
00445      *                  MAPSET ('ORCHSO2')
00446      *                  SET    (MAP2-POINTER)
00447      *      END-EXEC.
00448          MOVE 'ORCHMO2' TO DFHEIV1 MOVE 'ORCHSO2' TO DFHEIV2 MOVE '
00449      -      '            ' TO DFHEIVO CALL 'DFHEI1' USING DFHEIVO
00450          DFHEIV1 MAP2-POINTER DFHEIV98 DFHEIV2.
00451
00452
00453      VALIDATE-ALL-DATA.
00454          MOVE SPACES TO MAP2-ERRORS (1)
00455                         MAP2-ERRORS (2)
00456                         MAP2-ERRORS (3)
00457                         MAP2-ERRORS (4).
00458          SET ERROR-I  TO  ZEROES.

00460          IF MAP2-DOCUMENT NUMERIC
00461              NEXT SENTENCE
00462          ELSE SET ERROR-I UP BY 1
00463              MOVE 'INVALID DOCUMENT NUMBER' TO  MAP2-ERRORS (ERROR-I)
00464                      MOVE -1              TO  MAP2-DOCUMENT-L.

00466      *       HERE EDIT THE REST OF THE DATA.


00468      CHECK-IF-THERE-ARE-ERRORS.

00470          IF ERROR-I NOT EQUAL TO ZEROES
00471              GO TO DISPLAY-ERROR-SCREEN.


00473      NO-ERRORS-RTN.

00475          MOVE TSA-ORDER-NUMBER  TO  TWA-ORDER-RECORD-KEY.

00477      *      EXEC CICS
00478      *          HANDLE CONDITION
00479      *               NOTOPEN (FILE-NOT-OPEN)
00480      *               NOTFND  (RECORD-NOT-FOUND)
00481      *      END-EXEC.
00482          MOVE '                        ' TO DFHEIVO CALL 'DFHEI1' USING
00483          DFHEIVO GO TO FILE-NOT-OPEN RECORD-NOT-FOUND DEPENDING ON
00484          DFHEIGDI.
00485
```

Fig. 10.2. The DATA-VALIDATION section For A File Update Application.

```
14        ORCHO1A        16.20.58        12/27/80

00486


00488      *     EXEC CICS
00489      *          READ DATASET ('ORTEST')
00490      *               SET      (POM-POINTER)
00491      *               RIDFLD   (TWA-ORDER-RECORD-KEY)
00492      *               UPDATE
00493      *     END-EXEC.
00494            MOVE 'ORTEST' TO DFHEIV3 MOVE '            ' TO DFHEIVO CALL 'D
00495      -    'FHEI1' USING DFHEIVO DFHEIV3 POM-POINTER DFHEIV98
00496            TWA-ORDER-RECORD-KEY.
00497
00498
00499
00500      *          HERE MOVE CHANGES TO FILE RECORD DEFINITION.


00502            REWRITE-ORDER-RECORD.
00503            COMPUTE TWA-POM-LENGTH = 37 + ORDER-LINE-COUNT * 44.

00505      *     EXEC CICS
00506      *          REWRITE DATASET ('ORTEST')
00507      *               LENGTH   (TWA-POM-LENGTH)
00508      *               FROM     (ORDER-MASTER-RECORD)
00509      *     END-EXEC.
00510            MOVE 'ORTEST' TO DFHEIV3 MOVE '            ' TO DFHEIVO CALL 'D
00511      -    'FHEI1' USING DFHEIVO DFHEIV3 ORDER-MASTER-RECORD
00512            TWA-POM-LENGTH.
00513
00514
00515      *     EXEC CICS
00516      *          SEND MAP    ('ORCHM01')
00517      *               MAPSET ('ORCHS01')
00518      *               MAPONLY
00519      *               ERASE
00520      *     END-EXEC.
00521            MOVE 'ORCHM01' TO DFHEIV1 MOVE 'ORCHS01' TO DFHEIV2 MOVE '
00522      -    '            ' TO DFHEIVO CALL 'DFHEI1' USING DFHEIVO
00523            DFHEIV1 DFHEIV99 DFHEIV98 DFHEIV2.
00524
00525
00526
00527            MOVE  '1'  TO COMMAREA-PROCESS-SW.


00529            RETURN-AT-ORDER-VALIDATE.

00531      *     EXEC CICS
00532      *          RETURN TRANSID  (EIBTRNID)
00533      *                 COMMAREA (COMMUNICATION-AREA)
00534      *                 LENGTH   (1)
00535      *     END-EXEC.
```

Fig. 10.2. (Continued)

```
00536.              MOVE 1 TO DFHEIV11 MOVE '            ' TO DFHEIV0 CALL 'DFHEI1'
00537               USING DFHEIV0 EIBTRNID COMMUNICATION-AREA DFHEIV11.
00538
00539
00540
00541          DISPLAY-ERROR-SCREEN.

00543     *        EXEC CICS
00544     *           SEND  MAP        ('ORCHM02')
00545     *                 MAPSET     ('ORCHS02')
00546     *                 FROM       (MAP2-AREA)                              N
00547     *                 DATAONLY
00548     *                 CURSOR
00549     *        END-EXEC.
00550              MOVE 'ORCHM02' TO DFHEIV1 MOVE 'ORCHS02' TO DFHEIV2 MOVE -1
00551           TO DFHEIV11 MOVE '   J        ' TO DFHEIV0 CALL 'DFHEI1'
00552              USING DFHEIV0 DFHEIV1 MAP2-AREA DFHEIV98 DFHEIV2 DFHEIV99
00553              DFHEIV99 DFHEIV99 DFHEIV11.
00554
00555
00556                                                                        'D
00557              MOVE  '2'  TO  COMMAREA-PROCESS-SW.

00559              GO TO RETURN-AT-ORDER-VALIDATE.


00561          RECORD-NOT-FOUND.

00563              MOVE 'RECORD NOT FOUND' TO MAP2-ERRORS (1).
00564              MOVE -1        TO  MAP2-ORDER-NUMBER-L.
00565              GO TO DISPLAY-ERROR-SCREEN.
```

Fig. 10.2. (Continued)

File Add Application

1. RECEIVE MAP command to read the data entered by the operator.

2. Edits the data.

3. If there are no errors:
   a. GETMAIN command to secure main storage for the new record to be written out.
   b. Moves the data to the file record.
   c. HANDLE CONDITION command for NOTOPEN and DUPREC.* NOTOPEN will abnormally terminate the session while DUPREC will display the "DUPLICATE—NOT ACCEPTED" message to the operator.
   d. WRITE DATASET command to write the new record.
   e. SEND MAP command to display the next map required by the operator.
   f. Sets the communication area switch for the next section (this is generally the same DATA-VALIDATION section).**
   g. RETURN command to terminate the task.

4. If there are errors:
   a. SEND MAP command to display the error messages.
   b. Sets the communication area switch to reexecute the DATA-VALIDATION section to edit the corrections to be entered by the operator.
   c. RETURN command to terminate the task.

An example of this section is shown in Figure 10.3.

---

*The DUPREC option is specified to display an error message just in case the record to be created has an existing duplicate.

**In a File Add Application, the record key is generally validated in the same DATA-VALIDATION section. There is generally no need to check in a separate section if the record has a duplicate because this should rarely happen anyway.

```
   14        ORAD01A       16.16.28       12/27/80

00422      ****************************************************************
00423      *                                                             *
00424       DATA-VALIDATION SECTION.
00425      *                                                             *
00426      ****************************************************************

00428      *     EXEC CICS
00429      *         RECEIVE MAP    ('ORADM01')
00430      *                 MAPSET ('ORADS01')
00431      *                 SET    (MAP1-POINTER)
00432      *     END-EXEC.
00433            MOVE 'ORADM01' TO DFHEIV1 MOVE 'ORADS01' TO DFHEIV2 MOVE '
00434      -        '           ' TO DFHEIVO CALL 'DFHEI1' USING DFHEIVO
00435            DFHEIV1 MAP1-POINTER DFHEIV98 DFHEIV2.
00436
00437
00438       VALIDATE-ALL-DATA.
00439            MOVE SPACES TO MAP1-ERRORS (1)
00440                           MAP1-ERRORS (2)
00441                           MAP1-ERRORS (3)
00442                           MAP1-ERRORS (4).

00444            IF MAP1-ORDER-NUMBER NUMERIC
00445                MOVE MAP1-ORDER-NUMBER        TO  TSA-ORDER-NUMBER
00446            ELSE SET ERROR-I UP BY 1
00447                MOVE 'INVALID ORDER NUMBER'   TO  MAP1-ERRORS (ERROR-I)
00448                MOVE -1                       TO  MAP1-ORDER-NUMBER-L.

00450      *        HERE EDIT THE REST OF THE DATA.

00452       CHECK-IF-THERE-ARE-ERRORS.

00454            IF ERROR-I NOT EQUAL TO ZEROES
00455                GO TO DISPLAY-ERROR-SCREEN.

00457       NO-ERRORS-RTN.

00459      *     EXEC CICS
00460      *         GETMAIN
00461      *             SET    (POM-POINTER)
00462      *             LENGTH (433)
00463      *     END-EXEC.
00464            MOVE 433 TO DFHEIV11 MOVE '          ' TO DFHEIVO CALL 'DFHEI
00465      -     '1' USING DFHEIVO POM-POINTER DFHEIV11.
00466
00467
00468
00469            MOVE TSA-LINE-COUNT    TO  ORDER-LINE-COUNT.
00470            MOVE TSA-POMAST-RECORD TO  ORDER-MASTER-RECORD.
00471            COMPUTE TWA-POM-LENGTH = 37 + ORDER-LINE-COUNT * 44.
```

Fig. 10.3. The DATA-VALIDATION section For A File Add Application.

```
00472                    MOVE TSA-ORDER-NUMBER   TO  TWA-ORDER-RECORD-KEY.

00474          *    EXEC CICS
00475          *         HANDLE CONDITION
00476          *              NOTOPEN (FILE-NOT-OPEN)
00477          *              DUPREC  (DUPLICATE-RECORD)
00478          *    END-EXEC.
00479               MOVE '                    ' TO DFHEIVO CALL 'DFHEI1' USING
00480               DFHEIVO GO TO FILE-NOT-OPEN DUPLICATE-RECORD DEPENDING ON
00481               DFHEIGDI.
00482
00483
00484          *    EXEC CICS
00485          *         WRITE DATASET ('ORTEST')
00486          *               LENGTH (TWA-POM-LENGTH)
00487          *               FROM   (ORDER-MASTER-RECORD)
00488          *               RIDFLD (TWA-ORDER-RECORD-KEY)
00489          *    END-EXEC.
00490               MOVE 'ORTEST' TO DFHEIV3 MOVE '  C      ' TO DFHEIVO CALL 'D
00491          -    'FHEI1' USING DFHEIVO DFHEIV3 ORDER-MASTER-RECORD
00492               TWA-POM-LENGTH TWA-ORDER-RECORD-KEY.
00493
00494
00495
00496          DISPLAY-FRESH-SCREEN.

00498          *    EXEC CICS
00499          *         SEND MAP   ('ORADMO1')
00500          *              MAPSET ('ORADSO1')
00501          *              MAPONLY
00502          *              ERASE
00503          *    END-EXEC.
00504               MOVE 'ORADMO1' TO DFHEIV1 MOVE 'ORADSO1' TO DFHEIV2 MOVE '
00505          -    '              ' TO DFHEIVO CALL 'DFHEI1' USING DFHEIVO
00506               DFHEIV1 DFHEIV99 DFHEIV98 DFHEIV2.
00507
00508
00509
00510          RETURN-FOR-NEXT-ORDER.

00512               MOVE '1'  TO COMMAREA-PROCESS-SW.

00514          *    EXEC CICS
00515          *         RETURN TRANSID  (EIBTRNID)
00516          *                COMMAREA (COMMUNICATION-AREA)
00517          *                LENGTH   (1)
00518          *    END-EXEC.
00519               MOVE 1 TO DFHEIV11 MOVE '         ' TO DFHEIVO CALL 'DFHEI1'
00520               USING DFHEIVO EIBTRNID COMMUNICATION-AREA DFHEIV11.
00521
00522
00523
00524          DISPLAY-ERROR-SCREEN.
```

Fig. 10.3. (Continued)

```
     16          ORAD01A           16.16.28          12/27/80

00526        *      EXEC CICS
00527        *          SEND MAP        ('ORADM01')
00528        *              MAPSET      ('ORADS01')
00529        *              FROM        (MAP1-AREA)
00530        *              DATAONLY
00531        *              CURSOR
00532        *      END-EXEC
00533               MOVE 'ORADM01' TO DFHEIV1 MOVE 'ORADS01' TO DFHEIV2 MOVE -1
00534               TO DFHEIV11 MOVE '  J         ' TO DFHEIVO CALL 'DFHEI1'
00535               USING DFHEIVO DFHEIV1 MAP1-AREA DFHEIV98 DFHEIV2 DFHEIV99
00536               DFHEIV99 DFHEIV99 DFHEIV11
00537
00538
00539
00540               GO TO RETURN-FOR-NEXT-ORDER.


00542        DUPLICATE-RECORD.

00544               MOVE 'DUPLICATE -- NOT ACCEPTED' TO MAP1-ERRORS (1).
00545               MOVE -1      TO  MAP1-ORDER-NUMBER-L.
00546               GO TO DISPLAY-ERROR-SCREEN.
```

Fig. 10.3. (Continued)

BYPASS-INPUT SECTION

When data is entered for validation, the operator should have the option to discontinue whatever he is working on and start with a new record. This would normally be done only if he could not resolve a validation error message. Otherwise, he would never be able to get out of the DATA-VALIDATION section and continue the session.

I suggest the use of one or all of the programmer attention (PA) keys for this problem by specifying them in a HANDLE AID command. These keys do not allow the program to read data from the terminal on the RECEIVE MAP command (a MAPFAIL error will result) and are thus of limited use. This section does the following:

1. GETMAIN command to secure main storage for the map that will contain the message. This is because CICS/VS will get main storage for the symbolic description map only on a RECEIVE MAP command.

2. SEND MAP command to display the "RECORD BYPASSED—CONTINUE" message.

3. Set the communication area switch for the section that processes a new record.

4. RETURN command to terminate the task.

An example of this section is shown in Figure 10.4.

```
   17        ORA001A        16.16.28        12/27/80

00548     ***************************************************************************
00549     *                                                                         *
00550     BYPASS-INPUT SECTION.
00551     *                                                                         *
00552     ***************************************************************************

00554     *    EXEC CICS
00555     *        GETMAIN
00556     *            SET      (MAP1-POINTER)
00557     *            LENGTH  (958)
00558     *            INITIMG (HEX-ZEROES)
00559     *    END-EXEC.
00560          MOVE 958 TO DFHEIV11 MOVE '           ' TO DFHEIV0 CALL 'DFHEI
00561     -    '1' USING DFHEIV0 MAP1-POINTER DFHEIV11 HEX-ZEROES.
00562
00563
00564
00565
00566          MOVE 'ORDER BYPASSED - CONTINUE' TO MAP1-ERRORS (1).

00568     *    EXEC CICS
00569     *        SEND MAP     ('ORADM01')
00570     *             MAPSET  ('ORADS01')
00571     *             FROM    (MAP1-AREA)
00572     *             ERASE
00573     *    END-EXEC.
00574          MOVE 'ORADM01' TO DFHEIV1 MOVE 'ORADS01' TO DFHEIV2 MOVE '
00575     -    '   S   ' TO DFHEIV0 CALL 'DFHEI1' USING DFHEIV0
00576          DFHEIV1 MAP1-AREA DFHEIV98 DFHEIV2.
00577
00578
00579
00580          MOVE '1' TO COMMAREA-PROCESS-SW.

00582     *    EXEC CICS
00583     *        RETURN TRANSID   (EIBTRNID)
00584     *               COMMAREA  (COMMUNICATION-AREA)
00585     *               LENGTH    (1)
00586     *    END-EXEC.
00587          MOVE 1 TO DFHEIV11 MOVE '           ' TO DFHEIV0 CALL 'DFHEI1'
00588          USING DFHEIV0 EIBTRNID COMMUNICATION-AREA DFHEIV11.
00589
00590
00591
```

Fig. 10.4. The BYPASS-INPUT section.

WRONG-KEY-USED SECTION

In applications where there is no input data to be bypassed, the PA keys may be of no use. However, we still have to specify them in a HANDLE AID command to display an error message if they are used by the operator. This is because PA keys result in a MAPFAIL error that will terminate the session on a RECEIVE MAP command. This section does the following:

1. GETMAIN command to secure main storage for the map that will contain the message.

2. SEND MAP command to display the "WRONG-KEY-USED" message.

3. Set the communication area switch for the same section to give the operator the chance to use another key (maybe the ENTER key) to continue where he left off without having to reenter any data.

4. RETURN command to terminate the task.

An example of this section is given in Figure 10.5.

```
   12        ORIQO1A        16.10.10      12/27/80

00408      ***********************************************************
00409      *                                                        *
00410       WRONG-KEY-USED SECTION.                                 *
00411      *                                                        *
00412      ***********************************************************


00414      *     EXEC CICS
00415      *         GETMAIN
00416      *              SET     (MAP1-POINTER)
00417      *              LENGTH  (970)
00418      *              INITIMG (HEX-ZEROES)
00419      *     END-EXEC.
00420           MOVE 970 TO DFHEIV11 MOVE '          ' TO DFHEI
00421      -   '1' USING DFHEIVO MAP1-POINTER DFHEIV11 HEX-ZEROES.
00422
00423
00424
00425
00426           MOVE 'WRONG KEY USED' TO MAP1-ERROR.

00428      *     EXEC CICS
00429      *         SEND MAP    ('ORIQMO1')
00430      *              MAPSET  ('ORIQS01')
00431      *              FROM    (MAP1-AREA)
00432      *              DATAONLY
00433      *     END-EXEC.
00434           MOVE 'ORIQMO1' TO DFHEIV1 MOVE 'ORIQS01' TO DFHEIV2 MOVE '
00435      -   '          ' TO DFHEIVO CALL 'DFHEI1' USING DFHEIVO
00436           DFHEIV1 MAP1-AREA DFHEIV98 DFHEIV2.
00437
00438
00439
00440           MOVE '1' TO COMMAREA-PROCESS-SW.

00442      *     EXEC CICS
00443      *         RETURN TRANSID  (EIBTRNID)
00444      *                COMMAREA (COMMUNICATION-AREA)
00445      *                LENGTH   (1)
00446      *     END-EXEC.
00447           MOVE 1 TO DFHEIV11 MOVE '          ' TO DFHEIVO CALL 'DFHEI1'
00448           USING DFHEIVO EIBTRNID COMMUNICATION-AREA DFHEIV11.
00449
00450
00451
```

Fig. 10.5. The WRONG-KEY-USED section.

11

Terminal Input/Output Commands

INTRODUCTION

The most important commands in CICS/VS programs are the Terminal Input/Output commands because most programs read data entered by the operator and display data for the operator. Besides the HANDLE AID command, there are four other commands that are commonly used for terminal operations. To read the terminal data into the program, the RECEIVE MAP command is used; to display data on a terminal, the SEND MAP command is used; to display an unformatted message (a message that is not part of a map) for the operator, the SEND command is used; to save transmission time in a continuous entry application, the ISSUE ERASEUP command is used.

TERMINAL INPUT COMMAND

When the operator hits the ENTER or PF keys on the terminal, Terminal Control transmits data with the modified data tag "ON" into the terminal input/output area (TIOA). On a RECEIVE MAP command, CICS/VS secures main storage for the symbolic description map and moves user data from the TIOA into this area. It will also establish the address of the area to the program so it can be accessed.

The RECEIVE MAP command requires BMS modules, which provide the necessary formatting service for the program to interpret input data streams. BMS in turn uses Terminal Control facilities for data transmission.

The format of the command is:

```
RECEIVE    MAP      ('map name')
           MAPSET   ('mapset name')
           SET      (map-pointer)
```

118

The map name and mapset name are those specified in the map program. The SET operand specifies the linkage pointer that corresponds to the particular symbolic description map. As mentioned before, the use of linkage pointers to gain access to the corresponding main storage constitutes the locate-mode option and will be the one used in this book.

An example of the RECEIVE MAP command is:

```
RECEIVE   MAP      ('ORCHM01')
          MAPSET ('ORCHS01')
          SET      (MAP1-POINTER)
```

When this command is executed, CICS/VS secures main storage for the symbolic description map corresponding to MAP1-POINTER and moves data from the TIOA into this storage area where the format of the data is defined in the map program that has the mapset name (label) "ORCHS01" and map name (label) "ORCHM01".

The MAPFAIL exceptional condition can occur on this command if the TIOA contains no data. The programmer should specify it in a HANDLE CONDITION command (generally at the MAIN-LINE section) to specify a paragraph in the ABNORMAL-TERMINATION section that displays a message and terminates the session.

TERMINAL OUTPUT COMMAND

To display data on a terminal, the SEND MAP command is used. The command uses BMS modules for formatting output data streams, which in turn uses Terminal Control facilities for data transmission. There are three versions of this command: (1) Display initial information (fields defined with the INITIAL operand in the map program) from the physical map; (2) Display data only from the symbolic description map; (3) combine initial information from the physical map with data from the symbolic description map.

Physical Map Only

In many instances, the programmer just wants to display the screen title, the field identifiers, and any user data defined with an initial value. The operator may then start entering data on the terminal. Since only fields defined with the INITIAL operand in the map program are displayed, we are in fact displaying the physical map. The format of the command is:

            SEND MAP   ('map name')
                  MAPSET ('mapset name')
                  MAPONLY
                  ERASE

The MAPONLY operand specifies that only fields with initial values from the physical map are to be displayed. The ERASE operand specifies that the previous display on the screen will be erased before the new screen is displayed. This is useful if the previous display is a different map because it prevents mixing of displays that can confuse the operator.

An example of this command is:

            SEND MAP   ('ORCHM01')
                  MAPSET   ('ORCHS01')
                  MAPONLY
                  ERASE

This will erase the previous display and then display all fields defined with the INITIAL operand in the map program with the map name (label) "ORCHM01" and the mapset name (label) "ORCHS01".

Symbolic Description Map Only

Once the screen title, field identifiers, etc. have been displayed on the terminal on a MAPONLY option, we do not have to redisplay them on the next screen display as long as we are still using the same map. Current displays are never erased unless specified in the command. We thus save transmission time.

For instance, in an application with data editing, after the program has displayed the title and field identifiers, the operator starts entering data on the terminal. Once he hits the ENTER key or any PF key, the program may validate the data. If there are no errors, the data will presumably be used to update a file. The next map is then displayed. However, if there are any errors, the program has to display error messages along with what the operator entered so that corrections can be entered. We are in fact only displaying data from the symbolic description map. The format of the command is:

```
SEND  MAP         ('map name')
      MAPSET      ('mapset name')
      FROM        (map area)
      DATAONLY
```

The DATAONLY operand specifies that only data from map area (the symbolic description map) is to be displayed. We do not use the ERASE operand, so the original display (title, field identifiers) is not erased.

An example of this command is:

```
SEND  MAP         ('ORCHM01')
      MAPSET      ('ORCHS01')
      FROM        (MAP1-AREA)
      DATAONLY
```

All fields from MAP1-AREA where the first byte is not hexadecimal zeroes will be displayed on the terminal. Displayed fields will overlay the corresponding fields in the original display, leaving the rest of the original display untouched, unless the ERASE operand is specified.

MAP1-AREA must have main storage allocated to it before this command is given, otherwise the results are unpredictable. However, a RECEIVE MAP command is generally issued earlier in the task, which obtains the necessary storage area. If not, then the programmer has to secure his own main storage area using the GETMAIN command.

The attribute bytes of the fields will also be transmitted along with the fields. The attribute bytes are those transmitted to the symbolic description map on the RECEIVE MAP command, unless modified by the program.

Combined Version

In some applications, the displaying of initial values from the map program (hence from the physical map) is not enough when the map displayed is different from the previous display; the programmer may want to add his own display. For example, in an application involving multiple maps, an important field like record key may have been entered on the first map. But when the second map is displayed, this key will also have to appear for the benefit of the operator. Therefore, the first time the second map is displayed, the programmer will have to mix this field, which should be in the symbolic description map, with the title and field identifiers of a map.

The format of the command is:

```
SEND  MAP       ('map name')
      MAPSET    ('mapset name')
      FROM      (map area)
      ERASE
```

Note that we are omitting the MAPONLY and DATAONLY operands. If there is no RECEIVE MAP command earlier in the task for this map, the programmer has to use GETMAIN to secure main storage for the symbolic description map before the command is issued. Again, the ERASE option is used to erase the previous display.

Any data in the symbolic description map will override the corresponding data in the physical map, unless the former is hexadecimal zeroes; however, attributes from the physical map will be used before corresponding attributes in the symbolic description map, unless it is hexadecimal zeroes.

MODIFYING ATTRIBUTES

The attributes of fields (whether protected, of bright intensity, etc.) are generally those coming from the physical map as defined in the map program. For maps defined with MODE=INOUT, the programmer has the option to change the attributes from those specified in the map program. One instance occurs in a map that is used for file update: The operator enters the record key and it is verified correct. When the same map is displayed so that the operator can enter the data, the programmer should change the unprotected attribute of the record key to autoskip so the operator can no longer change it.

This is done by replacing the value of the attribute byte of the field in the symbolic description map, which was originally transmitted there on the RECEIVE MAP command. To standardize the data names used to modify attribute bytes, the installation should have a standard attribute list maintained in the source program library that is copied by the application programmer into his program (see Figure 5.3).

The programmer should understand that there is only one byte to represent the attributes of a field on any modification. The new attributes will completely replace the old ones.

Suppose the record key mentioned is defined as unprotected, numeric, and bright, and we want to modify this to autoskip and bright. We check Fig. 5.3 and verify that the dataname ATTR-PROT-ASKIP-BRT-PEN means autoskip (PROT being included in ASKIP), bright, and pen detectible (this extra attribute will just be ignored). Each field defined with a label (and thus having entries in the symbolic description map) actually has a halfword binary length field, a one-byte attribute field, and the actual field itself. The record key field may be represented in the symbolic description map as:

```
    . . . . .
    . . . . .
05   MAP1-RECORD-KEY-L     PIC  S9999  COMP.
05   MAP1-RECORD-KEY-A     PIC  X.
05   MAP1-RECORD-KEY       PIC  9 (6).
    . . . . .
    . . . . .
```

The process of changing the attributes in the program is illustrated in Figure 11.1.

The attributes of MAP1-RECORD-KEY are the ones transmitted to the symbolic description map on the RECEIVE MAP command. These are modified by the programmer before the next SEND MAP command. These modified attributes will be the new attributes until they are modified again or until the physical map is redisplayed as either the physical map only version or the combined version of the SEND MAP command.

After Figure 11.1 is executed, the record key entered by the operator will still show brightly on the screen, but it can not be changed anymore.

SYMBOLIC CURSOR POSITIONING

Every time a map is displayed on a screen, the field where the cursor is initially positioned may be controlled in two ways. The choice will always be that field that the operator enters or changes first.

When a new map is being displayed, the programmer generally knows the first field that may be entered or changed by the operator. He specifies this field with the IC (insert cursor) operand in the map program.

. . . . .

RECEIVE MAP command.

. . . . .

. . . . .

MOVE ATTR-PROT-ASKIP-BRT-PEN TO MAP1-RECORD-KEY-A.

. . . . .

. . . . .

SEND MAP command.

. . . . .

. . . . .

RETURN command (task terminates).

Fig. 11.1. Modifying Attributes.

However, in a map defined with MODE=INOUT, there are two reasons why the programmer has to control the initial position of the cursor every time the same map is redisplayed: (1) The IC operand is effective only when the physical map is included in the display. Thus, on successive displays of the same map (DATAONLY option), the cursor will be positioned at the start of the map (as specified by the LINE and COLUMN operands, else 1, 1 is the default). (2) An INOUT map is generally used interactively. The operator enters a set of data that is validated and redisplayed on the screen in a series of steps.

In a series of terminal inputs and outputs that validate data entered, it is always best to place the cursor on the next display, in case of errors, under the first field validated as an error. This will generally be the first field to be corrected by the operator. For instance, if the operator enters 20 fields and the first error detected was the fourth field entered, then the cursor should be placed under this field on the next display of the map. If the operator enters corrections and on the next display it is now the 15th field that is the first error, then the cursor will be placed under the 15th field.

The cursor can be placed under a specific field by using the symbolic cursor positioning technique. In this method, −1 is moved to the length field of that field in the symbolic description map and then specifying the CURSOR operand in the SEND MAP command.

For instance, assume that this is part of a symbolic description map:


```
01      MAP1-AREA.
          . . . . .

          . . . . .
        05   MAP1-NAME-L      PIC   S9999 COMP.
        05   MAP1-NAME-A      PIC   X.
        05   MAP1-NAME        PIC   X (30).
          . . . . .

          . . . . .
```


A typical use of the cursor positioning technique in an application is shown in Figure 11.2.

```
. . . .
RECEIVE  MAP  command.
. . . . .

. . . . .
MOVE  -1  TO MAP1-NAME-L.
. . . . .

. . . . .
EXEC  CICS
       SEND  MAP         ('ORCHM01')
             MAPSET      ('ORCHS01')
             FROM        (MAP1-AREA)
             DATAONLY
             CURSOR
END-EXEC.
. . . . .

. . . .
RETURN command (task terminates).
```

Fig. 11.2. Symbolic Cursor Positioning Technique.

When the SEND MAP command is executed, the CURSOR operand will cause the cursor to be placed under the field whose length field was set to -1. In this case, the field is MAP1-NAME. If we are using the combined version of the SEND MAP command, the symbolic cursor positioning technique will override the insert cursor (IC) specification in the map program.

The technique of cursor positioning may be combined with the technique of modifying attributes. For instance, on page 123 we mentioned a map where we change the attributes of the record key. Presumably, the programmer has specified the IC operand for the record key field in the map program so the cursor will fall under this field when the physical map is first displayed.

However, when the attributes are changed on the next display of the screen so the record key can no longer be modified by the operator, it is necessary to position the cursor on the next unprotected field that follows the record key. Assuming that MAP1-NAME is the next unprotected field, the procedure is given by Figure 11.3.

. . . . .

RECEIVE MAP command.

. . . . .

. . . . .

MOVE ATTR-PROT-ASKIP-BRT-PEN TO MAP1-RECORD-KEY-A.
MOVE –1 TO MAP1-NAME-L.
EXEC CICS
       SEND MAP   ('ORCHM01')
             MAPSET   ('ORCHS01')
             FROM   (MAP1-AREA)
             DATAONLY
             CURSOR
END-EXEC.

. . . . .

. . . . .

RETURN command (task terminates).

Fig. 11.3.   Modifying Attributes and Symbolic Cursor Positioning.

After the procedure in Figure 11.3 is executed, the attributes of
the field MAP1-RECORD-KEY are changed and the cursor is positioned under the field MAP1-NAME.

FSET OPERAND

All fields defined with labels in the map program have corresponding
modified data tags monitored by CICS/VS. Only fields with the modified data tags "ON" will be transmitted into the symbolic description map on a RECEIVE MAP command and thus be available in the
program.

Any field entered or modified by the operator will have its modified
data tag set "ON" to make it available to the program. This tag will
remain "ON" and the corresponding field will always be transmitted
to the symbolic description map on succeeding RECEIVE MAP commands as long as the same map is used.

Fields that are not entered on that particular map (although it may
have been entered in another map), which must be made available to

the program on a RECEIVE MAP command, must have the FSET attribute. For instance, in applications with multiple maps, where the operator has the option to recall the data entered in a previous map, (the data would have been saved in temporary storage in the meantime), when the program moves the fields that have been saved into the map being recalled, those fields must have the FSET attribute. Otherwise, the fields will not be transmitted into the symbolic description map on the RECEIVE MAP command *even if the fields will show on the screen.*

There are two ways of setting the attribute to FSET. First, it may be specified as one of the attributes when the field is specified in the map program. Second, the programmer may change the attributes of the field to include the FSET attribute.

UNFORMATTED MESSAGE

An unformatted message is one that is displayed on a screen but is not part of a map. Thus, the programmer does not have to have a map program to display the message. This is useful for messages sent to the operator when the session is terminated, either normally by the operator, or abnormally, as when a major error occurs on the execution of a command.

The format of the command is:


```
SEND  FROM    (message area)
      LENGTH (message length)
      ERASE
```


This command will display, starting at line 1, column 1 of the terminal, as many bytes of message area depending on the message length. ERASE is optional but is usually specified so that the previous display is erased.

For instance, to display the appropriate message when the operator terminates the job, we can code:

```
MOVE  JOB-NORMAL-END-MESSAGE TO TWA-OPERATOR-MESSAGE.
EXEC  CICS
        SEND  FROM     (TWA-OPERATOR-MESSAGE)
              LENGTH (31)
              ERASE
END-EXEC.
```

ISSUE ERASEAUP

In certain applications, the operator may enter data on a terminal that can be used, after validation, to update an on-line file and/or generate journal records. The SEND MAP* command with the ERASE operand are then used on a successful entry to enable the operator to enter the next set of data.

If the next map required is actually the same as the map being displayed, then we would actually be retransmitting fields like the title, the field identifiers, etc., which are already in the current map. The ISSUE ERASEAUP command avoids this retransmission by erasing all user-entered (unprotected) fields on the terminal and setting their modified data tags to "OFF". The operator may then continue entering the next set of data. This command is especially helpful if the terminals are at remote sites where transmission speeds (through modems) are slower than usual.

The format of this command is:

ISSUE ERASEAUP

There is, however, one limitation with the ISSUE ERASEAUP command. Since only unprotected fields are erased and message areas are defined as autoskip, the last set of error messages will remain on the screen, thus confusing the operator. The programmer may go around this problem by defining the message fields as unprotected (instead of the usual autoskip) so that they are erased along

---

*Usually with the MAPONLY option.

with the other unprotected fields on the ISSUE ERASEAUP command. But the problem is that the operator may inadvertently enter data on these fields.

Otherwise, I suggest that we redisplay the physical map instead of using ISSUE ERASEAUP to ensure a prompting message to the operator.

In spite of this, there are four reasons for using the ISSUE ERASEAUP command:

1. A large portion of the display consists of protected fields, with a corresponding large potential for savings.

2. Remote terminals are being used.

3. The application is heavily used.

4. There is an urgent need to save transmission time because the increase in response time is significant to the installation.

12

File Control Commands

INTRODUCTION

CICS/VS supports VSAM (virtual storage access method), ISAM (indexed sequential access method), and DAM (direct access method). This book, however, will show only operations on a VSAM file since it is the one used in the program examples. If the reader is interested in using ISAM or DAM files, he should refer to a regular CICS/VS manual. He will notice that the commands are very similar.

ON-LINE FILES

Application programs work with on-line files, and the programmer should know about their use in CICS/VS application programs. These are:

1. All on-line files must be defined (generally by the systems programmer) in the File Control Table. This table will specify, among other things, what actions (add a new record, delete an existing record, browse on the file, etc.) are allowed on the file.

2. Files are not opened and closed by the application program because such programs are used by many terminals that access these files at different times. They are instead opened and closed in the following manner:

   a. Files that are used by all applications (tables, etc.) may be opened when CICS/VS is initialized at the beginning of the day and closed when CICS/VS is terminated at the end of the day. The automatic opening and closing of files is part of the job steps that initialize or terminate CICS/VS.

   b. Files used only by certain applications are usually opened just before the first use of those applications but after

CICS/VS has been initialized, and are generally closed after the last use of those applications but before CICS/VS is terminated. The user may actually open and close files many times during the day, but this entails extra overhead and may not be necessary.

3. The programs that open or close on-line files require special CICS/VS macros and are generally written by the systems programmer. If used as in 2.b., these programs will have their own transaction identifiers. This enables the user to open or close files at the same terminal used for applications.

ALTERNATE INDEXES

CICS/VS gives the application programmer the facility to have alternate indexes (also known as secondary indexes) for VSAM files so an operator may do a read on or a browse through a file using keys independent of the primary key. For instance, a Purchase Order file may have a primary index based on the order number but may also have an alternate index based on the date of the order. The operator may then have the option of displaying a specific record using either the order number or the date of order or of using any of two browse programs, one using the order number to scan records in order number sequence, and another using the date of order to scan records in date of order sequence.

The primary key and alternate keys are specified when the file is defined (generally, by the systems programmer) and the corresponding indexes are automatically maintained up to date by CICS/VS on any file add, update, or delete operation.

A browse based on an alternate key is shown in the program example in Chapter 23.

FILE SERVICES

CICS/VS provides the application programmer with the facility to access on-line files using commands in the PROCEDURE DIVISION. Once a file has been opened, he may request a service any time he wants. The commands that provide the services are:

1. READ. Read a record from a file.

2. WRITE. Write a new record into a file.

3. REWRITE. Update an existing record in a file.

4. DELETE (VSAM only). Delete a single record or a group of records from a key-sequenced file.

5. UNLOCK. Release exclusive control over a record or a group of records.

6. STARTBR. Specify the starting point of a browse operation.

7. READNEXT. Read the next record in a file during a browse.

8. READPREV (VSAM only). Read the previous record in a file during a browse.

9. RESETBR. Reset the starting point of a browse.

10. ENDBR. End a browse.

READING INPUT RECORDS

The most common method for getting an input record is to read a specific record. The command for reading a specific record is:

```
read dataset ('file identifier')
     set     (file-pointer)
     ridfld  (data area)
```

The DATASET operand specifies the file identifier of the file in the File Control Table. If the RIDFLD operand specifies an alternate key, then the file identifier corresponds to that of the alternate index. The SET operand specifies the linkage pointer that points to the file record description in the LINKAGE section. The RIDFLD operand specifies the data area that contains the record identification field (key of the record, a relative byte address, or a relative record number).

An example of this command is:

```
MOVE  MAP1-RECORD-KEY TO TWA-RECORD-KEY.
EXEC  CICS
        READ  DATASET  ('POMAST')
              SET       (POMAST-POINTER)
              RIDFLD    (TWA-RECORD-KEY)
END-EXEC.
```

When the read command is executed, CICS/VS gets main storage for the file record description pointed to by POMAST-POINTER. Then, using the key equal to that contained in TWA-RECORD-KEY, CICS/VS moves the record from the file 'POMAST' to this storage area. The key value is set to what the operator presumably entered on the terminal (as MAP1-RECORD-KEY).

As another example, it is also possible to read a record using a generic key, that is, only part of the key will be used. The command may be coded as:

```
read  dataset    ('file identifier')
      set        (file-pointer)
      ridfld     (data area)
      generic
      keylength  (numeric literal)
      gteq
```

The DATASET operand specifies the file identifier of the file in the File Control Table. The SET operand specifies the linkage pointer that points to the file record description in the LINKAGE section. The RIDFLD operand specifies the data area that contains the record identification field (the generic key). The GENERIC operand specifies that we will be using only part of the key. The KEYLENGTH operand specifies the length of the generic key. And the GTEQ operand is optional and specifies that if the record cannot be found using the key (in this case generic), the next record will be used.

An example of this command is:

```
MOVE  MAP1-RECORD-KEY TO TWA-RECORD-KEY.
EXEC  CICS
      READ  DATASET       ('POMAST')
            SET           (POMAST-POINTER)
            RIDFLD        (TWA-RECORD-KEY)
            GENERIC
            KEYLENGTH   (5)
            GTEQ
END-EXEC.
```

When this command is executed, CICS/VS gets main storage for the file record description pointed to by POMAST-POINTER. Then it moves the first record from the file 'POMAST', whose first 5 bytes of the key are equal to or greater than the first 5 bytes of the value contained in TWA-RECORD-KEY, to this storage area.

The GTEQ operand is optional and is specified only if the programmer wants to get the first record with a higher key in case the record being requested is not in the file. Otherwise, the NOTFND condition occurs.

Reading For Update

For a record that will be updated or deleted (VSAM only) after it has been read, the UPDATE option must be specified. That record may then be rewritten or deleted.

CICS/VS will secure exclusive control of the record (ISAM) or of the whole block where the record belongs (DAM), or of the control interval where the record resides (VSAM), so that nobody else (that is, no other task) can access the same record or control interval until the record is rewritten, deleted (VSAM only), the program specifies the UNLOCK command, or the task terminates. This makes sure that no one else will modify or delete the same record until the operator either finishes modifying it, deletes it, or no longer needs it.

Exceptional Conditions

Of the many conditions that may occur on a READ command, the programmer should code two, and may code a third, in a HANDLE CONDITION command: NOTOPEN, NOTFND, and DUPKEY. The NOTOPEN condition should be specified to execute a paragraph in the ABNORMAL-TERMINATION section that displays a message and aborts the session. This condition should in fact always be specified for all commands for file access.

The NOTFND condition should likewise be coded to take care of the condition when a record is not in the file. Generally, this will not abort the session; for instance, in an inquiry or update application, the message that the record is not in the file should be displayed for the operator. He may then correct the record key or enter a new one.

If the READ command is using an alternate key, then the DUPKEY condition should likewise be coded because alternate keys generally have duplicates. Like NOTFND, this should not abort the session.

Other conditions should rarely, if ever, happen. Therefore, the programmer should not bother coding these conditions but instead allow them to be covered by the ERROR condition, which is the catchall condition.

WRITING OUTPUT RECORDS

Adding New Records

We use the WRITE command to add new records to an existing file. The command is:

```
write  dataset     ('file identifier')
       from        (file-area)
       ridfld      (data area)
       length      (data value)
```

The DATASET operand specifies the file identifier of the file in the File Control Table. The FROM operand specifies the file record description in the LINKAGE section. The RIDFLD operand specifies the data area that contains the record identification field (key of the record). The LENGTH operand is optional for fixed-length records when the file record description is of the correct size (generally, it is) but it is required for a variable-length record. This may be a numeric literal or a data area.

An example of this command is:

```
COMPUTE TWA-RECORD-LENGTH = 60 + 15 * NUMBER-OF-STORES.
EXEC CICS
        WRITE DATASET  ('POMAST')
              FROM     (POMAST-AREA)
              RIDFLD   (TWA-RECORD-KEY)
              LENGTH   (TWA-RECORD-LENGTH)
END-EXEC.
```

When the WRITE command is executed, CICS/VS will add into the file 'POMAST' a record with the data coming from POMAST-AREA and position it in the file according to the value of TWA-RECORD-KEY. The length of the record added (we assume a variable-length record) is contained in TWA-RECORD-LENGTH as computed before the WRITE command. Naturally, for fixed-length records, the LENGTH operand of the WRITE command and the COMPUTE statement used to compute the record length are not needed.

Securing Storage For The File Record Description

In the READ command, CICS/VS will automatically secure main storage for the file record description. This is not the case for the WRITE command because main storage must already be available for the file record description so that the record can be built up before the (WRITE) command. The programmer will have to use a GETMAIN command to secure an area large enough to contain the largest record to be written out.

The programmer may release the storage area acquired by using the FREEMAIN command when the WRITE command is finished or else let the task release the storage area when it terminates. It is more efficient for the programmer to release storage he has acquired when it is no longer required and the task is not yet about to be terminated.

Exceptional Conditions

Of the many conditions that may occur on a WRITE command, the programmer should code two in a HANDLE CONDITION command: NOTOPEN and DUPREC. The NOTOPEN condition should be specified to execute a paragraph in the ABNORMAL-TERMINATION section to display a message and abort the session. This condition should in fact always be specified for all commands for file access.

The DUPREC condition should likewise be coded to take care of the condition when the key of the record to be added to the file matches that of an existing record. A message should then be displayed for the operator, but the session should not be terminated.

Other conditions should rarely, if ever, happen. Therefore, the programmer should not bother coding these conditions but instead allow them to be covered by the ERROR condition, which is the catchall condition.

UPDATING EXISTING RECORDS

The REWRITE Command

The REWRITE command is used for rewriting (presumably after changes are made) records that were read in the same task, and thus is used to update existing records. The format of the command is:

```
rewrite  dataset   ('file identifier')
         from      (file-area)
         length    (data value)
```

The DATASET operand specifies the file identifier of the file in the File Control Table. The FROM operand specifies the file record description in the LINKAGE section. The LENGTH operand is optional for fixed-length records when the file record description is of the correct size (generally, it is), but is required for a variable-length record. This may be a numeric literal or a data area.

An example of this command is:

```
EXEC  CICS
      READ  DATASET  ('POMAST')
            SET       (POMAST-POINTER)
            RIDFLD    (TWA-RECORD-KEY)
            UPDATE
END-EXEC.
. . . . .
. . . . .
COMPUTE TWA-RECORD-LENGTH = 60 + 15 * NUMBER-OF-STORES.
EXEC  CICS
      REWRITE  DATASET  ('POMAST')
               FROM      (POMAST-AREA)
               LENGTH    (TWA-RECORD-LENGTH)
END-EXEC.
```

When the REWRITE command is executed, CICS/VS will rewrite into the file 'POMAST' the record in POMAST-AREA with the same RIDFLD field used in the previous READ with UPDATE option that secured the record. The LENGTH operand specifies the length (in bytes) of the rewritten record.

Exclusive Control

As we mentioned before, any record to be updated must be initially read with the UPDATE operand. When this is executed, CICS/VS secures the record for the programmer (if it is in the file) and then gets exclusive control of the record (ISAM), the whole block (DAM), or the whole control interval that contains the record (VSAM).

After CICS/VS gets exclusive control for VSAM files, an attempt by another task to use the same control interval before exclusive control is released (by the REWRITE, UNLOCK, or DELETE commands, or when the original task terminates) will cause the second task to go into a wait until exclusive control is released. If the same task does it, an INVREQ condition occurs.

For ISAM files, an attempt to read the same record before it is updated (REWRITE command), before exclusive control is purposely released (UNLOCK command), or before the original task terminates will cause a lockout.

Exceptional Conditions

There is no need to specify error conditions for this command because they will be covered by the corresponding READ for update command.

DELETING EXISTING RECORDS

Only for VSAM files can the programmer delete records in the file. He may choose to delete the record(s) immediately or to delete each record after it is read (he may want to sight verify if this is indeed the record to be deleted).

Immediate Delete

To delete a VSAM record or group of records without reading the record first, the command is:

```
delete  dataset     ('file identifier')
        ridfld      (data area)
        keylength   (data value)
        generic
```

The DATASET operand specifies the file identifier of the file in the File Control Table. The RIDFLD operand specifies the data area that contains the record identification field (key of the record, a relative byte address, or a relative record number). The KEYLENGTH operand is mandatory if GENERIC is specified. It specifies the length of the generic key used. The GENERIC operand is optional and specifies that we are deleting a group of records.

An example of this command is:

```
EXEC  CICS
        DELETE  DATASET      ('POMAST')
                RIDFLD        (TWA-RECORD-KEY)
END-EXEC.
```

This command will delete the specific record whose key is equal to that specified in TWA-RECORD-KEY.

Another example of the command is:

```
EXEC  CICS
        DELETE  DATASET      ('POMAST')
                RIDFLD        (TWA-RECORD-KEY)
                KEYLENGTH (5)
                GENERIC
END-EXEC.
```

This command will delete the group of records whose first 5 bytes of the key equals the value in TWA-RECORD-KEY.

Delete After Read

The programmer may also delete a specific record after the record has been read for update. The format of the command is similar to that of immediate delete but with the RIDFLD operand omitted since this is the same one specified in the READ for update command. An example is:

```
EXEC  CICS
        READ  DATASET      ('POMAST')
              SET           (POMAST-POINTER)
              RIDFLD        (TWA-RECORD-KEY)
              UPDATE
END-EXEC.
. . . . . . .
. . . . . . .
EXEC  CICS
        DELETE DATASET      ('POMAST')
END-EXEC.
```

Exceptional Conditions

Whether the programmer opts for an immediate delete or does a READ for update first, there should be two conditions specified in a HANDLE CONDITION command, NOTOPEN and NOTFND. The reasons are similar to those mentioned on page 136.

RELEASING EXCLUSIVE CONTROL

For a record read with the UPDATE operand, CICS/VS will secure exclusive control so that the record (along with the whole control interval or the whole block, as the case may be) can not be accessed until it has been updated, deleted (VSAM only), or the task has ended. If, however, the record will not be updated or deleted after all and the task is not about to end, the programmer should release exclusive control so the record can be accessed. This is done by using the UNLOCK command, and the format is:

unlock dataset ('file identifier')

An example of this command is:

```
EXEC  CICS
        READ  DATASET    ('POMAST')
              SET        (POMAST-POINTER)
              RIDFLD     (TWA-RECORD-KEY)
              UPDATE
END-EXEC.
. . . . . . .
. . . . . . .
EXEC  CICS
        UNLOCK  DATASET    ('POMAST')
END-EXEC.
```

After the unlock command is executed, the record (along with the whole control interval or the whole block, as the case may be) can then be accessed.

Exceptional Conditions

There is no need to specify exceptional conditions for this command because they will be covered by the corresponding READ for UPDATE command.

FILE BROWSE

In many instances where the operator wants to recall previously entered information, he simply enters the record identifier and the program uses this to get the corresponding record in the file and display it. This is known as the inquiry function. However, if the exact record identifier is not known, but can be approximated, then a browse application can be used to pinpoint the record.

In the browse application, the operator enters the approximate record identifier and this is used as the starting point of a search of the file index. By using a single key (the PF1 key is usually used), the operator can continuously scan forward through the file, in ascending sequence, without having to enter another record identifier. With another key (usually the PF2 key is used), he can do it in descending sequence (VSAM file only).

A browse can also be used when there is a need to know which records belong to a particular alternate key value. For instance, in a Purchase Order file with the date of order as an alternate key, there may be a need to see which orders were made on a specific date.

Since CICS/VS maintains pointers to records only within a task, the browse commands require that the task not be terminated for the whole browse session. Thus, this is the only application in CICS/VS where the design has to be pure conversational, not pseudoconversational.

However, this should not degrade the response time for the installation very much for two reasons: First, a browse application should be used rarely and avoided if possible. Secondly, browse applications are often used only for a short time because they are generally written so that only record summaries (but including the exact record identifier) are displayed, allowing many records to be displayed at the same time. Once the required record can be determined from the display, the operator may then terminate the browse and go to a regular inquiry, using the record identifier displayed at the browse to get the complete display of the record.

The application programmer can actually write a browse application using the pseudoconversational mode of processing. He can maintain the pointers to records in between task initiation and termination, but he can not use some of the powerful features available through the CICS/VS browse commands.

The browse function allows an operator to display a series of records singly or as a group. He has the option of starting the browse at any specific record in the file, reading the records in ascending sequence, reading them in descending sequence (VSAM only), restarting the browse at some other record, and terminating the browse.

Browse Starting Point

The STARTBR command specifies the starting point (but does not retrieve the record) of the browse and is usually based on a value entered by the operator. The format of the command is:

```
startbr  dataset     ('file identifier')
         ridfld      (data area)
         keylength   (data value)
         generic
         gteq
```

The DATASET operand specifies the file identifier of the file in the File Control Table. If the RIDFLD operand specifies an alternate key, then the file identifier corresponds to that of the alternate index. The RIDFLD operand specifies the data area that contains the record identification field (key of the record, a relative byte address, or a relative record number). The KEYLENGTH operand is mandatory if GENERIC is specified and specifies the length of the generic key used. The GENERIC operand is optional and specifies that we are using a generic key. The GTEQ operand is optional but is generally specified to select the next higher record in case the record specified does not exist (otherwise a NOTFND exceptional condition occurs).

An example of this command is:

```
EXEC CICS
        STARTBR  DATASET  ('POMAST')
                 RIDFLD   (TWA-RECORD-KEY)
                 GTEQ
END-EXEC.
```

When this command is executed, the browse starting point is at the record whose record identification field is equal to the value in TWA-RECORD-KEY or, if there is no such record, the next higher record. If TWA-RECORD-KEY is equal to HIGH-VALUES, then the end of the file is the starting point. A READPREV command will then retrieve the last record in the file.

Exceptional Conditions for Startbr

The programmer should code the NOTOPEN and NOTFND exceptional conditions in a HANDLE CONDITION command. As we mentioned before, the NOTOPEN condition is always specified for applications that use files; the NOTFND condition is used to display an error message in case the record specified does not exist or, in case GTEQ is specified, the starting record number is higher than the last record in the file. The NOTFND condition will not occur if RIDFLD specifies a field equal to HIGH-VALUES even if there is no such record.

Browse in Ascending Sequence

The READNEXT command is used to retrieve records in a forward sequence. It is used in the following ways: First, it will retrieve the record specified in the STARTBR or RESETBR command if they were the previous File Control command. Second, it will retrieve the next record in ascending sequence if the previous File Control command is another READNEXT or a READPREV (VSAM only). Third, for VSAM files, it can be used to skip forward to read a record beyond the next higher record in ascending sequence.

The format of the command is:

```
readnext  dataset    ('file identifier')
          set        (file-pointer)
          ridfld     (data area)
```

The DATASET operand specifies the file identifier of the file in the File Control Table. If the RIDFLD operand specifies an alternate key, then the file identifier corresponds to that of the alternate index. The SET operand specifies the linkage pointer that points to the file record description in the LINKAGE section. The RIDFLD operand specifies the data area that contains the record identification field (key of the record, a relative byte address, or a relative record number).

An example of this command is:

```
EXEC  CICS
      READNEXT  DATASET    ('POMAST')
                SET        (POM-POINTER)
                RIDFLD     (TWA-RECORD-KEY)
END-EXEC.
```

When this command is executed, a record is retrieved and TWA-RECORD-KEY will be set to the record identification field of the record.

If this command follows a READPREV command and we have not done a skip forward browse or a RESETBR command has not been executed in between, then the same record retrieved by the READPREV command will be retrieved by the READNEXT command. In this case, the programmer should do another READNEXT.

Skip Forward Browse

We mentioned before that the READNEXT command may be used right after a STARTBR or RESETBR command or right after another READNEXT or a READPREV command. A third use is for a skip forward browse, where the operator still retrieves the record in ascending sequence but skips records. In this technique, the operator enters a new record identification field corresponding to the next record to be retrieved, and this will be used on the READNEXT command to retrieve the next record required.

Exceptional Conditions for READNEXT

The programmer should code the NOTFND and ENDFILE exceptional conditions in a HANDLE CONDITION command. NOTFND is used in case the operator opts for the skip forward browse and the record cannot be found.* ENDFILE is used if, during normal browse in ascending sequence, the end of the file is reached. For both conditions, the message "END OF FILE" should be displayed to the operator to guide him in deciding what to do next.

If the browse is being made by using an alternate key, the DUPKEY exceptional condition should likewise be coded in case there are records with duplicate alternate keys; this condition occurs for all records retrieved, except the last duplicate.

Browse in Descending Sequence

The READPREV command (VSAM only) retrieves records in descending sequence. The format is:

```
readprev  dataset    ('file identifier')
          set        (file-pointer)
          ridfld     (data area)
```

The DATASET operand specifies the file identifier of the file in the File Control Table. If the RIDFLD operand specifies an alternate key, then the file identifier corresponds to that of the alternate index. The SET operand specifies the linkage pointer that points to the file record description in the LINKAGE section. The RIDFLD operand specifies the data area that contains the record identification field (key of the record, a relative byte address, or a relative record number).

An example of this command is:

---

*Since most browses specify the GTEQ operand for STARTBR and RESETBR, this will happen only if the record required is beyond the end of the file.

```
        EXEC CICS
             READPREV DATASET   ('POMAST')
                      SET       (POM-POINTER)
                      RIDFLD    (TWA-RECORD-KEY)
        END-EXEC.
```

When this command is executed, the record next in descending sequence is retrieved. TWA-RECORD-KEY will be set to the value of the record retrieved.

If this command follows a READNEXT command, then the very same records are retrieved for both commands. In this case, the programmer should do another READPREV.

Skip Backward Browse

There is no command to do a skip backward browse. If the operator wants to retrieve, in descending sequence, a record beyond the next record, he will have to enter a new record identification field, which will then be used for a RESETBR command, followed by a READNEXT command.

Exceptional Conditions for READPREV

The programmer should code the ENDFILE exceptional condition in a HANDLE CONDITION command. This is used if, during a browse in descending sequence, the end of the file is reached. The message "END OF FILE" should then be displayed to the operator to guide him in deciding what to do next.

If the GTEQ operand is specified in the STARTBR or RESETBR command (generally it is), then the NOTFND exceptional condition need not be coded since this will never happen.

If the browse is being made with the use of an alternate index, the DUPKEY exceptional condition should likewise be coded; in case of records with duplicate alternate keys, this error occurs for all records retrieved except for the last duplicate. Also, in case of duplicates, the records will be retrieved in the order they were added to the file and not in the reverse order.

Reset the Browse Starting Point

The RESETBR command resets the starting point of the browse (but does not retrieve the record) and is usually based on a value entered by the operator. The format is:

```
resetbr  dataset     ('file identifier')
         ridfld      (data area)
         keylength   (data value)
         generic
         gteq
```

The DATASET operand specifies the file identifier of the file in the File Control Table. If the RIDFLD operand specifies an alternate key, then the file identifier corresponds to that of the alternate index. The RIDFLD operand specifies the data area that contains the record identification field (key of the record, a relative byte address, or a relative recored record number). The KEYLENGTH operand is mandatory if GENERIC is specified and specifies the length of the generic key used. The GENERIC operand is optional and specifies that we are using a generic key. The GTEQ operand is optional but is generally specified to select the next higher record in case the record specified does not exist (otherwise a NOTFND exceptional condition occurs).

An example of this command is:

```
EXEC  CICS
        RESETBR  DATASET   ('POMAST')
                 RIDFLD    (TWA-RECORD-KEY)
                 GTEQ
END-EXEC.
```

When this command is executed, the browse starting point is reset to the value of TWA-RECORD-KEY, or if there is no such record, the next higher record. If TWA-RECORD-KEY is equal to HIGH-VALUES, then the end of the file is the starting point. A READPREV command will then retrieve the last record in the file.

Exceptional Conditions for RESETBR

The same exceptional conditions as for STARTBR should be specified.

Ending the Browse

The ENDBR command is used to end the browse function. The format of the command is:

endbr dataset ('file identifier')

Exceptional Conditions for ENDBR

There are no exceptional conditions specified for this command.

13

Temporary Storage Commands

INTRODUCTION

In the pseudoconversational mode of processing, a task is initiated and terminated many times during an application. The main reason for this is to free system resources, especially main storage, so that it may be used by other tasks while CICS/VS is waiting for action from the terminal operator. This helps optimize response time.

Temporary storage allows the programmer to save in either main storage or auxiliary storage (direct access storage device) data that would otherwise be lost when the task terminates. A good guide for determining which medium to use is this: If more than one second lapses between the time data is released by the previous program and the time it is used by the next program,* especially if the data is more than 300 bytes long, it should be in auxiliary storage. For the large majority of applications that use temporary storage, this is the medium to use. The installation should limit the use of main storage for temporary storage since this is a resource in demand by many tasks.

Temporary storage records are written out into a particular queue selected by the programmer according to a queue identifier (up to 8 bytes long). While he may write as many records in a queue as he wants and use as many queues as necessary, most applications need only one record in one queue. It is more efficient, for reasons of overhead, to have a single large record rather than several smaller ones.

The installation should standardize the specification for queue identifiers so no task may accidentally use or delete temporary storage queues belonging to somebody else. A common identifier used is

---

*In the pseudoconversational mode of processing, it generally takes some time for the operator to respond to and restart a task after it has been terminated; temporary storage in auxiliary storage is therefore often used to save data.

the combination of the terminal identification code and the transaction identifier.

Two typical uses of temporary storage are the following:

1. Scratchpad facility. An application may create a temporary storage queue and use it for data that must be saved for the next initiation of the task in pseudoconversational mode. At the end of the session, the application will generally delete the queue.

2. Suspend data set. In a data collection application, where there is a possibility of the application being suspended so the operator can switch to a higher-priority application, the incomplete data may be written out to temporary storage. After the higher-priority application is finished, the data collection application may then be continued, and all data already written out previously in temporary storage will just be recalled.

There are three commands used for temporary storage. The WRITEQ TS command writes or rewrites one record into a queue, the READQ TS command reads a particular record from a queue, and the DELETEQ TS command deletes the whole queue.

WRITING A NEW RECORD INTO A QUEUE

When a task has completed building up the temporary storage record to be used by another task, it is written out before the task terminates. The format of the command is:

```
writeq  ts
        from     (data area)
        queue    (symbolic name)*
        length   (data value)
        item     (data area)*
        main or auxiliary
```

---

*I suggest that these be defined in the Transaction Work Area.

The FROM operand specifies the main storage area to be written out. The QUEUE operand specifies the queue identification code of the queue. The LENGTH operand specifies the length of the record to be written out. The ITEM operand is optional and sets the half-word binary data area to the value that is set by CICS/VS for the record, depending on the position of the record in the queue. AUX-ILIARY is the default.

If the queue identification code is defined as:

```
01    TWA-AREA.
      05    . . . . . . .
      05    . . . . . . .
      05    TSA-QUEUE-ID.
         10    TSA-TERM-ID      PIC X (4).
         10    TSA-TRANS-ID     PIC X (4).
```

We can code the following:

```
set  tsa-queue-id to the proper value.
EXEC  CICS
      WRITEQ  TS
            FROM     (TSA-AREA)
            QUEUE   (TSA-QUEUE-ID)
            LENGTH (2000)
END-EXEC.
```

When this command is executed, CICS/VS assigns an item number for the record defined in TSA-AREA (if this record starts a new queue, the item number assigned is 1 and subsequent item numbers follow on sequentially), then writes out 2000 bytes of it into the queue identified by TSA-QUEUE-ID.

Note that for every new record written out, the main storage area defined by the FROM operand must be secured through a GETMAIN command so it may be made available to the program. The INITIMG operand is optional for the GETMAIN command and is generally not coded since the fields in the area will be set to the proper value in the program anyway.

READING A RECORD FROM A QUEUE

Whenever a task needs data stored in temporary storage, it must read the particular record where the data resides. The format of the command is:

```
readq  ts
    queue      (symbolic name)
    set        (tsa-pointer)
    length     (data area)*
    item       (data value) or next
```

The QUEUE operand specifies the queue identification code of the queue. The SET operand specifies the linkage pointer corresponding to the temporary storage area. The LENGTH operand specifies a halfword binary data area that will be set to the length of the particular record read. The ITEM operand specifies the item number of the record to be read. If ITEM is not specified, NEXT is the default, which means the next sequential record following the last record read (by any task) is read.

An example of the command is:

```
set  tsa-queue-id to the proper value.
EXEC  CICS
        READQ  TS
              QUEUE     (TSA-QUEUE-ID)
              SET       (TSA-POINTER)
              LENGTH    (TSA-LENGTH)
              ITEM      (1)
END-EXEC.
```

When this command is executed, CICS/VS will secure main storage for the area corresponding to TSA-POINTER and read the first record in the queue identified by TSA-QUEUE-ID into this area. TSA-LENGTH will be set to the length of the record read.

---

*This is generally defined in the Transaction Work Area.

REWRITING A RECORD IN A QUEUE

After a temporary storage record read in a task has been modified within that task, it should be rewritten in the same task so the changes will be reflected when the record is read by another task. The format of the command is:

```
writeq  ts
      from      (data area)
      queue     (symbolic name)
      length    (data area)
      item      (data area)
      rewrite
```

The FROM operand specifies the main storage area to be rewritten. The QUEUE operand specifies the queue identification code of the queue. The LENGTH operand specifies the same data area in the previous READQ TS command that read the particular record. The ITEM operand specifies a halfword binary area that contains the item number of the record to be rewritten. The REWRITE operand specifies that this is a rewrite operation.

An example of this command is:

```
MOVE  1  TO TSA-QUEUE-NO.
EXEC  CICS
      WRITEQ  TS
            FROM       (TSA-AREA)
            QUEUE      (TSA-QUEUE-ID)
            LENGTH     (TSA-LENGTH)
            ITEM       (TSA-QUEUE-NO)
            REWRITE
END-EXEC.
```

When this command is executed, the first record in the queue defined by TSA-QUEUE-ID is rewritten using the main storage area TSA-AREA and the length TSA-LENGTH. Any task may then access the updated temporary storage record.

DELETING A QUEUE

Any temporary storage queue that is no longer needed may be deleted
to free storage areas (main or auxiliary) corresponding to it. The
command deletes the whole queue and the format is:

```
deleteq  ts
         queue  (symbolic name)
```

The QUEUE operand specifies the queue identification code of
the queue to be deleted. There is no command to delete individual
records in a queue.

An example of the command is:

```
set  tsa-queue-id  to  the proper value.
EXEC  CICS
         DELETEQ  TS
                  QUEUE  (TSA-QUEUE-ID)
END-EXEC.
```

TEMPORARY STORAGE COMMAND
EXCEPTIONAL CONDITIONS

Scratchpad Facility

Temporary storage queues used as scratchpads, are usually created at
the INITIALIZATION section and deleted at the FINALIZATION
section. However, in case the FINALIZATION section is never executed, as would occur in a program abend, a CICS/VS abnormal termination, or a hardware error that needs the system to be powered
down, we should attempt to delete the queue at the beginning of the
INITIALIZATION section. In this case, QIDERR should be specified
in a HANDLE CONDITION command just in case the queue was
deleted after all to avoid a CICS/VS default that would abort the
session on the DELETEQ command.

Generally, this is the only exceptional condition that should be
specifically defined in a HANDLE CONDITION command because
if the program passed through the normal program test, the other
errors should not happen for other commands. If they do, they can
always be taken cared of by the catchall ERROR condition.

14

Program Control Commands

INTRODUCTION

Program Control commands allow the programmer to select the flow of control between application programs in CICS/VS. Specifically, they allow the programmer to do five things:

1. RETURN. Return control from one application program to another or to CICS/VS (in which case the task terminates).

2. XCTL. Transfer control from one application program to another with no return to the requesting program.

3. LINK. Effectively "call" another application program, and when the latter is finished, return control to the requesting program.

4. LOAD. Load an application program, table, or mapset into main storage and return control to the requesting program.

5. RELEASE. Delete a previously loaded application program, table, or mapset from main storage.

All programs executed through these commands must be entered in the Processing Program Table (PPT), usually maintained by the systems programmer.

APPLICATION PROGRAM LEVELS

Application programs running under CICS/VS execute at various logical levels. The first program to receive control in a task is at the highest logical level. On a XCTL command, both programs are at the same logical level. On a LINK command, the "called" program is at the next lower logical level. A RETURN command will always return control to the next higher logical level, or if the program is already at the highest logical level, to CICS/VS. In many instances, these commands can also pass data to the next program.

An example of this flow of control is shown in Figure 14.1.

When the task is initiated, application program A executes at the highest logical level. At some point, this issues a XCTL command for application program B, which then executes at the same logical level. This in turn issues a LINK command for application program C, which then executes at the next lower logical level. At some point, application program C in turn issues a XCTL command for application program D, which then executes at the same logical level. Program D in turn issues a LINK command for application program E, which then executes at the next lower logical level (in this example, the lowest logical level).

At some point, application program E issues a RETURN command, which returns control to the next higher logical level at the statement following the LINK command of application program D. At some point in application program D, a RETURN command is issued, which returns control to the next higher logical level at the statement following the LINK command of application program B. When this issues a RETURN command, the task is terminated since this is already at the highest logical level.

Note that only the last application program at each logical level issues the RETURN command.

THE RETURN COMMAND

The RETURN command returns control to another application program at the next higher logical level or to CICS/VS. When the command is issued in a lower logical level application program, the program to which control is returned will have at one point issued the LINK command and will be one logical level higher than the application program issuing the RETURN. When the application program issuing the command is at the highest logical level, control returns to CICS/VS and the task is terminated. The format of the command is:

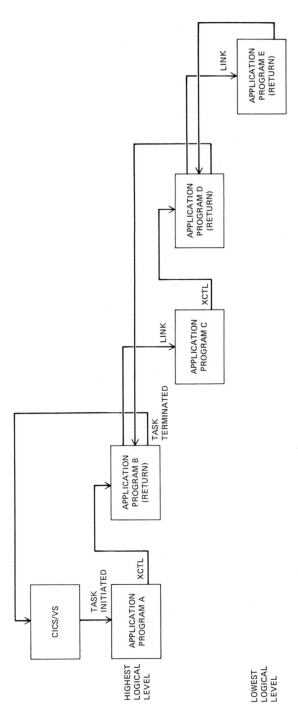

Fig. 14.1. Application Program Logical Levels.

return transid   (transaction identifier)
        commarea   (data area)
        length   (data value)

The TRANSID operand specifies the transaction identifier of the next program to execute on the same terminal (if the task is associated with a terminal).* The COMMAREA operand specifies the data area that will be passed on to the next program. The LENGTH operand specifies the length of the data passed. The COMMAREA and LENGTH operands are used only if we are returning to CICS/VS. Otherwise, the INVREQ exceptional condition will occur.

In the pseudoconversational mode of processing, I suggest the following techniques in the use of the transaction identifier:

1. At the INITIALIZATION section, always specify the literal comprising the transaction identifier. This standardizes the specification of the transaction identifier at this section because if a program is initiated by the XCTL command (as in the program examples), we cannot use the EIBTRNID field of the Execute Interface Block.

2. At the other sections, the EIBTRNID is used because we are using the same transaction identifier to implement the pseudo-conversational mode of processing.

We mentioned on page 89 that we use the first byte of the communication area as a switch to implement the pseudoconversational mode of processing.

THE XCTL COMMAND

The XCTL command transfers control from one application program to another at the same logical level. The program issuing the command is released and the next program is loaded into main storage if it is not yet there. The format of the command is:

---

*This is the case for most applications.

```
xctl  program    (name)
      commarea   (data area)
      length     (data value)
```

The PROGRAM operand specifies the phase name of the program that will take over control. The COMMAREA and LENGTH operands are used to pass data from the requesting program to the new program.

THE LINK COMMAND

The LINK command "calls" another program at the next lower logical level, after which the requesting program regains control when the last program to execute at the lower logical level executes a RETURN command.* The "called" program is loaded into main storage if it is not yet there, but the requesting program is not released. The format of the command is:

```
link  program    (name)
      commarea   (data area)
      length     (data value)
```

The operands specify the same things as are in the XCTL command. The "called" program will handle exceptional conditions (HANDLE CONDITION specifications), attention identifiers, and abends independently of the "calling" program. When control is returned to the "calling" program, the original HANDLE CONDITION commands are reset to what they were before the LINK command was issued.

THE LOAD COMMAND

The load command loads an application program, mapset, or table from the library where they reside into main storage. The format of the command is:

---

*The "called" program may itself issue a XCTL command to another program, in which case the latter program will issue the RETURN command.

load program   (name)
      set   (linkage-pointer)
      length   (data area)
      hold

The PROGRAM operand specifies the phase name of the application program, mapset, or the identifier of the table. The SET operand specifies the linkage pointer corresponding to the area where the application program, mapset, or table is loaded. The LENGTH operand is optional and will be set to the length involved. The HOLD operand is also optional and is used if the application program, mapset, or table is to remain in main storage until a RELEASE command is issued. Otherwise, the loaded application program, mapset, or table is released when the task issuing the LOAD command is terminated normally or abnormally.

This command is useful for doing a one-time load of a heavily used application program or mapset into main storage so that the overhead of repeated loading is eliminated. It is also useful in loading a table "as is" into main storage.

THE RELEASE COMMAND

The RELEASE command is used to delete from main storage any application program, mapset, or table previously loaded through a LOAD command. This command is effective regardless of whether the HOLD operand was specified in the corresponding LOAD command or not. The format of the command is:

release program (name)

15

Miscellaneous Commands

INTRODUCTION

The four most important sets of commands to learn are the Terminal Input/Output commands, the File Control commands, the Temporary Storage commands, and the Program Control commands. The program must be able to read data from and display data on terminals. It should be able to access on-line files easily. It should be able to save data in an environment where the program and main storage are purged many times in a session. The programmer should be able to cause programs to execute in an interactive environment.

However, there are other commands that are useful to the programmer. These commands (with the exception of those used for debugging, which will be discussed in Chapter 24) are presented in this chapter.

THE SUSPEND COMMAND

A task currently in control will remain in control until a command that causes a wait is executed. The task is then suspended and the highest priority task that is ready to execute will take over control. This is the CICS/VS multitasking feature.

However, multitasking can cause a problem because a CPU-intensive task will monopolize the CPU to the exclusion of other tasks. If that task is of low priority, it may cause tasks of higher priority to have slower response times.

To avoid this, the programmer has the option to suspend a program (and thus a task) even before a command that causes a wait is executed, so that the next highest priority task may execute. The suspended task is then placed in the wait queue. The format of the command is:

suspend

THE GETMAIN COMMAND

When a program first executes in a task, only the WORKING-STORAGE section, the Transaction Work Area, the Common Work Area, and the Terminal Control Table User Area will have main storage assigned to them. The rest of the LINKAGE section will not have corresponding main storage areas.

On an input command (RECEIVE MAP to read terminal data, READ DATASET to read a file record, etc.), CICS/VS will automatically secure main storage for the corresponding symbolic description map, file record description, etc. The programmer may then be able to access these areas.

On an output command (SEND MAP to display data on a terminal, WRITE DATASET to create a new record, etc.), the area to be used must be present since it must contain the data to be outputted. If the area is the same one acquired through an input command in the same task, then the same area is used; otherwise, the programmer has to get main storage for the area himself.

The format of the command is:

```
getmain
        set      (linkage-pointer)
        length   (data value)
        initimg  (data area)
```

The SET operand specifies the linkage pointer that corresponds to the area acquired. The LENGTH operand specifies the length in bytes of the area. The INITIMG operand is optional and specifies a data area whose value the acquired area will be set to.

An example of this command is:

```
EXEC  CICS
      GETMAIN
              SET       (MAP1-POINTER)
              LENGTH (900)
              INITIMG (HEX-ZEROES)
      END-EXEC.
```

When the command is executed, 900 bytes of main storage will be allocated for MAP1-AREA (area that corresponds to MAP1-POINTER), and the area will be set to the value of HEX-ZEROES (generally defined in the WORKING-STORAGE section). HEX-ZEROES will be propagated through the whole area acquired.

This command is most commonly used for:

1. A map to be displayed when part of the displayed information or attributes come from the application program and there is no RECEIVE MAP command for that map in that task. The area should be initialized to hexadecimal zeroes by using the INITIMG* option.

2. A record to be added to a file.

3. A new temporary storage record to be created.

4. A journal record to be written out.

5. Any area defined in the LINKAGE section when required in an application program.

THE FREEMAIN COMMAND

All main storage areas acquired through the GETMAIN command will not be released until the task terminates. Therefore, on those occasions when the output command that uses the area has already been executed and the task is still not about to be terminated, we may be wasting main storage. If the area is only a few bytes, however, the effort to purge the area may not be worth it; otherwise, the programmer may purge the area through the FREEMAIN command. The format is:

freemain data (data area)

---

*The area acquired for a symbolic description map should always be initialized to hexadecimal zeroes since BMS always displays data that is not hexadecimal zeroes. For other areas, INITIMG is optional and is generally not used because the fields will be filled up in the application program anyway.

An example of this command is:

```
EXEC  CICS
            FREEMAIN DATA  (MAP1-AREA)
     END-EXEC.
```

When this command is executed, the main storage corresponding to MAP1-AREA, which was acquired through a previous GETMAIN command, will be released.

WRITING JOURNAL RECORDS

CICS/VS provides special-purpose sequential data sets, called journals, which any task can write to anytime. Journal data sets accept records of varying length from various tasks, and these records generally contain information used either for statistical purposes, for file recovery, or for batch file update.

For instance, a File Add application may also generate a journal record, every time a record is written out, to contain information like operator initials, date, time of day, record number, dollar total of the record, etc. These records may then be used offline to prepare a statistical report as an audit trail.

The format of the command is:

```
journal  jfileid    (data value)
         jtypeid    (data value)
         from       (data area)
         length     (data value)
         wait
```

The JFILEID operand specifies the journal data set to be used (02 is the regular journal). The JTYPEID operand specifies a two-byte identifier for the journal record, which is specific for each application or group of applications. The FROM operand specifies the user data* to be included in the record written out. The LENGTH operand specifies the length of the user data. The use of the WAIT operand is

---

*CICS/VS adds a prefix to the journal record.

optional but is suggested so that the task does not continue until the journal record is completely written out.

The programmer should use the GETMAIN command to secure main storage for the journal record written out.

HANDLE ABEND COMMAND

On a program abend (not CICS/VS exceptional condition), the system default terminates the task with a dump printout used for debugging. However, if the programmer prefers to take care of an abend by executing his own routine in place of the system default, the HANDLE ABEND command can specify a program or label exit. The format of the command is:

```
handle abend
       program     (phase name)
       label       (paragraph/section)
       cancel
       reset
```

All the operands are mutually exclusive. The PROGRAM operand specifies the phase name of the program that will take control. The LABEL operand specifies the section or paragraph name if the same program is used. The CANCEL operand will cancel a previous HANDLE ABEND command at the same logical level of the application program in control. The RESET operand reactivates an exit cancelled by a HANDLE ABEND CANCEL command or by CICS/VS.

Generally, the programmer should opt for the system default instead of issuing this command himself because the dump printout includes the PSW that is used for debugging.

STARTING A TASK

In most applications, a session is initiated when the operator enters a transaction identifier on a terminal. However, if the user wants a session or a task to start at a specified time, the START command is used. The format of this command is:

```
start   transid   (transaction identifier)
        termid    (terminal identification code)
        interval  (hhmmss) / time (hhmmss)
        from      (data area)
```

The TRANSID operand specifies the transaction identifier of the task to be started. The TERMID operand is optional and specifies the terminal identifier if the task is associated with a terminal. The INTERVAL operand specifies the time interval in hours, minutes, and seconds from the time the command is executed to the time the task is started. The TIME operand, which is mutually exclusive with the INTERVAL operand, specifies the exact time in hours, minutes, and seconds the task is started. The FROM operand specifies the location of the data to be passed to the task.

If the INTERVAL operand specifies a zero or the TIME operand a value that is equal to the current time of day (or up to six hours preceding it), the task can be started immediately.

REQUESTING CURRENT TIME OF DAY

When a task is initiated, the EIBDATE and EIBTIME fields of the Execute Interface Block are updated by CICS/VS. The programmer may further update these fields during a task by using the ASKTIME command. The format of the command is:

```
asktime
```

The EIBDATE field is not often critical since the date will probably not have changed from the time the task was initiated. However, the time will have changed and this command may be useful when the programmer needs to use the exact time of day; for instance, when generating journal records.

16

Programming Techniques

INTRODUCTION

In addition to learning CICS/VS features and commands, the programmer needs to learn programming techniques so that he can use these features and commands in the best way possible. There is a need for him to understand security techniques to prevent the unauthorized use of files and applications, techniques for using maps and temporary storage, and techniques for passing data between application programs.

ESTABLISHING SECURITY AND PRIORITY

CICS/VS Sign-On

As an option, the user may require operators to use the CICS/VS sign-on procedure before he or she can use some or all of the applications in the installation. This procedure is used to establish whether the operator is authorized to use a given application and what priority, if any, be given to the tasks that will be initiated during the use of the application. The format of the sign-on entry is:

CSSN NAME=XXXXXXXXXXXXXXXXXXXX, PS=XXXX

The NAME operand is from 1 to 20 characters long. The PS (password) operand is four characters long. These are compared with the sign-on table that is maintained by the systems programmer. This table contains the following information:

1. operator name

2. operator identification

3. operator password

4. operator security codes

5. operator security class

6. operator priority

When the operator enters the name and password and then hits the ENTER key or any PF key, the CICS/VS sign-on program is initiated. The sign-on program loads the sign-on table and verifies whether the name and password match any entry in the table. If not, an error message is displayed.

If an entry is found, the operator identification (usually the operator's initials), security codes, security class, and priority are extracted from the table and moved to the terminal control table (TCT) entry for the terminal that has been signed on. This information remains in the TCT entry until the operator signs off. The message "SIGN ON IS COMPLETE" will be displayed on a successful sign on.

Operator identification (3 characters) is used for statistical purposes. When the operator signs off, a message containing operator identification, number of transactions entered, and number of transaction errors may be sent to transient data on disk, magnetic tape, line printer, or any other CICS/VS supported device. This information may then be used for evaluation or as an audit trail.

Authorization for application use is determined by comparing the operator security codes with the security code of the transaction identifier that corresponds to the required program. The operator may have more than one security code if he is authorized to use applications (hence programs) with different security codes. A security code of 1 generally implies the lowest security while a code of 24 implies the highest security. Thus, many File Inquiry applications (especially for non-sensitive data) will have low security codes while File Update or File Inquiry applications (sensitive data) will have high security codes.

If the transaction identifier is not authorized for the operator, CICS/VS will reject it and send an error message to the operator's terminal and the master terminal, indicating a security violation. Operator identification, terminal identification, and transaction identifier are included in the message. The master terminal operator may then take appropriate action.

The operator security class is used primarily in conjunction with the CICS/VS message routing facility. This facility will not be explained in this book. Let it suffice to say that messages through this facility will be sent to specific operators or specific operator classes only if they have signed on to CICS/VS.

The operator priority is added to the terminal priority and the transaction priority to establish the overall task priority. Each of them can have a value from 0 to 255. The terminal priority is specified in the TCT entry for the terminal. The transaction priority is specified in the PCT entry for the transaction identifier. A task priority number of 255 will have the highest priority while 0 will have the lowest priority. If the task priority as computed is greater than 255, 255 is used.

The use of three factors to establish task priority provides the user with considerable flexibility in selecting which application, operator, or terminal should have the shortest response time.

CICS/VS Sign Off

When the operator is finished, he should sign off so no other operator can use applications using his sign-on data. The format is:

CSSF

The operator should then get the message

"SIGN OFF IS COMPLETE".

Improving Security

While the CICS/VS sign-on procedure is necessary for establishing priority and is used by CICS/VS for statistical purposes and message routing, the security portion may be inadequate to the user. After all, all an operator has to know is the name and password to be able to use an application unauthorized to him.

The user may therefore use procedures in addition to or in place of the CICS/VS sign-on procedures. Some of these are:

1. The operator may be required to enter another password specifically for a particular application, and this password procedure may be as involved as the user wants. In the program examples (Chapter 17 to 23), all operators start a session by entering a password through a master sign-on program.

2. In addition to the password required for a particular application, the user may set up a table of terminal identifications for a given application defined in the application itself and check whether the terminal used (as identified in the EIBTRMID field of the Execute Interface Block) is allowed by the application.

3. An additional password may also be required in the program before an operator is allowed to use a file; optionally, the operator may be required to enter a password to be able to retrieve certain records in a file or even to access certain fields in a record.

4. The passwords or terminal identifications entered for 1, 2, and 3 may be changed dynamically by the operator through a special program. In this case, they should be in direct-access storage devices and not hard coded in the application program. As an option, the password and/or terminal identification file may be maintained in coded form so it cannot be easily deciphered by unauthorized personnel. Each application would then decode the password or terminal identifier through a table before it is evaluated in the application.

5. The sign-on table may be regenerated with new values at certain intervals of time so the password and name may be changed from time to time.

It is really up to the user to determine what level of security is needed for applications. Applications like File Inquiry, especially for non-sensitive data, may be given an easier-to-use security procedure while applications for files that are sensitive must be well protected against unauthorized use. It should be remembered that while there is such a thing as lax security, there is also such a thing as too much security.

FILE OPENING AND CLOSING

On-line files are not opened and closed in the application program because they are used by many tasks. Files that are often used in many applications, like tables, preferably are automatically opened when CICS/VS is initialized at the beginning of the day and automatically closed when CICS/VS is terminated at the end of the day. Files used only in certain applications preferably are opened just before the application is first used on a given day but after CICS/VS is initialized. They should be closed after the application is last used but before CICS/VS is terminated.

Such files are opened and closed by special programs coded with CICS/VS macros that are normally written by the systems programmer. The operator uses transaction identifiers for the programs in much the same way he uses them for applications.

However, during a testing process, if a file-opening program has not yet been coded, the programmer may still open the files and conduct the test by using the CICS/VS file opening service before the test. The format is:

CSMT   DAT, OPE, FILEID=file   identifier

The file identifier is the one specified in the File Control Table. The file would then be closed after the test using the CICS/VS service:

CSMT   DAT, CLO, FILEID=file   identifier

USING MAPS

1. On a map defined with mode IN or INOUT, it is a good idea to include a one-byte field labeled "DUMMY" with attributes ASKIP, DRK, and FSET and with any initial value. This will guarantee that the field is transmitted to the TIOA when the ENTER or any PF key is used. This will avoid the MAPFAIL

error if the operator does not enter anything. The programmer may use any unused position of the screen, usually the first position. See the map programs in Chapters 17 to 23.

2. On any GETMAIN command for the symbolic description map, the INITIMG operand should be specified to initialize the whole area to hexadecimal zeroes. This ensures that only data included in the program will ultimately be displayed on the terminal (on the SEND MAP command) since hexadecimal zeroes will not be transmitted from the symbolic description map to the terminal.

3. When an operator is entering data (File Add or File Update) on a map, it is useful to display an appropriate message when the data entered by the operator has been validated and used to add a new record or update an existing record. A typical message is:

"RECORD ACCEPTED (or UPDATED)–CONTINUE".

The operator then knows that everything he has entered has been accepted and he can continue with the next record. This message is best defined as part of the map program (hence physical map) so this will appear on the fresh screen that is displayed every time a record is finished. As a result, only the MAPONLY option need be specified for the fresh screen.

4. When a map that is being used as in (3) is first displayed in a session (at the INITIALIZATION section), it is best to temporarily replace the "RECORD ACCEPTED" message with a message like "ENTER FIRST RECORD" so that the operator will know that the terminal is ready for the first record. We have to use the GETMAIN command to secure main storage for the symbolic description map, then move the message to this area and display it in combination with the physical map.

5. Whenever a currently displayed map is different in format from the previous map displayed, it is wise to always use the

ERASE option so that the latter is completely erased and does not confuse the operator. The possibility of the display from the new map completely overlaying the old display (and thus making the ERASE option redundant) is extremely rare. Therefore, the ERASE option is always suggested in this instance.

6. After the physical map (titles, field identifiers, etc.) is displayed, on succeeding displays of the same map we do not have to include it since it can remain on the screen. We therefore use the DATAONLY option, without the ERASE option.

7. In certain applications, like File Inquiry or File Browse, where new data is continuously displayed, we can use the same technique as in (6). Only data is transmitted for display, saving transmission time. However, if the data displayed is of variable length, a new display will not overlay a previous display if it is shorter than the latter and will mislead the operator reading the data (the extra data coming from the previous display will be mistaken as coming from the current display). If this is so, we are forced to display the physical map with the symbolic description map every time we display the map by omitting MAPONLY and DATAONLY and specifying ERASE. This is shown in the program examples for File Inquiry and File Browse.

8. In many applications, the PF keys can function just like the ENTER key because they can also initiate a task and allow terminal data to be transmitted to the Terminal Input/Output Area. In this case we do not have to specify their use. However, the PA keys always have to be specified (generally in a HANDLE AID command) because they do not allow terminal data to be transmitted to the Terminal Input/Output Area and will result in a MAPFAIL error on the RECEIVE MAP command.

9. In an application where the operator enters data to be validated, the PA keys (or at least one of them, leaving the other

two as "wrong keys") may be used to leave the current entry if the operator cannot resolve a data validation error. Otherwise, the error will always appear and he will not be able to continue with the session without terminating it (generally by using the CLEAR key), then restarting it. The program should then issue a GETMAIN for the map to be displayed, then move the message "RECORD BYPASSED–CONTINUE" to the symbolic description map to be included in the next display. This is shown in the program examples in Chapters 19 and 20.

10.   In an application where there may not be any need to bypass input data already entered, the PA keys still have to be defined, and in this case they can be used to display the "WRONG KEY USED" message. In a technique similar to that in (9), the program issues a GETMAIN for the map to be displayed, then moves the message to the symbolic description map to be included in the next display. This is shown in the program examples in Chapters 18 and 21.

11.   The keyboard shift for a field entered by the operator (whether numeric or alphabetic) depends on whether the data entered is usually numeric or alphabetic. It is convenient for him to have the proper shift automatically provided for so he does not have to use the keyboard shift keys. However, the shift of the field is independent of the PICTURE specification of the field as defined in the symbolic description map. The attribute specification in the map program that provides either numeric (NUM specified) or alphabetic (NUM omitted) shift is different from the PICIN or PICOUT specification that provides the Cobol PICTURE specification. While numeric-shift fields that are used in computation (e.g. amounts) should be defined with PICTURE 9s, and fields with alphabetic shift should always be defined with PICTURE Xs, numeric-shift fields that are not used in computation may also be conveniently defined with PICTURE Xs. For instance, fields like item number or department numbers, which are in numeric shift, may be defined with PICTURE Xs to facilitate editing of these fields.

DATA VALIDATION TECHNIQUES

1. If the operator needs to enter a lot of data to be validated, the programmer should use several lines at the bottom of the screen for error messages. Since each message will usually be around 30 characters long or less, and each line has 80 characters,* there is space for two error messages per line. For most applications, the programmer can use two or three lines, for four or six error messages.

2. The programmer should validate as much data as possible, stopping only when the number of errors detected equals the number of error message positions. This is more efficient than having only one error message position. Otherwise, the operator would be forced to go through the editing steps again for other errors, thus resulting in the multiple reading and displaying of the same map and a delay in the completion of an entry.

3. The programmer should use the symbolic cursor positioning technique. As data is being validated, he should count the number of errors detected. When an error is detected for the first time, the literal –1 should be moved to the length of that field in the symbolic description map so that the cursor will be positioned under that field on the next display and the operator does not have to waste time positioning the cursor to correct the first error entry. This is shown in the DATA-VALIDATION SECTION of the File Add and File Update program examples.

4. The operator can also use the error count to terminate the editing steps when the number of errors detected equals the number of error message positions. There is no sense in further editing the data once we run out of error message positions because there is no place to put an error message anyway; we would also be wasting processing time. The programmer can effectively use a GO TO to bypass the editing of the rest of the data when this occurs. This is shown in the same program examples as in (3).

---

*The most popular CRT terminals have 80 columns.

5. To display the error messages and the data entered, the programmer simply has to display the symbolic description map without the ERASE operand; thus, the DATAONLY operand is specified. The CURSOR operand is also specified if the technique in (3) is used.

6. At the beginning of the editing steps, the error message positions should be blanked out (move spaces to them). This will make sure that messages from the previous editing steps, if this is not the first pass through the editing steps for the same set of data, will no longer be displayed. Thus, only error messages for the current editing steps will be displayed. This is more efficient than redisplaying the physical map with the symbolic description map and using the ERASE option.

7. If a field has to be entered (for instance, the record key in a File Add application), the programmer can immediately edit the field for validity. If it has not been entered, the field will contain LOW-VALUES.

8. If the field is optional, then the programmer should first check the length of the field for a value greater than ZERO; if so, data was entered on that field and can be edited.

USING TEMPORARY STORAGE

1. Temporary storage is very useful in passing data to another task (may be the same program in pseudoconversational mode). Since we can use direct access storage devices for this instead of main storage, we save a precious resource that otherwise would not be available to other tasks. A good guide is: Any group of data that will remain inactive for more than one second,* especially if it is longer than 300 bytes, should be placed in temporary storage, then read when needed.

2. The programmer may use as many temporary storage records as needed in a single queue and as many queues as he needs

---

*It is inactive from the time it is released by a program (WRITEQ TS) up to the time it is read by the next program (READQ TS).

for the application. For most applications, however, he will need only one record in a single queue if he uses temporary storage for a scratchpad. It is always more efficient to get a single, long, temporary storage record rather than many smaller ones because of the overhead in reading and rewriting it.

3. A very useful queue identification code consists of the terminal identification code and the transaction identifier. This way there is no danger that some other terminals or programs will, without permission, use or delete temporary storage queues belonging to somebody else.

4. If the application uses temporary storage for a scratchpad facility, it will no longer need it at the end of the session and should therefore delete it at the FINALIZATION section. At the INITIALIZATION section, this deletion should likewise be attempted since the FINALIZATION section may not have been executed in the previous session. This can happen if there was a program abend, if a hardware error forced the abnormal shutdown of the whole system, or if a CICS/VS error (probably nucleus) forces the termination of the whole CICS/VS partition. This can be seen in the File Add and File Update program examples.

5. At the INITIALIZATION section, after deleting any previous temporary storage queues, we have to do a GETMAIN for the new temporary storage record to be created. Here, the INITIMG operand is generally not coded since all fields will be set to the proper values in the program anyway. After setting the fields to their proper values, we then save the record for the next task by writing it out. The WRITEQ TS command is used.

6. Every time a record in the temporary storage queue is required, it has first to be read in the task. The ITEM operand has to be specified in the READQ TS command so the corresponding record in the queue will be read.

7. Every time a record in the temporary storage queue is updated for the next task, we have to rewrite it. The WRITEQ TS command is used with the ITEM and REWRITE operands.

8. When a temporary storage queue is deleted, all records in that queue are deleted since CICS/VS does not have the facility to delete individual records in a queue.

PASSING DATA BETWEEN PROGRAMS

Temporary Storage

Data may be passed from one application program to another in many ways, depending on the situation. The most common way of passing data from one task to another is through the use of temporary storage records. For example, in the pseudoconversational mode of processing, data may be passed from one execution of the program to the next by using temporary storage queues to implement a scratchpad facility. A good guide is: Data no longer needed by the previous program but which will not be required by the next program until more than one second later, especially if the data is more than 300 bytes long, should be maintained in temporary storage in a direct access storage device.

The Transaction Work Area (TWA)

Another method for passing data between programs employs the Transaction Work Area. However, the two programs involved must execute in the same task since the Transaction Work Area is released when a task terminates. This may be used, for instance, in an XCTL command where two programs have identical TWAs and the second program gets a copy of the first program's TWA and may access it after executing the ADDRESS command with the TWA operand.

The Terminal Control Table User Area

Data may also be passed through the Terminal Control Table User Area. This area is defined as an entry in the LINKAGE section and will have a corresponding linkage pointer. The application programmer establishes addressability to this area in the same ADDRESS command used to establish addressability to the Transaction Work Area and the Common Work Area.

This area can be passed only if the tasks execute at the same terminal. It may therefore be used in the pseudoconversational mode of processing to implement a scratchpad facility, but it does need main storage instead of a direct access storage device, so it may be wasting an important resource. Furthermore, it is limited to 255 bytes.

The Common Work Area

The Common Work Area is part of the Common Systems Area, and all programs in the installation can access it any time to read data from it or to change data in it. However, the user should control the use of this resource because if an error is made by a single application, the results for other applications are unpredictable. It is much easier to pass data through other means, like temporary storage, where applications are not affected by errors in other applications.

The Communication Area

The RETURN, XCTL, and LINK program control commands have the option of passing data to the next program. The data is defined in either the WORKING-STORAGE or LINKAGE section in the first program, but it must be defined in the second program as DFHCOMMAREA, which is the first entry in the LINKAGE section.

On a RETURN command to CICS/VS, the COMMAREA operand specifies the data area and the LENGTH operand the length of the area that is passed to the program that first executes on the next task to be initiated at the same terminal.

On the XCTL or LINK command, the COMMAREA and LENGTH operands pertain to the data area that will be passed to the program specified in the command.

17

Program Examples

INTRODUCTION

We will now present several programs built around a simplified Purchase Order system. The main purpose of the examples is not to show a typical Purchase Order system, but rather to show typical CICS/VS programs. The examples are in fact somewhat simplified and many requirements of a Purchase Order system are not reflected.

The following programs will be presented:

1. Sign-on Program
2. File Inquiry
3. File Add
4. File Update
5. File Delete
6. File Browse (Primary Key)
7. File Browse (Alternate Key)

THE MASTER SIGN-ON PROGRAM

In many applications, the user prefers that all operators start with a master Sign-on program so that the use of the various applications may be properly controlled. This program usually requires each operator to choose one application (add a new record, update an existing record, inquire through the file, etc.) and enter the password for that particular application. The program then validates the password against the particular application and if valid, executes a XCTL command to the particular application. If not, the Sign-on program will be aborted with a message.

The user may choose to have the program send a message to or ring a bell on a master terminal controlled by the user manager stating that there was an invalid sign-on attempt at a particular terminal. The user may also prefer to have all operators use a complicated password procedure to reduce the chance that an unauthorized person might accidentally discover the password. Such passwords (which never show on the terminal screen) may be used in conjunction with the regular CICS/VS sign-on service (CSSN).

In our program examples, the operator will start with the master Sign-on program and continue the session with the particular application selected until he decides to terminate it. A diagram of the procedure is shown in Figure 17.1.

PROGRAM SPECIFICATIONS

The program specifications are as follows:

1. Implement the program using the pseudoconversational mode of processing.

2. Use 'ORAP' as the transaction identifier to initiate the session.

3. The operator selects a particular application and enters the corresponding password for it.

4. If there is more than one application selected, abort the session with the message "JOB ABORTED–MULTIPLE FUNCTION NOT ALLOWED."

5. If there is no application selected, abort the session with the message "JOB ABORTED–NO FUNCTION SELECTED."

6. If the password entered is invalid, abort the session with the message "JOB ABORTED–INVALID PASSWORD."

7. The passwords required for each application are:

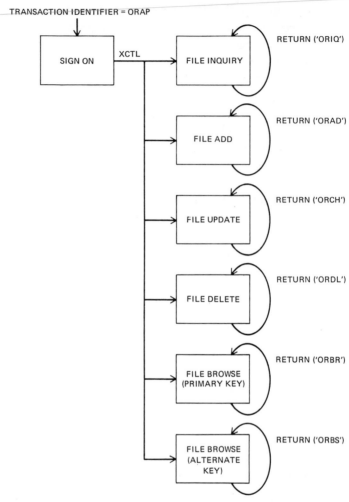

Fig. 17.1. General Procedure Of A Typical Application.

Application	Password
File Inquiry	MMDD* + 1111
File Add	MMDD + 2222
File Update	MMDD + 3333
File Delete	MMDD + 4444
File Browse (Primary key)	MMDD + 5555
File Browse (Alternate key)	MMDD + 6666

*MMDD is the current month and day.

8. The program will transfer control (do a XCTL) to the following programs if the password is valid for the application:

Application	Program
File Inquiry	ORIQ01A
File Add	ORAD01A
File Update	ORCH01A
File Delete	ORDL01A
File Browse (Primary key)	ORBR01A
File Browse (Alternate key)	ORBS01A

9. On any PA key, terminate the session.

SCREEN LAYOUT

The screen layout to be used in the program is shown in Figure 17.2. All 9s are numeric and Xs are alphanumeric fields.

MAP PROGRAM

The map program corresponding to the screen layout is shown in Figure 17.3.

PROGRAM LISTING

The program listing for the sign-on program is shown in Figure 17.4. All program listings in this book will be those of the compiler and

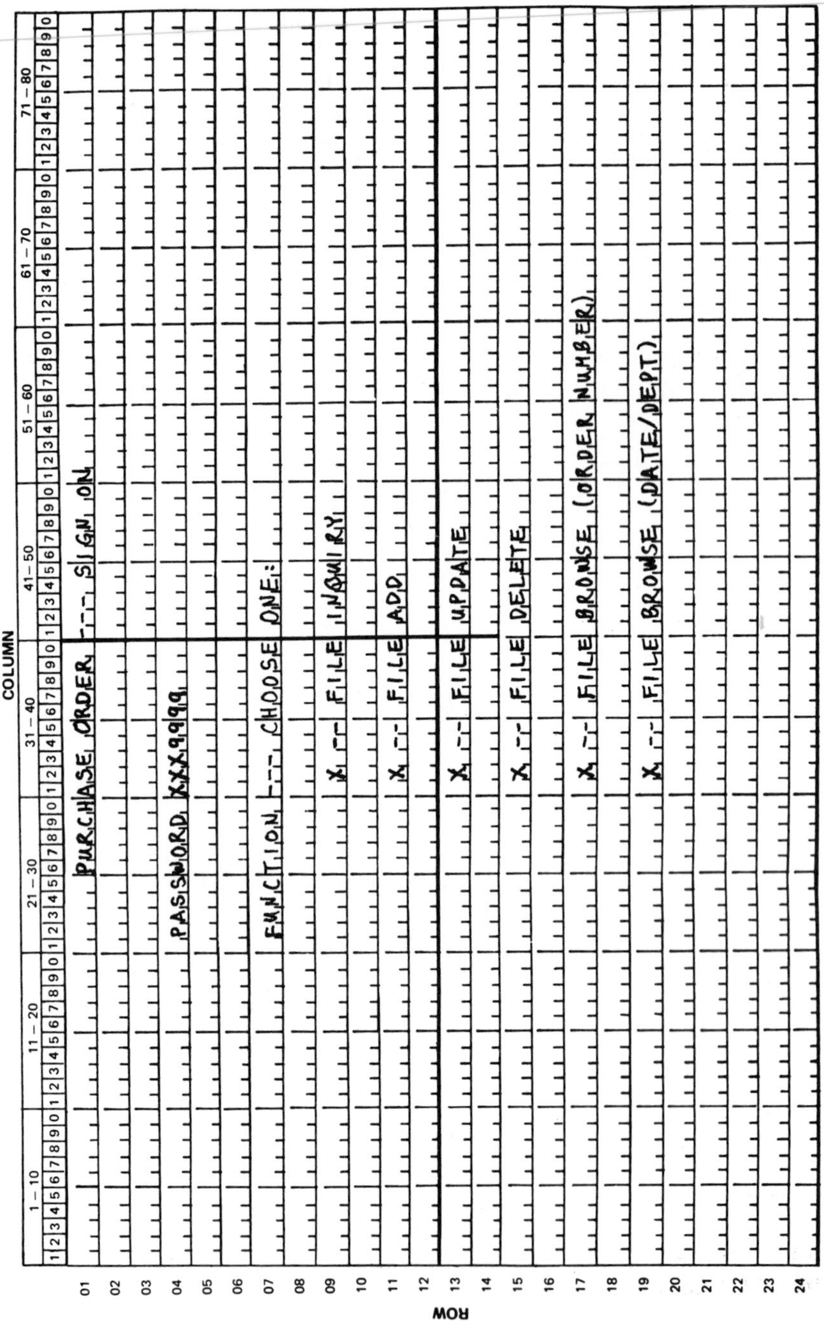
COLUMN
ROW
PURCHASE ORDER --- SIGN ON
PASSWORD XXX9999
FUNCTION --- CHOOSE ONE:
X --- FILE INQUIRY
X --- FILE ADD
X --- FILE UPDATE
X --- FILE DELETE
X --- FILE BROWSE (ORDER NUMBER)
X --- FILE BROWSE (DATE/DEPT.)

Fig. 17.2. Screen Layout – Sign On Program.

```
STMT    SOURCE STATEMENT                        DOS/VS ASSEMBLER REL 34.0 13.50
    1              PRINT NOGEN
    2 ORAPSO1      DFHMSD TYPE=MAP,MODE=INOUT,CTRL=FREEKB,LANG=COBOL,          X
                     TIOAPFX=YES
   12 ORAPMO1      DFHMDI SIZE=(24,80)
   40 DUMMY        DFHMDF POS=(01,01),LENGTH=01,ATTRB=(ASKIP,DRK,FSET),       X
                     INITIAL='1'
   52              DFHMDF POS=(01,25),LENGTH=26,ATTRB=(ASKIP,BRT),            X
                     INITIAL='PURCHASE ORDER --- SIGN ON'
   64              DFHMDF POS=(04,21),LENGTH=08,ATTRB=(ASKIP,BRT),            X
                     INITIAL='PASSWORD'
   76 PASSWRD      DFHMDF POS=(04,30),LENGTH=07,ATTRB=(UNPROT,DRK,IC)
   87              DFHMDF POS=(04,38),LENGTH=1
   98              DFHMDF POS=(07,21),LENGTH=24,ATTRB=(ASKIP,BRT),            X
                     INITIAL='FUNCTION --- CHOOSE ONE '
  110 INQUIRY      DFHMDF POS=(09,30),LENGTH=01,ATTRB=(UNPROT,BRT)
  121              DFHMDF POS=(09,32),LENGTH=16,ATTRB=(ASKIP,BRT),            X
                     INITIAL=' -- FILE INQUIRY'
  133 ADD          DFHMDF POS=(11,30),LENGTH=01,ATTRB=(UNPROT,BRT)
  144              DFHMDF POS=(11,32),LENGTH=12,ATTRB=(ASKIP,BRT),            X
                     INITIAL=' -- FILE ADD'
  156 UPDATE       DFHMDF POS=(13,30),LENGTH=01,ATTRB=(UNPROT,BRT)
  167              DFHMDF POS=(13,32),LENGTH=15,ATTRB=(ASKIP,BRT),            X
                     INITIAL=' -- FILE UPDATE'
  179 DELETE       DFHMDF POS=(15,30),LENGTH=01,ATTRB=(UNPROT,BRT)
  190              DFHMDF POS=(15,32),LENGTH=15,ATTRB=(ASKIP,BRT),            X
                     INITIAL=' -- FILE DELETE'
  202 BROWSE       DFHMDF POS=(17,30),LENGTH=01,ATTRB=(UNPROT,BRT)
  213              DFHMDF POS=(17,32),LENGTH=30,ATTRB=(ASKIP,BRT),            X
                     INITIAL=' -- FILE BROWSE (ORDER NUMBER)'
  225 BROWSE2      DFHMDF POS=(19,30),LENGTH=01,ATTRB=(UNPROT,BRT)
  236              DFHMDF POS=(19,32),LENGTH=27,ATTRB=(ASKIP,BRT),            X
                     INITIAL=' -- FILE BROWSE (DATE/DEPT)'
  248              DFHMSD TYPE=FINAL
  262              END
```

Fig. 17.3.   Map Program – Sign On Program.

1   IBM DOS VS COBOL

```
 CBL SUPMAP,STXIT,NOTRUNC,CSYNTAX,SXREF,OPT,VERB,CLIST,BUF=19069
 CBL NOOPT,LIB
00001              IDENTIFICATION DIVISION.

00003              PROGRAM-ID. ORAPO1A.


00005              ENVIRONMENT DIVISION.


00007         ***********************************************************
00008         *                                                         *
00009         *     1. THIS IS THE SIGN-ON PROGRAM FOR ALL PURCHASE ORDER *
00010         *        APPLICATIONS.                                     *
00011         *                                                         *
00012         *     2. THE PROGRAM WILL ALLOW THE OPERATOR TO ACCESS THE *
00013         *        PURCHASE ORDER FILE FOR THE FOLLOWING FUNCTIONS   *
00014         *                                                         *
00015         *              (A) INQUIRY (DISPLAY RECORD INFORMATION).   *
00016         *              (B) ADD NEW RECORDS.                        *
00017         *              (C) UPDATE EXISTING RECORDS.               *
00018         *              (D) DELETE EXISTING RECORDS.               *
00019         *              (E) DO A BROWSE VIA RECORD KEY (ORDER NUMBER). *
00020         *              (F) DO A BROWSE VIA ALTERNATE KEY,          *
00021         *                  (DATE OF ORDER WITHIN DEPARTMENT NUMBER). *
00022         *                                                         *
00023         *     3. THE FUNCTION SELECTED BY THE OPERATOR IS VALIDATED *
00024         *        AGAINST THE PASSWORD ENTERED.                    *
00025         *                                                         *
00026         ***********************************************************
```

Fig. 17.4.   Sign On Program.

```
    2        ORAPO1A         13.23.49        07/26/80

00028          DATA DIVISION.


00030          WORKING-STORAGE SECTION.


00032      01  COMMUNICATION-AREA.

00034          05  COMMAREA-PROCESS-SW          PIC X.

00036          05  COMMAREA-OPERATOR-INITIAL   PIC XXX.


00038      01  AREA1.


00040          05  JOB-NORMAL-END-MESSAGE  PIC X(23) VALUE
00041                  'JOB NORMALLY TERMINATED'.


00043          05  JOB-ABORTED-MESSAGE.
00044              10  FILLER              PIC X(15) VALUE 'JOB ABORTED --'.
00045              10  MAJOR-ERROR-MSG     PIC X(30).


00047          05  OLD-EIB-AREA.
00048              10  FILLER              PIC X(7) VALUE 'OLD EIB'.
00049              10  OLD-EIBFN           PIC XX.
00050              10  OLD-EIBRCODE        PIC X(6).
```

Fig. 17.4. (Continued)

```
      3          QRAPO1A          13.23.49          07/26/80

00052          01  DFHEIVAR COPY DFHEIVAR.
00053 C        01  DFHEIVAR.
00054 C            02    DFHEIV0   PICTURE X(26).
00055 C            02    DFHEIV1   PICTURE X(8).
00056 C            02    DFHEIV2   PICTURE X(8).
00057 C            02    DFHEIV3   PICTURE X(8).
00058 C            02    DFHEIV4   PICTURE X(6).
00059 C            02    DFHEIV5   PICTURE X(4).
00060 C            02    DFHEIV6   PICTURE X(4).
00061 C            02    DFHEIV7   PICTURE X(2).
00062 C            02    DFHEIV8   PICTURE X(2).
00063 C            02    DFHEIV9   PICTURE X(1).
00064 C            02    DFHEIV10  PICTURE S9(7) USAGE COMPUTATIONAL-3.
00065 C            02    DFHEIV11  PICTURE S9(4) USAGE COMPUTATIONAL.
00066 C            02    DFHEIV12  PICTURE S9(4) USAGE COMPUTATIONAL.
00067 C            02    DFHEIV13  PICTURE S9(4) USAGE COMPUTATIONAL.
00068 C            02    DFHEIV14  PICTURE S9(4) USAGE COMPUTATIONAL.
00069 C            02    DFHEIV15  PICTURE S9(4) USAGE COMPUTATIONAL.
00070 C            02    DFHEIV16  PICTURE S9(9) USAGE COMPUTATIONAL.
00071 C            02    DFHEIV17  PICTURE X(4).
00072 C            02    DFHEIV18  PICTURE X(4).
00073 C            02    DFHEIV19  PICTURE X(4).
00074 C            02    DFHEIV97  PICTURE S9(7) USAGE COMPUTATIONAL-3 VALUE ZERO.
00075 C            02    DFHEIV98  PICTURE S9(4) USAGE COMPUTATIONAL VALUE ZERO.
00076 C            02    DFHEIV99  PICTURE X(1)  VALUE SPACE.
00077          LINKAGE SECTION.
00078          01  DFHEIBLK COPY DFHEIBLK.
00079 C        *    EIBLK EXEC INTERFACE BLOCK
00080 C        01  DFHEIBLK.
00081 C        *         EIBTIME     TIME IN 0HHMMSS FORMAT
00082 C              02 EIBTIME     PICTURE S9(7) USAGE COMPUTATIONAL-3.
00083 C        *         EIBDATE     DATE IN 00YYDDD FORMAT
00084 C              02 EIBDATE     PICTURE S9(7) USAGE COMPUTATIONAL-3.
00085 C        *         EIBTRNID    TRANSACTION IDENTIFIER
00086 C              02 EIBTRNID    PICTURE X(4).
00087 C        *         EIBTASKN    TASK NUMBER
00088 C              02 EIBTASKN    PICTURE S9(7) USAGE COMPUTATIONAL-3.
00089 C        *         EIBTRMID    TERMINAL IDENTIFIER
00090 C              02 EIBTRMID    PICTURE X(4).
00091 C        *         DFHEIGDI    RESERVED
00092 C              02 DFHEIGDI    PICTURE S9(4) USAGE COMPUTATIONAL.
00093 C        *         EIBCPOSN    CURSOR POSITION
00094 C              02 EIBCPOSN    PICTURE S9(4) USAGE COMPUTATIONAL.
00095 C        *         EIBCALEN    COMMAREA LENGTH
00096 C              02 EIBCALEN    PICTURE S9(4) USAGE COMPUTATIONAL.
00097 C        *         EIBAID      ATTENTION IDENTIFIER
00098 C              02 EIBAID      PICTURE X(1).
00099 C        *         EIBFN       FUNCTION CODE
00100 C              02 EIBFN       PICTURE X(2).
00101 C        *         EIBRCODE    RESPONSE CODE
00102 C              02 EIBRCODE    PICTURE X(6).
00103 C        *         EIBDS       DATASET NAME
00104 C              02 EIBDS       PICTURE X(8).
```

Fig. 17.4. (Continued)

```
      4          ORAP01A          13.23.49          07/26/80


   00105 C     *         EIBREQID     REQUEST IDENTIFIER
   00106 C         02 EIBREQID   PICTURE X(8).
   00107      01  DFHCOMMAREA.

   00109         05  PROCESS-SW                 PIC X.
   00110            88  PASSWORD-VALIDATION-TIME     VALUE '1'.



   00112      01  LINKAGE-POINTERS.

   00114         05  FILLER              PIC S9(8) COMP.
   00115         05  MAP1-POINTER        PIC S9(8) COMP.
   00116         05  TWA-POINTER         PIC S9(8) COMP.




      5          ORAP01A          13.23.49          07/26/80

 00118      ***********************************************************
 00119      *                                                         *
 00120      *         SIGN-ON MAP AREA DESCRIPTION                     *
 00121      *                                                         *
 00122      ***********************************************************


 00124      01  MAP1-AREA.

 00126         05  FILLER              PIC X(12).
 00127         05  MAP1-DUMMY-L        PIC S9999 COMP.
 00128         05  MAP1-DUMMY-A        PIC X.
 00129         05  MAP1-DUMMY          PIC X.
 00130         05  MAP1-PASSWORD-L     PIC S9999 COMP.
 00131         05  MAP1-PASSWORD-A     PIC X.
 00132         05  MAP1-PASSWORD.
 00133            10  MAP1-PASSWORD-ALP    PIC XXX.
 00134            10  MAP1-PASSWORD-NUM    PIC 9999.
 00135         05  MAP1-INQUIRY-L      PIC S9999 COMP.
 00136         05  MAP1-INQUIRY-A      PIC X.
 00137         05  MAP1-INQUIRY        PIC X.
 00138         05  MAP1-ADD-L          PIC S9999 COMP.
 00139         05  MAP1-ADD-A          PIC X.
 00140         05  MAP1-ADD            PIC X.
 00141         05  MAP1-UPDATE-L       PIC S9999 COMP.
 00142         05  MAP1-UPDATE-A       PIC X.
 00143         05  MAP1-UPDATE         PIC X.
 00144         05  MAP1-DELETE-L       PIC S9999 COMP.
 00145         05  MAP1-DELETE-A       PIC X.
 00146         05  MAP1-DELETE         PIC X.
 00147         05  MAP1-BROWSE-L       PIC S9999 COMP.
 00148         05  MAP1-BROWSE-A       PIC X.
 00149         05  MAP1-BROWSE         PIC X.
 00150         05  MAP1-BROWSE-ALT-L   PIC S9999 COMP.
 00151         05  MAP1-BROWSE-ALT-A   PIC X.
 00152         05  MAP1-BROWSE-ALT     PIC X.
```

Fig. 17.4. (Continued)

```
00154          ****************************************************************
00155          *                                                              *
00156          *                 TRANSACTION WORK AREA                        *
00157          *                                                              *
00158          ****************************************************************


00160          01  TWA-AREA.

00162              05  TWA-CTR                    PIC S9999 COMP.

00164              05  TWA-OPERATOR-MESSAGE       PIC X(45).

00166              05  TWA-CURRENT-DATE.
00167                  10  TWA-CURRENT-MM         PIC 99.
00168                  10  FILLER                 PIC X.
00169                  10  TWA-CURRENT-DD         PIC 99.
00170                  10  FILLER                 PIC XXX.

00172              05  TWA-PASSWORD-DATE.
00173                  10  TWA-PASSWORD-DATE-MM   PIC 99.
00174                  10  TWA-PASSWORD-DATE-DD   PIC 99.

00176              05  TWA-DATE REDEFINES TWA-PASSWORD-DATE   PIC 9999.
```

Fig. 17.4. (Continued)

7   ORAPO1A   13.23.49   07/26/80

```
00178            PROCEDURE DIVISION USING DFHEIBLK DFHCOMMAREA.
00179                CALL 'DFHEI1'.


00181            ************************************************************************
00182            *                                                                    *
00183            MAIN-LINE SECTION.
00184            *                                                                    *
00185            ************************************************************************


00187        *     EXEC CICS
00188        *         ADDRESS TWA (TWA-POINTER)
00189        *     END-EXEC.
00190              MOVE '                ' TO DFHEIVO CALL 'DFHEI1' USING
00191              DFHEIVO TWA-POINTER.
00192
00193        *     EXEC CICS
00194        *         HANDLE AID
00195        *             CLEAR (FINALIZATION)
00196        *             PA1 (INITIALIZATION)
00197        *             PA2 (INITIALIZATION)
00198        *             PA3 (INITIALIZATION)
00199        *     END-EXEC.
00200              MOVE ' 0              ' TO DFHEIVO CALL 'DFHEI1' USING
00201              DFHEIVO GO TO FINALIZATION INITIALIZATION INITIALIZATION
00202              INITIALIZATION DEPENDING ON DFHEIGDI.
00203
00204
00205
00206
00207        *     EXEC CICS
00208        *         HANDLE CONDITION
00209        *             MAPFAIL (MAPFAIL-ERROR)
00210        *             ERROR   (MAJOR-ERROR)
00211        *     END-EXEC.
00212              MOVE '                ' TO DFHEIVO CALL 'DFHEI1' USING
00213              DFHEIVO GO TO MAPFAIL-ERROR MAJOR-ERROR DEPENDING ON
00214              DFHEIGDI.
00215
00216
00217              IF EIBCALEN NOT EQUAL TO ZEROES
00218                  GO TO PASSWORD-VALIDATION.

00220              IF EIBCALEN EQUAL TO ZEROES
00221                  GO TO INITIALIZATION.
```

Fig. 17.4. (Continued)

       8   ORAPO1A   13.23.49   07/26/80

```
00223        *******************************************************************
00224        *                                                                 *
00225        PASSWORD-VALIDATION SECTION.
00226        *                                                                 *
00227        *******************************************************************

00229        *    EXEC CICS
00230        *        RECEIVE MAP    ('ORAPMO1')
00231        *                MAPSET ('ORAPSO1')
00232        *                SET    (MAP1-POINTER)
00233        *    END-EXEC.
00234             MOVE 'ORAPMO1' TO DFHEIV1 MOVE 'ORAPSO1' TO DFHEIV2 MOVE '
00235        -    '        ' TO DFHEIVO CALL 'DFHEI1' USING DFHEIVO
00236             DFHEIV1 MAP1-POINTER DFHEIV98 DFHEIV2.
00237
00238
00239             MOVE ZEROES TO TWA-CTR.

00241             IF MAP1-INQUIRY-L     NOT EQUAL TO ZEROES
00242                 ADD 1 TO TWA-CTR.

00244             IF MAP1-ADD-L         NOT EQUAL TO ZEROES
00245                 ADD 2 TO TWA-CTR.

00247             IF MAP1-UPDATE-L      NOT EQUAL TO ZEROES
00248                 ADD 4 TO TWA-CTR.

00250             IF MAP1-DELETE-L      NOT EQUAL TO ZEROES
00251                 ADD 8 TO TWA-CTR.

00253             IF MAP1-BROWSE-L      NOT EQUAL TO ZEROES
00254                 ADD 16 TO TWA-CTR.

00256             IF MAP1-BROWSE-ALT-L  NOT EQUAL TO ZEROES
00257                 ADD 32 TO TWA-CTR.

00259             IF    TWA-CTR EQUAL TO 1
00260                OR TWA-CTR EQUAL TO 2
00261                OR TWA-CTR EQUAL TO 4
00262                OR TWA-CTR EQUAL TO 8
00263                OR TWA-CTR EQUAL TO 16
00264                OR TWA-CTR EQUAL TO 32
00265             THEN NEXT SENTENCE
00266             ELSE IF TWA-CTR EQUAL TO ZEROES
00267                      GO TO NO-FUNCTION-ERROR
00268                      ELSE GO TO MULTIPLE-FUNCTION-ERROR.

00270             MOVE CURRENT-DATE    TO  TWA-CURRENT-DATE.
00271             MOVE TWA-CURRENT-MM  TO  TWA-PASSWORD-DATE-MM.
00272             MOVE TWA-CURRENT-DD  TO  TWA-PASSWORD-DATE-DD.
```

Fig. 17.4. (Continued)

```
00274                 IF TWA-CTR EQUAL TO 1
00275                     IF MAP1-PASSWORD-L NOT EQUAL TO ZEROES
00276                         IF        (MAP1-PASSWORD-ALP EQUAL TO 'PAL'
00277                              OR MAP1-PASSWORD-ALP EQUAL TO 'ABC')

00279                              AND MAP1-PASSWORD-NUM NUMERIC
00280                              AND MAP1-PASSWORD-NUM EQUAL (TWA-DATE + 1111)

00282                         THEN GO TO INQUIRY-SELECTED
00283                         ELSE GO TO PASSWORD-ERROR
00284                     ELSE GO TO PASSWORD-ERROR.

00286                 IF TWA-CTR EQUAL TO 2
00287                     IF MAP1-PASSWORD-L NOT EQUAL TO ZEROES
00288                         IF        MAP1-PASSWORD-ALP EQUAL TO 'PAL'
00289                              AND MAP1-PASSWORD-NUM NUMERIC
00290                              AND MAP1-PASSWORD-NUM EQUAL (TWA-DATE + 2222)
00291                         THEN GO TO ADD-SELECTED
00292                         ELSE GO TO PASSWORD-ERROR
00293                     ELSE GO TO PASSWORD-ERROR.

00295                 IF TWA-CTR EQUAL TO 4
00296                     IF MAP1-PASSWORD-L NOT EQUAL TO ZEROES
00297                         IF        MAP1-PASSWORD-ALP EQUAL TO 'PAL'
00298                              AND MAP1-PASSWORD-NUM NUMERIC
00299                              AND MAP1-PASSWORD-NUM EQUAL (TWA-DATE + 3333)
00300                         THEN GO TO UPDATE-SELECTED
00301                         ELSE GO TO PASSWORD-ERROR
00302                     ELSE GO TO PASSWORD-ERROR.

00304                 IF TWA-CTR EQUAL TO 8
00305                     IF MAP1-PASSWORD-L NOT EQUAL TO ZEROES
00306                         IF        MAP1-PASSWORD-ALP EQUAL TO 'PAL'
00307                              AND MAP1-PASSWORD-NUM NUMERIC
00308                              AND MAP1-PASSWORD-NUM EQUAL (TWA-DATE + 4444)
00309                         THEN GO TO DELETE-SELECTED
00310                         ELSE GO TO PASSWORD-ERROR
00311                     ELSE GO TO PASSWORD-ERROR.

00313                 IF TWA-CTR EQUAL TO 16
00314                     IF MAP1-PASSWORD-L NOT EQUAL TO ZEROES
00315                         IF        (MAP1-PASSWORD-ALP EQUAL TO 'PAL'
00316                              OR   MAP1-PASSWORD-ALP EQUAL TO 'ABC'
00317                              OR   MAP1-PASSWORD-ALP EQUAL TO 'XYZ')

00319                              AND MAP1-PASSWORD-NUM NUMERIC
00320                              AND MAP1-PASSWORD-NUM EQUAL (TWA-DATE + 5555)

00322                         THEN GO TO REGULAR-BROWSE-SELECTED
00323                         ELSE GO TO PASSWORD-ERROR
00324                     ELSE GO TO PASSWORD-ERROR.
```

Fig. 17.4. (Continued)

```
     10          ORAPO1A            13.23.49          07/26/80

00326                    IF TWA-CTR EQUAL TO 32
00327                        IF MAP1-PASSWORD-L NOT EQUAL TO ZEROES
00328                           IF        (MAP1-PASSWORD-ALP EQUAL TO 'PAL'
00329                              OR   MAP1-PASSWORD-ALP EQUAL TO 'ABC'
00330                              OR   MAP1-PASSWORD-ALP EQUAL TO 'XYZ')

00332                           AND MAP1-PASSWORD-NUM NUMERIC
00333                           AND MAP1-PASSWORD-NUM EQUAL (TWA-DATE + 6666)

00335                           THEN GO TO ALTERNATE-BROWSE-SELECTED
00336                           ELSE GO TO PASSWORD-ERROR
00337                        ELSE GO TO PASSWORD-ERROR.
```

Fig. 17.4. (Continued)

11   ORAP01A   13.23.49   07/26/80   .

```
00339          SUCCESSFUL-SELECTION-ROUTINES.

00341          INQUIRY-SELECTED.

00343              MOVE '0'                TO COMMAREA-PROCESS-SW.
00344              MOVE MAP1-PASSWORD-ALP TO COMMAREA-OPERATOR-INITIAL.

00346      *     EXEC CICS
00347      *         XCTL PROGRAM  ('ORIQ01A')
00348      *              COMMAREA (COMMUNICATION-AREA)
00349      *              LENGTH   (4)
00350      *     END-EXEC.
00351            MOVE 'ORIQ01A' TO DFHEIV3 MOVE 4 TO DFHEIV11 MOVE '
00352      -     ' TO DFHEIV0 CALL 'DFHEI1' USING DFHEIV0 DFHEIV3
00353            COMMUNICATION-AREA DFHEIV11.
00354
00355


00357          ADD-SELECTED.

00359              MOVE '0'                TO COMMAREA-PROCESS-SW.
00360              MOVE MAP1-PASSWORD-ALP TO COMMAREA-OPERATOR-INITIAL.

00362      *     EXEC CICS
00363      *         XCTL PROGRAM  ('ORAD01A')
00364      *              COMMAREA (COMMUNICATION-AREA)
00365      *              LENGTH   (4)
00366      *     END-EXEC.
00367            MOVE 'ORAD01A' TO DFHEIV3 MOVE 4 TO DFHEIV11 MOVE '
00368      -     ' TO DFHEIV0 CALL 'DFHEI1' USING DFHEIV0 DFHEIV3
00369            COMMUNICATION-AREA DFHEIV11.
00370
00371


00373          UPDATE-SELECTED.

00375              MOVE '0'                TO COMMAREA-PROCESS-SW.
00376              MOVE MAP1-PASSWORD-ALP TO COMMAREA-OPERATOR-INITIAL.

00378      *     EXEC CICS
00379      *         XCTL PROGRAM  ('ORCH01A')
00380      *              COMMAREA (COMMUNICATION-AREA)
00381      *              LENGTH   (4)
00382      *     END-EXEC.
00383            MOVE 'ORCH01A' TO DFHEIV3 MOVE 4 TO DFHEIV11 MOVE '
00384      -     ' TO DFHEIV0 CALL 'DFHEI1' USING DFHEIV0 DFHEIV3
00385            COMMUNICATION-AREA DFHEIV11.
00386
00387
```

Fig. 17.4. (Continued)

```
     12          ORAPO1A        13.23.49          07/26/80


   00389          DELETE-SELECTED.

   00391              MOVE 'O'             TO COMMAREA-PROCESS-SW.
   00392              MOVE MAP1-PASSWORD-ALP TO COMMAREA-OPERATOR-INITIAL.

   00394     *        EXEC CICS
   00395     *            XCTL PROGRAM  ('ORDLO1A')
   00396     *                COMMAREA (COMMUNICATION-AREA)
   00397     *                LENGTH  (4)
   00398     *        END-EXEC.
   00399              MOVE 'ORDLO1A' TO DFHEIV3 MOVE 4 TO DFHEIV11 MOVE '
   00400     -        '' TO DFHEIVO CALL 'DFHEI1' USING DFHEIVO DFHEIV3
   00401              COMMUNICATION-AREA DFHEIV11.
   00402
   00403


   00405          REGULAR-BROWSE-SELECTED.

   00407              MOVE 'O'             TO COMMAREA-PROCESS-SW.
   00408              MOVE MAP1-PASSWORD-ALP TO COMMAREA-OPERATOR-INITIAL.

   00410     *        EXEC CICS
   00411     *            XCTL PROGRAM  ('ORBRO1A')
   00412     *                COMMAREA (COMMUNICATION-AREA)
   00413     *                LENGTH  (4)
   00414     *        END-EXEC.
   00415              MOVE 'ORBRO1A' TO DFHEIV3 MOVE 4 TO DFHEIV11 MOVE '
   00416     -        '' TO DFHEIVO CALL 'DFHEI1' USING DFHEIVO DFHEIV3
   00417              COMMUNICATION-AREA DFHEIV11.
   00418
   00419


   00421          ALTERNATE-BROWSE-SELECTED.

   00423              MOVE 'O'             TO COMMAREA-PROCESS-SW.
   00424              MOVE MAP1-PASSWORD-ALP TO COMMAREA-OPERATOR-INITIAL.

   00426     *        EXEC CICS
   00427     *            XCTL PROGRAM  ('ORBSO1A')
   00428     *                COMMAREA (COMMUNICATION-AREA)
   00429     *                LENGTH  (4)
   00430     *        END-EXEC.
   00431              MOVE 'ORBSO1A' TO DFHEIV3 MOVE 4 TO DFHEIV11 MOVE '
   00432     -        '' TO DFHEIVO CALL 'DFHEI1' USING DFHEIVO DFHEIV3
   00433              COMMUNICATION-AREA DFHEIV11.
   00434
   00435
```

Fig. 17.4. (Continued)

13   ORAPO1A   13.23.49   07/26/80

```
00437          *********************************************************************
00438          *                                                                   *
00439           INITIALIZATION SECTION.
00440          *                                                                   *
00441          *********************************************************************

00443          *     EXEC CICS
00444          *         SEND MAP     ('ORAPMO1')
00445          *               MAPSET ('ORAPSO1')
00446          *               MAPONLY
00447          *               ERASE
00448          *     END-EXEC.
00449                MOVE 'ORAPMO1' TO DFHEIV1 MOVE 'ORAPSO1' TO DFHEIV2 MOVE '
00450          -     '                ' TO DFHEIVO CALL 'DFHEI1' USING DFHEIVO
00451                DFHEIV1 DFHEIV99 DFHEIV98 DFHEIV2.
00452
00453
00454
00455                MOVE '1' TO COMMAREA-PROCESS-SW.

00457          *     EXEC CICS
00458          *         RETURN TRANSID   ('ORAP')
00459          *                COMMAREA (COMMUNICATION-AREA)
00460          *                LENGTH   (1)
00461          *     END-EXEC.
00462                MOVE 'ORAP' TO DFHEIV5 MOVE 1 TO DFHEIV11 MOVE '           '
00463                TO DFHEIVO CALL 'DFHEI1' USING DFHEIVO DFHEIV5
00464                COMMUNICATION-AREA DFHEIV11.
00465
00466
```

Fig. 17.4. (Continued)

```
00468          ********************************************************************
00469          *                                                                *
00470           FINALIZATION SECTION.
00471          *                                                                *
00472          ********************************************************************


00474           PREPARE-TERMINATION-MESSAGE.
00475               MOVE JOB-NORMAL-END-MESSAGE TO TWA-OPERATOR-MESSAGE.


00477           DISPLAY-OPERATOR-MESSAGE.

00479          *     EXEC CICS
00480          *         SEND FROM   (TWA-OPERATOR-MESSAGE)
00481          *              LENGTH (45)
00482          *              ERASE
00483          *     END-EXEC.
00484               MOVE 45 TO DFHEIV11 MOVE '              ' TO DFHEIVO CALL '
00485          -    'DFHEI1' USING DFHEIVO DFHEIV99 DFHEIV98 TWA-OPERATOR-MESSAGE
00486               DFHEIV11.
00487
00488


00490           END-OF-JOB.

00492          *     EXEC CICS
00493          *         RETURN
00494          *     END-EXEC.
00495               MOVE '          ' TO DFHEIVO CALL 'DFHEI1' USING DFHEIVO.
00496
00497
```

Fig. 17.4. (Continued)

15   ORAP01A   13.23.49   07/26/80

```
00499          *****************************************************************
00500          *                                                               *
00501           ABNORMAL-TERMINATION SECTION.
00502          *                                                               *
00503          *****************************************************************


00505           PASSWORD-ERROR.
00506               MOVE 'INVALID PASSWORD' TO MAJOR-ERROR-MSG.
00507               GO TO PREPARE-ABORT-MESSAGE.


00509           NO-FUNCTION-ERROR.
00510               MOVE 'NO FUNCTION CHOSEN' TO MAJOR-ERROR-MSG.
00511               GO TO PREPARE-ABORT-MESSAGE.


00513           MULTIPLE-FUNCTION-ERROR.
00514               MOVE 'MULTIPLE FUNCTIONS NOT ALLOWED' TO MAJOR-ERROR-MSG.
00515               GO TO PREPARE-ABORT-MESSAGE.


00517           MAPFAIL-ERROR.
00518               MOVE 'MAP FAILURE' TO MAJOR-ERROR-MSG.
00519               GO TO PREPARE-ABORT-MESSAGE.


00521           MAJOR-ERROR.
00522               MOVE  EIBFN     TO  OLD-EIBFN.
00523               MOVE  EIBRCODE  TO  OLD-EIBRCODE.

00525          *    EXEC CICS
00526          *        DUMP DUMPCODE ('ERRS')
00527          *    END-EXEC.
00528               MOVE 'ERRS' TO DFHEIV5 MOVE '         ' TO DFHEIVO CALL 'DFH
00529          -    'EI1' USING DFHEIVO DFHEIV5.
00530
00531               MOVE 'MAJOR ERROR' TO MAJOR-ERROR-MSG.
00532               GO TO PREPARE-ABORT-MESSAGE.


00534           PREPARE-ABORT-MESSAGE.
00535               MOVE JOB-ABORTED-MESSAGE TO TWA-OPERATOR-MESSAGE.
00536               GO TO DISPLAY-OPERATOR-MESSAGE.
```

Fig. 17.4. (Continued)

not the command-language translator, and thus the commands will already be as translated.

THE MAIN-LINE SECTION

1. Lines 187–191. ADDRESS command for the TWA.

2. Lines 193–202. HANDLE AID command. For this very simple program, the use of the PA keys to restart the session* saves coding extra statements.

3. Lines 207–214. HANDLE CONDITION command.

4. Lines 217–218. If this is not the first execution of the program in the session, the application selected and the corresponding password are validated.

5. Lines 220–221. If this is the first execution of the program in the session, the INITIALIZATION section is executed.

THE INITIALIZATION SECTION

1. Lines 443–451. Display the password map.

2. Line 455.   Set the communication area switch to 1.

3. Lines 457–464. Terminate the task.

THE PASSWORD-VALIDATION SECTION

1. Lines 229–236. Read the map containing the password and the application selected.

---

*The PA keys generally have different functions. See page 175 and the other program examples.

2. Lines 239–257. We use binary integers to detect which application was selected. This is a programming technique.

3. Lines 259–268. If there was more than one application selected, we have a "multiple function" error; if no function was selected, we have a "no function" error.

4. Lines 270–337. Check the password entered against the application selected. If valid, the particular application is selected through a XCTL command; otherwise, there is a password error.

5. Lines 341–433. The paragraphs to select the particular application. Note that a communication area switch with a value of '0' and the password are sent to the program selected.

THE FINALIZATION SECTION

1. Lines 474–486. Display the "JOB NORMALLY TERMINATED" message.

2. Lines 490–495. Terminate the session.

THE ABNORMAL-TERMINATION SECTION

These are the routines used to abnormally terminate the session on errors and CICS/VS command exceptional conditions not covered by a HANDLE CONDITION command.

EXAMPLE

The following are fascimiles of actual photographs taken of a CRT terminal during a session.

Fig. 17.5. The operator keys in the transaction identifier "ORAP," then hits the ENTER key.

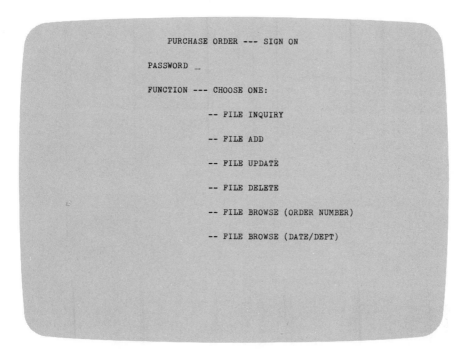

```
          PURCHASE ORDER --- SIGN ON

    PASSWORD _

    FUNCTION --- CHOOSE ONE:

                    -- FILE INQUIRY

                    -- FILE ADD

                    -- FILE UPDATE

                    -- FILE DELETE

                    -- FILE BROWSE (ORDER NUMBER)

                    -- FILE BROWSE (DATE/DEPT)
```

Fig. 17.6. The Sign On program executes and the Sign On map is displayed. The operator may now select the application he wants.

Fig. 17.7. If the operator keys in a transaction identifier not in the Program Control Table, then hits the ENTER key . . . . .

```
ORAQ   DFH2001   INVALID TRANSACTION IDENTIFICATION - PLEASE RESUBMIT
```

Fig. 17.8.   . . . . . Task Control terminates the task and the appropriate message is displayed.

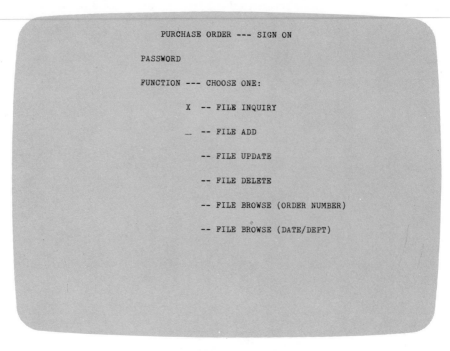

```
                    PURCHASE ORDER --- SIGN ON

          PASSWORD

          FUNCTION --- CHOOSE ONE:

                    X  -- FILE INQUIRY

                    _  -- FILE ADD

                       -- FILE UPDATE

                       -- FILE DELETE

                       -- FILE BROWSE (ORDER NUMBER)

                       -- FILE BROWSE (DATE/DEPT)
```

Fig. 17.9. If the operator keys in a password (defined with the DRK attribute) that is invalid for the application selected, then hits the ENTER key, ...

Fig. 17.10. . . . . . The Sign On program is aborted and the appropriate message is displayed.

18

The File Inquiry Program

INTRODUCTION

The File Inquiry program allows the operator to display information from a record selected by using its record key. It executes when selected by the Sign-on program and will continue executing in the session until terminated by the operator. The flow of control to execute this program is shown in Figure 18.1.

PROGRAM SPECIFICATION

The program specifications are as follows:

1. Implement the program using the pseudoconversational mode of processing.

2. Use 'ORIQ' as the transaction identifier. However, the session should not be started by using this identifier, but rather through an XCTL command from the Sign-on program.

3. If the session is started by using the transaction identifier, abort the session with the message "JOB ABORTED–SIGNON VIOLATION."

4. The record to be displayed is based on the order number.

5. If the order number entered is not numeric, display the message "INVALID ORDER NUMBER."

6. If the record is not in the file, display the message "RECORD NOT FOUND."

7. For (5) and (6), allow the operator to correct the order number.

8. If the record is in the file, display it.

9. On any PA key, display the message "WRONG KEY USED"; allow the operator to continue with the session.

SCREEN LAYOUT

The screen layout to be used in the program is shown in Figure 18.2. All 9s are numeric fields and Xs are alphanumeric fields.

MAP PROGRAM

The map program corresponding to the screen layout is Figure 18.3.

PROGRAM LISTING

The program listing for the File Inquiry program is shown in Figure 18.4. The listing is that of the compiler and not the command-language translator, and thus the commands are already as translated.

THE MAIN-LINE SECTION

1. Lines 267–271. ADDRESS command for the TWA.

2. Lines 273–282. HANDLE AID command. The PA keys will result in the "WRONG KEY USED" error.

3. Lines 287–294. HANDLE CONDITION command.

4. Lines 297–302. The selection of sections.

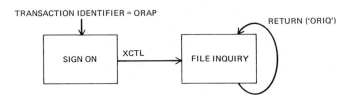

Fig. 18.1. File Inquiry Application.

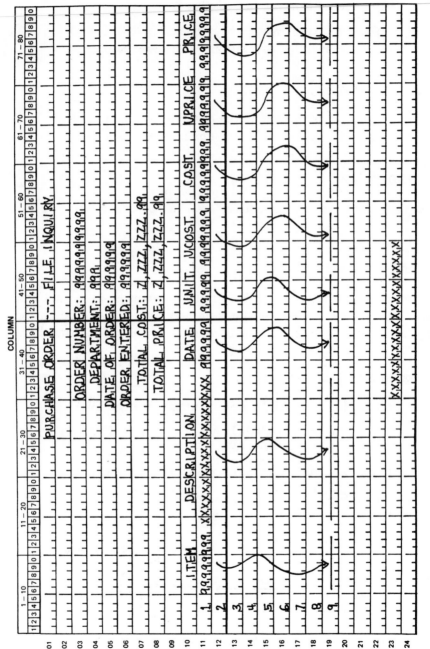

Fig. 18.2.   Screen Layout — File Inquiry.

```
STMT    SOURCE STATEMENT                        DOS/VS ASSEMBLER REL 34.0 14.03

   1              PRINT NOGEN
   2 ORIQSO1      DFHMSD TYPE=MAP,MODE=INOUT,CTRL=FREEKB,LANG=COBOL,TIOAPFX=YES
  12 ORIQMO1      DFHMDI SIZE=(24,80)
  40 DUMMY        DFHMDF POS=(01,01),LENGTH=01,ATTRB=(ASKIP,DRK,FSET),        X
                    INITIAL='1'
  52              DFHMDF POS=(01,25),LENGTH=31,ATTRB=(ASKIP,BRT),             X
                    INITIAL='PURCHASE ORDER --- FILE INQUIRY'
  64              DFHMDF POS=(03,30),LENGTH=13,ATTRB=ASKIP,                   X
                    INITIAL='ORDER NUMBER '
  76 ORDER        DFHMDF POS=(03,44),LENGTH=10,ATTRB=(NUM,BRT,IC)
  87              DFHMDF POS=(03,55),LENGTH=01,ATTRB=PROT
  98              DFHMDF POS=(04,32),LENGTH=11,ATTRB=ASKIP,INITIAL='DEPARTMENT '
 110 DEPT         DFHMDF POS=(04,44),LENGTH=03,ATTRB=(ASKIP,BRT)
 121              DFHMDF POS=(05,29),LENGTH=14,ATTRB=ASKIP,                   X
                    INITIAL='DATE OF ORDER '
 133 DATEOR       DFHMDF POS=(05,44),LENGTH=06,ATTRB=(ASKIP,BRT)
 144              DFHMDF POS=(06,29),LENGTH=14,ATTRB=ASKIP,                   X
                    INITIAL='ORDER ENTERED '
 156 DATEENT      DFHMDF POS=(06,44),LENGTH=06,ATTRB=(ASKIP,BRT)
 167              DFHMDF POS=(07,32),LENGTH=11,ATTRB=ASKIP,INITIAL='TOTAL COST '
 179 TOTCOST      DFHMDF POS=(07,44),LENGTH=12,ATTRB=(ASKIP,BRT),            X
                    PICOUT='Z,ZZZ,ZZZ.99'
 190              DFHMDF POS=(08,31),LENGTH=12,ATTRB=ASKIP,                   X
                    INITIAL='TOTAL PRICE '
 202 TOTPRCE      DFHMDF POS=(08,44),LENGTH=12,ATTRB=(ASKIP,BRT),            X
                    PICOUT='Z,ZZZ,ZZZ.99'
 213              DFHMDF POS=(10,07),LENGTH=04,ATTRB=ASKIP,INITIAL='ITEM'
 225              DFHMDF POS=(10,17),LENGTH=11,ATTRB=ASKIP,INITIAL='DESCRIPTION'
 237              DFHMDF POS=(10,35),LENGTH=04,ATTRB=ASKIP,INITIAL='DATE'
 249              DFHMDF POS=(10,42),LENGTH=04,ATTRB=ASKIP,INITIAL='UNIT '
 261              DFHMDF POS=(10,48),LENGTH=05,ATTRB=ASKIP,INITIAL='UCOST'
 273              DFHMDF POS=(10,57),LENGTH=04,ATTRB=ASKIP,INITIAL='COST '
 285              DFHMDF POS=(10,65),LENGTH=06,ATTRB=ASKIP,INITIAL='UPRICE'
 297              DFHMDF POS=(10,74),LENGTH=05,ATTRB=ASKIP,INITIAL='PRICE '
 309 LINE1        DFHMDF POS=(11,03),LENGTH=01,ATTRB=ASKIP
 320 ITEM1        DFHMDF POS=(11,05),LENGTH=08,ATTRB=(ASKIP,BRT),            X
                    PICIN='99999999',PICOUT='99999999'
 331 DESC1        DFHMDF POS=(11,14),LENGTH=19,ATTRB=(ASKIP,BRT)
 342 LNDATE1      DFHMDF POS=(11,34),LENGTH=06,ATTRB=(ASKIP,BRT)
 353 UNIT1        DFHMDF POS=(11,41),LENGTH=05,ATTRB=(ASKIP,BRT),            X
                    PICIN='99999',PICOUT='99999'
 364 UCOST1       DFHMDF POS=(11,47),LENGTH=07,ATTRB=(ASKIP,BRT),            X
                    PICIN='9999999',PICOUT='9999999'
 375 COST1        DFHMDF POS=(11,55),LENGTH=08,ATTRB=(ASKIP,BRT),            X
                    PICIN='99999999',PICOUT='99999999'
 386 UPRICE1      DFHMDF POS=(11,64),LENGTH=07,ATTRB=(ASKIP,BRT),            X
                    PICIN='9999999',PICOUT='9999999'
 397 PRICE1       DFHMDF POS=(11,72),LENGTH=08,ATTRB=(ASKIP,BRT),            X
                    PICIN='99999999',PICOUT='99999999'
 408 LINE2        DFHMDF POS=(12,03),LENGTH=01,ATTRB=ASKIP
 419 ITEM2        DFHMDF POS=(12,05),LENGTH=08,ATTRB=(ASKIP,BRT),            X
```

Fig. 18.3. Map Program — File Inquiry.

```
STMT     SOURCE STATEMENT                              DOS/VS ASSEMBLER REL 34.0 14.03

                 PICIN='99999999',PICOUT='99999999'
430 DESC2    DFHMDF POS=(12,14),LENGTH=19,ATTRB=(ASKIP,BRT)
441 LNDATE2  DFHMDF POS=(12,34),LENGTH=06,ATTRB=(ASKIP,BRT)
452 UNIT2    DFHMDF POS=(12,41),LENGTH=05,ATTRB=(ASKIP,BRT),              X
                 PICIN='99999',PICOUT='99999'
463 UCOST2   DFHMDF POS=(12,47),LENGTH=07,ATTRB=(ASKIP,BRT),             X
                 PICIN='9999999',PICOUT='9999999'
474 COST2    DFHMDF POS=(12,55),LENGTH=08,ATTRB=(ASKIP,BRT),             X
                 PICIN='99999999',PICOUT='99999999'
485 UPRICE2  DFHMDF POS=(12,64),LENGTH=07,ATTRB=(ASKIP,BRT),            X
                 PICIN='9999999',PICOUT='9999999'
496 PRICE2   DFHMDF POS=(12,72),LENGTH=08,ATTRB=(ASKIP,BRT),           X
                 PICIN='99999999',PICOUT='99999999'
507 LINE3    DFHMDF POS=(13,03),LENGTH=01,ATTRB=ASKIP
518 ITEM3    DFHMDF POS=(13,05),LENGTH=08,ATTRB=(ASKIP,BRT),             X
                 PICIN='99999999',PICOUT='99999999'
529 DESC3    DFHMDF POS=(13,14),LENGTH=19,ATTRB=(ASKIP,BRT)
540 LNDATE3  DFHMDF POS=(13,34),LENGTH=06,ATTRB=(ASKIP,BRT)
551 UNIT3    DFHMDF POS=(13,41),LENGTH=05,ATTRB=(ASKIP,BRT),             X
                 PICIN='99999',PICOUT='99999'
562 UCOST3   DFHMDF POS=(13,47),LENGTH=07,ATTRB=(ASKIP,BRT),            X
                 PICIN='9999999',PICOUT='9999999'
573 COST3    DFHMDF POS=(13,55),LENGTH=08,ATTRB=(ASKIP,BRT),            X
                 PICIN='99999999',PICOUT='99999999'
584 UPRICE3  DFHMDF POS=(13,64),LENGTH=07,ATTRB=(ASKIP,BRT),           X
                 PICIN='9999999',PICOUT='9999999'
595 PRICE3   DFHMDF POS=(13,72),LENGTH=08,ATTRB=(ASKIP,BRT),           X
                 PICIN='99999999',PICOUT='99999999'
606 LINE4    DFHMDF POS=(14,03),LENGTH=01,ATTRB=ASKIP
617 ITEM4    DFHMDF POS=(14,05),LENGTH=08,ATTRB=(ASKIP,BRT),            X
                 PICIN='99999999',PICOUT='99999999'
628 DESC4    DFHMDF POS=(14,14),LENGTH=19,ATTRB=(ASKIP,BRT)
639 LNDATE4  DFHMDF POS=(14,34),LENGTH=06,ATTRB=(ASKIP,BRT)
650 UNIT4    DFHMDF POS=(14,41),LENGTH=05,ATTRB=(ASKIP,BRT),            X
                 PICIN='99999',PICOUT='99999'
661 UCOST4   DFHMDF POS=(14,47),LENGTH=07,ATTRB=(ASKIP,BRT),           X
                 PICIN='9999999',PICOUT='9999999'
672 COST4    DFHMDF POS=(14,55),LENGTH=08,ATTRB=(ASKIP,BRT),           X
                 PICIN='99999999',PICOUT='99999999'
683 UPRICE4  DFHMDF POS=(14,64),LENGTH=07,ATTRB=(ASKIP,BRT),          X
                 PICIN='9999999',PICOUT='9999999'
694 PRICE4   DFHMDF POS=(14,72),LENGTH=08,ATTRB=(ASKIP,BRT),          X
                 PICIN='99999999',PICOUT='99999999'
705 LINE5    DFHMDF POS=(15,03),LENGTH=01,ATTRB=ASKIP
716 ITEM5    DFHMDF POS=(15,05),LENGTH=08,ATTRB=(ASKIP,BRT),          X
                 PICIN='99999999',PICOUT='99999999'
727 DESC5    DFHMDF POS=(15,14),LENGTH=19,ATTRB=(ASKIP,BRT)
738 LNDATE5  DFHMDF POS=(15,34),LENGTH=06,ATTRB=(ASKIP,BRT)
749 UNIT5    DFHMDF POS=(15,41),LENGTH=05,ATTRB=(ASKIP,BRT),          X
                 PICIN='99999',PICOUT='99999'
760 UCOST5   DFHMDF POS=(15,47),LENGTH=07,ATTRB=(ASKIP,BRT),         X
```

Fig. 18.3. Map Program – File Inquiry.

```
STMT    SOURCE STATEMENT                              DOS/VS ASSEMBLER REL 34.0 14.03
                PICIN='9999999',PICOUT='9999999'
 771 COST5    DFHMDF POS=(15,55),LENGTH=08,ATTRB=(ASKIP,BRT),                    X
                PICIN='99999999',PICOUT='99999999'
 782 UPRICE5  DFHMDF POS=(15,64),LENGTH=07,ATTRB=(ASKIP,BRT),                    X
                PICIN='9999999',PICOUT='9999999'
 793 PRICE5   DFHMDF POS=(15,72),LENGTH=08,ATTRB=(ASKIP,BRT),                    X
                PICIN='99999999',PICOUT='99999999'
 804 LINE6    DFHMDF POS=(16,03),LENGTH=01,ATTRB=ASKIP
 815 ITEM6    DFHMDF POS=(16,05),LENGTH=08,ATTRB=(ASKIP,BRT),                    X
                PICIN='99999999',PICOUT='99999999'
 826 DESC6    DFHMDF POS=(16,14),LENGTH=19,ATTRB=(ASKIP,BRT)
 837 LNDATE6  DFHMDF POS=(16,34),LENGTH=06,ATTRB=(ASKIP,BRT)
 848 UNIT6    DFHMDF POS=(16,41),LENGTH=05,ATTRB=(ASKIP,BRT),                    X
                PICIN='99999',PICOUT='99999'
 859 UCOST6   DFHMDF POS=(16,47),LENGTH=07,ATTRB=(ASKIP,BRT),                    X
                PICIN='9999999',PICOUT='9999999'
 870 COST6    DFHMDF POS=(16,55),LENGTH=08,ATTRB=(ASKIP,BRT),                    X
                PICIN='99999999',PICOUT='99999999'
 881 UPRICE6  DFHMDF POS=(16,64),LENGTH=07,ATTRB=(ASKIP,BRT),                    X
                PICIN='9999999',PICOUT='9999999'
 892 PRICE6   DFHMDF POS=(16,72),LENGTH=08,ATTRB=(ASKIP,BRT),                    X
                PICIN='99999999',PICOUT='99999999'
 903 LINE7    DFHMDF POS=(17,03),LENGTH=01,ATTRB=ASKIP
 914 ITEM7    DFHMDF POS=(17,05),LENGTH=08,ATTRB=(ASKIP,BRT),                    X
                PICIN='99999999',PICOUT='99999999'
 925 DESC7    DFHMDF POS=(17,14),LENGTH=19,ATTRB=(ASKIP,BRT)
 936 LNDATE7  DFHMDF POS=(17,34),LENGTH=06,ATTRB=(ASKIP,BRT)
 947 UNIT7    DFHMDF POS=(17,41),LENGTH=05,ATTRB=(ASKIP,BRT),                    X
                PICIN='99999',PICOUT='99999'
 958 UCOST7   DFHMDF POS=(17,47),LENGTH=07,ATTRB=(ASKIP,BRT),                    X
                PICIN='9999999',PICOUT='9999999'
 969 COST7    DFHMDF POS=(17,55),LENGTH=08,ATTRB=(ASKIP,BRT),                    X
                PICIN='99999999',PICOUT='99999999'
 980 UPRICE7  DFHMDF POS=(17,64),LENGTH=07,ATTRB=(ASKIP,BRT),                    X
                PICIN='9999999',PICOUT='9999999'
 991 PRICE7   DFHMDF POS=(17,72),LENGTH=08,ATTRB=(ASKIP,BRT),                    X
                PICIN='99999999',PICOUT='99999999'
1002 LINE8    DFHMDF POS=(18,03),LENGTH=01,ATTRB=ASKIP
1013 ITEM8    DFHMDF POS=(18,05),LENGTH=08,ATTRB=(ASKIP,BRT),                    X
                PICIN='99999999',PICOUT='99999999'
1024 DESC8    DFHMDF POS=(18,14),LENGTH=19,ATTRB=(ASKIP,BRT)
1035 LNDATE8  DFHMDF POS=(18,34),LENGTH=06,ATTRB=(ASKIP,BRT)
1046 UNIT8    DFHMDF POS=(18,41),LENGTH=05,ATTRB=(ASKIP,BRT),                    X
                PICIN='99999',PICOUT='99999'
1057 UCOST8   DFHMDF POS=(18,47),LENGTH=07,ATTRB=(ASKIP,BRT),                    X
                PICIN='9999999',PICOUT='9999999'
1068 COST8    DFHMDF POS=(18,55),LENGTH=08,ATTRB=(ASKIP,BRT),                    X
                PICIN='99999999',PICOUT='99999999'
1079 UPRICE8  DFHMDF POS=(18,64),LENGTH=07,ATTRB=(ASKIP,BRT),                    X
                PICIN='9999999',PICOUT='9999999'
1090 PRICE8   DFHMDF POS=(18,72),LENGTH=08,ATTRB=(ASKIP,BRT),                    X
```

Fig. 18.3. Map Program — File Inquiry.

```
STMT    SOURCE STATEMENT                              DOS/VS ASSEMBLER REL 34.0 14.03

                    PICIN='99999999',PICOUT='99999999'
1101 LINE9     DFHMDF POS=(19,03),LENGTH=01,ATTRB=ASKIP
1112 ITEM9     DFHMDF POS=(19,05),LENGTH=08,ATTRB=(ASKIP,BRT),           X
                    PICIN='99999999',PICOUT='99999999'
1123 DESC9     DFHMDF POS=(19,14),LENGTH=19,ATTRB=(ASKIP,BRT)
1134 LNDATE9   DFHMDF POS=(19,34),LENGTH=06,ATTRB=(ASKIP,BRT)
1145 UNIT9     DFHMDF POS=(19,41),LENGTH=05,ATTRB=(ASKIP,BRT),           X
                    PICIN='99999',PICOUT='99999'
1156 UCOST9    DFHMDF POS=(19,47),LENGTH=07,ATTRB=(ASKIP,BRT),           X
                    PICIN='9999999',PICOUT='9999999'
1167 COST9     DFHMDF POS=(19,55),LENGTH=08,ATTRB=(ASKIP,BRT),           X
                    PICIN='99999999',PICOUT='99999999'
1178 UPRICE9   DFHMDF POS=(19,64),LENGTH=07,ATTRB=(ASKIP,BRT),           X
                    PICIN='9999999',PICOUT='9999999'
1189 PRICE9    DFHMDF POS=(19,72),LENGTH=08,ATTRB=(ASKIP,BRT),           X
                    PICIN='99999999',PICOUT='99999999'
12CC ERROR     DFHMDF POS=(23,30),LENGTH=20,ATTRB=(ASKIP,BRT)
1211           DFHMSD TYPE=FINAL
1225           END
```

Fig. 18.3.　Map Program — File Inquiry.

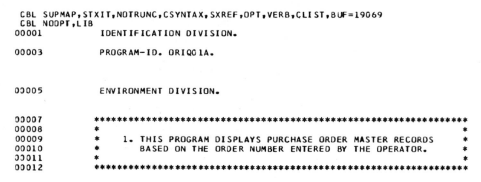

```
     1   IBM DOS VS COBOL

  CBL SUPMAP,STXIT,NOTRUNC,CSYNTAX,SXREF,OPT,VERB,CLIST,BUF=19069
  CBL NOOPT,LIB
00001          IDENTIFICATION DIVISION.

00003          PROGRAM-ID. ORIQ01A.


00005          ENVIRONMENT DIVISION.


00007          *************************************************************
00008          *                                                          *
00009          *      1. THIS PROGRAM DISPLAYS PURCHASE ORDER MASTER RECORDS   *
00010          *         BASED ON THE ORDER NUMBER ENTERED BY THE OPERATOR.    *
00011          *                                                          *
00012          *************************************************************
```

Fig. 18.4.　File Inquiry Program.

```
   2        ORIQ01A          12.55.39        08/02/80

00014        DATA DIVISION.


00016        WORKING-STORAGE SECTION.


00018        01  COMMUNICATION-AREA.

00020             05  COMMAREA-PROCESS-SW      PIC X.


00022        01  AREA1.

00024             05  JOB-NORMAL-END-MESSAGE  PIC X(23) VALUE
00025                 'JOB NORMALLY TERMINATED'.

00027             05  JOB-ABORTED-MESSAGE.
00028                 10  FILLER              PIC X(15) VALUE 'JOB ABORTED --'.
00029                 10  MAJOR-ERROR-MSG     PIC X(16).

00031             05  HEXADECIMAL-ZEROES      PIC 9999 COMP VALUE ZEROES.

00033             05  FILLER REDEFINES HEXADECIMAL-ZEROES.
00034                 10  FILLER              PIC X.
00035                 10  HEX-ZEROES          PIC X.

00037             05  OLD-EIB-AREA.
00038                 10  FILLER              PIC X(7) VALUE 'OLD EIB'.
00039                 10  OLD-EIBFN           PIC XX.
00040                 10  OLD-EIBRCODE        PIC X(6).
```

Fig. 18.4.   (Continued)

```
00042              01  DFHEIVAR COPY DFHEIVAR.
00043 C            01  DFHEIVAR.
00044 C                02  DFHEIV0   PICTURE X(26).
00045 C                02  DFHEIV1   PICTURE X(8).
00046 C                02  DFHEIV2   PICTURE X(8).
00047 C                02  DFHEIV3   PICTURE X(8).
00048 C                02  DFHEIV4   PICTURE X(6).
00049 C                02  DFHEIV5   PICTURE X(4).
00050 C                02  DFHEIV6   PICTURE X(4).
00051 C                02  DFHEIV7   PICTURE X(2).
00052 C                02  DFHEIV8   PICTURE X(2).
00053 C                02  DFHEIV9   PICTURE X(1).
00054 C                02  DFHEIV10  PICTURE S9(7) USAGE COMPUTATIONAL-3.
00055 C                02  DFHEIV11  PICTURE S9(4) USAGE COMPUTATIONAL.
00056 C                02  DFHEIV12  PICTURE S9(4) USAGE COMPUTATIONAL.
00057 C                02  DFHEIV13  PICTURE S9(4) USAGE COMPUTATIONAL.
00058 C                02  DFHEIV14  PICTURE S9(4) USAGE COMPUTATIONAL.
00059 C                02  DFHEIV15  PICTURE S9(4) USAGE COMPUTATIONAL.
00060 C                02  DFHEIV16  PICTURE S9(9) USAGE COMPUTATIONAL.
00061 C                02  DFHEIV17  PICTURE X(4).
00062 C                02  DFHEIV18  PICTURE X(4).
00063 C                02  DFHEIV19  PICTURE X(4).
00064 C                02  DFHEIV97  PICTURE S9(7) USAGE COMPUTATIONAL-3 VALUE ZERO.
00065 C                02  DFHEIV98  PICTURE S9(4) USAGE COMPUTATIONAL VALUE ZERO.
00066 C                02  DFHEIV99  PICTURE X(1) VALUE SPACE.
00067              LINKAGE SECTION.
00068              01  DFHEIBLK COPY DFHEIBLK.
00069 C            *     EIBLK EXEC INTERFACE BLOCK
00070 C            01  DFHEIBLK.
00071 C            *          EIBTIME     TIME IN 0HHMMSS FORMAT
00072 C                02 EIBTIME        PICTURE S9(7) USAGE COMPUTATIONAL-3.
00073 C            *          EIBDATE     DATE IN 00YYDDD FORMAT
00074 C                02 EIBDATE        PICTURE S9(7) USAGE COMPUTATIONAL-3.
00075 C            *          EIBTRNID    TRANSACTION IDENTIFIER
00076 C                02 EIBTRNID       PICTURE X(4).
00077 C            *          EIBTASKN    TASK NUMBER
00078 C                02 EIBTASKN       PICTURE S9(7) USAGE COMPUTATIONAL-3.
00079 C            *          EIBTRMID    TERMINAL IDENTIFIER
00080 C                02 EIBTRMID       PICTURE X(4).
00081 C            *          DFHEIGDI    RESERVED
00082 C                02 DFHEIGDI       PICTURE S9(4) USAGE COMPUTATIONAL.
00083 C            *          EIBCPOSN    CURSOR POSITION
00084 C                02 EIBCPOSN       PICTURE S9(4) USAGE COMPUTATIONAL.
00085 C            *          EIBCALEN    COMMAREA LENGTH
00086 C                02 EIBCALEN       PICTURE S9(4) USAGE COMPUTATIONAL.
00087 C            *          EIBAID      ATTENTION IDENTIFIER
00088 C                02 EIBAID         PICTURE X(1).
00089 C            *          EIBFN       FUNCTION CODE
00090 C                02 EIBFN          PICTURE X(2).
00091 C            *          EIBRCODE    RESPONSE CODE
00092 C                02 EIBRCODE       PICTURE X(6).
00093 C            *          EIBDS       DATASET NAME
00094 C                02 EIBDS          PICTURE X(8).
```

Fig. 18.4. (Continued)

```
     4          ORIQ01A          12.55.39          08/02/80

00095 C      *          EIBREQID     REQUEST IDENTIFIER
00096 C                 02 EIBREQID     PICTURE X(8).
00097              01  DFHCOMMAREA                  PIC X.

00099                    88  INITIAL-ENTRY-TIME        VALUE '0'.
00100                    88  ORDER-DISPLAY-TIME        VALUE '1'.


00102              01  LINKAGE-POINTERS.

00104                    05  FILLER              PIC S9(8) COMP.
00105                    05  MAP1-POINTER        PIC S9(8) COMP.
00106                    05  POM-POINTER         PIC S9(8) COMP.
00107                    05  TWA-POINTER         PIC S9(8) COMP.
```

Fig. 18.4.   (Continued)

```
        5          ORIQO1A            12.55.39         08/02/80

00109      ********************************************************************
00110      *                                                                *
00111      *                  DISPLAY MAP DESCRIPTION                       *
00112      *                                                                *
00113      ********************************************************************


00115          01  MAP1-AREA.
00116              05  FILLER                          PIC X(12).
00117              05  MAP1-DUMMY-L                    PIC S9999 COMP.
00118              05  MAP1-DUMMY-A                    PIC X.
00119              05  MAP1-DUMMY                      PIC X.
00120              05  MAP1-ORDER-NUMBER-L             PIC S9999 COMP.
00121              05  MAP1-ORDER-NUMBER-A             PIC X.
00122              05  MAP1-ORDER-NUMBER               PIC X(10).
00123              05  MAP1-DEPARTMENT-L               PIC S9999 COMP.
00124              05  MAP1-DEPARTMENT-A               PIC X.
00125              05  MAP1-DEPARTMENT                 PIC XXX.
00126              05  MAP1-ORDER-DATE-L               PIC S9999 COMP.
00127              05  MAP1-ORDER-DATE-A               PIC X.
00128              05  MAP1-ORDER-DATE.
00129                  10   MAP1-ORDER-DATE-MONTH      PIC XX.
00130                  10   MAP1-ORDER-DATE-DAY        PIC XX.
00131                  10   MAP1-ORDER-DATE-YEAR       PIC XX.
00132              05  MAP1-ORDER-DATE-ENTERED-L       PIC S9999 COMP.
00133              05  MAP1-ORDER-DATE-ENTERED-A       PIC X.
00134              05  MAP1-ORDER-DATE-ENTERED         PIC X(6).
00135              05  MAP1-TOTAL-COST-L               PIC S9999 COMP.
00136              05  MAP1-TOTAL-COST-A               PIC X.
00137              05  MAP1-TOTAL-COST                 PIC Z,ZZZ,ZZZ.99.
00138              05  MAP1-TOTAL-PRICE-L              PIC S9999 COMP.
00139              05  MAP1-TOTAL-PRICE-A              PIC X.
00140              05  MAP1-TOTAL-PRICE                PIC Z,ZZZ,ZZZ.99.
00141              05  MAP1-LINE-ITEM                  OCCURS 9
00142                                                  INDEXED BY MAP1-LINE-I.
00143                  10   MAP1-LINE-NUMBER-L         PIC S9999 COMP.
00144                  10   MAP1-LINE-NUMBER-A         PIC X.
00145                  10   MAP1-LINE-NUMBER           PIC 9.
00146                  10   MAP1-ITEM-NUMBER-L         PIC S9999 COMP.
00147                  10   MAP1-ITEM-NUMBER-A         PIC X.
00148                  10   MAP1-ITEM-NUMBER           PIC 9(8).
00149                  10   MAP1-ITEM-DESCRIPTION-L    PIC S9999 COMP.
00150                  10   MAP1-ITEM-DESCRIPTION-A    PIC X.
00151                  10   MAP1-ITEM-DESCRIPTION      PIC X(19).
00152                  10   MAP1-ITEM-DATE-L           PIC S9999 COMP.
00153                  10   MAP1-ITEM-DATE-A           PIC X.
00154                  10   MAP1-ITEM-DATE             PIC X(6).
00155                  10   MAP1-UNIT-L                PIC S9999 COMP.
00156                  10   MAP1-UNIT-A                PIC X.
00157                  10   MAP1-UNIT                  PIC 9(5).
00158                  10   MAP1-UNIT-COST-L           PIC S9999 COMP.
00159                  10   MAP1-UNIT-COST-A           PIC X.
```

Fig. 18.4.   (Continued)

```
00160                    10   MAP1-UNIT-COST           PIC 9(7).
00161                    10   MAP1-COST-L              PIC S9999 COMP.
00162                    10   MAP1-COST-A              PIC X.
00163                    10   MAP1-COST                PIC 9(8).
00164                    10   MAP1-UNIT-PRICE-L        PIC S9999 COMP.
00165                    10   MAP1-UNIT-PRICE-A        PIC X.
00166                    10   MAP1-UNIT-PRICE          PIC 9(7).
00167                    10   MAP1-PRICE-L             PIC S9999 COMP.
00168                    10   MAP1-PRICE-A             PIC X.
00169                    10   MAP1-PRICE               PIC 9(8).
00170                05   MAP1-ERROR-L                 PIC S9999 COMP.
00171                05   MAP1-ERROR-A                 PIC X.
00172                05   MAP1-ERROR                   PIC X(20).
```

Fig. 18.4. (Continued)

```
00174        ******************************************************************
00175        *                                                                *
00176        *        PURCHASE ORDER MASTER -- FILE LAYOUT                    *
00177        *                                                                *
00178        ******************************************************************

00180        01   ORDER-MASTER-RECORD.
00181             05   ORDER-NUMBER                PIC X(10).
00182             05   ORDER-ALT-KEY.
00183                  10   ORDER-DEPARTMENT       PIC XXX.
00184                  10   ORDER-DATE.
00185                       15   ORDER-DATE-YEAR        PIC XX.
00186                       15   ORDER-DATE-MONTH       PIC XX.
00187                       15   ORDER-DATE-DAY         PIC XX.
00188             05   ORDER-DATE-ENTERED.
00189                  10   ORDER-DATE-ENTERED-MONTH   PIC XX.
00190                  10   ORDER-DATE-ENTERED-DAY     PIC XX.
00191                  10   ORDER-DATE-ENTERED-YEAR    PIC XX.
00192             05   ORDER-TOTAL-COST            PIC S9(7)V99   COMP-3.
00193             05   ORDER-TOTAL-PRICE           PIC S9(7)V99   COMP-3.
00194             05   ORDER-LINE-COUNT            PIC S9999      COMP.
00195             05   ORDER-ALL-LINES.
00196                  10   ORDER-LINE-ITEM            OCCURS 1 TO 9
00197                                                  DEPENDING ON ORDER-LINE-COUNT
00198                                                  INDEXED BY ORDER-LINE-I.
00199                       15   ORDER-ITEM-NUMBER        PIC X(8).
00200                       15   ORDER-ITEM-DESCRIPTION   PIC X(19).
00201                       15   ORDER-ITEM-DATE.
00202                            20   ORDER-ITEM-DATE-MONTH   PIC XX.
00203                            20   ORDER-ITEM-DATE-DAY     PIC XX.
00204                            20   ORDER-ITEM-DATE-YEAR    PIC XX.
00205                       15   ORDER-UNIT               PIC S9(5)      COMP-3.
00206                       15   ORDER-UNIT-COST          PIC S9(5)V99   COMP-3.
00207                       15   ORDER-UNIT-PRICE         PIC S9(5)V99   COMP-3.
```

Fig. 18.4. (Continued)

```
00209        ****************************************************************
00210        *                                                              *
00211        *                  TRANSACTION WORK AREA                       *
00212        *                                                              *
00213        ****************************************************************


00215        01   TWA-AREA.

00217             05   TWA-LINE-ITEM-MAP.
00218                  10   TWA-LINE-NUMBER-MAP-L           PIC S9999 COMP.
00219                  10   TWA-LINE-NUMBER-MAP-A           PIC X.
00220                  10   TWA-LINE-NUMBER-MAP             PIC 9.
00221                  10   TWA-ITEM-NUMBER-MAP-L           PIC S9999 COMP.
00222                  10   TWA-ITEM-NUMBER-MAP-A           PIC X.
00223                  10   TWA-ITEM-NUMBER-MAP             PIC 9(8).
00224                  10   TWA-ITEM-DESCRIPTION-MAP-L      PIC S9999 COMP.
00225                  10   TWA-ITEM-DESCRIPTION-MAP-A      PIC X.
00226                  10   TWA-ITEM-DESCRIPTION-MAP        PIC X(19).
00227                  10   TWA-ITEM-DATE-MAP-L             PIC S9999 COMP.
00228                  10   TWA-ITEM-DATE-MAP-A             PIC X.
00229                  10   TWA-ITEM-DATE-MAP               PIC X(6).
00230                  10   TWA-UNIT-MAP-L                  PIC S9999 COMP.
00231                  10   TWA-UNIT-MAP-A                  PIC X.
00232                  10   TWA-UNIT-MAP                    PIC 9(5).
00233                  10   TWA-UNIT-COST-MAP-L             PIC S9999 COMP.
00234                  10   TWA-UNIT-COST-MAP-A             PIC X.
00235                  10   TWA-UNIT-COST-MAP               PIC 9(7).
00236                  10   TWA-COST-MAP-L                  PIC S9999 COMP.
00237                  10   TWA-COST-MAP-A                  PIC X.
00238                  10   TWA-COST-MAP                    PIC 9(8).
00239                  10   TWA-UNIT-PRICE-MAP-L            PIC S9999 COMP.
00240                  10   TWA-UNIT-PRICE-MAP-A            PIC X.
00241                  10   TWA-UNIT-PRICE-MAP              PIC 9(7).
00242                  10   TWA-PRICE-MAP-L                 PIC S9999 COMP.
00243                  10   TWA-PRICE-MAP-A                 PIC X.
00244                  10   TWA-PRICE-MAP                   PIC 9(8).


00246             05   TWA-LINE-ITEM-ORDER.
00247                  10   TWA-ITEM-NUMBER-ORDER           PIC X(8).
00248                  10   TWA-ITEM-DESCRIPTION-ORDER      PIC X(19).
00249                  10   TWA-ITEM-DATE-ORDER             PIC X(6).
00250                  10   TWA-UNIT-ORDER                  PIC S9(5)        COMP-3.
00251                  10   TWA-UNIT-COST-ORDER             PIC S9(5)V99 COMP-3.
00252                  10   TWA-UNIT-PRICE-ORDER            PIC S9(5)V99 COMP-3.


00254             05   TWA-OPERATOR-MESSAGE               PIC X(31).


00256             05   TWA-ORDER-RECORD-KEY              PIC X(10).
```

Fig. 18.4.   (Continued)

```
    9          ORIQ01A          12.55.39          08/02/80

00258              PROCEDURE DIVISION USING DFHEIBLK DFHCOMMAREA.
00259                  CALL 'DFHEI1'.


00261              ****************************************************************
00262              *                                                            *
00263              MAIN-LINE SECTION.
00264              *                                                            *
00265              ****************************************************************


00267          *      EXEC CICS
00268          *          ADDRESS TWA (TWA-POINTER)
00269          *      END-EXEC.
00270                 MOVE '8B  DC              ' TO DFHEIVO CALL 'DFHEI1' USING
00271                 DFHEIVO TWA-POINTER.
00272
00273          *      EXEC CICS
00274          *          HANDLE AID
00275          *              CLEAR (FINALIZATION)
00276          *              PA1 (WRONG-KEY-USED)
00277          *              PA2 (WRONG-KEY-USED)
00278          *              PA3 (WRONG-KEY-USED)
00279          *      END-EXEC.
00280                 MOVE 'BFO DEDFC           ' TO DFHEIVO CALL 'DFHEI1' USING
00281                 DFHEIVO GO TO FINALIZATION WRONG-KEY-USED WRONG-KEY-USED
00282                 WRONG-KEY-USED DEPENDING ON DFHEIGDI.



00286
00287          *      EXEC CICS
00288          *          HANDLE CONDITION
00289          *              MAPFAIL (MAPFAIL-ERROR)
00290          *              ERROR   (MAJOR-ERROR)
00291          *      END-EXEC.
00292                 MOVE 'BD  DUA             ' TO DFHEIVO CALL 'DFHEI1' USING
00293                 DFHEIVO GO TO MAPFAIL-ERROR MAJOR-ERROR DEPENDING ON
00294                 DFHEIGDI.

00296
00297              IF EIBCALEN NOT EQUAL TO ZEROES
00298                  IF ORDER-DISPLAY-TIME
00299                      GO TO ORDER-DISPLAY
00300                  ELSE IF INITIAL-ENTRY-TIME
00301                      GO TO INITIALIZATION
00302                  ELSE GO TO PROCESS-SWITCH-ERROR.

00304              IF EIBCALEN EQUAL TO ZEROES
00305                  GO TO SIGN-ON-VIOLATION.
```

Fig. 18.4.   (Continued)

```
      10        ORIQO1A        12.55.39      08/02/80

00307        ************************************************************************
00308        *                                                                     *
00309          ORDER-DISPLAY SECTION.
00310        *                                                                     *
00311        ************************************************************************


00313     *     EXEC CICS
00314     *         HANDLE CONDITION
00315     *             NOTOPEN (FILE-NOT-OPEN)
00316     *             NOTFND  (RECORD-NOT-FOUND)
00317     *     END-EXEC.
00318           MOVE 'BD  DL(              ' TO DFHEIVO CALL 'DFHEI1' USING
00319           DFHEIVO GO TO FILE-NOT-OPEN RECORD-NOT-FOUND DEPENDING ON
00320           DFHEIGDI.
00321
00322
00323     *     EXEC CICS
00324     *         RECEIVE MAP   ('ORIQM01')
00325     *                 MAPSET ('ORIQSO1')
00326     *                 SET    (MAP1-POINTER)
00327     *     END-EXEC.
00328            MOVE 'ORIQM01' TO DFHEIV1 MOVE 'ORIQSO1' TO DFHEIV2 MOVE 'QB
00329     -    '& DA   EI  -' TO DFHEIVO CALL 'DFHEI1' USING DFHEIVO
00330           DFHEIV1 MAP1-POINTER DFHEIV98 DFHEIV2.
00331
00332
00333           IF MAP1-ORDER-NUMBER NOT NUMERIC
00334               GO TO INVALID-ORDER-RTN.

00336           MOVE MAP1-ORDER-NUMBER TO TWA-ORDER-RECORD-KEY.

00338     *     EXEC CICS
00339     *         READ DATASET ('ORTEST')
00340     *              SET     (POM-POINTER)
00341     *              RIDFLD  (TWA-ORDER-RECORD-KEY)
00342     *     END-EXEC.
00343           MOVE 'ORTEST' TO DFHEIV3 MOVE 'FB& DA   ' TO DFHEIVO CALL 'D
00344     -    'FHEI1' USING DFHEIVO DFHEIV3 POM-POINTER DFHEIV98
00345           TWA-ORDER-RECORD-KEY.
00346
00347
00348           MOVE ORDER-NUMBER          TO  MAP1-ORDER-NUMBER.
00349           MOVE ORDER-DEPARTMENT      TO  MAP1-DEPARTMENT.
00350           MOVE ORDER-DATE-MONTH      TO  MAP1-ORDER-DATE-MONTH.
00351           MOVE ORDER-DATE-DAY        TO  MAP1-ORDER-DATE-DAY.
00352           MOVE ORDER-DATE-YEAR       TO  MAP1-ORDER-DATE-YEAR.
00353           MOVE ORDER-DATE-ENTERED    TO  MAP1-ORDER-DATE-ENTERED.
00354           MOVE ORDER-TOTAL-COST      TO  MAP1-TOTAL-COST.
00355           MOVE ORDER-TOTAL-PRICE     TO  MAP1-TOTAL-PRICE.
00356           MOVE SPACES                TO  MAP1-ERROR.
00357           SET ORDER-LINE-I           TO  1.
00358           PERFORM LAYOUT-EACH-LINE
```

Fig. 18.4.   (Continued)

11   ORIQ01A   12.55.39   08/02/80

```
00359                      UNTIL ORDER-LINE-I GREATER THAN ORDER-LINE-COUNT.
00360                  GO TO DISPLAY-ORDER.


00362          LAYOUT-EACH-LINE.
00363              SET MAP1-LINE-I                          TO ORDER-LINE-I.
00354              MOVE ORDER-LINE-ITEM (ORDER-LINE-I) TO TWA-LINE-ITEM-ORDER.
00355              MOVE MAP1-LINE-ITEM (MAP1-LINE-I)   TO TWA-LINE-ITEM-MAP.
00366              SET TWA-LINE-NUMBER-MAP                  TO ORDER-LINE-I.
00367              MOVE TWA-ITEM-NUMBER-ORDER     TO   TWA-ITEM-NUMBER-MAP.
00368              MOVE TWA-ITEM-DESCRIPTION-ORDER TO TWA-ITEM-DESCRIPTION-MAP.
00369              MOVE TWA-ITEM-DATE-ORDER        TO    TWA-ITEM-DATE-MAP.
00370              MOVE TWA-UNIT-ORDER             TO    TWA-UNIT-MAP.
00371              MOVE TWA-UNIT-COST-ORDER        TO    TWA-UNIT-COST-MAP.
00372              COMPUTE TWA-COST-MAP = TWA-UNIT-ORDER * TWA-UNIT-COST-ORDER.
00373              MOVE TWA-UNIT-PRICE-ORDER       TO    TWA-UNIT-PRICE-MAP.
00374              COMPUTE TWA-PRICE-MAP =
00375                         TWA-UNIT-ORDER * TWA-UNIT-PRICE-ORDER.
00376              MOVE TWA-LINE-ITEM-MAP     TO   MAP1-LINE-ITEM (MAP1-LINE-I).
00377              SET ORDER-LINE-I UP BY 1.


00379          DISPLAY-ORDER.

00381      *       EXEC CICS
00382      *           SEND MAP    ('ORIQM01')
00383      *                MAPSET ('ORIQS01')
00384      *                FROM   (MAP1-AREA)
00385      *                ERASE
00386      *       END-EXEC.
00387             MOVE 'ORIQM01' TO DFHEIV1 MOVE 'ORIQS01' TO DFHEIV2 MOVE 'QD
00388      -      '& D    ESD -' TO DFHEIVO CALL 'DFHEI1' USING DFHEIVO
00389             DFHEIV1 MAP1-AREA DFHEIV98 DFHEIV2.
00390
00391
00392
00393          RETURN-FOR-NEXT-ORDER.

00395             MOVE '1' TO COMMAREA-PROCESS-SW.

00397      *       EXEC CICS
00398      *           RETURN TRANSID  (EIBTRNID)
00399      *                  COMMAREA (COMMUNICATION-AREA)
00400      *                  LENGTH   (1)
00401      *       END-EXEC.
00402             MOVE 1 TO DFHEIV11 MOVE '+H- D  & ' TO DFHEIVO CALL 'DFHEI1'
00403             USING DFHEIVO EIBTRNID COMMUNICATION-AREA DFHEIV11.
00404
00405
00406
00407          RECORD-NOT-FOUND.

00409             MOVE 'RECORD NOT FOUND' TO MAP1-ERROR.
```

Fig. 18.4.   (Continued)

```
    12          OR IQO1A        12.55.39        08/02/80


00410                GO TO DISPLAY-INVALID-ORDER-MESSAGE.


00412            DISPLAY-INVALID-ORDER-MESSAGE.

00414        *     EXEC CICS
00415        *         SEND MAP    ('ORIQMO1')
00416        *              MAPSET ('ORIQSO1')
00417        *              FROM   (MAP1-AREA)
00418        *              ERASE
00419        *     END-EXEC.
00420              MOVE 'ORIQMO1' TO DFHEIV1 MOVE 'ORIQSO1' TO DFHEIV2 MOVE 'QD
00421        -    '& D    ESD -' TO DFHEIVO CALL 'DFHEI1' USING DFHEIVO
00422             DFHEIV1 MAP1-AREA DFHEIV98 DFHEIV2.
00423
00424
00425
00426                GO TO RETURN-FOR-NEXT-ORDER.


00428            INVALID-ORDER-RTN.

00430                MOVE 'INVALID ORDER NUMBER' TO MAP1-ERROR.
00431                GO TO DISPLAY-INVALID-ORDER-MESSAGE.



    13          OR IQO1A        12.55.39        08/02/80

00433        ****************************************************************
00434        *                                                              *
00435         WRONG-KEY-USED SECTION.
00436        *                                                              *
00437        ****************************************************************

00439        *     EXEC CICS
00440        *         GETMAIN
00441        *              SET     (MAP1-POINTER)
00442        *              LENGTH  (970)
00443        *              INITIMG (HEX-ZEROES)
00444        *     END-EXEC.
00445              MOVE 970 TO DFHEIV11 MOVE ' B- D   ' TO DFHEIVO CALL 'DFHEI
00446        -    '1' USING DFHEIVO MAP1-POINTER DFHEIV11 HEX-ZEROES.
00447
00448
00449
00450
00451                MOVE 'WRONG KEY USED' TO MAP1-ERROR.

00453        *     EXEC CICS
00454        *         SEND MAP    ('ORIQMO1')
00455        *              MAPSET ('ORIQSO1')
00456        *              FROM   (MAP1-AREA)
00457        *              DATAONLY
00458        *     END-EXEC.
00459              MOVE 'ORIQMO1' TO DFHEIV1 MOVE 'ORIQSO1' TO DFHEIV2 MOVE 'QD
00460        -    '& D    E-D -' TO DFHEIVO CALL 'DFHEI1' USING DFHEIVO
00461             DFHEIV1 MAP1-AREA DFHEIV98 DFHEIV2.
00462
00463
00464
00465                GO TO RETURN-FOR-NEXT-ORDER.
```

Fig. 18.4. (Continued)

14   ORIQ01A   12.55.39   08/02/80

```
00467      ****************************************************************
00468      *                                                              *
00469       INITIALIZATION SECTION.
00470      *                                                              *
00471      ****************************************************************

00473      *     EXEC CICS
00474      *         SEND MAP     ('ORIQM01')
00475      *              MAPSET ('ORIQS01')
00476      *              MAPONLY
00477      *              ERASE
00478      *     END-EXEC.
00479         MOVE 'ORIQM01' TO DFHEIV1 MOVE 'ORIQS01' TO DFHEIV2 MOVE 'QD
00480      -  '& D    ESD  -' TO DFHEIVO CALL 'DFHEI1' USING DFHEIVO
00481         DFHEIV1 DFHEIV99 DFHEIV98 DFHEIV2.
00482
00483
00484
00485         MOVE '1' TO COMMAREA-PROCESS-SW.

00487      *     EXEC CICS
00488      *         RETURN TRANSID   ('ORIQ')
00489      *              COMMAREA (COMMUNICATION-AREA)
00490      *              LENGTH    (1)
00491      *     END-EXEC.
00492         MOVE 'ORIQ' TO DFHEIV5 MOVE 1 TO DFHEIV11 MOVE '+H- D & '
00493         TO DFHEIVO CALL 'DFHEI1' USING DFHEIVO DFHEIV5
00494         COMMUNICATION-AREA DFHEIV11.
00495
00496
```

Fig. 18.4.   (Continued)

```
00498        ***********************************************************************
00499        *                                                                     *
00500         FINALIZATION SECTION.
00501        *                                                                     *
00502        ***********************************************************************


00504         PREPARE-TERMINATION-MESSAGE.

00506            MOVE JOB-NORMAL-END-MESSAGE TO TWA-OPERATOR-MESSAGE.


00508         JOB-TERMINATED.

00510        *    EXEC CICS
00511        *        SEND FROM    (TWA-OPERATOR-MESSAGE)
00512        *             LENGTH (31)
00513        *             ERASE
00514        *    END-EXEC.
00515             MOVE 31 TO DFHEIV11 MOVE 'DDO D   A       ' TO DFHEIVO CALL '
00516        -   'DFHEI1' USING DFHEIVO DFHEIV99 DFHEIV98 TWA-OPERATOR-MESSAGE
00517             DFHEIV11.
00518
00519


00521         END-OF-JOB.

00523        *    EXEC CICS
00524        *        RETURN
00525        *    END-EXEC.
00526             MOVE '+H   D  & ' TO DFHEIVO CALL 'DFHEI1' USING DFHEIVO.
00527
00528
```

Fig. 18.4. (Continued)

```
   16        ORIQO1A         12.55.39        08/02/80

00530      *****************************************************************
00531      *                                                              *
00532       ABNORMAL-TERMINATION SECTION.
00533      *                                                            *
00534      *****************************************************************


00536       FILE-NOT-OPEN.

00538      *     EXEC CICS
00539      *         XCTL PROGRAM ('TEL2OPEN')
00540      *     END-EXEC.
00541             MOVE 'TEL2OPEN' TO DFHEIV3 MOVE '+D   D   B ' TO DFHEIVO CALL
00542            'DFHEI1' USING DFHEIVO DFHEIV3.
00543


00545       MAPFAIL-ERROR.
00546             MOVE 'MAP FAILURE' TO MAJOR-ERROR-MSG.
00547             GO TO PREPARE-ABORT-MESSAGE.


00549       PROCESS-SWITCH-ERROR.
00550             MOVE 'PROCESS ERROR' TO MAJOR-ERROR-MSG.
00551             GO TO PREPARE-ABORT-MESSAGE.


00553       SIGN-ON-VIOLATION.
00554             MOVE 'SIGNON VIOLATION' TO MAJOR-ERROR-MSG.
00555             GO TO PREPARE-ABORT-MESSAGE.


00557       MAJOR-ERROR.
00558             MOVE  EIBFN      TO  OLD-EIBFN.
00559             MOVE  EIBRCODE   TO  OLD-EIBRCODE.

00561      *     EXEC CICS
00562      *         DUMP DUMPCODE ('ERRS')
00563      *     END-EXEC.
00564             MOVE 'ERRS' TO DFHEIV5 MOVE '*B   D   = ' TO DFHEIVO CALL 'DFH
00565      -      'EI1' USING DFHEIVO DFHEIV5.
00566
00567             MOVE 'MAJOR ERROR' TO MAJOR-ERROR-MSG.
00568             GO TO PREPARE-ABORT-MESSAGE.


00570       PREPARE-ABORT-MESSAGE.
00571             MOVE JOB-ABORTED-MESSAGE TO TWA-OPERATOR-MESSAGE.
00572             GO TO JOB-TERMINATED.
```

Fig. 18.4. (Continued)

5. Lines 304–305. If the program is executed at the start of the session by an operator-entered transaction identifier instead of through an XCTL command from the Sign-on program, a sign-on violation occurs. This is so if EIBCALEN is equal to zero.

THE INITIALIZATION SECTION

1. Lines 473–481. Display the inquiry map.

2. Line 485.   Set the communication area switch to 1.

3. Lines 487–494. Terminate the task.

THE ORDER-DISPLAY SECTION

1. Lines 313–320. HANDLE CONDITION command for the order file.

2. Lines 323–330. Read the map that contains the order number entered by the operator.

3. Lines 333–345. Read the order file using the order number entered.

4. If the record is found:
    a. Lines 348–377. Lay out the fields of the record in the area secured by CICS/VS for the symbolic description map. Note the GO TO of line 360 to keep the code in a "straight line."
    b. Lines 379–389. Display the record. The ERASE option is specified since the data is variable (from 1 to 9 lines). If the data were fixed, this would not be required and DATAONLY would then be specified.
    c. Line 395.   Set the communication area switch to 1.
    d. Lines 397–403. Terminate the task.

5. If the record is not found:
    a. Line 409.   Lay out the "RECORD NOT FOUND" message in the area secured by CICS/VS for the symbolic description map.

b. Lines 412–422. Display the message. In this case, the ERASE option is mandatory to erase data from the previous display.

c. Line 426.   Set the communication area switch to 1 and terminate the task.

THE WRONG-KEY-USED SECTION

1. Lines 439–446. GETMAIN command to secure main storage for the map that will contain the error message. This is because the PA keys do not allow CICS/VS to secure main storage for the symbolic description map through a RECEIVE MAP command.

2. Line 451.   Move the "WRONG KEY USED" message into the area secured.

3. Lines 453–461. Display the error message.

4. Line 465.   Set the communication area switch to 1 and terminate the task. This GO TO should be of no concern because this section will rarely be executed.

THE FINALIZATION SECTION

1. Lines 504–517. Display the "JOB NORMALLY TERMINATED" message.

2. Lines 521–526. Terminate the session.

THE ABNORMAL-TERMINATION SECTION

These are the routines used to abnormally terminate the session on errors and CICS/VS command exceptional conditions not covered by a HANDLE CONDITION command.

EXAMPLE

The following are facsimiles of actual photographs taken of a CRT terminal during a session.

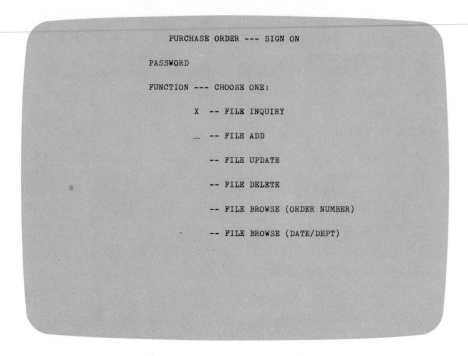

```
                    PURCHASE ORDER --- SIGN ON

          PASSWORD

          FUNCTION --- CHOOSE ONE:

                        X  -- FILE INQUIRY

                        _  -- FILE ADD

                           -- FILE UPDATE

                           -- FILE DELETE

                           -- FILE BROWSE (ORDER NUMBER)

                           -- FILE BROWSE (DATE/DEPT)
```

Fig. 18.5. The File Inquiry application is selected by keying in an "X" on the File Inquiry line and the corresponding password, then hitting the ENTER key.

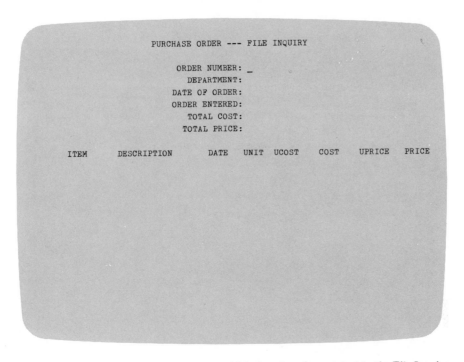

```
              PURCHASE ORDER --- FILE INQUIRY

                     ORDER NUMBER: _
                      DEPARTMENT:
                     DATE OF ORDER:
                     ORDER ENTERED:
                       TOTAL COST:
                       TOTAL PRICE:


    ITEM       DESCRIPTION       DATE   UNIT  UCOST    COST    UPRICE   PRICE
```

Fig. 18.6. The Sign On program executes which then transfers control to the File Inquiry program. This displays the File Inquiry map.

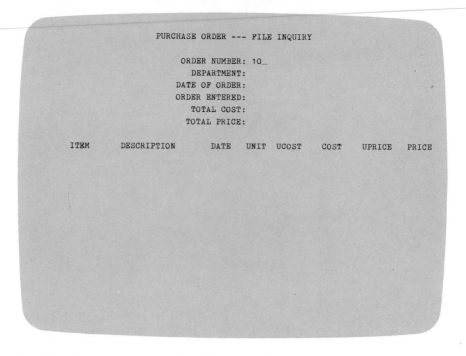

Fig. 18.7.   The operator keys in the order number of the record to be displayed, then hits the ENTER key.

```
              PURCHASE ORDER --- FILE INQUIRY

                    ORDER NUMBER: Q000000010
                      DEPARTMENT: 003
                   DATE OF ORDER: 122480
                   ORDER ENTERED: 122680
                      TOTAL COST:    1,600.00
                     TOTAL PRICE:    3,200.00


    ITEM        DESCRIPTION       DATE   UNIT  UCOST    COST    UPRICE   PRICE
  1 00087632 12-INCH CRESCENT   122480 00100 0000600 00060000 0001200 00120000
  2 00063271 BENCH VISE         122480 00050 0002000 00100000 0004000 00200000
```

Fig. 18.8.   The program displays the record.

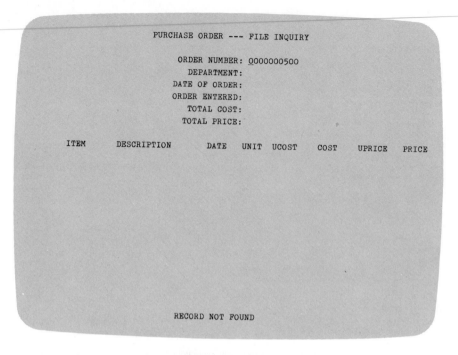

Fig. 18.9. If the record corresponding to the order number entered is not in the file, the "RECORD NOT FOUND" message is displayed.

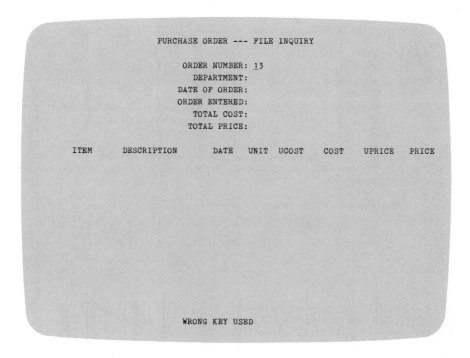

```
         PURCHASE ORDER --- FILE INQUIRY

              ORDER NUMBER: 13
               DEPARTMENT:
             DATE OF ORDER:
             ORDER ENTERED:
                TOTAL COST:
               TOTAL PRICE:

  ITEM      DESCRIPTION      DATE   UNIT  UCOST    COST   UPRICE   PRICE














              WRONG KEY USED
```

Fig. 18.10. If the operator keys in an order number but then hits one of the PA keys instead of the ENTER key, the "WRONG KEY USED" message is displayed.

```
                    PURCHASE ORDER --- FILE INQUIRY

                    ORDER NUMBER: 0000000013
                      DEPARTMENT: 003
                    DATE OF ORDER: 122680
                    ORDER ENTERED: 122680
                       TOTAL COST:      1,850.00
                      TOTAL PRICE:      3,700.00


   ITEM        DESCRIPTION       DATE   UNIT  UCOST     COST    UPRICE    PRICE
 1 00081667 1/2 HP CHAIN SAW    122680 00025 0005000 00125000 0010000 00250000
 2 00009152 7 1/4 IN. CIRCL SAW 122680 00040 0001500 00060000 0003000 00120000
```

Fig. 18.11. If the operator then hits the ENTER key, the session continues. The record selected in Fig. 18.10 is now displayed.

19

The File Add Program

INTRODUCTION

This program allows the operator to add new records to the Purchase Order file according to the record key entered. The program executes when selected by the Sign-on program and will continue the session until terminated by the operator. The flow of control to execute this program is shown in Figure 19.1.

PROGRAM SPECIFICATIONS

The program specifications are as follows:

1. Implement the program using the pseudoconversational mode of processing.

2. Use 'ORAD' as the transaction identifier. However, the session should not be started by using this identifier, but rather through an XCTL command from the Sign-on program.

3. If the session is started by using the transaction identifier, abort the session with the message "JOB ABORTED–SIGNON VIOLATION."

4. Edit the data using page 177 as a guide.

5. On any PA key, bypass the input data and display the next fresh screen for the next set of data.

SCREEN LAYOUT

The screen layout to be used in the program is shown in Figure 19.2. All 9s are numeric fields and Xs are alphanumeric fields.

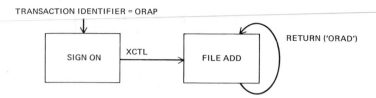

Fig. 19.1. File Add Application.

MAP PROGRAM

The map program corresponding to the screen layout is shown in Figure 19.3.

PROGRAM LISTING

The program listing for the File Add program is shown in Figure 19.4.

MAIN-LINE SECTION

1. Lines 382–386. ADDRESS command for the TWA.

2. Lines 388–397. HANDLE AID command. The PA keys will execute the BYPASS-INPUT section.

3. Lines 402–409. HANDLE CONDITION command.

4. Lines 412–417. The selection of sections.

5. Lines 419–420. If the program is executed at the start of the session by an operator-entered transaction identifier instead of through an XCTL program from the Sign-on program, a sign-on violation occurs. This is so if EIBCALEN is equal to zero.

THE INITIALIZATION SECTION

1. Lines 883–888. HANDLE CONDITION command for the deletion of a specific temporary storage queue.

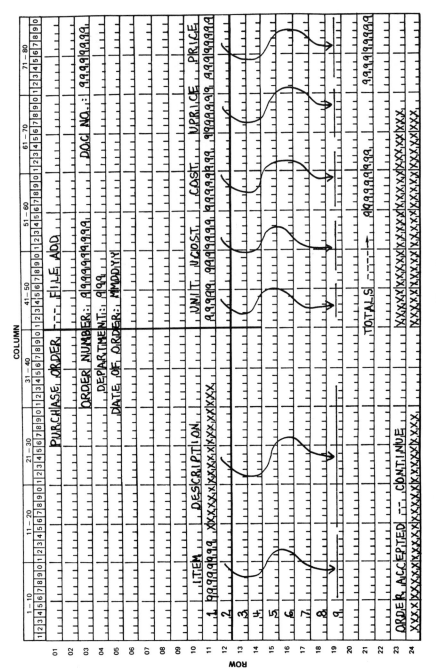

Fig. 19.2. Screen Layout — File Add.

```
STMT     SOURCE STATEMENT                                    DOS/VS ASSEMBLER REL 34.0 13.10

   1                      PRINT NOGEN
   2 ORADSO1             DFHMSD TYPE=MAP,MODE=INOUT,CTRL=FREEKB,LANG=COBOL,TIOAPFX=YES
  12 ORADMO1             DFHMDI SIZE=(24,80)
  40 DUMMY               DFHMDF POS=(01,01),LENGTH=01,ATTRB=(ASKIP,DRK,FSET),          X
                               INITIAL='1'
  52                     DFHMDF POS=(01,25),LENGTH=27,ATTRB=(ASKIP,BRT),               X
                               INITIAL='PURCHASE ORDER --- FILE ADD'
  64                     DFHMDF POS=(03,30),LENGTH=13,ATTRB=ASKIP,                      X
                               INITIAL='ORDER NUMBER '
  76 ORDER               DFHMDF POS=(03,44),LENGTH=10,ATTRB=(NUM,BRT,IC)
  87                     DFHMDF POS=(03,55),LENGTH=01,ATTRB=PROT
  98                     DFHMDF POS=(03,62),LENGTH=08,ATTRB=ASKIP,INITIAL='DOC NO. '
 110 DOCNO               DFHMDF POS=(03,71),LENGTH=08,ATTRB=(NUM,BRT)
 121                     DFHMDF POS=(03,80),LENGTH=01,ATTRB=PROT
 132                     DFHMDF POS=(04,32),LENGTH=11,ATTRB=ASKIP,INITIAL='DEPARTMENT '
 144 DEPT                DFHMDF POS=(04,44),LENGTH=03,ATTRB=(NUM,BRT)
 155                     DFHMDF POS=(04,48),LENGTH=01,ATTRB=ASKIP
 166                     DFHMDF POS=(05,29),LENGTH=14,ATTRB=ASKIP,                      X
                               INITIAL='DATE OF ORDER '
 178 DATEOR              DFHMDF POS=(05,44),LENGTH=06,ATTRB=(NUM,BRT),INITIAL='MMDDYY'
 190                     DFHMDF POS=(05,51),LENGTH=01,ATTRB=ASKIP
 201                     DFHMDF POS=(10,07),LENGTH=04,ATTRB=ASKIP,INITIAL='ITEM'
 213                     DFHMDF POS=(10,17),LENGTH=11,ATTRB=ASKIP,INITIAL='DESCRIPTION'
 225                     DFHMDF POS=(10,42),LENGTH=04,ATTRB=ASKIP,INITIAL='UNIT'
 237                     DFHMDF POS=(10,48),LENGTH=05,ATTRB=ASKIP,INITIAL='UCOST'
 249                     DFHMDF POS=(10,57),LENGTH=04,ATTRB=ASKIP,INITIAL='COST'
 261                     DFHMDF POS=(10,65),LENGTH=06,ATTRB=ASKIP,INITIAL='UPRICE'
 273                     DFHMDF POS=(10,74),LENGTH=05,ATTRB=ASKIP,INITIAL='PRICE'
 285                     DFHMDF POS=(11,03),LENGTH=01,ATTRB=ASKIP,INITIAL='1'
 297 ITEM1               DFHMDF POS=(11,05),LENGTH=08,ATTRB=(NUM,BRT),                  X
                               PICIN='99999999',PICOUT='99999999'
 308 DESC1               DFHMDF POS=(11,14),LENGTH=19,ATTRB=(UNPROT,BRT)
 319                     DFHMDF POS=(11,34),LENGTH=01,ATTRB=PROT
 330 UNIT1               DFHMDF POS=(11,41),LENGTH=05,ATTRB=(NUM,BRT),                  X
                               PICIN='99999',PICOUT='99999'
 341 UCOST1              DFHMDF POS=(11,47),LENGTH=07,ATTRB=(NUM,BRT),                  X
                               PICIN='9999999',PICOUT='9999999'
 352 COST1               DFHMDF POS=(11,55),LENGTH=08,ATTRB=(NUM,BRT),                  X
                               PICIN='99999999',PICOUT='99999999'
 363 UPRICE1             DFHMDF POS=(11,64),LENGTH=07,ATTRB=(NUM,BRT),                  X
                               PICIN='9999999',PICOUT='9999999'
 374 PRICE1              DFHMDF POS=(11,72),LENGTH=08,ATTRB=(NUM,BRT),                  X
                               PICIN='99999999',PICOUT='99999999'
 385                     DFHMDF POS=(12,01),LENGTH=01,ATTRB=PROT
 396                     DFHMDF POS=(12,03),LENGTH=01,ATTRB=ASKIP,INITIAL='2'
 408 ITEM2               DFHMDF POS=(12,05),LENGTH=08,ATTRB=(NUM,BRT),                  X
                               PICIN='99999999',PICOUT='99999999'
 419 DESC2               DFHMDF POS=(12,14),LENGTH=19,ATTRB=(UNPROT,BRT)
 430                     DFHMDF POS=(12,34),LENGTH=01,ATTRB=PROT
 441 UNIT2               DFHMDF POS=(12,41),LENGTH=05,ATTRB=(NUM,BRT),                  X
                               PICIN='99999',PICOUT='99999'
```

Fig. 19.3. Map Program — File Add.

```
STMT    SOURCE STATEMENT                        DOS/VS ASSEMBLER REL 34.0 13.10

452 UCOST2   DFHMDF POS=(12,47),LENGTH=07,ATTRB=(NUM,BRT),             X
                    PICIN='9999999',PICOUT='9999999'
463 COST2    DFHMDF POS=(12,55),LENGTH=08,ATTRB=(NUM,BRT),             X
                    PICIN='99999999',PICOUT='99999999'
474 UPRICE2  DFHMDF POS=(12,64),LENGTH=07,ATTRB=(NUM,BRT),            X
                    PICIN='9999999',PICOUT='9999999'
485 PRICE2   DFHMDF POS=(12,72),LENGTH=08,ATTRB=(NUM,BRT),            X
                    PICIN='99999999',PICOUT='99999999'
496          DFHMDF POS=(13,01),LENGTH=01,ATTRB=PROT
507          DFHMDF POS=(13,03),LENGTH=01,ATTRB=ASKIP,INITIAL='3'
519 ITEM3    DFHMDF POS=(13,05),LENGTH=08,ATTRB=(NUM,BRT),            X
                    PICIN='99999999',PICOUT='99999999'
530 DESC3    DFHMDF POS=(13,14),LENGTH=19,ATTRB=(UNPROT,BRT)
541          DFHMDF POS=(13,34),LENGTH=01,ATTRB=PROT
552 UNIT3    DFHMDF POS=(13,41),LENGTH=05,ATTRB=(NUM,BRT),            X
                    PICIN='99999',PICOUT='99999'
563 UCOST3   DFHMDF POS=(13,47),LENGTH=07,ATTRB=(NUM,BRT),            X
                    PICIN='9999999',PICOUT='9999999'
574 COST3    DFHMDF POS=(13,55),LENGTH=08,ATTRB=(NUM,BRT),            X
                    PICIN='99999999',PICOUT='99999999'
585 UPRICE3  DFHMDF POS=(13,64),LENGTH=07,ATTRB=(NUM,BRT),            X
                    PICIN='9999999',PICOUT='9999999'
596 PRICE3   DFHMDF POS=(13,72),LENGTH=08,ATTRB=(NUM,BRT),            X
                    PICIN='99999999',PICOUT='99999999'
607          DFHMDF POS=(14,01),LENGTH=01,ATTRB=PROT
618          DFHMDF POS=(14,03),LENGTH=01,ATTRB=ASKIP,INITIAL='4'
630 ITEM4    DFHMDF POS=(14,05),LENGTH=08,ATTRB=(NUM,BRT),            X
                    PICIN='99999999',PICOUT='99999999'
641 DESC4    DFHMDF POS=(14,14),LENGTH=19,ATTRB=(UNPROT,BRT)
652          DFHMDF POS=(14,34),LENGTH=01,ATTRB=PROT
663 UNIT4    DFHMDF POS=(14,41),LENGTH=05,ATTRB=(NUM,BRT),            X
                    PICIN='99999',PICOUT='99999'
674 UCOST4   DFHMDF POS=(14,47),LENGTH=07,ATTRB=(NUM,BRT),            X
                    PICIN='9999999',PICOUT='9999999'
685 COST4    DFHMDF POS=(14,55),LENGTH=08,ATTRB=(NUM,BRT),            X
                    PICIN='99999999',PICOUT='99999999'
696 UPRICE4  DFHMDF POS=(14,64),LENGTH=07,ATTRB=(NUM,BRT),            X
                    PICIN='9999999',PICOUT='9999999'
707 PRICE4   DFHMDF POS=(14,72),LENGTH=08,ATTRB=(NUM,BRT),            X
                    PICIN='99999999',PICOUT='99999999'
718          DFHMDF POS=(15,01),LENGTH=01,ATTRB=PROT
729          DFHMDF POS=(15,03),LENGTH=01,ATTRB=ASKIP,INITIAL='5'
741 ITEM5    DFHMDF POS=(15,05),LENGTH=08,ATTRB=(NUM,BRT),            X
                    PICIN='99999999',PICOUT='99999999'
752 DESC5    DFHMDF POS=(15,14),LENGTH=19,ATTRB=(UNPROT,BRT)
763          DFHMDF POS=(15,34),LENGTH=01,ATTRB=PROT
774 UNIT5    DFHMDF POS=(15,41),LENGTH=05,ATTRB=(NUM,BRT),            X
                    PICIN='99999',PICOUT='99999'
785 UCOST5   DFHMDF POS=(15,47),LENGTH=07,ATTRB=(NUM,BRT),            X
                    PICIN='9999999',PICOUT='9999999'
796 COST5    DFHMDF POS=(15,55),LENGTH=08,ATTRB=(NUM,BRT),            X
```

Fig. 19.3. (Continued)

STMT   SOURCE STATEMENT   DOS/VS ASSEMBLER REL 34.0 13.10

```
                         PIC IN='99999999',PICOUT='99999999'
 807 UPRICE5  DFHMDF POS=(15,64),LENGTH=07,ATTRB=(NUM,BRT),                       X
                         PICIN='9999999',PICOUT='9999999'
 818 PRICE5   DFHMDF POS=(15,72),LENGTH=08,ATTRB=(NUM,BRT),                       X
                         PIC IN='99999999',PICOUT='99999999'
 829          DFHMDF POS=(16,01),LENGTH=01,ATTRB=PROT
 840          DFHMDF POS=(16,03),LENGTH=01,ATTRB=ASKIP,INITIAL='6'
 852 ITEM6    DFHMDF POS=(16,05),LENGTH=08,ATTRB=(NUM,BRT),                       X
                         PIC IN='99999999',PICOUT='99999999'
 863 DESC6    DFHMDF POS=(16,14),LENGTH=19,ATTRB=(UNPROT,BRT)
 874          DFHMDF POS=(16,34),LENGTH=01,ATTRB=PROT
 885 UNIT6    DFHMDF POS=(16,41),LENGTH=05,ATTRB=(NUM,BRT),                       X
                         PIC IN='99999',PICOUT='99999'
 896 UCOST6   DFHMDF POS=(16,47),LENGTH=07,ATTRB=(NUM,BRT),                       X
                         PIC IN='9999999',PICOUT='9999999'
 907 COST6    DFHMDF POS=(16,55),LENGTH=08,ATTRB=(NUM,BRT),                       X
                         PIC IN='99999999',PICOUT='99999999'
 918 UPRICE6  DFHMDF POS=(16,64),LENGTH=07,ATTRB=(NUM,BRT),                       X
                         PIC IN='9999999',PICOUT='9999999'
 929 PRICE6   DFHMDF POS=(16,72),LENGTH=08,ATTRB=(NUM,BRT),                       X
                         PIC IN='99999999',PICOUT='99999999'
 940          DFHMDF POS=(17,01),LENGTH=01,ATTRB=PROT
 951          DFHMDF POS=(17,03),LENGTH=01,ATTRB=ASKIP,INITIAL='7'
 963 ITEM7    DFHMDF POS=(17,05),LENGTH=08,ATTRB=(NUM,BRT),                       X
                         PIC IN='99999999',PICOUT='99999999'
 974 DESC7    DFHMDF POS=(17,14),LENGTH=19,ATTRB=(UNPROT,BRT)
 985          DFHMDF POS=(17,34),LENGTH=01,ATTRB=PROT
 996 UNIT7    DFHMDF POS=(17,41),LENGTH=05,ATTRB=(NUM,BRT),                       X
                         PIC IN='99999',PICOUT='99999'
1007 UCOST7   DFHMDF POS=(17,47),LENGTH=07,ATTRB=(NUM,BRT),                       X
                         PIC IN='9999999',PICOUT='9999999'
1018 COST7    DFHMDF POS=(17,55),LENGTH=08,ATTRB=(NUM,BRT),                       X
                         PIC IN='99999999',PICOUT='99999999'
1029 UPRICE7  DFHMDF POS=(17,64),LENGTH=07,ATTRB=(NUM,BRT),                       X
                         PIC IN='9999999',PICOUT='9999999'
1040 PRICE7   DFHMDF POS=(17,72),LENGTH=08,ATTRB=(NUM,BRT),                       X
                         PIC IN='99999999',PICOUT='99999999'
1051          DFHMDF POS=(18,01),LENGTH=01,ATTRB=PROT
1062          DFHMDF POS=(18,03),LENGTH=01,ATTRB=ASKIP,INITIAL='8'
1074 ITEM8    DFHMDF POS=(18,05),LENGTH=08,ATTRB=(NUM,BRT),                       X
                         PIC IN='99999999',PICOUT='99999999'
1085 DESC8    DFHMDF POS=(18,14),LENGTH=19,ATTRB=(UNPROT,BRT)
1096          DFHMDF POS=(18,34),LENGTH=01,ATTRB=PROT
1107 UNIT8    DFHMDF POS=(18,41),LENGTH=05,ATTRB=(NUM,BRT),                       X
                         PIC IN='99999',PICOUT='99999'
1118 UCOST8   DFHMDF POS=(18,47),LENGTH=07,ATTRB=(NUM,BRT),                       X
                         PIC IN='9999999',PICOUT='9999999'
1129 COST8    DFHMDF POS=(18,55),LENGTH=08,ATTRB=(NUM,BRT),                       X
                         PIC IN='99999999',PICOUT='99999999'
1140 UPRICE8  DFHMDF POS=(18,64),LENGTH=07,ATTRB=(NUM,BRT),                       X
                         PIC IN='9999999',PICOUT='9999999'
```

Fig. 19.3.   (Continued)

```
STMT    SOURCE STATEMENT                          DOS/VS ASSEMBLER REL 34.0 13.10

1151 PRICE8    DFHMDF POS=(18,72),LENGTH=08,ATTRB=(NUM,BRT),                    X
                      PICIN='99999999',PICOUT='99999999'
1162           DFHMDF POS=(19,01),LENGTH=01,ATTRB=PROT
1173           DFHMDF POS=(19,03),LENGTH=01,ATTRB=ASKIP,INITIAL='9'
1185 ITEM9     DFHMDF POS=(19,05),LENGTH=08,ATTRB=(NUM,BRT),                    X
                      PICIN='99999999',PICOUT='99999999'
1196 DESC9     DFHMDF POS=(19,14),LENGTH=19,ATTRB=(UNPROT,BRT)
1207           DFHMDF POS=(19,34),LENGTH=01,ATTRB=PROT
1218 UNIT9     DFHMDF POS=(19,41),LENGTH=05,ATTRB=(NUM,BRT),                    X
                      PICIN='99999',PICOUT='99999'
1229 UCOST9    DFHMDF POS=(19,47),LENGTH=07,ATTRB=(NUM,BRT),                    X
                      PICIN='9999999',PICOUT='9999999'
1240 COST9     DFHMDF POS=(19,55),LENGTH=08,ATTRB=(NUM,BRT),                    X
                      PICIN='99999999',PICOUT='99999999'
1251 UPRICE9   DFHMDF POS=(19,64),LENGTH=07,ATTRB=(NUM,BRT),                    X
                      PICIN='9999999',PICOUT='9999999'
1262 PRICE9    DFHMDF POS=(19,72),LENGTH=08,ATTRB=(NUM,BRT),                    X
                      PICIN='99999999',PICOUT='99999999'
1273           DFHMDF POS=(20,01),LENGTH=01,ATTRB=PROT
1284           DFHMDF POS=(21,39),LENGTH=13,ATTRB=ASKIP,                        X
                      INITIAL='TOTALS ----- '
1296 TOTCOST   DFHMDF POS=(21,54),LENGTH=09,ATTRB=(NUM,BRT),                    X
                      PICIN='999999999',PICOUT='999999999'
1307           DFHMDF POS=(21,64),LENGTH=01,ATTRB=PROT
1318 TOTPRCE   DFHMDF POS=(21,71),LENGTH=09,ATTRB=(NUM,BRT),                    X
                      PICIN='999999999',PICOUT='999999999'
1329           DFHMDF POS=(22,01),LENGTH=01,ATTRB=PROT
1340 ERR1      DFHMDF POS=(23,01),LENGTH=28,ATTRB=(ASKIP,BRT),                  X
                      INITIAL='ORDER ACCEPTED -- CONTINUE'
1352 ERR2      DFHMDF POS=(23,40),LENGTH=28,ATTRB=(ASKIP,BRT)
1363 ERR3      DFHMDF POS=(24,01),LENGTH=28,ATTRB=(ASKIP,BRT)
1374 ERR4      DFHMDF POS=(24,40),LENGTH=28,ATTRB=(ASKIP,BRT)
1385           DFHMSD TYPE=FINAL
1399           END
```

Fig. 19.3.   (Continued)

```
             1   IBM DOS VS COBOL


 CBL SUPMAP,STXIT,NOTRUNC,CSYNTAX,SXREF,OPT,VERB,CLIST,BUF=19069
 CBL NOOPT,LIB
 00001              IDENTIFICATION DIVISION.

 00003              PROGRAM-ID. ORAD01A.


 00005              ENVIRONMENT DIVISION.


 00007      *****************************************************************
 00008      *                                                              *
 00009      *   1. THIS PROGRAM ADDS NEW ORDERS INTO THE PURCHASE ORDER    *
 00010      *      MASTER FILE.                                            *
 00011      *                                                              *
 00012      *   2. AT LEAST ONE LINE ITEM MUST BE PRESENT FOR EACH ORDER.  *
 00013      *                                                              *
 00014      *   3. A JOURNAL RECORD IS GENERATED FOR EACH NEW ORDER        *
 00015      *      ENTERED.  THE JOURNAL DETAILS ARE                       *
 00016      *                 A) OPERATOR INITIAL.                         *
 00017      *                 B) DATE ENTERED.                             *
 00018      *                 C) ORDER NUMBER.                             *
 00019      *                 D) DOCUMENT NUMBER.                          *
 00020      *                 E) TOTAL COST OF ORDER.                      *
 00021      *                 F) TOTAL PRICE OF ORDER.                     *
 00022      *                                                              *
 00023      *****************************************************************
```

Fig. 19.4. File Add Program.

```
   2         ORADO1A          15.54.49        12/27/80

00025         DATA DIVISION.


00027         WORKING-STORAGE SECTION.


00029      01  COMMUNICATION-AREA.

00031          05  COMMAREA-PROCESS-SW            PIC X.


00033      01  AREA1.


00035          05  VALIDATION-ERROR-MESSAGE.
00036              10  FILLER                     PIC X(5) VALUE 'LINE'.
00037              10  VALIDATION-ERROR-LINE      PIC 9.
00038              10  FILLER                     PIC XXX   VALUE ' - '.
00039              10  VALIDATION-ERROR-MSG       PIC X(19).


00041          05  JOB-NORMAL-END-MESSAGE  PIC X(23) VALUE
00042              'JOB NORMALLY TERMINATED'.


00044          05  JOB-ABORTED-MESSAGE.
00045              10  FILLER                PIC X(15) VALUE 'JOB ABORTED --'.
00046              10  MAJOR-ERROR-MSG       PIC X(16).


00048          05  HEXADECIMAL-ZEROES        PIC 9999 COMP VALUE ZEROES.


00050          05  FILLER REDEFINES HEXADECIMAL-ZEROES.
00051              10  FILLER                PIC X.
00052              10  HEX-ZEROES            PIC X.


00054          05  OLD-EIB-AREA.
00055              10  FILLER                PIC X(7) VALUE 'OLD EIB'.
00056              10  OLD-EIBFN             PIC XX.
00057              10  OLD-EIBRCODE          PIC X(6).
```

Fig. 19.4.   (Continued)

```
00059              01  DFHEIVAR COPY DFHEIVAR.
00060 C            01  DFHEIVAR.
00061 C                02   DFHEIV0   PICTURE X(26).
00062 C                02   DFHEIV1   PICTURE X(8).
00063 C                02   DFHEIV2   PICTURE X(8).
00064 C                02   DFHEIV3   PICTURE X(8).
00065 C                02   DFHEIV4   PICTURE X(6).
00066 C                02   DFHEIV5   PICTURE X(4).
00067 C                02   DFHEIV6   PICTURE X(4).
00068 C                02   DFHEIV7   PICTURE X(2).
00069 C                02   DFHEIV8   PICTURE X(2).
00070 C                02   DFHEIV9   PICTURE X(1).
00071 C                02   DFHEIV10  PICTURE S9(7) USAGE COMPUTATIONAL-3.
00072 C                02   DFHEIV11  PICTURE S9(4) USAGE COMPUTATIONAL.
00073 C                02   DFHEIV12  PICTURE S9(4) USAGE COMPUTATIONAL.
00074 C                02   DFHEIV13  PICTURE S9(4) USAGE COMPUTATIONAL.
00075 C                02   DFHEIV14  PICTURE S9(4) USAGE COMPUTATIONAL.
00076 C                02   DFHEIV15  PICTURE S9(4) USAGE COMPUTATIONAL.
00077 C                02   DFHEIV16  PICTURE S9(9) USAGE COMPUTATIONAL.
00078 C                02   DFHEIV17  PICTURE X(4).
00079 C                02   DFHEIV18  PICTURE X(4).
00080 C                02   DFHEIV19  PICTURE X(4).
00081 C                02   DFHEIV97  PICTURE S9(7) USAGE COMPUTATIONAL-3 VALUE ZERO.
00082 C                02   DFHEIV98  PICTURE S9(4) USAGE COMPUTATIONAL VALUE ZERO.
00083 C                02   DFHEIV99  PICTURE X(1)  VALUE SPACE.
00084              LINKAGE SECTION.
00085              01  DFHEIBLK COPY DFHEIBLK.
00086 C            *    EIBLK EXEC INTERFACE BLOCK
00087 C            01  DFHEIBLK.
00088 C            *        EIBTIME      TIME IN OHHMMSS FORMAT
00089 C                02 EIBTIME       PICTURE S9(7) USAGE COMPUTATIONAL-3.
00090 C            *        EIBDATE      DATE IN OOYYDDD FORMAT
00091 C                02 EIBDATE       PICTURE S9(7) USAGE COMPUTATIONAL-3.
00092 C            *        EIBTRNID     TRANSACTION IDENTIFIER
00093 C                02 EIBTRNID      PICTURE X(4).
00094 C            *        EIBTASKN     TASK NUMBER
00095 C                02 EIBTASKN      PICTURE S9(7) USAGE COMPUTATIONAL-3.
00096 C            *        EIBTRMID     TERMINAL IDENTIFIER
00097 C                02 EIBTRMID      PICTURE X(4).
00098 C            *        DFHEIGDI     RESERVED
00099 C                02 DFHEIGDI      PICTURE S9(4) USAGE COMPUTATIONAL.
00100 C            *        EIBCPOSN     CURSOR POSITION
00101 C                02 EIBCPOSN      PICTURE S9(4) USAGE COMPUTATIONAL.
00102 C            *        EIBCALEN     COMMAREA LENGTH
00103 C                02 EIBCALEN      PICTURE S9(4) USAGE COMPUTATIONAL.
00104 C            *        EIBAID       ATTENTION IDENTIFIER
00105 C                02 EIBAID        PICTURE X(1).
00106 C            *        EIBFN        FUNCTION CODE
00107 C                02 EIBFN         PICTURE X(2).
00108 C            *        EIBRCODE     RESPONSE CODE
00109 C                02 EIBRCODE      PICTURE X(6).
00110 C            *        EIBDS        DATASET NAME
00111 C                02 EIBDS         PICTURE X(8).
```

Fig. 19.4.   (Continued)

4   ORAD01A   15.54.49   12/27/80

```
00112 C    *          EIBREQID      REQUEST IDENTIFIER
00113 C               02 EIBREQID   PICTURE X(8).
00114           01  DFHCOMMAREA.

00116               05  PROCESS-SW              PIC X.
00117                   88  INITIAL-ENTRY-TIME            VALUE '0'.
00118                   88  ORDER-VALIDATION-TIME         VALUE '1'.


00120               05  OPERATOR-INITIAL        PIC XXX.



00122           01  LINKAGE-POINTERS.

00124               05  FILLER              PIC S9(8) COMP.
00125               05  MAP1-POINTER        PIC S9(8) COMP.
00126               05  POM-POINTER         PIC S9(8) COMP.
00127               05  TWA-POINTER         PIC S9(8) COMP.
00128               05  TSA-POINTER         PIC S9(8) COMP.
00129               05  JOURNAL-POINTER     PIC S9(8) COMP.
00130               05  TABLE-POINTER       PIC S9(8) COMP.
```

Fig. 19.4.   (Continued)

```
00132     *********************************************************************
00133     *                                                                   *
00134     *                   ORDER ENTRY MAP DESCRIPTION                     *
00135     *                                                                   *
00136     *********************************************************************


00138        01   MAP1-AREA.

00140             05   FILLER                           PIC X(12).
00141             05   MAP1-DUMMY-L                     PIC S9999 COMP.
00142             05   MAP1-DUMMY-A                     PIC X.
00143             05   MAP1-DUMMY                       PIC X.
00144             05   MAP1-ORDER-NUMBER-L              PIC S9999 COMP.
00145             05   MAP1-ORDER-NUMBER-A              PIC X.
00146             05   MAP1-ORDER-NUMBER                PIC X(10).
00147             05   MAP1-DOCUMENT-L                  PIC S9999 COMP.
00148             05   MAP1-DOCUMENT-A                  PIC X.
00149             05   MAP1-DOCUMENT                    PIC X(8).
00150             05   MAP1-DEPARTMENT-L                PIC S9999 COMP.
00151             05   MAP1-DEPARTMENT-A                PIC X.
00152             05   MAP1-DEPARTMENT                  PIC XXX.
00153             05   MAP1-ORDER-DATE-L                PIC S9999 COMP.
00154             05   MAP1-ORDER-DATE-A                PIC X.
00155             05   MAP1-ORDER-DATE.
00156                  10   MAP1-ORDER-DATE-MONTH       PIC XX.
00157                  10   MAP1-ORDER-DATE-DAY         PIC XX.
00158                  10   MAP1-ORDER-DATE-YEAR        PIC XX.
00159             05   MAP1-LINE-ITEM             OCCURS 9
00160                                             INDEXED BY MAP1-LINE-I.
00161                  10   MAP1-ITEM-NUMBER-L          PIC S9999 COMP.
00162                  10   MAP1-ITEM-NUMBER-A          PIC X.
00163                  10   MAP1-ITEM-NUMBER            PIC 9(8).
00164                  10   MAP1-ITEM-DESCRIPTION-L     PIC S9999 COMP.
00165                  10   MAP1-ITEM-DESCRIPTION-A     PIC X.
00166                  10   MAP1-ITEM-DESCRIPTION       PIC X(19).
00167                  10   MAP1-UNIT-L                 PIC S9999 COMP.
00168                  10   MAP1-UNIT-A                 PIC X.
00169                  10   MAP1-UNIT                   PIC 9(5).
00170                  10   MAP1-UNIT-COST-L            PIC S9999 COMP.
00171                  10   MAP1-UNIT-COST-A            PIC X.
00172                  10   MAP1-UNIT-COST              PIC 9(5)V99.
00173                  10   MAP1-COST-L                 PIC S9999 COMP.
00174                  10   MAP1-COST-A                 PIC X.
00175                  10   MAP1-COST                   PIC 9(6)V99.
00176                  10   MAP1-UNIT-PRICE-L           PIC S9999 COMP.
00177                  10   MAP1-UNIT-PRICE-A           PIC X.
00178                  10   MAP1-UNIT-PRICE             PIC 9(5)V99.
00179                  10   MAP1-PRICE-L                PIC S9999 COMP.
00180                  10   MAP1-PRICE-A                PIC X.
00181                  10   MAP1-PRICE                  PIC 9(6)V99.
00182             05   MAP1-TOTAL-COST-L               PIC S9999 COMP.
```

Fig. 19.4.   (Continued)

```
6           ORAD01A          15.54.49        12/27/80

00183                    05   MAP1-TOTAL-COST-A          PIC X.
00184                    05   MAP1-TOTAL-COST            PIC 9(7)V99.
00185                    05   MAP1-TOTAL-PRICE-L         PIC S9999 COMP.
00186                    05   MAP1-TOTAL-PRICE-A         PIC X.
00187                    05   MAP1-TOTAL-PRICE           PIC 9(7)V99.
00188                    05   FILLER                     OCCURS 4
00189                                                    INDEXED BY ERROR-I.
00190                        10   MAP1-ERRORS-L          PIC S9999 COMP.
00191                        10   MAP1-ERRORS-A          PIC X.
00192                        10   MAP1-ERRORS            PIC X(28).


7           ORAD01A          15.54.49        12/27/80

00194       ***************************************************************
00195       *                                                             *
00196       *        PURCHASE ORDER MASTER -- FILE LAYOUT                 *
00197       *                                                             *
00198       ***************************************************************

00200       01   ORDER-MASTER-RECORD.
00201            05   ORDER-NUMBER                       PIC X(10).
00202            05   ORDER-ALT-KEY.
00203                10   ORDER-DEPARTMENT               PIC XXX.
00204                10   ORDER-DATE.
00205                    15   ORDER-DATE-YEAR            PIC XX.
00206                    15   ORDER-DATE-MONTH           PIC XX.
00207                    15   ORDER-DATE-DAY             PIC XX.
00208            05   ORDER-DATE-ENTERED.
00209                10   ORDER-DATE-ENTERED-MONTH       PIC XX.
00210                10   ORDER-DATE-ENTERED-DAY         PIC XX.
00211                10   ORDER-DATE-ENTERED-YEAR        PIC XX.
00212            05   ORDER-TOTAL-COST                   PIC S9(7)V99   COMP-3.
00213            05   ORDER-TOTAL-PRICE                  PIC S9(7)V99   COMP-3.
00214            05   ORDER-LINE-COUNT                   PIC S9999      COMP.
00215            05   ORDER-ALL-LINES.
00216                10   ORDER-LINE-ITEM                OCCURS 1 TO 9
00217                                                    DEPENDING ON ORDER-LINE-COUNT
00218                                                    INDEXED BY ORDER-LINE-I.
00219                    15   ORDER-ITEM-NUMBER          PIC X(8).
00220                    15   ORDER-ITEM-DESCRIPTION     PIC X(19).
00221                    15   ORDER-ITEM-DATE.
00222                        20   ORDER-ITEM-DATE-MONTH  PIC XX.
00223                        20   ORDER-ITEM-DATE-DAY    PIC XX.
00224                        20   ORDER-ITEM-DATE-YEAR   PIC XX.
00225                    15   ORDER-UNIT                 PIC S9(5)      COMP-3.
00226                    15   ORDER-UNIT-COST            PIC S9(5)V99   COMP-3.
00227                    15   ORDER-UNIT-PRICE           PIC S9(5)V99   COMP-3.
```

Fig. 19.4.   (Continued)

```
      8        ORADO1A        15.54.49        12/27/80

00229          ****************************************************************************
00230          *                                                                          *
00231          *                    TRANSACTION WORK AREA                                 *
00232          *                                                                          *
00233          ****************************************************************************


00235          01   TWA-AREA.


00237              05   TWA-LINE-ITEM-MAP.
00238                  10   TWA-ITEM-NUMBER-MAP-L              PIC S9999 COMP.
00239                  10   TWA-ITEM-NUMBER-MAP-A             PIC X.
00240                  10   TWA-ITEM-NUMBER-MAP               PIC X(8).
00241                  10   TWA-ITEM-DESCRIPTION-MAP-L        PIC S9999 COMP.
00242                  10   TWA-ITEM-DESCRIPTION-MAP-A        PIC X.
00243                  10   TWA-ITEM-DESCRIPTION-MAP.
00244                     15   TWA-DESCRIPTION-FIRST-MAP      PIC X.
00245                     15   FILLER                         PIC X(18).
00246                  10   TWA-UNIT-MAP-L                    PIC S9999 COMP.
00247                  10   TWA-UNIT-MAP-A                    PIC X.
00248                  10   TWA-UNIT-MAP                      PIC 9(5).
00249                  10   TWA-UNIT-COST-MAP-L               PIC S9999 COMP.
00250                  10   TWA-UNIT-COST-MAP-A               PIC X.
00251                  10   TWA-UNIT-COST-MAP                 PIC 9(5)V99.
00252                  10   TWA-COST-MAP-L                    PIC S9999 COMP.
00253                  10   TWA-COST-MAP-A                    PIC X.
00254                  10   TWA-COST-MAP                      PIC 9(6)V99.
00255                  10   TWA-UNIT-PRICE-MAP-L              PIC S9999 COMP.
00256                  10   TWA-UNIT-PRICE-MAP-A              PIC X.
00257                  10   TWA-UNIT-PRICE-MAP                PIC 9(5)V99.
00258                  10   TWA-PRICE-MAP-L                   PIC S9999 COMP.
00259                  10   TWA-PRICE-MAP-A                   PIC X.
00260                  10   TWA-PRICE-MAP                     PIC 9(6)V99.


00262              05   TWA-LINE-ITEM-ORDER.
00263                  10   TWA-ITEM-NUMBER-ORDER             PIC X(8).
00264                  10   TWA-ITEM-DESCRIPTION-ORDER        PIC X(19).
00265                  10   TWA-ITEM-DATE-ORDER               PIC X(6).
00266                  10   TWA-UNIT-ORDER                    PIC S9(5)       COMP-3.
00267                  10   TWA-UNIT-COST-ORDER               PIC S9(5)V99    COMP-3.
00268                  10   TWA-UNIT-PRICE-ORDER              PIC S9(5)V99    COMP-3.


00270              05   TWA-TOTAL-COST                        PIC S9(7)V99    COMP-3.


00272              05   TWA-TOTAL-PRICE                       PIC S9(7)V99    COMP-3.


00274              05   TWA-ORDER-RECORD-KEY                  PIC X(10).
```

Fig. 19.4.   (Continued)

```
00276                   05   TSA-QUEUE-ID.
00277                        10   TSA-TERM-ID                        PIC  XXXX.
00278                        10   TSA-TRANS-ID                       PIC  XXXX.


00280                   05   TWA-BINARY-FIELDS   COMP.
00281                        10   TWA-LINE-DATA-CNT                  PIC  S9(8).
00282                        10   TWA-JOURNAL-ID                     PIC  S9(8).
00283                        10   TWA-POM-LENGTH                     PIC  S9(4).
00284                        10   TSA-LENGTH                         PIC  S9(4).
00285                        10   TSA-QUEUE-NO                       PIC  S9(4).
00286                        10   TWA-JOURNAL-LENGTH                 PIC  S9(4).


00288                   05   TWA-OPERATOR-MESSAGE                    PIC  X(31).


00290                   05   TWA-CURRENT-DATE.
00291                        10   TWA-CURRENT-DATE-MONTH             PIC  XX.
00292                        10   FILLER                             PIC  X.
00293                        10   TWA-CURRENT-DATE-DAY               PIC  XX.
00294                        10   FILLER                             PIC  X.
00295                        10   TWA-CURRENT-DATE-YEAR              PIC  XX.


00297                   05   TWA-DEPT-TABLE-KEY.
00298                        10   TWA-DEPT-TABLE-KEY-CODE            PIC  X.
00299                        10   TWA-DEPT-TABLE-KEY-NUMBER          PIC  9(7)  COMP-3.
```

Fig. 19.4. (Continued)

```
      10         ORAD01A         15.54.49        12/27/80

 00301         *************************************************************
 00302         *                                                           *
 00303         *              TEMPORARY STORAGE AREA                        *
 00304         *                                                           *
 00305         *************************************************************


 00307         01  TSA-AREA.

 00309             05  TSA-POMAST-RECORD.
 00310                 10  TSA-ORDER-NUMBER            PIC X(10).
 00311                 10  TSA-DEPARTMENT              PIC XXX.
 00312                 10  TSA-ORDER-DATE.
 00313                     15  TSA-ORDER-DATE-YEAR         PIC XX.
 00314                     15  TSA-ORDER-DATE-MONTH        PIC XX.
 00315                     15  TSA-ORDER-DATE-DAY          PIC XX.
 00316                 10  TSA-ORDER-ENTERED.
 00317                     15  TSA-ORDER-ENTERED-MONTH     PIC XX.
 00318                     15  TSA-ORDER-ENTERED-DAY       PIC XX.
 00319                     15  TSA-ORDER-ENTERED-YEAR      PIC XX.
 00320                 10  TSA-TOTAL-COST              PIC S9(7)V99 COMP-3.
 00321                 10  TSA-TOTAL-PRICE             PIC S9(7)V99 COMP-3.
 00322                 10  TSA-LINE-COUNT              PIC S9999    COMP.
 00323                 10  TSA-LINE-ITEM            OCCURS 9
 00324                                              INDEXED BY TSA-LINE-I.
 00325                     15  TSA-ITEM-NUMBER             PIC X(8).
 00326                     15  TSA-ITEM-DESCRIPTION        PIC X(19).
 00327                     15  TSA-ITEM-DATE               PIC X(6).
 00328                     15  TSA-UNIT                    PIC S9(5)    COMP-3.
 00329                     15  TSA-UNIT-COST               PIC S9(5)V99 COMP-3.
 00330                     15  TSA-UNIT-PRICE              PIC S9(5)V99 COMP-3.


 00332             05  TSA-OPERATOR-INITIAL           PIC XXX.


 00334             05  TSA-DEPT-CNT                   PIC S9(8)    COMP.


 00336             05  TSA-DEPTS                   OCCURS 300
 00337                                             DEPENDING ON TSA-DEPT-CNT
 00338                                             ASCENDING KEY TSA-DEPT-NO
 00339                                             INDEXED BY DEPT-I.
 00340                 10  TSA-DEPT-NO                 PIC XXX.
```

Fig. 19.4. (Continued)

```
   11          ORAD01A          15.54.49        12/27/80

00342        *************************************************************
00343        *                                                           *
00344        *           JOURNAL  RECORD  LAYOUT                         *
00345        *                                                           *
00346        *************************************************************


00348        01   JOURNAL-RECORD.

00350             05   JOURNAL-OPERATOR-INITIAL      PIC XXX.
00351             05   JOURNAL-DATE-ENTERED          PIC X(6).
00352             05   JOURNAL-ORDER-NUMBER          PIC X(10).
00353             05   JOURNAL-DOCUMENT-NUMBER       PIC X(8).
00354             05   JOURNAL-TOTAL-COST            PIC S9(7)V99 COMP-3.
00355             05   JOURNAL-TOTAL-PRICE           PIC S9(7)V99 COMP-3.




   12          ORAD01A          15.54.49        12/27/80

00357        *************************************************************
00358        *                                                           *
00359        *           DEPARTMENT  TABLE  ---  RECORD  LAYOUT          *
00360        *                                                           *
00361        *************************************************************


00363        01   DEPT-TABLE-RECORD.
00364             05   DEPT-TABLE-KEY.
00365                  10   DEPT-TABLE-KEY-CODE      PIC X.
00366                       88  DEPT-RECORD              VALUE 'D'.
00367                  10   DEPT-TABLE-KEY-NUMBER    PIC 9(7) COMP-3.
00368             05   DEPT-NO                       PIC XXX.
00369             05   FILLER                        PIC X(30).
00370             05   DEPT-DIVISION                 PIC XX.
00371             05   FILLER                        PIC X(45).
```

Fig. 19.4.   (Continued)

```
00373               PROCEDURE DIVISION USING DFHEIBLK DFHCOMMAREA.
00374                    CALL 'DFHEI1'.

00376               ****************************************************************
00377               *                                                              *
00378               MAIN-LINE SECTION.
00379               *                                                              *
00380               ****************************************************************

00382          *    EXEC CICS
00383          *        ADDRESS TWA (TWA-POINTER)
00384          *    END-EXEC.
00385               MOVE '                    ' TO DFHEIVO CALL 'DFHEI1' USING
00386               DFHEIVO TWA-POINTER.
00387
00388          *    EXEC CICS
00389          *        HANDLE AID
00390          *            CLEAR (FINALIZATION)
00391          *            PA1 (BYPASS-INPUT)
00392          *            PA2 (BYPASS-INPUT)
00393          *            PA3 (BYPASS-INPUT)
00394          *    END-EXEC.
00395               MOVE ' 0                  ' TO DFHEIVO CALL 'DFHEI1' USING
00396               DFHEIVO GO TO FINALIZATION BYPASS-INPUT BYPASS-INPUT
00397               BYPASS-INPUT DEPENDING ON DFHEIGDI.
00398
00399
00400
00401
00402          *    EXEC CICS
00403          *        HANDLE CONDITION
00404          *            MAPFAIL (MAPFAIL-ERROR)
00405          *            ERROR   (MAJOR-ERROR)
00406          *    END-EXEC.
00407               MOVE '                  ' TO DFHEIVO CALL 'DFHEI1' USING
00408               DFHEIVO GO TO MAPFAIL-ERROR MAJOR-ERROR DEPENDING ON
00409               DFHEIGDI.
00410
00411
00412               IF EIBCALEN NOT EQUAL TO ZEROES
00413                   IF ORDER-VALIDATION-TIME
00414                       GO TO ORDER-VALIDATION
00415                   ELSE IF INITIAL-ENTRY-TIME
00416                       GO TO INITIALIZATION
00417                   ELSE GO TO PROCESS-SWITCH-ERROR.

00419               IF EIBCALEN EQUAL TO ZEROES
00420                   GO TO SIGN-ON-VIOLATION.
```

Fig. 19.4. (Continued)

14   ORADO1A   15.54.49   12/27/80

```
00422          ***************************************************************
00423          *                                                             *
00424          ORDER-VALIDATION SECTION.
00425          *                                                             *
00426          ***************************************************************

00428     *     EXEC CICS
00429     *          RECEIVE MAP     ('ORADMO1')
00430     *                  MAPSET  ('ORADSO1')
00431     *                  SET     (MAP1-POINTER)
00432     *     END-EXEC.
00433          MOVE 'ORADMO1' TO DFHEIV1 MOVE 'ORADSO1' TO DFHEIV2 MOVE '
00434     -        '          ' TO DFHEIVO CALL 'DFHEI1' USING DFHEIVO
00435          DFHEIV1 MAP1-POINTER DFHEIV98 DFHEIV2.
00436
00437
00438          MOVE EIBTRMID    TO  TSA-TERM-ID.
00439          MOVE EIBTRNID    TO  TSA-TRANS-ID.

00441     *     EXEC CICS
00442     *          READQ TS
00443     *               QUEUE  (TSA-QUEUE-ID)
00444     *               SET    (TSA-POINTER)
00445     *               LENGTH (TSA-LENGTH)
00446     *               ITEM   (1)
00447     *     END-EXEC.
00448          MOVE 1 TO DFHEIV11 MOVE '  Y       ' TO DFHEIVO CALL 'DFHEI1'
00449          USING DFHEIVO TSA-QUEUE-ID TSA-POINTER TSA-LENGTH DFHEIV99
00450          DFHEIV11.
00451
00452
00453
00454
00455          MOVE SPACES TO MAP1-ERRORS (1)
00456                         MAP1-ERRORS (2)
00457                         MAP1-ERRORS (3)
00458                         MAP1-ERRORS (4).
00459          SET ERROR-I    TO  ZEROES.


00461     VALIDATE-FIXED-DATA.

00463          IF MAP1-ORDER-NUMBER NUMERIC
00464               MOVE MAP1-ORDER-NUMBER         TO  TSA-ORDER-NUMBER
00465          ELSE SET ERROR-I UP BY 1
00466               MOVE 'INVALID ORDER NUMBER'  TO  MAP1-ERRORS (ERROR-I)
00467               MOVE -1                      TO  MAP1-ORDER-NUMBER-L.

00469          IF MAP1-DOCUMENT NUMERIC
00470               NEXT SENTENCE
00471          ELSE SET ERROR-I UP BY 1
00472               MOVE 'INVALID DOCUMENT NUMBER' TO  MAP1-ERRORS (ERROR-I)
```

Fig. 19.4. (Continued)

```
00473                     IF ERROR-I EQUAL TO 1
00474                         MOVE -1                      TO   MAP1-DOCUMENT-L.

00476                 SEARCH ALL TSA-DEPTS
00477                     AT END
00478                         GO TO DEPARTMENT-ERROR-RTN
00479                     WHEN MAP1-DEPARTMENT EQUAL   TO   TSA-DEPT-NO (DEPT-I)
00480                         MOVE MAP1-DEPARTMENT     TO   TSA-DEPARTMENT
00481                         GO TO EDIT-ORDER-DATE.


00483                 DEPARTMENT-ERROR-RTN.

00485                     SET ERROR-I UP BY 1.
00486                     MOVE 'INVALID DEPARTMENT NUMBER' TO MAP1-ERRORS (ERROR-I).
00487                     IF ERROR-I EQUAL TO 1
00488                         MOVE -1                      TO   MAP1-DEPARTMENT-L.


00490                 EDIT-ORDER-DATE.

00492                     IF      MAP1-ORDER-DATE-MONTH (GREATER '00' AND LESS '13')
00493                         AND MAP1-ORDER-DATE-DAY   (GREATER '00' AND LESS '32')
00494                         AND MAP1-ORDER-DATE-YEAR   NUMERIC
00495                     THEN MOVE MAP1-ORDER-DATE-MONTH   TO   TSA-ORDER-DATE-MONTH
00496                          MOVE MAP1-ORDER-DATE-DAY     TO   TSA-ORDER-DATE-DAY
00497                          MOVE MAP1-ORDER-DATE-YEAR    TO   TSA-ORDER-DATE-YEAR
00498                     ELSE SET ERROR-I UP BY 1
00499                          MOVE 'INVALID ORDER-DATE'    TO   MAP1-ERRORS (ERROR-I)
00500                          IF ERROR-I EQUAL TO 1
00501                              MOVE -1                  TO   MAP1-ORDER-DATE-L.


00503                 VALIDATE-FIXED-DATA-END.

00505                     IF ERROR-I EQUAL TO 4
00506                         GO TO DISPLAY-ERROR-SCREEN.


00508                 VALIDATE-VARIABLE-DATA.

00510                     SET MAP1-LINE-I      TO  1.
00511                     MOVE +99             TO  TWA-LINE-DATA-CNT.
00512                     MOVE MAP1-ORDER-DATE TO  TWA-ITEM-DATE-ORDER.
00513                     MOVE ZEROES          TO  TWA-TOTAL-COST
00514                                              TWA-TOTAL-PRICE.
00515                     PERFORM VALIDATE-EACH-LINE THRU VALIDATE-EACH-LINE-EXIT
00516                         UNTIL TWA-LINE-DATA-CNT EQUAL TO ZEROES
00517                             OR ERROR-I          EQUAL TO 4
00518                             OR MAP1-LINE-I      GREATER THAN 9.
00519                     GO TO VALIDATE-TOTALS.
```

Fig. 19.4.   (Continued)

```
00521          VALIDATE-EACH-LINE.

00523              MOVE ZEROES                         TO  TWA-LINE-DATA-CNT.
00524              SET VALIDATION-ERROR-LINE  TO  MAP1-LINE-I.
00525              MOVE MAP1-LINE-ITEM (MAP1-LINE-I) TO TWA-LINE-ITEM-MAP.

00527              IF TWA-ITEM-NUMBER-MAP-L NOT EQUAL TO ZEROES
00528              THEN IF TWA-ITEM-NUMBER-MAP NUMERIC
00529                      MOVE TWA-ITEM-NUMBER-MAP TO TWA-ITEM-NUMBER-ORDER
00530                      ADD 1 TO TWA-LINE-DATA-CNT
00531              ELSE MOVE 'INVALID ITEM NUMBER' TO VALIDATION-ERROR-MSG
00532                      SET ERROR-I UP BY 1
00533                      MOVE VALIDATION-ERROR-MESSAGE
00534                                      TO MAP1-ERRORS (ERROR-I)
00535                      IF ERROR-I EQUAL TO 1
00536                          MOVE -1 TO MAP1-ITEM-NUMBER-L (MAP1-LINE-I)
00537                      ELSE IF ERROR-I EQUAL TO 4
00538                              GO TO VALIDATE-EACH-LINE-EXIT.

00540              IF TWA-ITEM-DESCRIPTION-MAP-L EQUAL TO ZEROES
00541                  MOVE SPACES TO TWA-ITEM-DESCRIPTION-ORDER
00542              ELSE IF TWA-DESCRIPTION-FIRST-MAP EQUAL TO SPACES
00543                      MOVE 'INVALID DESCRIPTION'
00544                                      TO VALIDATION-ERROR-MSG
00545                      SET ERROR-I UP BY 1
00546                      MOVE VALIDATION-ERROR-MESSAGE
00547                                      TO MAP1-ERRORS (ERROR-I)
00548                      IF ERROR-I EQUAL TO 1
00549                          MOVE -1
00550                              TO MAP1-ITEM-DESCRIPTION-L (MAP1-LINE-I)
00551                      ELSE IF ERROR-I EQUAL TO 4
00552                              GO TO VALIDATE-EACH-LINE-EXIT
00553                          ELSE NEXT SENTENCE
00554              ELSE MOVE TWA-ITEM-DESCRIPTION-MAP
00555                                      TO TWA-ITEM-DESCRIPTION-ORDER
00556                      ADD 2          TO TWA-LINE-DATA-CNT.

00558              IF TWA-UNIT-MAP-L NOT EQUAL TO ZEROES
00559              THEN IF TWA-UNIT-MAP NUMERIC
00560                      MOVE TWA-UNIT-MAP          TO  TWA-UNIT-ORDER
00561                      ADD 4 TO TWA-LINE-DATA-CNT
00562              ELSE MOVE ZEROES                   TO  TWA-UNIT-ORDER
00563                      MOVE 'INVALID UNIT'        TO  VALIDATION-ERROR-MSG
00564                      SET ERROR-I UP BY 1
00565                      MOVE VALIDATION-ERROR-MESSAGE
00566                                      TO  MAP1-ERRORS (ERROR-I)
00567                      IF ERROR-I EQUAL TO 1
00568                          MOVE -1           TO  MAP1-UNIT-L (MAP1-LINE-I)
00569                      ELSE IF ERROR-I EQUAL TO 4
00570                              GO TO VALIDATE-EACH-LINE-EXIT.

00572              IF TWA-UNIT-COST-MAP-L NOT EQUAL TO ZEROES
00573              THEN IF TWA-UNIT-COST-MAP NUMERIC
```

Fig. 19.4.   (Continued)

```
00574                        MOVE TWA-UNIT-COST-MAP   TO   TWA-UNIT-COST-ORDER
00575                        ADD 8 TO TWA-LINE-DATA-CNT
00576                   ELSE MOVE ZEROES              TO   TWA-UNIT-COST-ORDER
00577                        MOVE 'INVALID UNIT COST'
00578                                             TO   VALIDATION-ERROR-MSG
00579                        SET ERROR-I UP BY 1
00580                        MOVE VALIDATION-ERROR-MESSAGE
00581                                             TO   MAP1-ERRORS (ERROR-I)
00582                   IF ERROR-I EQUAL TO 1
00583                        MOVE -1   TO   MAP1-UNIT-COST-L (MAP1-LINE-I)
00584                   ELSE IF ERROR-I EQUAL TO 4
00585                             GO TO VALIDATE-EACH-LINE-EXIT.

00587              IF TWA-COST-MAP-L NOT EQUAL TO ZEROES
00588              THEN IF    TWA-COST-MAP  NUMERIC
00589                   AND TWA-COST-MAP =
00590                        TWA-UNIT-ORDER * TWA-UNIT-COST-ORDER
00591                   THEN ADD TWA-COST-MAP  TO   TWA-TOTAL-COST
00592                        ADD 16            TO   TWA-LINE-DATA-CNT
00593                   ELSE MOVE 'INVALID COST'  TO VALIDATION-ERROR-MSG
00594                        SET ERROR-I UP BY 1
00595                        MOVE VALIDATION-ERROR-MESSAGE
00596                                          TO MAP1-ERRORS (ERROR-I)
00597                   IF ERROR-I EQUAL TO 1
00598                        MOVE -1 TO MAP1-COST-L (MAP1-LINE-I)
00599                   ELSE IF ERROR-I EQUAL TO 4
00600                             GO TO VALIDATE-EACH-LINE-EXIT.

00602              IF TWA-UNIT-PRICE-MAP-L NOT EQUAL TO ZEROES
00603              THEN IF TWA-UNIT-PRICE-MAP  NUMERIC
00604                        MOVE TWA-UNIT-PRICE-MAP   TO   TWA-UNIT-PRICE-ORDER
00605                        ADD 32 TO TWA-LINE-DATA-CNT
00606                   ELSE MOVE ZEROES             TO   TWA-UNIT-PRICE-ORDER
00607                        MOVE 'INVALID UNIT PRICE'
00608                                             TO   VALIDATION-ERROR-MSG
00609                        SET ERROR-I UP BY 1
00610                        MOVE VALIDATION-ERROR-MESSAGE
00611                                             TO   MAP1-ERRORS (ERROR-I)
00612                   IF ERROR-I EQUAL TO 1
00613                        MOVE -1 TO MAP1-UNIT-PRICE-L (MAP1-LINE-I)
00614                   ELSE IF ERROR-I EQUAL TO 4
00615                             GO TO VALIDATE-EACH-LINE-EXIT.

00617              IF TWA-PRICE-MAP-L NOT EQUAL TO ZEROES
00618              THEN IF    TWA-PRICE-MAP  NUMERIC
00619                   AND TWA-PRICE-MAP =
00620                        TWA-UNIT-ORDER * TWA-UNIT-PRICE-ORDER
00621                   THEN ADD TWA-PRICE-MAP  TO   TWA-TOTAL-PRICE
00622                        ADD 64            TO   TWA-LINE-DATA-CNT
00623                   ELSE MOVE 'INVALID PRICE'  TO VALIDATION-ERROR-MSG
00624                        SET ERROR-I UP BY 1
00625                        MOVE VALIDATION-ERROR-MESSAGE
00626                                          TO   MAP1-ERRORS (ERROR-I)
```

Fig. 19.4. (Continued)

18   ORAD01A   15.54.49   12/27/80

```
00627                         IF ERROR-I EQUAL TO 1
00628                             MOVE -1 TO MAP1-PRICE-L (MAP1-LINE-I)
00629                         ELSE IF ERROR-I EQUAL TO 4
00630                             GO TO VALIDATE-EACH-LINE-EXIT.

00632              IF TWA-LINE-DATA-CNT EQUAL TO (125 OR 127)
00633                  IF ERROR-I EQUAL TO ZEROES
00634                      SET TSA-LINE-I    TO MAP1-LINE-I
00635                      MOVE TWA-LINE-ITEM-ORDER
00636                                     TO TSA-LINE-ITEM (TSA-LINE-I)
00637                  ELSE NEXT SENTENCE
00638              ELSE IF TWA-LINE-DATA-CNT EQUAL TO ZEROES
00639                  NEXT SENTENCE
00640              ELSE SET ERROR-I UP BY 1
00641                      MOVE 'INCOMPLETE DATA' TO VALIDATION-ERROR-MSG
00642                      MOVE VALIDATION-ERROR-MESSAGE
00643                                     TO MAP1-ERRORS (ERROR-I)
00644                         IF ERROR-I EQUAL TO 1
00645                             MOVE -1
00646                                     TO MAP1-ITEM-NUMBER-L (MAP1-LINE-I)
00647                         ELSE IF ERROR-I EQUAL TO 4
00648                             GO TO VALIDATE-EACH-LINE-EXIT.

00650              SET MAP1-LINE-I UP BY 1.
00651      VALIDATE-EACH-LINE-EXIT.   EXIT.


00653      VALIDATE-TOTALS.

00655          IF ERROR-I EQUAL TO 4
00656              GO TO DISPLAY-ERROR-SCREEN.

00658          IF     MAP1-LINE-I EQUAL TO 2
00659             AND TWA-LINE-DATA-CNT EQUAL TO ZEROES
00660          THEN SET ERROR-I UP BY 1
00661              MOVE 'NO LINE ITEM ENTERED' TO MAP1-ERRORS (ERROR-I)
00662              IF ERROR-I EQUAL TO 1
00663                  MOVE -1 TO MAP1-ITEM-NUMBER-L (1)
00664              ELSE IF ERROR-I EQUAL TO 4
00665                      GO TO VALIDATE-TOTALS-EXIT.

00667          IF     MAP1-TOTAL-COST NUMERIC
00668             AND MAP1-TOTAL-COST = TWA-TOTAL-COST
00669          THEN MOVE TWA-TOTAL-COST          TO  TSA-TOTAL-COST
00670          ELSE SET ERROR-I UP BY 1
00671              MOVE 'INCORRECT TOTAL COST'  TO  MAP1-ERRORS (ERROR-I)
00672              IF ERROR-I EQUAL TO 1
00673                  MOVE -1              TO  MAP1-TOTAL-COST-L
00674              ELSE IF ERROR-I EQUAL TO 4
00675                      GO TO VALIDATE-TOTALS-EXIT.

00677          IF     MAP1-TOTAL-PRICE NUMERIC
00678             AND MAP1-TOTAL-PRICE = TWA-TOTAL-PRICE
```

Fig. 19.4.   (Continued)

```
00679                 THEN MOVE TWA-TOTAL-PRICE              TO   TSA-TOTAL-PRICE
00680                 ELSE SET ERROR-I UP BY 1
00681                      MOVE 'INCORRECT TOTAL PRICE'  TO   MAP1-ERRORS (ERROR-I)
00682                      IF ERROR-I EQUAL TO 1
00683                          MOVE -1                     TO   MAP1-TOTAL-PRICE-L
00684                      ELSE IF ERROR-I EQUAL TO 4
00685                              GO TO VALIDATE-TOTALS-EXIT.
00686             VALIDATE-TOTALS-EXIT.   EXIT.


00688             CHECK-IF-THERE-ARE-ERRORS.

00690                     IF ERROR-I NOT EQUAL TO ZEROES
00691                         GO TO DISPLAY-ERROR-SCREEN.


00693             NO-ERRORS-RTN.

00695                     SET TSA-LINE-COUNT TO MAP1-LINE-I.

00697                     IF TSA-LINE-COUNT GREATER THAN 9
00698                         IF TWA-LINE-DATA-CNT EQUAL TO ZEROES
00699                             SUBTRACT 2 FROM TSA-LINE-COUNT
00700                         ELSE SUBTRACT 1 FROM TSA-LINE-COUNT
00701                     ELSE SUBTRACT 2 FROM TSA-LINE-COUNT.

00703         *     EXEC CICS
00704         *         GETMAIN
00705         *             SET    (POM-POINTER)
00706         *             LENGTH (433)
00707         *     END-EXEC.
00708               MOVE 433 TO DFHEIV11 MOVE '            ' TO DFHEIVO CALL 'DFHEI
00709         -     '1' USING DFHEIVO POM-POINTER DFHEIV11.
00710
00711
00712
00713               MOVE TSA-LINE-COUNT      TO   ORDER-LINE-COUNT.
00714               MOVE TSA-POMAST-RECORD   TO   ORDER-MASTER-RECORD.
00715               COMPUTE TWA-POM-LENGTH = 37 + ORDER-LINE-COUNT * 44.
00716               MOVE TSA-ORDER-NUMBER    TO   TWA-ORDER-RECORD-KEY.

00718         *     EXEC CICS
00719         *         HANDLE CONDITION
00720         *             NOTOPEN (FILE-NOT-OPEN)
00721         *             DUPREC  (DUPLICATE-RECORD)
00722         *     END-EXEC.
00723               MOVE '                    ' TO DFHEIVO CALL 'DFHEI1' USING
00724         DFHEIVO GO TO FILE-NOT-OPEN DUPLICATE-RECORD DEPENDING ON
00725         DFHEIGDI.
00726
00727
00728         *     EXEC CICS
00729         *         WRITE DATASET ('ORTEST')
```

Fig. 19.4.   (Continued)

```
00730        *                    LENGTH   (TWA-POM-LENGTH)
00731        *                    FROM     (ORDER-MASTER-RECORD)
00732        *                    RIDFLD   (TWA-ORDER-RECORD-KEY)
00733        *       END-EXEC.
00734                MOVE 'ORTEST' TO DFHEIV3 MOVE '   0       ' TO DFHEIVO CALL 'D
00735        -     'FHEI1' USING DFHEIVO DFHEIV3 ORDER-MASTER-RECORD
00736              TWA-POM-LENGTH TWA-ORDER-RECORD-KEY.
00737
00738
00739
00740        *       EXEC CICS
00741        *          FREEMAIN DATA (ORDER-MASTER-RECORD)
00742        *       END-EXEC.
00743                MOVE '          ' TO DFHEIVO CALL 'DFHEI1' USING DFHEIVO
00744              ORDER-MASTER-RECORD.
00745
00746        *       EXEC CICS
00747        *          GETMAIN
00748        *              SET     (JOURNAL-POINTER)
00749        *              LENGTH (37)
00750        *       END-EXEC
00751                MOVE 37 TO DFHEIV11 MOVE '        ' TO DFHEIVO CALL 'DFHEI1
00752        -     '' USING DFHEIVO JOURNAL-POINTER DFHEIV11
00753
00754
00755
00756                MOVE TSA-OPERATOR-INITIAL    TO   JOURNAL-OPERATOR-INITIAL.
00757                MOVE TSA-ORDER-ENTERED       TO   JOURNAL-DATE-ENTERED.
00758                MOVE TSA-ORDER-NUMBER        TO   JOURNAL-ORDER-NUMBER.
00759                MOVE TSA-TOTAL-COST          TO   JOURNAL-TOTAL-COST.
00760                MOVE TSA-TOTAL-PRICE         TO   JOURNAL-TOTAL-PRICE.
00761                MOVE MAP1-DOCUMENT           TO   JOURNAL-DOCUMENT-NUMBER.
00762                MOVE 37                      TO   TWA-JOURNAL-LENGTH.

00764        *       EXEC CICS
00765        *          JOURNAL JFILEID (02)
00766        *                  JTYPEID ('01')
00767        *                  FROM    (JOURNAL-RECORD)
00768        *                  LENGTH  (TWA-JOURNAL-LENGTH)
00769        *                  REQID   (TWA-JOURNAL-ID)
00770        *                  WAIT
00771        *       END-EXEC.
00772                MOVE 02 TO DFHEIV11 MOVE '01' TO DFHEIV7 MOVE '  8       ' TO
00773              DFHEIVO CALL 'DFHEI1' USING DFHEIVO DFHEIV11 TWA-JOURNAL-ID
00774              DFHEIV7 JOURNAL-RECORD TWA-JOURNAL-LENGTH.
00775
00776
00777
00778
00779
00780              DISPLAY-FRESH-SCREEN.

00782        *       EXEC CICS
```

Fig. 19.4.   (Continued)

```
    21          ORAD01A        15.54.49        12/27/80

00783         *          SEND MAP     ('ORADM01')
00784         *                    MAPSET ('ORADS01')
00785         *                    MAPONLY
00786         *                    ERASE
00787         *       END-EXEC.
00788            MOVE 'ORADM01' TO DFHEIV1 MOVE 'ORADS01' TO DFHEIV2 MOVE '
00789         -         '          ' TO DFHEIVO CALL 'DFHEI1' USING DFHEIVO
00790            DFHEIV1 DFHEIV99 DFHEIV98 DFHEIV2.
00791
00792
00793
00794          RETURN-FOR-NEXT-ORDER.

00796            MOVE '1' TO COMMAREA-PROCESS-SW.

00798         *    EXEC CICS
00799         *        RETURN TRANSID  (EIBTRNID)
00800         *                   COMMAREA (COMMUNICATION-AREA)
00801         *                   LENGTH   (1)
00802         *       END-EXEC.
00803            MOVE 1 TO DFHEIV11 MOVE '         ' TO DFHEIVO CALL 'DFHEI1'
00804            USING DFHEIVO EIBTRNID COMMUNICATION-AREA DFHEIV11.
00805
00806
00807
00808          DISPLAY-ERROR-SCREEN.

00810         *    EXEC CICS
00811         *        SEND MAP     ('ORADM01')
00812         *                   MAPSET ('ORADS01')
00813         *                   FROM   (MAP1-AREA)
00814         *                   DATAONLY
00815         *                   CURSOR
00816         *       END-EXEC
00817            MOVE 'ORADM01' TO DFHEIV1 MOVE 'ORADS01' TO DFHEIV2 MOVE -1
00818            TO DFHEIV11 MOVE '  J          ' TO DFHEIVO CALL 'DFHEI1'
00819            USING DFHEIVO DFHEIV1 MAP1-AREA DFHEIV98 DFHEIV2 DFHEIV99
00820            DFHEIV99 DFHEIV99 DFHEIV11
00821
00822
00823
00824            GO TO RETURN-FOR-NEXT-ORDER.

00826          DUPLICATE-RECORD.

00828            MOVE 'DUPLICATE -- NOT ACCEPTED' TO MAP1-ERRORS (1).
00829            MOVE -1       TO MAP1-ORDER-NUMBER-L.
00830            GO TO DISPLAY-ERROR-SCREEN.
```

Fig. 19.4.   (Continued)

22   ORADO1A   15.54.49   12/27/80

```
00832        ******************************************************************
00833        *                                                                *
00834        BYPASS-INPUT SECTION.
00835        *                                                                *
00836        ******************************************************************


00838        *    EXEC CICS
00839        *        GETMAIN
 00840       *            SET      (MAP1-POINTER)
 0841       *            LENGTH   (958)
0 942       *            INITIMG  (HEX-ZEROES)
0u343       *    END-EXEC.
00844             MOVE 958 TO DFHEIV11 MOVE '            ' TO DFHEIVO CALL 'DFHEI
00845        -    '1' USING DFHEIVO MAP1-POINTER DFHEIV11 HEX-ZEROES.
00846
00847
00848
00849
00850             MOVE 'ORDER BYPASSED - CONTINUE' TO MAP1-ERRORS (1).


00852        *    EXEC CICS
00853        *        SEND MAP    ('ORADMO1')
00854        *             MAPSET ('ORADSO1')
00855        *             FROM   (MAP1-AREA)
00856        *             ERASE
00857        *    END-EXEC.
00858             MOVE 'ORADMO1' TO DFHEIV1 MOVE 'ORADSO1' TO DFHEIV2 MOVE '
00859        -    '     S    ' TO DFHEIVO CALL 'DFHEI1' USING DFHEIVO
00860             DFHEIV1 MAP1-AREA DFHEIV98 DFHEIV2.
00861
00862
00863
00864             MOVE '1' TO COMMAREA-PROCESS-SW.

00866        *    EXEC CICS
00867        *        RETURN TRANSID   (EIBTRNID)
00868        *               COMMAREA  (COMMUNICATION-AREA)
00869        *               LENGTH    (1)
00870        *    END-EXEC.
00871             MOVE 1 TO DFHEIV11 MOVE '            ' TO DFHEIVO CALL 'DFHEI1'
00872             USING DFHEIVO EIBTRNID COMMUNICATION-AREA DFHEIV11.
00873
00874
00875
```

```
00877          **********************************************************************
00878          *                                                                    *
00879           INITIALIZATION SECTION.
00880          *                                                                    *
00881          **********************************************************************


00883          *      EXEC CICS
00884          *          HANDLE CONDITION
00885          *              QIDERR (GET-STORAGE-FOR-TSA)
00886          *      END-EXEC.
00887                 MOVE '                   ' TO DFHEIVO CALL 'DFHEI1' USING
00888                 DFHEIVO GO TO GET-STORAGE-FOR-TSA DEPENDING ON DFHEIGDI.
00889
00890
00891                 MOVE EIBTRMID    TO  TSA-TERM-ID.
00892                 MOVE 'ORAD'      TO  TSA-TRANS-ID.

00894          *      EXEC CICS
00895          *          DELETEQ TS
00896          *              QUEUE (TSA-QUEUE-ID)
00897          *      END-EXEC.
00898                 MOVE '         ' TO DFHEIVO CALL 'DFHEI1' USING DFHEIVO
00899                 TSA-QUEUE-ID.
00900
00901
00902           GET-STORAGE-FOR-TSA.

00904          *      EXEC CICS
00905          *          GETMAIN
00906          *              SET     (TSA-POINTER)
00907          *              LENGTH  (1340)
00908          *      END-EXEC.
00909                 MOVE 1340 TO DFHEIV11 MOVE '         ' TO DFHEIVO CALL 'DFHE
00910          -      'I1' USING DFHEIVO TSA-POINTER DFHEIV11.
00911
00912
00913
00914           LOAD-DEPARTMENT-TABLE.

00916                 SET DEPT-I       TO  ZEROES.
00917                 MOVE 'D'         TO  TWA-DEPT-TABLE-KEY-CODE.
00918                 MOVE 1           TO  TWA-DEPT-TABLE-KEY-NUMBER.

00920          *      EXEC CICS
00921          *          HANDLE CONDITION
00922          *              ENDFILE (READ-DEPT-TABLE-EXIT)
00923          *      END-EXEC.
00924                 MOVE '                   ' TO DFHEIVO CALL 'DFHEI1' USING
00925                 DFHEIVO GO TO READ-DEPT-TABLE-EXIT DEPENDING ON DFHEIGDI.
00926
00927
00928          *      EXEC CICS
```

Fig. 19.4. (Continued)

```
00929    *            STARTBR DATASET ('DSXTABS')
00930    *                    RIDFLD  (TWA-DEPT-TABLE-KEY)
00931    *                    GTEQ
00932    *        END-EXEC.
00933             MOVE 'DSXTABS' TO DFHEIV3 MOVE '          ' TO DFHEIVO CALL '
00934    -      'DFHEI1' USING DFHEIVO DFHEIV3 DFHEIV99 DFHEIV98
00935             TWA-DEPT-TABLE-KEY.
00936
00937
00938        READ-DEPT-TABLE.

00940    *        EXEC CICS
00941    *            READNEXT DATASET ('DSXTABS')
00942    *                     SET     (TABLE-POINTER)
00943    *                     RIDFLD  (TWA-DEPT-TABLE-KEY)
00944    *        END-EXEC.
00945             MOVE 'DSXTABS' TO DFHEIV3 MOVE '  M      ' TO DFHEIVO CALL '
00946    -      'DFHEI1' USING DFHEIVO DFHEIV3 TABLE-POINTER DFHEIV98
00947             TWA-DEPT-TABLE-KEY DFHEIV98 DFHEIV98.
00948
00949
00950             IF DEPT-RECORD
00951             THEN IF DEPT-NO EQUAL '999'
00952                     GO TO READ-DEPT-TABLE-EXIT
00953                 ELSE IF DEPT-DIVISION LESS THAN '85'
00954                          SET DEPT-I UP BY 1
00955                          MOVE DEPT-NO TO TSA-DEPT-NO (DEPT-I).

00957             GO TO READ-DEPT-TABLE.
00958        READ-DEPT-TABLE-EXIT.  EXIT.


00960        CHECK-IF-TABLE-LOADED.

00962             IF DEPT-I EQUAL TO ZEROES
00963                     GO TO TABLE-NOT-LOADED-ERROR
00964             ELSE SET TSA-DEPT-CNT TO DEPT-I.


00966        INITIALIZE-TSA.

00968             MOVE CURRENT-DATE             TO  TWA-CURRENT-DATE.
00969             MOVE TWA-CURRENT-DATE-MONTH   TO  TSA-ORDER-ENTERED-MONTH.
00970             MOVE TWA-CURRENT-DATE-DAY     TO  TSA-ORDER-ENTERED-DAY.
00971             MOVE TWA-CURRENT-DATE-YEAR    TO  TSA-ORDER-ENTERED-YEAR.
00972             MOVE OPERATOR-INITIAL         TO  TSA-OPERATOR-INITIAL.
00973             MOVE 1340                     TO  TSA-LENGTH.

00975    *        EXEC CICS
00976    *            WRITEQ TS
00977    *                QUEUE  (TSA-QUEUE-ID)
00978    *                FROM   (TSA-AREA)
00979    *                LENGTH (TSA-LENGTH)
```

Fig. 19.4. (Continued)

```
00980        *    END-EXEC.
00981             MOVE '          ' TO DFHEIVO CALL 'DFHEI1' USING DFHEIVO
00982             TSA-QUEUE-ID TSA-AREA TSA-LENGTH.
00983
00984
00985
00986
00987        *    EXEC CICS
00988        *        FREEMAIN DATA (TSA-AREA)
00989        *    END-EXEC.
00990             MOVE '          ' TO DFHEIVO CALL 'DFHEI1' USING DFHEIVO
00991             TSA-AREA.
00992
00993        *    EXEC CICS
00994        *        GETMAIN
00995        *            SET     (MAP1-POINTER)
00996        *            LENGTH  (958)
00997        *            INITIMG (HEX-ZEROES)
00998        *    END-EXEC.
00999             MOVE 958 TO DFHEIV11 MOVE '          ' TO DFHEIVO CALL 'DFHEI
01000        -    '1' USING DFHEIVO MAP1-POINTER DFHEIV11 HEX-ZEROES.
01001
01002
01003
01004
01005             MOVE 'ENTER FIRST ORDER' TO MAP1-ERRORS (1).

01007        *    EXEC CICS
01008        *        SEND MAP   ('ORADMO1')
01009        *             MAPSET ('ORADSO1')
01010        *             FROM   (MAP1-AREA)
01011        *             ERASE
01012        *    END-EXEC.
01013             MOVE 'ORADMO1' TO DFHEIV1 MOVE 'ORADSO1' TO DFHEIV2 MOVE '
01014        -    '      S    ' TO DFHEIVO CALL 'DFHEI1' USING DFHEIVO
01015             DFHEIV1 MAP1-AREA DFHEIV98 DFHEIV2.
01016
01017
01018
01019             MOVE '1' TO COMMAREA-PROCESS-SW.

01021        *    EXEC CICS
01022        *        RETURN TRANSID  ('ORAD')
01023        *               COMMAREA (COMMUNICATION-AREA)
01024        *               LENGTH   (1)
01025        *    END-EXEC.
01026             MOVE 'ORAD' TO DFHEIV5 MOVE 1 TO DFHEIV11 MOVE '          '
01027             TO DFHEIVO CALL 'DFHEI1' USING DFHEIVO DFHEIV5
01028             COMMUNICATION-AREA DFHEIV11.
01029
01030
```

Fig. 19.4.   (Continued)

26   ORAD01A   15.54.49   12/27/80

```
01032      ***************************************************************
01033      *                                                             *
01034       FINALIZATION SECTION.
01035      *                                                             *
01036      ***************************************************************


01038       PREPARE-TERMINATION-MESSAGE.
01039           MOVE JOB-NORMAL-END-MESSAGE TO TWA-OPERATOR-MESSAGE.


01041       JOB-TERMINATED.

01043      *    EXEC CICS
01044      *        SEND FROM   (TWA-OPERATOR-MESSAGE)
01045      *             LENGTH (31)
01046      *             ERASE
01047      *    END-EXEC.
01048           MOVE 31 TO DFHEIV11 MOVE '                ' TO DFHEIVO CALL '
01049      -   'DFHEI1' USING DFHEIVO DFHEIV99 DFHEIV98 TWA-OPERATOR-MESSAGE
01050           DFHEIV11.
01051
01052
01053      *    EXEC CICS
01054      *        HANDLE CONDITION
01055      *             QIDERR (END-OF-JOB)
01056      *    END-EXEC.
01057           MOVE '                ' TO DFHEIVO CALL 'DFHEI1' USING
01058           DFHEIVO GO TO END-OF-JOB DEPENDING ON DFHEIGDI.
01059
01060
01061           MOVE EIBTRMID  TO   TSA-TERM-ID.
01062           MOVE EIBTRNID  TO   TSA-TRANS-ID.

01064      *    EXEC CICS
01065      *        DELETEQ TS
01066      *             QUEUE (TSA-QUEUE-ID)
01067      *    END-EXEC.
01068           MOVE '           ' TO DFHEIVO CALL 'DFHEI1' USING DFHEIVO
01069           TSA-QUEUE-ID.
01070
01071


01073       END-OF-JOB.

01075      *    EXEC CICS
01076      *        RETURN
01077      *    END-EXEC.
01078           MOVE '           ' TO DFHEIVO CALL 'DFHEI1' USING DFHEIVO.
01079
01080
```

Fig. 19.4.   (Continued)

```
01082         **************************************************************************
01083         *                                                                      *
01084          ABNORMAL-TERMINATION SECTION.
01085         *                                                                      *
01086         **************************************************************************


01088          FILE-NOT-OPEN.

01090         *     EXEC CICS
01091         *         XCTL PROGRAM ('TEL2OPEN')
01092         *     END-EXEC.
01093                   MOVE 'TEL2OPEN' TO DFHEIV3 MOVE '           ' TO DFHEIVO CALL
01094               'DFHEI1' USING DFHEIVO DFHEIV3.
01095
01096          MAPFAIL-ERROR.
01097                   MOVE 'MAP FAILURE' TO MAJOR-ERROR-MSG.
01098                   GO TO PREPARE-ABORT-MESSAGE.


01100          PROCESS-SWITCH-ERROR.
01101                   MOVE 'PROCESS ERROR' TO MAJOR-ERROR-MSG.
01102                   GO TO PREPARE-ABORT-MESSAGE.


01104          SIGN-ON-VIOLATION.
01105                   MOVE 'SIGNON VIOLATION' TO MAJOR-ERROR-MSG.
01106                   GO TO PREPARE-ABORT-MESSAGE.


01108          TABLE-NOT-LOADED-ERROR.
01109                   MOVE 'TABLE NOT LOADED' TO MAJOR-ERROR-MSG.
01110                   GO TO PREPARE-ABORT-MESSAGE.


01112          MAJOR-ERROR.
01113                   MOVE   EIBFN      TO   OLD-EIBFN.
01114                   MOVE   EIBRCODE   TO   OLD-EIBRCODE.

01116         *     EXEC CICS
01117         *         DUMP DUMPCODE ('ERRS')
01118         *     END-EXEC.
01119                   MOVE 'ERRS' TO DFHEIV5 MOVE '           ' TO DFHEIVO CALL 'DFH
01120          -    'EI1' USING DFHEIVO DFHEIV5.
01121
01122                   MOVE 'MAJOR ERROR' TO MAJOR-ERROR-MSG.
01123                   GO TO PREPARE-ABORT-MESSAGE.


01125          PREPARE-ABORT-MESSAGE.
01126                   MOVE JOB-ABORTED-MESSAGE TO TWA-OPERATOR-MESSAGE.
01127                   GO TO JOB-TERMINATED.
```

Fig. 19.4.   (Continued)

2. Lines 891–899. Delete the old temporary storage queue.*

3. Lines 902–910. GETMAIN command to secure main storage for the new temporary storage record to be created.

4. Lines 917–918. The record identification field of a file to be browsed is set to the proper values. We browse this file to load a table of valid department numbers into the temporary storage record to be created.

5. Lines 920–925. HANDLE CONDITION command for the file.

6. Lines 928–958. The table is moved to the temporary storage record.

7. Lines 975–982. WRITEQ TS command to create the new temporary storage record.

8. Lines 987–991. FREEMAIN DATA command to release main storage secured for the temporary storage record by the GETMAIN command in lines 902–910.

9. Lines 993–1000. GETMAIN command to secure main storage for the map to be displayed, which will include a program-generated message.

10. Lines 1007–1015. SEND MAP command to display the map. The "ENTER FIRST ORDER" message is inlcuded in the display.

11. Line 1019.   Set the communication area switch to 1.

12. Lines 1021–1028. RETURN command to terminate the task.

THE ORDER-VALIDATION SECTION

1. Lines 428–435. READ MAP command to read the data entered by the operator.

2. Lines 441–450. READQ TS command to read the temporary storage record that will be used as a scratchpad.

*This is a precautionary measure. See page 179.

3. Lines 455–686. The editing of the data.

4. If there are no errors:
    a. Lines 703–709. GETMAIN command to secure main storage for the new record to be written out.
    b. Lines 713–715. Move the data to the file record.
    c. Lines 718–725. HANDLE CONDITION command for the order file.
    d. Lines 728–736. WRITE DATASET command to write the new record.
    e. Lines 740–744. FREEMAIN DATA command to release main storage secured for the order record by the GETMAIN command in lines 703–709.
    f. Lines 746–752. GETMAIN command to secure main storage for the journal record to be written out.
    g. Lines 756–762. Move the data into the journal record.
    h. Lines 764–774. JOURNAL command to write out the journal record.
    i. Lines 782–790. SEND MAP command to display the next map required by the operator.
    j. Line 796.   Set the communication area switch to 1.
    k. Lines 798–804. RETURN command to terminate the task.

5. If there are errors:
    a. Lines 810–820. SEND MAP command to display the error messages.
    b. Line 824. Set the communication area switch to 1 and RETURN command to terminate the task.

THE BYPASS-INPUT SECTION

1. Lines 838–845. GETMAIN command to secure main storage for the map that will contain the message.

2. Lines 852–860. SEND MAP command to display the "ORDER BYPASSED–CONTINUE" message.

3. Line 864. Set the communication area switch to 1.

4. Lines 866–872. RETURN command to terminate the task.

THE FINALIZATION SECTION

1. Lines 1043–1050. Display the "JOB NORMALLY TERMI-NATED" message.

2. Lines 1053–1058. HANDLE CONDITION command for the temporary storage queue.

3. Lines 1064–1069. DELETEQ TS command to delete the temporary storage queue used as a scratchpad.

4. Lines 1075–1078. RETURN command to terminate the session.

THE ABNORMAL-TERMINATION SECTION

These are the routines used to abnormally terminate the session on errors and CICS/VS exceptional conditions not covered by a HANDLE CONDITION command.

THE JOURNAL RECORDS

This example of the File Add program generates journal records (see Figure 19.5). We will print these records in hexadecimal format. The system prefix is 72 bytes long and bytes 73 to 109 correspond to statements 350 to 355 of Figure 19.4. The four records correspond to order numbers 10, 11, 12, and 13. The operator initial is PAL and the entry date is December 26, 1980.

EXAMPLE

The following are facsimiles of actual photographs taken of a CRT terminal during a session.

BLOCK   1   DATA   1C9

```
CHAR                                                   ORADL770PAL12268C0000000010000C110
ZONE   0600020084000100010831010000012291201083104000DF201000008122BDJCCDFFFDCDFFFFFFFFFFFFFF0
NUMR   0D0006000500C200C006F0C000C00792F752F006F03000061000400200C791F69143770713122680000001000001100
       1...5...10...15...20...25...30...35...40...45...50...55...60...65...70...75...80...85...90...95.....
```

```
CHAR   -
ZONE   060000200
NUMR   100C0300C
       101...5...1
```

BLOCK   2   DATA   109

```
CHAR                                                   01        ORADL770PAL1226800000000011000C0111
ZONE   060002008400010002083101000045132912010831040000DF02010000091318DDCCDFFFDCDFFFFFFFFFFFFFFF0
NUMR   0D000600050002200C006F0C0B0197720F752F006F03000036010C040020C729F69143770713122680000011000001100
       1...5...10...15...20...25...30...35...40...45...50...55...60...65...70...75...80...85...90...95.....
```

```
CHAR
ZONE   020000500
NUMR   060C0020C
       101...5...1
```

BLOCK   3   DATA   109

```
CHAR                                                   01        ORADL770PAL1226800000000012000C112
ZONE   0600020084000100030831010000C43131712010831040000DF02010000001307DDCCDFFFDCDFFFFFFFFFFFFFFF0
NUMR   0D0006000500C200C006F0C0B0281730F752F006F03000061000400201C739F69143770713122680000000012000001120
       1...5...10...15...20...25...30...35...40...45...50...55...60...65...70...75...80...85...90...95.....
```

```
CHAR
ZONE   020000400
NUMR   100C0200C
       101...5...1
```

BLOCK   4   DATA   1C9

```
CHAR                                                   01        ORADL770PAL1226800000000013000C113
ZONE   060002008400010004083101000040131912010831040000DF0201030001316DDCCDFFFDCDFFFFFFFFFFFFFFF0
NUMR   0D0006000500C200C006F0C0B0037B756F752F006F03000061000400201C755F69143770713122680000000013000001130
       1...5...10...15...20...25...30...35...40...45...50...55...60...65...70...75...80...85...90...95.....
```

```
CHAR
ZONE   080000700
NUMR   150C0300C
       101...5...1
```

Fig. 19.5.   Journal Records In Hexadecimal Format.

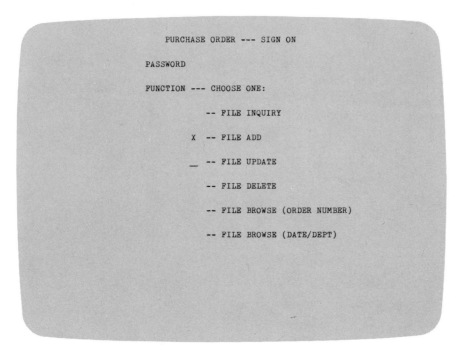

Fig. 19.6. The File Add application is selected by keying in an "X" on the File Add line and the corresponding password, then hitting the ENTER key.

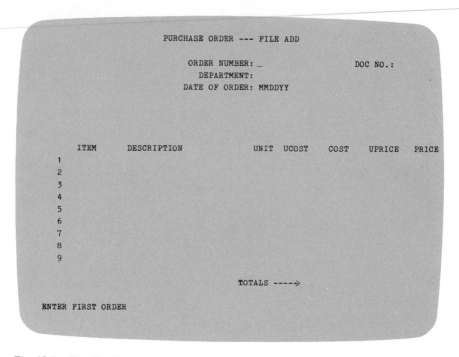

```
                    PURCHASE ORDER --- FILE ADD

                         ORDER NUMBER: _              DOC NO.:
                         DEPARTMENT:
                         DATE OF ORDER: MMDDYY



         ITEM      DESCRIPTION           UNIT  UCOST   COST   UPRICE   PRICE
      1
      2
      3
      4
      5
      6
      7
      8
      9

                                   TOTALS ---->

 ENTER FIRST ORDER
```

Fig. 19.7. The Sign On program executes which then transfers control to the File Add program. This displays the File Add map.

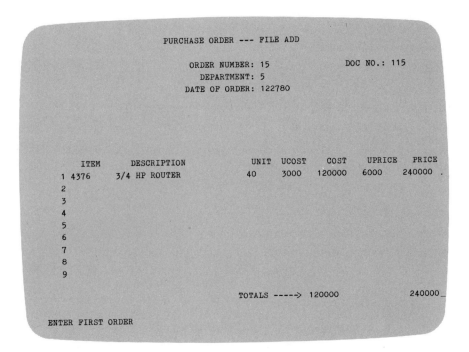

Fig. 19.8. The operator keys in the order to be added to the file, then hits the ENTER key.

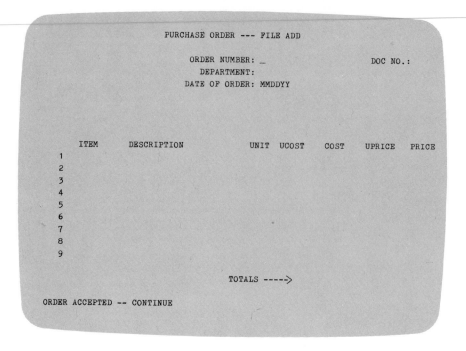

Fig. 19.9.   If there are no errors from Fig. 19.8, the order is added to the file. The "ORDER ACCEPTED – CONTINUE" message is then displayed on a fresh map to inform the operator. He may then continue with the next order.

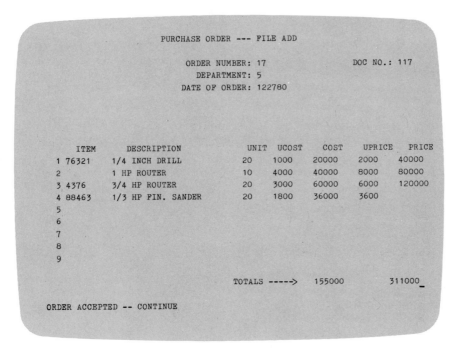

```
                    PURCHASE ORDER --- FILE ADD

                    ORDER NUMBER: 17              DOC NO.: 117
                    DEPARTMENT: 5
                    DATE OF ORDER: 122780



      ITEM      DESCRIPTION          UNIT  UCOST   COST    UPRICE   PRICE
  1 76321    1/4 INCH DRILL          20    1000   20000    2000    40000
  2          1 HP ROUTER             10    4000   40000    8000    80000
  3 4376     3/4 HP ROUTER           20    3000   60000    6000   120000
  4 88463    1/3 HP FIN. SANDER      20    1800   36000    3600
  5
  6
  7
  8
  9

                              TOTALS ----->   155000          311000_

  ORDER ACCEPTED -- CONTINUE
```

Fig. 19.10. The operator keys in the next order to be added to the file, then hits the ENTER key.

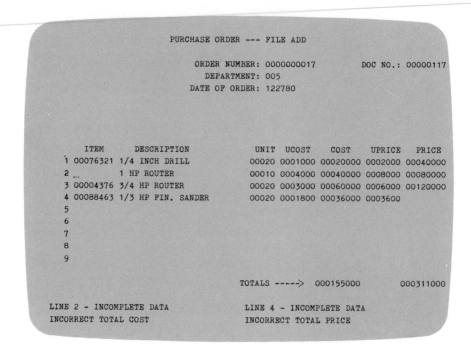

```
                    PURCHASE ORDER --- FILE ADD

                        ORDER NUMBER: 0000000017         DOC NO.: 00000117
                         DEPARTMENT: 005
                       DATE OF ORDER: 122780




        ITEM        DESCRIPTION              UNIT  UCOST     COST    UPRICE    PRICE
     1 00076321 1/4 INCH DRILL               00020 0001000 00020000 0002000 00040000
     2 _          1 HP ROUTER                00010 0004000 00040000 0008000 00080000
     3 00004376 3/4 HP ROUTER                00020 0003000 00060000 0006000 00120000
     4 00088463 1/3 HP FIN. SANDER           00020 0001800 00036000 0003600
     5
     6
     7
     8
     9

                                     TOTALS -----> 000155000          000311000

 LINE 2 - INCOMPLETE DATA            LINE 4 - INCOMPLETE DATA
 INCORRECT TOTAL COST                INCORRECT TOTAL PRICE
```

Fig. 19.11.   Four errors are detected. Note that the cursor is under the first error detected.

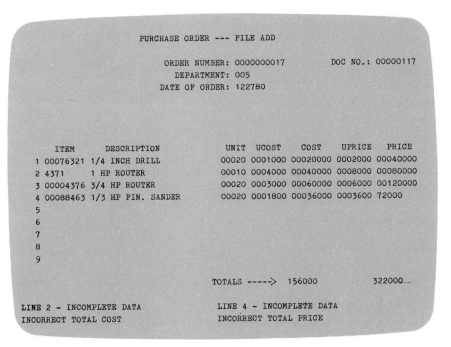

```
              PURCHASE ORDER --- FILE ADD

                  ORDER NUMBER: 0000000017        DOC NO.: 00000117
                  DEPARTMENT: 005
                  DATE OF ORDER: 122780




     ITEM        DESCRIPTION         UNIT  UCOST    COST    UPRICE    PRICE
1 00076321 1/4 INCH DRILL           00020 0001000 00020000 0002000 00040000
2 4371       1 HP ROUTER            00010 0004000 00040000 0008000 00080000
3 00004376 3/4 HP ROUTER            00020 0003000 00060000 0006000 00120000
4 00088463 1/3 HP FIN. SANDER       00020 0001800 00036000 0003600 72000
5
6
7
8
9

                         TOTALS ----->  156000             322000_
```

LINE 2 - INCOMPLETE DATA   LINE 4 - INCOMPLETE DATA
INCORRECT TOTAL COST   INCORRECT TOTAL PRICE

Fig. 19.12.   The operator keys in the corrections, then hits the ENTER key.

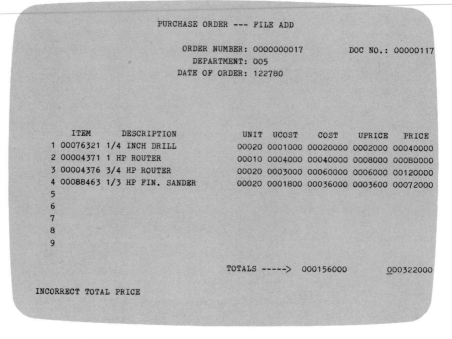

```
            PURCHASE ORDER --- FILE ADD

                ORDER NUMBER: 0000000017          DOC NO.: 00000117
                  DEPARTMENT: 005
                DATE OF ORDER: 122780




        ITEM        DESCRIPTION        UNIT  UCOST    COST    UPRICE    PRICE
    1 00076321 1/4 INCH DRILL          00020 0001000 00020000 0002000 00040000
    2 00004371 1 HP ROUTER             00010 0004000 00040000 0008000 00080000
    3 00004376 3/4 HP ROUTER           00020 0003000 00060000 0006000 00120000
    4 00088463 1/3 HP FIN. SANDER      00020 0001800 00036000 0003600 00072000
    5
    6
    7
    8
    9

                                 TOTALS -----> 000156000       000322000

INCORRECT TOTAL PRICE
```

Fig. 19.13.   One error is left. Note again that the cursor is under this field.

```
                    PURCHASE ORDER --- FILE ADD

                       ORDER NUMBER: _                    DOC NO.:
                       DEPARTMENT:
                       DATE OF ORDER: MMDDYY




        ITEM      DESCRIPTION          UNIT  UCOST   COST   UPRICE   PRICE
    1
    2
    3
    4
    5
    6
    7
    8
    9

                            TOTALS ---->

ORDER ACCEPTED -- CONTINUE
```

Fig. 19.14.   After the operator enters the corrections, the order is added to the file.

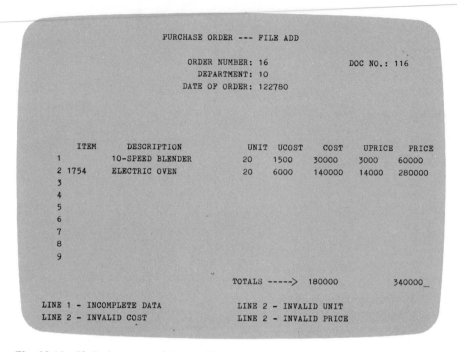

```
                      PURCHASE ORDER --- FILE ADD

                      ORDER NUMBER: 16                    DOC NO.: 116
                      DEPARTMENT: 10
                      DATE OF ORDER: 122780



        ITEM        DESCRIPTION        UNIT  UCOST    COST    UPRICE    PRICE
     1              10-SPEED BLENDER     20   1500    30000    3000     60000
     2  1754        ELECTRIC OVEN        20   6000   140000   14000    280000
     3
     4
     5
     6
     7
     8
     9

                                      TOTALS ----->  180000            340000_

LINE 1 - INCOMPLETE DATA           LINE 2 - INVALID UNIT
LINE 2 - INVALID COST              LINE 2 - INVALID PRICE
```

Fig. 19.15. If the operator wishes to discontinue the processing of an order after errors
have been detected, he hits any PA key.

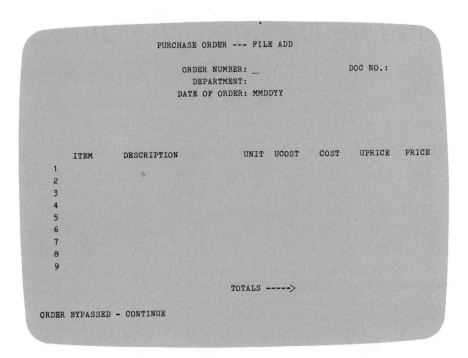

Fig. 19.16. A fresh map is then displayed with the message "ORDER BYPASSED – CONTINUE". The operator may then continue with the next order.

20

The File Update Program

INTRODUCTION

The File Update program allows the operator to change certain fields in an existing order record. The program executes when selected by the Sign-on program and will continue executing in the session until terminated by the operator. The flow of control to execute this program is shown in Figure 20.1.

PROGRAM SPECIFICATIONS

The File Update program specifications are as follows:

1. Implement the program using the pseudoconversational mode of processing.

2. Use 'ORCH' as the transaction identifier. However, the session should not be started by using this identifier, but rather through an XTCL command from the Sign-on program.

3. If the session is started by using the transaction identifier, abort the session with the message "JOB ABORTED— SIGNON VIOLATION."

4. Edit the data using page 177 as a guide.

5. On any PA key, bypass the input data and display the next fresh screen for the next order to be updated.

SCREEN LAYOUTS

These are the screen layouts to be used in the program. Figure 20.2 is for the order number of the order that will be modified, and Figure 20.3 is for the changes themselves. All 9s are numeric fields and Xs are alphanumeric fields.

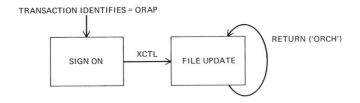

Fig. 20.1. File Update Application.

MAP PROGRAMS

These are the map programs corresponding to the screen layouts. Figure 20.4 corresponds to Figure 20.2 and Figure 20.5 corresponds to Figure 20.3.

PROGRAM LISTING

The program listing for the File Update program is shown in Figure 20.6.

MAIN-LINE SECTION

1. Lines 395–399. ADDRESS command for the TWA.

2. Lines 401–410. HANDLE AID command. The PA keys will execute the BYPASS-INPUT section.

3. Lines 415–422. HANDLE CONDITION command.

4. Lines 425–432. The selection of sections.

5. Lines 434–435. If the program is executed at the start of a session by an operator-entered transaction identifier instead of through an XCTL command from the Sign-on program, a sign-on violation occurs. This is so if EIBCALEN is equal to zero.

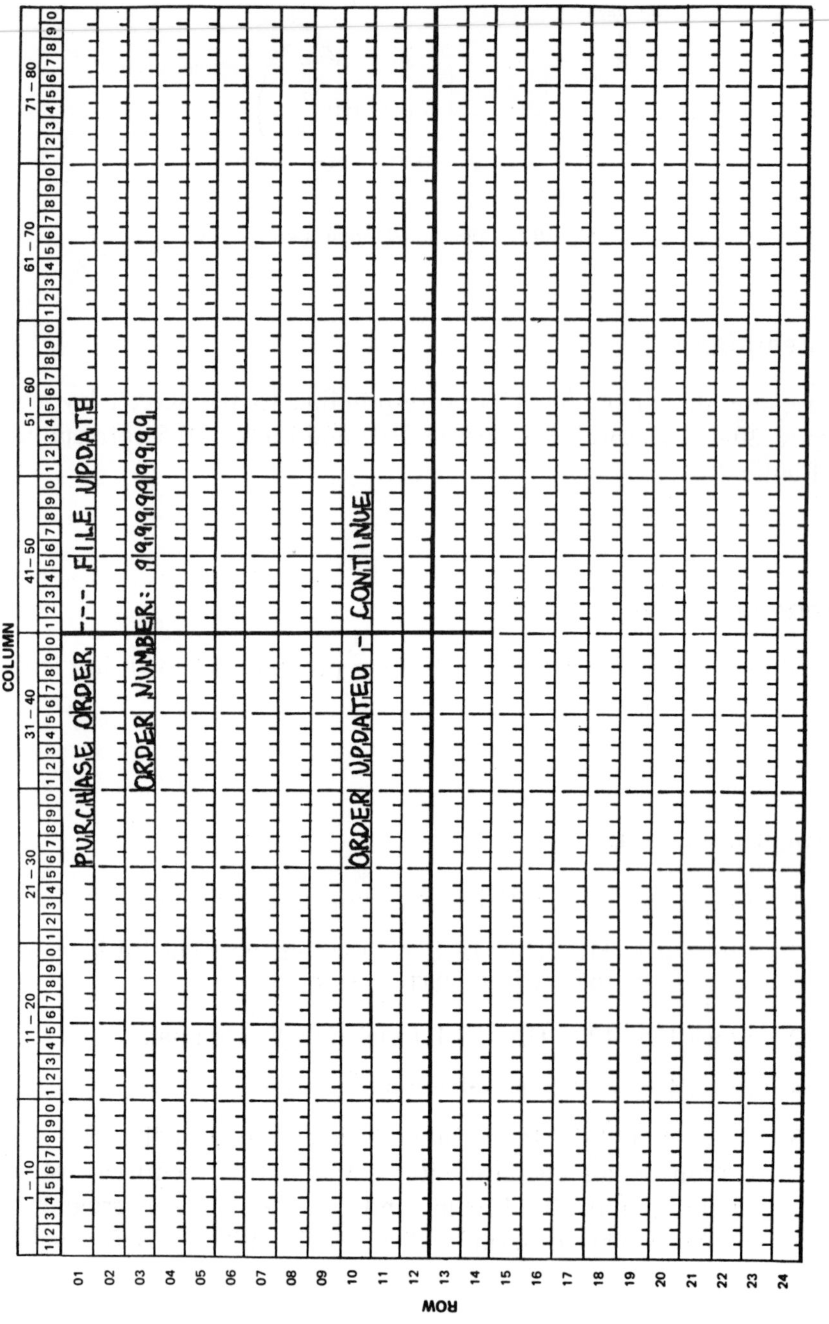

Fig. 20.2.   Order Screen Layout – File Update.

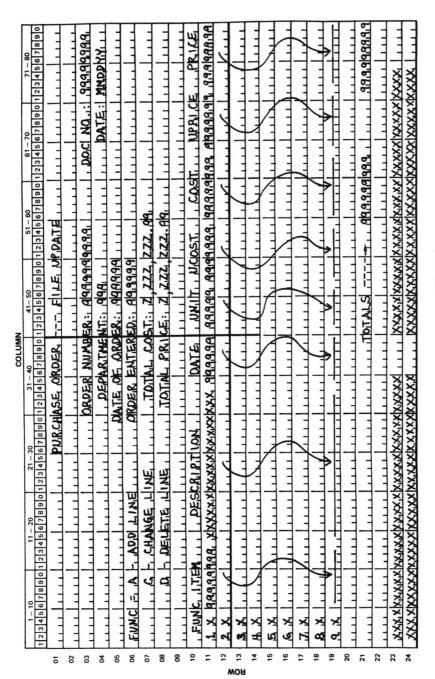

Fig. 20.3.   Data Screen Layout – File Update.

```
STMT     SOURCE STATEMENT                              DOS/VS ASSEMBLER REL 34.0 14.10

    1                PRINT NOGEN
    2 ORCHS01        DFHMSD TYPE=MAP,MODE=INOUT,CTRL=FREEKB,LANG=COBOL,TIOAPFX=YES
   12 ORCHM01        DFHMDI SIZE=(24,80)
   40 DUMMY          DFHMDF POS=(01,01),LENGTH=01,ATTRB=(ASKIP,DRK,FSET),         X
                       INITIAL='1'
   52                DFHMDF POS=(01,25),LENGTH=30,ATTRB=(ASKIP,BRT),              X
                       INITIAL='PURCHASE ORDER --- FILE UPDATE'
   64                DFHMDF POS=(03,30),LENGTH=13,ATTRB=ASKIP,                    X
                       INITIAL='ORDER NUMBER '
   76 ORDER          DFHMDF POS=(03,44),LENGTH=10,ATTRB=(NUM,BRT,IC)
   87                DFHMDF POS=(03,55),LENGTH=01,ATTRB=PROT
   98 ERROR          DFHMDF POS=(10,25),LENGTH=25,ATTRB=(ASKIP,BRT),             X
                       INITIAL='ORDER UPDATED - CONTINUE'
  110                DFHMSD TYPE=FINAL
  124                END
```

Fig. 20.4.   Order Screen Map Program — File Update.

```
STMT      SOURCE STATEMENT                              DOS/VS ASSEMBLER REL 34.0 14.50

   1                  PRINT NOGEN
   2 ORCHS02          DFHMSD TYPE=MAP,MODE=INOUT,CTRL=FREEKB,LANG=COBOL,TIOAPFX=YES
  12 ORCHMO2          DFHMDI SIZE=(24,80)
  40 DUMMY            DFHMDF POS=(01,01),LENGTH=01,ATTRB=(ASKIP,DRK,FSET),             X
                             INITIAL='1'
  52                  DFHMDF POS=(01,25),LENGTH=30,ATTRB=(ASKIP,BRT),                  X
                             INITIAL='PURCHASE ORDER --- FILE UPDATE'
  64                  DFHMDF POS=(03,30),LENGTH=13,ATTRB=ASKIP,                        X
                             INITIAL='ORDER NUMBER '
  76 ORDER           DFHMDF POS=(03,44),LENGTH=10,ATTRB=(ASKIP,BRT)
  87                  DFHMDF POS=(03,62),LENGTH=08,ATTRB=ASKIP,INITIAL='DOC NO. '
  99 DOCNO           DFHMDF POS=(03,71),LENGTH=08,ATTRB=(NUM,BRT,IC)
 110                  DFHMDF POS=(03,80),LENGTH=01,ATTRB=PROT
 121                  DFHMDF POS=(04,32),LENGTH=11,ATTRB=ASKIP,INITIAL='DEPARTMENT '
 133 DEPT            DFHMDF POS=(04,44),LENGTH=03,ATTRB=(ASKIP,BRT)
 144                  DFHMDF POS=(04,65),LENGTH=05,ATTRB=ASKIP,INITIAL='DATE '
 156 DATEUPD         DFHMDF POS=(04,71),LENGTH=06,ATTRB=(NUM,BRT),INITIAL='MMDDYY'
 168                  DFHMDF POS=(04,78),LENGTH=01,ATTRB=ASKIP
 179                  DFHMDF POS=(05,29),LENGTH=14,ATTRB=ASKIP,                        X
                             INITIAL='DATE OF ORDER '
 191 DATEOR          DFHMDF POS=(05,44),LENGTH=06,ATTRB=(ASKIP,BRT)
 202                  DFHMDF POS=(06,01),LENGTH=06,ATTRB=ASKIP,INITIAL='FUNC ='
 214                  DFHMDF POS=(06,08),LENGTH=12,ATTRB=ASKIP,                        X
                             INITIAL='A - ADD LINE'
 226                  DFHMDF POS=(06,29),LENGTH=14,ATTRB=ASKIP,                        X
                             INITIAL='ORDER ENTERED '
 238 DATEENT         DFHMDF POS=(06,44),LENGTH=06,ATTRB=(ASKIP,BRT)
 249                  DFHMDF POS=(07,08),LENGTH=15,ATTRB=ASKIP,                        X
                             INITIAL='C - CHANGE LINE'
 261                  DFHMDF POS=(07,32),LENGTH=11,ATTRB=ASKIP,INITIAL='TOTAL COST '
 273 TOTCOST         DFHMDF POS=(07,44),LENGTH=12,ATTRB=(ASKIP,BRT),                  X
                             PICOUT='Z,ZZZ,ZZZ.99'
 284                  DFHMDF POS=(08,08),LENGTH=15,ATTRB=ASKIP,                        X
                             INITIAL='D - DELETE LINE'
 296                  DFHMDF POS=(08,31),LENGTH=12,ATTRB=ASKIP,                        X
                             INITIAL='TOTAL PRICE '
 308 TOTPRCE         DFHMDF POS=(08,44),LENGTH=12,ATTRB=(ASKIP,BRT),                  X
                             PICOUT='Z,ZZZ,ZZZ.99'
 319                  DFHMDF POS=(10,02),LENGTH=04,ATTRB=ASKIP,INITIAL='FUNC'
 331                  DFHMDF POS=(10,07),LENGTH=04,ATTRB=ASKIP,INITIAL='ITEM'
 343                  DFHMDF POS=(10,17),LENGTH=11,ATTRB=ASKIP,INITIAL='DESCRIPTION'
 355                  DFHMDF POS=(10,35),LENGTH=04,ATTRB=ASKIP,INITIAL='DATE'
 367                  DFHMDF POS=(10,42),LENGTH=04,ATTRB=ASKIP,INITIAL='UNIT'
 379                  DFHMDF POS=(10,48),LENGTH=05,ATTRB=ASKIP,INITIAL='UCOST'
 391                  DFHMDF POS=(10,57),LENGTH=04,ATTRB=ASKIP,INITIAL='COST'
 403                  DFHMDF POS=(10,65),LENGTH=06,ATTRB=ASKIP,INITIAL='UPRICE'
 415                  DFHMDF POS=(10,74),LENGTH=05,ATTRB=ASKIP,INITIAL='PRICE'
 427                  DFHMDF POS=(11,01),LENGTH=01,ATTRB=ASKIP,INITIAL='1'
 439 FUNC1           DFHMDF POS=(11,03),LENGTH=01,ATTRB=(UNPROT,BRT)
 450 ITEM1           DFHMDF POS=(11,05),LENGTH=08,ATTRB=(NUM,BRT),                     X
                             PICIN='99999999',PICOUT='99999999'
```

Fig. 20.5. Data Screen Map Program — File Update.

```
STMT    SOURCE STATEMENT                              DOS/VS ASSEMBLER REL 34.0 14.50

 461 DESC1     DFHMDF POS=(11,14),LENGTH=19,ATTRB=(UNPROT,BRT)
 472 LNDATE1   DFHMDF POS=(11,34),LENGTH=06,ATTRB=(ASKIP,BRT)
 483 UNIT1     DFHMDF POS=(11,41),LENGTH=05,ATTRB=(NUM,BRT),                    X
                      PICIN='99999',PICOUT='99999'
 494 UCOST1    DFHMDF POS=(11,47),LENGTH=07,ATTRB=(NUM,BRT),                    X
                      PICIN='9999999',PICOUT='9999999'
 505 COST1     DFHMDF POS=(11,55),LENGTH=08,ATTRB=(NUM,BRT),                    X
                      PICIN='99999999',PICOUT='99999999'
 516 UPRICE1   DFHMDF POS=(11,64),LENGTH=07,ATTRB=(NUM,BRT),                    X
                      PICIN='9999999',PICOUT='9999999'
 527 PRICE1    DFHMDF POS=(11,72),LENGTH=08,ATTRB=(NUM,BRT),                    X
                      PICIN='99999999',PICOUT='99999999'
 538           DFHMDF POS=(12,01),LENGTH=01,ATTRB=ASKIP,INITIAL='2'
 550 FUNC2     DFHMDF POS=(12,03),LENGTH=01,ATTRB=(UNPROT,BRT)
 561 ITEM2     DFHMDF POS=(12,05),LENGTH=08,ATTRB=(NUM,BRT),                    X
                      PICIN='99999999',PICOUT='99999999'
 572 DESC2     DFHMDF POS=(12,14),LENGTH=19,ATTRB=(UNPROT,BRT)
 583 LNDATE2   DFHMDF POS=(12,34),LENGTH=06,ATTRB=(ASKIP,BRT)
 594 UNIT2     DFHMDF POS=(12,41),LENGTH=05,ATTRB=(NUM,BRT),                    X
                      PICIN='99999',PICOUT='99999'
 605 UCOST2    DFHMDF POS=(12,47),LENGTH=07,ATTRB=(NUM,BRT),                    X
                      PICIN='9999999',PICOUT='9999999'
 616 COST2     DFHMDF POS=(12,55),LENGTH=08,ATTRB=(NUM,BRT),                    X
                      PICIN='99999999',PICOUT='99999999'
 627 UPRICE2   DFHMDF POS=(12,64),LENGTH=07,ATTRB=(NUM,BRT),                    X
                      PICIN='9999999',PICOUT='9999999'
 638 PRICE2    DFHMDF POS=(12,72),LENGTH=08,ATTRB=(NUM,BRT),                    X
                      PICIN='99999999',PICOUT='99999999'
 649           DFHMDF POS=(13,01),LENGTH=01,ATTRB=ASKIP,INITIAL='3'
 661 FUNC3     DFHMDF POS=(13,03),LENGTH=01,ATTRB=(UNPROT,BRT)
 672 ITEM3     DFHMDF POS=(13,05),LENGTH=08,ATTRB=(NUM,BRT),                    X
                      PICIN='99999999',PICOUT='99999999'
 683 DESC3     DFHMDF POS=(13,14),LENGTH=19,ATTRB=(UNPROT,BRT)
 694 LNDATE3   DFHMDF POS=(13,34),LENGTH=06,ATTRB=(ASKIP,BRT)
 705 UNIT3     DFHMDF POS=(13,41),LENGTH=05,ATTRB=(NUM,BRT),                    X
                      PICIN='99999',PICOUT='99999'
 716 UCOST3    DFHMDF POS=(13,47),LENGTH=07,ATTRB=(NUM,BRT),                    X
                      PICIN='9999999',PICOUT='9999999'
 727 COST3     DFHMDF POS=(13,55),LENGTH=08,ATTRB=(NUM,BRT),                    X
                      PICIN='99999999',PICOUT='99999999'
 738 UPRICE3   DFHMDF POS=(13,64),LENGTH=07,ATTRB=(NUM,BRT),                    X
                      PICIN='9999999',PICOUT='9999999'
 749 PRICE3    DFHMDF POS=(13,72),LENGTH=08,ATTRB=(NUM,BRT),                    X
                      PICIN='99999999',PICOUT='99999999'
 760           DFHMDF POS=(14,01),LENGTH=01,ATTRB=ASKIP,INITIAL='4'
 772 FUNC4     DFHMDF POS=(14,03),LENGTH=01,ATTRB=(UNPROT,BRT)
 783 ITEM4     DFHMDF POS=(14,05),LENGTH=08,ATTRB=(NUM,BRT),                    X
                      PICIN='99999999',PICOUT='99999999'
 794 DESC4     DFHMDF POS=(14,14),LENGTH=19,ATTRB=(UNPROT,BRT)
 805 LNDATE4   DFHMDF POS=(14,34),LENGTH=06,ATTRB=(ASKIP,BRT)
 816 UNIT4     DFHMDF POS=(14,41),LENGTH=05,ATTRB=(NUM,BRT),                    X
```

Fig. 20.5.   (Continued)

```
                   PICIN='99999',PICOUT='99999'
 827 UCOST4        DFHMDF POS=(14,47),LENGTH=07,ATTRB=(NUM,BRT),           X
                   PICIN='9999999',PICOUT='9999999'
 838 COST4         DFHMDF POS=(14,55),LENGTH=08,ATTRB=(NUM,BRT),           X
                   PICIN='99999999',PICOUT='99999999'
 849 UPRICE4       DFHMDF POS=(14,64),LENGTH=07,ATTRB=(NUM,BRT),           X
                   PICIN='9999999',PICOUT='9999999'
 860 PRICE4        DFHMDF POS=(14,72),LENGTH=08,ATTRB=(NUM,BRT),           X
                   PICIN='99999999',PICOUT='99999999'
 871               DFHMDF POS=(15,01),LENGTH=01,ATTRB=ASKIP,INITIAL='5'
 883 FUNC5         DFHMDF POS=(15,03),LENGTH=01,ATTRB=(UNPROT,BRT)
 894 ITEM5         DFHMDF POS=(15,05),LENGTH=08,ATTRB=(NUM,BRT),           X
                   PICIN='99999999',PICOUT='99999999'
 905 DESC5         DFHMDF POS=(15,14),LENGTH=19,ATTRB=(UNPROT,BRT)
 916 LNDATE5       DFHMDF POS=(15,34),LENGTH=06,ATTRB=(ASKIP,BRT)
 927 UNIT5         DFHMDF POS=(15,41),LENGTH=05,ATTRB=(NUM,BRT),           X
                   PICIN='99999',PICOUT='99999'
 938 UCOST5        DFHMDF POS=(15,47),LENGTH=07,ATTRB=(NUM,BRT),           X
                   PICIN='9999999',PICOUT='9999999'
 949 COST5         DFHMDF POS=(15,55),LENGTH=08,ATTRB=(NUM,BRT),           X
                   PICIN='99999999',PICOUT='99999999'
 960 UPRICE5       DFHMDF POS=(15,64),LENGTH=07,ATTRB=(NUM,BRT),           X
                   PICIN='9999999',PICOUT='9999999'
 971 PRICE5        DFHMDF POS=(15,72),LENGTH=08,ATTRB=(NUM,BRT),           X
                   PICIN='99999999',PICOUT='99999999'
 982               DFHMDF POS=(16,01),LENGTH=01,ATTRB=ASKIP,INITIAL='6'
 994 FUNC6         DFHMDF POS=(16,03),LENGTH=01,ATTRB=(UNPROT,BRT)
1005 ITEM6         DFHMDF POS=(16,05),LENGTH=08,ATTRB=(NUM,BRT),           X
                   PICIN='99999999',PICOUT='99999999'
1016 DESC6         DFHMDF POS=(16,14),LENGTH=19,ATTRB=(UNPROT,BRT)
1027 LNDATE6       DFHMDF POS=(16,34),LENGTH=06,ATTRB=(ASKIP,BRT)
1038 UNIT6         DFHMDF POS=(16,41),LENGTH=05,ATTRB=(NUM,BRT),           X
                   PICIN='99999',PICOUT='99999'
1049 UCOST6        DFHMDF POS=(16,47),LENGTH=07,ATTRB=(NUM,BRT),           X
                   PICIN='9999999',PICOUT='9999999'
1060 COST6         DFHMDF POS=(16,55),LENGTH=08,ATTRB=(NUM,BRT),           X
                   PICIN='99999999',PICOUT='99999999'
1071 UPRICE6       DFHMDF POS=(16,64),LENGTH=07,ATTRB=(NUM,BRT),           X
                   PICIN='9999999',PICOUT='9999999'
1082 PRICE6        DFHMDF POS=(16,72),LENGTH=08,ATTRB=(NUM,BRT),           X
                   PICIN='99999999',PICOUT='99999999'
1093               DFHMDF POS=(17,01),LENGTH=01,ATTRB=ASKIP,INITIAL='7'
1105 FUNC7         DFHMDF POS=(17,03),LENGTH=01,ATTRB=(UNPROT,BRT)
1116 ITEM7         DFHMDF POS=(17,05),LENGTH=08,ATTRB=(NUM,BRT),           X
                   PICIN='99999999',PICOUT='99999999'
1127 DESC7         DFHMDF POS=(17,14),LENGTH=19,ATTRB=(UNPROT,BRT)
1138 LNDATE7       DFHMDF POS=(17,34),LENGTH=06,ATTRB=(ASKIP,BRT)
1149 UNIT7         DFHMDF POS=(17,41),LENGTH=05,ATTRB=(NUM,BRT),           X
                   PICIN='99999',PICOUT='99999'
1160 UCOST7        DFHMDF POS=(17,47),LENGTH=07,ATTRB=(NUM,BRT),           X
                   PICIN='9999999',PICOUT='9999999'
```

Fig. 20.5. (Continued)

```
STMT    SOURCE STATEMENT                              DOS/VS ASSEMBLER REL 34.0 14.50

1171 COST7     DFHMDF POS=(17,55),LENGTH=08,ATTRB=(NUM,BRT),              X
                      PICIN='99999999',PICOUT='99999999'
1182 UPRICE7   DFHMDF POS=(17,64),LENGTH=07,ATTRB=(NUM,BRT),             X
                      PICIN='9999999',PICOUT='9999999'
1193 PRICE7    DFHMDF POS=(17,72),LENGTH=08,ATTRB=(NUM,BRT),             X
                      PICIN='99999999',PICOUT='99999999'
1204           DFHMDF POS=(18,01),LENGTH=01,ATTRB=ASKIP,INITIAL='8'
1216 FUNC8     DFHMDF POS=(18,03),LENGTH=01,ATTRB=(UNPROT,BRT)
1227 ITEM8     DFHMDF POS=(18,05),LENGTH=08,ATTRB=(NUM,BRT),             X
                      PICIN='99999999',PICOUT='99999999'
1238 DESC8     DFHMDF POS=(18,14),LENGTH=19,ATTRB=(UNPROT,BRT)
1249 LNDATE8   DFHMDF POS=(18,34),LENGTH=06,ATTRB=(ASKIP,BRT)
1260 UNIT8     DFHMDF POS=(18,41),LENGTH=05,ATTRB=(NUM,BRT),             X
                      PICIN='99999',PICOUT='99999'
1271 UCOST8    DFHMDF POS=(18,47),LENGTH=07,ATTRB=(NUM,BRT),             X
                      PICIN='9999999',PICOUT='9999999'
1282 COST8     DFHMDF POS=(18,55),LENGTH=08,ATTRB=(NUM,BRT),             X
                      PICIN='99999999',PICOUT='99999999'
1293 UPRICE8   DFHMDF POS=(18,64),LENGTH=07,ATTRB=(NUM,BRT),             X
                      PICIN='9999999',PICOUT='9999999'
1304 PRICE8    DFHMDF POS=(18,72),LENGTH=08,ATTRB=(NUM,BRT),             X
                      PICIN='99999999',PICOUT='99999999'
1315           DFHMDF POS=(19,01),LENGTH=01,ATTRB=ASKIP,INITIAL='9'
1327 FUNC9     DFHMDF POS=(19,03),LENGTH=01,ATTRB=(UNPROT,BRT)
1338 ITEM9     DFHMDF POS=(19,05),LENGTH=08,ATTRB=(NUM,BRT),             X
                      PICIN='99999999',PICOUT='99999999'
1349 DESC9     DFHMDF POS=(19,14),LENGTH=19,ATTRB=(UNPROT,BRT)
1360 LNDATE9   DFHMDF POS=(19,34),LENGTH=06,ATTRB=(ASKIP,BRT)
1371 UNIT9     DFHMDF POS=(19,41),LENGTH=05,ATTRB=(NUM,BRT),             X
                      PICIN='99999',PICOUT='99999'
1382 UCOST9    DFHMDF POS=(19,47),LENGTH=07,ATTRB=(NUM,BRT),             X
                      PICIN='9999999',PICOUT='9999999'
1393 COST9     DFHMDF POS=(19,55),LENGTH=08,ATTRB=(NUM,BRT),             X
                      PICIN='99999999',PICOUT='99999999'
1404 UPRICE9   DFHMDF POS=(19,64),LENGTH=07,ATTRB=(NUM,BRT),             X
                      PICIN='9999999',PICOUT='9999999'
1415 PRICE9    DFHMDF POS=(19,72),LENGTH=08,ATTRB=(NUM,BRT),             X
                      PICIN='99999999',PICOUT='99999999'
1426           DFHMDF POS=(20,01),LENGTH=01,ATTRB=PROT
1437           DFHMDF POS=(21,39),LENGTH=13,ATTRB=ASKIP,                 X
                      INITIAL='TOTALS ----- '
1449 TOTEDCS   DFHMDF POS=(21,54),LENGTH=09,ATTRB=(NUM,BRT),             X
                      PICIN='999999999',PICOUT='999999999'
1460           DFHMDF POS=(21,64),LENGTH=01,ATTRB=PROT
1471 TOTEDPR   DFHMDF POS=(21,71),LENGTH=09,ATTRB=(NUM,BRT),             X
                      PICIN='999999999',PICOUT='999999999'
1482           DFHMDF POS=(22,01),LENGTH=01,ATTRB=PROT
1493 ERR1      DFHMDF POS=(23,01),LENGTH=34,ATTRB=(ASKIP,BRT)
1504 ERR2      DFHMDF POS=(23,40),LENGTH=34,ATTRB=(ASKIP,BRT)
1515 ERR3      DFHMDF POS=(24,01),LENGTH=34,ATTRB=(ASKIP,BRT)
1526 ERR4      DFHMDF POS=(24,40),LENGTH=34,ATTRB=(ASKIP,BRT)


STMT    SOURCE STATEMENT                              DOS/VS ASSEMBLER REL 34.0 14.50

1537           DFHMSD TYPE=FINAL
1551           END
```

Fig. 20.5. (Continued)

```
 1   IBM DOS VS COBOL

CBL SUPMAP,STXIT,NOTRUNC,CSYNTAX,SXREF,OPT,VERB,CLIST,BUF=19069
CBL NOOPT,LIB
00001              IDENTIFICATION DIVISION.

00003              PROGRAM-ID. ORCHO1A.


00005              ENVIRONMENT DIVISION.


00007         ****************************************************************
00008         *                                                              *
00009         *      1. THIS PROGRAM UPDATES EXISTING ORDERS IN THE PURCHASE  *
00010         *         ORDER MASTER FILE.                                    *
00011         *                                                              *
00012         *      2. THE FIXED DATA AREA WILL REMAIN UNCHANGED.            *
00013         *                                                              *
00014         *      3. THE OPERATOR MAY DO THE FOLLOWING.                    *
00015         *            A) ADD A NEW LINE.                                 *
00016         *            B) CHANGE AN EXISTING LINE.                        *
00017         *            C) DELETE AN EXISTING LINE.                        *
00018         *                                                              *
00019         ****************************************************************
```

Fig. 20.6.   File Update Program.

```
  2        ORCHO1A          15.48.02        12/27/80

00021          DATA DIVISION.

00023          WORKING-STORAGE SECTION.

00025          01  COMMUNICATION-AREA.

00027              05  COMMAREA-PROCESS-SW           PIC X.

00029          01  AREA1.


00031              05  VALIDATION-ERROR-MESSAGE.
00032                  10  FILLER                    PIC X(5) VALUE 'LINE'.
00033                  10  VALIDATION-ERROR-LINE      PIC 9.
00034                  10  FILLER                    PIC XXX   VALUE ' - '.
00035                  10  VALIDATION-ERROR-MSG       PIC X(25).

00037              05  JOB-NORMAL-END-MESSAGE  PIC X(23) VALUE
00038                  'JOB NORMALLY TERMINATED'.

00040              05  JOB-ABORTED-MESSAGE.
00041                  10  FILLER                    PIC X(15) VALUE 'JOB ABORTED --'.
00042                  10  MAJOR-ERROR-MSG            PIC X(16).

00044              05  HEXADECIMAL-ZEROES            PIC 9999 COMP VALUE ZEROES.

00046              05  FILLER REDEFINES HEXADECIMAL-ZEROES.
00047                  10  FILLER                    PIC X.
00048                  10  HEX-ZEROES                PIC X.

00050              05  OLD-EIB-AREA.
00051                  10  FILLER                    PIC X(7) VALUE 'OLD EIB'.
00052                  10  OLD-EIBFN                  PIC XX.
00053                  10  OLD-EIBRCODE               PIC X(6).
```

Fig. 20.6. (Continued)

3   ORCHO1A   15.48.02   12/27/80

```
00055          01  DFHEIVAR COPY DFHEIVAR.
00056 C        01  DFHEIVAR.
00057 C            02    DFHEIVO   PICTURE X(26).
00058 C            02    DFHEIV1   PICTURE X(8).
00059 C            02    DFHEIV2   PICTURE X(8).
00060 C            02    DFHEIV3   PICTURE X(8).
00061 C            02    DFHEIV4   PICTURE X(6).
00062 C            02    DFHEIV5   PICTURE X(4).
00063 C            02    DFHEIV6   PICTURE X(4).
00064 C            02    DFHEIV7   PICTURE X(2).
00065 C            02    DFHEIV8   PICTURE X(2).
00066 C            02    DFHEIV9   PICTURE X(1).
00067 C            02    DFHEIV10  PICTURE S9(7) USAGE COMPUTATIONAL-3.
00068 C            02    DFHEIV11  PICTURE S9(4) USAGE COMPUTATIONAL.
00069 C            02    DFHEIV12  PICTURE S9(4) USAGE COMPUTATIONAL.
00070 C            02    DFHEIV13  PICTURE S9(4) USAGE COMPUTATIONAL.
00071 C            02    DFHEIV14  PICTURE S9(4) USAGE COMPUTATIONAL.
00072 C            02    DFHEIV15  PICTURE S9(4) USAGE COMPUTATIONAL.
00073 C            02    DFHEIV16  PICTURE S9(9) USAGE COMPUTATIONAL.
00074 C            02    DFHEIV17  PICTURE X(4).
00075 C            02    DFHEIV18  PICTURE X(4).
00076 C            02    DFHEIV19  PICTURE X(4).
00077 C            02    DFHEIV97  PICTURE S9(7) USAGE COMPUTATIONAL-3 VALUE ZERO.
00078 C            02    DFHEIV98  PICTURE S9(4) USAGE COMPUTATIONAL VALUE ZERO.
00079 C            02    DFHEIV99 PICTURE X(1)   VALUE SPACE.
00080          LINKAGE SECTION.
00081          01  DFHEIBLK COPY DFHEIBLK.
00082 C        *     EIBLK EXEC INTERFACE BLOCK
00083 C        01  DFHEIBLK.
00084 C        *         EIBTIME       TIME IN 0HHMMSS FORMAT
00085 C            02 EIBTIME       PICTURE S9(7) USAGE COMPUTATIONAL-3.
00086 C        *         EIBDATE       DATE IN 00YYDDD FORMAT
00087 C            02 EIBDATE       PICTURE S9(7) USAGE COMPUTATIONAL-3.
00088 C        *         EIBTRNID      TRANSACTION IDENTIFIER
00089 C            02 EIBTRNID      PICTURE X(4).
00090 C        *         EIBTASKN      TASK NUMBER
00091 C            02 EIBTASKN      PICTURE S9(7) USAGE COMPUTATIONAL-3.
00092 C        *         EIBTRMID      TERMINAL IDENTIFIER
00093 C            02 EIBTRMID      PICTURE X(4).
00094 C        *         DFHEIGDI      RESERVED
00095 C            02 DFHEIGDI      PICTURE S9(4) USAGE COMPUTATIONAL.
00096 C        *         EIBCPOSN      CURSOR POSITION
00097 C            02 EIBCPOSN      PICTURE S9(4) USAGE COMPUTATIONAL.
00098 C        *         EIBCALEN      COMMAREA LENGTH
00099 C            02 EIBCALEN      PICTURE S9(4) USAGE COMPUTATIONAL.
00100 C        *         EIBAID        ATTENTION IDENTIFIER
00101 C            02 EIBAID        PICTURE X(1).
00102 C        *         EIBFN         FUNCTION CODE
00103 C            02 EIBFN         PICTURE X(2).
00104 C        *         EIBRCODE      RESPONSE CODE
00105 C            02 EIBRCODE      PICTURE X(6).
00106 C        *         EIBDS         DATASET NAME
00107 C            02 EIBDS         PICTURE X(8).
```

Fig. 20.6. (Continued)

```
            4         ORCH01A        15.48.02        12/27/80

        00108 C      *         EIBREQID    REQUEST IDENTIFIER
        00109 C                02 EIBREQID  PICTURE X(8).
        00110            01  DFHCOMMAREA.

        00112               05  PROCESS-SW              PIC X.
        00113                   88  INITIAL-ENTRY-TIME        VALUE '0'.
        00114                   88  ORDER-VERIFICATION-TIME   VALUE '1'.
        00115                   88  ORDER-VALIDATION-TIME     VALUE '2'.


        00117            01  LINKAGE-POINTERS.

        00119               05  FILLER             PIC S9(8) COMP.
        00120               05  MAP1-POINTER       PIC S9(8) COMP.
        00121               05  MAP2-POINTER       PIC S9(8) COMP.
        00122               05  POM-POINTER        PIC S9(8) COMP.
        00123               05  TWA-POINTER        PIC S9(8) COMP.
        00124               05  TSA-POINTER        PIC S9(8) COMP.
```

Fig. 20.6. (Continued)

```
            5         ORCH01A        15.48.02        12/27/80

        00126    *******************************************************************
        00127    *                                                                 *
        00128    *            ORDER VERIFICATION MAP DESCRIPTION                    *
        00129    *                                                                 *
        00130    *******************************************************************


        00132       01  MAP1-AREA.

        00134          05  FILLER                PIC X(12).
        00135          05  MAP1-DUMMY-L          PIC S9999 COMP.
        00136          05  MAP1-DUMMY-A          PIC X.
        00137          05  MAP1-DUMMY            PIC X.
        00138          05  MAP1-ORDER-NUMBER-L   PIC S9999 COMP.
        00139          05  MAP1-ORDER-NUMBER-A   PIC X.
        00140          05  MAP1-ORDER-NUMBER     PIC X(10).
        00141          05  MAP1-ERROR-L          PIC S9999 COMP.
        00142          05  MAP1-ERROR-A          PIC X.
        00143          05  MAP1-ERROR            PIC X(25).
```

Fig. 20.6. (Continued)

6   ORCHO1A   15.48.02   12/27/80

```
00145          ******************************************************************
00146          *                                                                *
00147          *                ORDER VALIDATION MAP DESCRIPTION                *
00148          *                                                                *
00149          ******************************************************************


00151          01  MAP2-AREA.

00153              05  FILLER                      PIC X(12).
00154              05  MAP2-DUMMY-L                PIC S9999 COMP.
00155              05  MAP2-DUMMY-A                PIC X.
00156              05  MAP2-DUMMY                  PIC X.
00157              05  MAP2-ORDER-NUMBER-L         PIC S9999 COMP.
00158              05  MAP2-ORDER-NUMBER-A         PIC X.
00159              05  MAP2-ORDER-NUMBER           PIC X(10).
00160              05  MAP2-DOCUMENT-L             PIC S9999 COMP.
00161              05  MAP2-DOCUMENT-A             PIC X.
00162              05  MAP2-DOCUMENT               PIC X(8).
00163              05  MAP2-DEPARTMENT-L           PIC S9999 COMP.
00164              05  MAP2-DEPARTMENT-A           PIC X.
00165              05  MAP2-DEPARTMENT             PIC XXX.
00166              05  MAP2-CHANGE-DATE-L          PIC S9999 COMP.
00167              05  MAP2-CHANGE-DATE-A          PIC X.
00168              05  MAP2-CHANGE-DATE.
00169                  10  MAP2-CHANGE-DATE-MONTH  PIC XX.
00170                  10  MAP2-CHANGE-DATE-DAY    PIC XX.
00171                  10  MAP2-CHANGE-DATE-YEAR   PIC XX.
00172              05  MAP2-ORDER-DATE-L           PIC S9999 COMP.
00173              05  MAP2-ORDER-DATE-A           PIC X.
00174              05  MAP2-ORDER-DATE.
00175                  10  MAP2-ORDER-DATE-MONTH   PIC XX.
00176                  10  MAP2-ORDER-DATE-DAY     PIC XX.
00177                  10  MAP2-ORDER-DATE-YEAR    PIC XX.
00178              05  MAP2-ORDER-DATE-ENTERED-L   PIC S9999 COMP.
00179              05  MAP2-ORDER-DATE-ENTERED-A   PIC X.
00180              05  MAP2-ORDER-DATE-ENTERED     PIC X(6).
00181              05  MAP2-TOTAL-COST-L           PIC S9999 COMP.
00182              05  MAP2-TOTAL-COST-A           PIC X.
00183              05  MAP2-TOTAL-COST             PIC Z,ZZZ,ZZZ.99.
00184              05  MAP2-TOTAL-PRICE-L          PIC S9999 COMP.
00185              05  MAP2-TOTAL-PRICE-A          PIC X.
00186              05  MAP2-TOTAL-PRICE            PIC Z,ZZZ,ZZZ.99.
00187              05  MAP2-LINE-ITEM              OCCURS 9
00188                                             INDEXED BY MAP2-LINE-I.
00189                  10  MAP2-ITEM-FUNCTION-L      PIC S9999 COMP.
00190                  10  MAP2-ITEM-FUNCTION-A      * PIC X.
00191                  10  MAP2-ITEM-FUNCTION        PIC X.
00192                  10  MAP2-ITEM-NUMBER-L        PIC S9999 COMP.
00193                  10  MAP2-ITEM-NUMBER-A        PIC X.
00194                  10  MAP2-ITEM-NUMBER          PIC 9(8).
00195                  10  MAP2-ITEM-DESCRIPTION-L   PIC S9999 COMP.
```

Fig. 20.6. (Continued)

```
00196              10   MAP2-ITEM-DESCRIPTION-A      PIC X.
00197              10   MAP2-ITEM-DESCRIPTION        PIC X(19).
00198              10   MAP2-ITEM-DATE-L             PIC S9999 COMP.
00199              10   MAP2-ITEM-DATE-A             PIC X.
00200              10   MAP2-ITEM-DATE               PIC X(6).
00201              10   MAP2-UNIT-L                  PIC S9999 COMP.
00202              10   MAP2-UNIT-A                  PIC X.
00203              10   MAP2-UNIT                    PIC 9(5).
00204              10   MAP2-UNIT-COST-L             PIC S9999 COMP.
00205              10   MAP2-UNIT-COST-A             PIC X.
00206              10   MAP2-UNIT-COST               PIC 9(5)V99.
00207              10   MAP2-COST-L                  PIC S9999 COMP.
00208              10   MAP2-COST-A                  PIC X.
00209              10   MAP2-COST                    PIC 9(6)V99.
00210              10   MAP2-UNIT-PRICE-L            PIC S9999 COMP.
00211              10   MAP2-UNIT-PRICE-A            PIC X.
00212              10   MAP2-UNIT-PRICE              PIC 9(5)V99.
00213              10   MAP2-PRICE-L                 PIC S9999 COMP.
00214              10   MAP2-PRICE-A                 PIC X.
00215              10   MAP2-PRICE                   PIC 9(6)V99.
00216         05   MAP2-EDIT-TOTAL-COST-L           PIC S9999 COMP.
00217         05   MAP2-EDIT-TOTAL-COST-A           PIC X.
00218         05   MAP2-EDIT-TOTAL-COST             PIC 9(7)V99.
00219         05   MAP2-EDIT-TOTAL-PRICE-L          PIC S9999 COMP.
00220         05   MAP2-EDIT-TOTAL-PRICE-A          PIC X.
00221         05   MAP2-EDIT-TOTAL-PRICE            PIC 9(7)V99.
00222         05   FILLER                       OCCURS 4
00223                                           INDEXED BY ERROR-I.
00224              10   MAP2-ERRORS-L                -PIC S9999 COMP.
00225              10   MAP2-ERRORS-A                PIC X.
00226              10   MAP2-ERRORS                  PIC X(34).
```

Fig. 20.6. (Continued)

8   ORCHO1A   15.48.02   12/27/80

```
00228        ********************************************************************
00229        *                                                                  *
00230        *            PURCHASE ORDER MASTER -- FILE LAYOUT                   *
00231        *                                                                  *
00232        ********************************************************************

00234        01   ORDER-MASTER-RECORD.
00235             05   ORDER-NUMBER                     PIC X(10).
00236             05   ORDER-ALT-KEY.
00237                  10   ORDER-DEPARTMENT            PIC XXX.
00238                  10   ORDER-DATE.
00239                       15   ORDER-DATE-YEAR        PIC XX.
00240                       15   ORDER-DATE-MONTH       PIC XX.
00241                       15   ORDER-DATE-DAY         PIC XX.
00242             05   ORDER-DATE-ENTERED.
00243                  10   ORDER-DATE-ENTERED-MONTH    PIC XX.
00244                  10   ORDER-DATE-ENTERED-DAY      PIC XX.
00245                  10   ORDER-DATE-ENTERED-YEAR     PIC XX.
00246             05   ORDER-TOTAL-COST                 PIC S9(7)V99    COMP-3.
00247             05   ORDER-TOTAL-PRICE                PIC S9(7)V99    COMP-3.
00248             05   ORDER-LINE-COUNT                 PIC S9999       COMP.
00249             05   ORDER-ALL-LINES.
00250                  10   ORDER-LINE-ITEM        OCCURS 1 TO 9
00251                                              DEPENDING ON ORDER-LINE-COUNT
00252                                              INDEXED BY ORDER-LINE-I.
00253                       15   ORDER-ITEM-NUMBER        PIC X(8).
00254                       15   ORDER-ITEM-DESCRIPTION   PIC X(19).
00255                       15   ORDER-ITEM-DATE.
00256                            20   ORDER-ITEM-DATE-MONTH    PIC XX.
00257                            20   ORDER-ITEM-DATE-DAY      PIC XX.
00258                            20   ORDER-ITEM-DATE-YEAR     PIC XX.
00259                       15   ORDER-UNIT               PIC S9(5)      COMP-3.
00260                       15   ORDER-UNIT-COST          PIC S9(5)V99   COMP-3.
00261                       15   ORDER-UNIT-PRICE         PIC S9(5)V99   COMP-3.
```

Fig. 20.6. (Continued)

```
    9          ORCHO1A          15.48.02        12/27/80

00263         ****************************************************************
00264         *
00265         *                    TRANSACTION WORK AREA                     *
00266         *                                                              *
00267         ****************************************************************


00269         01   TWA-AREA.


00271              05   TWA-LINE-ITEM-MAP.
00272                   10   TWA-ITEM-FUNCTION-MAP-L          PIC S9999 COMP.
00273                   10   TWA-ITEM-FUNCTION-MAP-A          PIC X.
00274                   10   TWA-ITEM-FUNCTION-MAP            PIC X.
00275                        88   SCREEN-FUNCTION-IS-ADD           VALUE 'A'.
00276                        88   SCREEN-FUNCTION-IS-CHANGE        VALUE 'C'.
00277                        88   SCREEN-FUNCTION-IS-DELETE        VALUE 'D'.
00278                   10   TWA-ITEM-NUMBER-MAP-L           PIC S9999 COMP.
00279                   10   TWA-ITEM-NUMBER-MAP-A           PIC X.
00280                   10   TWA-ITEM-NUMBER-MAP             PIC X(8).
00281                   10   TWA-ITEM-DESCRIPTION-MAP-L      PIC S9999 COMP.
00282                   10   TWA-ITEM-DESCRIPTION-MAP-A      PIC X.
00283                   10   TWA-ITEM-DESCRIPTION-MAP.
00284                        15   TWA-DESCRIPTION-FIRST-MAP  PIC X.
00285                        15   FILLER                     PIC X(18).
00286                   10   TWA-ITEM-DATE-MAP-L            PIC S9999 COMP.
00287                   10   TWA-ITEM-DATE-MAP-A            PIC X.
00288                   10   TWA-ITEM-DATE-MAP              PIC X(6).
00289                   10   TWA-UNIT-MAP-L                 PIC S9999 COMP.
00290                   10   TWA-UNIT-MAP-A                 PIC X.
00291                   10   TWA-UNIT-MAP                   PIC 9(5).
00292                   10   TWA-UNIT-COST-MAP-L            PIC S9999 COMP.
00293                   10   TWA-UNIT-COST-MAP-A            PIC X.
00294                   10   TWA-UNIT-COST-MAP              PIC 9(5)V99.
00295                   10   TWA-COST-MAP-L                 PIC S9999 COMP.
00296                   10   TWA-COST-MAP-A                 PIC X.
00297                   10   TWA-COST-MAP                   PIC 9(6)V99.
00298                   10   TWA-UNIT-PRICE-MAP-L           PIC S9999 COMP.
00299                   10   TWA-UNIT-PRICE-MAP-A           PIC X.
00300                   10   TWA-UNIT-PRICE-MAP             PIC 9(5)V99.
00301                   10   TWA-PRICE-MAP-L                PIC S9999 COMP.
00302                   10   TWA-PRICE-MAP-A                PIC X.
00303                   10   TWA-PRICE-MAP                  PIC 9(6)V99.


00305              05   TWA-LINE-ITEM-ORDER.
00306                   10   TWA-ITEM-NUMBER-ORDER           PIC X(8).
00307                   10   TWA-ITEM-DESCRIPTION-ORDER      PIC X(19).
00308                   10   TWA-ITEM-DATE-ORDER             PIC X(6).
00309                   10   TWA-UNIT-ORDER                  PIC S9(5)    COMP-3.
00310                   10   TWA-UNIT-COST-ORDER             PIC S9(5)V99 COMP-3.
00311                   10   TWA-UNIT-PRICE-ORDER            PIC S9(5)V99 COMP-3.
```

Fig. 20.6. (Continued)

```
    10         ORCH01A           15.48.02         12/27/80

00313              05   TWA-TOTAL-COST                    PIC S9(7)V99   COMP-3.

00315              C5   TWA-TOTAL-PRICE                   PIC S9(7)V99   COMP-3.

00317              05   TWA-FUNCTION-COUNTS   COMP.
00318                   10   TWA-FUNCTION-ADD-COUNT       PIC S9(8).
00319                   10   TWA-FUNCTION-CHANGE-COUNT    PIC S9(8).
00320                   10   TWA-FUNCTION-DELETE-COUNT    PIC S9(8).

00322              05   TWA-EDITING-SWITCHES.
00323                   10   TWA-UNIT-SW                  PIC X.
00324                     88   UNIT-WAS-ENTERED                VALUE 'Y'.
00325                   10   TWA-UNIT-COST-SW             PIC X.
00326                     88   UNIT-COST-WAS-ENTERED           VALUE 'Y'.
00327                   10   TWA-UNIT-PRICE-SW            PIC X.
00328                     88   UNIT-PRICE-WAS-ENTERED          VALUE 'Y'.

00330              05   TWA-DELETE-SWITCH                 PIC X.
00331                   88   NO-DELETE-SO-FAR                  VALUE 'N'.

00333              05   TWA-ORDER-RECORD-KEY              PIC X(10).

00335              05   TSA-QUEUE-ID.
00336                   10   TSA-TERM-ID                  PIC XXXX.
00337                   10   TSA-TRANS-ID                 PIC XXXX.

00339              05   TWA-BINARY-FIELDS   COMP.
00340                   10   TWA-LINE-DATA-CNT            PIC S9(8).
00341                   10   TWA-POM-LENGTH               PIC S9(4).
00342                   10   TSA-LENGTH                   PIC S9(4).
00343                   10   TSA-QUEUE-NO                 PIC S9(4).

00345              05   TWA-OPERATOR-MESSAGE              PIC X(31).

00347              05   TWA-CURRENT-DATE.
00348                   10   TWA-CURRENT-DATE-MONTH       PIC XX.
00349                   10   FILLER                       PIC X.
00350                   10   TWA-CURRENT-DATE-DAY         PIC XX.
00351                   10   FILLER                       PIC X.
00352                   10   TWA-CURRENT-DATE-YEAR        PIC XX.
```

Fig. 20.6. (Continued)

```
    11          ORCH01A          15.48.02      12/27/8?

00354          ************************************************************
00355          *                                                          *
00356          *                  TEMPORARY STORAGE AREA                  *
00357          *                                                          *
00358          ************************************************************


00360          01   TSA-AREA.


00362               05   TSA-ORDER-NUMBER                PIC X(10).


00364               05   TSA-ORDER-ALL-LINES.
00365                  10   TSA-LINE-ITEM            OCCURS 9
00366                                                INDEXED BY TSA-LINE-I.
00367                     15   TSA-LINE-FUNCTION     PIC X.
00368                        88   LINE-IS-UNCHANGED        VALUE SPACE.
00369                        88   LINE-IS-ADDED            VALUE 'A'.
00370                        88   LINE-IS-CHANGED          VALUE 'C'.
00371                        88   LINE-IS-DELETED          VALUE 'D'.
00372                     15   TSA-ORDER-LINE.
00373                        20   TSA-ITEM-NUMBER       PIC X(8).
00374                        20   TSA-ITEM-DESCRIPTION  PIC X(19).
00375                        20   TSA-ITEM-DATE         PIC X(6).
00376                        20   TSA-UNIT              PIC S9(5)    COMP-3.
00377                        20   TSA-UNIT-COST         PIC S9(5)V99 COMP-3.
00378                        20   TSA-UNIT-PRICE        PIC S9(5)V99 COMP-3.


00380               05   TSA-POM-NUMBER-OF-LINES         PIC S9(8) COMP.


00382               05   TSA-SCREEN-NUMBER-OF-LINES      PIC S9(8) COMP.


00384               05   TSA-CHANGE-DATE                 PIC X(6).
```

Fig. 20.6. (Continued)

```
    12          ORCHO1A          15.48.02          12/27/80


00386                PROCEDURE DIVISION USING DFHEIBLK DFHCOMMAREA.
00387                    CALL 'DFHEI1'.

00389                ************************************************************
00390                *                                                        *
00391                MAIN-LINE SECTION.
00392                *                                                        *
00393                ************************************************************

00395           *    EXEC CICS
00396           *        ADDRESS TWA (TWA-POINTER)
00397           *    END-EXEC.
00398                MOVE '                    ' TO DFHEIVO CALL 'DFHEI1' USING
00399                DFHEIVO TWA-POINTER.
00400
00401           *    EXEC CICS
00402           *        HANDLE AID
00403           *            CLEAR (FINALIZATION)
00404           *            PA1 (BYPASS-INPUT)
00405           *            PA2 (BYPASS-INPUT)
00406           *            PA3 (BYPASS-INPUT)
00407           *    END-EXEC.
00408                MOVE ' 0                  ' TO DFHEIVO CALL 'DFHEI1' USING
00409                DFHEIVO GO TO FINALIZATION BYPASS-INPUT BYPASS-INPUT
00410                BYPASS-INPUT DEPENDING ON DFHEIGDI.
00411
00412
00413
00414
00415           *    EXEC CICS
00416           *        HANDLE CONDITION
00417           *            MAPFAIL (MAPFAIL-ERROR)
00418           *            ERROR   (MAJOR-ERROR)
00419           *    END-EXEC.
00420                MOVE '                    ' TO DFHEIVO CALL 'DFHEI1' USING
00421                DFHEIVO GO TO MAPFAIL-ERROR MAJOR-ERROR DEPENDING ON
00422                DFHEIGDI.
00423
00424
00425                IF EIBCALEN NOT EQUAL TO ZEROES
00426                    IF ORDER-VALIDATION-TIME
00427                        GO TO ORDER-VALIDATION
00428                    ELSE IF ORDER-VERIFICATION-TIME
00429                        GO TO ORDER-VERIFICATION
00430                    ELSE IF INITIAL-ENTRY-TIME
00431                        GO TO INITIALIZATION
00432                    ELSE GO TO PROCESS-SWITCH-ERROR.

00434                IF EIBCALEN EQUAL TO ZEROES
00435                    GO TO SIGN-ON-VIOLATION.
```

Fig. 20.6. (Continued)

```
    13         ORCH01A          15.48.02        12/27/80


00437        ******************************************************************
00438        *                                                                *
00439         ORDER-VALIDATION SECTION.
00440        *                                                                *
00441        ******************************************************************


00443        *      EXEC CICS
00444        *           RECEIVE MAP    ('ORCHMO2')
00445        *                   MAPSET ('ORCHS02')
00446        *                   SET    (MAP2-POINTER)
00447        *      END-EXEC.
00448               MOVE 'ORCHMO2' TO DFHEIV1 MOVE 'ORCHS02' TO DFHEIV2 MOVE '
00449        -    '                 ' TO DFHEIVO CALL 'DFHEI1' USING DFHEIVO
00450               DFHEIV1 MAP2-POINTER DFHEIV98 DFHEIV2.
00451
00452
00453               MOVE EIBTRMID    TO   TSA-TERM-ID.
00454               MOVE EIBTRNID    TO   TSA-TRANS-ID.

00456        *      EXEC CICS
00457        *           READQ TS
00458        *                 QUEUE  (TSA-QUEUE-ID)
00459        *                 SET    (TSA-POINTER)
00460        *                 LENGTH (TSA-LENGTH)
00461        *                 ITEM   (1)
00462        *      END-EXEC.
00463               MOVE 1 TO DFHEIV11 MOVE '  Y      ' TO DFHEIVO CALL 'DFHEI1'
00464               USING DFHEIVO TSA-QUEUE-ID TSA-POINTER TSA-LENGTH DFHEIV99
00465               DFHEIV11.
00466
00467
00468
00469
00470               MOVE SPACES TO MAP2-ERRORS (1)
00471                              MAP2-ERRORS (2)
00472                              MAP2-ERRORS (3)
00473                              MAP2-ERRORS (4).
00474               SET ERROR-I   TO  ZEROES.

00476               IF MAP2-DOCUMENT NUMERIC
00477                  NEXT SENTENCE
00478               ELSE SET ERROR-I UP BY 1
00479                    MOVE 'INVALID DOCUMENT NUMBER' TO  MAP2-ERRORS (ERROR-I)
00480                    MOVE -1                        TO  MAP2-DOCUMENT-L.

00482               IF    MAP2-CHANGE-DATE-MONTH (GREATER '00' AND LESS '13')
00483               AND  MAP2-CHANGE-DATE-DAY   (GREATER '00' AND LESS '32')
00484               AND  MAP2-CHANGE-DATE-YEAR   NUMERIC
00485               THEN MOVE MAP2-CHANGE-DATE  TO  TSA-CHANGE-DATE
00486               ELSE SET ERROR-I UP BY 1
00487                    MOVE 'INVALID DATE' TO MAP2-ERRORS (ERROR-I)
```

Fig. 20.6. (Continued)

```
   14          ORCH01A          15.48.02          12/27/80


00488                   IF ERROR-I EQUAL TO 1
00489                        MOVE -1 TO MAP2-CHANGE-DATE-L.


00491          VALIDATE-VARIABLE-DATA.

00493          SET MAP2-LINE-I       TO  1.
00494          MOVE ZEROES           TO  TWA-LINE-DATA-CNT.
00495          MOVE ZEROES           TO  TWA-FUNCTION-ADD-COUNT
00496                                     TWA-FUNCTION-CHANGE-COUNT
00497                                     TWA-FUNCTION-DELETE-COUNT.
00498          MOVE ZEROES           TO  TWA-TOTAL-COST
00499                                     TWA-TOTAL-PRICE.
00500          PERFORM VALIDATE-EACH-LINE THRU VALIDATE-EACH-LINE-EXIT
00501               UNTIL    (TWA-LINE-DATA-CNT EQUAL TO ZEROES
00502                    AND MAP2-LINE-I GREATER
00503                                    (TSA-POM-NUMBER-OF-LINES + 1))
00504               OR ERROR-I              EQUAL TO 4
00505               OR MAP2-LINE-I         GREATER THAN 9.
00506          GO TO CHECK-IF-ANY-DATA-ENTERED.


00508          VALIDATE-EACH-LINE.
00509          MOVE SPACES                    TO  TWA-UNIT-SW
00510                                             TWA-UNIT-COST-SW
00511                                             TWA-UNIT-PRICE-SW.
00512          MOVE ZEROES                    TO  TWA-LINE-DATA-CNT.
00513          SET VALIDATION-ERROR-LINE  TO  MAP2-LINE-I.
00514          MOVE MAP2-LINE-ITEM (MAP2-LINE-I) TO TWA-LINE-ITEM-MAP.
00515          SET TSA-LINE-I             TO  MAP2-LINE-I.
00516          MOVE TSA-ORDER-LINE (TSA-LINE-I) TO TWA-LINE-ITEM-ORDER.

00518          IF TWA-ITEM-FUNCTION-MAP-L NOT EQUAL TO ZEROES
00519               IF SCREEN-FUNCTION-IS-ADD
00520                    ADD 1 TO TWA-FUNCTION-ADD-COUNT
00521                    IF MAP2-LINE-I GREATER TSA-POM-NUMBER-OF-LINES
00522                        NEXT SENTENCE
00523                    ELSE MOVE 'INVALID ADD FUNCTION'
00524                                        TO VALIDATION-ERROR-MSG
00525                        GO TO ERROR-FUNCTION-RTN
00526               ELSE IF SCREEN-FUNCTION-IS-CHANGE
00527                    ADD 1 TO TWA-FUNCTION-CHANGE-COUNT
00528                    IF MAP2-LINE-I
00529                              NOT GREATER TSA-POM-NUMBER-OF-LINES
00530                        NEXT SENTENCE
00531                    ELSE MOVE 'INVALID CHANGE FUNCTION'
00532                                        TO VALIDATION-ERROR-MSG
00533                        GO TO ERROR-FUNCTION-RTN
00534               ELSE IF SCREEN-FUNCTION-IS-DELETE
00535                    ADD 1 TO TWA-FUNCTION-DELETE-COUNT
00536                    IF MAP2-LINE-I
00537                              NOT GREATER TSA-POM-NUMBER-OF-LINES
00538                        NEXT SENTENCE
```

Fig. 20.6. (Continued)

```
00539                                              ELSE MOVE 'INVALID DELETE FUNCTION'
00540                                                        TO VALIDATION-ERROR-MSG
00541                                                   GO TO ERROR-FUNCTION-RTN
00542                                         ELSE MOVE 'INVALID FUNCTION CODE'
00543                                                        TO VALIDATION-ERROR-MSG
00544                                              GO TO ERROR-FUNCTION-RTN.

00546             GO TO VALIDATE-ITEM-NUMBER.


00548        ERROR-FUNCTION-RTN.
00549             SET ERROR-I UP BY 1.
00550             MOVE VALIDATION-ERROR-MESSAGE TO MAP2-ERRORS (ERROR-I).
00551             IF ERROR-I EQUAL TO 1
00552                 MOVE -1 TO MAP2-ITEM-FUNCTION-L (MAP2-LINE-I).
00553             SET MAP2-LINE-I UP BY 1.
00554             GO TO VALIDATE-EACH-LINE-EXIT.


00556        VALIDATE-ITEM-NUMBER.


00558             IF TWA-ITEM-NUMBER-MAP-L NOT EQUAL TO ZEROES
00559                 IF     SCREEN-FUNCTION-IS-ADD
00560                     OR SCREEN-FUNCTION-IS-CHANGE
00561                     THEN IF TWA-ITEM-NUMBER-MAP NUMERIC
00562                              MOVE TWA-ITEM-NUMBER-MAP
00563                                        TO TWA-ITEM-NUMBER-ORDER
00564                              ADD 1 TO TWA-LINE-DATA-CNT
00565                         ELSE MOVE 'INVALID ITEM NUMBER'
00566                                        TO VALIDATION-ERROR-MSG
00567                              GO TO ERROR-ITEM-NUMBER-RTN
00568                     ELSE MOVE 'INVALID ITEM NUMBER ENTRY'
00569                                   TO VALIDATION-ERROR-MSG
00570                         GO TO ERROR-ITEM-NUMBER-RTN.

00572             GO TO VALIDATE-ITEM-DESCRIPTION.


00574        ERROR-ITEM-NUMBER-RTN.
00575             SET ERROR-I UP BY 1.
00576             MOVE VALIDATION-ERROR-MESSAGE TO MAP2-ERRORS (ERROR-I).
00577             IF ERROR-I EQUAL TO 1
00578                 MOVE -1 TO MAP2-ITEM-NUMBER-L (MAP2-LINE-I)
00579             ELSE IF ERROR-I EQUAL TO 4
00580                     GO TO VALIDATE-EACH-LINE-EXIT.


00582        VALIDATE-ITEM-DESCRIPTION.

00584             IF TWA-ITEM-DESCRIPTION-MAP-L EQUAL TO ZEROES
00585                 IF SCREEN-FUNCTION-IS-ADD
00586                     MOVE SPACES TO TWA-ITEM-DESCRIPTION-ORDER
00587                 ELSE NEXT SENTENCE
```

Fig. 20.6. (Continued)

```
00588                    ELSE IF    SCREEN-FUNCTION-IS-ADD
00589                       OR SCREEN-FUNCTION-IS-CHANGE
00590                    THEN IF TWA-DESCRIPTION-FIRST-MAP EQUAL TO SPACES
00591                            MOVE 'INVALID DESCRIPTION'
00592                                      TO VALIDATION-ERROR-MSG
00593                         GO TO ERROR-ITEM-DESCRIPTION-RTN
00594                    ELSE MOVE TWA-ITEM-DESCRIPTION-MAP
00595                                      TO TWA-ITEM-DESCRIPTION-ORDER
00596                         ADD 2           TO TWA-LINE-DATA-CNT
00597                 ELSE MOVE 'INVALID ITEM DESC ENTRY'
00598                                      TO  VALIDATION-ERROR-MSG
00599                         GO TO ERROR-ITEM-DESCRIPTION-RTN.

00601           GO TO VALIDATE-UNIT.


00603      ERROR-ITEM-DESCRIPTION-RTN.
00604           SET ERROR-I UP BY 1.
00605           MOVE VALIDATION-ERROR-MESSAGE  TO  MAP2-ERRORS (ERROR-I).
00606           IF ERROR-I EQUAL TO 1
00607                MOVE -1 TO MAP2-ITEM-DESCRIPTION-L (MAP2-LINE-I)
00608           ELSE IF ERROR-I EQUAL TO 4
00609                    GO TO VALIDATE-EACH-LINE-EXIT.


00611      VALIDATE-UNIT.

00613           IF TWA-UNIT-MAP-L NOT EQUAL TO ZEROES
00614                IF    SCREEN-FUNCTION-IS-ADD
00615                   OR SCREEN-FUNCTION-IS-CHANGE
00616                THEN IF TWA-UNIT-MAP NUMERIC
00617                         MOVE TWA-UNIT-MAP         TO  TWA-UNIT-ORDER
00618                         ADD 4 TO TWA-LINE-DATA-CNT
00619                         MOVE 'Y' TO TWA-UNIT-SW
00620                    ELSE MOVE ZEROES             TO  TWA-UNIT-ORDER
00621                         MOVE 'INVALID UNIT' TO  VALIDATION-ERROR-MSG
00622                         GO TO ERROR-UNIT-RTN
00623                ELSE MOVE 'INVALID UNIT ENTRY' TO VALIDATION-ERROR-MSG
00624                     GO TO ERROR-UNIT-RTN.

00626           GO TO VALIDATE-UNIT-COST.


00628      ERROR-UNIT-RTN.
00629           SET ERROR-I UP BY 1.
00630           MOVE VALIDATION-ERROR-MESSAGE TO MAP2-ERRORS (ERROR-I).
00631           IF ERROR-I EQUAL TO 1
00632                MOVE -1 TO MAP2-UNIT-L (MAP2-LINE-I)
00633           ELSE IF ERROR-I EQUAL TO 4
00634                    GO TO VALIDATE-EACH-LINE-EXIT.


00636      VALIDATE-UNIT-COST.
```

Fig. 20.6. (Continued)

```
      17              ORCHO1A          15.48.02      12/27/80

00638          IF TWA-UNIT-COST-MAP-L NOT EQUAL TO ZEROES
00639              IF   SCREEN-FUNCTION-IS-ADD
00640            OR SCREEN-FUNCTION-IS-CHANGE
00641            THEN IF TWA-UNIT-COST-MAP NUMERIC
00642                    MOVE TWA-UNIT-COST-MAP
00643                              TO TWA-UNIT-COST-ORDER
00644                    ADD 8 TO TWA-LINE-DATA-CNT
00645                    MOVE 'Y' TO TWA-UNIT-COST-SW
00646              ELSE MOVE 'INVALID UNIT COST'
00647                              TO  VALIDATION-ERROR-MSG
00648                GO TO ERROR-UNIT-COST-RTN
00649            ELSE MOVE 'INVALID UNIT COST ENTRY'
00650                              TO VALIDATION-ERROR-MSG
00651                GO TO ERROR-UNIT-COST-RTN.

00653          GO TO VALIDATE-LINE-COST.


00655      ERROR-UNIT-COST-RTN.
00656          SET ERROR-I UP BY 1.
00657          MOVE VALIDATION-ERROR-MESSAGE TO MAP2-ERRORS (ERROR-I).
00658          IF ERROR-I EQUAL TO 1
00659              MOVE -1 TO MAP2-UNIT-COST-L (MAP2-LINE-I)
00660          ELSE IF ERROR-I EQUAL TO 4
00661                  GO TO VALIDATE-EACH-LINE-EXIT.


00663      VALIDATE-LINE-COST.

00665          IF TWA-COST-MAP-L NOT EQUAL TO ZEROES
00666              IF   SCREEN-FUNCTION-IS-ADD
00667            OR SCREEN-FUNCTION-IS-CHANGE
00668            THEN IF   TWA-COST-MAP  NUMERIC
00669                AND TWA-COST-MAP =
00670                          TWA-UNIT-ORDER * TWA-UNIT-COST-ORDER
00671              THEN ADD TWA-COST-MAP  TO  TWA-TOTAL-COST
00672                    ADD 16         TO  TWA-LINE-DATA-CNT
00673              ELSE MOVE 'INVALID COST' TO VALIDATION-ERROR-MSG
00674                GO TO ERROR-LINE-COST-RTN
00675            ELSE MOVE 'INVALID COST ENTRY'
00676                              TO VALIDATION-ERROR-MSG
00677                GO TO ERROR-LINE-COST-RTN
00678          ELSE IF SCREEN-FUNCTION-IS-DELETE
00679              COMPUTE TWA-TOTAL-COST = TWA-TOTAL-COST
00680                    + TWA-UNIT-ORDER * TWA-UNIT-COST-ORDER
00681              ELSE IF    SCREEN-FUNCTION-IS-CHANGE
00682                  AND  (UNIT-WAS-ENTERED
00683                    OR UNIT-COST-WAS-ENTERED)
00684              THEN MOVE 'COST NOT ENTERED'
00685                              TO VALIDATION-ERROR-MSG
00686                GO TO ERROR-LINE-COST-RTN.
```

Fig. 20.6. (Continued)

18   ORCH01A   15.48.02   12/27/80

```
00688              GO TO VALIDATE-UNIT-PRICE.


00690       ERROR-LINE-COST-RTN.
00691              SET ERROR-I UP BY 1.
00692              MOVE VALIDATION-ERROR-MESSAGE TO MAP2-ERRORS (ERROR-I).
00693              IF ERROR-I EQUAL TO 1
00694                  MOVE -1 TO MAP2-COST-L (MAP2-LINE-I)
00695              ELSE IF ERROR-I EQUAL TO 4
00696                      GO TO VALIDATE-EACH-LINE-EXIT.


00698       VALIDATE-UNIT-PRICE.

00700              IF TWA-UNIT-PRICE-MAP-L NOT EQUAL TO ZEROES
00701                  IF    SCREEN-FUNCTION-IS-ADD
00702                  OR SCREEN-FUNCTION-IS-CHANGE
00703                  THEN IF TWA-UNIT-PRICE-MAP   NUMERIC
00704                          MOVE TWA-UNIT-PRICE-MAP
00705                                  TO TWA-UNIT-PRICE-ORDER
00706                          ADD 32 TO TWA-LINE-DATA-CNT
00707                          MOVE 'Y' TO TWA-UNIT-PRICE-SW
00708                      ELSE MOVE 'INVALID UNIT PRICE'
00709                                          TO  VALIDATION-ERROR-MSG
00710                          GO TO ERROR-UNIT-PRICE-RTN
00711                  ELSE MOVE 'INVALID UNIT PRICE ENTRY'
00712                                          TO  VALIDATION-ERROR-MSG
00713                      GO TO ERROR-UNIT-PRICE-RTN.


00715              GO TO VALIDATE-LINE-PRICE.


00717       ERROR-UNIT-PRICE-RTN.
00718              SET ERROR-I UP BY 1.
00719              MOVE VALIDATION-ERROR-MESSAGE TO MAP2-ERRORS (ERROR-I).
00720              IF ERROR-I EQUAL TO 1
00721                  MOVE -1 TO MAP2-UNIT-PRICE-L (MAP2-LINE-I)
00722              ELSE IF ERROR-I EQUAL TO 4
00723                      GO TO VALIDATE-EACH-LINE-EXIT.


00725       VALIDATE-LINE-PRICE.

00727              IF TWA-PRICE-MAP-L NOT EQUAL TO ZEROES
00728                  IF    SCREEN-FUNCTION-IS-ADD
00729                  OR SCREEN-FUNCTION-IS-CHANGE
00730                  THEN IF    TWA-PRICE-MAP   NUMERIC
00731                          AND TWA-PRICE-MAP =
00732                                  TWA-UNIT-ORDER * TWA-UNIT-PRICE-ORDER
00733                          THEN ADD TWA-PRICE-MAP   TO   TWA-TOTAL-PRICE
00734                              ADD 64           TO   TWA-LINE-DATA-CNT
00735                          ELSE MOVE 'INVALID PRICE' TO VALIDATION-ERROR-MSG
00736                              GO TO ERROR-LINE-PRICE-RTN
```

Fig. 20.6. (Continued)

19   ORCH01A   15.48.02   12/27/80

```
00737                         ELSE MOVE 'INVALID PRICE ENTRY' TO VALIDATION-ERROR-MSG
00738                              GO TO ERROR-LINE-PRICE-RTN
00739                    ELSE IF SCREEN-FUNCTION-IS-DELETE
00740                         COMPUTE TWA-TOTAL-PRICE = TWA-TOTAL-PRICE
00741                              + TWA-UNIT-ORDER * TWA-UNIT-PRICE-ORDER
00742                    ELSE IF     SCREEN-FUNCTION-IS-CHANGE
00743                         AND    (UNIT-WAS-ENTERED
00744                              OR UNIT-PRICE-WAS-ENTERED)
00745                         THEN MOVE 'PRICE NOT ENTERED'
00746                                        TO VALIDATION-ERROR-MSG
00747                              GO TO ERROR-LINE-PRICE-RTN.

00749              GO TO CHECK-FOR-DATA-COMPLETION.


00751         ERROR-LINE-PRICE-RTN.
00752              SET ERROR-I UP BY 1.
00753              MOVE VALIDATION-ERROR-MESSAGE TO MAP2-ERRORS (ERROR-I).
00754              IF ERROR-I EQUAL TO 1
00755                   MOVE -1 TO MAP2-PRICE-L (MAP2-LINE-I)
00756              ELSE IF ERROR-I EQUAL TO 4
00757                        GO TO VALIDATE-EACH-LINE-EXIT.


00759         CHECK-FOR-DATA-COMPLETION.

00761              IF SCREEN-FUNCTION-IS-ADD
00762                   IF TWA-LINE-DATA-CNT EQUAL TO (125 OR 127)
00763                        IF ERROR-I EQUAL TO ZEROES
00764                             MOVE TSA-CHANGE-DATE
00765                                       TO TWA-ITEM-DATE-ORDER
00766                             SET TSA-LINE-I   TO MAP2-LINE-I
00767                             MOVE TWA-LINE-ITEM-ORDER
00768                                       TO TSA-ORDER-LINE (TSA-LINE-I)
00769                             MOVE TWA-ITEM-FUNCTION-MAP
00770                                       TO TSA-LINE-FUNCTION (TSA-LINE-I)
00771                        ELSE NEXT SENTENCE
00772                   ELSE MOVE 'INCOMPLETE ADD' TO VALIDATION-ERROR-MSG
00773                        GO TO ERROR-INCOMPLETE-DATA-RTN
00774              ELSE IF SCREEN-FUNCTION-IS-CHANGE
00775                   IF TWA-LINE-DATA-CNT EQUAL TO ZEROES
00776                        MOVE 'NO CHANGE DATA' TO VALIDATION-ERROR-MSG
00777                        GO TO ERROR-INCOMPLETE-DATA-RTN
00778                   ELSE IF ERROR-I EQUAL TO ZEROES
00779                             MOVE TSA-CHANGE-DATE
00780                                       TO TWA-ITEM-DATE-ORDER
00781                             SET TSA-LINE-I TO MAP2-LINE-I
00782                             MOVE TWA-LINE-ITEM-ORDER
00783                                       TO TSA-ORDER-LINE (TSA-LINE-I)
00784                             MOVE TWA-ITEM-FUNCTION-MAP
00785                                       TO TSA-LINE-FUNCTION (TSA-LINE-I)
00786                        ELSE NEXT SENTENCE
00787              ELSE IF SCREEN-FUNCTION-IS-DELETE
```

Fig. 20.6. (Continued)

```
    20          ORCH01A          15.48.02          12/27/80

00788                              MOVE TWA-ITEM-FUNCTION-MAP
00789                                   TO TSA-LINE-FUNCTION (TSA-LINE-I

00791              GO TO VALIDATE-LINE-END.


00793         ERROR-INCOMPLETE-DATA-RTN.
00794              SET ERROR-I UP BY 1.
00795              MOVE VALIDATION-ERROR-MESSAGE TO MAP2-ERRORS (ERROR-I).
00796              IF ERROR-I EQUAL TO 1
00797                   MOVE -1 TO MAP2-ITEM-NUMBER-L (MAP2-LINE-I)
00798              ELSE IF ERROR-I EQUAL TO 4
00799                   GO TO VALIDATE-EACH-LINE-EXIT.


00801         VALIDATE-LINE-END.
00802              SET MAP2-LINE-I UP BY 1.
00803         VALIDATE-EACH-LINE-EXIT.   EXIT.


00805         CHECK-IF-ANY-DATA-ENTERED.

00807              IF ERROR-I EQUAL TO 4
00808                   GO TO DISPLAY-ERROR-SCREEN.

00810              IF  (TWA-FUNCTION-ADD-COUNT
00811               + TWA-FUNCTION-CHANGE-COUNT
00812               + TWA-FUNCTION-DELETE-COUNT) EQUAL TO ZEROES
00813              THEN SET ERROR-I UP BY 1
00814                   MOVE 'NO UPDATE ENTERED' TO MAP2-ERRORS (ERROR-I)
00815                   IF ERROR-I EQUAL TO 1
00816                        MOVE -1 TO MAP2-ITEM-FUNCTION-L (1)
00817                   ELSE IF ERROR-I EQUAL TO 4
00818                        GO TO CHECK-IF-ANY-DATA-ENTERED-EXIT
00819                   ELSE NEXT SENTENCE
00820              ELSE IF  (TSA-POM-NUMBER-OF-LINES
00821                   + TWA-FUNCTION-ADD-COUNT
00822                   - TWA-FUNCTION-DELETE-COUNT) EQUAL TO ZEROES
00823              THEN SET ERROR-I UP BY 1
00824                   MOVE 'NO LINE ITEM TO BE LEFT'
00825                                  TO MAP2-ERRORS (ERROR-I)
00826                   IF ERROR-I EQUAL TO 1
00827                        MOVE -1 TO MAP2-ITEM-FUNCTION-L (1)
00828                   ELSE IF ERROR-I EQUAL TO 4
00829                        GO TO CHECK-IF-ANY-DATA-ENTERED-EXIT.

00831              IF    MAP2-EDIT-TOTAL-COST NUMERIC
00832               AND MAP2-EDIT-TOTAL-COST = TWA-TOTAL-COST
00833              THEN NEXT SENTENCE
00834              ELSE SET ERROR-I UP BY 1
00835                   MOVE 'INCORRECT TOTAL COST'  TO  MAP2-ERRORS (ERROR-I)
00836                   IF ERROR-I EQUAL TO 1
00837                        MOVE -1                 TO  MAP2-EDIT-TOTAL-COST-L
```

Fig. 20.6. (Continued)

```
        21              ORCH01A            15.48.02        12/27/80

    00838                         ELSE IF ERROR-I EQUAL TO 4
    00839                              GO TO CHECK-IF-ANY-DATA-ENTERED-EXIT.

    00841                  IF     MAP2-EDIT-TOTAL-PRICE NUMERIC
    00842                  AND MAP2-EDIT-TOTAL-PRICE = TWA-TOTAL-PRICE
    00843                  THEN NEXT SENTENCE
    00844                  ELSE SET ERROR-I UP BY 1
    00845                       MOVE 'INCORRECT TOTAL PRICE' TO MAP2-ERRORS (ERROR-I)
    00846                       IF ERROR-I EQUAL TO 1
    00847                            MOVE -1                TO MAP2-EDIT-TOTAL-PRICE-L
    00848                       ELSE IF ERROR-I EQUAL TO 4
    00849                              GO TO CHECK-IF-ANY-DATA-ENTERED-EXIT.
    00850            CHECK-IF-ANY-DATA-ENTERED-EXIT.  EXIT.


    00852            CHECK-IF-THERE-ARE-ERRORS.

    00854                  IF ERROR-I NOT EQUAL TO ZEROES
    00855                       GO TO DISPLAY-ERROR-SCREEN.


    00857            NO-ERRORS-RTN.

    00859                  SET TSA-SCREEN-NUMBER-OF-LINES   TO  MAP2-LINE-I.

    00861                  IF MAP2-LINE-I GREATER THAN 9
    00862                       IF TWA-ITEM-FUNCTION-MAP-L NOT EQUAL TO ZEROES
    00863                            SUBTRACT 1 FROM TSA-SCREEN-NUMBER-OF-LINES
    00864                       ELSE SUBTRACT 2 FROM TSA-SCREEN-NUMBER-OF-LINES
    00865                  ELSE SUBTRACT 2 FROM TSA-SCREEN-NUMBER-OF-LINES.

    00867                  MOVE TSA-ORDER-NUMBER   TO   TWA-ORDER-RECORD-KEY.

    00869       *     EXEC CICS
    00870       *          HANDLE CONDITION
    00871       *               NOTOPEN (FILE-NOT-OPEN)
    00872       *               NOTFND  (RECORD-NOT-FOUND)
    00873       *     END-EXEC.
    00874             MOVE '                     ' TO DFHEIVO CALL 'DFHEI1' USING
    00875             DFHEIVO GO TO FILE-NOT-OPEN RECORD-NOT-FOUND DEPENDING ON
    00876             DFHEIGDI.
    00877
    00878


    00880       *     EXEC CICS
    00881       *          READ DATASET ('ORTEST')
    00882       *               SET     (POM-POINTER)
    00883       *               RIDFLD  (TWA-ORDER-RECORD-KEY)
    00884       *               UPDATE
    00885       *     END-EXEC.
    00886             MOVE 'ORTEST' TO DFHEIV3 MOVE '          ' TO DFHEIVO CALL 'D
    00887       -     'FHEI1' USING DFHEIVO DFHEIV3 POM-POINTER DFHEIV98
```

Fig. 20.6. (Continued)

```
00888                    TWA-ORDER-RECORD-KEY.
00889
00890
00891
00892                    MOVE 'N' TO TWA-DELETE-SWITCH.
00893                    SET TSA-LINE-I   TO 1.
00894                    SET ORDER-LINE-I   TO 1.
00895                    PERFORM REFORMAT-ORDER-RECORD
00896                        UNTIL TSA-LINE-I GREATER TSA-SCREEN-NUMBER-OF-LINES.
00897                    GO TO READJUST-ORDER-TOTALS.


00899             REFORMAT-ORDER-RECORD.
00900                 IF LINE-IS-UNCHANGED (TSA-LINE-I)
00901                     IF NO-DELETE-SO-FAR
00902                         SET TSA-LINE-I   UP  BY 1
00903                         SET ORDER-LINE-I  UP  BY 1
00904                     ELSE MOVE TSA-ORDER-LINE (TSA-LINE-I)
00905                                       TO ORDER-LINE-ITEM (ORDER-LINE-I)
00906                         SET TSA-LINE-I    UP  BY 1
00907                         SET ORDER-LINE-I  UP  BY 1
00908                 ELSE IF    LINE-IS-ADDED (TSA-LINE-I)
00909                     OR LINE-IS-CHANGED (TSA-LINE-I)
00910                     THEN MOVE TSA-ORDER-LINE (TSA-LINE-I)
00911                                       TO ORDER-LINE-ITEM (ORDER-LINE-I)
00912                         SET TSA-LINE-I    UP  BY 1
00913                         SET ORDER-LINE-I  UP  BY 1
00914                     ELSE SET TSA-LINE-I UP BY 1
00915                         MOVE 'Y' TO TWA-DELETE-SWITCH.


00917             READJUST-ORDER-TOTALS.
00918                 SET ORDER-LINE-COUNT TO  ORDER-LINE-I.
00919                 SUBTRACT 1 FROM ORDER-LINE-COUNT.
00920                 MOVE ZEROES          TO   ORDER-TOTAL-COST
00921                                           ORDER-TOTAL-PRICE.
00922                 SET ORDER-LINE-I TO 1.
00923                 PERFORM READJUST-ORDER-TOTALS2
00924                     UNTIL ORDER-LINE-I GREATER ORDER-LINE-COUNT.
00925                 GO TO REWRITE-ORDER-RECORD.


00927             READJUST-ORDER-TOTALS2.
00928                 COMPUTE ORDER-TOTAL-COST = ORDER-TOTAL-COST
00929                         + (ORDER-UNIT (ORDER-LINE-I)
00930                             * ORDER-UNIT-COST (ORDER-LINE-I)).
00931                 COMPUTE ORDER-TOTAL-PRICE = ORDER-TOTAL-PRICE
00932                         + (ORDER-UNIT (ORDER-LINE-I)
00933                             * ORDER-UNIT-PRICE (ORDER-LINE-I)).
00934                 SET ORDER-LINE-I UP BY 1.


00936             REWRITE-ORDER-RECORD.
```

Fig. 20.6. (Continued)

```
00937                    COMPUTE TWA-POM-LENGTH = 37 + ORDER-LINE-COUNT * 44.

00939        *     EXEC CICS
00940        *         REWRITE DATASET ('ORTEST')
00941        *                 LENGTH  (TWA-POM-LENGTH)
00942        *                 FROM    (ORDER-MASTER-RECORD)
00943        *     END-EXEC.
00944              MOVE 'ORTEST' TO DFHEIV3 MOVE '            ' TO DFHEIVO CALL 'D
00945        -    'FHEI1' USING DFHEIVO DFHEIV3 ORDER-MASTER-RECORD
00946              TWA-POM-LENGTH.
00947
00948
00949        *     EXEC CICS
00950        *         SEND MAP    ('ORCHMO1')
00951        *              MAPSET ('ORCHSO1')
00952        *              MAPONLY
00953        *              ERASE
00954        *     END-EXEC.
00955              MOVE 'ORCHMO1' TO DFHEIV1 MOVE 'ORCHSO1' TO DFHEIV2 MOVE '
00956        -    '          ' TO DFHEIVO CALL 'DFHEI1' USING DFHEIVO
00957              DFHEIV1 DFHEIV99 DFHEIV98 DFHEIV2.
00958
00959
00960
00961              MOVE  '1'  TO COMMAREA-PROCESS-SW.


00963        RETURN-AT-ORDER-VALIDATE.

00965        *     EXEC CICS
00966        *         RETURN TRANSID (EIBTRNID)
00967        *                COMMAREA (COMMUNICATION-AREA)
00968        *                LENGTH  (1)
00969        *     END-EXEC.
00970              MOVE 1 TO DFHEIV11 MOVE '          ' TO DFHEIVO CALL 'DFHEI1'
00971              USING DFHEIVO EIBTRNID COMMUNICATION-AREA DFHEIV11.
00972
00973
00974
00975        DISPLAY-ERROR-SCREEN.

00977        *     EXEC CICS
00978        *         SEND MAP    ('ORCHMO2')
00979        *              MAPSET ('ORCHSO2')
00980        *              FROM   (MAP2-AREA)
00981        *              DATAONLY
00982        *              CURSOR
00983        *     END-EXEC.
00984              MOVE 'ORCHMO2' TO DFHEIV1 MOVE 'ORCHSO2' TO DFHEIV2 MOVE -1
00985              TO DFHEIV11 MOVE '  J          ' TO DFHEIVO CALL 'DFHEI1'
00986              USING DFHEIVO DFHEIV1 MAP2-AREA DFHEIV98 DFHEIV2 DFHEIV99
00987              DFHEIV99 DFHEIV99 DFHEIV11.
00988
```

Fig. 20.6. (Continued)

```
    24          ORCH01A            15.48.02            12/27/80

00989
00990
00991                MOVE  '2'  TO  COMMAREA-PROCESS-SW.

00993                GO TO RETURN-AT-ORDER-VALIDATE.


00995          RECORD-NOT-FOUND.

00997                MOVE 'RECORD NOT FOUND' TO MAP2-ERRORS (1).
00998                MOVE -1        TO  MAP2-ORDER-NUMBER-L.
00999                GO TO DISPLAY-ERROR-SCREEN.
```

Fig. 20.6. (Continued)

```
    25        ORCH01A        15.48.02        12/27/80


01001          *******************************************************************
01002          *                                                                 *
01003           ORDER-VERIFICATION SECTION.
01004          *                                                                 *
01005          *******************************************************************


01007          *     EXEC CICS
01008          *         RECEIVE MAP    ('ORCHM01')
01009          *                 MAPSET ('ORCHS01')
01010          *                 SET    (MAP1-POINTER)
01011          *     END-EXEC.
01012                MOVE 'ORCHM01' TO DFHEIV1 MOVE 'ORCHS01' TO DFHEIV2 MOVE '
01013          -     '            ' TO DFHEIV0 CALL 'DFHEI1' USING DFHEIV0
01014                DFHEIV1 MAP1-POINTER DFHEIV98 DFHEIV2.

01016
01017                IF MAP1-ORDER-NUMBER NOT NUMERIC
01018                    GO TO INVALID-ORDER-NUMBER.

01020                MOVE MAP1-ORDER-NUMBER TO TWA-ORDER-RECORD-KEY.

01022          *     EXEC CICS
01023          *         HANDLE CONDITION
01024          *                 NOTOPEN (FILE-NOT-OPEN)
01025          *                 NOTFND  (RECORD-NOT-FOUND-VERIFY)
01026          *     END-EXEC.
01027                MOVE '                    ' TO DFHEIV0 CALL 'DFHEI1' USING
01028                DFHEIV0 GO TO FILE-NOT-OPEN RECORD-NOT-FOUND-VERIFY
01029                DEPENDING ON DFHEIGDI.
01030
01031
01032          *     EXEC CICS
01033          *         READ DATASET ('ORTEST')
01034          *              SET     (POM-POINTER)
01035          *              RIDFLD  (TWA-ORDER-RECORD-KEY)
01036          *     END-EXEC.
01037                MOVE 'ORTEST' TO DFHEIV3 MOVE '          ' TO DFHEIV0 CALL 'D
01038          -     'FHEI1' USING DFHEIV0 DFHEIV3 POM-POINTER DFHEIV98
01039                TWA-ORDER-RECORD-KEY.
01040
01041
01042           SECURE-DATA-MAP.

01044          *     EXEC CICS
01045          *         GETMAIN
01046          *             SET     (MAP2-POINTER)
01047          *             LENGTH  (1139)
01048          *             INITIMG (HEX-ZEROES)
01049          *     END-EXEC.
01050                MOVE 1139 TO DFHEIV11 MOVE '          ' TO DFHEIV0 CALL 'DFHE
01051          -     'I1' USING DFHEIV0 MAP2-POINTER DFHEIV11 HEX-ZEROES.
01052
```

Fig. 20.6. (Continued)

```
  26        ORCHO1A          15.48.02        12/27/80

01053
01054
01055
01056            MOVE ORDER-NUMBER          TO   MAP2-ORDER-NUMBER.
01057            MOVE ORDER-DEPARTMENT      TO   MAP2-DEPARTMENT.
01058            MOVE ORDER-DATE-MONTH      TO   MAP2-ORDER-DATE-MONTH.
01059            MOVE ORDER-DATE-DAY        TO   MAP2-ORDER-DATE-DAY.
01060            MOVE ORDER-DATE-YEAR       TO   MAP2-ORDER-DATE-YEAR.
01061            MOVE ORDER-DATE-ENTERED    TO   MAP2-ORDER-DATE-ENTERED.
01062            MOVE ORDER-TOTAL-COST      TO   MAP2-TOTAL-COST.
01063            MOVE ORDER-TOTAL-PRICE     TO   MAP2-TOTAL-PRICE.
01064            SET ORDER-LINE-I           TO   1.
01065            PERFORM LAYOUT-EACH-LINE
01066               UNTIL ORDER-LINE-I GREATER THAN ORDER-LINE-COUNT.
01067            GO TO DISPLAY-ORDER.


01069        LAYOUT-EACH-LINE.
01070            SET MAP2-LINE-I                         TO ORDER-LINE-I.
01071            MOVE ORDER-LINE-ITEM (ORDER-LINE-I) TO TWA-LINE-ITEM-ORDER.
01072            MOVE MAP2-LINE-ITEM (MAP2-LINE-I)   TO TWA-LINE-ITEM-MAP.
01073            MOVE TWA-ITEM-NUMBER-ORDER     TO  TWA-ITEM-NUMBER-MAP.
01074            MOVE TWA-ITEM-DESCRIPTION-ORDER TO TWA-ITEM-DESCRIPTION-MAP.
01075            MOVE TWA-ITEM-DATE-ORDER       TO  TWA-ITEM-DATE-MAP.
01076            MOVE TWA-UNIT-ORDER            TO  TWA-UNIT-MAP.
01077            MOVE TWA-UNIT-COST-ORDER       TO  TWA-UNIT-COST-MAP.
01078            COMPUTE TWA-COST-MAP = TWA-UNIT-ORDER * TWA-UNIT-COST-ORDER.
01079            MOVE TWA-UNIT-PRICE-ORDER      TO  TWA-UNIT-PRICE-MAP.
01080            COMPUTE TWA-PRICE-MAP =
01081                    TWA-UNIT-ORDER * TWA-UNIT-PRICE-ORDER.
01082            MOVE TWA-LINE-ITEM-MAP    TO  MAP2-LINE-ITEM (MAP2-LINE-I).
01083            SET ORDER-LINE-I UP BY 1.


01085        DISPLAY-ORDER.

01087      *     EXEC CICS
01088      *         SEND MAP    ('ORCHMO2')
01089      *              MAPSET ('ORCHSO2')
01090      *              FROM   (MAP2-AREA)
01091      *              ERASE
01092      *     END-EXEC.
01093            MOVE 'ORCHMO2' TO DFHEIV1 MOVE 'ORCHSO2' TO DFHEIV2 MOVE '
01094      -      '      S    ' TO DFHEIVO CALL 'DFHEI1' USING DFHEIVO
01095            DFHEIV1 MAP2-AREA DFHEIV98 DFHEIV2.
01096
01097
01098
01099      *     EXEC CICS
01100      *         FREEMAIN DATA (MAP2-AREA)
01101      *     END-EXEC.
01102            MOVE '          ' TO DFHEIVO CALL 'DFHEI1' USING DFHEIVO
01103            MAP2-AREA.
```

Fig. 20.6. (Continued)

```
    27        ORCH01A        15.48.02        12/27/80

01104
01105                   MOVE EIBTRMID    TO   TSA-TERM-ID.
01106                   MOVE EIBTRNID    TO   TSA-TRANS-ID.

01108        *      EXEC CICS
01109        *         READQ TS
01110        *              QUEUE  (TSA-QUEUE-ID)
01111        *              SET    (TSA-POINTER)
01112        *              LENGTH (TSA-LENGTH)
01113        *              ITEM   (1)
01114        *      END-EXEC.
01115               MOVE 1 TO DFHEIV11 MOVE '  Y       ' TO DFHEIVO CALL 'DFHEI1'
01116               USING DFHEIVO TSA-QUEUE-ID TSA-POINTER TSA-LENGTH DFHEIV99
01117               DFHEIV11.
01118
01119
01120
01121
01122               MOVE TWA-ORDER-RECORD-KEY  TO   TSA-ORDER-NUMBER.
01123               MOVE ORDER-LINE-COUNT      TO   TSA-POM-NUMBER-OF-LINES.
01124               SET ORDER-LINE-I           TO   1.
01125               PERFORM MOVE-ORDER-LINES-TO-TSA
01126                   UNTIL ORDER-LINE-I GREATER THAN ORDER-LINE-COUNT.
01127               GO TO REWRITE-TSA-AT-VERIFY.


01129          MOVE-ORDER-LINES-TO-TSA.
01130               SET TSA-LINE-I         TO   ORDER-LINE-I.
01131               MOVE ORDER-LINE-ITEM (ORDER-LINE-I)
01132                                     TO   TSA-ORDER-LINE (TSA-LINE-I).
01133               MOVE SPACE            TO   TSA-LINE-FUNCTION (TSA-LINE-I).
01134               SET ORDER-LINE-I UP BY 1.


01136          REWRITE-TSA-AT-VERIFY.

01138               MOVE 1   TO   TSA-QUEUE-NO.

01140        *      EXEC CICS
01141        *         WRITEQ TS
01142        *              QUEUE  (TSA-QUEUE-ID)
01143        *              FROM   (TSA-AREA)
01144        *              LENGTH (TSA-LENGTH)
01145        *              ITEM   (TSA-QUEUE-NO)
01146        *              REWRITE
01147        *      END-EXEC.
01148               MOVE '  Y       ' TO DFHEIVO CALL 'DFHEI1' USING DFHEIVO
01149               TSA-QUEUE-ID TSA-AREA TSA-LENGTH DFHEIV99 TSA-QUEUE-NO.
01150
01151
01152
01153
01154
```

Fig. 20.6. (Continued)

28   ORCH01A   15.48.02   12/27/80

```
01155
01156              MOVE '2' TO  COMMAREA-PROCESS-SW.

01158          RETURN-AT-ORDER-VERIFY.
01159      *     EXEC CICS
01160      *        RETURN TRANSID  (EIBTRNID)
01161      *              COMMAREA (COMMUNICATION-AREA)
01162      *              LENGTH   (1)
01163      *     END-EXEC.
01164            MOVE 1 TO DFHEIV11 MOVE '          ' TO DFHEIVO CALL 'DFHEI1'
01165            USING DFHEIVO EIBTRNID COMMUNICATION-AREA DFHEIV11.
01166
01167
01168


01170          RECORD-NOT-FOUND-VERIFY.
01171            MOVE 'RECORD NOT FOUND' TO  MAP1-ERROR.
01172            GO TO SEND-MAP-VERIFY-ERROR.


01174          SEND-MAP-VERIFY-ERROR.

01176      *     EXEC CICS
01177      *        SEND MAP    ('ORCHM01')
01178      *             MAPSET ('ORCHS01')
01179      *             FROM   (MAP1-AREA)
01180      *             DATAONLY
01181      *     END-EXEC.
01182            MOVE 'ORCHM01' TO DFHEIV1 MOVE 'ORCHS01' TO DFHEIV2 MOVE '
01183      -     '               ' TO DFHEIVO CALL 'DFHEI1' USING DFHEIVO
01184            DFHEIV1 MAP1-AREA DFHEIV98 DFHEIV2.
01185
01186
01187
01188            MOVE '1' TO  COMMAREA-PROCESS-SW.
01189            GO TO RETURN-AT-ORDER-VERIFY.


01191          INVALID-ORDER-NUMBER.
01192            MOVE 'INVALID ORDER NUMBER' TO MAP1-ERROR.
01193            GO TO SEND-MAP-VERIFY-ERROR.
```

Fig. 20.6. (Continued)

```
01195          *****************************************************************
01196          *                                                               *
01197           BYPASS-INPUT SECTION.
01198          *                                                               *
01199          *****************************************************************

01201          *    EXEC CICS
01202          *       GETMAIN
01203          *           SET      (MAP1-POINTER)
01204          *           LENGTH   (57)
01205          *           INITIMG  (HEX-ZEROES)
01206          *    END-EXEC.
01207               MOVE 57 TO DFHEIV11 MOVE '            ' TO DFHEIVO CALL 'DFHEI1
01208          -    '' USING DFHEIVO MAP1-POINTER DFHEIV11 HEX-ZEROES.
01209
01210
01211
01212
01213               MOVE 'ORDER BYPASSED - CONTINUE' TO MAP1-ERROR.


01215          *    EXEC CICS
01216          *       SEND MAP   ('ORCHMO1')
01217          *           MAPSET  ('ORCHSO1')
01218          *           FROM    (MAP1-AREA)
01219          *           ERASE
01220          *    END-EXEC.
01221               MOVE 'ORCHMO1' TO DFHEIV1 MOVE 'ORCHSO1' TO DFHEIV2 MOVE '
01222          -    '        S   ' TO DFHEIVO CALL 'DFHEI1' USING DFHEIVO
01223               DFHEIV1 MAP1-AREA DFHEIV98 DFHEIV2.
01224
01225
01226
01227               MOVE '1' TO COMMAREA-PROCESS-SW.

01229          *    EXEC CICS
01230          *       RETURN TRANSID   (EIBTRNID)
01231          *           COMMAREA (COMMUNICATION-AREA)
01232          *           LENGTH   (1)
01233          *    END-EXEC.
01234               MOVE 1 TO DFHEIV11 MOVE '            ' TO DFHEIVO CALL 'DFHEI1'
01235               USING DFHEIVO EIBTRNID COMMUNICATION-AREA DFHEIV11.
01236
01237
01238
```

Fig. 20.6. (Continued)

```
   30        ORCH01A        15.48.02        12/27/80

01240       ***************************************************************
01241       *                                                             *
01242       INITIALIZATION SECTION.
01243       *                                                             *
01244       ***************************************************************

01246       *    EXEC CICS
01247       *        HANDLE CONDITION
01248       *            QIDERR (GET-STORAGE-FOR-TSA)
01249       *    END-EXEC.
01250            MOVE '                    ' TO DFHEIVO CALL 'DFHEI1' USING
01251            DFHEIVO GO TO GET-STORAGE-FOR-TSA DEPENDING ON DFHEIGDI.
01252
01253
01254            MOVE EIBTRMID    TO   TSA-TERM-ID.
01255            MOVE 'ORCH'      TO   TSA-TRANS-ID.

01257       *    EXEC CICS
01258       *        DELETEQ TS
01259       *            QUEUE (TSA-QUEUE-ID)
01260       *    END-EXEC.
01261            MOVE '             ' TO DFHEIVO CALL 'DFHEI1' USING DFHEIVO
01262            TSA-QUEUE-ID.

01263
01264
01265        GET-STORAGE-FOR-TSA.

01267       *    EXEC CICS
01268       *        GETMAIN
01269       *            SET    (TSA-POINTER)
01270       *            LENGTH (429)
01271       *    END-EXEC.
01272            MOVE 429 TO DFHEIV11 MOVE '        ' TO DFHEIVO CALL 'DFHEI
01273       -    '1' USING DFHEIVO TSA-POINTER DFHEIV11.
01274
01275
01276
01277            MOVE 429                        TO   TSA-LENGTH.

01279       *    EXEC CICS
01280       *        WRITEQ TS
01281       *            QUEUE  (TSA-QUEUE-ID)
01282       *            FROM   (TSA-AREA)
01283       *            LENGTH (TSA-LENGTH)
01284       *    END-EXEC.
01285            MOVE '           ' TO DFHEIVO CALL 'DFHEI1' USING DFHEIVO
01286            TSA-QUEUE-ID TSA-AREA TSA-LENGTH.
01287
01288
01289
01290
01291       *    EXEC CICS
01292       *        FREEMAIN DATA (TSA-AREA)
```

Fig. 20.6. (Continued)

```
01293      *      END-EXEC.
01294             MOVE '          ' TO DFHEIVO CALL 'DFHEI1' USING DFHEIVO
01295             TSA-AREA.
01296
01297      *      EXEC CICS
01298      *          GETMAIN
01299      *              SET     (MAP1-POINTER)
01300      *              LENGTH  (57)
01301      *              INITIMG (HEX-ZEROES)
01302      *      END-EXEC.
01303             MOVE 57 TO DFHEIV11 MOVE '          ' TO DFHEIVO CALL 'DFHEI1
01304      -      '' USING DFHEIVO MAP1-POINTER DFHEIV11 HEX-ZEROES.
01305
01306
01307
01308
01309             MOVE 'ENTER FIRST ORDER' TO MAP1-ERROR.

01311      *      EXEC CICS
01312      *          SEND MAP    ('ORCHM01')
01313      *              MAPSET  ('ORCHSC1')
01314      *              FROM    (MAP1-AREA)
01315      *              ERASE
01316      *      END-EXEC.
01317             MOVE 'ORCHM01' TO DFHEIV1 MOVE 'ORCHS01' TO DFHEIV2 MOVE '
01318      -      '      S     ' TO DFHEIVO CALL 'DFHEI1' USING DFHEIVO
01319             DFHEIV1 MAP1-AREA DFHEIV98 DFHEIV2.
01320
01321
01322
01323             MOVE '1' TO COMMAREA-PROCESS-SW.

01325      *      EXEC CICS
01326      *          RETURN TRANSID  ('ORCH')
01327      *              COMMAREA (COMMUNICATION-AREA)
01328      *              LENGTH   (1)
01329      *      END-EXEC.
01330             MOVE 'ORCH' TO DFHEIV5 MOVE 1 TO DFHEIV11 MOVE '
01331             TO DFHEIVO CALL 'DFHEI1' USING DFHEIVO DFHEIV5
01332             COMMUNICATION-AREA DFHEIV11.
01333
01334
```

Fig. 20.6. (Continued)

```
01336      ***********************************************************************
01337      *                                                                     *
01338      FINALIZATION SECTION.
01339      *                                                                     *
01340      ***********************************************************************

01342      PREPARE-TERMINATION-MESSAGE.
01343          MOVE JOB-NORMAL-END-MESSAGE TO TWA-OPERATOR-MESSAGE.


01345      JOB-TERMINATED.

01347      *    EXEC CICS
01348      *        SEND FROM   (TWA-OPERATOR-MESSAGE)
01349      *             LENGTH (31)
01350      *             ERASE
01351      *    END-EXEC.
01352           MOVE 31 TO DFHEIV11 MOVE '               ' TO DFHEIVO CALL '
01353      -   'DFHEI1' USING DFHEIVO DFHEIV99 DFHEIV98 TWA-OPERATOR-MESSAGE
01354           DFHEIV11.
01355
01356
01357      *    EXEC CICS
01358      *        HANDLE CONDITION
01359      *             QIDERR (END-OF-JOB)
01360      *    END-EXEC.
01361           MOVE '                   ' TO DFHEIVO CALL 'DFHEI1' USING
01362           DFHEIVO GO TO END-OF-JOB DEPENDING ON DFHEIGDI.
01363
01364
01365           MOVE EIBTRMID  TO  TSA-TERM-ID.
01366           MOVE EIBTRNID  TO  TSA-TRANS-ID.

01368      *    EXEC CICS
01369      *        DELETEQ TS
01370      *             QUEUE (TSA-QUEUE-ID)
01371      *    END-EXEC.
01372           MOVE '           ' TO DFHEIVO CALL 'DFHEI1' USING DFHEIVO
01373           TSA-QUEUE-ID.
01374
01375


01377      END-OF-JOB.

01379      *    EXEC CICS
01380      *        RETURN
01381      *    END-EXEC.
01382           MOVE '         ' TO DFHEIVO CALL 'DFHEI1' USING DFHEIVO.
01383
01384
```

Fig. 20.6. (Continued)

        33   ORCH01A   15.48.02   12/27/80

```
01386          ****************************************************************
01387          *                                                              *
01388          ABNORMAL-TERMINATION SECTION.
01389          *                                                              *
01390          ****************************************************************

01392          FILE-NOT-OPEN.

01394      *      EXEC CICS
01395      *          XCTL PROGRAM ('TEL20PEN')
01396      *      END-EXEC.
01397              MOVE 'TEL20PEN' TO DFHEIV3 MOVE '            ' TO DFHEIVO CALL
01398          'DFHEI1' USING DFHEIVO DFHEIV3.
01399
01400          MAPFAIL-ERROR.
01401              MOVE 'MAP FAILURE' TO MAJOR-ERROR-MSG.
01402              GO TO PREPARE-ABORT-MESSAGE.


01404          PROCESS-SWITCH-ERROR.
01405              MOVE 'PROCESS ERROR' TO MAJOR-ERROR-MSG.
01406              GO TO PREPARE-ABORT-MESSAGE.


01408          SIGN-ON-VIOLATION.
01409              MOVE 'SIGNON VIOLATION' TO MAJOR-ERROR-MSG.
01410              GO TO PREPARE-ABORT-MESSAGE.


01412          MAJOR-ERROR.
01413              MOVE  EIBFN      TO  OLD-EIBFN.
01414              MOVE  EIBRCODE   TO  OLD-EIBRCODE.

01416      *      EXEC CICS
01417      *          DUMP DUMPCODE ('ERRS')
01418      *      END-EXEC.
01419              MOVE 'ERRS' TO DFHEIV5 MOVE '          ' TO DFHEIVO CALL 'DFH
01420      -      'EI1' USING DFHEIVO DFHEIV5.
01421
01422              MOVE 'MAJOR ERROR' TO MAJOR-ERROR-MSG.
01423              GO TO PREPARE-ABORT-MESSAGE.


01425          PREPARE-ABORT-MESSAGE.
01426              MOVE JOB-ABORTED-MESSAGE TO TWA-OPERATOR-MESSAGE.
01427              GO TO JOB-TERMINATED.
```

Fig. 20.6. (Continued)

THE INITIALIZATION SECTION

1. Lines 1246–1251. HANDLE CONDITION command for the temporary storage queue to be deleted.

2. Lines 1257–1262. Delete the old temporary storage queue.*

3. Lines 1267–1273. GETMAIN command to secure main storage for the new temporary storage record to be created.

4. Lines 1279–1286. WRITEQ TS command to write the temporary storage record that will be used as a scratchpad.

5. Lines 1291–1295. FREEMAIN DATA command to release main storage for the temporary storage record secured through the GETMAIN command in lines 1267–1273.

6. Lines 1297–1304. GETMAIN command to secure main storage for the map to be displayed, which will include a program-generated message.

7. Lines 1311–1319. SEND MAP command to display the map. The "ENTER FIRST ORDER" message is included in the display.

8. Line 1323.   Set the communication area switch to 1.

9. Lines 1325–1332. RETURN command to terminate the task.

THE ORDER-VERIFICATION SECTION

1. Lines 1007–1014. RECEIVE MAP command to read the order number entered by the operator.

2. Lines 1022–1029. HANDLE CONDITION command for the order file.

3. Lines 1032–1039. READ DATASET command to read the file.

---

*This is a precautionary measure. See page 179.

   4. If the record is in the file:

      a. Lines 1044–1051. GETMAIN command for the map that will contain the data from the record just read.

      b. Lines 1056–1083. Move the data from the record into the map to be displayed.

      c. Lines 1087–1095. SEND MAP command to display the data from the record.

      d. Lines 1099–1103. FREEMAIN DATA command to release main storage secured for the map in the GETMAIN command in lines 1044–1051.

      e. Lines 1108–1117. READQ TS command to read the temporary storage record to be used as a scratchpad.

      f. Lines 1122–1134. Move the data from the record into the temporary storage record.

      g. Lines 1140–1149. WRITEQ TS command with the REWRITE option to rewrite the temporary storage record.

      h. Line 1156.   Set the communication area switch to 2.

      i. Lines 1158–1165. RETURN command to terminate the task.

   5. If the record is not in the file:

      a. Lines 1176–1184. SEND MAP command to display the "RECORD NOT FOUND" message.

      b. Line 1188.   Set the communication area switch to 1.

      c. Line 1189.   RETURN command to terminate the task.

THE ORDER-VALIDATION SECTION

1. Lines 443–450. RECEIVE MAP command to read the data entered by the operator.

2. Lines 456–465. READQ TS command to read the temporary storage record to be used as a scratchpad.

3. Lines 470–850. The editing of the data.

4. If there are no errors:
   a. Lines 869–876. HANDLE CONDITION command for the order file.
   b. Lines 880–888. READ DATASET command with the UPDATE option to make the record available for update.
   c. Lines 892–934. Move the changes to the order record.
   d. Lines 939–946. REWRITE DATASET command to update the record.
   e. Lines 949–957. SEND MAP command to display the next map required by the operator.
   f. Line 961.   Set the communication area switch to 1.
   g. Lines 965–971. RETURN command to terminate the task.

5. If there are errors:
   a. Lines 977–987. SEND MAP command to display the error messages.
   b. Line 991.   Set the communication area switch to 2.
   c. Line 993.   RETURN command to terminate the task.

THE BYPASS-INPUT SECTION

1. Lines 1201–1208. GETMAIN command to secure main storage for the map that will contain the message.

2. Lines 1215–1223. SEND MAP command to display the "ORDER BYPASSED – CONTINUE" message.

3. Line 1227.   Set the communication area switch to 1.

4. Lines 1229–1235. RETURN command to terminate the task.

THE FINALIZATION SECTION

1. Lines 1347–1354. Display the "JOB NORMALLY TERMINATED" message.

2. Lines 1357–1362. HANDLE CONDITION command for the temporary storage queue.

3. Lines 1368–1373. DELETEQ TS command to delete the temporary storage queue used as a scratchpad.

4. Lines 1379–1382. RETURN command to terminate the session.

THE ABNORMAL-TERMINATION SECTION

These are the routines used to abnormally terminate the session on errors and CICS/VS exceptional conditions not covered by a HANDLE CONDITION command.

EXAMPLE

The following are facsimiles of actual photographs taken of a CRT terminal during a session.

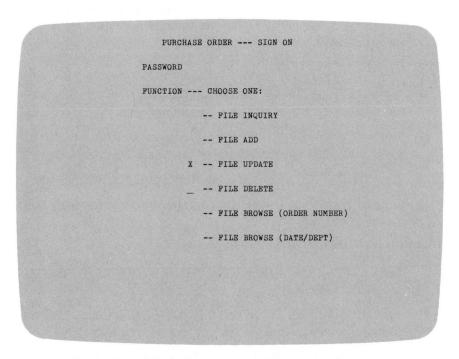

```
                    PURCHASE ORDER --- SIGN ON

         PASSWORD

         FUNCTION --- CHOOSE ONE:

                        -- FILE INQUIRY

                        -- FILE ADD

              X   -- FILE UPDATE

              _   -- FILE DELETE

                        -- FILE BROWSE (ORDER NUMBER)

                        -- FILE BROWSE (DATE/DEPT)
```

Fig. 20.7. The File Update application is selected by keying in an "X" on the File Update line and the corresponding password, then hitting the ENTER key.

```
        PURCHASE ORDER --- FILE UPDATE

             ORDER NUMBER: _



        ENTER FIRST ORDER
```

Fig. 20.8. The Sign On program executes which then transfers control to the File Update program. This displays the order number map.

```
            PURCHASE ORDER --- FILE UPDATE

               ORDER NUMBER: 5_




        ENTER FIRST ORDER
```

Fig. 20.9. The operator keys in the order number of the record to be updated, then hits the ENTER key.

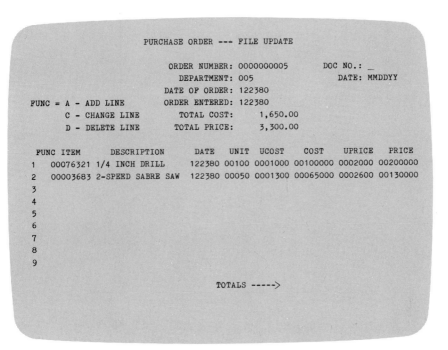

```
                    PURCHASE ORDER --- FILE UPDATE

                         ORDER NUMBER: 0000000005        DOC NO.: _
                         DEPARTMENT: 005                 DATE: MMDDYY
                         DATE OF ORDER: 122380
FUNC = A - ADD LINE      ORDER ENTERED: 122380
       C - CHANGE LINE      TOTAL COST:     1,650.00
       D - DELETE LINE      TOTAL PRICE:    3,300.00

 FUNC ITEM       DESCRIPTION       DATE   UNIT  UCOST    COST    UPRICE   PRICE
 1   00076321 1/4 INCH DRILL      122380 00100 0001000 00100000 0002000 00200000
 2   00003683 2-SPEED SABRE SAW   122380 00050 0001300 00065000 0002600 00130000
 3
 4
 5
 6
 7
 8
 9

                              TOTALS ----->
```

Fig. 20.10.   The program displays the record.

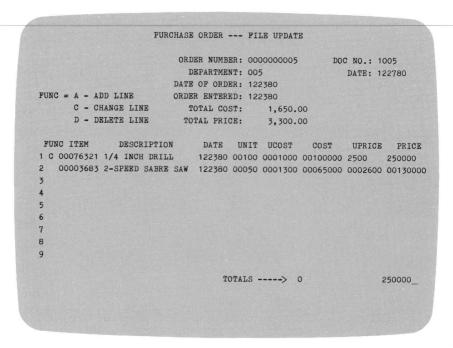

```
                    PURCHASE ORDER --- FILE UPDATE

                    ORDER NUMBER: 0000000005      DOC NO.: 1005
                    DEPARTMENT: 005                  DATE: 122780
                 DATE OF ORDER: 122380
FUNC = A - ADD LINE        ORDER ENTERED: 122380
       C - CHANGE LINE        TOTAL COST:    1,650.00
       D - DELETE LINE       TOTAL PRICE:    3,300.00

  FUNC ITEM        DESCRIPTION      DATE   UNIT  UCOST    COST   UPRICE   PRICE
1 C 00076321 1/4 INCH DRILL       122380 00100 0001000 00100000 2500    250000
2   00003683 2-SPEED SABRE SAW    122380 00050 0001300 00065000 0002600 00130000
3
4
5
6
7
8
9

                            TOTALS -----> 0                      250000_
```

Fig. 20.11. The operator keys in the changes to the record, then hits the ENTER key.

```
            PURCHASE ORDER --- FILE UPDATE

                ORDER NUMBER: _




            ORDER UPDATED - CONTINUE
```

Fig. 20.12. If there are no errors from Fig. 20.11, the order is updated. The "ORDER UPDATED – CONTINUE" message is then displayed to inform the operator. He may then continue with the next order.

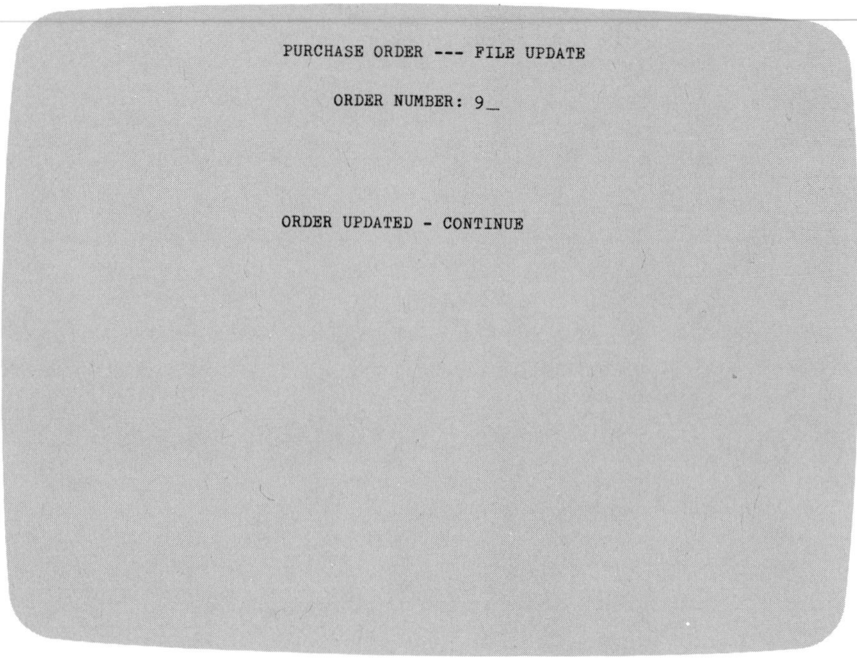

```
                    PURCHASE ORDER --- FILE UPDATE

                      ORDER NUMBER: 9_




               ORDER UPDATED - CONTINUE
```

Fig. 20.13. The operator keys in the order number of the next order to be updated, then hits the ENTER key.

```
                  PURCHASE ORDER --- FILE UPDATE

                     ORDER NUMBER: 0000000009      DOC NO.: _
                      DEPARTMENT: 003                DATE: MMDDYY
                    DATE OF ORDER: 122480
FUNC = A - ADD LINE     ORDER ENTERED: 122480
       C - CHANGE LINE     TOTAL COST:      890.00
       D - DELETE LINE    TOTAL PRICE:    1,700.00

  FUNC ITEM       DESCRIPTION       DATE   UNIT  UCOST    COST    UPRICE   PRICE
1  00093762 BLOCK PLANE          122780 00010 0000900 00009000 0001600 00016000
2  00001877 1 INCH CHISEL        122480 00050 0000300 00015000 0000500 00025000
3  00003663 26 IN. CROSSCUT SAW  122480 00100 0000600 00060000 0001200 00120000
4  00054976 FILE SET             122780 00010 0000500 00005000 0000900 00009000
5
6
7
8
9

                         TOTALS ----->
```

Fig. 20.14.   The program displays the record.

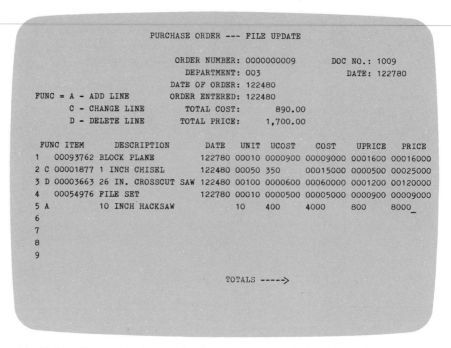

```
                      PURCHASE ORDER --- FILE UPDATE

                         ORDER NUMBER: 0000000009      DOC NO.: 1009
                          DEPARTMENT: 003                DATE: 122780
                       DATE OF ORDER: 122480
  FUNC = A - ADD LINE   ORDER ENTERED: 122480
         C - CHANGE LINE    TOTAL COST:        890.00
         D - DELETE LINE   TOTAL PRICE:      1,700.00

   FUNC ITEM      DESCRIPTION       DATE   UNIT  UCOST     COST    UPRICE   PRICE
   1    00093762 BLOCK PLANE       122780 00010 0000900 00009000 0001600 00016000
   2 C  00001877 1 INCH CHISEL     122480 00050 350      00015000 0000500 00025000
   3 D  00003663 26 IN. CROSSCUT SAW 122480 00100 0000600 00060000 0001200 00120000
   4    00054976 FILE SET          122780 00010 0000500 00005000 0000900 00009000
   5 A           10 INCH HACKSAW           10    400     4000     800     8000_
   6
   7
   8
   9


                              TOTALS ----->
```

Fig. 20.15.   The operator keys in the changes to the record, then hits the ENTER key.

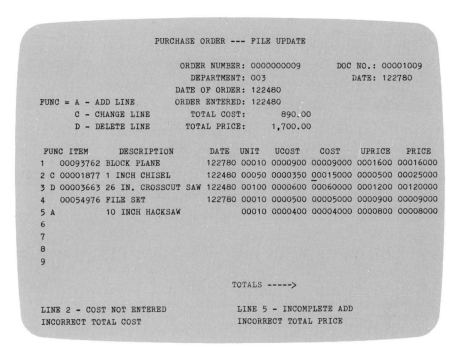

```
                    PURCHASE ORDER --- FILE UPDATE

                    ORDER NUMBER: 0000000009      DOC NO.: 00001009
                    DEPARTMENT: 003                  DATE: 122780
                 DATE OF ORDER: 122480
FUNC = A - ADD LINE   ORDER ENTERED: 122480
       C - CHANGE LINE    TOTAL COST:      890.00
       D - DELETE LINE    TOTAL PRICE:   1,700.00

 FUNC ITEM      DESCRIPTION      DATE  UNIT  UCOST    COST     UPRICE   PRICE
 1    00093762 BLOCK PLANE      122780 00010 0000900 00009000 0001600 00016000
 2 C  00001877 1 INCH CHISEL    122480 00050 0000350 00015000 0000500 00025000
 3 D  00003663 26 IN. CROSSCUT SAW 122480 00100 0000600 00060000 0001200 00120000
 4    00054976 FILE SET         122780 00010 0000500 00005000 0000900 00009000
 5 A           10 INCH HACKSAW         00010 0000400 00004000 0000800 00008000
 6
 7
 8
 9

                          TOTALS ----->

 LINE 2 - COST NOT ENTERED        LINE 5 - INCOMPLETE ADD
 INCORRECT TOTAL COST             INCORRECT TOTAL PRICE
```

Fig. 20.16.   Four errors are detected.   Note that the cursor is under the first error detected.

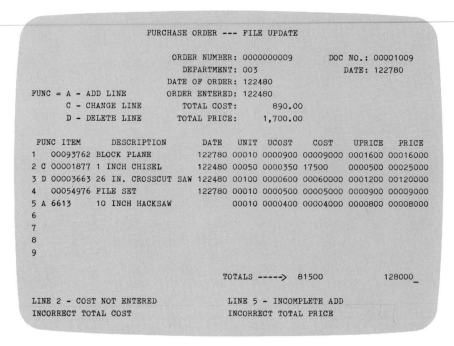

```
                    PURCHASE ORDER --- FILE UPDATE

                        ORDER NUMBER: 0000000009        DOC NO.: 00001009
                        DEPARTMENT: 003                   DATE: 122780
                        DATE OF ORDER: 122480
FUNC = A - ADD LINE     ORDER ENTERED: 122480
       C - CHANGE LINE     TOTAL COST:       890.00
       D - DELETE LINE     TOTAL PRICE:    1,700.00

  FUNC ITEM       DESCRIPTION      DATE   UNIT  UCOST    COST    UPRICE   PRICE
  1    00093762 BLOCK PLANE        122780 00010 0000900 00009000 0001600 00016000
  2 C  00001877 1 INCH CHISEL      122480 00050 0000350 17500    0000500 00025000
  3 D  00003663 26 IN. CROSSCUT SAW 122480 00100 0000600 00060000 0001200 00120000
  4    00054976 FILE SET           122780 00010 0000500 00005000 0000900 00009000
  5 A  6613      10 INCH HACKSAW           00010 0000400 00004000 0000800 00008000
  6
  7
  8
  9

                                  TOTALS ----->  81500              128000_

LINE 2 - COST NOT ENTERED              LINE 5 - INCOMPLETE ADD
INCORRECT TOTAL COST                   INCORRECT TOTAL PRICE
```

Fig. 20.17. The operator keys in the corrections, then hits the ENTER key.

```
PURCHASE ORDER --- FILE UPDATE

   ORDER NUMBER: _



ORDER UPDATED - CONTINUE
```

Fig. 20.18. If there are no more errors, the order is updated.

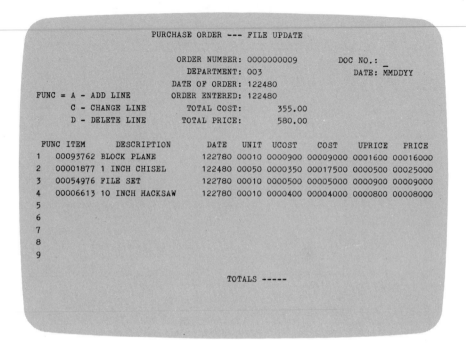

```
                    PURCHASE ORDER --- FILE UPDATE

                    ORDER NUMBER: 0000000009        DOC NO.: _
                    DEPARTMENT: 003                 DATE: MMDDYY
                    DATE OF ORDER: 122480
FUNC = A - ADD LINE     ORDER ENTERED: 122480
       C - CHANGE LINE     TOTAL COST:      355.00
       D - DELETE LINE     TOTAL PRICE:     580.00

FUNC ITEM      DESCRIPTION      DATE   UNIT  UCOST    COST    UPRICE   PRICE
 1   00093762 BLOCK PLANE      122780 00010 0000900 00009000 0001600 00016000
 2   00001877 1 INCH CHISEL    122480 00050 0000350 00017500 0000500 00025000
 3   00054976 FILE SET         122780 00010 0000500 00005000 0000900 00009000
 4   00006613 10 INCH HACKSAW  122780 00010 0000400 00004000 0000800 00008000
 5
 6
 7
 8
 9

                         TOTALS -----
```

Fig. 20.19.   The just-updated order is redisplayed. Note that the changes in Fig. 20.15 are reflected.

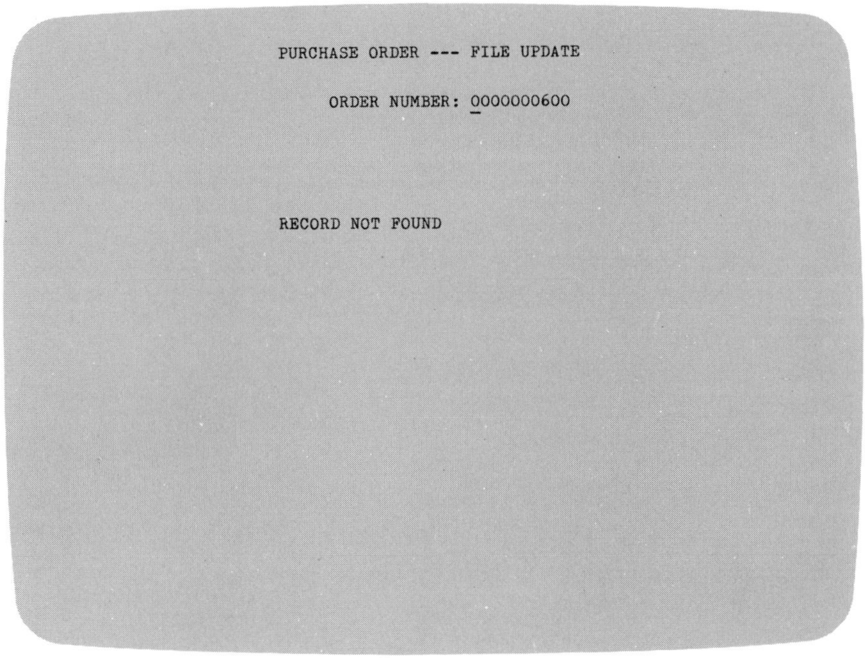

Fig. 20.20. If the record corresponding to the order number entered is not in the file, the "RECORD NOT FOUND" message is displayed.

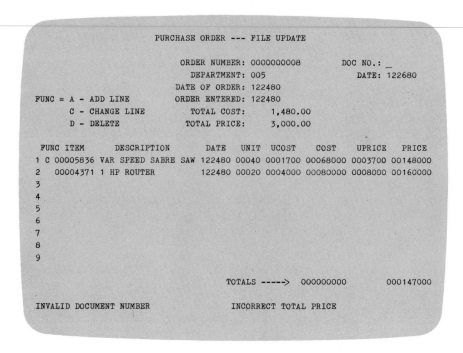

```
                    PURCHASE ORDER --- FILE UPDATE

                    ORDER NUMBER: 0000000008        DOC NO.: _
                    DEPARTMENT: 005                  DATE: 122680
                    DATE OF ORDER: 122480
FUNC = A - ADD LINE    ORDER ENTERED: 122480
       C - CHANGE LINE    TOTAL COST:    1,480.00
       D - DELETE         TOTAL PRICE:   3,000.00

  FUNC ITEM      DESCRIPTION      DATE   UNIT  UCOST    COST     UPRICE    PRICE
1 C 00005836 VAR SPEED SABRE SAW 122480 00040 0001700 00068000 0003700 00148000
2   00004371 1 HP ROUTER         122480 00020 0004000 00080000 0008000 00160000
3
4
5
6
7
8
9

                              TOTALS ----->  000000000        000147000

INVALID DOCUMENT NUMBER              INCORRECT TOTAL PRICE
```

Fig. 20.21. If the operator wishes to discontinue the processing of an order after it has been displayed, he hits any PA key.

```
            PURCHASE ORDER --- FILE UPDATE

                ORDER NUMBER: __



            ORDER BYPASSED - CONTINUE
```

Fig. 20.22. A fresh order map is then displayed, along with the message "ORDER BY-PASSED – CONTINUE". The operator may then continue with the next order.

21

The File Delete Program

INTRODUCTION

The File Delete program allows the operator to delete records from the order file according to the record key entered. The program executes when selected by the Sign-on program and will continue executing in the session until terminated by the operator. The flow of control to execute this program is shown in Figure 21.1.

PROGRAM SPECIFICATION

The File Delete program specifications are as follows:

1. Implement the program using the pseudoconversational mode of processing.

2. Use 'ORDL' as the transaction identifier. However, the session should not be started by using this identifier, but rather through an XCTL command from the Sign-on program.

3. If the session is started by using the transaction identifier, abort the session with the message "JOB ABORTED – SIGN-ON VIOLATION."

4. The record to be deleted is based on the order number.

5. If the order number entered is not numeric, display the message "INVALID ORDER NUMBER."

6. If the record is not in the file, display the message "RECORD NOT FOUND."

7. For (5) and (6), allow the operator to correct the order number.

8. If the record is in the file, delete it.

9. On any PA key, display the message "WRONG KEY USED"; allow the operator to continue with the session.

SCREEN LAYOUT

The screen layout to be used in the program is shown in Figure 21.2. All 9s are numeric fields and Xs are alphanumeric fields.

MAP PROGRAM

The map program corresponding to the screen layout is shown in Figure 21.3.

PROGRAM LISTING

The program listing for the File Delete program is given in Figure 21.4. The listing is that of the compiler and not the command-language translator, and thus the commands are already as translated.

THE MAIN-LINE SECTION

1. Lines 148–152. ADDRESS command for the TWA.
2. Lines 154–163. HANDLE AID command. The PA keys will result in the "WRONG KEY USED" error.
3. Lines 168–175. HANDLE CONDITION command.
4. Lines 178–183. The selection of sections.
5. Lines 185–186. If the program is executed at the start of the session by an operator-entered transaction identifier instead of through an XCTL command from the Sign-on program, a sign-on violation occurs. This is so if EIBCALEN is equal to zero.

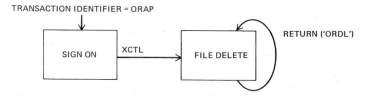

Fig. 21.1. File Delete Application.

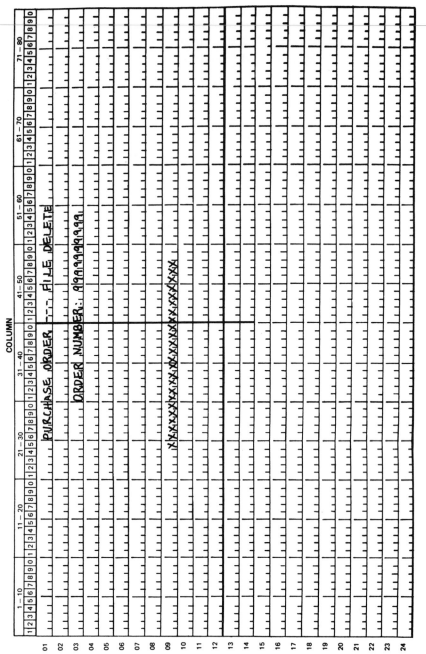

Fig. 21.2.   Screen Layout – File Delete.

```
STMT    SOURCE STATEMENT                              DOS/VS ASSEMBLER REL 34.0 14.14

   1              PRINT NOGEN
   2 ORDLSO1      DFHMSD TYPE=MAP,MODE=INOUT,CTRL=FREEKB,LANG=COBOL,TIOAPFX=YES
  12 ORDLMO1      DFHMDI SIZE=(24,80)
  40 DUMMY        DFHMDF POS=(01,01),LENGTH=01,ATTRB=(ASKIP,DRK,FSET),          X
                         INITIAL='1'
  52              DFHMDF POS=(01,25),LENGTH=30,ATTRB=(ASKIP,BRT),               X
                         INITIAL='PURCHASE ORDER --- FILE DELETE'
  64              DFHMDF POS=(03,30),LENGTH=13,ATTRB=ASKIP,                     X
                         INITIAL='ORDER NUMBER '
  76 ORDER        DFHMDF POS=(03,44),LENGTH=10,ATTRB=(NUM,BRT,IC)
  87              DFHMDF POS=(03,55),LENGTH=01,ATTRB=PROT
  98 ERROR        DFHMDF POS=(09,24),LENGTH=24,ATTRB=(ASKIP,BRT)
 109              DFHMSD TYPE=FINAL
 123              END
```

Fig. 21.3. Map Program — File Delete.

```
   1   IBM DOS VS COBOL


CBL SUPMAP,STXIT,NOTRUNC,CSYNTAX,SXREF,OPT,VERB,CLIST,BUF=19069
CBL NOOPT,LIB
00001           IDENTIFICATION DIVISION.

00003           PROGRAM-ID. ORDLO1A.


00005           ENVIRONMENT DIVISION.

00007           **********************************************************************
00008           *                                                                    *
00009           *    1. THIS PROGRAM DELETES RECORDS FROM THE PURCHASE  ORDER        *
00010           *       MASTER FILE.                                                 *
00011           *                                                                    *
00012           **********************************************************************
```

Fig. 21.4.   File Delete Program.

```
00014           DATA DIVISION.


00016           WORKING-STORAGE SECTION.


00018           01  COMMUNICATION-AREA.

00020               05  COMMAREA-PROCESS-SW     PIC X.


00022           01  AREA1.


00024               05  JOB-NORMAL-END-MESSAGE  PIC X(23) VALUE
00025                   'JOB NORMALLY TERMINATED'.

00027               05  JOB-ABORTED-MESSAGE.
00028                   10  FILLER              PIC X(15) VALUE 'JOB ABORTED --'.
00029                   10  MAJOR-ERROR-MSG     PIC X(16).


00031               05  HEXADECIMAL-ZEROES      PIC 9999 COMP VALUE ZEROES.


00033               05  FILLER REDEFINES HEXADECIMAL-ZEROES.
00034                   10  FILLER              PIC X.
00035                   10  HEX-ZEROES          PIC X.


00037               05  OLD-EIB-AREA.
00038                   10  FILLER              PIC X(7) VALUE 'OLD EIB'.
00039                   10  OLD-EIBFN           PIC XX.
00040                   10  OLD-EIBRCODE        PIC X(6).
```

Fig. 21.4.   (Continued)

3   ORDLO1A   13.02.04   08/02/80

```
00042          01  DFHEIVAR COPY DFHEIVAR.
00043 C        01  DFHEIVAR.
00044 C            02    DFHEIVO  PICTURE X(26).
00045 C            02    DFHEIV1  PICTURE X(8).
00046 C            02    DFHEIV2  PICTURE X(8).
00047 C            02    DFHEIV3  PICTURE X(8).
00048 C            02    DFHEIV4  PICTURE X(6).
00049 C            02    DFHEIV5  PICTURE X(4).
00050 C            02    DFHEIV6  PICTURE X(4).
00051 C            02    DFHEIV7  PICTURE X(2).
00052 C            02    DFHEIV8  PICTURE X(2).
00053 C            02    DFHEIV9  PICTURE X(1).
00054 C            02    DFHEIV10 PICTURE S9(7) USAGE COMPUTATIONAL-3.
00055 C            02    DFHEIV11 PICTURE S9(4) USAGE COMPUTATIONAL.
00056 C            02    DFHEIV12 PICTURE S9(4) USAGE COMPUTATIONAL.
00057 C            02    DFHEIV13 PICTURE S9(4) USAGE COMPUTATIONAL.
00058 C            02    DFHEIV14 PICTURE S9(4) USAGE COMPUTATIONAL.
00059 C            02    DFHEIV15 PICTURE S9(4) USAGE COMPUTATIONAL.
00060 C            02    DFHEIV16 PICTURE S9(9) USAGE COMPUTATIONAL.
00061 C            02    DFHEIV17 PICTURE X(4).
00062 C            02    DFHEIV18 PICTURE X(4).
00063 C            02    DFHEIV19 PICTURE X(4).
00064 C            02    DFHEIV97 PICTURE S9(7) USAGE COMPUTATIONAL-3 VALUE ZERO.
00065 C            02    DFHEIV98 PICTURE S9(4) USAGE COMPUTATIONAL VALUE ZERO.
00066 C            02    DFHEIV99 PICTURE X(1)  VALUE SPACE.
00067          LINKAGE SECTION.
00068          01  DFHEIBLK COPY DFHEIBLK.
00069 C        *     EIBLK EXEC INTERFACE BLOCK
00070 C        01    DFHEIBLK.
00071 C        *        EIBTIME     TIME IN OHHMMSS FORMAT
00072 C                 02 EIBTIME  PICTURE S9(7) USAGE COMPUTATIONAL-3.
00073 C        *        EIBDATE     DATE IN OOYYDDD FORMAT
00074 C                 02 EIBDATE  PICTURE S9(7) USAGE COMPUTATIONAL-3.
00075 C        *        EIBTRNID    TRANSACTION IDENTIFIER
00076 C                 02 EIBTRNID PICTURE X(4).
00077 C        *        EIBTASKN    TASK NUMBER
00078 C                 02 EIBTASKN PICTURE S9(7) USAGE COMPUTATIONAL-3.
00079 C        *        EIBTRMID    TERMINAL IDENTIFIER
00080 C                 02 EIBTRMID PICTURE X(4).
00081 C        *        DFHEIGDI    RESERVED
00082 C                 02 DFHEIGDI PICTURE S9(4) USAGE COMPUTATIONAL.
00083 C        *        EIBCPOSN    CURSOR POSITION
00084 C                 02 EIBCPOSN PICTURE S9(4) USAGE COMPUTATIONAL.
00085 C        *        EIBCALEN    COMMAREA LENGTH
00086 C                 02 EIBCALEN PICTURE S9(4) USAGE COMPUTATIONAL.
00087 C        *        EIBAID      ATTENTION IDENTIFIER
00088 C                 02 EIBAID   PICTURE X(1).
00089 C        *        EIBFN       FUNCTION CODE
00090 C                 02 EIBFN    PICTURE X(2).
00091 C        *        EIBRCODE    RESPONSE CODE
00092 C                 02 EIBRCODE PICTURE X(6).
00093 C        *        EIBDS       DATASET NAME
00094 C                 02 EIBDS    PICTURE X(8).
```

Fig. 21.4. (Continued)

```
        4          ORDLO1A          13.02.04          08/02/80

00095 C      *         EIBREQID     REQUEST IDENTIFIER
00096 C                02 EIBREQID  PICTURE X(8).
00097            01  DFHCOMMAREA.

00099                05  PROCESS-SW                PIC X.
00100                    88  INITIAL-ENTRY-TIME              VALUE '0'.
00101                    88  DELETE-TIME                     VALUE '1'.


00103            01  LINKAGE-POINTERS.

00105                05  FILLER                    PIC S9(8) COMP.
00106                05  MAP1-POINTER              PIC S9(8) COMP.
00107                05  TWA-POINTER               PIC S9(8) COMP.



        5          ORDLO1A          13.02.04          08/02/80

00109        *********************************************************************
00110        *                                                                  *
00111        *                DELETE MAP DESCRIPTION                            *
00112        *                                                                  *
00113        *********************************************************************


00115            01  MAP1-AREA.
00116                05  FILLER                    PIC X(12).
00117                05  MAP1-DUMMY-L              PIC S9999 COMP.
00118                05  MAP1-DUMMY-A              PIC X.
00119                05  MAP1-DUMMY                PIC X.
00120                05  MAP1-ORDER-NUMBER-L       PIC S9999 COMP.
00121                05  MAP1-ORDER-NUMBER-A       PIC X.
00122                05  MAP1-ORDER-NUMBER         PIC X(10).
00123                05  MAP1-ERROR-L              PIC S9999 COMP.
00124                05  MAP1-ERROR-A              PIC X.
00125                05  MAP1-ERROR                PIC X(24).



        6          ORDLO1A          13.02.04          08/02/80

00127        *********************************************************************
00128        *                                                                  *
00129        *                TRANSACTION WORK AREA                             *
00130        *                                                                  *
00131        *********************************************************************


00133            01  TWA-AREA.

00135                05  TWA-OPERATOR-MESSAGE     PIC X(31).

00137                05  TWA-ORDER-RECORD-KEY     PIC X(10).
```

Fig. 21.4. (Continued)

```
    7        ORDLO1A          13.02.04         08/02/80


00139              PROCEDURE DIVISION USING DFHEIBLK DFHCOMMAREA.
00140                  CALL 'DFHEI1'.


00142              *************************************************************
00143              *                                                           *
00144              MAIN-LINE SECTION.
00145              *                                                           *
00146              *************************************************************


00148         *        EXEC CICS
00149         *            ADDRESS TWA (TWA-POINTER)
00150         *        END-EXEC.
00151                  MOVE 'BB  DC               ' TO DFHEIVO CALL 'DFHEI1' USING
00152                  DFHEIVO TWA-POINTER.
00153
00154         *        EXEC CICS
00155         *            HANDLE AID
00156         *                CLEAR (FINALIZATION)
00157         *                PA1 (WRONG-KEY-USED)
00158         *                PA2 (WRONG-KEY-USED)
00159         *                PA3 (WRONG-KEY-USED)
00160         *        END-EXEC.
00161                  MOVE 'BFO DEDFC            ' TO DFHEIVO CALL 'DFHEI1' USING
00162                  DFHEIVO GO TO FINALIZATION WRONG-KEY-USED WRONG-KEY-USED
00163                  WRONG-KEY-USED DEPENDING ON DFHEIGDI.
00164
00165
00166
00167
00168         *        EXEC CICS
00169         *            HANDLE CONDITION
00170         *                MAPFAIL (MAPFAIL-ERROR)
00171         *                ERROR   (MAJOR-ERROR)
00172         *        END-EXEC.
00173                  MOVE 'BD  DUA              ' TO DFHEIVO CALL 'DFHEI1' USING
00174                  DFHEIVO GO TO MAPFAIL-ERROR MAJOR-ERROR DEPENDING ON
00175                  DFHEIGDI.
00176
00177
00178                  IF EIBCALEN NOT EQUAL TO ZEROES
00179                      IF DELETE-TIME
00180                          GO TO DELETE-THE-RECORD
00181                      ELSE IF INITIAL-ENTRY-TIME
00182                          GO TO INITIALIZATION
00183                      ELSE GO TO PROCESS-SWITCH-ERROR.

00185                  IF EIBCALEN EQUAL TO ZEROES
00186                      GO TO SIGN-ON-VIOLATION.
```

Fig. 21.4. (Continued)

8   ORDLO1A   13-02-04   08/02/80

```
00188          ****************************************************************
00189          *                                                              *
00190           DELETE-THE-RECORD SECTION.
00191          *                                                              *
00192          ****************************************************************

00194          *     EXEC CICS
00195          *         HANDLE CONDITION
00196          *             NOTOPEN (FILE-NOT-OPEN)
00197          *             NOTFND  (RECORD-NOT-FOUND)
00198          *     END-EXEC.
00199                MOVE 'BD   DL(              ' TO DFHEIVO CALL 'DFHEI1' USING
00200                DFHEIVO GO TO FILE-NOT-OPEN RECORD-NOT-FOUND DEPENDING ON
00201                DFHEIGDI.
00202
00203
00204          *     EXEC CICS
00205          *         RECEIVE MAP    ('ORDLMO1')
00206          *                 MAPSET ('ORDLSO1')
00207          *                 SET    (MAP1-POINTER)
00208          *     END-EXEC.
00209                MOVE 'ORDLMO1' TO DFHEIV1 MOVE 'ORDLSO1' TO DFHEIV2 MOVE 'QB
00210          -     '& DA   EI  -' TO DFHEIVO CALL 'DFHEI1' USING DFHEIVO
00211                DFHEIV1 MAP1-POINTER DFHEIV98 DFHEIV2.
00212
00213
00214                IF MAP1-ORDER-NUMBER NOT NUMERIC
00215                    GO TO INVALID-ORDER-RTN.

00217                MOVE MAP1-ORDER-NUMBER TO TWA-ORDER-RECORD-KEY.

00219          *     EXEC CICS
00220          *         DELETE DATASET ('ORTEST')
00221          *                RIDFLD  (TWA-ORDER-RECORD-KEY)
00222          *     END-EXEC.
00223                MOVE 'ORTEST' TO DFHEIV3 MOVE 'FH& D  A ' TO DFHEIVO CALL 'D
00224          -     'FHEI1' USING DFHEIVO DFHEIV3 DFHEIV99 DFHEIV98
00225                TWA-ORDER-RECORD-KEY.
00226
00227                MOVE 'ORDER DELETED - CONTINUE' TO MAP1-ERROR.

00229          *     EXEC CICS
00230          *         SEND MAP    ('ORDLMO1')
00231          *              MAPSET ('ORDLSO1')
00232          *              FROM   (MAP1-AREA)
00233          *              DATAONLY
00234          *     END-EXEC.
00235                MOVE 'ORDLMO1' TO DFHEIV1 MOVE 'ORDLSO1' TO DFHEIV2 MOVE 'QD
00236          -     '& D   E-D  -' TO DFHEIVO CALL 'DFHEI1' USING DFHEIVO
00237                DFHEIV1 MAP1-AREA DFHEIV98 DFHEIV2.
00238
00239
```

Fig. 21.4. (Continued)

```
00240
00241        RETURN-FOR-NEXT-ORDER.

00243           MOVE '1' TO COMMAREA-PROCESS-SW.

00245    *      EXEC CICS
00246    *          RETURN TRANSID  (EIBTRNID)
00247    *                  COMMAREA (COMMUNICATION-AREA)
00248    *                  LENGTH   (1)
00249    *      END-EXEC.
00250           MOVE 1 TO DFHEIV11 MOVE '+H- D  & ' TO DFHEIVO CALL 'DFHEI1'
00251           USING DFHEIVO EIBTRNID COMMUNICATION-AREA DFHEIV11.
00252
00253
00254


00256        RECORD-NOT-FOUND.
00257           MOVE 'RECORD NOT FOUND' TO MAP1-ERROR.
00258           GO TO DISPLAY-INVALID-ORDER-MESSAGE.


00260        DISPLAY-INVALID-ORDER-MESSAGE.

00262    *      EXEC CICS
00263    *          SEND MAP    ('ORDLM01')
00264    *               MAPSET ('ORDLS01')
00265    *               FROM   (MAP1-AREA)
00266    *               DATAONLY
00267    *      END-EXEC.
00268           MOVE 'ORDLM01' TO DFHEIV1 MOVE 'ORDLS01' TO DFHEIV2 MOVE 'QD
00269    -      '& D    E-D  -' TO DFHEIVO CALL 'DFHEI1' USING DFHEIVO
00270           DFHEIV1 MAP1-AREA DFHEIV98 DFHEIV2.
00271
00272
00273
00274           GO TO RETURN-FOR-NEXT-ORDER.


00276        INVALID-ORDER-RTN.

00278           MOVE 'INVALID ORDER NUMBER' TO MAP1-ERROR.
00279           GO TO DISPLAY-INVALID-ORDER-MESSAGE.
```

Fig. 21.4. (Continued)

```
  10          ORDL01A          13.02.04          08/02/80

00281           *********************************************************************
00282           *                                                                   *
00283            WRONG-KEY-USED SECTION.
00284           *                                                                   *
00285           *********************************************************************

00287           *     EXEC CICS
00288           *         GETMAIN
00289           *             SET     (MAP1-POINTER)
00290           *             LENGTH  (56)
00291           *             INITIMG (HEX-ZEROES)
00292           *     END-EXEC.
00293               MOVE 56 TO DFHEIV11 MOVE 'aB- D  a ' TO DFHEIVO CALL 'DFHEI1
00294           -   '' USING DFHEIVO MAP1-POINTER DFHEIV11 HEX-ZEROES.
00295
00296
00297
00298
00299               MOVE 'WRONG KEY USED' TO MAP1-ERROR.

00301           *     EXEC CICS
00302           *         SEND MAP    ('ORDLM01')
00303           *             MAPSET ('ORDLS01')
00304           *             FROM   (MAP1-AREA)
00305           *             DATAONLY
00306           *     END-EXEC.
00307               MOVE 'ORDLM01' TO DFHEIV1 MOVE 'ORDLS01' TO DFHEIV2 MOVE 'QD
00308           -   '& D   E-D -' TO DFHEIVO CALL 'DFHEI1' USING DFHEIVO
00309               DFHEIV1 MAP1-AREA DFHEIV98 DFHEIV2.
00310
00311
00312
00313               GO TO RETURN-FOR-NEXT-ORDER.
```

Fig. 21.4.   (Continued)

```
   11        ORDL01A        13.02.04       08/02/80

00315        *************************************************************
00316        *                                                          *
00317        INITIALIZATION SECTION.
00318        *                                                          *
00319        *************************************************************

00321        *    EXEC CICS
00322        *        SEND MAP     ('ORDLM01')
00323        *                MAPSET ('ORDLS01')
00324        *                MAPONLY
00325        *                ERASE
00326        *    END-EXEC.
00327             MOVE 'ORDLM01' TO DFHEIV1 MOVE 'ORDLS01' TO DFHEIV2 MOVE 'QD
00328        -    '& D    ESD -' TO DFHEIVO CALL 'DFHEI1' USING DFHEIVO
00329             DFHEIV1 DFHEIV99 DFHEIV98 DFHEIV2.
00330
00331
00332
00333             MOVE '1' TO COMMAREA-PROCESS-SW.

00335        *    EXEC CICS
00336        *        RETURN TRANSID ('ORDL')
00337        *                COMMAREA (COMMUNICATION-AREA)
00338        *                LENGTH    (1)
00339        *    END-EXEC.
00340             MOVE 'ORDL' TO DFHEIV5 MOVE 1 TO DFHEIV11 MOVE '+H- D   & '
00341             TO DFHEIVO CALL 'DFHEI1' USING DFHEIVO DFHEIV5
00342             COMMUNICATION-AREA DFHEIV11.
00343
00344
```

Fig. 21.4. (Continued)

```
    12          ORDLO1A          13.02.04          08/02/80

00346          ****************************************************************
00347          *                                                              *
00348          FINALIZATION SECTION.
00349          *                                                              *
00350          ****************************************************************

00352             PREPARE-TERMINATION-MESSAGE.
00353                 MOVE JOB-NORMAL-END-MESSAGE TO TWA-OPERATOR-MESSAGE.

00355             JOB-TERMINATED.
00356          *      EXEC CICS
00357          *          SEND FROM   (TWA-OPERATOR-MESSAGE)
00358          *               LENGTH (31)
00359          *               ERASE
00360          *      END-EXEC.
00361              MOVE 31 TO DFHEIV11 MOVE 'DDO D    A      ' TO DFHEIVO CALL '
00362          -   'DFHEI1' USING DFHEIVO DFHEIV99 DFHEIV98 TWA-OPERATOR-MESSAGE
00363              DFHEIV11.
00364
00365

00367             END-OF-JOB.
00368          *      EXEC CICS
00369          *          RETURN
00370          *      END-EXEC.
00371              MOVE '+H  D  & ' TO DFHEIVO CALL 'DFHEI1' USING DFHEIVO.
00372
00373
```

Fig. 21.4.   (Continued)

13   OR DLOlA   13.02.04   08/02/80

```
00375         *****************************************************************
00376         *                                                              *
00377          ABNORMAL-TERMINATION SECTION.
00378         *                                                              *
00379         *****************************************************************


00381          FILE-NOT-OPEN.

00383         *    EXEC CICS
00384         *       XCTL PROGRAM ('TEL2OPEN')
00385         *    END-EXEC.
03386              MOVE 'TEL2OPEN' TO DFHEIV3 MOVE '+D  D  B ' TO DFHEIVO CALL
00387              'DFHEI1' USING DFHEIVO DFHEIV3.

00388
00389          MAPFAIL-ERROR.
00390              MOVE 'MAP FAILURE' TO MAJOR-ERROR-MSG.
00391              GO TO PREPARE-ABORT-MESSAGE.


00393          PROCESS-SWITCH-ERROR.
00394              MOVE 'PROCESS ERROR' TO MAJOR-ERROR-MSG.
00395              GO TO PREPARE-ABORT-MESSAGE.


00397          SIGN-ON-VIOLATION.
00398              MOVE 'SIGNON VIOLATION' TO MAJOR-ERROR-MSG.
00399              GO TO PREPARE-ABORT-MESSAGE.


00401          MAJOR-ERROR.
00402              MOVE  EIBFN      TO   OLD-EIBFN.
00403              MOVE  EIBRCODE   TO   OLD-EIBRCODE.

00405         *    EXEC CICS
00406         *       DUMP DUMPCODE ('ERRS')
00407         *    END-EXEC.
00408              MOVE 'ERRS' TO DFHEIV5 MOVE '*B  D  = ' TO DFHEIVO CALL 'DFH
00409         -    'EI1' USING DFHEIVO DFHEIV5.
00410
00411              MOVE 'MAJOR ERROR' TO MAJOR-ERROR-MSG.
00412              GO TO PREPARE-ABORT-MESSAGE.


00414          PREPARE-ABORT-MESSAGE.
03415              MOVE JOB-ABORTED-MESSAGE TO TWA-OPERATOR-MESSAGE.
00416              GO TO JOB-TERMINATED.
```

Fig. 21.4.   (Continued)

THE INITIALIZATION SECTION

1. Lines 321–329. Display the delete map.

2. Line 333.   Set the communication area switch to 1.

3. Lines 335–342. Terminate the task.

THE DELETE-THE-RECORD SECTION

1. Lines 194–201. HANDLE CONDITION command for the order file.

2. Lines 204–211. Read the map that contains the order number entered by the operator.

3. Lines 214–225. Delete the record using the order number entered.

4. If the record is found:
   a. Line 227.   Lay out the "ORDER DELETED – CONTINUE" message in the area secured by CICS/VS for the symbolic description map.
   b. Lines 229–237. Display the message.
   c. Line 243.   Set the communication area switch to 1.
   d. Lines 245–251. Terminate the task.

5. If the record is not found:
   a. Line 257.   Lay out the "RECORD NOT FOUND" message in the area secured by CICS/VS for the symbolic description map.
   b. Lines 260–270. Display the message.
   c. Line 243.   Set the communication area switch to 1.
   d. Lines 245–251. Terminate the task.

THE WRONG-KEY-USED SECTION

1. Lines 287–294. GETMAIN command to secure main storage for the map that will contain the error message. This is because the PA keys do not allow CICS/VS to secure main storage for the symbolic description map through a RECEIVE MAP command.

2. Line 299.   Move the "WRONG KEY USED" message into the area secured.

3. Lines 301–309. Display the error message.

4. Line 313.   Set the communication area switch to 1 and terminate the task. This GO TO should be of no concern because this section will rarely be executed.

THE FINALIZATION SECTION

1. Lines 352–363. Display the "JOB NORMALLY TERMI-NATED" message.

2. Lines 367–371. Terminate the session.

THE ABNORMAL-TERMINATION SECTION

These are the routines used to abnormally terminate the session on errors and CICS/VS command exceptional conditions not covered by a HANDLE CONDITION command.

EXAMPLE

The following are facsimiles of actual photographs taken of a CRT terminal during a session.

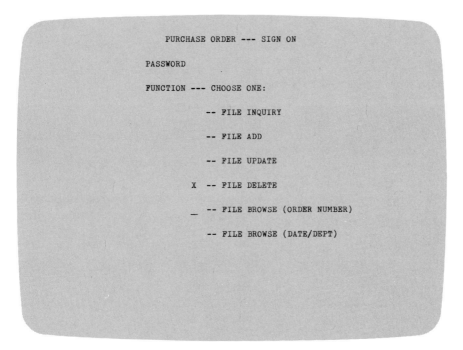

```
          PURCHASE ORDER --- SIGN ON

    PASSWORD

    FUNCTION --- CHOOSE ONE:

                -- FILE INQUIRY

                -- FILE ADD

                -- FILE UPDATE

        X   -- FILE DELETE

        _   -- FILE BROWSE (ORDER NUMBER)

                -- FILE BROWSE (DATE/DEPT)
```

Fig. 21.5. The File Delete application is selected by keying in an "X" on the File Delete line and the corresponding password, then hitting the ENTER key.

Fig. 21.6.   The Sign On program executes which then transfers control to the File Delete program. This displays the File Delete map.

Fig. 21.7. The operator keys in the order number of the record to be deleted, then hits the ENTER key.

```
            PURCHASE ORDER --- FILE DELETE

            ORDER NUMBER: 0000000200



      ORDER DELETED - CONTINUE
```

Fig. 21.8. The program deletes the record. The "ORDER DELETED – CONTINUE" message is then displayed to inform the operator. He may then continue with the next order.

```
        PURCHASE ORDER --- FILE DELETE

          ORDER NUMBER: 0000000200



      RECORD NOT FOUND
```

Fig. 21.9. If the record to be deleted is not in the file (as for example the previously deleted record), the "RECORD NOT FOUND" message is displayed.

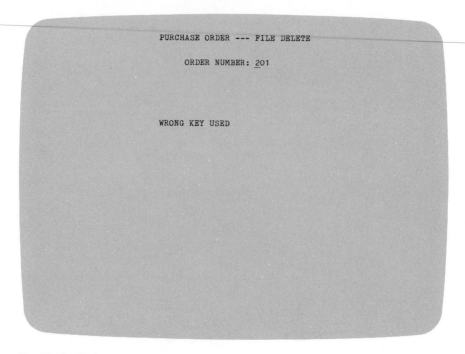

Fig. 21.10. If the operator keys in an order number but hits one of the PA keys instead of the ENTER key, the "WRONG KEY USED" message is displayed.

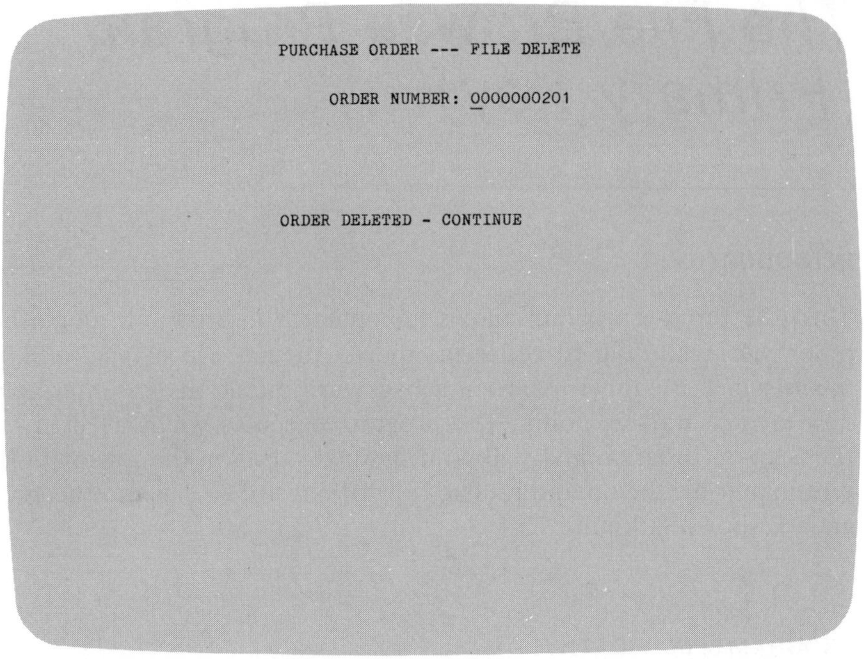

```
        PURCHASE ORDER --- FILE DELETE

           ORDER NUMBER: 0000000201




        ORDER DELETED - CONTINUE
```

Fig. 21.11. If the operator then hits the ENTER key, the session continues. The record selected in Fig. 21.10 is now deleted.

22

The File Browse Program (Primary Key)

INTRODUCTION

This File Browse program allows the operator to browse through the order file according to order number sequence. He may also skip records in both the forward and backward directions by entering a new browse starting point. The program executes when selected by the Sign-on program and will continue executing in the session until terminated by the operator. The flow of control to execute this program is shown in Figure 22.1.

PROGRAM SPECIFICATION

The File Browse program (primary key) specifications are as follows:

1. Implement the program using the conversational mode of processing.

2. Use 'ORBR' as the transaction identifier. However, the session should be started not by this identifier, but rather through an XCTL command from the Sign-on program.

3. If the session is started by using the transaction identifier, abort the session with the message "JOB ABORTED — SIGNON VIOLATION."

4. The browse starting point is the order number entered by the operator; if the record is not in the file, the record next in ascending sequence is used; if the order number is higher than the last record in the file, the last record is used.

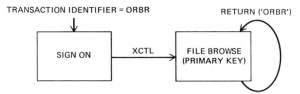

Fig. 22.1. File Browse Application (Primary Key).

5. On the PF1 key, display the record next in ascending sequence.

6. On the PF2 key, display the record next in descending sequence.

7. The operator may restart the browse at some other point by entering a new order number.

8. On any PA key, display the message "WRONG KEY USED"; allow the operator to continue on with the session.

9. In this example, display only one record per page.

SCREEN LAYOUT

The screen layout to be used in the program is shown in Figure 22.2. All 9s are numeric fields and Xs are alphanumeric fields.

MAP PROGRAM

The map program corresponding to the screen layout is shown in Figure 22.3.

PROGRAM LISTING

The program listing for the File Browse program (primary key) is shown in Figure 22.4. The listing is that of the compiler and not the command-language translator, and thus the commands are already as translated.

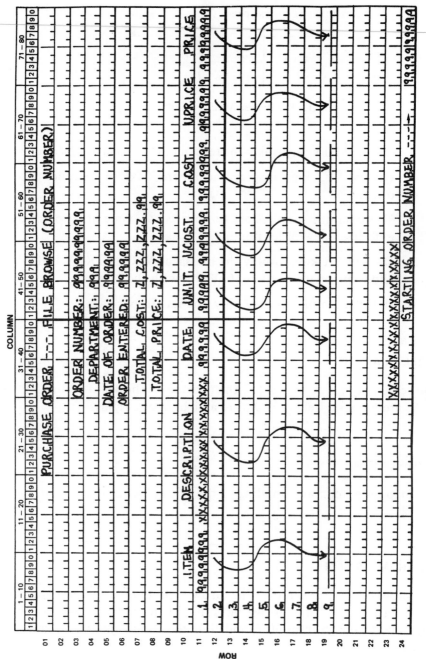

Fig. 22.2. Screen Layout – File Browse (Primary Key).

```
STMT    SOURCE STATEMENT                        DOS/VS ASSEMBLER REL 34.0 14.07

   1                 PRINT NOGEN
   2 ORBRSO1         DFHMSD TYPE=MAP,MODE=INOUT,CTRL=FREEKB,LANG=COBOL,TIOAPFX=YES
  12 ORBRMO1         DFHMDI SIZE=(24,80)
  40 DUMMY           DFHMDF POS=(01,01),LENGTH=01,ATTRB=(ASKIP,DRK,FSET),          X
                       INITIAL='1'
  52                 DFHMDF POS=(01,20),LENGTH=45,ATTRB=(ASKIP,BRT),               X
                       INITIAL='PURCHASE ORDER --- FILE BROWSE (ORDER NUMBER)'
  64                 DFHMDF POS=(03,30),LENGTH=13,ATTRB=ASKIP,                     X
                       INITIAL='ORDER NUMBER '
  76 ORDER           DFHMDF POS=(03,44),LENGTH=10,ATTRB=(ASKIP,BRT)
  87                 DFHMDF POS=(04,32),LENGTH=11,ATTRB=ASKIP,INITIAL='DEPARTMENT '
  99 DEPT            DFHMDF POS=(04,44),LENGTH=03,ATTRB=(ASKIP,BRT)
 110                 DFHMDF POS=(05,29),LENGTH=14,ATTRB=ASKIP,                     X
                       INITIAL='DATE OF ORDER '
 122 DATEOR          DFHMDF POS=(05,44),LENGTH=06,ATTRB=(ASKIP,BRT)
 133                 DFHMDF POS=(06,29),LENGTH=14,ATTRB=ASKIP,                     X
                       INITIAL='ORDER ENTERED '
 145 DATEENT         DFHMDF POS=(06,44),LENGTH=06,ATTRB=(ASKIP,BRT)
 156                 DFHMDF POS=(07,32),LENGTH=11,ATTRB=ASKIP,INITIAL='TOTAL COST '
 168 TOTCOST         DFHMDF POS=(07,44),LENGTH=12,ATTRB=(ASKIP,BRT),              X
                       PICOUT='Z,ZZZ,ZZZ.99'
 179                 DFHMDF POS=(08,31),LENGTH=12,ATTRB=ASKIP,                     X
                       INITIAL='TOTAL PRICE '
 191 TOTPRCE         DFHMDF POS=(08,44),LENGTH=12,ATTRB=(ASKIP,BRT),              X
                       PICOUT='Z,ZZZ,ZZZ.99'
 202                 DFHMDF POS=(10,07),LENGTH=04,ATTRB=ASKIP,INITIAL='ITEM'
 214                 DFHMDF POS=(10,17),LENGTH=11,ATTRB=ASKIP,INITIAL='DESCRIPTION'
 226                 DFHMDF POS=(10,35),LENGTH=04,ATTRB=ASKIP,INITIAL='DATE'
 238                 DFHMDF POS=(10,42),LENGTH=04,ATTRB=ASKIP,INITIAL='UNIT'
 250                 DFHMDF POS=(10,48),LENGTH=05,ATTRB=ASKIP,INITIAL='UCOST'
 262                 DFHMDF POS=(10,57),LENGTH=04,ATTRB=ASKIP,INITIAL='COST'
 274                 DFHMDF POS=(10,65),LENGTH=06,ATTRB=ASKIP,INITIAL='UPRICE'
 286                 DFHMDF POS=(10,74),LENGTH=05,ATTRB=ASKIP,INITIAL='PRICE'
 298 LINE1           DFHMDF POS=(11,03),LENGTH=01,ATTRB=ASKIP
 309 ITEM1           DFHMDF POS=(11,05),LENGTH=08,ATTRB=(ASKIP,BRT),              X
                       PICIN='99999999',PICOUT='99999999'
 320 DESC1           DFHMDF POS=(11,14),LENGTH=19,ATTRB=(ASKIP,BRT)
 331 LNDATE1         DFHMDF POS=(11,34),LENGTH=06,ATTRB=(ASKIP,BRT)
 342 UNIT1           DFHMDF POS=(11,41),LENGTH=05,ATTRB=(ASKIP,BRT),              X
                       PICIN='99999',PICOUT='99999'
 353 UCOST1          DFHMDF POS=(11,47),LENGTH=07,ATTRB=(ASKIP,BRT),              X
                       PICIN='9999999',PICOUT='9999999'
 364 COST1           DFHMDF POS=(11,55),LENGTH=08,ATTRB=(ASKIP,BRT),              X
                       PICIN='99999999',PICOUT='99999999'
 375 UPRICE1         DFHMDF POS=(11,64),LENGTH=07,ATTRB=(ASKIP,BRT),              X
                       PICIN='9999999',PICOUT='9999999'
 386 PRICE1          DFHMDF POS=(11,72),LENGTH=08,ATTRB=(ASKIP,BRT),              X
                       PICIN='99999999',PICOUT='99999999'
 397 LINE2           DFHMDF POS=(12,03),LENGTH=01,ATTRB=ASKIP
 408 ITEM2           DFHMDF POS=(12,05),LENGTH=08,ATTRB=(ASKIP,BRT),              X
                       PICIN='99999999',PICOUT='99999999'
```

Fig. 22.3. Map Program — File Browse (Primary Key).

```
STMT     SOURCE STATEMENT                              DOS/VS ASSEMBLER REL 34.0 14.07

419 DESC2     DFHMDF POS=(12,14),LENGTH=19,ATTRB=(ASKIP,BRT)
430 LNDATE2   DFHMDF POS=(12,34),LENGTH=06,ATTRB=(ASKIP,BRT)
441 UNIT2     DFHMDF POS=(12,41),LENGTH=05,ATTRB=(ASKIP,BRT),              X
                 PICIN='99999',PICOUT='99999'
452 UCOST2    DFHMDF POS=(12,47),LENGTH=07,ATTRB=(ASKIP,BRT),              X
                 PICIN='9999999',PICOUT='9999999'
463 COST2     DFHMDF POS=(12,55),LENGTH=08,ATTRB=(ASKIP,BRT),              X
                 PICIN='99999999',PICOUT='99999999'
474 UPRICE2   DFHMDF POS=(12,64),LENGTH=07,ATTRB=(ASKIP,BRT),             X
                 PICIN='9999999',PICOUT='9999999'
485 PRICE2    DFHMDF POS=(12,72),LENGTH=08,ATTRB=(ASKIP,BRT),             X
                 PICIN='99999999',PICOUT='99999999'
496 LINE3     DFHMDF POS=(13,03),LENGTH=01,ATTRB=ASKIP
507 ITEM3     DFHMDF POS=(13,05),LENGTH=08,ATTRB=(ASKIP,BRT),             X
                 PICIN='99999999',PICOUT='99999999'
518 DESC3     DFHMDF POS=(13,14),LENGTH=19,ATTRB=(ASKIP,BRT)
529 LNDATE3   DFHMDF POS=(13,34),LENGTH=06,ATTRB=(ASKIP,BRT)
540 UNIT3     DFHMDF POS=(13,41),LENGTH=05,ATTRB=(ASKIP,BRT),             X
                 PICIN='99999',PICOUT='99999'
551 UCOST3    DFHMDF POS=(13,47),LENGTH=07,ATTRB=(ASKIP,BRT),             X
                 PICIN='9999999',PICOUT='9999999'
562 COST3     DFHMDF POS=(13,55),LENGTH=08,ATTRB=(ASKIP,BRT),             X
                 PICIN='99999999',PICOUT='99999999'
573 UPRICE3   DFHMDF POS=(13,64),LENGTH=07,ATTRB=(ASKIP,BRT),            X
                 PICIN='9999999',PICOUT='9999999'
584 PRICE3    DFHMDF POS=(13,72),LENGTH=08,ATTRB=(ASKIP,BRT),            X
                 PICIN='99999999',PICOUT='99999999'
595 LINE4     DFHMDF POS=(14,03),LENGTH=01,ATTRB=ASKIP
606 ITEM4     DFHMDF POS=(14,05),LENGTH=08,ATTRB=(ASKIP,BRT),            X
                 PICIN='99999999',PICOUT='99999999'
617 DESC4     DFHMDF POS=(14,14),LENGTH=19,ATTRB=(ASKIP,BRT)
628 LNDATE4   DFHMDF POS=(14,34),LENGTH=06,ATTRB=(ASKIP,BRT)
639 UNIT4     DFHMDF POS=(14,41),LENGTH=05,ATTRB=(ASKIP,BRT),            X
                 PICIN='99999',PICOUT='99999'
650 UCOST4    DFHMDF POS=(14,47),LENGTH=07,ATTRB=(ASKIP,BRT),            X
                 PICIN='9999999',PICOUT='9999999'
661 COST4     DFHMDF POS=(14,55),LENGTH=08,ATTRB=(ASKIP,BRT),            X
                 PICIN='99999999',PICOUT='99999999'
672 UPRICE4   DFHMDF POS=(14,64),LENGTH=07,ATTRB=(ASKIP,BRT),           X
                 PICIN='9999999',PICOUT='9999999'
683 PRICE4    DFHMDF POS=(14,72),LENGTH=08,ATTRB=(ASKIP,BRT),           X
                 PICIN='99999999',PICOUT='99999999'
694 LINE5     DFHMDF POS=(15,03),LENGTH=01,ATTRB=ASKIP
705 ITEM5     DFHMDF POS=(15,05),LENGTH=08,ATTRB=(ASKIP,BRT),           X
                 PICIN='99999999',PICOUT='99999999'
716 DESC5     DFHMDF POS=(15,14),LENGTH=19,ATTRB=(ASKIP,BRT)
727 LNDATE5   DFHMDF POS=(15,34),LENGTH=06,ATTRB=(ASKIP,BRT)
738 UNIT5     DFHMDF POS=(15,41),LENGTH=05,ATTRB=(ASKIP,BRT),           X
                 PICIN='99999',PICOUT='99999'
749 UCOST5    DFHMDF POS=(15,47),LENGTH=07,ATTRB=(ASKIP,BRT),           X
                 PICIN='9999999',PICOUT='9999999'
```

Fig. 22.3.   (Continued)

```
STMT     SOURCE STATEMENT                              DOS/VS ASSEMBLER REL 34.0 14.07

 760 COST5     DFHMDF  POS=(15,55),LENGTH=08,ATTRB=(ASKIP,BRT),          X
                       PICIN='99999999',PICOUT='99999999'
 771 UPRICE5   DFHMDF  POS=(15,64),LENGTH=07,ATTRB=(ASKIP,BRT),          X
                       PICIN='9999999',PICOUT='9999999'
 782 PRICE5    DFHMDF  POS=(15,72),LENGTH=08,ATTRB=(ASKIP,BRT),          X
                       PICIN='99999999',PICOUT='99999999'
 793 LINE6     DFHMDF  POS=(16,03),LENGTH=01,ATTRB=ASKIP
 804 ITEM6     DFHMDF  POS=(16,05),LENGTH=08,ATTRB=(ASKIP,BRT),          X
                       PICIN='99999999',PICOUT='99999999'
 815 DESC6     DFHMDF  POS=(16,14),LENGTH=19,ATTRB=(ASKIP,BRT)
 826 LNDATE6   DFHMDF  POS=(16,34),LENGTH=06,ATTRB=(ASKIP,BRT)
 837 UNIT6     DFHMDF  POS=(16,41),LENGTH=05,ATTRB=(ASKIP,BRT),          X
                       PICIN='99999',PICOUT='99999'
 848 UCOST6    DFHMDF  POS=(16,47),LENGTH=07,ATTRB=(ASKIP,BRT),          X
                       PICIN='9999999',PICOUT='9999999'
 859 COST6     DFHMDF  POS=(16,55),LENGTH=08,ATTRB=(ASKIP,BRT),          X
                       PICIN='99999999',PICOUT='99999999'
 870 UPRICE6   DFHMDF  POS=(16,64),LENGTH=07,ATTRB=(ASKIP,BRT),          X
                       PICIN='9999999',PICOUT='9999999'
 881 PRICE6    DFHMDF  POS=(16,72),LENGTH=08,ATTRB=(ASKIP,BRT),          X
                       PICIN='99999999',PICOUT='99999999'
 892 LINE7     DFHMDF  POS=(17,03),LENGTH=01,ATTRB=ASKIP
 903 ITEM7     DFHMDF  POS=(17,05),LENGTH=08,ATTRB=(ASKIP,BRT),          X
                       PICIN='99999999',PICOUT='99999999'
 914 DESC7     DFHMDF  POS=(17,14),LENGTH=19,ATTRB=(ASKIP,BRT)
 925 LNDATE7   DFHMDF  POS=(17,34),LENGTH=06,ATTRB=(ASKIP,BRT)
 936 UNIT7     DFHMDF  POS=(17,41),LENGTH=05,ATTRB=(ASKIP,BRT),          X
                       PICIN='99999',PICOUT='99999'
 947 UCOST7    DFHMDF  POS=(17,47),LENGTH=07,ATTRB=(ASKIP,BRT),          X
                       PICIN='9999999',PICOUT='9999999'
 958 COST7     DFHMDF  POS=(17,55),LENGTH=08,ATTRB=(ASKIP,BRT),          X
                       PICIN='99999999',PICOUT='99999999'
 969 UPRICE7   DFHMDF  POS=(17,64),LENGTH=07,ATTRB=(ASKIP,BRT),          X
                       PICIN='9999999',PICOUT='9999999'
 980 PRICE7    DFHMDF  POS=(17,72),LENGTH=08,ATTRB=(ASKIP,BRT),          X
                       PICIN='99999999',PICOUT='99999999'
 991 LINE8     DFHMDF  POS=(18,03),LENGTH=01,ATTRB=ASKIP
1002 ITEM8     DFHMDF  POS=(18,05),LENGTH=08,ATTRB=(ASKIP,BRT),          X
                       PICIN='99999999',PICOUT='99999999'
1013 DESC8     DFHMDF  POS=(18,14),LENGTH=19,ATTRB=(ASKIP,BRT)
1024 LNDATE8   DFHMDF  POS=(18,34),LENGTH=06,ATTRB=(ASKIP,BRT)
1035 UNIT8     DFHMDF  POS=(18,41),LENGTH=05,ATTRB=(ASKIP,BRT),          X
                       PICIN='99999',PICOUT='99999'
1046 UCOST8    DFHMDF  POS=(18,47),LENGTH=07,ATTRB=(ASKIP,BRT),          X
                       PICIN='9999999',PICOUT='9999999'
1057 COST8     DFHMDF  POS=(18,55),LENGTH=08,ATTRB=(ASKIP,BRT),          X
                       PICIN='99999999',PICOUT='99999999'
1068 UPRICE8   DFHMDF  POS=(18,64),LENGTH=07,ATTRB=(ASKIP,BRT),          X
                       PICIN='9999999',PICOUT='9999999'
1079 PRICE8    DFHMDF  POS=(18,72),LENGTH=08,ATTRB=(ASKIP,BRT),          X
                       PICIN='99999999',PICOUT='99999999'
```

Fig. 22.3.   (Continued)

```
STMT    SOURCE STATEMENT                           DOS/VS ASSEMBLER REL 34.0 14.07 .

1090 LINE9      DFHMDF POS=(19,03),LENGTH=01,ATTRB=ASKIP
1101 ITEM9      DFHMDF POS=(19,05),LENGTH=08,ATTRB=(ASKIP,BRT),           X
                       PICIN='99999999',PICOUT='99999999'
1112 DESC9      DFHMDF POS=(19,14),LENGTH=19,ATTRB=(ASKIP,BRT)
1123 LNDATE9    DFHMDF POS=(19,34),LENGTH=06,ATTRB=(ASKIP,BRT)
1134 UNIT9      DFHMDF POS=(19,41),LENGTH=05,ATTRB=(ASKIP,BRT),           X
                       PICIN='99999',PICOUT='99999'
1145 UCOST9     DFHMDF POS=(19,47),LENGTH=07,ATTRB=(ASKIP,BRT),           X
                       PICIN='9999999',PICOUT='9999999'
1156 COST9      DFHMDF POS=(19,55),LENGTH=08,ATTRB=(ASKIP,BRT),           X
                       PICIN='99999999',PICOUT='99999999'
1167 UPRICE9    DFHMDF POS=(19,64),LENGTH=07,ATTRB=(ASKIP,BRT),           X
                       PICIN='9999999',PICOUT='9999999'
1178 PRICE9     DFHMDF POS=(19,72),LENGTH=08,ATTRB=(ASKIP,BRT),           X
                       PICIN='99999999',PICOUT='99999999'
1189 ERROR      DFHMDF POS=(23,30),LENGTH=20,ATTRB=(ASKIP,BRT)
1200            DFHMDF POS=(24,40),LENGTH=27,ATTRB=ASKIP,                 X
                       INITIAL='STARTING ORDER NUMBER ---- '
1212 STARTOR    DFHMDF POS=(24,70),LENGTH=10,ATTRB=(NUM,BRT,FSET,IC)
1223            DFHMSD TYPE=FINAL
1237            END
```

Fig. 22.3. (Continued)

```
     1   IBM DOS VS COBOL


CBL SUPMAP,STXIT,NOTRUNC,CSYNTAX,SXREF,OPT,VERB,CLIST,BUF=19069
CBL NOOPT,LIB
00001          IDENTIFICATION DIVISION.

00003          PROGRAM-ID. ORBRO1A.


00005          ENVIRONMENT DIVISION.


00007          ***********************************************************************
00008          *                                                                     *
00009          *    1. THIS PROGRAM ALLOWS A BROWSE (BY ORDER NUMBER) ON THE         *
00010          *       PURCHASE ORDER MASTER FILE.                                   *
00011          *                                                                     *
00012          *    2. THE OPERATOR MAY START AT THE BEGINNING OF THE FILE           *
00013          *       BY ENTERING ALL ZEROES ON THE STARTING ORDER NUMBER           *
00014          *       FIELD.                                                        *
00015          *                                                                     *
00016          *    3. SHE MAY ALSO START AT THE END OF THE FILE (FOR A              *
00017          *       BROWSE BACKWARDS) BY ENTERING ALL NINES.                      *
00018          *                                                                     *
00019          *    4. BROWSE FORWARD -   PF1 OR ENTER KEY.                          *
00020          *                                                                     *
00021          *    5. BROWSE BACKWARDS - PF2 KEY.                                   *
00022          *                                                                     *
00023          ***********************************************************************
```

Fig. 22.4. File Browse Program (Primary Key).

```
 2          ORBRO1A          12.59.17         08/02/80

00025          DATA DIVISION.

00027          WORKING-STORAGE SECTION.

00029          01  COMMUNICATION-AREA.

00031              05  COMMAREA-PROCESS-SW      PIC X.


00033          01  AREA1.

00035              05  JOB-NORMAL-END-MESSAGE  PIC X(23) VALUE
00036                  'JOB NORMALLY TERMINATED'.


00038              05  JOB-ABORTED-MESSAGE.
00039                  10  FILLER                PIC X(15) VALUE 'JOB ABORTED --'.
00040                  10  MAJOR-ERROR-MSG       PIC X(16).


00042              05  HEXADECIMAL-ZEROES        PIC 9999 COMP VALUE ZEROES.


00044              05  FILLER REDEFINES HEXADECIMAL-ZEROES.
00045                  10  FILLER                PIC X.
00046                  10  HEX-ZEROES            PIC X.


00048              05  OLD-EIB-AREA.
00049                  10  FILLER                PIC X(7) VALUE 'OLD EIB'.
00050                  10  OLD-EIBFN             PIC XX.
00051                  10  OLD-EIBRCODE          PIC X(6).


00053          01  DFHAID COPY DFHAID.
00054 C        01      DFHAID.
00055 C            02  DFHNULL   PIC  X   VALUE IS ' '.
00056 C            02  DFHENTER  PIC  X   VALUE IS QUOTE.
00057 C            02  DFHCLEAR  PIC  X   VALUE IS ' '.
00058 C            02  DFHPEN    PIC  X   VALUE IS '='.
00059 C            02  DFHOPID   PIC  X   VALUE IS 'W'.
00060 C            02  DFHPA1    PIC  X   VALUE IS '%'.
00061 C            02  DFHPA2    PIC  X   VALUE IS ' '.
00062 C            02  DFHPA3    PIC  X   VALUE IS ','.
00063 C            02  DFHPF1    PIC  X   VALUE IS '1'.
00064 C            02  DFHPF2    PIC  X   VALUE IS '2'.
00065 C            02  DFHPF3    PIC  X   VALUE IS '3'.
00066 C            02  DFHPF4    PIC  X   VALUE IS '4'.
```

Fig. 22.4. (Continued)

```
00067 C          02  DFHPF5   PIC  X  VALUE IS '5'.
00068 C          02  DFHPF6   PIC  X  VALUE IS '6'.
00069 C          02  DFHPF7   PIC  X  VALUE IS '7'.
00070 C          02  DFHPF8   PIC  X  VALUE IS '8'.
00071 C          02  DFHPF9   PIC  X  VALUE IS '9'.
00072 C          02  DFHPF10  PIC  X  VALUE IS ' '.
00073 C          02  DFHPF11  PIC  X  VALUE IS '#'.
00074 C          02  DFHPF12  PIC  X  VALUE IS 'a'.
00075 C          02  DFHPF13  PIC  X  VALUE IS 'A'.
00076 C          02  DFHPF14  PIC  X  VALUE IS 'B'.
00077 C          02  DFHPF15  PIC  X  VALUE IS 'C'.
00078 C          02  DFHPF16  PIC  X  VALUE IS 'D'.
00079 C          02  DFHPF17  PIC  X  VALUE IS 'E'.
00080 C          02  DFHPF18  PIC  X  VALUE IS 'F'.
00081 C          02  DFHPF19  PIC  X  VALUE IS 'G'.
00082 C          02  DFHPF20  PIC  X  VALUE IS 'H'.
00083 C          02  DFHPF21  PIC  X  VALUE IS 'I'.
00084 C          02  DFHPF22  PIC  X  VALUE IS ' '.
00085 C          02  DFHPF23  PIC  X  VALUE IS '.'.
00086 C          02  DFHPF24  PIC  X  VALUE IS 'a'.
```

Fig. 22.4.   (Continued)

```
00088            01  DFHEIVAR COPY DFHEIVAR.
00089 C          01  DFHEIVAR.
00090 C              02    DFHEIVO   PICTURE X(26).
00091 C              02    DFHEIV1   PICTURE X(8).
00092 C              02    DFHEIV2   PICTURE X(8).
00093 C              02    DFHEIV3   PICTURE X(8).
00094 C              02    DFHEIV4   PICTURE X(6).
00095 C              02    DFHEIV5   PICTURE X(4).
00096 C              02    DFHEIV6   PICTURE X(4).
00097 C              02    DFHEIV7   PICTURE X(2).
00098 C              02    DFHEIV8   PICTURE X(2).
00099 C              02    DFHEIV9   PICTURE X(1).
00100 C              02    DFHEIV10  PICTURE S9(7) USAGE COMPUTATIONAL-3.
00101 C              02    DFHEIV11  PICTURE S9(4) USAGE COMPUTATIONAL.
00102 C              02    DFHEIV12  PICTURE S9(4) USAGE COMPUTATIONAL.
00103 C              02    DFHEIV13  PICTURE S9(4) USAGE COMPUTATIONAL.
00104 C              02    DFHEIV14  PICTURE S9(4) USAGE COMPUTATIONAL.
00105 C              02    DFHEIV15  PICTURE S9(4) USAGE COMPUTATIONAL.
00106 C              02    DFHEIV16  PICTURE S9(9) USAGE COMPUTATIONAL.
00107 C              02    DFHEIV17  PICTURE X(4).
00108 C              02    DFHEIV18  PICTURE X(4).
00109 C              02    DFHEIV19  PICTURE X(4).
00110 C              02    DFHEIV97  PICTURE S9(7) USAGE COMPUTATIONAL-3 VALUE ZERO.
00111 C              02    DFHEIV98  PICTURE S9(4) USAGE COMPUTATIONAL VALUE ZERO.
00112 C              02    DFHEIV99  PICTURE X(1)  VALUE SPACE.
00113            LINKAGE SECTION.

00115            01  DFHEIBLK COPY DFHEIBLK.
00116 C          *   EIBLK EXEC INTERFACE BLOCK
00117 C          01  DFHEIBLK.
00118 C          *       EIBTIME       TIME IN 0HHMMSS FORMAT
00119 C              02 EIBTIME    PICTURE S9(7) USAGE COMPUTATIONAL-3.
00120 C          *       EIBDATE       DATE IN 00YYDDD FORMAT
00121 C              02 EIBDATE    PICTURE S9(7) USAGE COMPUTATIONAL-3.
00122 C          *       EIBTRNID      TRANSACTION IDENTIFIER
00123 C              02 EIBTRNID   PICTURE X(4).
00124 C          *       EIBTASKN      TASK NUMBER
00125 C              02 EIBTASKN   PICTURE S9(7) USAGE COMPUTATIONAL-3.
00126 C          *       EIBTRMID      TERMINAL IDENTIFIER
00127 C              02 EIBTRMID   PICTURE X(4).
00128 C          *       DFHEIGDI      RESERVED
00129 C              02 DFHEIGDI   PICTURE S9(4) USAGE COMPUTATIONAL.
00130 C          *       EIBCPOSN      CURSOR POSITION
00131 C              02 EIBCPOSN   PICTURE S9(4) USAGE COMPUTATIONAL.
00132 C          *       EIBCALEN      COMMAREA LENGTH
00133 C              02 EIBCALEN   PICTURE S9(4) USAGE COMPUTATIONAL.
00134 C          *       EIBAID        ATTENTION IDENTIFIER
00135 C              02 EIBAID     PICTURE X(1).
00136 C          *       EIBFN         FUNCTION CODE
00137 C              02 EIBFN      PICTURE X(2).
00138 C          *       EIBRCODE      RESPONSE CODE
00139 C              02 EIBRCODE   PICTURE X(6).
```

Fig. 22.4.   (Continued)

```
        5           ORBRO1A              12.59.17          08/02/80
```

```
00140 C    *         EIBDS       DATASET NAME
00141 C         02 EIBDS       PICTURE X(8).
00142 C    *         EIBREQID    REQUEST IDENTIFIER
00143 C         02 EIBREQID    PICTURE X(8).
00144      01  DFHCOMMAREA                     PIC X.

00146         88  INITIAL-ENTRY-TIME          VALUE '0'.
00147         88  BROWSE-START-TIME           VALUE '1'.


00149      01  LINKAGE-POINTERS.

00151         05  FILLER            PIC S9(8) COMP.
00152         05  MAP1-POINTER      PIC S9(8) COMP.
00153         05  POM-POINTER       PIC S9(8) COMP.
00154         05  TWA-POINTER       PIC S9(8) COMP.
```

Fig. 22.4.   (Continued)

6   OR BRO1A   12.59.17   08/02/80

```
00156      **********************************************************************
00157      *                                                                    *
00158      *                DISPLAY MAP DESCRIPTION                             *
00159      *                                                                    *
00160      **********************************************************************


00162      01   MAP1-AREA.
00163           05   FILLER                    PIC X(12).
00164           05   MAP1-DUMMY-L              PIC S9999 COMP.
00165           05   MAP1-DUMMY-A              PIC X.
00166           05   MAP1-DUMMY                PIC X.
00167           05   MAP1-ORDER-NUMBER-L       PIC S9999 COMP.
00168           05   MAP1-ORDER-NUMBER-A       PIC X.
00169           05   MAP1-ORDER-NUMBER         PIC X(10).
00170           05   MAP1-DEPARTMENT-L         PIC S9999 COMP.
00171           05   MAP1-DEPARTMENT-A         PIC X.
00172           05   MAP1-DEPARTMENT           PIC XXX.
00173           05   MAP1-ORDER-DATE-L         PIC S9999 COMP.
00174           05   MAP1-ORDER-DATE-A         PIC X.
00175           05   MAP1-ORDER-DATE.
00176             10   MAP1-ORDER-DATE-MONTH   PIC XX.
00177             10   MAP1-ORDER-DATE-DAY     PIC XX.
00178             10   MAP1-ORDER-DATE-YEAR    PIC XX.
00179           05   MAP1-ORDER-DATE-ENTERED-L PIC S9999 COMP.
00180           05   MAP1-ORDER-DATE-ENTERED-A PIC X.
00181           05   MAP1-ORDER-DATE-ENTERED   PIC X(6).
00182           05   MAP1-TOTAL-COST-L         PIC S9999 COMP.
00183           05   MAP1-TOTAL-COST-A         PIC X.
00184           05   MAP1-TOTAL-COST           PIC Z,ZZZ,ZZZ.99.
00185           05   MAP1-TOTAL-PRICE-L        PIC S9999 COMP.
00186           05   MAP1-TOTAL-PRICE-A        PIC X.
00187           05   MAP1-TOTAL-PRICE          PIC Z,ZZZ,ZZZ.99.
00188           05   MAP1-LINE-ITEM            OCCURS 9
00189                                          INDEXED BY MAP1-LINE-I.
00190             10   MAP1-LINE-NUMBER-L      PIC S9999 COMP.
00191             10   MAP1-LINE-NUMBER-A      PIC X.
00192             10   MAP1-LINE-NUMBER        PIC 9.
00193             10   MAP1-ITEM-NUMBER-L      PIC S9999 COMP.
00194             10   MAP1-ITEM-NUMBER-A      PIC X.
00195             10   MAP1-ITEM-NUMBER        PIC X(8).
00196             10   MAP1-ITEM-DESCRIPTION-L PIC S9999 COMP.
00197             10   MAP1-ITEM-DESCRIPTION-A PIC X.
00198             10   MAP1-ITEM-DESCRIPTION   PIC X(19).
00199             10   MAP1-ITEM-DATE-L        PIC S9999 COMP.
00200             10   MAP1-ITEM-DATE-A        PIC X.
00201             10   MAP1-ITEM-DATE          PIC X(6).
00202             10   MAP1-UNIT-L             PIC S9999 COMP.
00203             10   MAP1-UNIT-A             PIC X.
00204             10   MAP1-UNIT               PIC 9(5).
00205             10   MAP1-UNIT-COST-L        PIC S9999 COMP.
00206             10   MAP1-UNIT-COST-A        PIC X.
```

Fig. 22.4.   (Continued)

```
         7          ORBRO1A        12.59.17        08/02/80


00207                    10  MAP1-UNIT-COST              PIC 9(7).
00208                    10  MAP1-COST-L                 PIC S9999 COMP.
00209                    10  MAP1-COST-A                 PIC X.
00210                    10  MAP1-COST                   PIC 9(8).
00211                    10  MAP1-UNIT-PRICE-L           PIC S9999 COMP.
00212                    10  MAP1-UNIT-PRICE-A           PIC X.
00213                    10  MAP1-UNIT-PRICE             PIC 9(7).
00214                    10  MAP1-PRICE-L                PIC S9999 COMP.
00215                    10  MAP1-PRICE-A                PIC X.
00216                    10  MAP1-PRICE                  PIC 9(8).
00217                05  MAP1-ERROR-L                    PIC S9999 COMP.
00218                05  MAP1-ERROR-A                    PIC X.
00219                05  MAP1-ERROR                      PIC X(20).
00220                05  MAP1-START-ORDER-L              PIC S9999 COMP.
00221                05  MAP1-START-ORDER-A              PIC X.
00222                05  MAP1-START-ORDER                PIC X(10).




         8          ORBRO1A        12.59.17        08/02/80


00224      ***************************************************************
00225      *                                                             *
00226      *          PURCHASE ORDER MASTER -- FILE LAYOUT               *
00227      *                                                             *
00228      ***************************************************************


00230      01  ORDER-MASTER-RECORD.
00231          05  ORDER-NUMBER                  PIC X(10).
00232          05  ORDER-ALT-KEY.
00233              10  ORDER-DEPARTMENT          PIC XXX.
00234              10  ORDER-DATE.
00235                  15  ORDER-DATE-YEAR       PIC XX.
00236                  15  ORDER-DATE-MONTH      PIC XX.
00237                  15  ORDER-DATE-DAY        PIC XX.
00238          05  ORDER-DATE-ENTERED.
00239              10  ORDER-DATE-ENTERED-MONTH  PIC XX.
00240              10  ORDER-DATE-ENTERED-DAY    PIC XX.
00241              10  ORDER-DATE-ENTERED-YEAR   PIC XX.
00242          05  ORDER-TOTAL-COST             PIC S9(7)V99   COMP-3.
00243          05  ORDER-TOTAL-PRICE            PIC S9(7)V99   COMP-3.
00244          05  ORDER-LINE-COUNT             PIC S9999      COMP.
00245          05  ORDER-ALL-LINES.
00246              10  ORDER-LINE-ITEM
00247                                      DEPENDING ON ORDER-LINE-COUNT
00248                                      INDEXED BY ORDER-LINE-I.
00249                  15  ORDER-ITEM-NUMBER       PIC X(8).
00250                  15  ORDER-ITEM-DESCRIPTION  PIC X(19).
00251                  15  ORDER-ITEM-DATE.
00252                      20  ORDER-ITEM-DATE-MONTH   PIC XX.
00253                      20  ORDER-ITEM-DATE-DAY     PIC XX.
00254                      20  ORDER-ITEM-DATE-YEAR    PIC XX.
00255                  15  ORDER-UNIT              PIC S9(5)    COMP-3.
00256                  15  ORDER-UNIT-COST         PIC S9(5)V99 COMP-3.
00257                  15  ORDER-UNIT-PRICE        PIC S9(5)V99 COMP-3.
```

Line 00246 continues: `10  ORDER-LINE-ITEM          OCCURS 1 TO 9`

Fig. 22.4.   (Continued)

9   OR BRO1A   12.59.17   08/02/80

```
00259        ***********************************************************************
00260        *                                                                     *
00261        *                    TRANSACTION WORK AREA                            *
00262        *                                                                     *
00263        ***********************************************************************


00265        01   TWA-AREA.


00267             05   TWA-LINE-ITEM-MAP.
00268                  10   TWA-LINE-NUMBER-MAP-L          PIC S9999 COMP.
00269                  10   TWA-LINE-NUMBER-MAP-A          PIC X.
00270                  10   TWA-LINE-NUMBER-MAP            PIC 9.
00271                  10   TWA-ITEM-NUMBER-MAP-L          PIC S9999 COMP.
00272                  10   TWA-ITEM-NUMBER-MAP-A          PIC X.
00273                  10   TWA-ITEM-NUMBER-MAP            PIC X(8).
00274                  10   TWA-ITEM-DESCRIPTION-MAP-L     PIC S9999 COMP.
00275                  10   TWA-ITEM-DESCRIPTION-MAP-A     PIC X.
00276                  10   TWA-ITEM-DESCRIPTION-MAP       PIC X(19).
00277                  10   TWA-ITEM-DATE-MAP-L            PIC S9999 COMP.
00278                  10   TWA-ITEM-DATE-MAP-A            PIC X.
00279                  10   TWA-ITEM-DATE-MAP              PIC X(6).
00280                  10   TWA-UNIT-MAP-L                 PIC S9999 COMP.
00281                  10   TWA-UNIT-MAP-A                 PIC X.
00282                  10   TWA-UNIT-MAP                   PIC 9(5).
00283                  10   TWA-UNIT-COST-MAP-L            PIC S9999 COMP.
00284                  10   TWA-UNIT-COST-MAP-A            PIC X.
00285                  10   TWA-UNIT-COST-MAP              PIC 9(7).
00286                  10   TWA-COST-MAP-L                 PIC S9999 COMP.
00287                  10   TWA-COST-MAP-A                 PIC X.
00288                  10   TWA-COST-MAP                   PIC 9(8).
00289                  10   TWA-UNIT-PRICE-MAP-L           PIC S9999 COMP.
00290                  10   TWA-UNIT-PRICE-MAP-A           PIC X.
00291                  10   TWA-UNIT-PRICE-MAP             PIC 9(7).
00292                  10   TWA-PRICE-MAP-L                PIC S9999 COMP.
00293                  10   TWA-PRICE-MAP-A                PIC X.
00294                  10   TWA-PRICE-MAP                  PIC 9(8).


00296             05   TWA-LINE-ITEM-ORDER.
00297                  10   TWA-ITEM-NUMBER-ORDER          PIC X(8).
00298                  10   TWA-ITEM-DESCRIPTION-ORDER     PIC X(19).
00299                  10   TWA-ITEM-DATE-ORDER            PIC X(6).
00300                  10   TWA-UNIT-ORDER                 PIC S9(5)       COMP-3.
00301                  10   TWA-UNIT-COST-ORDER            PIC S9(5)V99 COMP-3.
00302                  10   TWA-UNIT-PRICE-ORDER           PIC S9(5)V99 COMP-3.


00304             05   TWA-OPERATOR-MESSAGE               PIC X(31).
```

Fig. 22.4.   (Continued)

```
     10          ORBRO1A          12.59.17         08/02/80
```

```
00306              05  TWA-ORDER-RECORD-KEY            PIC X(10).


00308              05  PREV-ACTION                     PIC X.
00309                  88   PREV-ACTION-FORWARD              VALUE '1'.
00310                  88   PREV-ACTION-BACKWARDS            VALUE '2'.
00311                  88   PREV-ACTION-FORWARD-EOF          VALUE '3'.
00312                  88   PREV-ACTION-BACKWARDS-EOF        VALUE '4'.
00313                  88   PREV-ACTION-FORWARD-NOTFOUND     VALUE '5'.
00314                  88   PREV-ACTION-IMMATERIAL           VALUE '9'.
```

```
     11          ORBRO1A          12.59.17         08/02/80
```

```
00316          PROCEDURE DIVISION USING DFHEIBLK DFHCOMMAREA.
00317              CALL 'DFHEI1'.


00319          ******************************************************************
00320          *                                                                *
00321          MAIN-LINE SECTION.
00322          *                                                                *
00323          ******************************************************************

00325          *     EXEC CICS
00326          *         ADDRESS TWA (TWA-POINTER)
00327          *     END-EXEC.
00328                MOVE 'BB  DC           ' TO DFHEIVO CALL 'DFHEI1' USING
00329                DFHEIVO TWA-POINTER.
00330
00331          *     EXEC CICS
00332          *         HANDLE AID
00333          *             CLEAR (FINALIZATION)
00334          *                PA1 (WRONG-KEY-USED)
00335          *                PA2 (WRONG-KEY-USED)
00336          *                PA3 (WRONG-KEY-USED)
00337          *     END-EXEC.
00338                MOVE 'BFO DEDFC         ' TO DFHEIVO CALL 'DFHEI1' USING
00339                DFHEIVO GO TO FINALIZATION WRONG-KEY-USED WRONG-KEY-USED
00340                WRONG-KEY-USED DEPENDING ON DFHEIGDI.
00341
00342
00343
00344
00345          *     EXEC CICS
00346          *         HANDLE CONDITION
00347          *             MAPFAIL (MAPFAIL-ERROR)
00348          *             NOTOPEN (FILE-NOT-OPEN)
00349          *             ERROR   (MAJOR-ERROR)
00350          *     END-EXEC.
00351                MOVE 'BD- DULA          ' TO DFHEIVO CALL 'DFHEI1' USING
00352                DFHEIVO GO TO MAPFAIL-ERROR FILE-NOT-OPEN MAJOR-ERROR
00353                DEPENDING ON DFHEIGDI.
00354
00355
00356
00357                IF EIBCALEN NOT EQUAL TO ZEROES
00358                    IF BROWSE-START-TIME
00359                        GO TO BROWSE-START
00360                    ELSE IF INITIAL-ENTRY-TIME
00361                        GO TO INITIALIZATION
00362                    ELSE GO TO PROCESS-SWITCH-ERROR.

00364                IF EIBCALEN EQUAL TO ZEROES
00365                    GO TO SIGN-ON-VIOLATION.
```

Fig. 22.4. (Continued)

```
  12         ORBRO1A        12.59.17        08/02/80


00367       ****************************************************************
00368       *                                                              *
00369       BROWSE-CONTINUE SECTION.
00370       *                                                              *
00371       ****************************************************************

00373       *    EXEC CICS
00374       *        RECEIVE MAP    ('ORBRMO1')
00375       *                MAPSET ('ORBRSO1')
00376       *                SET    (MAP1-POINTER)
00377       *    END-EXEC.
00378            MOVE 'ORBRMO1' TO DFHEIV1 MOVE 'ORBRSO1' TO DFHEIV2 MOVE 'QB
00379       -   '& DA   EI  -' TO DFHEIVO CALL 'DFHEI1' USING DFHEIVO
00380            DFHEIV1 MAP1-POINTER DFHEIV98 DFHEIV2.
00381
00382
00383            IF MAP1-START-ORDER NOT NUMERIC
00384               GO TO INVALID-ORDER.

00386            IF MAP1-START-ORDER EQUAL TO TWA-ORDER-RECORD-KEY
00387               IF     EIBAID EQUAL TO DFHPF1
00388               OR EIBAID EQUAL TO DFHENTER
00389               THEN GO TO BROWSE-FORWARD
00390               ELSE IF EIBAID EQUAL TO DFHPF2
00391                       IF PREV-ACTION-FORWARD-NOTFOUND
00392                           MOVE HIGH-VALUES TO TWA-ORDER-RECORD-KEY

00394       *                     EXEC CICS
00395       *                         RESETBR
00396       *                             DATASET ('ORTEST')
00397       *                             RIDFLD  (TWA-ORDER-RECORD-KEY)
00398       *                             GTEQ
00399       *                     END-EXEC
00400                             MOVE 'ORTEST' TO DFHEIV3 MOVE 'FMO D -U
00401       -   '' TO DFHEIVO CALL 'DFHEI1' USING DFHEIVO DFHEIV3 DFHEIV99
00402            DFHEIV98 TWA-ORDER-RECORD-KEY
00403
00404
00405
00406                             GO TO BROWSE-BACKWARD
00407                         ELSE GO TO BROWSE-BACKWARD
00408                     ELSE GO TO WRONG-KEY-USED
00409            ELSE MOVE '9' TO PREV-ACTION
00410               IF MAP1-START-ORDER GREATER THAN TWA-ORDER-RECORD-KEY
00411                   MOVE MAP1-START-ORDER TO TWA-ORDER-RECORD-KEY
00412                   GO TO BROWSE-FORWARD
00413               ELSE MOVE MAP1-START-ORDER TO TWA-ORDER-RECORD-KEY
00414       *           EXEC CICS
00415       *               RESETBR
00416       *                   DATASET ('ORTEST')
00417       *                   RIDFLD  (TWA-ORDER-RECORD-KEY)
00418       *                   GTEQ
00419       *           END-EXEC


  13         ORBRO1A        12.59.17        08/02/80


00420                   MOVE 'ORTEST' TO DFHEIV3 MOVE 'FMO D -U ' TO
00421            DFHEIVO CALL 'DFHEI1' USING DFHEIVO DFHEIV3 DFHEIV99
00422            DFHEIV98 TWA-ORDER-RECORD-KEY
00423
00424
00425
00426                   GO TO BROWSE-FORWARD.
```

Fig. 22.4.   (Continued)

```
00428          ***********************************************************************
00429          *                                                                    *
00430           BROWSE-FORWARD SECTION.
00431          *                                                                    *
00432          ***********************************************************************


00434          *    EXEC CICS
00435          *        HANDLE CONDITION
00436          *            ENDFILE (END-OF-FILE-FORWARD)
00437          *            NOTFND  (RECORD-NOT-FOUND-FORWARD)
00438          *    END-EXEC.
00439               MOVE 'BD    DN(              ' TO DFHEIVO CALL 'DFHEI1' USING
00440               DFHEIVO GO TO END-OF-FILE-FORWARD RECORD-NOT-FOUND-FORWARD
00441               DEPENDING ON DFHEIGDI.


00444           READ-NEXT-RECORD.

00446          *    EXEC CICS
00447          *        READNEXT DATASET ('ORTEST')
00448          *                 SET     (PON-POINTER)
00449          *                 RIDFLD  (TWA-ORDER-RECORD-KEY)
00450          *    END-EXEC.
00451               MOVE 'ORTEST' TO DFHEIV3 MOVE 'F+M DA 0 ' TO DFHEIVO CALL 'D
00452          -    'FHEI1' USING DFHEIVO DFHEIV3 PON-POINTER DFHEIV98
00453               TWA-ORDER-RECORD-KEY DFHEIV98 DFHEIV98.


00456               IF PREV-ACTION-BACKWARDS
00457                   MOVE '1' TO PREV-ACTION
00458                   GO TO READ-NEXT-RECORD.


00460           LAYOUT-ORDER-SCREEN.
00461               MOVE TWA-ORDER-RECORD-KEY   TO  MAP1-START-ORDER.
00462               MOVE ORDER-NUMBER           TO  MAP1-ORDER-NUMBER.
00463               MOVE ORDER-DEPARTMENT       TO  MAP1-DEPARTMENT.
00464               MOVE ORDER-DATE-MONTH       TO  MAP1-ORDER-DATE-MONTH.
00465               MOVE ORDER-DATE-DAY         TO  MAP1-ORDER-DATE-DAY.
00466               MOVE ORDER-DATE-YEAR        TO  MAP1-ORDER-DATE-YEAR.
00467               MOVE ORDER-DATE-ENTERED     TO  MAP1-ORDER-DATE-ENTERED.
00468               MOVE ORDER-TOTAL-COST       TO  MAP1-TOTAL-COST.
00469               MOVE ORDER-TOTAL-PRICE      TO  MAP1-TOTAL-PRICE.
00470               MOVE SPACES                 TO  MAP1-ERROR.
00471               SET ORDER-LINE-I            TO  1.
00472               PERFORM LAYOUT-EACH-LINE
00473                   UNTIL ORDER-LINE-I GREATER THAN ORDER-LINE-COUNT.
00474               GO TO DISPLAY-ORDER.


00476           LAYOUT-EACH-LINE.
00477               SET MAP1-LINE-I                         TO ORDER-LINE-I.
```

Fig. 22.4.   (Continued)

```
00478                    MOVE ORDER-LINE-ITEM (ORDER-LINE-I) TO TWA-LINE-ITEM-ORDER.
00479                    MOVE MAP1-LINE-ITEM (MAP1-LINE-I)   TO TWA-LINE-ITEM-MAP.
00480                    SET TWA-LINE-NUMBER-MAP            TO ORDER-LINE-I.
00481                    MOVE TWA-ITEM-NUMBER-ORDER       TO  TWA-ITEM-NUMBER-MAP.
00482                    MOVE TWA-ITEM-DESCRIPTION-ORDER TO TWA-ITEM-DESCRIPTION-MAP.
00483                    MOVE TWA-ITEM-DATE-ORDER       TO  TWA-ITEM-DATE-MAP.
00484                    MOVE TWA-UNIT-ORDER            TO  TWA-UNIT-MAP.
00485                    MOVE TWA-UNIT-COST-ORDER       TO  TWA-UNIT-COST-MAP.
00486                    COMPUTE TWA-COST-MAP = TWA-UNIT-ORDER * TWA-UNIT-COST-ORDER.
00487                    MOVE TWA-UNIT-PRICE-ORDER       TO  TWA-UNIT-PRICE-MAP.
00488                    COMPUTE TWA-PRICE-MAP =
00489                                 TWA-UNIT-ORDER * TWA-UNIT-PRICE-ORDER.
00490                    MOVE TWA-LINE-ITEM-MAP     TO  MAP1-LINE-ITEM (MAP1-LINE-I).
00491                    SET ORDER-LINE-I UP BY 1.


00493            DISPLAY-ORDER.

00495        *       EXEC CICS
00496        *           SEND MAP   ('ORBRMO1')
00497        *                MAPSET ('ORBRSO1')
00498        *                FROM   (MAP1-AREA)
00499        *                ERASE
00500        *       END-EXEC.
00501                 MOVE 'ORBRMO1' TO DFHEIV1 MOVE 'ORBRSO1' TO DFHEIV2 MOVE 'QD
00502        -        '& D   ESD -' TO DFHEIVO CALL 'DFHEI1' USING DFHEIVO
00503                 DFHEIV1 MAP1-AREA DFHEIV98 DFHEIV2.
00504
00505
00506
00507            AFTER-DISPLAY.
00508                 MOVE '1' TO PREV-ACTION.
00509                 GO TO BROWSE-CONTINUE.


00511            END-OF-FILE-FORWARD.
00512                 MOVE TWA-ORDER-RECORD-KEY   TO  MAP1-START-ORDER.
00513                 MOVE   '3'               TO  PREV-ACTION.
00514                 GO TO END-OF-FILE-FORWARD-MESSAGE.


00516            END-OF-FILE-FORWARD-MESSAGE.
00517                 MOVE 'END OF FILE' TO MAP1-ERROR.

00519        *       EXEC CICS
00520        *           SEND MAP   ('ORBRMO1')
00521        *                MAPSET ('ORBRSO1')
00522        *                FROM   (MAP1-AREA)
00523        *                ERASE
00524        *       END-EXEC.
00525                 MOVE 'ORBRMO1' TO DFHEIV1 MOVE 'ORBRSO1' TO DFHEIV2 MOVE 'QD
00526        -        '& D   ESD -' TO DFHEIVO CALL 'DFHEI1' USING DFHEIVO
00527                 DFHEIV1 MAP1-AREA DFHEIV98 DFHEIV2.
```

Fig. 22.4.   (Continued)

```
   16           ORBRO1A          12.59.17         08/02/80

00528
00529
00530
00531              GO TO BROWSE-CONTINUE.


00533          RECORD-NOT-FOUND-FORWARD.
00534              MOVE TWA-ORDER-RECORD-KEY  TO  MAP1-START-ORDER.
00535              MOVE   '5'                 TO  PREV-ACTION.
00536              GO TO END-OF-FILE-FORWARD-MESSAGE.


   17           ORBRO1A          12.59.17         08/02/80

00538          *************************************************************
00539          *                                                           *
00540          BROWSE-BACKWARD SECTION.
00541          *                                                           *
00542          *************************************************************

00544          *    EXEC CICS
00545          *        HANDLE CONDITION
00546          *            ENDFILE (END-OF-FILE-BACKWARDS)
00547          *    END-EXEC.
00548               MOVE 'BD  DM              ' TO DFHEIVO CALL 'DFHEI1' USING
00549               DFHEIVO GO TO END-OF-FILE-BACKWARDS DEPENDING ON DFHEIGDI.
00550
00551
00552          READ-PREVIOUS-RECORD.
00553          *    EXEC CICS
00554          *        READPREV DATASET ('ORTEST')
00555          *                 SET     (POM-POINTER)
00556          *                 RIDFLD  (TWA-ORDER-RECORD-KEY)
00557          *    END-EXEC.
00558               MOVE 'ORTEST' TO DFHEIV3 MOVE 'F&M DA 4 ' TO DFHEIVO CALL 'D
00559          -    'FHEI1' USING DFHEIVO DFHEIV3 POM-POINTER DFHEIV98
00560               TWA-ORDER-RECORD-KEY DFHEIV98 DFHEIV98.
00561
00562
00563              IF PREV-ACTION-FORWARD
00564                  MOVE '2' TO PREV-ACTION
00565                  GO TO READ-PREVIOUS-RECORD.

00567              PERFORM LAYOUT-ORDER-SCREEN THRU DISPLAY-ORDER.
00568              MOVE '2' TO PREV-ACTION.
00569              GO TO BROWSE-CONTINUE.


00571          END-OF-FILE-BACKWARDS.
00572              MOVE TWA-ORDER-RECORD-KEY   TO  MAP1-START-ORDER.
00573              MOVE   'END OF FILE'        TO  MAP1-ERROR.
00574              MOVE   '4'                  TO  PREV-ACTION.

00576          *    EXEC CICS
00577          *        SEND MAP   ('ORBRM01')
00578          *             MAPSET ('ORBRS01')
00579          *             FROM   (MAP1-AREA)
00580          *             ERASE
00581          *    END-EXEC.
00582               MOVE 'ORBRM01' TO DFHEIV1 MOVE 'ORBRS01' TO DFHEIV2 MOVE 'QD
00583          -    '& 0    ESD -' TO DFHEIVO CALL 'DFHEI1' USING DFHEIVO
00584               DFHEIV1 MAP1-AREA DFHEIV98 DFHEIV2.
00585
00586
00587
00588              GO TO BROWSE-CONTINUE.
```

Fig. 22.4.   (Continued)

```
  18        ORBRO1A        12.59.17        08/02/80


00590          INVALID-ORDER.
00591              MOVE 'INVALID ORDER NUMBER' TO MAP1-ERROR.

00593      *      EXEC CICS
00594      *          SEND MAP     ('ORBRMO1')
00595      *              MAPSET ('ORBRSO1')
00596      *              FROM   (MAP1-AREA)
00597      *              ERASE
00598      *      END-EXEC.
00599              MOVE 'ORBRMO1' TO DFHEIV1 MOVE 'ORBRSO1' TO DFHEIV2 MOVE 'QD
00600      -      '& D    ESD  -' TO DFHEIVO CALL 'DFHEI1' USING DFHEIVO
00601              DFHEIV1 MAP1-AREA DFHEIV98 DFHEIV2.
00602
00603
00604

00606              GO TO BROWSE-CONTINUE.




  19        ORBRO1A        12.59.17        08/02/80


00608      ***************************************************************
00609      *                                                             *
00610          WRONG-KEY-USED SECTION.
00611      *                                                             *
00612      ***************************************************************

00614      *      EXEC CICS
00615      *          GETMAIN
00616      *              SET      (MAP1-POINTER)
00617      *              LENGTH   (983)
00618      *              INITIMG (HEX-ZEROES)
00619      *      END-EXEC.
00620              MOVE 983 TO DFHEIV11 MOVE 'αB- D  α ' TO DFHEIVO CALL 'DFHEI
00621      -      '1' USING DFHEIVO MAP1-POINTER DFHEIV11 HEX-ZEROES.
00622
00623
00624
00625
00626              MOVE 'WRONG KEY USED' TO MAP1-ERROR.

00628      *      EXEC CICS
00629      *          SEND MAP     ('ORBRMO1')
00630      *              MAPSET ('ORBRSO1')
00631      *              FROM   (MAP1-AREA)
00632      *              DATAONLY
00633      *      END-EXEC.
00634              MOVE 'ORBRMO1' TO DFHEIV1 MOVE 'ORBRSO1' TO DFHEIV2 MOVE 'QD
00635      -      '& D    E-D  -' TO DFHEIVO CALL 'DFHEI1' USING DFHEIVO
00636              DFHEIV1 MAP1-AREA DFHEIV98 DFHEIV2.
00637
00638
00639
00640      *      EXEC CICS
00641      *          FREEMAIN DATA (MAP1-AREA)
00642      *      END-EXEC.
00643              MOVE 'αD  D    ' TO DFHEIVO CALL 'DFHEI1' USING DFHEIVO
00644              MAP1-AREA.
00645
00646              GO TO BROWSE-CONTINUE.
```

Fig. 22.4.   (Continued)

```
00648          *****************************************************************
00649          *                                                               *
00650          BROWSE-START SECTION.
00651          *                                                               *
00652          *****************************************************************


00654      *      EXEC CICS
00655      *          RECEIVE MAP    ('ORBRM01')
00656      *                  MAPSET ('ORBRS01')
00657      *                  SET    (MAP1-POINTER)
00658      *      END-EXEC.
00659             MOVE 'ORBRM01' TO DFHEIV1 MOVE 'ORBRS01' TO DFHEIV2 MOVE 'QB
00660      -     '& DA    EI   -' TO DFHEIVO CALL 'DFHEI1' USING DFHEIVO
00661             DFHEIV1 MAP1-POINTER DFHEIV98 DFHEIV2.
00662
00663
00664          BROWSE-STARTING-RECORD.

00666             IF MAP1-START-ORDER NOT NUMERIC
00667                 GO TO INVALID-ORDER-NUMBER-START.

00669             MOVE MAP1-START-ORDER   TO   TWA-ORDER-RECORD-KEY.

00671      *      EXEC CICS
00672      *          HANDLE CONDITION
00673      *              NOTFND (RECORD-NOT-FOUND-STARTBROWSE)
00674      *      END-EXEC.
00675             MOVE 'BD  D(                ' TO DFHEIVO CALL 'DFHEI1' USING
00676             DFHEIVO GO TO RECORD-NOT-FOUND-STARTBROWSE DEPENDING ON
00677             DFHEIGDI.
00678
00679          BROWSE-COMMAND.

00681      *      EXEC CICS
00682      *          STARTBR DATASET ('ORTEST')
00683      *                  RIDFLD  (TWA-ORDER-RECORD-KEY)
00684      *                  GTEQ
00685      *      END-EXEC.
00686             MOVE 'ORTEST' TO DFHEIV3 MOVE 'F¤O D -- ' TO DFHEIVO CALL 'D
00687      -     'FHEI1' USING DFHEIVO DFHEIV3 DFHEIV99 DFHEIV98
00688             TWA-ORDER-RECORD-KEY.
00689
00690
00691             IF TWA-ORDER-RECORD-KEY NUMERIC
00692                 GO TO BROWSE-FORWARD
00693             ELSE GO TO BROWSE-BACKWARD.


00695          RECORD-NOT-FOUND-STARTBROWSE.
00696             MOVE HIGH-VALUES TO TWA-ORDER-RECORD-KEY.
00697             GO TO BROWSE-COMMAND.
```

Fig. 22.4.   (Continued)

```
   21          ORBRO1A          12.59.17          08/02/80


00699              INVALID-ORDER-NUMBER-START.
00700                   MOVE 'INVALID ORDER NUMBER' TO MAP1-ERROR.

00702         *     EXEC CICS
00703         *         SEND MAP    ('ORBRMO1')
00704         *              MAPSET ('ORBRSO1')
00705         *              FROM   (MAP1-AREA)
00706         *              DATAONLY
00707         *     END-EXEC.
00708                   MOVE 'ORBRMO1' TO DFHEIV1 MOVE 'ORBRSO1' TO DFHEIV2 MOVE 'QD
00709         -       '& D    E-D -' TO DFHEIVO CALL 'DFHEI1' USING DFHEIVO
00710                   DFHEIV1 MAP1-AREA DFHEIV98 DFHEIV2.
00711
00712
00713
00714                   MOVE  '1'  TO COMMAREA-PROCESS-SW.

00716         *     EXEC CICS
00717         *         RETURN TRANSID  (EIBTRNID)
00718         *                COMMAREA (COMMUNICATION-AREA)
00719         *                LENGTH   (1)
00720         *     END-EXEC.
00721                   MOVE 1 TO DFHEIV11 MOVE '+H- D  & ' TO DFHEIVO CALL 'DFHEI1'
00722                   USING DFHEIVO EIBTRNID COMMUNICATION-AREA DFHEIV11.
00723
00724
00725


   22          ORBRO1A          12.59.17          08/02/80


00727              ***************************************************************
00728              *                                                             *
00729              INITIALIZATION SECTION.
00730              *                                                             *
00731              ***************************************************************

00733         *     EXEC CICS
00734         *         SEND MAP    ('ORBRMO1')
00735         *              MAPSET ('ORBRSO1')
00736         *              MAPONLY
00737         *              ERASE
00738         *     END-EXEC.
00739                   MOVE 'ORBRMO1' TO DFHEIV1 MOVE 'ORBRSO1' TO DFHEIV2 MOVE 'QD
00740         -       '& D    ESD -' TO DFHEIVO CALL 'DFHEI1' USING DFHEIVO
00741                   DFHEIV1 DFHEIV99 DFHEIV98 DFHEIV2.
00742
00743
00744
00745                   MOVE  '1'  TO  COMMAREA-PROCESS-SW.

00747         *     EXEC CICS
00748         *         RETURN TRANSID  ('ORBR')
00749         *                COMMAREA (COMMUNICATION-AREA)
00750         *                LENGTH   (1)
00751         *     END-EXEC.
00752                   MOVE 'ORBR' TO DFHEIV5 MOVE 1 TO DFHEIV11 MOVE '+H- D  & '
00753                   TO DFHEIVO CALL 'DFHEI1' USING DFHEIVO DFHEIV5
00754                   COMMUNICATION-AREA DFHEIV11.
00755
00756
```

Fig. 22.4. (Continued)

```
   23          ORBR01A        12.59.17        08/02/80


00758          ***********************************************************************
00759          *                                                                    *
00760           FINALIZATION SECTION.
00761          *                                                                    *
00762          ***********************************************************************


00764          PREPARE-TERMINATION-MESSAGE.
00765              MOVE JOB-NORMAL-END-MESSAGE TO TWA-OPERATOR-MESSAGE.

00767          JOB-TERMINATED.
00768          *    EXEC CICS
00769          *        SEND FROM   (TWA-OPERATOR-MESSAGE)
00770          *             LENGTH (31)
00771          *             ERASE
00772          *    END-EXEC.
00773              MOVE 31 TO DFHEIV11 MOVE 'DDO D     A      ' TO DFHEIVO CALL '
00774          -  'DFHEI1' USING DFHEIVO DFHEIV99 DFHEIV98 TWA-OPERATOR-MESSAGE
00775              DFHEIV11.
00776
00777


00779          END-OF-JOB.
00780          *    EXEC CICS
00781          *        RETURN
00782          *    END-EXEC.
00783              MOVE '+H  D  & ' TO DFHEIVO CALL 'DFHEI1' USING DFHEIVO.
00784
00785
```

Fig. 22.4.   (Continued)

```
   24        ORBRO1A         12.59.17        08/02/80


00787        ******************************************************************
00788        *                                                                *
00789        ABNORMAL-TERMINATION SECTION.
00790        *                                                                *
00791        ******************************************************************


00793        FILE-NOT-OPEN.

00795        *     EXEC CICS
00796        *         XCTL PROGRAM ('TEL2OPEN')
00797        *     END-EXEC.
00798              MOVE 'TEL2OPEN' TO DFHEIV3 MOVE '+0   D   B ' TO DFHEIVO CALL
00799              'DFHEI1' USING DFHEIVO DFHEIV3.
00800


00802        MAPFAIL-ERROR.
00803              MOVE 'MAP FAILURE' TO MAJOR-ERROR-MSG.
00804              GO TO PREPARE-ABORT-MESSAGE.


00806        PROCESS-SWITCH-ERROR.
00807              MOVE 'PROCESS ERROR' TO MAJOR-ERROR-MSG.
00808              GO TO PREPARE-ABORT-MESSAGE.


00810        SIGN-ON-VIOLATION.
00811              MOVE 'SIGNON VIOLATION' TO MAJOR-ERROR-MSG.
00812              GO TO PREPARE-ABORT-MESSAGE.


00814        MAJOR-ERROR.
00815              MOVE   EIBFN      TO   OLD-EIBFN.
00816              MOVE   EIBRCODE   TO   OLD-EIBRCODE.

00818        *     EXEC CICS
00819        *         DUMP DUMPCODE ('ERRS')
00820        *     END-EXEC.
00821              MOVE 'ERRS' TO DFHEIV5 MOVE '*B   D  = ' TO DFHEIVO CALL 'DFH
00822        -     'EI1' USING DFHEIVO DFHEIV5.
00823
00824              MOVE 'MAJOR ERROR' TO MAJOR-ERROR-MSG.
00825              GO TO PREPARE-ABORT-MESSAGE.


00827        PREPARE-ABORT-MESSAGE.
00828              MOVE JOB-ABORTED-MESSAGE TO TWA-OPERATOR-MESSAGE.
00829              GO TO JOB-TERMINATED.
```

Fig. 22.4.   (Continued)

THE MAIN-LINE SECTION

1. Lines 325–329. ADDRESS command for the TWA.

2. Lines 331–340. HANDLE AID command. The PA keys will result in the "WRONG KEY USED" error.

3. Lines 345–353. HANDLE CONDITION command. The NOTOPEN condition for the order file is specified here rather than in other sections because the program is in conversational mode and this specification will not change during the session.

4. Lines 357–362. The selection of sections.

5. Lines 364–365. If the program is executed at the start of the session by an operator-entered transaction identifier instead of through an XCTL command from the Sign-on program, a sign-on violation occurs. This is so if EIBCALEN is equal to zero.

THE INITIALIZATION SECTION

1. Lines 733–741. Display the browse map.

2. Line 745.   Set the communication area switch to 1.

3. Lines 747–754. Terminate the task. This section is implemented in the pseudoconversational mode so the task is terminated while the operator enters the browse starting point.

THE BROWSE-START SECTION

1. Lines 654–661. Read the map that contains the order number that is the starting point of the browse.

2. Lines 671–677. HANDLE CONDITION command for the order file.

3. Lines 679–688. STARTBR command to establish the starting point of the browse.

4. Lines 691–693. Line 691 will be executed if a record was found based on the order number and is always executed be-

   cause of the GTEQ operand of STARTBR unless the order number entered is greater than the last order number in the file. We then go into a forward browse to display this record. Line 693 will be executed if a record was not found, in which case lines 696–697 would have been executed to mark the end of the file. We therefore go into a backward browse to display the last record in the file.

5. Line 696.   If the record is not found, we set the key to HIGH-VALUES to mark the end of the file as the starting point of the browse (in this case, we have to browse backwards).

6. If the order number (as entered by the operator) is not numeric:
   a. Line 700.   Lay out the message "INVALID ORDER NUMBER" in the area secured by CICS/VS for the symbolic description map.
   b. Lines 702–710. Display the error message.
   c. Line 714.   Set the communication area switch to 1.
   d. Lines 716–722. Terminate the task.

THE BROWSE-FORWARD SECTION

1. Lines 434–441. HANDLE CONDITION command for the order file. The ENDFILE option is for the routine if the end of the file is reached in a normal forward browse. The NOTFND option is for the routine if we do not find a record during skip-browse forward.

2. Lines 444–453. Read the next record in ascending sequence.

3. Lines 456–458. If the previous File read was a READPREV command, then we bypass this record; otherwise we would be displaying the same record as in the previous display.

4. Lines 460–491. Move the record data into the symbolic description map.

5. Lines 493–503. Display the record. The ERASE option is specified since the data is variable (from 1 to 9 lines). If the data were fixed, this would not be required and DATAONLY would then be specified.

6. Lines 508–509. The forward browse is finished; wait for the next action from the operator.

7. Lines 512–531. If the end of the file is reached during normal forward browse, we display the "END OF FILE" message.

8. Lines 534–536. If the record is not found in a skip-forward browse, we likewise display the "END OF FILE" message.

THE BROWSE-BACKWARD SECTION

1. Lines 544–549. HANDLE CONDITION command for the order file. The ENDFILE option is for the routine if the end of the file is reached in a normal backward browse. The NOTFND option is not specified because it will never happen in a READPREV command if the GTEQ operand is specified in the browse.

2. Lines 552–560. Read the next record in descending sequence.

3. Lines 563–565. If the previous File read was a READNEXT command, then we bypass this record; otherwise we would be displaying the same record as in the previous display.

4. Line 567. Display the record.

5. Lines 568–569. The backward browse is finished; wait for the next action from the operator.

6. Lines 571–588. If the end of the file is reached during normal backward browse, we display the "END OF FILE" message.

7. Lines 593–601. If any new browse starting point entered is not numeric, we display the "INVALID ORDER NUMBER" message.

THE BROWSE-CONTINUE SECTION

1. Lines 373–380. Read the map containing the record key.

2. If a new order number was not entered:
   a. Lines 387–389. If the PF1 or ENTER key was used, do a forward browse.
   b. If the PF2 key was used:
      1. Lines 391–406. If the previous action was a skip-forward browse and the record was not found (this can happen if the last order number entered by the operator was higher than the last record in the file), the browse is reset to the end of the file and the last record is displayed.
      2. Line 407. Otherwise, do a backward browse.
   c. Line 408.   Otherwise, the wrong key was used.

3. If a new order number was entered:
   a. Lines 410–412. If the new order number is greater than the previously displayed order, then do a skip-forward browse.
   b. Lines 413–426. Otherwise, the browse starting point is reset using the new order number, and do a forward browse.

THE WRONG-KEY-USED SECTION

1. Lines 614–621. GETMAIN command to secure main storage for the map that will contain the error message. This is because the PA keys do not allow CICS/VS to secure main storage for the symbolic description map through a RECEIVE MAP command.

2. Line 626.   Move the "WRONG KEY USED" message into the area secured.

3. Lines 628–636. Display the error message.

4. Lines 640–644. FREEMAIN command to free main storage secured in the previous GETMAIN command. We have to do this to save main storage because, since we are using the conversational mode of processing, the area will not otherwise be freed through task termination.

5. Line 646.   The operator may continue the browse.

THE FINALIZATION SECTION

1. Lines 768–775. Display the "JOB NORMALLY TERMI-
   NATED" message.

2. Lines 780–783. Terminate the session.

THE ABNORMAL-TERMINATION SECTION

These are the routines used to abnormally terminate the session on
errors and CICS/VS command exceptional conditions not covered by
a HANDLE CONDITION command.

EXAMPLE

The following are facsimiles of actual photographs taken of a CRT
terminal during a session.

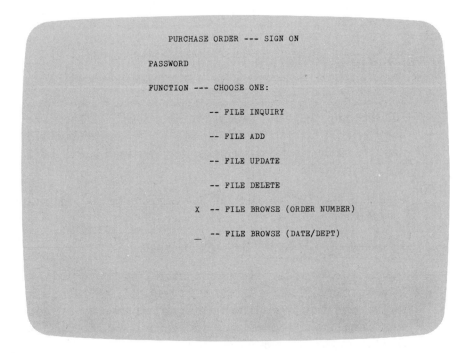

```
              PURCHASE ORDER --- SIGN ON

      PASSWORD

      FUNCTION --- CHOOSE ONE:

                   -- FILE INQUIRY

                   -- FILE ADD

                   -- FILE UPDATE

                   -- FILE DELETE

          X  -- FILE BROWSE (ORDER NUMBER)

          _  -- FILE BROWSE (DATE/DEPT)
```

Fig. 22.5. The File Browse (by order number) application is selected by keying in an "X"
on the File Browse line and the corresponding password, then hitting the ENTER key.

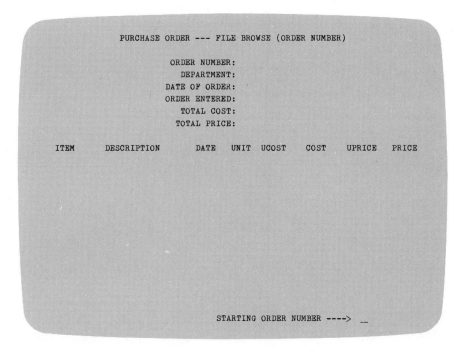

```
        PURCHASE ORDER --- FILE BROWSE (ORDER NUMBER)

                    ORDER NUMBER:
                    DEPARTMENT:
                    DATE OF ORDER:
                    ORDER ENTERED:
                       TOTAL COST:
                      TOTAL PRICE:

 ITEM      DESCRIPTION       DATE   UNIT  UCOST    COST    UPRICE   PRICE












                    STARTING ORDER NUMBER ---->  _
```

Fig. 22.6. The Sign On program executes which then transfers control to the File Browse program. This displays the File Browse map.

```
            PURCHASE ORDER --- FILE BROWSE (ORDER NUMBER)

                        ORDER NUMBER:
                         DEPARTMENT:
                       DATE OF ORDER:
                       ORDER ENTERED:
                          TOTAL COST:
                         TOTAL PRICE:


    ITEM       DESCRIPTION        DATE   UNIT  UCOST    COST    UPRICE   PRICE

















                            STARTING ORDER NUMBER ----> O
```

Fig. 22.7.   The operator keys in the browse starting point, then hits the ENTER key.

```
              PURCHASE ORDER --- FILE BROWSE (ORDER NUMBER)

                       ORDER NUMBER: 0000000001
                        DEPARTMENT: 003
                      DATE OF ORDER: 122280
                      ORDER ENTERED: 122280
                         TOTAL COST:      200.00
                        TOTAL PRICE:      400.00


     ITEM       DESCRIPTION      DATE   UNIT  UCOST    COST   UPRICE   PRICE
   1 00000100 CHISEL SET        122280 00050 0000400 00020000 0000800 00040000










                          STARTING ORDER NUMBER ----> 0000000001
```

Fig. 22.8. The program displays the record whose order number is equal to the starting
point. Since the record does not exist, the next higher one is used.

```
                 PURCHASE ORDER --- FILE BROWSE (ORDER NUMBER)

                        ORDER NUMBER: 0000000002
                         DEPARTMENT: 005
                      DATE OF ORDER: 122280
                      ORDER ENTERED: 122280
                         TOTAL COST:     3,600.00
                        TOTAL PRICE:     7,200.00


     ITEM      DESCRIPTION      DATE   UNIT  UCOST     COST    UPRICE    PRICE
   1 00005450 3/8 INCH REV DRILL 122280 00030 0002000 00060000 0004000 00120000
   2 00077321 1/4 INCH DRILL     122280 00100 0001000 00100000 0002000 00200000
   3 00004371 1 HP ROUTER        122280 00050 0004000 00200000 0008000 00400000









                        STARTING ORDER NUMBER ---->    0000000002
```

Fig. 22.9. The operator hits the PF1 key, which results in the display of the record next in ascending sequence.

```
         PURCHASE ORDER --- FILE BROWSE (ORDER NUMBER)


              ORDER NUMBER: 0000000002
               DEPARTMENT: 005
            DATE OF ORDER: 122280
            ORDER ENTERED: 122280
                TOTAL COST:      3,600.00
               TOTAL PRICE:      7,200.00


    ITEM       DESCRIPTION      DATE   UNIT  UCOST     COST     UPRICE    PRICE
  1 00005450 3/8 INCH REV DRILL 122280 00030 0002000 00060000 0004000 00120000
  2 00076321 1/4 INCH DRILL     122280 00100 0001000 00100000 0002000 00200000
  3 00004371 1 HP ROUTER        122280 00050 0004000 00200000 0008000 00400000








                        STARTING ORDER NUMBER ---->   16_
```

Fig. 22.10. The operator keys in another browse starting point, then hits the ENTER key.

```
              PURCHASE ORDER --- FILE BROWSE (ORDER NUMBER)

                         ORDER NUMBER: 0000000016
                         DEPARTMENT: 010
                      DATE OF ORDER: 122780
                      ORDER ENTERED: 122780
                          TOTAL COST:     1,700.00
                          TOTAL PRICE:    3,400.00


      ITEM       DESCRIPTION      DATE    UNIT  UCOST    COST    UPRICE    PRICE
   1 00000163 10-SPEED BLENDER   122780  00020 0001500 00030000 0003000 00060000
   2 00001754 ELECTRIC OVEN      122780  00020 0007000 00140000 0014000 00280000









                              STARTING ORDER NUMBER ----> 0000000016
```

Fig. 22.11. The program displays the record whose order number is equal to the new starting point. The skip-forward function is executed to do this.

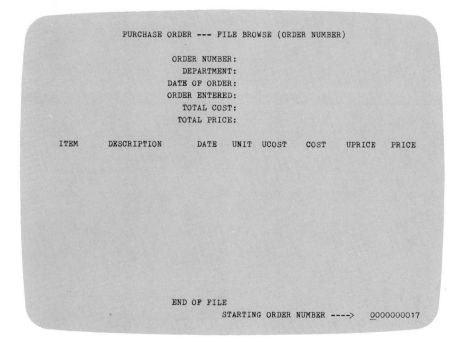

```
        PURCHASE ORDER --- FILE BROWSE (ORDER NUMBER)

                    ORDER NUMBER:
                     DEPARTMENT:
                    DATE OF ORDER:
                    ORDER ENTERED:
                       TOTAL COST:
                      TOTAL PRICE:

ITEM      DESCRIPTION      DATE   UNIT  UCOST    COST    UPRICE   PRICE
```

```
        END OF FILE
                      STARTING ORDER NUMBER ----->   0000000017
```

Fig. 22.12. After repeated PF1's, the end of the file is reached. Order number 17 was the last order displayed.

```
              PURCHASE ORDER --- FILE BROWSE (ORDER NUMBER)

                        ORDER NUMBER: 0000000017
                         DEPARTMENT: 005
                       DATE OF ORDER: 122780
                       ORDER ENTERED: 122780
                          TOTAL COST:      1,560.00
                         TOTAL PRICE:      3,120.00


     ITEM        DESCRIPTION        DATE   UNIT  UCOST    COST    UPRICE    PRICE
 1 00076321 1/4 INCH DRILL        122780 00020 0001000 00020000 0002000 00040000
 2 00004371 1 HP ROUTER           122780 00010 0004000 00040000 0008000 00080000
 3 00004376 3/4 HP ROUTER         122780 00020 0003000 00060000 0006000 00120000
 4 00088463 1/3 HP FIN. SANDER    122780 00020 0001800 00036000 0003600 00072000






                            STARTING ORDER NUMBER ---->   0000000017
```

Fig. 22.13. The operator hits the PF2 key, which results in the display of the record next in descending sequence.

```
          PURCHASE ORDER --- FILE BROWSE (ORDER NUMBER)

                    ORDER NUMBER: 0000000017
                    DEPARTMENT: 005
                 DATE OF ORDER: 122780
                 ORDER ENTERED: 122780
                    TOTAL COST:    1,560.00
                    TOTAL PRICE:   3,120.00


   ITEM        DESCRIPTION      DATE   UNIT  UCOST    COST   UPRICE    PRICE
1 00076321 1/4 INCH DRILL      122780 00020 0001000 00020000 0002000 00040000
2 00004371 1 HP ROUTER         122780 00010 0004000 00040000 0008000 00080000
3 00004376 3/4 HP ROUTER       122780 00020 0003000 00060000 0006000 00120000
4 00088463 1/3 HP FIN. SANDER  122780 00020 0001800 00036000 0003600 00072000








                     STARTING ORDER NUMBER ---->    1_
```

Fig. 22.14.   The operator keys in another browse starting point, then hits the ENTER key.

```
              PURCHASE ORDER --- FILE BROWSE (ORDER NUMBER)

                    ORDER NUMBER: 0000000001
                    DEPARTMENT: 003
                  DATE OF ORDER: 122280
                  ORDER ENTERED: 122280
                     TOTAL COST:      200.00
                    TOTAL PRICE:      400.00


       ITEM      DESCRIPTION      DATE   UNIT  UCOST    COST    UPRICE    PRICE
     1 00000100  CHISEL SET      122280  00050 0000400 00020000 0000800 00040000















                            STARTING ORDER NUMBER ----> 0000000001
```

Fig. 22.15.   The program displays the record whose order number is equal to the new start-ing point. The skip-backward function is executed to do this.

```
          PURCHASE ORDER --- FILE BROWSE (ORDER NUMBER)

                  ORDER NUMBER: 0000000001
                  DEPARTMENT: 003
                DATE OF ORDER: 122280
                ORDER ENTERED: 122280
                    TOTAL COST:      200.00
                   TOTAL PRICE:      400.00


      ITEM      DESCRIPTION      DATE    UNIT  UCOST    COST   UPRICE   PRICE
   1 00000100 CHISEL SET       122280 00050 0000400 00020000 0000800 00040000












                   WRONG KEY USED
                        STARTING ORDER NUMBER ----    0000000009
```

Fig. 22.16. If the operator keys in another browse starting point but then hits one of the PA keys instead of the ENTER key, the "WRONG KEY USED" message is displayed.

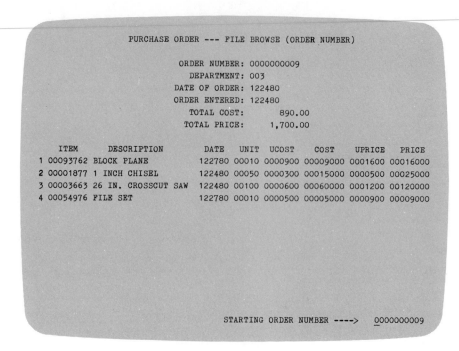

```
              PURCHASE ORDER --- FILE BROWSE (ORDER NUMBER)

                      ORDER NUMBER: 0000000009
                        DEPARTMENT: 003
                     DATE OF ORDER: 122480
                     ORDER ENTERED: 122480
                        TOTAL COST:      890.00
                       TOTAL PRICE:    1,700.00

        ITEM      DESCRIPTION        DATE   UNIT  UCOST    COST    UPRICE   PRICE
     1 00093762 BLOCK PLANE          122780 00010 0000900 00009000 0001600 00016000
     2 00001877 1 INCH CHISEL        122480 00050 0000300 00015000 0000500 00025000
     3 00003663 26 IN. CROSSCUT SAW  122480 00100 0000600 00060000 0001200 00120000
     4 00054976 FILE SET             122780 00010 0000500 00005000 0000900 00009000




                              STARTING ORDER NUMBER ----> 0000000009
```

Fig. 22.17. If the operator then hits the **ENTER** key, the session continues. The record selected in Fig. 22.16 is now displayed.

23

The File Browse Program (Alternate Key)

INTRODUCTION

This File Browse program allows the operator to browse through the order file according to order date within department number sequence (alternate key). He may also skip records in both the forward and backward directions by entering a new browse starting point. The program executes when selected by the Sign-on program and will continue executing in the session until terminated by the operator. The flow of control to execute this program is shown in Figure 23.1.

PROGRAM SPECIFICATION

The File Browse program (alternate key) specifications are as follows:

1. Implement the program using the conversational mode of processing.

2. Use 'ORBS' as the transaction identifier. However, the session should not be started by using this identifier, but rather through an XCTL command from the Sign-on program.

3. If the session is started by using the transaction identifier, abort the session with the message "JOB ABORTED — SIGNON VIOLATION."

4. The browse starting point is based on the order date within the department number entered by the operator. If the record is not in the file, the record next in ascending sequence is used. If the starting point is higher than the last record in the file, the last record is used.

5. On the PF1 key, display the record next in ascending sequence.

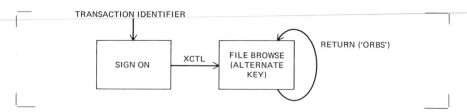

Fig. 23.1. File Browse Application (Alternate Key).

6. On the PF2 key, display the record next in descending sequence.

7 The operator may restart the browse at some other point by entering a new starting point.

8. On any PA key, display the message "WRONG KEY USED"; allow the operator to continue on with the session.

9. In this example, display only one record per page.

SCREEN LAYOUT

The screen layout to be used in the program is shown in Figure 23.2. All 9s are numeric fields and Xs are alphanumeric fields.

MAP PROGRAM

The map program corresponding to the screen layout is shown in Figure 23.3.

PROGRAM LISTING

The program listing for the File Browse program (date of order within department number) is shown in Figure 23.4. The listing is that of the compiler and not the command-language translator, and thus the commands are already as translated.

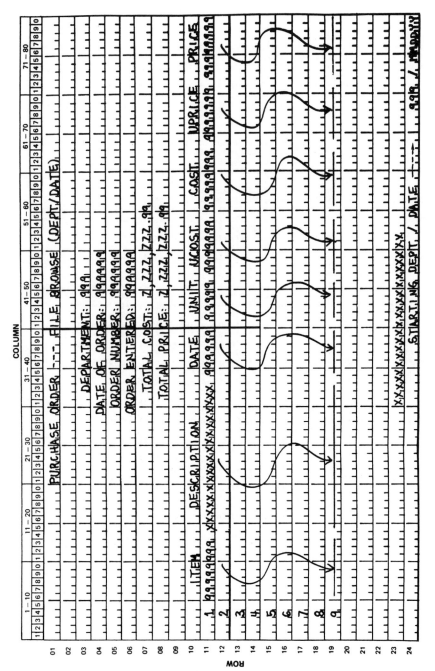

Fig. 23.2.   Screen Layout – File Browse (Alternate Key).

```
STMT    SOURCE STATEMENT                              DOS/VS ASSEMBLER REL 34.0 13.13

    1              PRINT NOGEN
    2 ORBSSO1      DFHMSD TYPE=MAP,MODE=INOUT,CTRL=FREEKB,LANG=COBOL,TIOAPFX=YES
   12 ORBSMO1      DFHMDI SIZE=(24,80)
   40 DUMMY        DFHMDF POS=(01,01),LENGTH=01,ATTRB=(ASKIP,DRK,FSET),          X
                          INITIAL='1'
   52              DFHMDF POS=(01,20),LENGTH=42,ATTRB=(ASKIP,BRT),               X
                          INITIAL='PURCHASE ORDER --- FILE BROWSE (DEPT/DATE)'
   64              DFHMDF POS=(03,32),LENGTH=11,ATTRB=ASKIP,INITIAL='DEPARTMENT '
   76 DEPT         DFHMDF POS=(03,44),LENGTH=03,ATTRB=(ASKIP,BRT)
   87              DFHMDF POS=(04,29),LENGTH=14,ATTRB=ASKIP,                     X
                          INITIAL='DATE OF ORDER '
   99 DATEOR       DFHMDF POS=(04,44),LENGTH=06,ATTRB=(ASKIP,BRT)
  110              DFHMDF POS=(05,30),LENGTH=13,ATTRB=ASKIP,                     X
                          INITIAL='ORDER NUMBER '
  122 ORDER        DFHMDF POS=(05,44),LENGTH=10,ATTRB=(ASKIP,BRT)
  133              DFHMDF POS=(06,29),LENGTH=14,ATTRB=ASKIP,                     X
                          INITIAL='ORDER ENTERED '
  145 DATEENT      DFHMDF POS=(06,44),LENGTH=06,ATTRB=(ASKIP,BRT)
  156              DFHMDF POS=(07,32),LENGTH=11,ATTRB=ASKIP,INITIAL='TOTAL COST '
  168 TOTCOST      DFHMDF POS=(07,44),LENGTH=12,ATTRB=(ASKIP,BRT),              X
                          PICOUT='Z,ZZZ,ZZZ.99'
  179              DFHMDF POS=(08,31),LENGTH=12,ATTRB=ASKIP,                     X
                          INITIAL='TOTAL PRICE '
  191 TOTPRCE      DFHMDF POS=(08,44),LENGTH=12,ATTRB=(ASKIP,BRT),              X
                          PICOUT='Z,ZZZ,ZZZ.99'
  202              DFHMDF POS=(10,07),LENGTH=04,ATTRB=ASKIP,INITIAL='ITEM'
  214              DFHMDF POS=(10,17),LENGTH=11,ATTRB=ASKIP,INITIAL='DESCRIPTION'
  226              DFHMDF POS=(10,35),LENGTH=04,ATTRB=ASKIP,INITIAL='DATE'
  238              DFHMDF POS=(10,42),LENGTH=04,ATTRB=ASKIP,INITIAL='UNIT'
  250              DFHMDF POS=(10,48),LENGTH=05,ATTRB=ASKIP,INITIAL='UCOST'
  262              DFHMDF POS=(10,57),LENGTH=04,ATTRB=ASKIP,INITIAL='COST'
  274              DFHMDF POS=(10,65),LENGTH=06,ATTRB=ASKIP,INITIAL='UPRICE'
  286              DFHMDF POS=(10,74),LENGTH=05,ATTRB=ASKIP,INITIAL='PRICE'
  298 LINE1        DFHMDF POS=(11,03),LENGTH=01,ATTRB=ASKIP
  309 ITEM1        DFHMDF POS=(11,05),LENGTH=08,ATTRB=(ASKIP,BRT),              X
                          PICIN='99999999',PICOUT='99999999'
  320 DESC1        DFHMDF POS=(11,14),LENGTH=19,ATTRB=(ASKIP,BRT)
  331 LNDATE1      DFHMDF POS=(11,34),LENGTH=06,ATTRB=(ASKIP,BRT)
  342 UNIT1        DFHMDF POS=(11,41),LENGTH=05,ATTRB=(ASKIP,BRT),              X
                          PICIN='99999',PICOUT='99999'
  353 UCOST1       DFHMDF POS=(11,47),LENGTH=07,ATTRB=(ASKIP,BRT),              X
                          PICIN='9999999',PICOUT='9999999'
  364 COST1        DFHMDF POS=(11,55),LENGTH=08,ATTRB=(ASKIP,BRT),              X
                          PICIN='99999999',PICOUT='99999999'
  375 UPRICE1      DFHMDF POS=(11,64),LENGTH=07,ATTRB=(ASKIP,BRT),              X
                          PICIN='9999999',PICOUT='9999999'
  386 PRICE1       DFHMDF POS=(11,72),LENGTH=08,ATTRB=(ASKIP,BRT),              X
                          PICIN='99999999',PICOUT='99999999'
  397 LINE2        DFHMDF POS=(12,03),LENGTH=01,ATTRB=ASKIP
  408 ITEM2        DFHMDF POS=(12,05),LENGTH=08,ATTRB=(ASKIP,BRT),              X
                          PICIN='99999999',PICOUT='99999999'
```

Fig. 23.3. Map Program – File Browse (Alternate Key).

```
419 DESC2      DFHMDF POS=(12,14),LENGTH=19,ATTRB=(ASKIP,BRT)
430 LNDATE2    DFHMDF POS=(12,34),LENGTH=06,ATTRB=(ASKIP,BRT)
441 UNIT2      DFHMDF POS=(12,41),LENGTH=05,ATTRB=(ASKIP,BRT),       X
               PICIN='99999',PICOUT='99999'
452 UCOST2     DFHMDF POS=(12,47),LENGTH=07,ATTRB=(ASKIP,BRT),       X
               PICIN='9999999',PICOUT='9999999'
463 COST2      DFHMDF POS=(12,55),LENGTH=08,ATTRB=(ASKIP,BRT),       X
               PICIN='99999999',PICOUT='99999999'
474 UPRICE2    DFHMDF POS=(12,64),LENGTH=07,ATTRB=(ASKIP,BRT),       X
               PICIN='9999999',PICOUT='9999999'
485 PRICE2     DFHMDF POS=(12,72),LENGTH=08,ATTRB=(ASKIP,BRT),       X
               PICIN='99999999',PICOUT='99999999'
496 LINE3      DFHMDF POS=(13,03),LENGTH=01,ATTRB=ASKIP
507 ITEM3      DFHMDF POS=(13,05),LENGTH=08,ATTRB=(ASKIP,BRT),       X
               PICIN='99999999',PICOUT='99999999'
518 DESC3      DFHMDF POS=(13,14),LENGTH=19,ATTRB=(ASKIP,BRT)
529 LNDATE3    DFHMDF POS=(13,34),LENGTH=06,ATTRB=(ASKIP,BRT)
540 UNIT3      DFHMDF POS=(13,41),LENGTH=05,ATTRB=(ASKIP,BRT),       X
               PICIN='99999',PICOUT='99999'
551 UCOST3     DFHMDF POS=(13,47),LENGTH=07,ATTRB=(ASKIP,BRT),       X
               PICIN='9999999',PICOUT='9999999'
562 COST3      DFHMDF POS=(13,55),LENGTH=08,ATTRB=(ASKIP,BRT),       X
               PICIN='99999999',PICOUT='99999999'
573 UPRICE3    DFHMDF POS=(13,64),LENGTH=07,ATTRB=(ASKIP,BRT),       X
               PICIN='9999999',PICOUT='9999999'
584 PRICE3     DFHMDF POS=(13,72),LENGTH=08,ATTRB=(ASKIP,BRT),       X
               PICIN='99999999',PICOUT='99999999'
595 LINE4      DFHMDF POS=(14,03),LENGTH=01,ATTRB=ASKIP
606 ITEM4      DFHMDF POS=(14,05),LENGTH=08,ATTRB=(ASKIP,BRT),       X
               PICIN='99999999',PICOUT='99999999'
617 DESC4      DFHMDF POS=(14,14),LENGTH=19,ATTRB=(ASKIP,BRT)
628 LNDATE4    DFHMDF POS=(14,34),LENGTH=06,ATTRB=(ASKIP,BRT)
639 UNIT4      DFHMDF POS=(14,41),LENGTH=05,ATTRB=(ASKIP,BRT),       X
               PICIN='99999',PICOUT='99999'
650 UCOST4     DFHMDF POS=(14,47),LENGTH=07,ATTRB=(ASKIP,BRT),       X
               PICIN='9999999',PICOUT='9999999'
661 COST4      DFHMDF POS=(14,55),LENGTH=08,ATTRB=(ASKIP,BRT),       X
               PICIN='99999999',PICOUT='99999999'
672 UPRICE4    DFHMDF POS=(14,64),LENGTH=07,ATTRB=(ASKIP,BRT),       X
               PICIN='9999999',PICOUT='9999999'
683 PRICE4     DFHMDF POS=(14,72),LENGTH=08,ATTRB=(ASKIP,BRT),       X
               PICIN='99999999',PICOUT='99999999'
694 LINE5      DFHMDF POS=(15,03),LENGTH=01,ATTRB=ASKIP
705 ITEM5      DFHMDF POS=(15,05),LENGTH=08,ATTRB=(ASKIP,BRT),       X
               PICIN='99999999',PICOUT='99999999'
716 DESC5      DFHMDF POS=(15,14),LENGTH=19,ATTRB=(ASKIP,BRT)
727 LNDATE5    DFHMDF POS=(15,34),LENGTH=06,ATTRB=(ASKIP,BRT)
738 UNIT5      DFHMDF POS=(15,41),LENGTH=05,ATTRB=(ASKIP,BRT),       X
               PICIN='99999',PICOUT='99999'
749 UCOST5     DFHMDF POS=(15,47),LENGTH=07,ATTRB=(ASKIP,BRT),       X
               PICIN='9999999',PICOUT='9999999'
```

Fig. 23.3.   (Continued)

```
 760 COST5    DFHMDF POS=(15,55),LENGTH=08,ATTRB=(ASKIP,BRT),        X
              PICIN='99999999',PICOUT='99999999'
 771 UPRICE5  DFHMDF POS=(15,64),LENGTH=07,ATTRB=(ASKIP,BRT),        X
              PICIN='9999999',PICOUT='9999999'
 782 PRICE5   DFHMDF POS=(15,72),LENGTH=08,ATTRB=(ASKIP,BRT),        X
              PICIN='99999999',PICOUT='99999999'
 793 LINE6    DFHMDF POS=(16,03),LENGTH=01,ATTRB=ASKIP
 804 ITEM6    DFHMDF POS=(16,05),LENGTH=08,ATTRB=(ASKIP,BRT),        X
              PICIN='99999999',PICOUT='99999999'
 815 DESC6    DFHMDF POS=(16,14),LENGTH=19,ATTRB=(ASKIP,BRT)
 826 LNDATE6  DFHMDF POS=(16,34),LENGTH=06,ATTRB=(ASKIP,BRT)
 837 UNIT6    DFHMDF POS=(16,41),LENGTH=05,ATTRB=(ASKIP,BRT),        X
              PICIN='99999',PICOUT='99999'
 848 UCOST6   DFHMDF POS=(16,47),LENGTH=07,ATTRB=(ASKIP,BRT),        X
              PICIN='9999999',PICOUT='9999999'
 859 COST6    DFHMDF POS=(16,55),LENGTH=08,ATTRB=(ASKIP,BRT),        X
              PICIN='99999999',PICOUT='99999999'
 870 UPRICE6  DFHMDF POS=(16,64),LENGTH=07,ATTRB=(ASKIP,BRT),        X
              PICIN='9999999',PICOUT='9999999'
 881 PRICE6   DFHMDF POS=(16,72),LENGTH=08,ATTRB=(ASKIP,BRT),        X
              PICIN='99999999',PICOUT='99999999'
 892 LINE7    DFHMDF POS=(17,03),LENGTH=01,ATTRB=ASKIP
 903 ITEM7    DFHMDF POS=(17,05),LENGTH=08,ATTRB=(ASKIP,BRT),        X
              PICIN='99999999',PICOUT='99999999'
 914 DESC7    DFHMDF POS=(17,14),LENGTH=19,ATTRB=(ASKIP,BRT)
 925 LNDATE7  DFHMDF POS=(17,34),LENGTH=06,ATTRB=(ASKIP,BRT)
 936 UNIT7    DFHMDF POS=(17,41),LENGTH=05,ATTRB=(ASKIP,BRT),        X
              PICIN='99999',PICOUT='99999'
 947 UCOST7   DFHMDF POS=(17,47),LENGTH=07,ATTRB=(ASKIP,BRT),        X
              PICIN='9999999',PICOUT='9999999'
 958 COST7    DFHMDF POS=(17,55),LENGTH=08,ATTRB=(ASKIP,BRT),        X
              PICIN='99999999',PICOUT='99999999'
 969 UPRICE7  DFHMDF POS=(17,64),LENGTH=07,ATTRB=(ASKIP,BRT),        X
              PICIN='9999999',PICOUT='9999999'
 980 PRICE7   DFHMDF POS=(17,72),LENGTH=08,ATTRB=(ASKIP,BRT),        X
              PICIN='99999999',PICOUT='99999999'
 991 LINE8    DFHMDF POS=(18,03),LENGTH=01,ATTRB=ASKIP
1002 ITEM8    DFHMDF POS=(18,05),LENGTH=08,ATTRB=(ASKIP,BRT),        X
              PICIN='99999999',PICOUT='99999999'
1013 DESC8    DFHMDF POS=(18,14),LENGTH=19,ATTRB=(ASKIP,BRT)
1024 LNDATE8  DFHMDF POS=(18,34),LENGTH=06,ATTRB=(ASKIP,BRT)
1035 UNIT8    DFHMDF POS=(18,41),LENGTH=05,ATTRB=(ASKIP,BRT),        X
              PICIN='99999',PICOUT='99999'
1046 UCOST8   DFHMDF POS=(18,47),LENGTH=07,ATTRB=(ASKIP,BRT),        X
              PICIN='9999999',PICOUT='9999999'
1057 COST8    DFHMDF POS=(18,55),LENGTH=08,ATTRB=(ASKIP,BRT),        X
              PICIN='99999999',PICOUT='99999999'
1068 UPRICE8  DFHMDF POS=(18,64),LENGTH=07,ATTRB=(ASKIP,BRT),        X
              PICIN='9999999',PICOUT='9999999'
1079 PRICE8   DFHMDF POS=(18,72),LENGTH=08,ATTRB=(ASKIP,BRT),        X
              PICIN='99999999',PICOUT='99999999'
```

Fig. 23.3. (Continued)

```
STMT    SOURCE STATEMENT                        DOS/VS ASSEMBLER REL 34.0 13.13

1090 LINE9     DFHMDF POS=(19,03),LENGTH=01,ATTRB=ASKIP
1101 ITEM9     DFHMDF POS=(19,05),LENGTH=08,ATTRB=(ASKIP,BRT),          X
               PICIN='99999999',PICOUT='99999999'
1112 DESC9     DFHMDF POS=(19,14),LENGTH=19,ATTRB=(ASKIP,BRT)
1123 LNDATE9   DFHMDF POS=(19,34),LENGTH=06,ATTRB=(ASKIP,BRT)
1134 UNIT9     DFHMDF POS=(19,41),LENGTH=05,ATTRB=(ASKIP,BRT),          X
               PICIN='99999',PICOUT='99999'
1145 UCOST9    DFHMDF POS=(19,47),LENGTH=07,ATTRB=(ASKIP,BRT),          X
               PICIN='9999999',PICOUT='9999999'
1156 COST9     DFHMDF POS=(19,55),LENGTH=08,ATTRB=(ASKIP,BRT),          X
               PICIN='99999999',PICOUT='99999999'
1167 UPRICE9   DFHMDF POS=(19,64),LENGTH=07,ATTRB=(ASKIP,BRT),          X
               PICIN='9999999',PICOUT='9999999'
1178 PRICE9    DFHMDF POS=(19,72),LENGTH=08,ATTRB=(ASKIP,BRT),          X
               PICIN='99999999',PICOUT='99999999'
1189 ERROR     DFHMDF POS=(23,30),LENGTH=22,ATTRB=(ASKIP,BRT)
1200           DFHMDF POS=(24,38),LENGTH=26,ATTRB=ASKIP,                X
               INITIAL='STARTING DEPT / DATE ---- '
1212 STRDEPT   DFHMDF POS=(24,68),LENGTH=03,ATTRB=(NUM,BRT,FSET,IC),    X
               INITIAL='999'
1224           DFHMDF POS=(24,72),LENGTH=01,ATTRB=ASKIP,INITIAL='/'
1236 STRDATE   DFHMDF POS=(24,74),LENGTH=06,ATTRB=(NUM,BRT,FSET),       X
               INITIAL='MMDDYY'
1248           DFHMSD TYPE=FINAL
1262           END
```

Fig. 23.3. (Continued)

```
  1  IBM DOS VS COBOL


CBL SUPMAP,STXIT,NOTRUNC,CSYNTAX,SXREF,OPT,VERB,CLIST,BUF=19069
CBL NOOPT,LIB
00001           IDENTIFICATION DIVISION.

00003           PROGRAM-ID. ORBSO1A.


00005           ENVIRONMENT DIVISION.


00007      ************************************************************
00008      *                                                         *
00009      *     1. THIS PROGRAM ALLOWS A BROWSE (BY ORDER DATE WITHIN *
00010      *        DEPARTMENT NUMBER) ON THE PURCHASE ORDER MASTER FILE. *
00011      *                                                         *
00012      *     2. THE OPERATOR MAY START AT THE EARLIEST ORDER DATE OF *
00013      *        THE LOWEST DEPARTMENT NUMBER BY ENTERING ALL ZEROES *
00014      *        ON THE DEPT/DATE STARTING FIELD.                  *
00015      *                                                         *
00016      *     3. SHE MAY ALSO START AT THE LATEST DATE OF THE HIGHEST *
00017      *        DEPARTMENT NUMBER (FOR A BROWSE BACKWARDS) BY ENTERING *
00018      *        ALL NINES.                                        *
00019      *                                                         *
00020      *     4. BROWSE FORWARD -   PF1 OR ENTER KEY.             *
00021      *                                                         *
00022      *     5. BROWSE BACKWARDS - PF2 KEY.                      *
00023      *                                                         *
00024      ************************************************************
```

Fig. 23.4. File Browse Program (Alternate Key).

```
2         ORBS01A          15.59.55        12/27/80

00026         DATA DIVISION.

00028         WORKING-STORAGE SECTION.

00030         01  COMMUNICATION-AREA.

00032             05  COMMAREA-PROCESS-SW      PIC X.


00034         01  AREA1.

00036             05  JOB-NORMAL-END-MESSAGE  PIC X(23) VALUE
00037                 'JOB NORMALLY TERMINATED'.

00039             05  JOB-ABORTED-MESSAGE.
00040                 10  FILLER              PIC X(15) VALUE 'JOB ABORTED --'.
00041                 10  MAJOR-ERROR-MSG     PIC X(16).

00043             05  HEXADECIMAL-ZEROES      PIC 9999 COMP VALUE ZEROES.

00045             05  FILLER REDEFINES HEXADECIMAL-ZEROES.
00046                 10  FILLER              PIC X.
00047                 10  HEX-ZEROES          PIC X.

00049             05  OLD-EIB-AREA.
00050                 10  FILLER              PIC X(7) VALUE 'OLD EIB'.
00051                 10  OLD-EIBFN           PIC XX.
00052                 10  OLD-EIBRCODE        PIC X(6).

00054             05  DUPLICATE-MESSAGE.
00055                 10  FILLER              PIC X(12) VALUE 'DUPLICATE - '.
00056                 10  DUPLICATE-COUNT     PIC 999.
00057                 10  DUPLICATE-LAST      PIC X(7).


00059         01  DFHAID COPY DFHAID.
00060 C       01      DFHAID.
00061 C           02  DFHNULL   PIC  X   VALUE IS ' '.
00062 C           02  DFHENTER  PIC  X   VALUE IS QUOTE.
00063 C           02  DFHCLEAR  PIC  X   VALUE IS ' '.
00064 C           02  DFHPEN    PIC  X   VALUE IS '='.
00065 C           02  DFHOPID   PIC  X   VALUE IS 'W'.
00066 C           02  DFHPA1    PIC  X   VALUE IS 'Z'.
```

Fig. 23.4. (Continued)

```
00067 C        02  DFHPA2    PIC  X  VALUE IS ' '.
00068 C        02  DFHPA3    PIC  X  VALUE IS ','.
00069 C        02  DFHPF1    PIC  X  VALUE IS '1'.
00070 C        02  DFHPF2    PIC  X  VALUE IS '2'.
00071 C        02  DFHPF3    PIC  X  VALUE IS '3'.
00072 C        02  DFHPF4    PIC  X  VALUE IS '4'.
00073 C        02  DFHPF5    PIC  X  VALUE IS '5'.
00074 C        02  DFHPF6    PIC  X  VALUE IS '6'.
00075 C        02  DFHPF7    PIC  X  VALUE IS '7'.
00076 C        02  DFHPF8    PIC  X  VALUE IS '8'.
00077 C        02  DFHPF9    PIC  X  VALUE IS '9'.
00078 C        02  DFHPF10   PIC  X  VALUE IS ' '.
00079 C        02  DFHPF11   PIC  X  VALUE IS '#'.
00080 C        02  DFHPF12   PIC  X  VALUE IS 'a'.
00081 C        02  DFHPF13   PIC  X  VALUE IS 'A'.
00082 C        02  DFHPF14   PIC  X  VALUE IS 'B'.
00083 C        02  DFHPF15   PIC  X  VALUE IS 'C'.
00084 C        02  DFHPF16   PIC  X  VALUE IS 'D'.
00085 C        02  DFHPF17   PIC  X  VALUE IS 'E'.
00086 C        02  DFHPF18   PIC  X  VALUE IS 'F'.
00087 C        02  DFHPF19   PIC  X  VALUE IS 'G'.
00088 C        02  DFHPF20   PIC  X  VALUE IS 'H'.
00089 C        02  DFHPF21   PIC  X  VALUE IS 'I'.
00090 C        02  DFHPF22   PIC  X  VALUE IS ' '.
00091 C        02  DFHPF23   PIC  X  VALUE IS '.'.
00092 C        02  DFHPF24   PIC  X  VALUE IS '¤'.
```

Fig. 23.4. (Continued)

```
00094              01   DFHEIVAR COPY DFHEIVAR.
00095 C            01   DFHEIVAR.
00096 C                 02    DFHEIV0   PICTURE X(26).
00097 C                 02    DFHEIV1   PICTURE X(8).
00098 C                 02    DFHEIV2   PICTURE X(8).
00099 C                 02    DFHEIV3   PICTURE X(8).
00100 C                 02    DFHEIV4   PICTURE X(6).
00101 C                 02    DFHEIV5   PICTURE X(4).
00102 C                 02    DFHEIV6   PICTURE X(4).
00103 C                 02    DFHEIV7   PICTURE X(2).
00104 C                 02    DFHEIV8   PICTURE X(2).
00105 C                 02    DFHEIV9   PICTURE X(1).
00106 C                 02    DFHEIV10  PICTURE S9(7) USAGE COMPUTATIONAL-3.
00107 C                 02    DFHEIV11  PICTURE S9(4) USAGE COMPUTATIONAL.
00108 C                 02    DFHEIV12  PICTURE S9(4) USAGE COMPUTATIONAL.
00109 C                 02    DFHEIV13  PICTURE S9(4) USAGE COMPUTATIONAL.
00110 C                 02    DFHEIV14  PICTURE S9(4) USAGE COMPUTATIONAL.
00111 C                 02    DFHEIV15  PICTURE S9(4) USAGE COMPUTATIONAL.
00112 C                 02    DFHEIV16  PICTURE S9(9) USAGE COMPUTATIONAL.
00113 C                 02    DFHEIV17  PICTURE X(4).
00114 C                 02    DFHEIV18  PICTURE X(4).
00115 C                 02    DFHEIV19  PICTURE X(4).
00116 C                 02    DFHEIV97  PICTURE S9(7) USAGE COMPUTATIONAL-3 VALUE ZERO.
00117 C                 02    DFHEIV98  PICTURE S9(4) USAGE COMPUTATIONAL VALUE ZERO.
00118 C                 02    DFHEIV99  PICTURE X(1)  VALUE SPACE.
00119              LINKAGE SECTION.

00121              01   DFHEIBLK COPY DFHEIBLK.
00122 C            *        EIBLK EXEC INTERFACE BLOCK
00123 C            01   DFHEIBLK.
00124 C            *        EIBTIME     TIME IN 0HHMMSS FORMAT
00125 C                 02 EIBTIME     PICTURE S9(7) USAGE COMPUTATIONAL-3.
00126 C            *        EIBDATE     DATE IN 00YYDDD FORMAT
00127 C                 02 EIBDATE     PICTURE S9(7) USAGE COMPUTATIONAL-3.
00128 C            *        EIBTRNID    TRANSACTION IDENTIFIER
00129 C                 02 EIBTRNID    PICTURE X(4).
00130 C            *        EIBTASKN    TASK NUMBER
00131 C                 02 EIBTASKN    PICTURE S9(7) USAGE COMPUTATIONAL-3.
00132 C            *        EIBTRMID    TERMINAL IDENTIFIER
00133 C                 02 EIBTRMID    PICTURE X(4).
00134 C            *        DFHEIGDI    RESERVED
00135 C                 02 DFHEIGDI    PICTURE S9(4) USAGE COMPUTATIONAL.
00136 C            *        EIBCPOSN    CURSOR POSITION
00137 C                 02 EIBCPOSN    PICTURE S9(4) USAGE COMPUTATIONAL.
00138 C            *        EIBCALEN    COMMAREA LENGTH
00139 C                 02 EIBCALEN    PICTURE S9(4) USAGE COMPUTATIONAL.
00140 C            *        EIBAID      ATTENTION IDENTIFIER
00141 C                 02 EIBAID      PICTURE X(1).
00142 C            *        EIBFN       FUNCTION CODE
00143 C                 02 EIBFN       PICTURE X(2).
00144 C            *        EIBRCODE    RESPONSE CODE
00145 C                 02 EIBRCODE    PICTURE X(6).
```

Fig. 23.4. (Continued)

```
      5         ORBS01A           15.59.55          12/27/80

00146 C        *         EIBDS        DATASET NAME
00147 C                  02 EIBDS     PICTURE X(8).
00148 C        *         EIBREQID     REQUEST IDENTIFIER
00149 C                  02 EIBREQID  PICTURE X(8).
00150          01  DFHCOMMAREA                     PIC X.

00152              88  INITIAL-ENTRY-TIME          VALUE '0'.
00153              88  BROWSE-START-TIME           VALUE '1'.


00155          01  LINKAGE-POINTERS.

00157              05  FILLER                      PIC S9(8) COMP.
00158              05  MAP1-POINTER                PIC S9(8) COMP.
00159              05  POM-POINTER                 PIC S9(8) COMP.
00160              05  TWA-POINTER                 PIC S9(8) COMP.
```

Fig. 23.4. (Continued)

```
00162        ***********************************************************************
00163        *                                                                     *
00164        *                    DISPLAY MAP DESCRIPTION                          *
00165        *                                                                     *
00166        ***********************************************************************


00168        01  MAP1-AREA.
00169            05  FILLER                        PIC X(12).
00170            05  MAP1-DUMMY-L                  PIC S9999 COMP.
00171            05  MAP1-DUMMY-A                  PIC X.
00172            05  MAP1-DUMMY                    PIC X.
00173            05  MAP1-DEPARTMENT-L             PIC S9999 COMP.
00174            05  MAP1-DEPARTMENT-A             PIC X.
00175            05  MAP1-DEPARTMENT               PIC XXX.
00176            05  MAP1-ORDER-DATE-L             PIC S9999 COMP.
00177            05  MAP1-ORDER-DATE-A             PIC X.
00178            05  MAP1-ORDER-DATE.
00179                10  MAP1-ORDER-DATE-MONTH     PIC XX.
00180                10  MAP1-ORDER-DATE-DAY       PIC XX.
00181                10  MAP1-ORDER-DATE-YEAR      PIC XX.
00182            05  MAP1-ORDER-NUMBER-L           PIC S9999 COMP.
00183            05  MAP1-ORDER-NUMBER-A           PIC X.
00184            05  MAP1-ORDER-NUMBER             PIC X(10).
00185            05  MAP1-ORDER-DATE-ENTERED-L     PIC S9999 COMP.
00186            05  MAP1-ORDER-DATE-ENTERED-A     PIC X.
00187            05  MAP1-ORDER-DATE-ENTERED       PIC X(6).
00188            05  MAP1-TOTAL-COST-L             PIC S9999 COMP.
00189            05  MAP1-TOTAL-COST-A             PIC X.
00190            05  MAP1-TOTAL-COST               PIC Z,ZZZ,ZZZ.99.
00191            05  MAP1-TOTAL-PRICE-L            PIC S9999 COMP.
00192            05  MAP1-TOTAL-PRICE-A            PIC X.
00193            05  MAP1-TOTAL-PRICE              PIC Z,ZZZ,ZZZ.99.
00194            05  MAP1-LINE-ITEM                OCCURS 9
00195                                              INDEXED BY MAP1-LINE-I.
00196                10  MAP1-LINE-NUMBER-L        PIC S9999 COMP.
00197                10  MAP1-LINE-NUMBER-A        PIC X.
00198                10  MAP1-LINE-NUMBER          PIC 9.
00199                10  MAP1-ITEM-NUMBER-L        PIC S9999 COMP.
00200                10  MAP1-ITEM-NUMBER-A        PIC X.
00201                10  MAP1-ITEM-NUMBER          PIC X(8).
00202                10  MAP1-ITEM-DESCRIPTION-L   PIC S9999 COMP.
00203                10  MAP1-ITEM-DESCRIPTION-A   PIC X.
00204                10  MAP1-ITEM-DESCRIPTION     PIC X(19).
00205                10  MAP1-ITEM-DATE-L          PIC S9999 COMP.
00206                10  MAP1-ITEM-DATE-A          PIC X.
00207                10  MAP1-ITEM-DATE            PIC X(6).
00208                10  MAP1-UNIT-L               PIC S9999 COMP.
00209                10  MAP1-UNIT-A               PIC X.
00210                10  MAP1-UNIT                 PIC 9(5).
00211                10  MAP1-UNIT-COST-L          PIC S9999 COMP.
00212                10  MAP1-UNIT-COST-A          PIC X.
```

Fig. 23.4. (Continued)

```
   7          ORBSO1A            15.59.55          12/27/80


00213                    10   MAP1-UNIT-COST              PIC 9(5)V99.
00214                    10   MAP1-COST-L                 PIC S9999 COMP.
00215                    10   MAP1-COST-A                 PIC X.
00216                    10   MAP1-COST                   PIC 9(6)V99.
00217                    10   MAP1-UNIT-PRICE-L           PIC S9999 COMP.
00218                    10   MAP1-UNIT-PRICE-A           PIC X.
00219                    10   MAP1-UNIT-PRICE             PIC 9(5)V99.
00220                    10   MAP1-PRICE-L                PIC S9999 COMP.
00221                    10   MAP1-PRICE-A                PIC X.
00222                    10   MAP1-PRICE                  PIC 9(6)V99.
00223                 05   MAP1-ERROR-L                   PIC S9999 COMP.
00224                 05   MAP1-ERROR-A                   PIC X.
00225                 05   MAP1-ERROR                     PIC X(22).
00226                 05   MAP1-START-DEPARTMENT-L        PIC S9999 COMP.
00227                 05   MAP1-START-DEPARTMENT-A        PIC X.
00228                 05   MAP1-START-DEPARTMENT          PIC XXX.
00229                 05   MAP1-START-DATE-L              PIC S9999 COMP.
00230                 05   MAP1-START-DATE-A              PIC X.
00231                 05   MAP1-START-DATE.
00232                    10   MAP1-START-DATE-MONTH       PIC XX.
00233                    10   MAP1-START-DATE-DAY         PIC XX.
00234                    10   MAP1-START-DATE-YEAR        PIC XX.


   8          ORBSO1A            15.59.55          12/27/80


00236          ****************************************************************
00237          *                                                              *
00238          *         PURCHASE ORDER MASTER -- FILE LAYOUT                 *
00239          *                                                              *
00240          ****************************************************************


00242          01   ORDER-MASTER-RECORD.
00243               05   ORDER-NUMBER                   PIC X(10).
00244               05   ORDER-ALT-KEY.
00245                  10   ORDER-DEPARTMENT            PIC XXX.
00246                  10   ORDER-DATE.
00247                     15   ORDER-DATE-YEAR          PIC XX.
00248                     15   ORDER-DATE-MONTH         PIC XX.
00249                     15   ORDER-DATE-DAY           PIC XX.
00250               05   ORDER-DATE-ENTERED.
00251                  10   ORDER-DATE-ENTERED-MONTH    PIC XX.
00252                  10   ORDER-DATE-ENTERED-DAY      PIC XX.
00253                  10   ORDER-DATE-ENTERED-YEAR     PIC XX.
00254               05   ORDER-TOTAL-COST              PIC S9(7)V99  COMP-3.
00255               05   ORDER-TOTAL-PRICE             PIC S9(7)V99  COMP-3.
00256               05   ORDER-LINE-COUNT              PIC S9999     COMP.
00257               05   ORDER-ALL-LINES.
00258                  10   ORDER-LINE-ITEM             OCCURS 1 TO 9
00259                                                  DEPENDING ON ORDER-LINE-COUNT
00260                                                  INDEXED BY ORDER-LINE-I.
00261                     15   ORDER-ITEM-NUMBER        PIC X(8).
00262                     15   ORDER-ITEM-DESCRIPTION   PIC X(19).
00263                     15   ORDER-ITEM-DATE.
00264                        20   ORDER-ITEM-DATE-MONTH PIC XX.
00265                        20   ORDER-ITEM-DATE-DAY   PIC XX.
00266                        20   ORDER-ITEM-DATE-YEAR  PIC XX.
00267                     15   ORDER-UNIT               PIC S9(5)     COMP-3.
00268                     15   ORDER-UNIT-COST          PIC S9(5)V99  COMP-3.
00269                     15   ORDER-UNIT-PRICE         PIC S9(5)V99  COMP-3.
```

Fig. 23.4. (Continued)

```
00271      ***********************************************************************
00272      *                                                                     *
00273      *                   TRANSACTION WORK AREA                             *
00274      *                                                                     *
00275      ***********************************************************************


00277      01   TWA-AREA.


00279           05   TWA-LINE-ITEM-MAP.
00280                10   TWA-LINE-NUMBER-MAP-L          PIC S9999 COMP.
00281                10   TWA-LINE-NUMBER-MAP-A          PIC X.
00282                10   TWA-LINE-NUMBER-MAP            PIC 9.
00283                10   TWA-ITEM-NUMBER-MAP-L          PIC S9999 COMP.
00284                10   TWA-ITEM-NUMBER-MAP-A          PIC X.
00285                10   TWA-ITEM-NUMBER-MAP            PIC X(8).
00286                10   TWA-ITEM-DESCRIPTION-MAP-L     PIC S9999 COMP.
00287                10   TWA-ITEM-DESCRIPTION-MAP-A     PIC X.
00288                10   TWA-ITEM-DESCRIPTION-MAP       PIC X(19).
00289                10   TWA-ITEM-DATE-MAP-L            PIC S9999 COMP.
00290                10   TWA-ITEM-DATE-MAP-A            PIC X.
00291                10   TWA-ITEM-DATE-MAP              PIC X(6).
00292                10   TWA-UNIT-MAP-L                 PIC S9999 COMP.
00293                10   TWA-UNIT-MAP-A                 PIC X.
00294                10   TWA-UNIT-MAP                   PIC 9(5).
00295                10   TWA-UNIT-COST-MAP-L            PIC S9999 COMP.
00296                10   TWA-UNIT-COST-MAP-A            PIC X.
00297                10   TWA-UNIT-COST-MAP              PIC 9(5)V99.
00298                10   TWA-COST-MAP-L                 PIC S9999 COMP.
00299                10   TWA-COST-MAP-A                 PIC X.
00300                10   TWA-COST-MAP                   PIC 9(6)V99.
00301                10   TWA-UNIT-PRICE-MAP-L           PIC S9999 COMP.
00302                10   TWA-UNIT-PRICE-MAP-A           PIC X.
00303                10   TWA-UNIT-PRICE-MAP             PIC 9(5)V99.
00304                10   TWA-PRICE-MAP-L                PIC S9999 COMP.
00305                10   TWA-PRICE-MAP-A                PIC X.
00306                10   TWA-PRICE-MAP                  PIC 9(6)V99.


00308           05   TWA-LINE-ITEM-ORDER.
00309                10   TWA-ITEM-NUMBER-ORDER          PIC X(8).
00310                10   TWA-ITEM-DESCRIPTION-ORDER     PIC X(19).
00311                10   TWA-ITEM-DATE-ORDER            PIC X(6).
00312                10   TWA-UNIT-ORDER                 PIC S9(5)     COMP-3.
00313                10   TWA-UNIT-COST-ORDER            PIC S9(5)V99 COMP-3.
00314                10   TWA-UNIT-PRICE-ORDER           PIC S9(5)V99 COMP-3.


00316           05   TWA-OPERATOR-MESSAGE               PIC X(31).
```

Fig. 23.4. (Continued)

```
10         ORBS01A          15.59.55        12/27/80


00318                   05   TWA-ALTERNATE-KEY.
00319                        10   TWA-ALTERNATE-KEY-DEPT           PIC XXX.
00320                        10   TWA-ALTERNATE-KEY-DATE.
00321                             15   TWA-ALTERNATE-KEY-DATE-YEAR      PIC XX.
00322                             15   TWA-ALTERNATE-KEY-DATE-MONTH     PIC XX.
00323                             15   TWA-ALTERNATE-KEY-DATE-DAY       PIC XX.


00325                   05   TWA-PREV-ALTERNATE-KEY            PIC X(9).


00327                   05   TWA-START-ALTERNATE-KEY.
00328                        10   TWA-START-DEPARTMENT             PIC XXX.
00329                        10   TWA-START-DATE.
00330                             15   TWA-START-DATE-YEAR         PIC XX.
00331                             15   TWA-START-DATE-MONTH        PIC XX.
00332                             15   TWA-START-DATE-DAY          PIC XX.


00334                   05   TWA-DUPLICATE-COUNT              PIC S999 COMP-3.


00336                   05   PREV-ACTION                      PIC X.
00337                        88   PREV-ACTION-FORWARD               VALUE '1'.
00338                        88   PREV-ACTION-BACKWARDS             VALUE '2'.
00339                        88   PREV-ACTION-FORWARD-EOF           VALUE '3'.
00340                        88   PREV-ACTION-BACKWARDS-EOF         VALUE '4'.
00341                        88   PREV-ACTION-FORWARD-NOTFOUND      VALUE '5'.
00342                        88   PREV-ACTION-IMMATERIAL            VALUE '9'.
```

Fig. 23.4. (Continued)

```
        11          ORBS01A         15.59.55        12/27/80

00344              PROCEDURE DIVISION USING DFHEIBLK DFHCOMMAREA.
00345                   CALL 'DFHEI1'.


00347              ****************************************************************
00348              *                                                              *
00349              MAIN-LINE SECTION.
00350              *                                                              *
00351              ****************************************************************

00353              *    EXEC CICS
00354              *        ADDRESS TWA (TWA-POINTER)
00355              *    END-EXEC.
00356                   MOVE '              ' TO DFHEIVO CALL 'DFHEI1' USING
00357                   DFHEIVO TWA-POINTER.
00358
00359              *    EXEC CICS
00360              *        HANDLE AID
00361              *            CLEAR (FINALIZATION)
00362              *            PA1 (WRONG-KEY-USED)
00363              *            PA2 (WRONG-KEY-USED)
00364              *            PA3 (WRONG-KEY-USED)
00365              *    END-EXEC.
00366                   MOVE '  0            ' TO DFHEIVO CALL 'DFHEI1' USING
00367                   DFHEIVO GO TO FINALIZATION WRONG-KEY-USED WRONG-KEY-USED
00368                   WRONG-KEY-USED DEPENDING ON DFHEIGDI.
00369
00370
00371
00372
00373              *    EXEC CICS
00374              *        HANDLE CONDITION
00375              *            MAPFAIL (MAPFAIL-ERROR)
00376              *            NOTOPEN (FILE-NOT-OPEN)
00377              *            ERROR   (MAJOR-ERROR)
00378              *    END-EXEC.
00379                   MOVE '              ' TO DFHEIVO CALL 'DFHEI1' USING
00380                   DFHEIVO GO TO MAPFAIL-ERROR FILE-NOT-OPEN MAJOR-ERROR
00381                   DEPENDING ON DFHEIGDI.
00382
00383
00384
00385                   IF EIBCALEN NOT EQUAL TO ZEROES
00386                       IF BROWSE-START-TIME
00387                           GO TO BROWSE-START
00388                       ELSE IF INITIAL-ENTRY-TIME
00389                           GO TO INITIALIZATION
00390                       ELSE GO TO PROCESS-SWITCH-ERROR.

00392                   IF EIBCALEN EQUAL TO ZEROES
00393                       GO TO SIGN-ON-VIOLATION.
```

Fig. 23.4. (Continued)

```
00395        *****************************************************************
00396        *                                                               *
00397        BROWSE-CONTINUE SECTION.
00398        *                                                               *
00399        *****************************************************************

00401    *      EXEC CICS
00402    *          RECEIVE MAP    ('ORBSM01')
00403    *                  MAPSET ('ORBSS01')
00404    *                  SET    (MAP1-POINTER)
00405    *      END-EXEC.
00406           MOVE 'ORBSM01' TO DFHEIV1 MOVE 'ORBSS01' TO DFHEIV2 MOVE '
00407    -      '            ' TO DFHEIVO CALL 'DFHEI1' USING DFHEIVO
00408           DFHEIV1 MAP1-POINTER DFHEIV98 DFHEIV2.
00409
00410
00411           IF    MAP1-START-DEPARTMENT NOT NUMERIC
00412              OR MAP1-START-DATE       NOT NUMERIC
00413           THEN GO TO INVALID-START-KEY.

00415           MOVE MAP1-START-DEPARTMENT   TO   TWA-START-DEPARTMENT.
00416           MOVE MAP1-START-DATE-MONTH   TO   TWA-START-DATE-MONTH.
00417           MOVE MAP1-START-DATE-DAY     TO   TWA-START-DATE-DAY.
00418           MOVE MAP1-START-DATE-YEAR    TO   TWA-START-DATE-YEAR.

00420           IF TWA-START-ALTERNATE-KEY = TWA-ALTERNATE-KEY
00421                   IF    EIBAID EQUAL TO DFHPF1
00422                     OR  EIBAID EQUAL TO DFHENTER
00423                   THEN GO TO BROWSE-FORWARD
00424                   ELSE IF EIBAID EQUAL TO DFHPF2
00425                           IF PREV-ACTION-FORWARD-NOTFOUND
00426                               MOVE ZEROES TO TWA-DUPLICATE-COUNT
00427                               MOVE SPACES TO TWA-PREV-ALTERNATE-KEY
00428                               MOVE HIGH-VALUES TO TWA-ALTERNATE-KEY

00430    *                         EXEC CICS
00431    *                             RESETBR
00432    *                                 DATASET ('ORTAIX')
00433    *                                 RIDFLD  (TWA-ALTERNATE-KEY)
00434    *                                 GTEQ
00435    *                         END-EXEC
00436                               MOVE 'ORTAIX' TO DFHEIV3 MOVE '
00437    -      '' TO DFHEIVO CALL 'DFHEI1' USING DFHEIVO DFHEIV3 DFHEIV99
00438           DFHEIV98 TWA-ALTERNATE-KEY
00439
00440
00441
00442                               GO TO BROWSE-BACKWARD
00443                           ELSE GO TO BROWSE-BACKWARD
00444                   ELSE GO TO WRONG-KEY-USED
00445           ELSE MOVE ZEROES            TO   TWA-DUPLICATE-COUNT
00446                MOVE SPACES            TO   TWA-PREV-ALTERNATE-KEY
00447                MOVE '9'               TO   PREV-ACTION
```

Fig. 23.4. (Continued)

```
00448                       IF TWA-START-ALTERNATE-KEY GREATER TWA-ALTERNATE-KEY
00449                           MOVE TWA-START-ALTERNATE-KEY TO TWA-ALTERNATE-KEY
00450                           GO TO BROWSE-FORWARD
00451                       ELSE MOVE TWA-START-ALTERNATE-KEY TO TWA-ALTERNATE-KEY

00453             *             EXEC CICS
00454             *                 RESETBR
00455             *                     DATASET ('ORTAIX')
00456             *                     RIDFLD  (TWA-ALTERNATE-KEY)
00457             *                     GTEQ
00458             *             END-EXEC
00459                           MOVE 'ORTAIX' TO DFHEIV3 MOVE '          ' TO
00460             DFHEIV0 CALL 'DFHEI1' USING DFHEIV0 DFHEIV3 DFHEIV99
00461             DFHEIV98 TWA-ALTERNATE-KEY
00462
00463
00464
00465                           GO TO BROWSE-FORWARD.
```

Fig. 23.4. (Continued)

```
    14          ORBSO1A          15.59.55          12/27/80

00467          ****************************************************************
00468          *                                                              *
00469           BROWSE-FORWARD SECTION.
00470          *                                                              *
00471          ****************************************************************

00473          *     EXEC CICS
00474          *         HANDLE CONDITION
00475          *                 ENDFILE (END-OF-FILE-FORWARD)
00476          *                 NOTFND  (RECORD-NOT-FOUND-FORWARD)
00477          *                 DUPKEY  (DUPLICATE-KEY-FORWARD)
00478          *     END-EXEC.
00479                MOVE '                       ' TO DFHEIVO CALL 'DFHEI1' USING
00480                DFHEIVO GO TO END-OF-FILE-FORWARD RECORD-NOT-FOUND-FORWARD
00481                DUPLICATE-KEY-FORWARD DEPENDING ON DFHEIGDI.
00482
00483
00484
00485           READ-NEXT-RECORD.

00487          *     EXEC CICS
00488          *         READNEXT DATASET ('ORTAIX')
00489          *                  SET     (POM-POINTER)
00490          *                  RIDFLD  (TWA-ALTERNATE-KEY)
00491          *     END-EXEC.
00492                MOVE 'ORTAIX' TO DFHEIV3 MOVE '  M       ' TO DFHEIVO CALL 'D
00493          -    'FHEI1' USING DFHEIVO DFHEIV3 POM-POINTER DFHEIV98
00494                TWA-ALTERNATE-KEY DFHEIV98 DFHEIV98.
00495
00496
00497               IF PREV-ACTION-BACKWARDS
00498                   MOVE '1' TO PREV-ACTION
00499                   GO TO READ-NEXT-RECORD.

00501               IF TWA-ALTERNATE-KEY EQUAL TWA-PREV-ALTERNATE-KEY
00502                   ADD 1                      TO  TWA-DUPLICATE-COUNT
00503                   MOVE TWA-DUPLICATE-COUNT   TO  DUPLICATE-COUNT
00504                   MOVE ZEROES                TO  TWA-DUPLICATE-COUNT
00505                   MOVE ' / LAST'             TO  DUPLICATE-LAST
00506                   MOVE DUPLICATE-MESSAGE     TO  MAP1-ERROR
00507               ELSE MOVE TWA-ALTERNATE-KEY    TO  TWA-PREV-ALTERNATE-KEY
00508                   MOVE SPACES                TO  MAP1-ERROR.

00510           LAYOUT-ORDER-SCREEN.
00511               MOVE TWA-ALTERNATE-KEY-DEPT        TO  MAP1-START-DEPARTMENT.
00512               MOVE TWA-ALTERNATE-KEY-DATE-MONTH  TO  MAP1-START-DATE-MONTH.
00513               MOVE TWA-ALTERNATE-KEY-DATE-DAY    TO  MAP1-START-DATE-DAY.
00514               MOVE TWA-ALTERNATE-KEY-DATE-YEAR   TO  MAP1-START-DATE-YEAR.
00515               MOVE ORDER-NUMBER                  TO  MAP1-ORDER-NUMBER.
00516               MOVE ORDER-DEPARTMENT              TO  MAP1-DEPARTMENT.
00517               MOVE ORDER-DATE-MONTH              TO  MAP1-ORDER-DATE-MONTH.
```

Fig. 23.4. (Continued)

```
00518                MOVE ORDER-DATE-DAY                   TO  MAP1-ORDER-DATE-DAY.
00519                MOVE ORDER-DATE-YEAR                  TO  MAP1-ORDER-DATE-YEAR.
00520                MOVE ORDER-DATE-ENTERED            TO  MAP1-ORDER-DATE-ENTERED.
00521                MOVE ORDER-TOTAL-COST                 TO  MAP1-TOTAL-COST.
00522                MOVE ORDER-TOTAL-PRICE                TO  MAP1-TOTAL-PRICE.
00523                SET ORDER-LINE-I                      TO  1.
00524                PERFORM LAYOUT-EACH-LINE
00525                     UNTIL ORDER-LINE-I GREATER THAN ORDER-LINE-COUNT.
00526                GO TO DISPLAY-ORDER.


00528            LAYOUT-EACH-LINE.
00529                SET MAP1-LINE-I                      TO ORDER-LINE-I.
00530                MOVE ORDER-LINE-ITEM (ORDER-LINE-I) TO TWA-LINE-ITEM-ORDER.
00531                MOVE MAP1-LINE-ITEM (MAP1-LINE-I)    TO TWA-LINE-ITEM-MAP.
00532                SET TWA-LINE-NUMBER-MAP              TO ORDER-LINE-I.
00533                MOVE TWA-ITEM-NUMBER-ORDER      TO  TWA-ITEM-NUMBER-MAP.
00534                MOVE TWA-ITEM-DESCRIPTION-ORDER TO TWA-ITEM-DESCRIPTION-MAP.
00535                MOVE TWA-ITEM-DATE-ORDER       TO  TWA-ITEM-DATE-MAP.
00536                MOVE TWA-UNIT-ORDER            TO  TWA-UNIT-MAP.
00537                MOVE TWA-UNIT-COST-ORDER       TO  TWA-UNIT-COST-MAP.
00538                COMPUTE TWA-COST-MAP = TWA-UNIT-ORDER * TWA-UNIT-COST-ORDER.
00539                MOVE TWA-UNIT-PRICE-ORDER      TO  TWA-UNIT-PRICE-MAP.
00540                COMPUTE TWA-PRICE-MAP =
00541                     TWA-UNIT-ORDER * TWA-UNIT-PRICE-ORDER.
00542                MOVE TWA-LINE-ITEM-MAP     TO  MAP1-LINE-ITEM (MAP1-LINE-I).
00543                SET ORDER-LINE-I UP BY 1.


00545            DISPLAY-ORDER.

00547        *       EXEC CICS
00548        *          SEND MAP    ('ORBSM01')
00549        *               MAPSET ('ORBSS01')
00550        *               FROM   (MAP1-AREA)
00551        *               ERASE
00552        *       END-EXEC.
00553                MOVE 'ORBSM01' TO DFHEIV1 MOVE 'ORBSS01' TO DFHEIV2 MOVE '
00554        -       '  S   ' TO DFHEIVO CALL 'DFHEI1' USING DFHEIVO
00555                DFHEIV1 MAP1-AREA DFHEIV98 DFHEIV2.
00556
00557
00558
00559            AFTER-DISPLAY.
00560                MOVE '1' TO PREV-ACTION.
00561                GO TO BROWSE-CONTINUE.


00563            DUPLICATE-KEY-FORWARD.
00564                ADD 1                                 TO  TWA-DUPLICATE-COUNT.
00565                MOVE TWA-DUPLICATE-COUNT            TO  DUPLICATE-COUNT.
00566                MOVE SPACES                          TO  DUPLICATE-LAST.
00567                MOVE DUPLICATE-MESSAGE               TO  MAP1-ERROR.
```

Fig. 23.4. (Continued)

```
16          ORBS01A          15.59.55          12/27/80

00568                    IF TWA-DUPLICATE-COUNT EQUAL    TO  1
00569                        MOVE TWA-ALTERNATE-KEY      TO  TWA-PREV-ALTERNATE-KEY.
00570                    GO TO LAYOUT-ORDER-SCREEN.


00572          END-OF-FILE-FORWARD.
00573                    MOVE TWA-ALTERNATE-KEY-DEPT       TO  MAP1-START-DEPARTMENT.
00574                    MOVE TWA-ALTERNATE-KEY-DATE-MONTH TO  MAP1-START-DATE-MONTH.
00575                    MOVE TWA-ALTERNATE-KEY-DATE-DAY   TO  MAP1-START-DATE-DAY.
00576                    MOVE TWA-ALTERNATE-KEY-DATE-YEAR  TO  MAP1-START-DATE-YEAR.
00577                    MOVE SPACES                       TO  TWA-PREV-ALTERNATE-KEY.
00578                    MOVE  '3'                         TO  PREV-ACTION.
00579                    GO TO END-OF-FILE-FORWARD-MESSAGE.


00581          END-OF-FILE-FORWARD-MESSAGE.
00582                    MOVE 'END OF FILE' TO MAP1-ERROR.

00584      *    EXEC CICS
00585      *        SEND MAP   ('ORBSM01')
00586      *             MAPSET ('ORBSS01')
00587      *             FROM   (MAP1-AREA)
00588      *             ERASE
00589      *    END-EXEC.
00590           MOVE 'ORBSM01' TO DFHEIV1 MOVE 'ORBSS01' TO DFHEIV2 MOVE '
00591      -        '    S    ' TO DFHEIVO CALL 'DFHEI1' USING DFHEIVO
00592           DFHEIV1 MAP1-AREA DFHEIV98 DFHEIV2.
00593
00594
00595
00596           GO TO BROWSE-CONTINUE.


00598          RECORD-NOT-FOUND-FORWARD.
00599                    MOVE TWA-ALTERNATE-KEY-DEPT       TO  MAP1-START-DEPARTMENT.
00600                    MOVE TWA-ALTERNATE-KEY-DATE-MONTH TO  MAP1-START-DATE-MONTH.
00601                    MOVE TWA-ALTERNATE-KEY-DATE-DAY   TO  MAP1-START-DATE-DAY.
00602                    MOVE TWA-ALTERNATE-KEY-DATE-YEAR  TO  MAP1-START-DATE-YEAR.
00603                    MOVE SPACES                       TO  TWA-PREV-ALTERNATE-KEY.
00604                    MOVE  '5'                         TO  PREV-ACTION.
00605                    GO TO END-OF-FILE-FORWARD-MESSAGE.
```

Fig. 23.4. (Continued)

```
     17          ORBS01A         15.59.55        12/27/80

00607        **********************************************************************
00608        *                                                                    *
00609         BROWSE-BACKWARD SECTION.
00610        *                                                                    *
00611        **********************************************************************


00613        *      EXEC CICS
00614        *          HANDLE CONDITION
00615        *              ENDFILE (END-OF-FILE-BACKWARDS)
00616        *              DUPKEY  (DUPLICATE-KEY-BACKWARDS)
00617        *      END-EXEC.
00618               MOVE '                          ' TO DFHEIVO CALL 'DFHEI1' USING
00619               DFHEIVO GO TO END-OF-FILE-BACKWARDS DUPLICATE-KEY-BACKWARDS
00620               DEPENDING ON DFHEIGDI.
00621
00622
00623         READ-PREVIOUS-RECORD.
00624        *      EXEC CICS
00625        *          READPREV DATASET ('ORTAIX')
00626        *              SET     (POM-POINTER)
00627        *              RIDFLD  (TWA-ALTERNATE-KEY)
00628        *      END-EXEC.
00629               MOVE 'ORTAIX' TO DFHEIV3 MOVE '  M    ' TO DFHEIVO CALL 'D
00630        -      'FHEI1' USING DFHEIVO DFHEIV3 POM-POINTER DFHEIV98
00631               TWA-ALTERNATE-KEY DFHEIV98 DFHEIV98.
00632
00633
00634               IF PREV-ACTION-FORWARD
00635                    MOVE '2' TO PREV-ACTION
00636                    GO TO READ-PREVIOUS-RECORD.

00638               IF TWA-ALTERNATE-KEY  EQUAL    TO  TWA-PREV-ALTERNATE-KEY
00639                    ADD 1                     TO  TWA-DUPLICATE-COUNT
00640                    MOVE TWA-DUPLICATE-COUNT  TO  DUPLICATE-COUNT
00641                    MOVE ZEROES               TO  TWA-DUPLICATE-COUNT
00642                    MOVE ' / LAST'            TO  DUPLICATE-LAST
00643                    MOVE DUPLICATE-MESSAGE    TO  MAP1-ERROR
00644               ELSE MOVE TWA-ALTERNATE-KEY   TO  TWA-PREV-ALTERNATE-KEY
00645                    MOVE SPACES               TO  MAP1-ERROR.


00647         LAYOUT-ORDER-SCREEN-BACKWARDS.
00648               PERFORM LAYOUT-ORDER-SCREEN THRU DISPLAY-ORDER.
00649               MOVE '2' TO PREV-ACTION.
00650               GO TO BROWSE-CONTINUE.


00652         DUPLICATE-KEY-BACKWARDS.
00653               ADD 1                          TO  TWA-DUPLICATE-COUNT.
00654               MOVE TWA-DUPLICATE-COUNT       TO  DUPLICATE-COUNT.
00655               MOVE SPACES                    TO  DUPLICATE-LAST.
00656               MOVE DUPLICATE-MESSAGE         TO  MAP1-ERROR.
```

Fig. 23.4. (Continued)

```
   18          ORBSO1A         15.59.55        12/27/80


00657                    IF TWA-DUPLICATE-COUNT EQUAL  TO  1
00658                        MOVE TWA-ALTERNATE-KEY   TO  TWA-PREV-ALTERNATE-KEY.
00659                    GO TO LAYOUT-ORDER-SCREEN-BACKWARDS.


00661          END-OF-FILE-BACKWARDS.
00662              MOVE TWA-ALTERNATE-KEY-DEPT        TO  MAP1-START-DEPARTMENT.
00663              MOVE TWA-ALTERNATE-KEY-DATE-MONTH TO  MAP1-START-DATE-MONTH.
00664              MOVE TWA-ALTERNATE-KEY-DATE-DAY   TO  MAP1-START-DATE-DAY.
00665              MOVE TWA-ALTERNATE-KEY-DATE-YEAR  TO  MAP1-START-DATE-YEAR.
00666              MOVE SPACES                       TO  TWA-PREV-ALTERNATE-KEY.
00667              MOVE  '4'                         TO  PREV-ACTION.
00668              MOVE 'END OF FILE' TO MAP1-ERROR.

00670        *     EXEC CICS
00671        *         SEND MAP   ('ORBSM01')
00672        *              MAPSET ('ORBSS01')
00673        *                 FROM  (MAP1-AREA)
00674        *                 ERASE
00675        *     END-EXEC.
00676              MOVE 'ORBSM01' TO DFHEIV1 MOVE 'ORBSS01' TO DFHEIV2 MOVE '
00677        -      '    S    ' TO DFHEIVO CALL 'DFHEI1' USING DFHEIVO
00678              DFHEIV1 MAP1-AREA DFHEIV98 DFHEIV2.
00679
00680
00681
00682              GO TO BROWSE-CONTINUE.


00684          INVALID-START-KEY.
00685              MOVE 'INVALID ALTERNATE KEY' TO MAP1-ERROR.

00687        *     EXEC CICS
00688        *         SEND MAP   ('ORBSM01')
00689        *              MAPSET ('ORBSS01')
00690        *                 FROM  (MAP1-AREA)
00691        *                 ERASE
00692        *     END-EXEC.
00693              MOVE 'ORBSM01' TO DFHEIV1 MOVE 'ORBSS01' TO DFHEIV2 MOVE '
00694        -      '    S    ' TO DFHEIVO CALL 'DFHEI1' USING DFHEIVO
00695              DFHEIV1 MAP1-AREA DFHEIV98 DFHEIV2.
00696
00697
00698

00700              GO TO BROWSE-CONTINUE.
```

Fig. 23.4. (Continued)

```
    19          ORBSO1A          15.59.55          12/27/80

00702          ********************************************************************
00703          *                                                                  *
00704           WRONG-KEY-USED SECTION.
00705          *                                                                  *
00706          ********************************************************************

00708          *     EXEC CICS
00709          *         GETMAIN
00710          *             SET      (MAP1-POINTER)
00711          *             LENGTH   (987)
00712          *             INITIMG  (HEX-ZEROES)
00713          *     END-EXEC.
00714                MOVE 987 TO DFHEIV11 MOVE '          ' TO DFHEIVO CALL 'DFHEI
00715          -     '1' USING DFHEIVO MAP1-POINTER DFHEIV11 HEX-ZEROES.
00716
00717
00718
00719
00720                MOVE 'WRONG KEY USED' TO MAP1-ERROR.

00722          *     EXEC CICS
00723          *         SEND MAP    ('ORBSMO1')
00724          *             MAPSET  ('ORBSSO1')
00725          *             FROM    (MAP1-AREA)
00726          *             DATAONLY
00727          *     END-EXEC.
00728                MOVE 'ORBSMO1' TO DFHEIV1 MOVE 'ORBSSO1' TO DFHEIV2 MOVE '
00729          -     '          ' TO DFHEIVO CALL 'DFHEI1' USING DFHEIVO
00730                DFHEIV1 MAP1-AREA DFHEIV98 DFHEIV2.
00731
00732
00733
00734          *     EXEC CICS
00735          *         FREEMAIN DATA (MAP1-AREA)
00736          *     END-EXEC.
00737                MOVE '          ' TO DFHEIVO CALL 'DFHEI1' USING DFHEIVO
00738                MAP1-AREA.
00739
00740                GO TO BROWSE-CONTINUE.
```

Fig. 23.4. (Continued)

```
20          ORBS01A        15.59.55        12/27/80


00742       **************************************************************
00743       *                                                            *
00744        BROWSE-START SECTION.
00745       *                                                            *
00746       **************************************************************


00748       *     EXEC CICS
00749       *         RECEIVE MAP     ('ORBSM01')
00750       *                 MAPSET  ('ORBSS01')
00751       *                 SET     (MAP1-POINTER)
00752       *     END-EXEC.
00753            MOVE 'ORBSM01' TO DFHEIV1 MOVE 'ORBSS01' TO DFHEIV2 MOVE '
00754       -          '        ' TO DFHEIV0 CALL 'DFHEI1' USING DFHEIV0
00755            DFHEIV1 MAP1-POINTER DFHEIV98 DFHEIV2.
00756
00757
00758        BROWSE-STARTING-RECORD.

00760            IF   MAP1-START-DEPARTMENT   NOT   NUMERIC
00761               OR MAP1-START-DATE        NOT   NUMERIC
00762            THEN GO TO INVALID-ALTERNATE-KEY-START.

00764            MOVE MAP1-START-DEPARTMENT    TO   TWA-START-DEPARTMENT.
00765            MOVE MAP1-START-DATE-MONTH    TO   TWA-START-DATE-MONTH.
00766            MOVE MAP1-START-DATE-DAY      TO   TWA-START-DATE-DAY.
00767            MOVE MAP1-START-DATE-YEAR     TO   TWA-START-DATE-YEAR.
00768            MOVE TWA-START-ALTERNATE-KEY  TO   TWA-ALTERNATE-KEY.

00770       *     EXEC CICS
00771       *         HANDLE CONDITION
00772       *             NOTFND (RECORD-NOT-FOUND-STARTBROWSE)
00773       *     END-EXEC.
00774            MOVE '                  ' TO DFHEIV0 CALL 'DFHEI1' USING
00775            DFHEIV0 GO TO RECORD-NOT-FOUND-STARTBROWSE DEPENDING ON
00776            DFHEIGDI.
00777
00778        BROWSE-COMMAND.

00780       *     EXEC CICS
00781       *         STARTBR DATASET ('ORTAIX')
00782       *                 RIDFLD  (TWA-ALTERNATE-KEY)
00783       *                 GTEQ
00784       *     END-EXEC.
00785            MOVE 'ORTAIX' TO DFHEIV3 MOVE '          ' TO DFHEIV0 CALL 'D
00786       -    'FHEI1' USING DFHEIV0 DFHEIV3 DFHEIV99 DFHEIV98
00787            TWA-ALTERNATE-KEY.
00788
00789
00790            MOVE ZEROES TO TWA-DUPLICATE-COUNT.

00792            IF TWA-ALTERNATE-KEY NUMERIC
00793               GO TO BROWSE-FORWARD
```

Fig. 23.4. (Continued)

```
00794                    ELSE GO TO BROWSE-BACKWARD.


00796           RECORD-NOT-FOUND-STARTBROWSE.
00797               MOVE HIGH-VALUES TO TWA-ALTERNATE-KEY.
00798               GO TO BROWSE-COMMAND.


00800           INVALID-ALTERNATE-KEY-START.
00801               MOVE 'INVALID ALTERNATE KEY' TO MAP1-ERROR.

00803       *       EXEC CICS
00804       *           SEND MAP     ('ORBSM01')
00805       *                MAPSET  ('ORBSS01')
00806       *                FROM    (MAP1-AREA)
00807       *                DATAONLY
00808       *       END-EXEC.
00809               MOVE 'ORBSM01' TO DFHEIV1 MOVE 'ORBSS01' TO DFHEIV2 MOVE '
00810       -           ' TO DFHEIVO CALL 'DFHEI1' USING DFHEIVO
00811               DFHEIV1 MAP1-AREA DFHEIV98 DFHEIV2.
00812
00813
00814
00815               MOVE '1'  TO COMMAREA-PROCESS-SW.

00817       *       EXEC CICS
00818       *           RETURN TRANSID  (EIBTRNID)
00819       *                  COMMAREA (COMMUNICATION-AREA)
00820       *                  LENGTH   (1)
00821       *       END-EXEC.
00822               MOVE 1 TO DFHEIV11 MOVE '          ' TO DFHEIVO CALL 'DFHEI1'
00823               USING DFHEIVO EIBTRNID COMMUNICATION-AREA DFHEIV11.
00824
00825
00826
```

Fig. 23.4. (Continued)

```
 22        ORBSO1A        15.59.55        12/27/80


00828           *********************************************************************
00829           *                                                                   *
00830           ( INITIALIZATION SECTION.
00831           *                                                                   *
00832           *********************************************************************


00834      *       EXEC CICS
00835      *           SEND MAP     ('ORBSM01')
00836      *                MAPSET ('ORBSS01')
00837      *                MAPONLY
00838      *                ERASE
00839      *       END-EXEC.
00840            MOVE 'ORBSM01' TO DFHEIV1 MOVE 'ORBSS01' TO DFHEIV2 MOVE '
00841      -      '             ' TO DFHEIVO CALL 'DFHEI1' USING DFHEIVO
00842           DFHEIV1 DFHEIV99 DFHEIV98 DFHEIV2.
00843
00844
00845
00846           MOVE  '1'   TO  COMMAREA-PROCESS-SW.

00848      *       EXEC CICS
00849      *           RETURN TRANSID  ('ORBS')
00850      *                   COMMAREA (COMMUNICATION-AREA)
00851      *                   LENGTH   (1)
00852      *       END-EXEC.
00853            MOVE 'ORBS' TO DFHEIV5 MOVE 1 TO DFHEIV11 MOVE '
00854           TO DFHEIVO CALL 'DFHEI1' USING DFHEIVO DFHEIV5
00855           COMMUNICATION-AREA DFHEIV11.
00856
00857
```

Fig. 23.4. (Continued)

```
   23          ORBS01A        15.59.55        12/27/80

00859       ******************************************************************
00860       *                                                                *
00861        FINALIZATION SECTION.
00862       *                                                                *
00863       ******************************************************************


00865        PREPARE-TERMINATION-MESSAGE.
00866            MOVE JOB-NORMAL-END-MESSAGE TO TWA-OPERATOR-MESSAGE.


00868        JOB-TERMINATED.
00869       *    EXEC CICS
00870       *        SEND FROM   (TWA-OPERATOR-MESSAGE)
00871       *            LENGTH (31)
00872       *            ERASE
00873       *    END-EXEC.
00874            MOVE 31 TO DFHEIV11 MOVE '               ' TO DFHEIVO CALL '
00875       -    'DFHEI1' USING DFHEIVO DFHEIV99 DFHEIV98 TWA-OPERATOR-MESSAGE
00876            DFHEIV11.
00877
00878


00880        END-OF-JOB.
00881       *    EXEC CICS
00882       *        RETURN
00883       *    END-EXEC.
00884            MOVE '         ' TO DFHEIVO CALL 'DFHEI1' USING DFHEIVO.
00885
00886
```

Fig. 23.4. (Continued)

```
   24        ORBS01A        15.59.55        12/27/80

00888     ****************************************************************
00889     *                                                              *
00890     ABNORMAL-TERMINATION SECTION.
00891     *                                                              *
00892     ****************************************************************


00894     FILE-NOT-OPEN.

00896     *    EXEC CICS
00897     *         XCTL PROGRAM ('TEL2OPEN')
00898     *    END-EXEC.
00899          MOVE 'TEL2OPEN' TO DFHEIV3 MOVE '        ' TO DFHEIVO CALL
00900          'DFHEI1' USING DFHEIVO DFHEIV3.
00901


00903     MAPFAIL-ERROR.
00904          MOVE 'MAP FAILURE' TO MAJOR-ERROR-MSG.
00905          GO TO PREPARE-ABORT-MESSAGE.


00907     PROCESS-SWITCH-ERROR.
00908          MOVE 'PROCESS ERROR' TO MAJOR-ERROR-MSG.
00909          GO TO PREPARE-ABORT-MESSAGE.


00911     SIGN-ON-VIOLATION.
00912          MOVE 'SIGNON VIOLATION' TO MAJOR-ERROR-MSG.
00913          GO TO PREPARE-ABORT-MESSAGE.


00915     MAJOR-ERROR.
00916          MOVE  EIBFN    TO  OLD-EIBFN.
00917          MOVE  EIBRCODE  TO  OLD-EIBRCODE.

00919     *    EXEC CICS
00920     *         DUMP DUMPCODE ('ERRS')
00921     *    END-EXEC.
00922          MOVE 'ERRS' TO DFHEIV5 MOVE '          ' TO DFHEIVO CALL 'DFH
00923     -    'EI1' USING DFHEIVO DFHEIV5.
00924
00925          MOVE 'MAJOR ERROR' TO MAJOR-ERROR-MSG.
00926          GO TO PREPARE-ABORT-MESSAGE.


00928     PREPARE-ABORT-MESSAGE.
00929          MOVE JOB-ABORTED-MESSAGE TO TWA-OPERATOR-MESSAGE.
00930          GO TO JOB-TERMINATED.
```

Fig. 23.4. (Continued)

THE MAIN-LINE SECTION

1. Lines 353–357. ADDRESS command for the TWA.

2. Lines 359–368. HANDLE AID command. The PA keys will result in the "WRONG KEY USED" error.

3. Lines 373–381. HANDLE CONDITION command. The NOT-OPEN condition for the order file is specified here rather than in other sections because the program is in the conversational mode and this specification will not change during the session.

4. Lines 385–390. The selection of sections.

5. Lines 392–393. If the program is executed at the start of the session by an operator-entered transaction identifier instead of through an XCTL command from the Sign-on program, a sign-on violation occurs. This is so if EIBCALEN is equal to zero.

THE INITIALIZATION SECTION

1. Lines 834–842. SEND MAP command to display the browse map.

2. Line 846.   Set the communication area switch to 1.

3. Lines 848–855. RETURN command to terminate the task. This section is implemented in the pseudoconversational mode so the task is terminated while the operator enters the browse starting point.

THE BROWSE-START SECTION

1. Lines 748–755. RECEIVE MAP command to read the map that contains the department number and date of order that is the starting point of the browse.

2. Lines 770–776. HANDLE CONDITION command for the order file.

3. Lines 780–787. STARTBR command to establish the starting point of the browse.

4. Lines 792–794. Line 792 will be executed if a record was found, which was based on the starting point, and is always executed because of the GTEQ operand of STARTBR unless the starting point is greater than the last record in the file. We then go into a forward browse to display this record. Line 794 will be executed if a record was not found, in which case lines 797–798 would have been executed to mark the end of the file. We therefore go into a backward browse to display the last record in the file.

5. Line 797.   If the record is not found, we set the key to HIGH-VALUES to mark the end of the file as the starting point of the browse (in this case, we have to browse backwards).

6. If the department number and date of order (as entered by the operator) are not numeric:
   a. Lines 803–811. Display the error message "INVALID ALTERNATE KEY."
   b. Line 815.   Set the communication area switch to 1.
   c. Lines 817–823. RETURN command to terminate the task.

THE BROWSE-FORWARD SECTION

1. Lines 473–481. HANDLE CONDITION command for the order file. The ENDFILE option is for the routine if the end of the file is reached in a normal forward browse. The NOTFND option is for the routine if we do not find a record during skip-forward browse. The DUPKEY option is for the routine if the alternate key is a duplicate.

2. Lines 487–494. Read the next record in ascending sequence.

3. Lines 497–499. If the previous File read was a READPREV command, then we bypass this record; otherwise we would be displaying the same record as in the previous display.

4. Lines 511–543. Move the record data into the symbolic description map.

5. Lines 547–555. Display the record. The ERASE option is specified since the data is variable (from 1 to 9 lines). If the

data were fixed, this would not be required and DATAONLY would then be specified.

6. Lines 560–561. The forward browse is finished; wait for the next action from the operator.

7. Lines 584–592. If the end of the file is reached during normal forward browse, we display the "END OF FILE" message.

8. Lines 599–605. If the record is not found in a skip-forward browse, we likewise display the "END OF FILE" message.

THE BROWSE-BACKWARD SECTION

1. Lines 613–620. HANDLE CONDITION command for the order file. The ENDFILE option is for the routine if the end of the file is reached in a normal backward browse. The DUPKEY option is for the routine in case of duplicate alternate keys. The NOTFND option is not specified because it will never happen in a READPREV command if the GTEQ operand is specified in the browse.

2. Lines 624–631. Read the next record in descending sequence.

3. Lines 634–636. If the previous File read was a READNEXT command, then we bypass this record; otherwise, we would be displaying the same record as in the previous display.

4. Line 648.   Display the record.

5. Lines 649–650. The backward browse is finished; wait for the next action from the operator.

6. Lines 670–678. If the end of the file is reached during normal backward browse, we display the "END OF FILE" message.

7. Lines 687–695. If any new browse starting point entered is invalid in format, we display the "INVALID ALTERNATE KEY" message.

THE BROWSE-CONTINUE SECTION

1. Lines 401–408. Read the map containing the alternate key.

2. If a new starting point was not entered:
   a. Lines 421–423. If the PF1 or ENTER key was used, do a forward browse.
   b. If the PF2 key was used:
      1. Lines 425–442. If the previous action was a skip-forward browse and the record was not found (this can happen if the starting point entered by the operator was higher than the last record in the file), the browse is reset to the end of the file and the last record is displayed.
      2. Line 443.   Otherwise, do a backward browse.
   c. Line 444.   Otherwise, the wrong key was used.

3. If a new starting point was entered:
   a. Lines 448–450. If the new starting point is greater than the previously displayed order, do a skip-forward browse.
   b. Lines 451–465. Otherwise, the browse starting point is reset and do a forward browse.

THE WRONG-KEY-USED SECTION

1. Lines 708–715. GETMAIN command to secure main storage for the map that will contain the error message. This is because the PA keys do not allow CICS/VS to secure main storage for the symbolic description map through the RECEIVE MAP command.

2. Line 720.   Move the "WRONG KEY USED" message into the area secured.

3. Lines 722–730. Display the error message.

4. Lines 734–738. FREEMAIN command to free main storage secured in the previous GETMAIN command. We have to do this to save main storage because, since we are using the conversational mode of processing, the area will not otherwise be freed by task termination.

5. Line 740.   The operator may continue the browse.

THE FINALIZATION SECTION

1. Lines 869–876. Display the "JOB NORMALLY TERMI-NATED" message.

2. Lines 881–884. Terminate the session.

THE ABNORMAL-TERMINATION SECTION

These are the routines to abnormally terminate the session on errors and CICS/VS command exceptional conditions not covered by a HANDLE CONDITION command.

EXAMPLE

The following are facsimiles of actual photographs taken of a CRT terminal during a session.

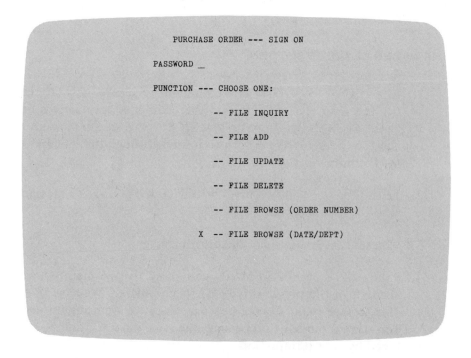

```
                    PURCHASE ORDER --- SIGN ON

          PASSWORD _

          FUNCTION --- CHOOSE ONE:

                         -- FILE INQUIRY

                         -- FILE ADD

                         -- FILE UPDATE

                         -- FILE DELETE

                         -- FILE BROWSE (ORDER NUMBER)

                    X  -- FILE BROWSE (DATE/DEPT)
```

Fig. 23.5. The File Browse (by date/department number) application is selected by keying in an "X" on the File Browse line and the corresponding password, then hitting the ENTER key.

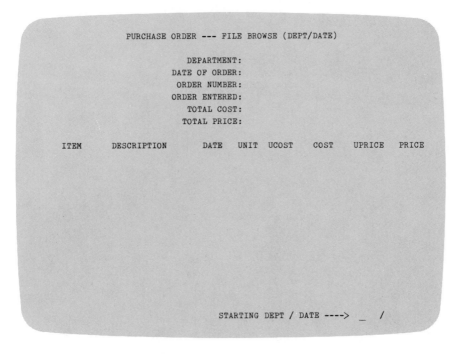

```
            PURCHASE ORDER --- FILE BROWSE (DEPT/DATE)

                        DEPARTMENT:
                      DATE OF ORDER:
                       ORDER NUMBER:
                      ORDER ENTERED:
                         TOTAL COST:
                        TOTAL PRICE:

  ITEM      DESCRIPTION      DATE    UNIT  UCOST    COST    UPRICE    PRICE
```

```
                        STARTING DEPT / DATE ----> _   /
```

Fig. 23.6. The Sign On program executes which then transfers control to the File Browse program. This displays the File Browse map.

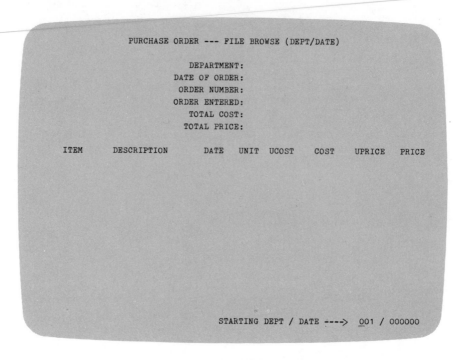

Fig. 23.7. The operator keys in the browse starting point, then hits the ENTER key.

```
         PURCHASE ORDER --- FILE BROWSE (DEPT/DATE)

                    DEPARTMENT: 003
                    DATE OF ORDER: 122280
                    ORDER NUMBER: 0000000001
                    ORDER ENTERED: 122280
                       TOTAL COST:      200.00
                       TOTAL PRICE:     400.00


   ITEM      DESCRIPTION      DATE   UNIT  UCOST     COST    UPRICE   PRICE
 1 00000100 CHISEL SET       122280 00050 0000400 00020000 0000800 00040000











                         STARTING DEPT / DATE ----> 003 / 122280
```

Fig. 23.8. The program displays the record whose date and department number are equal to the starting point. Since the record does not exist, the next higher one is used.

```
            PURCHASE ORDER --- FILE BROWSE (DEPT/DATE)

                        DEPARTMENT: 003
                      DATE OF ORDER: 122280
                       ORDER NUMBER: 0000000001
                      ORDER ENTERED: 122280
                         TOTAL COST:      200.00
                        TOTAL PRICE:      400.00


    ITEM       DESCRIPTION       DATE   UNIT  UCOST    COST   UPRICE   PRICE
 1 00000100 CHISEL SET          122280 00050 0000400 00020000 0000800 00040000













                       STARTING DEPT / DATE ----> 003 / 122480
```

Fig. 23.9. The operator keys in another browse starting point, then hits the ENTER key.

```
                PURCHASE ORDER --- FILE BROWSE (DEPT/DATE)

                        DEPARTMENT: 003
                        DATE OF ORDER: 122480
                        ORDER NUMBER: 0000000007
                        ORDER ENTERED: 122480
                            TOTAL COST:      600.00
                            TOTAL PRICE:   1,200.00

     ITEM       DESCRIPTION        DATE   UNIT  UCOST     COST     UPRICE    PRICE
   1 00037216 10-FEET STEEL TAPE   122480 00100 0000600 00060000 0001200 00120000




                DUPLICATE - 001
                        STARTING DEPT / DATE ----> 003 / 122480
```

Fig. 23.10. The program displays the record whose date and department number are equal to the new starting point. This is the first record in a set of duplicates. The skip-forward function is executed to do this.

```
                    PURCHASE ORDER --- FILE BROWSE (DEPT/DATE)

                        DEPARTMENT: 003
                    DATE OF ORDER: 122480
                    ORDER NUMBER: 0000000009
                    ORDER ENTERED: 122480
                        TOTAL COST:        890.00
                       TOTAL PRICE:      1,700.00


      ITEM       DESCRIPTION        DATE   UNIT  UCOST      COST    UPRICE     PRICE
   1 00093762 BLOCK PLANE           122780 00010 0000900 00009000 0001600 00016000
   2 00001877 1 INCH CHISEL         122480 00050 0000300 00015000 0000500 00025000
   3 00003663 26 IN. CROSSCUT SAW   122480 00100 0000600 00060000 0001200 00120000
   4 00054976 FILE SET              122780 00010 0000500 00005000 0000900 00009000






                   DUPLICATE - 002
                       STARTING DEPT / DATE ----> 003 / 122480
```

Fig. 23.11. The operator hits the PF1 key, which results in the display of the record next in ascending sequence. This is the second record in a set of duplicates.

```
          PURCHASE ORDER --- FILE BROWSE (DEPT/DATE)

                       DEPARTMENT: 003
                    DATE OF ORDER: 122480
                    ORDER NUMBER: 0000000010
                    ORDER ENTERED: 122680
                       TOTAL COST:     1,600.00
                      TOTAL PRICE:     3,200.00


   ITEM       DESCRIPTION      DATE   UNIT  UCOST    COST    UPRICE    PRICE
 1 00087632 12-INCH CRESCENT  122480 00100 0000600 00060000 0001200 00120000
 2 00063271 BENCH VISE        122480 00050 0002000 00100000 0004000 00200000




                    DUPLICATE - 003 / LAST
                        STARTING DEPT / DATE ----> 003 / 122480
```

Fig. 23.12.   The operator hits the PF1 key, which results in the display of the record next in ascending sequence. This is the third (and last) record in a set of duplicates.

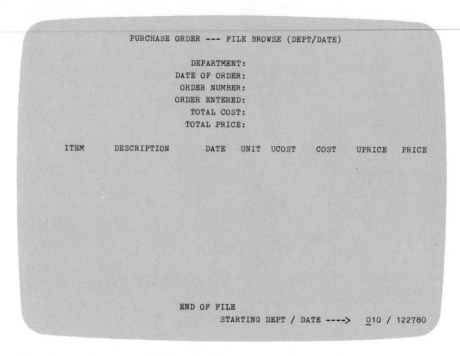

Fig. 23.13.   After repeated PF1's, the end of the file is reached. The record with department number of 010 and date of 122780 was the last record displayed.

```
              PURCHASE ORDER --- FILE BROWSE (DEPT/DATE)

                        DEPARTMENT: 010
                      DATE OF ORDER: 122780
                       ORDER NUMBER: 0000000016
                      ORDER ENTERED: 122780
                          TOTAL COST:     1,700.00
                          TOTAL PRICE:    3,400.00


    ITEM       DESCRIPTION      DATE   UNIT  UCOST    COST    UPRICE   PRICE
  1 00000163 10-SPEED BLENDER  122780 00020 0001500 00030000 0003000 00060000
  2 00001754 ELECTRIC OVEN     122780 00020 0007000 00140000 0014000 00280000




                              STARTING DEPT / DATE ----->   010 / 122780
```

Fig. 23.14. The operator hits the PF2 key, which results in the display of the record next in descending sequence.

```
              PURCHASE ORDER --- FILE BROWSE (DEPT/DATE)

                        DEPARTMENT: 010
                      DATE OF ORDER: 122680
                      ORDER NUMBER: 0000000012
                      ORDER ENTERED: 122680
                         TOTAL COST:     1,200.00
                         TOTAL PRICE:    2,400.00


     ITEM      DESCRIPTION      DATE   UNIT  UCOST    COST    UPRICE   PRICE
  1 00018834 ELECTRIC OVEN     122680 00030 0004000 00120000 0008000 00240000










                        STARTING DEPT / DATE ----> 001 / 000000
```

Fig. 23.15.   The operator keys in another browse starting point, then hits the ENTER key.

```
            PURCHASE ORDER --- FILE BROWSE (DEPT/DATE)

                      DEPARTMENT: 003
                    DATE OF ORDER: 122280
                     ORDER NUMBER: 0000000001
                    ORDER ENTERED: 122280
                        TOTAL COST:      200.00
                        TOTAL PRICE:     400.00


   ITEM      DESCRIPTION       DATE   UNIT  UCOST     COST    UPRICE    PRICE
 1 00000100 CHISEL SET        122280 00050 0000400 00020000 0000800 00040000






                         STARTING DEPT / DATE ----> 003 / 122280
```

Fig. 23.16. The program displays the record whose date and department number are equal to the new starting point. Since the record does not exist, the next higher one is used.

```
              PURCHASE ORDER --- FILE BROWSE (DEPT/DATE)

                        DEPARTMENT: 003
                        DATE OF ORDER: 122280
                        ORDER NUMBER: 0000000001
                        ORDER ENTERED: 122280
                            TOTAL COST:      200.00
                            TOTAL PRICE:     400.00


     ITEM       DESCRIPTION       DATE   UNIT  UCOST    COST    UPRICE   PRICE
   1 00000100 CHISEL SET        122280 00050 0000400 00020000 0000800 00040000












                        WRONG KEY USED
                          STARTING DEPT / DATE ---->   005 / 122480
```

Fig. 23.17. If the operator keys in another browse starting point but then hits one of the PA keys instead of the ENTER key, the "WRONG KEY USED" message is displayed.

```
           PURCHASE ORDER --- FILE BROWSE (DEPT/DATE)

                    DEPARTMENT: 005
                    DATE OF ORDER: 122480
                    ORDER NUMBER: 0000000008
                    ORDER ENTERED: 122480
                       TOTAL COST:    1,480.00
                       TOTAL PRICE:   3,080.00


   ITEM      DESCRIPTION       DATE   UNIT  UCOST    COST    UPRICE    PRICE
 1 00005836 VAR SPEED SABRE SAW 122680 00040 0001700 00068000 0003700 00148000
 2 00004371 1 HP ROUTER         122480 00020 0004000 00080000 0008000 00160000









                          STARTING DEPT / DATE ----->   005 / 122480
```

Fig. 23.18. If the operator then hits the ENTER key, the session continues. The record selected in Fig. 23.17 is now displayed.

24

General Debugging Techniques

INTRODUCTION

CICS/VS programs may be tested in three ways. The first way is by the Execution Diagnostic Facility (EDF), which allows the programmer to, among other things, temporarily modify commands, results of commands, certain data areas, etc., interactively during testing. We will not, however, discuss the details of the EDF because such a discussion is beyond the scope of this book. Also, the EDF is really best learned through actual use.

The second method for testing CICS/VS programs is this: the programmer may simulate a terminal on a sequential device such as a card reader, magnetic tape, or disk. Then he prepares test data and tests the program as if it were a batch program. I do not recommend this method because the EDF method and the next method are superior; they allow the programmer to change test data during the test, making the test easier to conduct.

In the third method, the programmer can test the program interactively in the same manner that it would be used "live." He could then debug it using the terminal screen, and interpret a trace and a dump. This is the method that will be shown.

SCREEN DEBUGGING

Unlike batch programs, where the programmer has to prepare data in advance of the testing process, CICS/VS programs may be tested extemporaneously. The programmer should, however, have a plan to enable him to test as many functions as possible in a single sitting. He should also develop troubleshooting techniques. He can do both because a CICS/VS application program can be tested for as long as desired in a single sitting; after all, in case of an abend (*ab*normal *end*), the session can be restarted.

The first step in debugging is to make a visual inspection of how the terminal screen displays and accepts information. For instance, after each new map is displayed on the screen, the programmer may check:

Before Entering Data

1. Is the screen correct as far as display is concerned? Are all titles, field identifiers, etc., complete, correctly placed, and of the right intensity (bright, normal, dark)? If not, the map program has to be corrected.

2. Is there "garbage" showing? If so, maybe the previous SEND MAP command did not specify ERASE? Or maybe the map program itself has extra fields defined?

3. Is the cursor under the first field to be entered or modified? If not, maybe the IC operand was not specified or was misplaced in the map program.

While Entering Data

1. Are the shift (alphabetic or numeric) and intensity correct as you enter each unprotected field? If not, the attributes of the corresponding fields in the map program may have been incorrectly specified.

2. As you enter each unprotected field completely, does the cursor automatically go to the next unprotected field? If not, there may be something wrong with the use of SKIP or STOPPER fields in the map program.

3. On using the SKIP key continuously, does the cursor only fall under unprotected fields? If not, there is again something wrong with the use of SKIP or STOPPER fields.

4. After entering the last unprotected field on the screen, does the cursor wrap around to the first unprotected field? If not, there is no SKIP or STOPPER field after the last unprotected field.

5. Are there areas in the screen where the cursor goes to and it should not? If so, those fields may have been defined as un-protected erroneously.

On a terminal where a lot of data is to be entered for validation, the programmer should have a general plan of action. I suggest that the following sets of data mix be entered separately:

1. The minimum amount of data that will be accepted as complete by the program, with no errors entered.

2. All data that will be accepted by the program, with no errors entered.

3. Data entered with the number of errors equal to the maximum number of error message positions.

4. Data entered with the number of errors greater than the maximum number of error message positions.

5. No data entered.

After the programmer has entered the data mix, the ENTER key is then used to initiate the task. He may then check the following:

Data Without Errors (Data mix 1 and 2 above)

1. Does the program accept all data as correct? If so, the program probably will display a message like "DATA ACCEPTED – CONTINUE" on a fresh screen.

2. Is there some data that should be edited as correct but is treated as an error?

3. Is there a program check or a CICS/VS command error that aborts the session?

Data With Errors (Data mix 3 and 4)

1. Does the program really validate the errors as errors? If not, there is a logic error.

2. Is the cursor placed under the very first error detected? If not, there is probably something wrong with the use of the symbolic cursor positioning technique.

3. As you correct the data one by one (do not correct all of them at the same time; you want to see the effect of various combinations of error data), does the cursor remain under the very first error detected each time the data is validated? If not, we have the same problem as in 2.

4. For data mix 4, does the program easily deal with the extra errors, bypassing the editing of further errors as it should?

5. For data mix 4 again, when you correct all errors detected on the first pass, do the other errors appear on the second pass?

6. Is there a program check or a CICS/VS command error that aborts the session?

No Data Entered (Data Set 5)

1. Does the program catch this as an error? It should.

2. Is there a program check or a CICS/VS command error that aborts the session?

In addition, the operator may check the following:

PA Key Used After Data Entry

1. Do the messages "DATA BYPASSED – CONTINUE" or "WRONG KEY USED" appear when appropriate?

2. On the first message, is the screen that goes with the message a fresh screen so that the operator may enter a new set of data? If not, there is an error.

3. On the second message, does the screen remain the same? Also, when the operator uses the correct key (generally the ENTER key), does the program proceed from where it left off, accepting the data already entered?

After The Data Has Been Accepted

1. When the record is displayed (for instance, in a File Update application, the very same record just updated may be immediately recalled), does the display show that the input was indeed accepted? If not, something went wrong in writing out the record after data validation.

PROGRAM TRACE

Trace Tables

CICS/VS provides a facility to have trace entries generated as a debugging aid. A "regular" trace table in main storage is always maintained as part of the CICS/VS nucleus. All tasks generate entries on this table, which is automatically printed out only in cases involving most CICS/VS command exceptional conditions,* a transaction abend, or commands that request a dump (DUMP command for instance). Entries on this table are written in a wrap-around manner; that is, when the end of the table is reached, the next entry replaces the first entry of the table.

In addition, an auxiliary trace facility allows tasks to write the very same entries, time-stamped, into a trace table on a sequential device (generally a magnetic tape or disk), which may be printed out offline through the CICS/VS Trace Utility program. Unlike the regular trace table, this one will contain all entries written to it once CICS/VS is initialized. It is useful during a program test if the regular trace table is inadequate (in size) or if the programmer wants a trace independent of the result of the test. This may also be used for performance analysis to identify potential bottlenecks, because entries are time-stamped, and for other statistical analysis.

The auxiliary trace facility is activated only if the auxiliary trace program has been generated. Activation is done by the programmer through the master terminal using this CICS/VS service:

$$CSMT \ ATR, ON$$

---

*If a HANDLE CONDITION command was specified for the error or the ERROR condition was specified, the corresponding routine will be executed instead.

He should then get the message:

"AUXILIARY TRACE FUNCTION ACTIVATED"

The trace facility may also be deactivated by:

CSMT ATR, OFF

He should then get the message:

"AUXILIARY TRACE FUNCTION DEACTIVATED"

Trace Entries

There are two types of entries in trace tables. The system trace entries are totally CICS/VS controlled and include Execute Interface Program trace points (the only one really of importance to the application programmer) every time a CICS/VS command is executed. Two entries are made for most commands: first, when the command is issued; second, when the functions required in the command have been performed and control is about to be returned to the application program. In between these two entries, the flow of control, especially the control programs* that were executed, can be traced.

The user trace entry point is generated on the ENTER command and is used to provide a trace of the program in between CICS/VS commands. This command is generally used only during testing and should be removed when the program is released to production. The format of the command is:

enter traceid (data value)
from   (data area)

The TRACEID operand is the trace identifier with value from 0 to 199 and appears in the first byte of the entry; the FROM operand is optional and places the value of the data area in bytes 8-15 of the entry.

---

*Many commands require several CICS/VS control programs.

Trace Header

All entries in the trace tables are 16 bytes long. The regular trace table contains a header that contains the following information:

Bytes	Contents
0–3	Address of the last-used entry.
4–7	Address of the beginning of the table.
8–11	Address of the end of the table.
12–15	Reserved.

A listing of the regular trace table is shown in Figure 24.1.

A points to the trace header; B is the address of the last entry used, which is 00146410; C is the address of the beginning of the table, which is 001457FO; D is the address of the end of the table, which is 00146460.

Execute Interface Trace Entry At Issuance

As we said before, of the system entries, the only ones of importance to the application programmer are the Execute Interface Program trace points. Most CICS/VS commands create two entries. The entry when the command is issued contains the following:

Bytes	Contents
0	X'E1' trace identifier.
1–3	Return point in the application program.
4	Not used.
5 (bits 0–3)	X'0', identifying the first entry for the command.
6–7	User task sequence number (packed decimal).
8–11	Address of the Working-Storage section (this is for ANS Cobol).
12, 13	Not used.
14, 15	Code identifying the CICS/VS command. This is identical to the EIBFN field codes of Fig. 24.7.

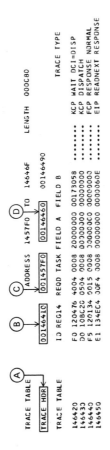

Fig. 24.1. The Regular Trace Table.

CUSTOMER INFORMATION CONTROL SYSTEM STORAGE DUMP   CODE=ERRS   TASK=ORAD   DATE=08/02/80   TIME=17 03 35   PAGE   3

TRACE TABLE

Address	ID	REG14	REQD	TASK	FIELD A	FIELD B		TRACE TYPE
146460	E1	134EC4	0004	0008	0012FA2C	0000060E	....	EIP READNEXT ENTRY
1457F0	F5	11E9C8	8003	0008	C4E2E7E3	C1C2E240	DSXTABS	FCP GETNEXT
145800	F0	120476	4004	0008	20000000	00173058	....	KCP WAIT DCI=DISP
145810	D0	10BC20	05C4	0038	00000000	00C00000	....	KCP DISPATCH
145820	F5	120134	0015	0008	00000000	0000060E	....	FCP RESPONSE NORMAL
145830	E1	134EC4	00F4	0008	00000000	0000060E	....	EIP READNEXT RESPONSE
145840	E1	134EC4	0004	0008	0012FA2C	0000060E	....	EIP READNEXT ENTRY
145850	F5	11E9C8	00F4	0008	C4E2E7E3	C1C2E240	DSXTABS	FCP GETNEXT
145860	F0	120476	4004	0008	20000000	00173058	....	KCP WAIT DCI=DISP
145870	D0	10BC20	0504	TC	00000000	00173058	....	KCP DISPATCH
145880	F0	10DB88	4004	TC	44000000	001007F8	8	KCP WAIT
145890	D0	10BC20	0504	0008	00000000	00000000	....	KCP DISPATCH
1458A0	F5	120134	0015	0008	00000000	0000060E	....	FCP RESPONSE NORMAL
1458B0	E1	134EC4	00F4	0008	00000000	0000060E	....	EIP READNEXT RESPONSE
1458C0	E1	134EC4	0004	0008	0012FA2C	0000060E	....	EIP READNEXT ENTRY
1458D0	F5	11E9C8	8003	0008	C4E2E7E3	C1C2E240	DSXTABS	FCP GETNEXT
1458E0	F0	120476	4004	0008	20000000	00173058	....	KCP WAIT DCI=DISP
1458F0	D0	10BC20	0504	0008	00000000	00000000	....	KCP DISPATCH
145900	F5	120134	0015	0008	00000000	0000060E	....	FCP RESPONSE NORMAL
145910	E1	134EC4	00F4	0008	00000000	0000060E	....	EIP READNEXT RESPONSE
145920	E1	134EC4	0004	0008	0012FA2C	0000060E	....	EIP READNEXT ENTRY
145930	F5	11E9C8	8003	0008	C4E2E7E3	C1C2E240	DSXTABS	FCP GETNEXT
145940	F0	120476	4004	0008	20000000	00173058	....	KCP WAIT DCI=DISP
145950	D0	10BC20	0504	0008	00000000	00000000	....	KCP DISPATCH
145960	F5	120134	0015	0008	00000000	0000060E	....	FCP RESPONSE NORMAL
145970	E1	134EC4	00F4	0008	00000000	0000060E	....	EIP READNEXT RESPONSE
145980	E1	134EC4	0004	0008	0012FA2C	0000060E	....	EIP READNEXT ENTRY
145990	F5	11E9C8	8003	0008	C4E2E7E3	C1C2E240	DSXTABS	FCP GETNEXT
1459A0	F0	120476	4004	0008	20000000	00173058	....	KCP WAIT DCI=DISP
1459B0	D0	10BC20	0504	0008	00000000	00000000	....	KCP DISPATCH
1459C0	F5	120134	0015	0008	00000000	0000060E	....	FCP RESPONSE NORMAL
1459D0	E1	134EC4	00F4	0008	00000000	0000060E	....	EIP READNEXT RESPONSE
1459E0	E1	12187A	8E04	0008	0012FA2C	00000A02	....	EIP WRITEQ-TS ENTRY
1459F0	C8	115222	0004	0008	00130540	8E130548	....	SCP GETMAIN
145A00	F7	1218C6	4103	0008	00130740	8E130548	L7700RAD	SCP ACQUIRED TEMPSTRG STORAGE
145A10	F1	12231A	F804	0008	03FF7FF0	00000038	....	TSP PUTQ
145A20	C8	115222	0004	0008	0012C000	01100660	....	SCP GETMAIN-COND-INIT
145A30	C8	121AEA	0004	0008	0012C055	98000040	....	SCP ACQUIRED TSTABLE STORAGE
145A40	C8	115222	8704	0008	0012C040	01130660	....	SCP GETMAIN-CONDITIONAL
145A50	F7	121FCC	0004	0008	0012C040	97120560	....	SCP ACQUIRED TSMAIN STORAGE
145A60	F7	12183E	0015	0008	00000000	00000000	....	TSP RESPONSE
145A70	C9	115222	4004	0008	00130740	01100660	....	SCP FREEMAIN
145A80	E1	134FDA	00C4	0008	00130740	8E130548	....	SCP RELEASED TEMPSTRG STORAGE
145A90	E1	135012	0004	0008	0012FA2C	00000A02	....	EIP WRITEQ-TS RESPONSE
145AA0	F1	11508A	0004	0008	0012FF90	00000C04	....	EIP FREEMAIN ENTRY
145AB0	C9	135012	4004	0008	0012FF90	01100660	....	SCP FREEMAIN
145AC0	E1	11530C	0004	0008	00900000	8C120548	....	SCP RELEASED USER STORAGE
145AD0	C9	135012	00F4	0008	0012FF90	00000C04	....	EIP FREEMAIN RESPONSE
145AE0	E1	135060	0004	0008	0012FA2C	00000C02	....	EIP GETMAIN ENTRY

Fig. 24.1.   (Continued)

```
CUSTOMER INFORMATION CONTROL SYSTEM STORAGE DUMP   CODE=ERRS   TASK=ORAD   DATE=08/02/80   TIME=17 03 35   PAGE  4

145AF0  F1 115052 CC04 0008 000003BE 01100660  ........    SCP GETMAIN-INIT
145B00  C8 115222 0004 0008 00130800 0C0003C8  .......H    SCP ACQUIRED USER STORAGE
145B10  E1 135060 00F4 0008 00000000 00000C02  ........    EIP GETMAIN RESPONSE
145B20 (E) 1350CE 0004 0008 0012FA2C 00001804  ........    EIP SEND-MAP ENTRY
145B30  FA 124FFE 0003 0008 00005E2  04000020  ...S..      BMS OUT MAP MAPSET SAVE ERASE
145B40  F2 1261AC 0804 0008 D609C1D7 E2F0F140  ORAPSO1     PCP DELETE
145B50  F2 126200 04C4 0008 D609C1C4 E2F0F140  ORADSO1     PCP LOAD
145B60  F1 118572 8804 0008 00130096 01100660  ........    SCP GETMAIN
145B70  FD 00001C 0204 0008 E3C904C5 1702279F  TIME....    TIMING TRACE 17/02/27.9
145B80  C8 115222 0004 0008 00132800 88000800  ........    SCP ACQUIRED PGM STORAGE
145B90  F0 11862A 4004 0008 88000000 0011A746  ........    KCP WAIT DCI=CICS
145BA0  D0 10BC20 0904 0008 0004A746 EDC00000  ........    KCP SYSTEM RESUME
145BB0  D0 10BC20 0504 0008 00000000 00000000  ........    KCP DISPATCH
145BC0  F1 127F3A 9E04 0008 00130856 01100660  ........    SCP GETMAIN
145BD0  C8 115222 0004 0008 0012C800 9E130868  ..H.....    SCP ACQUIRED MAPCOPY STORAGE
145BE0  F1 124578 CC04 0008 00000460 01100660  ........    SCP GETMAIN-INIT
145BF0  C8 115222 0004 0008 0012D070 8C0004E8  ........    SCP ACQUIRED USER STORAGE
145C00  F1 124846 8504 0008 001205D3 01100660  ..L...      SCP GETMAIN
145C10  C8 115222 0004 0008 00129170 85120SE8  ......Y     SCP ACQUIRED TERMINAL STORAGE
145C20  F1 124A00 4004 0008 0012D070 01100660  ........    SCP RELEASED USER STORAGE
145C30  C9 11530C 0004 0008 0012D070 01100660  ......Y     SCP FREEMAIN
145C40  F1 124A00 4004 0008 0012C800 9E130868  ..H...      SCP FREEMAIN
145C50  C9 11530C 0004 0008 0012C800 9E130868  ..H...      SCP RELEASED MAPCOPY STORAGE
145C60  FC 126CA8 0103 0008 00810000 00100660  ........    ZCP ZARQ APPL REQ ERASE WRITE
145C70 (F) 125EE6 0005 0008 00000000 00000000  ........    BMS RESPONSE
145C80  E1 1350CE 00F4 0008 00000000 00001804  ........    EIP SEND-MAP RESPONSE
145C90  E1 13511C 0004 0008 0012FA2C 0012FE08  ........    EIP RETURN ENTRY
145CA0  F1 11970C 9304 0008 00120019 01100660  ........    SCP GETMAIN
145CB0  C8 115222 0004 0008 0012C5A0 93120020  ..E...      SCP ACQUIRED SHARED STORAGE
145CC0  F2 119760 1004 0008 D609C1C4 F0F1C140  ORAD01A     PCP RETURN
145CD0  F1 11844A 4004 0008 0012F9E0 01100660  ..9...      SCP FREEMAIN
145CE0  C9 11530C 0004 0008 0012F9E0 8C1303C8  ..9....H    SCP RELEASED USER STORAGE
145CF0  F0 118992 8004 0008 00000000 00000000  ........    KCP DETACH
145D00  D8 10AC20 0203 0008 02000000 00130580  ........    SPP SYSTEM
145D10  F5 10D7F0 0003 0008 00130580 00130580  ........    FCP DME PROCESSOR
145D20  F1 120070 4004 0008 00130580 01100660  ........    SCP FREEMAIN
145D30  C9 11530C 0004 0008 00130580 9D130038  ........    SCP RELEASED DME STORAGE
145D40  F1 120070 4004 0008 001305F0 01100660  ...0....    SCP FREEMAIN
145D50  C9 11530C 0004 0008 001305F0 8F1300C8  ...0...H    SCP RELEASED FILE STORAGE
145D60  F5 120134 0004 0008 00000000 00000000  ........    FCP RESPONSE NORMAL
145D70  D8 10D95C 0015 0008 00000000 00000000  ........    SPP RESPONSE
145D80  F0 10AC2A 0304 0008 0011A746 00000000  ..y...      KCP DEQALL
145D90  D0 10BC20 0504 0008 00000000 00000000  ........    KCP DISPATCH
145DA0  D0 10BC20 0704 0008 02C80400 00000000  ..H...      KCP TERMINATE
145DB0  F1 10ADAD 4A04 0008 0012E800 00000000  ..Y...      SCP FREEMAIN
145DC0  C9 11530C 0004 0008 00130800 8C0003C8  .......H    SCP RELEASED USER STORAGE
145DD0  C9 11530C 0004 0008 001306C0 8F130078  ........    SCP RELEASED FILE STORAGE
145DE0  C9 11530C 0004 0008 00130530 8C000078  ........    SCP RELEASED USER STORAGE
145DF0  C9 11530C 0004 0008 001304E0 8C0000C8  ........    SCP RELEASED USER STORAGE
145E00  C9 11530C 0004 0008 0012F4F0 8C000048  ..0...      SCP RELEASED USER STORAGE
145E10  C9 11530C 0004 0008 0012FEF0 8C000048  ...0...      SCP RELEASED USER STORAGE
145E20  C9 11530C 0004 0008 0012FE70 8C000078  ........    SCP RELEASED USER STORAGE
145E30  C9 11530C 0004 0008 0012FE20 8C000048  ........    SCP RELEASED USER STORAGE
```

Fig. 24.1. (Continued)

```
CUSTOMER INFORMATION CONTROL SYSTEM STORAGE DUMP      CODE=ERRS      TASK=DRAD      DATE=08/02/80   TIME=17 03 35   PAGE   5

145E40  C9 11530C 0004 KC 0012FDB0 8C000068  .......    SCP RELEASED USER STORAGE
145E50  C9 11530C 0004 KC 0012F9C0 8C120018  ....9..    SCP RELEASED USER STORAGE
145E60  C9 11530C 0004 KC 0012F930 8C000088  ....9..    SCP RELEASED USER STORAGE
145E70  C9 11530C 0004 KC 0012F6A0 8C000288  ....6..    SCP RELEASED USER STORAGE
145E80  C9 11530C 0004 KC 0012F290 8C000408  ....2..    SCP RELEASED USER STORAGE
145E90  C9 11530C 0004 KC 0012E800 8A030598  ...Y...    SCP RELEASED TCA STORAGE
145EA0  D0 10BC20 0204 TC 00000000 00000000  .......    KCP DISPATCH
145EB0  F0 10DB88 4004 TC 44000000 001107F8  .......8   KCP WAIT
145EC0  D0 10BC20 9904 JJ 0000CC20 88A00000  .......    KCP SYSTEM RESUME
145ED0  D0 10BC20 0904 JJ 0000CC20 C2B00000  ...a...    KCP SYSTEM RESUME
145EE0  D0 10BC20 0904 JJ 0000CC20 38700000  .......    KCP SYSTEM RESUME
145EF0  D0 10BC20 0504 TC 00000000 00000000  .......    KCP DISPATCH
145F00  F1 10EA54 4004 TC 00129170 80100660  .......    SCP FREEMAIN
145F10  C9 11530C 0004 TC 00129170 851205E8  ......Y    SCP RELEASED TERMINAL STORAGE
145F20  F1 10EAF8 6004 TC 00129120 85000048  .......    SCP FREEMAIN ALL
145F30  C9 11530C 0004 TC 0000010F 80100660  .......    SCP RELEASED TERMINAL STORAGE
145F40  F1 10E9F0 E404 TC 00129000 80100660  .......8   SCP GETMAIN-COND-INIT
145F50  C8 115222 0004 TC 00129000 84000118  .......8   SCP ACQUIRED LINE STORAGE
145F60  F0 10DB88 4004 TC 00000000 001107F8  .......    KCP WAIT
145F70  D0 10BC20 0904 JJ 0000CC20 D1200000  ...J...    KCP SYSTEM RESUME
145F80  D0 10BC20 0504 TC 00000000 00000000  .......    KCP DISPATCH
145F90  F0 10DB88 4004 TC 44000000 001107F8  .......8   KCP WAIT
145FA0  D0 10BC20 0904 JJ 0000CC20 A6A00000  .......    KCP SYSTEM RESUME
145FB0  D0 10BC20 0504 TC 00000000 00000000  .......    KCP DISPATCH
145FC0  F0 10DB88 4004 TC 44000000 001107F8  .......8   KCP WAIT
145FD0  D0 10BC20 0504 TC 00000000 00000000  .......    KCP DISPATCH
145FE0  D0 10BC20 0504 TC 0000CC20 0E000000  .......    KCP SYSTEM RESUME
145FF0  F0 113464 1104 TC 01100660 D6D9C1C4  ...ORAD    KCP ATTACH-CONDITIONAL
146000  F1 10A91E EA04 TC 000807B0 80100660  .......Q   SCP GETMAIN-COND-INIT
146010  C8 115222 0604 0009 0012D800 8A0307B8 ...Q...   SCP ACQUIRED TCA STORAGE
146020  D0 10BC20 4004 TC D3F7F7F0 D6D9C1C4  L77ORAD    KCP CREATE
146030  D0 10BC20 0504 TC 00000000 001107F8  .......8   KCP DISPATCH
146040  F0 10DB88 4004 TC 44000000 00000000  .......    KCP WAIT
146350  D0 10BC20 0504 0009 00000000 00000000 .......   KCP DISPATCH
146060  F2 11880A 0204 0009 D6D9C1C4 F0F1C140 QRAD01A   PCP XCTL
146070  F1 1190FC 8C04 0009 0000003B 01100660 .......H  SCP GETMAIN
146080  C8 115222 CC04 0009 0012DFC0 8C0003C8 .......    SCP ACQUIRED USER STORAGE
146090  F1 10C2A6 CC04 0009 00000128 01100660 .......    SCP GETMAIN-INIT
1460A0  F1 115222 0004 0009 0012E390 8C000138 ...T...    SCP ACQUIRED USER STORAGE
1460B0  E1 1339C2 00F4 0009 0012E00C 00000202 .......    EIP ADDRESS ENTRY
1460C0  E1 1339C2 00F4 0009 00000000 00000202 .......    EIP ADDRESS ENTRY
1460D0  E1 1339C2 CC04 0009 0012E00C 00000206 .......    EIP ADDRESS RESPONSE
1460E0  C8 10BC96 CC04 0009 00000059 01100660 .......    SCP HANDLE-AID ENTRY
1460F0  C8 115222 CC04 0009 0012E4D0 8C000068 ...U...    SCP GETMAIN-INIT
146100  F1 10BD98 CC04 0009 00000040 01100660 ...,...    SCP ACQUIRED USER STORAGE
146110  C8 115222 00F4 0009 0012E540 8C000048 ...V...    SCP GETMAIN-INIT
146120  E1 1339C2 00F4 0009 00000000 00000206 .......    EIP HANDLE-AID RESPONSE
146130  E1 133A1C 00F4 0009 0012E00C 00000204 .......    EIP HANDLE-CONDITION ENTRY
146140  F1 10BC96 CC04 0009 00000070 01100660 ...V...    SCP GETMAIN-INIT
146150  C8 115222 0004 0009 0012E590 8C000078 .......    SCP ACQUIRED USER STORAGE
146160  F1 10BD98 CC04 0009 00000040 01100660 ...V...    SCP GETMAIN-INIT
146170  C8 115222 0004 0009 0012E610 8C000048 ...M...    SCP ACQUIRED USER STORAGE
146180  E1 133A1C 00F4 0009 00000000 8C000204 .......    EIP HANDLE-CONDITION RESPONSE
```

Fig. 24.1.   (Continued)

```
CUSTOMER INFORMATION CONTROL SYSTEM STORAGE DUMP    CODE=ERRS    TASK=DRAD    DATE=08/02/80    TIME=17 03 35    PAGE   6

                                                                      (G)
146190  E1 133ADC 0004 0009 0012E00C 0001A04   ........   EIP ENTER ENTRY
1461A0  6F 133ADC 0002 0009 0012E00C 00000000   ........   USER 111
1461B0  E1 133ADC 00F4 0009 0012E00C 00001A04   ........   EIP ENTER RESPONSE
1461C0  E1 133B3A 0004 0009 0012E00C 00001802   ........   EIP RECEIVE-MAP ENTRY
1461D0  FA 125080 0003 0009 00000505 00000020   ........   BMS MAP MAPSET MAP IN
1461E0  F1 12537E CC04 0009 00000274 01100660   ........   SCP GETMAIN-INIT
1461F0  C8 115222 0004 0009 0012E660 8C000288   .M....     SCP ACQUIRED USER STORAGE
146200  F1 15AD78 CC04 0009 00000074 01100660   ........   SCP GETMAIN-INIT
146210  C8 115222 0004 0009 0012E8F0 8C000088   .Y0....    SCP ACQUIRED USER STORAGE
146220  F2 126200 0404 0009 D6D9C1C4 E2F0F140   ORADS01    PCP LOAD
146230  F1 1244AC C504 0009 000003B1 01100660   ........   SCP GETMAIN-INIT
146240  C8 115222 0004 0009 00129120 85003C8    ......H    SCP ACQUIRED TERMINAL STORAGE
146250  F1 124E88 4004 0009 00129000 01100660   ........   SCP FREEMAIN
146260  C9 11530C 0005 0009 00129000 85000118   ........   SCP RELEASED TERMINAL STORAGE
146270  FA 125EE6 0005 0009 00000000 00000000   ........   BMS RESPONSE
146280  E1 133B3A 00F4 0009 0012E00C 00001802   ........   EIP RECEIVE-MAP RESPONSE
146290  E1 133BAA 0004 0009 0012E00C 00000A04   ........   EIP READQ-TS ENTRY
1462A0  F7 12192C 8903 0009 D3F7F7F0 D6D9C1C4   L770ORAD   TSP GETQ
1462B0  F1 121C38 AE04 0009 00120540 01100660   ........   SCP GETMAIN-CONDITIONAL
1462C0  C8 115222 0004 0009 0012E980 8E120548   .Z....     SCP ACQUIRED TEMPSTRG STORAGE
1462D0  F7 121FCC 0015 0009 00000000 00000A04   ........   TSP RESPONSE
1462E0  E1 133BAA 00F4 0009 0012E00C 00000A04   ........   EIP READQ-TS RESPONSE
1462F0  F1 115052 8C04 0009 00120181 01100660   ........   SCP GETMAIN ENTRY
146310  C8 115222 0004 0009 0012EED0 8C1201C8   ......H    SCP ACQUIRED USER STORAGE
146320  E1 1347D8 00F4 0009 00000000 0000C02    ........   EIP GETMAIN RESPONSE
146330  E1 13486E 0004 0009 0012E00C 00001A04   ........   EIP ENTER ENTRY
146340  E1 12E610 02F4 0009 E0000000 00001A04   ........   EIP ENTER RESPONSE
146350  E1 1352F8 0004 0009 0012E00C 00001C02   ........   EIP DUMP ENTRY
146360  F4 1597FC FE04 0009 00000000 C5D9D9E2   ...ERRS    DCP TRANSACTION
146370  F0 155C58 4004 0009 80000000 00155E78   ........   KCP WAIT DCI=SINGLE
146380  FD 00001C 0204 0009 E3C904C5 1703355F   TIME...    TIMING TRACE 17/03/35.5
146390  D0 10BC20 0504 TC   00000000 001007F8   ........8  KCP DISPATCH
1463A0  F0 10DBB8 4004 TC   44000000 6AA00000   ........   KCP WAIT
1463B0  D0 10BC20 0904 0009 00005E78 6AA00000   ........   KCP SYSTEM RESUME
1463C0  D0 10BC20 0504 TC   00000000 001007F8   ........8  KCP DISPATCH
1463D0  F0 10DBB8 4004 TC   44000000 001007F8   ........   KCP WAIT
1463E0  D0 10BC20 0504 0009 00000000 00000000   ........   KCP DISPATCH
1463F0  F0 155C58 4004 0009 80000000 00155E78   ........   KCP WAIT DCI=SINGLE
146400  D0 10BC20 0904 0009 00005E78 73000000   ........   KCP SYSTEM RESUME
146410  D0 10BC20 0504 0009 00000000 00000000   ........   KCP DISPATCH
```

Fig. 24.1. (Continued)

An example of this is E on page 465. You will notice that on the right is a description of the entry. It is always the literal "EIP" (*E*xecute *I*nterface *P*rogram), followed by the command (in this case "SEND MAP"), followed by the literal "ENTRY," meaning that this is the issuance of the command.

Execute Interface Trace Entry At Completion

The trace entry upon completion of the command contains the following:

Bytes	Contents
0	X'E1' trace identifier.
1–3	Return point in the application program; if the response code in bytes 8–13 is nonzero and an appropriate HANDLE CONDITION command is active, these bytes will contain the address of the label specified in the HANDLE CONDITION command.
4	EIBGDI.
5 (bits 0–3)	X'F', identifying the second entry for the command.
5 (bits 4–7)	Not used.
6–7	User task sequence number (packed decimal).
8–13	Response code. Zero response code signifies that no exceptional condition occurred during execution of the command. If the response is nonzero, Figure 24.8 will identify the problem.
14, 15	Code identifying the CICS/VS command. Same as for Entry at Issuance.

An example of this is F on page 465, and you will notice that the description of the entry is now "RESPONSE," meaning the command has been completed. This entry will appear regardless whether there was a CICS/VS command exceptional condition or not. Bytes 8–13 will signify an exceptional condition if it is not zeroes, and the EIBRCODE field of the Execute Interface Block should then be investigated.

The specific control programs executed in a CICS/VS command are really only of academic importance to the programmer since they are provided automatically when required by the command. However,

	Description	Trace Identifier	Program
1.	BFP	X'FB'	Built-in Function
2.	BMP	X'FA', X'CD', X'CF'	Basic Mapping Support
3.	DCP	X'F4'	Dump Control
4.	DIP	X'D7'	Batch Data Interchange
5.	EIP	X'E1'	Execute Interface
6.	FCP	X'F5'	File Control
7.	ICP	X'F3'	Interval Control
8.	JCP	X'F9'	Journal Control
9.	KCP	X'F0', X'D0'	Task Control
10.	PCP	X'F2'	Program Control
11.	SCP	X'F1', X'C8', X'C9', X'CA'	Storage Control
12.	SPC	X'D8'	Sync Point
13.	TCP	X'FC'	Terminal Control
14.	TDP	X'F6'	Transient Data
15.	TSP	X'F7'	Temporary Storage
16.	USER	user specified	User Trace Entry

Fig. 24.2. Table of Trace Identifiers.

if the programmer is interested in knowing what they are, he may use
the guide in Figure 24.2.

User Trace

The third trace entry of importance to the application programmer is
the user trace entry and this is generated on the ENTER command.
It contains the following information:

Bytes	Contents
0	Trace identifier, the hexadecimal equivalent of the data value specified in the TRACEID operand.
1–3	Return point in the application program.
4	Not used.
5 (bits 0–3)	Not used.
5 (bits 4–7)	X'2', identifying this entry as a user entry.

6–7	User task sequence number (packed decimal).
8–15	Value of the data area specified in the FROM operand.

An example of this is G on page 467. The description is the literal "USER" followed by the value specified in the TRACEID operand of the ENTER command. You will also notice that it is bracketed by the two Execute Interface entries.

TRANSACTION DUMP

While the trace tables provide the programmer with a trace of the programs as they execute, a transaction dump provides him with the contents of CICS/VS data blocks at the time the dump was initiated. This shows, among other things, the WORKING-STORAGE section, main storage corresponding to entries in the LINKAGE section, the Execute Interface Block, etc., all of which may be used in debugging.

The transaction dump is automatically generated on a program check; it is also the default in most CICS/VS command exceptional conditions not specified in a HANDLE CONDITION command, unless the ERROR condition is specified; it is an option in certain commands like DUMP or ABEND.

We will now show the procedure in debugging a program check. The program used is basically the File Add program but with certain statements removed to get the abend. The program and Data Division Map listing is shown in Figure 24.3.

The Procedure Division condensed listing is given in Figure 24.4.

The resulting transaction dump is shown in Figure 24.5.

The Transaction Work Area

The Transaction Work Area is part of the Task Control Area and always prints on page 1 of the transaction dump. It always starts at byte X'100' of the data block labeled "TASK CONTROL AREA (USER AREA)." This is A in Fig. 24.5 (page 504).

```
  1   IBM DOS VS COBOL                    REL 2.5 + PTF51   PP NO. 5746-CB1                    18.38.45   07/27/80

CBL SUPMAP,STXIT,NOTRUNC,CSYNTAX,SXREF,OPT,VERB,CLIST,BUF=19069
CBL NOOPT,LIB
00001      IDENTIFICATION DIVISION.                                                00000030

00003      PROGRAM-ID. ORADC1A.                                                    00000050

00005      ENVIRONMENT DIVISION.                                                   00000070

00007      **********************************************************              00000090
00008      *                                                        *              00000100
00009      *   1. THIS PROGRAM ADDS NEW ORDERS INTO THE PURCHASE ORDER *           00000110
00010      *      MASTER FILE.                                       *              00000120
00011      *                                                        *              00000130
00012      *   2. AT LEAST ONE LINE ITEM MUST BE PRESENT FOR EACH ORDER. *         00000140
00013      *                                                        *              00000150
00014      *   3. A JOURNAL RECORD IS GENERATED FOR EACH NEW ORDER   *             00000160
00015      *      ENTERED.  THE JOURNAL DETAILS ARE                  *             00000170
00016      *         A) OPERATOR INITIAL.                            *             00000180
00017      *         B) DATE ENTERED.                                *             00000190
00018      *         C) ORDER NUMBER.                                *             00000200
00019      *         D) DOCUMENT NUMBER.                             *             00000210
00020      *         E) TOTAL COST OF ORDER.                         *             00000220
00021      *         F) TOTAL PRICE OF ORDER.                        *             00000230
00022      *                                                        *              00000240
00023      **********************************************************              00000250
```

Fig. 24.3. Program Listing And Data Division Map.

```
   2    ORAD01A        18.38.45      07/27/80

00025   DATA DIVISION.                                                   00000270

00027   WORKING-STORAGE SECTION.                                         00000290

00029   01  COMMUNICATION-AREA.                                          00000310
00031       05  COMMAREA-PROCESS-SW            PIC X.                     00000330

00033   01  AREA1.                                                       00000350

00035       05  VALIDATION-ERROR-MESSAGE.                                00000370
00036           10  FILLER                     PIC X(5) VALUE 'LINE'.    00000380
00037           10  VALIDATION-ERROR-LINE      PIC 9.                    00000390
00038           10  FILLER                     PIC XXX  VALUE ' - '.     00000400
00039           10  VALIDATION-ERROR-MSG       PIC X(19).                00000410

00041       05  JOB-NORMAL-END-MESSAGE PIC X(23) VALUE                   00000430
00042           'JOB NORMALLY TERMINATED'.                              00000440

00044       05  JOB-ABORTED-MESSAGE.                                     00000460
00045           10  FILLER       PIC X(15) VALUE 'JOB ABORTED ---'.      00000470
00046           10  MAJOR-ERROR-MSG    PIC X(16).                        00000480

00048       05  HEXADECIMAL-ZEROES     PIC 9999 COMP VALUE ZEROES.       00000500

00050       05  FILLER REDEFINES HEXADECIMAL-ZEROES.                     00000520
00051           10  FILLER                 PIC X.                        00000530
00052           10  HEX-ZEROES             PIC X.                        00000540

00054       05  OLD-EIB-AREA.                                            00000560
00055           10  FILLER           PIC X(7) VALUE 'OLD EIB'.           00000570
00056           10  OLD-EIBFN        PIC XX.                             00000580
00057           10  OLD-EIBRCODE     PIC X(6).                           00000590
```

Fig. 24.3. (Continued)

```
ORADOIA        18.38.45        07/27/80                                                        3

00059 C    01  DFHEIVAR COPY DFHEIVAR.                                                 04000000
00060 C    01  DFHEIVAR.                                                               08000000
00061 C        02  DFHEIV0    PICTURE X(26).                                           12000000
00062 C        02  DFHEIV1    PICTURE X(8).                                            16000000
00063 C        02  DFHEIV2    PICTURE X(8).                                            20000000
00064 C        02  DFHEIV3    PICTURE X(8).                                            24000000
00065 C        02  DFHEIV4    PICTURE X(6).                                            28000000
00066 C        02  DFHEIV5    PICTURE X(4).                                            32000000
00067 C        02  DFHEIV6    PICTURE X(4).                                            36000000
00068 C        02  DFHEIV7    PICTURE X(2).                                            40000000
00069 C        02  DFHEIV8    PICTURE X(2).                                            45000000
00070 C        02  DFHEIV9    PICTURE X(1).                                            50000000
00071 C        02  DFHEIV10   PICTURE S9(7) USAGE COMPUTATIONAL-3.                     55000000
00072 C        02  DFHEIV11   PICTURE S9(4) USAGE COMPUTATIONAL.                       60000000
00073 C        02  DFHEIV12   PICTURE S9(4) USAGE COMPUTATIONAL.                       65000000
00074 C        02  DFHEIV13   PICTURE S9(4) USAGE COMPUTATIONAL.                       70000000
00075 C        02  DFHEIV14   PICTURE S9(4) USAGE COMPUTATIONAL.                       75000000
00076 C        02  DFHEIV15   PICTURE S9(4) USAGE COMPUTATIONAL.                       80000000
00077 C        02  DFHEIV16   PICTURE S9(9) USAGE COMPUTATIONAL.                       81000000
00078 C        02  DFHEIV17   PICTURE X(4).                                            82000000
00079 C        02  DFHEIV18   PICTURE X(4).                                            83000000
00080 C        02  DFHEIV19   PICTURE X(4).                                            85000000
00081 C        02  DFHEIV97   PICTURE S9(7) USAGE COMPUTATIONAL-3 VALUE ZERO.          90000000
00082 C        02  DFHEIV98   PICTURE S9(4) USAGE COMPUTATION VALUE ZERO.              95000000
00083 C        02  DFHEIV99   PICTURE X(1)  VALUE SPACE.                               00000610
00084 C    LINKAGE SECTION.
00085 C    01  DFHEIBLK COPY DFHEIBLK.                                                 02000000
00086 C    *  EIBLK EXEC INTERFACE BLOCK                                               04000000
00087 C    01  DFHEIBLK.                                                               06000000
00088 C        02  EIBTIME    TIME IN 0HHMMSS FORMAT                                   08000000
00089 C                       PICTURE S9(7) USAGE COMPUTATIONAL-3.                     10000000
00090 C    *                                                                          13000000
00091 C        02  EIBDATE    DATE IN 00YYDDD FORMAT                                   16000000
00092 C                       PICTURE S9(7) USAGE COMPUTATIONAL-3.                     19000000
00093 C    *  TRANSACTION IDENTIFIER                                                   24000000
00094 C        02  EIBTRNID   PICTURE X(4).                                            29000000
00095 C    *  TASK NUMBER                                                              34000000
00096 C        02  EIBTASKN   PICTURE S9(7) USAGE COMPUTATIONAL-3.                     37000000
00097 C    *  TERMINAL IDENTIFIER                                                      40000000
00098 C        02  EIBTRMID   PICTURE X(4).                                            43000000
00099 C        02  DFHEIGDI   RESERVED                                                 46000000
00100 C        02  EIBCPOSN   CURSOR POSITION                                          49000000
00101 C                       PICTURE S9(4) USAGE COMPUTATIONAL.                       52000000
00102 C        02  EIBCALEN   COMMAREA LENGTH                                          55000000
00103 C                       PICTURE S9(4) USAGE COMPUTATIONAL.                       70000000
00104 C    *  ATTENTION IDENTIFIER                                                     73000000
00105 C        02  EIBAID     PICTURE X(1).                                            76000000
00106 C    *  FUNCTION CODE                                                            79000000
00107 C        02  EIBFN      PICTURE X(2).                                            82000000
00108 C    *  RESPONSE CODE                                                            85000000
00109 C        02  EIBRCODE   PICTURE X(6).                                            88000000
00110 C    *  DATASET NAME                                                             91000000
00111 C        02  EIBDS      PICTURE X(8).
```

Fig. 24.3. (Continued)

```
ORAD01A              18.38.45      07/27/80

*         EIBREQID   REQUEST IDENTIFIER                      94000000
          02 EIBREQID  PICTURE X(8).                         97000000
    01 DFHCOMMAREA.                                          00000620

    05  PROCESS-SW                   PIC X.                   00000640
        88  INITIAL-ENTRY-TIME       VALUE '0'.              00000650
        88  ORDER-VALIDATION-TIME    VALUE '1'.              00000660

    05  OPERATOR-INITIAL             PIC XXX.                00000680

    01 LINKAGE-POINTERS.                                     00000700

    05  FILLER           PIC S9(8) COMP.                     00000720
    05  MAP1-POINTER     PIC S9(8) COMP.                     00000730
    05  POM-POINTER      PIC S9(8) COMP.                     00000740
    05  TWA-POINTER      PIC S9(8) COMP.                     00000750
    05  TSA-POINTER      PIC S9(8) COMP.                     00000760
    05  JOURNAL-POINTER  PIC S9(8) COMP.                     00000770
    05  TABLE-POINTER    PIC S9(8) COMP.                     00000780
```

4

00112 C
00113 C
00114

00116
00117
00118

00120

00122

00124
00125
00126
00127
00128
00129
00130

Fig. 24.3. (Continued)

```
5        ORADO1A         18.38.45      07/27/80

00132  ****************************************************************   00000800
00133  *  *                                                         *   00000810
00134  *        ORDER ENTRY MAP DESCRIPTION                         *   00000820
00135  *  *                                                         *   00000830
00136  ****************************************************************   00000840

00138  01  MAP1-AREA.                                                    00000860
00140      05  FILLER                     PIC X(12).                     00000880
00141      05  MAP1-DUMMY-L               PIC S9999 COMP.                00000890
00142      05  MAP1-DUMMY-A               PIC X.                         00000900
00143      05  MAP1-DUMMY                 PIC X.                         00000910
00144      05  MAP1-ORDER-NUMBER-L        PIC S9999 COMP.                00000920
00145      05  MAP1-ORDER-NUMBER-A        PIC X.                         00000930
00146      05  MAP1-ORDER-NUMBER          PIC X(10).                     00000940
00147      05  MAP1-DOCUMENT-L            PIC S9999 COMP.                00000950
00148      05  MAP1-DOCUMENT-A            PIC X.                         00000960
00149      05  MAP1-DOCUMENT              PIC X(8).                      00000970
00150      05  MAP1-DEPARTMENT-L          PIC S9999 COMP.                00000980
00151      05  MAP1-DEPARTMENT-A          PIC X.                         00000990
00152      05  MAP1-DEPARTMENT            PIC XXX.                       00001000
00153      05  MAP1-ORDER-DATE-L          PIC S9999 COMP.                00001010
00154      05  MAP1-ORDER-DATE-A          PIC X.                         00001020
00155      05  MAP1-ORDER-DATE.                                          00001030
00156          10  MAP1-ORDER-DATE-MONTH  PIC XX.                        00001040
00157          10  MAP1-ORDER-DATE-DAY    PIC XX.                        00001050
00158          10  MAP1-ORDER-DATE-YEAR   PIC XX.                        00001060
00159      05  MAP1-LINE-ITEM             OCCURS 9                       00001070
                                          INDEXED BY MAP1-LINE-I.        00001080
00161          10  MAP1-ITEM-NUMBER-L     PIC S9999 COMP.                00001090
00162          10  MAP1-ITEM-NUMBER-A     PIC X.                         00001100
00163          10  MAP1-ITEM-NUMBER       PIC 9(8).                      00001110
00164          10  MAP1-ITEM-DESCRIPTION-L PIC S9999 COMP.               00001120
00165          10  MAP1-ITEM-DESCRIPTION-A PIC X.                        00001130
00166          10  MAP1-ITEM-DESCRIPTION  PIC X(19).                     00001140
00167          10  MAP1-UNIT-L            PIC S9999 COMP.                00001150
00168          10  MAP1-UNIT-A            PIC X.                         00001160
00169          10  MAP1-UNIT              PIC 9(5).                      00001170
00170          10  MAP1-UNIT-COST-L       PIC S9999 COMP.                00001180
00171          10  MAP1-UNIT-COST-A       PIC X.                         00001190
00172          10  MAP1-UNIT-COST         PIC 9(5)V99.                   00001200
00173          10  MAP1-COST-L            PIC S9999 COMP.                00001210
00174          10  MAP1-COST-A            PIC X.                         00001220
00175          10  MAP1-COST              PIC 9(6)V99.                   00001230
00176          10  MAP1-UNIT-PRICE-L      PIC S9999 COMP.                00001240
00177          10  MAP1-UNIT-PRICE-A      PIC X.                         00001250
00178          10  MAP1-UNIT-PRICE        PIC 9(5)V99.                   00001260
00179          10  MAP1-PRICE-L           PIC S9999 COMP.                00001270
00180          10  MAP1-PRICE-A           PIC X.                         00001280
00181          10  MAP1-PRICE             PIC 9(6)V99.                   00001290
00182      05  MAP1-TOTAL-COST-L          PIC S9999 COMP.                00001300
```

Fig. 24.3. (Continued)

```
6       ORAD01A        18.38.45        07/27/80

00183        05  MAP1-TOTAL-COST-A        PIC X.                    00001310
00184        05  MAP1-TOTAL-COST          PIC 9(7)V99.              00001320
00185        05  MAP1-TOTAL-PRICE-L       PIC S9999 COMP.          00001330
00186        05  MAP1-TOTAL-PRICE-A       PIC X.                   00001340
00187        05  MAP1-TOTAL-PRICE         PIC 9(7)V99.             00001350
00188        05  FILLER                   OCCURS 4                 00001360
00189                                     INDEXED BY ERROR-I.      00001370
00190            10  MAP1-ERRORS-L        PIC S9999 COMP.          00001380
00191            10  MAP1-ERRORS-A        PIC X.                   00001390
00192            10  MAP1-ERRORS          PIC X(28).               00001400


7       ORAD01A        18.38.45        07/27/80

00194   ****************************************************        00000010
00195   *                                                *        00000020
00196   *    PURCHASE ORDER MASTER -- FILE LAYOUT        *        00000030
00197   *                                                *        00000040
00198   ****************************************************        00000050

00200   01  ORDER-MASTER-RECORD.                                   00000070
00201        05  ORDER-NUMBER                PIC X(10).            00000080
00202        05  ORDER-ALT-KEY.                                    00000090
00203            10  ORDER-DEPARTMENT        PIC XXX.              00000100
00204            10  ORDER-DATE.                                   00000110
00205                15  ORDER-DATE-YEAR     PIC XX.               00000120
00206                15  ORDER-DATE-MONTH    PIC XX.               00000130
00207                15  ORDER-DATE-DAY      PIC XX.               00000140
00208        05  ORDER-DATE-ENTERED.                               00000150
00209            10  ORDER-DATE-ENTERED-MONTH   PIC XX.            00000160
00210            10  ORDER-DATE-ENTERED-DAY     PIC XX.            00000170
00211            10  ORDER-DATE-ENTERED-YEAR    PIC XX.            00000180
00212        05  ORDER-TOTAL-COST        PIC S9(7)V99    COMP-3.   00000190
00213        05  ORDER-TOTAL-PRICE       PIC S9(7)V99    COMP-3.   00000200
00214        05  ORDER-LINE-COUNT        PIC S9999       COMP.     00000210
00215        05  ORDER-ALL-LINES.                                  00000220
00216            10  ORDER-LINE-ITEM     OCCURS 1 TO 9             00000230
00217                                    DEPENDING ON ORDER-LINE-COUNT  00000240
00218                                    INDEXED BY ORDER-LINE-I.  00000250
00219                15  ORDER-ITEM-NUMBER        PIC X(8).        00000260
00220                15  ORDER-ITEM-DESCRIPTION   PIC X(19).       00000270
00221                15  ORDER-ITEM-DATE.                          00000280
00222                    20  ORDER-ITEM-DATE-MONTH PIC XX.         00000290
00223                    20  ORDER-ITEM-DATE-DAY   PIC XX.         00000300
00224                    20  ORDER-ITEM-DATE-YEAR  PIC XX.         00000310
00225                15  ORDER-UNIT       PIC S9(5)       COMP-3.  00000320
00226                15  ORDER-UNIT-COST  PIC S9(5)V99    COMP-3.  00000330
00227                15  ORDER-UNIT-PRICE PIC S9(5)V99    COMP-3.  00000340
```

Fig. 24.3. (Continued)

```
8        ORAD01A        18.38.45        07/27/80

                **********************************************************
                *                                                        *   00001440
                *                  TRANSACTION WORK AREA                  *   00001450
                *                                                        *   00001460
                *                                                        *   00001470
                **********************************************************   00001480

00229                                                                        00001480
00230
00231
00232
00233

00235    01  TWA-AREA.                                                       00001500

00237    05  TWA-LINE-ITEM-MAP.                                             00001520
00238        10  TWA-ITEM-NUMBER-MAP-L       PIC S9999 COMP.               00001530
00239        10  TWA-ITEM-NUMBER-MAP-A       PIC X.                        00001540
00240        10  TWA-ITEM-NUMBER-MAP         PIC X(8).                     00001550
00241        10  TWA-ITEM-DESCRIPTION-MAP-L  PIC S9999 COMP.               00001560
00242        10  TWA-ITEM-DESCRIPTION-MAP-A  PIC X.                        00001570
00243        10  TWA-ITEM-DESCRIPTION-MAP.                                 00001580
00244            15  TWA-DESCRIPTION-FIRST-MAP                             00001590
                                              PIC X.                        00001600
00245            15  FILLER                   PIC X(18).                    00001610
00246        10  TWA-UNIT-MAP-L              PIC S9999 COMP.               00001620
00247        10  TWA-UNIT-MAP-A             PIC X.                        00001630
00248        10  TWA-UNIT-MAP               PIC 9(5).                     00001640
00249        10  TWA-UNIT-COST-MAP-L        PIC S9999 COMP.               00001650
00250        10  TWA-UNIT-COST-MAP-A        PIC X.                        00001660
00251        10  TWA-UNIT-COST-MAP          PIC 9(5)V99.                  00001670
00252        10  TWA-COST-MAP-L             PIC S9999 COMP.               00001680
00253        10  TWA-COST-MAP-A             PIC X.                        00001690
00254        10  TWA-COST-MAP               PIC 9(6)V99.                  00001700
00255        10  TWA-UNIT-PRICE-MAP-L       PIC S9999 COMP.               00001710
00256        10  TWA-UNIT-PRICE-MAP-A       PIC X.                        00001720
00257        10  TWA-UNIT-PRICE-MAP         PIC 9(5)V99.                  00001730
00258        10  TWA-PRICE-MAP-L            PIC S9999 COMP.               00001740
00259        10  TWA-PRICE-MAP-A            PIC X.                        00001750
00260        10  TWA-PRICE-MAP              PIC 9(6)V99.

00262    05  TWA-LINE-ITEM-ORDER.                                          00001770
00263        10  TWA-ITEM-NUMBER-ORDER       PIC X(8).                     00001780
00264        10  TWA-ITEM-DESCRIPTION-ORDER  PIC X(19).                    00001790
00265        10  TWA-ITEM-DATE-ORDER         PIC X(6).                     00001800
00266        10  TWA-UNIT-ORDER              PIC S9(5)      COMP-3.        00001810
00267        10  TWA-UNIT-COST-ORDER         PIC S9(5)V99   COMP-3.        00001820
00268        10  TWA-UNIT-PRICE-ORDER        PIC S9(5)V99   COMP-3.        00001830

00270    05  TWA-TOTAL-COST                  PIC S9(7)V99   COMP-3.        00001850

00272    05  TWA-TOTAL-PRICE                 PIC S9(7)V99   COMP-3.        00001870

00274    05  TWA-ORDER-RECORD-KEY            PIC X(10).                    00001890
```

Fig. 24.3. (Continued)

```
9        ORADO1A      18.38.45      07/27/80

00276  A    05  TSA-QUEUE-ID.                                    00001910
00277           10  TSA-TERM-ID              PIC XXXX.           00001920
00278           10  TSA-TRANS-ID             PIC XXXX.           00001930

00280       05  TWA-BINARY-FIELDS  COMP.                         00001950
00281           10  TWA-LINE-DATA-CNT        PIC S9(8).          00001960
00282           10  TWA-JOURNAL-ID           PIC S9(8).          00001970
00283           10  TWA-POM-LENGTH           PIC S9(4).          00001980
00284           10  TSA-LENGTH               PIC S9(4).          00001990
00285           10  TSA-QUEUE-NO             PIC S9(4).          00002000
00286           10  TWA-JOURNAL-LENGTH       PIC S9(4).          00002010

00288       05  TWA-OPERATOR-MESSAGE         PIC X(31).          00002030

00290       05  TWA-CURRENT-DATE.                                00002050
00291           10  TWA-CURRENT-DATE-MONTH   PIC XX.             00002060
00292           10  FILLER                   PIC X.              00002070
00293           10  TWA-CURRENT-DATE-DAY     PIC XX.             00002080
00294           10  FILLER                   PIC X.              00002090
00295           10  TWA-CURRENT-DATE-YEAR    PIC XX.             00002100

00297       05  TWA-DEPT-TABLE-KEY.                              00002120
00298           10  TWA-DEPT-TABLE-KEY-CODE     PIC X.           00002130
00299           10  TWA-DEPT-TABLE-KEY-NUMBER  PIC 9(7) COMP-3.  00002140
```

Fig. 24.3. (Continued)

```
  10          ORADO1A        18.38.45       07/27/80

00301   *****************************************************     *       00002160
00302   *                                                  *     *       00002170
00303   *              TEMPORARY STORAGE AREA              *     *       00002180
00304   *                                                  *     *       00002190
00305   *****************************************************     *       00002200

00307   01  TSA-AREA.                                                    00002220

00309       05  TSA-POMAST-RECORD.                                       00002240
00310           10  TSA-ORDER-NUMBER           PIC X(10).                00002250
00311           10  TSA-DEPARTMENT             PIC XXX.                  00002260
00312           10  TSA-ORDER-DATE.                                      00002270
00313               15  TSA-ORDER-DATE-YEAR    PIC XX.                   00002280
00314               15  TSA-ORDER-DATE-MONTH   PIC XX.                   00002290
00315               15  TSA-ORDER-DATE-DAY     PIC XX.                   00002300
00316           10  TSA-ORDER-ENTERED.                                   00002310
00317               15  TSA-ORDER-ENTERED-MONTH  PIC XX.                 00002320
00318               15  TSA-ORDER-ENTERED-DAY    PIC XX.                 00002330
00319               15  TSA-ORDER-ENTERED-YEAR   PIC XX.                 00002340
00320           10  TSA-TOTAL-COST             PIC S9(7)V99 COMP-3.      00002350
00321           10  TSA-TOTAL-PRICE            PIC S9(7)V99 COMP-3.      00002360
00322           10  TSA-LINE-COUNT             PIC S9999 COMP.           00002370
00323           10  TSA-LINE-ITEM             OCCURS 9                   00002380
00324                             INDEXED BY TSA-LINE-I.                 00002390
00325               15  TSA-ITEM-NUMBER        PIC X(8).                 00002400
00326               15  TSA-ITEM-DESCRIPTION   PIC X(19).                00002410
00327               15  TSA-ITEM-DATE          PIC X(6).                 00002420
00328               15  TSA-UNIT               PIC X(5)       COMP-3.    00002430
00329               15  TSA-UNIT-COST          PIC S9(5)V99   COMP-3.    00002440
00330               15  TSA-UNIT-PRICE         PIC S9(5)V99   COMP-3.    00002450

00332       05  TSA-OPERATOR-INITIAL           PIC XXX.                  00002470

00334       05  TSA-DEPT-CNT                   PIC S9(8)    COMP.        00002490

00336       05  TSA-DEPTS                     OCCURS 300                 00002510
00337                             DEPENDING ON TSA-DEPT-CNT              00002520
00338                             ASCENDING KEY TSA-DEPT-NO              00002530
00339                             INDEXED BY DEPT-I.                     00002540
00340           10  TSA-DEPT-NO                PIC XXX.                  00002550
```

Fig. 24.3. (Continued)

11   ORAD01A   18.38.45   07/27/80

```
     ****************************************************        00002570
     *                                                  *        00002580
     *              JOURNAL RECORD LAYOUT               *        00002590
     *                                                  *        00002600
     ****************************************************        00002610

      01  JOURNAL-RECORD.                                        00002630

          05  JOURNAL-OPERATOR-INITIAL    PIC XXX.              00002650
          05  JOURNAL-DATE-ENTERED        PIC X(6).             00002660
          05  JOURNAL-ORDER-NUMBER        PIC X(10).            00002670
          05  JOURNAL-DOCUMENT-NUMBER     PIC X(8).             00002680
          05  JOURNAL-TOTAL-COST          PIC S9(7)V99 COMP-3.  00002690
          05  JOURNAL-TOTAL-PRICE         PIC S9(7)V99 COMP-3.  00002700
```

(00342, 00343, 00344, 00345, 00346, 00348, 00350, 00351, 00352, 00353, 00354, 00355)

12   ORAD01A   18.38.45   07/27/80

```
     ****************************************************        00002720
     *                                                  *        00002730
     *          DEPARTMENT TABLE --- RECORD LAYOUT      *        00002740
     *                                                  *        00002750
     ****************************************************        00002763

      01  DEPT-TABLE-RECORD.                                     00002780
          05  DEPT-TABLE-KEY.                                    00002790
              10  DEPT-TABLE-KEY-CODE     PIC X.                00002800
                  88  DEPT-RECORD             VALUE 'D'.        00002810
              10  DEPT-TABLE-KEY-NUMBER   PIC 9(7) COMP-3.      00002820
          05  DEPT-NO                     PIC XXX.              00002830
          05  FILLER                      PIC X(30).            00002840
          05  DEPT-DIVISION               PIC XX.               00002850
          05  FILLER                      PIC X(45).            00002860
```

(00357, 00358, 00359, 00360, 00361, 00363, 00364, 00365, 00366, 00367, 00368, 00369, 00370, 00371)

Fig. 24.3. (Continued)

```
13   ORAD01A      18.38.45     07/27/80

00373  PROCEDURE DIVISION USING DFHEIBLK DFHCOMMAREA.                          00002880
00374      CALL 'DFHEI1'.

00376  ****************************************************************          00002900
00377  *                                                              *        00002910
00378  *  MAIN-LINE SECTION.                                          *        00002920
00379  *                                                              *        00002930
00380  ****************************************************************          00002940

00382  *     EXEC CICS
00383  *         ADDRESS TWA (TWA-POINTER)
00384  *     END-EXEC.
00385        MOVE ' '          ' TO DFHEIVO CALL 'DFHEI1' USING                00002960
00386        DFHEIVO TWA-POINTER.
00387
00388  *     EXEC CICS
00389  *         HANDLE AID
00390  *             CLEAR (FINALIZATION)
00391  *             PA1 (BYPASS-INPUT)
00392  *             PA2 (BYPASS-INPUT)
00393  *             PA3 (BYPASS-INPUT)
00394  *     END-EXEC.
00395        MOVE ' 0           ' TO DFHEIVO CALL 'DFHEI1' USING               00002990
00396        DFHEIVO GO TO FINALIZATION BYPASS-INPUT BYPASS-INPUT
00397        BYPASS-INPUT DEPENDING ON DFHEIGDI.
00398
00399
00400
00401
00402  *     EXEC CICS
00403  *         HANDLE CONDITION
00404  *             MAPFAIL (MAPFAIL-ERROR)
00405  *             ERROR (MAJOR-ERROR)
00406  *     END-EXEC.
00407        MOVE ' '          ' TO DFHEIVO CALL 'DFHEI1' USING                00003060
00408        DFHEIVO GO TO MAPFAIL-ERROR MAJOR-ERROR DEPENDING ON
00409        DFHEIGDI.
00410
00411        IF EIBCALEN NOT EQUAL TO ZEROES                                   00003110
00412            IF ORDER-VALIDATION-TIME                                      00003120
00413                GO TO ORDER-VALIDATION                                    00003130
00414            ELSE IF INITIAL-ENTRY-TIME                                    00003140
00415                GO TO INITIALIZATION                                      00003150
00416            ELSE GO TO PROCESS-SWITCH-ERROR.                              00003160
00417
00419        IF EIBCALEN EQUAL TO ZEROES                                       00003180
00420            GO TO SIGN-ON-VIOLATION.                                      00003190
```

Fig. 24.3. (Continued)

```
14          ORADO1A          18.38.45      07/27/80

00422       ***********************************************************    00003210
00423        ORDER-VALIDATION SECTION.                                 *   00003220
00424       *                                                              0C003230
00425       *                                                          *   00003240
00426       ***********************************************************    00003250

00428   *    EXEC CICS
00429   *       RECEIVE MAP    ('ORADMO1')
00430   *               MAPSET ('ORADSO1')
00431   *               SET    (MAP1-POINTER)
00432   *    END-EXEC.
00433        MOVE 'ORADMO1' TO DFHEIV1 MOVE 'ORADSO1' TO DFHEIV2 MOVE '    00003270
00434   -    ' TO DFHEIV0 CALL 'DFHEI1' USING DFHEIV0
00435        DFHEIV1 MAP1-POINTER DFHEIV98 DFHEIV2.
00436
00437        MOVE EIBTRMID    TO   TSA-TERM-ID.                            00003320
00438        MOVE EIBTRNID    TO   TSA-TRANS-ID.                           00003330

00441   *    EXEC CICS
00442   *      READQ TS
00443   *          QUEUE  (TSA-QUEUE-ID)
00444   *          SET    (TSA-POINTER)
00445   *          LENGTH (TSA-LENGTH)
00446   *          ITEM   (1)
00447   *    END-EXEC.
00448        MOVE 1 TO DFHEIV11 MOVE ' '        ' TO DFHEIV0 CALL 'DFHEI1' 00003350
00449        USING DFHEIV0 TSA-QUEUE-ID TSA-POINTER TSA-LENGTH DFHEIV99
00451        DFHEIV11.
00452
00453
00454
00455        MOVE SPACES TO MAP1-ERRORS (1)                                00003420
00456                       MAP1-ERRORS (2)                                00003430
00457                       MAP1-ERRORS (3)                                00003440
00458                       MAP1-ERRORS (4).                               00003450
00459        SET ERROR-I    TO ZEROES.                                     00003460

00461    VALIDATE-FIXED-DATA.                                              00003480

00463        IF MAP1-ORDER-NUMBER NUMERIC                                  00003500
00464           MOVE MAP1-ORDER-NUMBER         TO   TSA-ORDER-NUMBER       00003510
00465        ELSE SET ERROR-I UP BY 1                                      00003520
00466           MOVE 'INVALID ORDER NUMBER'    TO   MAP1-ERRORS (ERROR-I)  00003530
00467           MOVE -1                        TO   MAP1-ORDER-NUMBER-L.   00003540

00469        IF MAP1-DOCUMENT NUMERIC                                      00003560
00470           NEXT SENTENCE                                             00003570
00471        ELSE SET ERROR-I UP BY 1                                      00003580
00472           MOVE 'INVALID DOCUMENT NUMBER' TO  MAP1-ERRORS (ERROR-I)   00003590
```

Fig. 24.3. (Continued)

```
15        ORAD01A          18.38.45      07/27/80

00473              IF ERROR-I EQUAL TO 1                                    00003600
00474                  MOVE -1                       TO  MAP1-DOCUMENT-L.   00003610

00476              SEARCH ALL TSA-DEPTS                                     00003630
00477                  AT END                                              00003640
00478                      GO TO DEPARTMENT-ERROR-RTN                      00003650
00479                  WHEN MAP1-DEPARTMENT EQUAL    TO  TSA-DEPT-NO (DEPT-I) 00003660
00480                      MOVE MAP1-DEPARTMENT      TO  TSA-DEPARTMENT     00003670
00481                      GO TO EDIT-ORDER-DATE.                          00003680

00483          DEPARTMENT-ERROR-RTN.                                       00003700

00485              SET ERROR-I UP BY 1.                                    00003720
00486              MOVE 'INVALID DEPARTMENT NUMBER' TO MAP1-ERRORS (ERROR-I). 00003730
00487              IF ERROR-I EQUAL TO 1                                   00003740
00488                  MOVE -1                       TO  MAP1-DEPARTMENT-L. 00003750

00490          EDIT-ORDER-DATE.                                           00003770

00492              IF    MAP1-ORDER-DATE-MONTH (GREATER '00' AND LESS '13') 00003790
00493                AND MAP1-ORDER-DATE-DAY   (GREATER '00' AND LESS '32') 00003800
00494                AND MAP1-ORDER-DATE-YEAR   NUMERIC                    00003810
00495              THEN MOVE MAP1-ORDER-DATE-MONTH TO  TSA-ORDER-DATE-MONTH 00003820
00496                   MOVE MAP1-ORDER-DATE-DAY   TO  TSA-ORDER-DATE-DAY  00003830
00497                   MOVE MAP1-ORDER-DATE-YEAR  TO  TSA-ORDER-DATE-YEAR 00003840
00498              ELSE SET ERROR-I UP BY 1                                00003850
00499                   MOVE 'INVALID ORDER-DATE'  TO  MAP1-ERRORS (ERROR-I) 00003860
00500                   IF ERROR-I EQUAL TO 1                              00003870
00501                       MOVE -1                TO  MAP1-ORDER-DATE-L.  00003880

00503          VALIDATE-FIXED-DATA-END.                                    00003900

00505              IF ERROR-I EQUAL TO 4                                   00003920
00506                  GO TO DISPLAY-ERROR-SCREEN.                         00003930

00508          VALIDATE-VARIABLE-DATA.                                     00003950

00510              SET MAP1-LINE-I            TO  1.                       00003970
00511              MOVE +99                   TO  TWA-LINE-DATA-CNT.        00003980
00512              MOVE MAP1-ORDER-DATE       TO  TWA-ITEM-DATE-ORDER.     00003990
00513              PERFORM VALIDATE-EACH-LINE THRU VALIDATE-EACH-LINE-EXIT 00004000
00514                  UNTIL TWA-LINE-DATA-CNT EQUAL TO ZEROES             00004010
00515                  OR ERROR-I             EQUAL TO 4                   00004020
00516                  OR MAP1-LINE-I         GREATER THAN 9.              00004030
00517              GO TO VALIDATE-TOTALS.                                  00004040

00519          VALIDATE-EACH-LINE.                                         00004060
```

Fig. 24.3. (Continued)

```
16        ORADO1A        18.38.45        07/27/80

00521          MOVE ZEROES                 TO  TWA-LINE-DATA-CNT.                00004080
00522          SET VALIDATION-ERROR-LINE   TO  MAP1-LINE-I.                      00004090
00523          MOVE MAP1-LINE-ITEM (MAP1-LINE-I) TO TWA-LINE-ITEM-MAP.           00004100

00525      IF TWA-ITEM-NUMBER-MAP-L NOT EQUAL TO ZEROES                          00004120
00526      THEN IF TWA-ITEM-NUMBER-MAP NUMERIC                                   00004130
00527             MOVE TWA-ITEM-NUMBER-MAP TO TWA-ITEM-NUMBER-ORDER              00004140
00528             ADD 1 TO TWA-LINE-DATA-CNT                                     00004150
00530          ELSE MOVE 'INVALID ITEM NUMBER' TO VALIDATION-ERROR-MSG          00004160
00531             SET ERROR-I UP BY 1                                           00004170
00532             MOVE VALIDATION-ERROR-MESSAGE                                  00004180
00533                               TO MAP1-ERRORS (ERROR-I)                     00004190
00534             IF ERROR-I EQUAL TO 1                                          00004200
00535                MOVE -1 TO MAP1-ITEM-NUMBER-L (MAP1-LINE-I)                 00004210
00536             ELSE IF ERROR-I EQUAL TO 4                                     00004220
                         GO TO VALIDATE-EACH-LINE-EXIT.                          00004230

00538      IF TWA-ITEM-DESCRIPTION-MAP-L EQUAL TO ZEROES                         00004250
00539          MOVE SPACES TO TWA-ITEM-DESCRIPTION-ORDER                         00004260
00540      ELSE IF TWA-DESCRIPTION-FIRST-MAP EQUAL TO SPACES                     00004270
00541             MOVE 'INVALID DESCRIPTION'                                     00004280
00542                               TO VALIDATION-ERROR-MSG                      00004290
00543             SET ERROR-I UP BY 1                                           00004300
00544             MOVE VALIDATION-ERROR-MESSAGE                                  00004310
00545                               TO MAP1-ERRORS (ERROR-I)                     00004320
00546             IF ERROR-I EQUAL TO 1                                          00004330
00547                MOVE -1                                                     00004340
00548                   TO MAP1-ITEM-DESCRIPTION-L (MAP1-LINE-I)                 00004350
00549             ELSE IF ERROR-I EQUAL TO 4                                     00004360
00550                      GO TO VALIDATE-EACH-LINE-EXIT                         00004370
00551             ELSE NEXT SENTENCE                                            00004380
00552      ELSE MOVE TWA-ITEM-DESCRIPTION-MAP                                    00004390
00553                   TO TWA-ITEM-DESCRIPTION-ORDER                           00004400
00554          ADD 2                      TO TWA-LINE-DATA-CNT.                  00004410

00556      IF TWA-UNIT-MAP-L NOT EQUAL TO ZEROES                                00004430
00557      THEN IF TWA-UNIT-MAP NUMERIC                                         00004440
00558             MOVE TWA-UNIT-MAP         TO  TWA-UNIT-ORDER                   00004450
00559             ADD 4 TO TWA-LINE-DATA-CNT                                    00004460
00560          ELSE MOVE ZEROES            TO  TWA-UNIT-ORDER                    00004470
00561             MOVE 'INVALID UNIT'      TO  VALIDATION-ERROR-MSG              00004480
00562             SET ERROR-I UP BY 1                                           00004490
00563             MOVE VALIDATION-ERROR-MESSAGE                                  00004500
00564                               TO  MAP1-ERRORS (ERROR-I)                    00004510
00565             IF ERROR-I EQUAL TO 1                                          00004520
00566                MOVE -1      TO MAP1-UNIT-L (MAP1-LINE-I)                   00004530
00567             ELSE IF ERROR-I EQUAL TO 4                                     00004540
00568                      GO TO VALIDATE-EACH-LINE-EXIT.                        00004550

00570      IF TWA-UNIT-COST-MAP-L NOT EQUAL TO ZEROES                           00004570
00571      THEN IF TWA-UNIT-COST-MAP NUMERIC                                    00004580
00572             MOVE TWA-UNIT-COST-MAP TO TWA-UNIT-COST-ORDER                  00004590
00573             ADD 8 TO TWA-LINE-DATA-CNT                                    00004600
```

Fig. 24.3. (Continued)

17   ORAD01A   18.38.45   07/27/80

```
00574       ELSE MOVE ZEROES              TO  TWA-UNIT-COST-ORDER    00004610
00575       MOVE 'INVALID UNIT COST'      TO  VALIDATION-ERROR-MSG   00004620
00576                                                                00004630
00577       SET ERROR-I UP BY 1                                      00004640
00578       MOVE VALIDATION-ERROR-MESSAGE                            00004650
00579                                     TO  MAP1-ERRORS (ERROR-I)  00004660
00580       IF ERROR-I EQUAL TO 1                                    00004670
00581           MOVE -1  TO MAP1-UNIT-COST-L (MAP1-LINE-I)           00004680
00582       ELSE IF ERROR-I EQUAL TO 4                               00004690
00583                       GO TO VALIDATE-EACH-LINE-EXIT.           00004700

00585   IF TWA-COST-MAP-L NOT EQUAL TO ZEROES                        00004720
00586   THEN IF   TWA-COST-MAP NUMERIC                               00004730
00587            AND TWA-COST-MAP =                                  00004740
00588                 TWA-UNIT-ORDER * TWA-UNIT-COST-ORDER           00004750
00589            THEN ADD TWA-COST-MAP TO TWA-TOTAL-COST             00004760
00590                 ADD 16           TO  TWA-LINE-DATA-CNT          00004770
00591            ELSE MOVE 'INVALID COST' TO VALIDATION-ERROR-MSG    00004780
00592                 SET ERROR-I UP BY 1                            00004790
00593                 MOVE VALIDATION-ERROR-MESSAGE                  00004800
00594                                   TO MAP1-ERRORS (ERROR-I)     00004810
00595                 IF ERROR-I EQUAL TO 1                          00004820
00596                     MOVE -1 TO MAP1-COST-L (MAP1-LINE-I)       00004830
00597                 ELSE IF ERROR-I EQUAL TO 4                     00004840
00598                       GO TO VALIDATE-EACH-LINE-EXIT.           00004850

00600   IF TWA-UNIT-PRICE-MAP-L NOT EQUAL TO ZEROES                  00004870
00601   THEN IF TWA-UNIT-PRICE-MAP NUMERIC                           00004880
00602            MOVE TWA-UNIT-PRICE-MAP TO  TWA-UNIT-PRICE-ORDER    00004890
00603            ADD 32 TO TWA-LINE-DATA-CNT                         00004900
00604       ELSE MOVE ZEROES            TO  TWA-UNIT-PRICE-ORDER     00004910
00605       MOVE 'INVALID UNIT PRICE'   TO  VALIDATION-ERROR-MSG     00004920
00606                                                                00004930
00607       SET ERROR-I UP BY 1                                      00004940
00608       MOVE VALIDATION-ERROR-MESSAGE                            00004950
00609                                   TO  MAP1-ERRORS (ERROR-I)    00004960
00610       IF ERROR-I EQUAL TO 1                                    00004970
00611           MOVE -1 TO MAP1-UNIT-PRICE-L (MAP1-LINE-I)           00004980
00612       ELSE IF ERROR-I EQUAL TO 4                               00004990
00613               GO TO VALIDATE-EACH-LINE-EXIT.                   00005000

00615   IF TWA-PRICE-MAP-L NOT EQUAL TO ZEROES                       00005020
00616   THEN IF   TWA-PRICE-MAP =                                    00005030
00617            AND TWA-PRICE-MAP NUMERIC                           00005040
00618                 TWA-UNIT-ORDER * TWA-UNIT-PRICE-ORDER          00005050
00619            THEN ADD TWA-PRICE-MAP TO TWA-TOTAL-PRICE           00005060
00620                 ADD 64           TO  TWA-LINE-DATA-CNT          00005070
00621            ELSE MOVE 'INVALID PRICE' TO VALIDATION-ERROR-MSG   00005080
00622                 SET ERROR-I UP BY 1                            00005090
00623                 MOVE VALIDATION-ERROR-MESSAGE                  00005100
00624                                   TO MAP1-ERRORS (ERROR-I)     00005110
00625                 IF ERROR-I EQUAL TO 1                          00005120
00626                     MOVE -1 TO MAP1-PRICE-L (MAP1-LINE-I)      00005130
```

Fig. 24.3. (Continued)

```
18         ORAD01A              18.38.45      07/27/80

00627            ELSE IF ERROR-I EQUAL TO 4                               00005140
00628               GO TO VALIDATE-EACH-LINE-EXIT.                        00005150

00630        IF TWA-LINE-DATA-CNT EQUAL TO (125 OR 127)                   00005170
00631           IF ERROR-I EQUAL TO ZEROES                                00005180
00632              SET TSA-LINE-I TO MAP1-LINE-I                          00005190
00633              MOVE TWA-LINE-ITEM-ORDER                               00005200
00634                  TO TSA-LINE-ITEM (TSA-LINE-I)                      00005210
00635           ELSE NEXT SENTENCE                                        00005220
00636        ELSE IF TWA-LINE-DATA-CNT EQUAL TO ZEROES                    00005230
00637              NEXT SENTENCE                                          00005240
00638           ELSE SET ERROR-I UP BY 1                                  00005250
00639              MOVE 'INCOMPLETE DATA' TO VALIDATION-ERROR-MSG         00005260
00640              MOVE VALIDATION-ERROR-MESSAGE                          00005270
00641                  TO MAP1-ERRORS (ERROR-I)                           00005280
00642              IF ERROR-I EQUAL TO 1                                  00005290
00643                 MOVE -1                                             00005300
00644                    TO MAP1-ITEM-NUMBER-L (MAP1-LINE-I)              00005310
00645              ELSE IF ERROR-I EQUAL TO 4                             00005320
00646                 GO TO VALIDATE-EACH-LINE-EXIT.                      00005330

00648        SET MAP1-LINE-I UP BY 1.                                     00005350
00649    VALIDATE-EACH-LINE-EXIT.  EXIT.                                  00005360

00651    VALIDATE-TOTALS.                                                 00005380

00653        IF ERROR-I EQUAL TO 4                                        00005400
00654           GO TO DISPLAY-ERROR-SCREEN.                               00005410

00656        IF    MAP1-LINE-I EQUAL TO 2                                 00005430
00657           AND TWA-LINE-DATA-CNT EQUAL TO ZEROES                     00005440
00658        THEN SET ERROR-I UP BY 1                                     00005450
00659           MOVE 'NO LINE ITEM ENTERED' TO MAP1-ERRORS (ERROR-I)      00005460
00660           IF ERROR-I EQUAL TO 1                                     00005470
00661              MOVE -1 TO MAP1-ITEM-NUMBER-L (1)                      00005480
00662           ELSE IF ERROR-I EQUAL TO 4                                00005490
00663              GO TO VALIDATE-TOTALS-EXIT.                            00005500

00665        IF    MAP1-TOTAL-COST NUMERIC                               00005520
00666           AND MAP1-TOTAL-COST = TWA-TOTAL-COST                      00005530
00667        THEN MOVE TWA-TOTAL-COST          TO TSA-TOTAL-COST          00005540
00668        ELSE SET ERROR-I UP BY 1                                     00005550
00669           MOVE 'INCORRECT TOTAL COST' TO MAP1-ERRORS (ERROR-I)      00005560
00670           IF ERROR-I EQUAL TO 1                                     00005570
00671              MOVE -1                    TO MAP1-TOTAL-COST-L         00005580
00672           ELSE IF ERROR-I EQUAL TO 4                                00005590
00673              GO TO VALIDATE-TOTALS-EXIT.                            00005600

00675        IF    MAP1-TOTAL-PRICE NUMERIC                              00005620
00676           AND MAP1-TOTAL-PRICE = TWA-TOTAL-PRICE                    00005630
00677        THEN MOVE TWA-TOTAL-PRICE         TO TSA-TOTAL-PRICE         00005640
00678        ELSE SET ERROR-I UP BY 1                                     00005650
```

Fig. 24.3. (Continued)

```
  19    ORADO1A          18.38.45     07/27/80

00679          MOVE 'INCORRECT TOTAL PRICE'  TO  MAP1-ERRORS (ERROR-I)   00005660
00680          IF ERROR-I EQUAL TO 1                TO  MAP1-TOTAL-PRICE-L 00005670
00681              MOVE -1                                                 00005680
00682          ELSE IF ERROR-I EQUAL TO 4                                  00005690
00683              GO TO VALIDATE-TOTALS-EXIT.                             00005700
00684      VALIDATE-TOTALS-EXIT.  EXIT.                                    00005713

00686      CHECK-IF-THERE-ARE-ERRORS.                                      00005730

00688          IF ERROR-I NOT EQUAL TO ZEROES                             00005750
00689              GO TO DISPLAY-ERROR-SCREEN.                            00005760

00691      NO-ERRORS-RTN.                                                 00005780

00693          SET TSA-LINE-COUNT TO MAP1-LINE-I.                         00005800

00695          IF TSA-LINE-COUNT GREATER THAN 9                           00005820
00696              IF TWA-LINE-DATA-CNT EQUAL TO ZEROES                   00005830
00697                  SUBTRACT 2 FROM TSA-LINE-COUNT                     00005840
00698              ELSE SUBTRACT 1 FROM TSA-LINE-COUNT                    00005850
00699          ELSE SUBTRACT 2 FROM TSA-LINE-COUNT.                       00005860

00701  *       EXEC CICS
00702  *           GETMAIN
00703  *               SET  (POM-POINTER)
00704  *               LENGTH (433)
00705  *       END-EXEC.
00706   -      MOVE 433 TO DFHEIV11 MOVE ' '   ' TO DFHEIV0 CALL 'DFHEI1' 00005880
00707          '1' USING DFHEIV0 POM-POINTER DFHEIV11.
00708
00709
00710          MOVE TSA-LINE-COUNT    TO  ORDER-LINE-COUNT.               00005930
00711          MOVE TSA-POMAST-RECORD TO  ORDER-MASTER-RECORD.            00005940
00712          COMPUTE TWA-POM-LENGTH = 37 + ORDER-LINE-COUNT * 44.       00005950
00713
00714          MOVE TSA-ORDER-NUMBER  TO  TWA-ORDER-RECORD-KEY.           00005960

00716  *       EXEC CICS
00717  *           HANDLE CONDITION
00718  *               NOTOPEN (FILE-NOT-OPEN)
00719  *               DUPREC  (DUPLICATE-RECORD)
00720  *       END-EXEC.
00721          MOVE ' '     ' TO DFHEIV0 CALL 'DFHEI1' USING              00005980
00722          DFHEIV0 GO TO FILE-NOT-OPEN DUPLICATE-RECORD DEPENDING ON
00723          DFHEIGDI.
00724
00725
00726  *       EXEC CICS
00727  *           WRITE DATASET ('ORTEST')
00728  *               LENGTH (TWA-POM-LENGTH)
00729  *               FROM (ORDER-MASTER-RECORD)
```

Fig. 24.3. (Continued)

```
20        GRADO1A        18.38.45        07/27/80

00730  *        END-EXEC.    RIDFLD  (TWA-ORDER-RECORD-KEY)
00731  *        MOVE 'ORTEST' TO DFHEIV3 MOVE + O       ' TO DFHEIVO CALL 'D00006030
00732  -        'FHEII' USING DFHEIVO DFHEIV3 ORDER-MASTER-RECORD
00733           TWA-POM-LENGTH TWA-ORDER-RECORD-KEY.
00734
00735
00736
00737           EXEC CICS
00738  *           FREEMAIN DATA (ORDER-MASTER-RECORD)
00739  *        END-EXEC.
00740           MOVE ' ' TO DFHEIVO CALL 'DFHEII' USING DFHEIVO        00006090
00741           ORDER-MASTER-RECORD.
00742
00743
00744           EXEC CICS
00745  *           GETMAIN
00746  *              SET     (JOURNAL-POINTER)
00747  *              LENGTH (37)
00748  *        END-EXEC.
00749  -        MOVE 37 TO DFHEIV11 MOVE ' '   ' TO DFHEIVO CALL 'DFHEII00006120
00750           '' USING DFHEIVO JOURNAL-POINTER DFHEIV11
00751
00752
00753           MOVE TSA-OPERATOR-INITIAL    TO JOURNAL-OPERATOR-INITIAL.    00006170
00754           MOVE TSA-ORDER-ENTERED       TO JOURNAL-DATE-ENTERED.        00006180
00755           MOVE TSA-ORDER-NUMBER        TO JOURNAL-ORDER-NUMBER.        00006190
00756           MOVE TSA-TOTAL-COST          TO JOURNAL-TOTAL-COST.          00006200
00757           MOVE TSA-TOTAL-PRICE         TO JOURNAL-TOTAL-PRICE.         00006210
00758           MOVE MAP1-DOCUMENT           TO JOURNAL-DOCUMENT-NUMBER.     00006220
00759           MOVE 37                      TO TWA-JOURNAL-LENGTH.          00006230
00760
00762           EXEC CICS
00763  *           JOURNAL JFILEID (02)
00764  *              JTYPEID ('01')
00765  *              FROM    (JOURNAL-RECORD)
00766  *              LENGTH  (TWA-JOURNAL-LENGTH)
00767  *              REQID   (TWA-JOURNAL-ID)
00768  *              WAIT
00769  *        END-EXEC.
00770  *        MOVE 02 TO DFHEIV11 MOVE '01' TO DFHEIV7 MOVE + 8      ' T000006250
00771           DFHEIVO CALL 'DFHEII' USING DFHEIV11 TWA-JOURNAL-ID
00772           DFHEIV7 JOURNAL-RECORD TWA-JOURNAL-LENGTH.
00773
00774
00775
00776
00777
00778           DISPLAY-FRESH-SCREEN.
00780  *        EXEC CICS
00781  *           SEND    MAP    ('ORADMO1')
00782  *              MAPSET ('ORADSO1')                                      00006330
```

Fig. 24.3. (Continued)

```
21    ORADO1A              18.38.45        07/27/80

00783   *          MAPONLY
00784   *          ERASE
00785   *       END-EXEC.
00786           MOVE 'ORADMO1' TO DFHEIV1 MOVE 'ORADSO1' TO DFHEIV2 MOVE '   00006350
00787   -       ' TO DFHEIVO CALL 'DFHEI1' USING DFHEIVO
00788           DFHEIV1 DFHEIV99 DFHEIV98 DFHEIV2.
00789
00790
00791                                                                         00006410
00792   RETURN-FOR-NEXT-ORDER.
00793
00794           MOVE '1' TO COMMAREA-PROCESS-SW.                              00006430
00795
00796   *       EXEC CICS
00797   *          RETURN TRANSID (EIBTRNID)
00798   *          COMMAREA (COMMUNICATION-AREA)
00799   *          LENGTH   (1)
00800   *       END-EXEC.
00801           MOVE 1 TO DFHEIV11 MOVE '         ' TO DFHEIVO CALL 'DFHEI1'00006450
00802           USING DFHEIVO EIBTRNID COMMUNICATION-AREA DFHEIV11.
00803
00804
00805
00806   DISPLAY-ERROR-SCREEN.                                                 00006500
00807
00808   *       EXEC CICS
00809   *          SEND MAP    ('ORADMO1')
00810   *          MAPSET      ('ORADSO1')
00811   *          FROM        (MAP1-AREA)
00812   *          DATAONLY
00813   *          CURSOR
00814   *       END-EXEC.
00815           MOVE 'ORADMO1' TO DFHEIV1 MOVE 'ORADSO1' TO DFHEIV2 MOVE -1 00006520
00816   TO DFHEIV11 MOVE '  J        ' TO DFHEIVO CALL 'DFHEI1'
00817           USING DFHEIVO DFHEIV1 MAP1-AREA DFHEIV98 DFHEIV99
00818           DFHEIV99 DFHEIV99 DFHEIV11
00819
00820
00821
00822           GO TO RETURN-FOR-NEXT-ORDER.                                  00006590
00823
00824   DUPLICATE-RECORD.                                                     00006610
00825
00826           MOVE 'DUPLICATE -- NOT ACCEPTED' TO MAP1-ERRORS (1).          00006630
00827           MOVE -1 TO MAP1-ORDER-NUMBER-L.                              00006640
00828           GO TO DISPLAY-ERROR-SCREEN.                                   00006650
```

Fig. 24.3. (Continued)

```
22        ORADO1A        18.38.45        07/27/80

00830     **************************************************************   00006670
00831     *                                                           *        00006680
00832     BYPASS-INPUT SECTION.                                       *        00006690
00833     *                                                           *        00006700
00834     **************************************************************   00006710

00836     EXEC CICS
00837         GETMAIN
00838             SET      (MAP1-POINTER)
00839             LENGTH   (958)
00840             INITIMG  (HEX-ZEROES)
00841     END-EXEC.
00842         MOVE 958 TO DFHEIV11 MOVE ' '     TO DFHEIVO CALL 'DFHEIO00006730
00843     '1' USING DFHEIVO MAP1-POINTER DFHEIV11 HEX-ZEROES.
00844   -
00845
00846
00847
00848     MOVE 'ORDER BYPASSED - CONTINUE' TO MAP1-ERRORS (1).            00006790

00850     EXEC CICS
00851         SEND MAP  ('ORADMO1')
00852             MAPSET ('ORADSO1')
00853             FROM   (MAP1-AREA)
00854             ERASE
00855     END-EXEC.
00856         MOVE 'ORADMO1' TO DFHEIV1 MOVE 'ORADSO1' TO DFHEIV2 MOVE '   00006810
00857     '     S   ' TO DFHEIVO CALL 'DFHEII' USING DFHEIVO
00858     DFHEIV1 MAP1-AREA DFHEIV98 DFHEIV2.
00859   -
00860
00861
00862     MOVE '1' TO COMMAREA-PROCESS-SW.                                00006870

00864     EXEC CICS
00865         RETURN TRANSID (EIBTRNID)
00866             COMMAREA (COMMUNICATION-AREA)
00867             LENGTH   (1)
00868     END-EXEC.
00869         MOVE 1 TO DFHEIV11 MOVE ' '     TO DFHEIVO CALL 'DFHEII'00006890
00870     USING DFHEIVO EIBTRNID COMMUNICATION-AREA DFHEIV11.
00871   -
00872
00873
```

Fig. 24.3. (Continued)

```
23          ORAD01A     18.38.45     07/27/80

00875   ************************************************************   00006950
00876   *                                                        *   00006960
00877   * INITIALIZATION SECTION.                                    00006970
00878   *                                                        *   00006980
00879   ************************************************************   00006990

00881   *    EXEC CICS
00882   *        HANDLE CONDITION
00883   *            QIDERR (GET-STORAGE-FOR-TSA)
00884        END-EXEC.
00885        MOVE ' '       ' TO DFHEIVO CALL 'DFHEI1' USING        00007010
00886        DFHEIVO GO TO GET-STORAGE-FOR-TSA DEPENDING ON DFHEIGDI.
00887
00888
00889        MOVE EIBTRMID     TO   TSA-TERM-ID.                    00007050
00890        MOVE 'ORAD'       TO   TSA-TRANS-ID.                   00007060

00892   *    EXEC CICS
00893   *        DELETEQ TS
00894   *            QUEUE (TSA-QUEUE-ID)
00895        END-EXEC.
00896        MOVE ' '       ' TO DFHEIVO CALL 'DFHEI1' USING DFHEIVO   00007080
00897        TSA-QUEUE-ID.

00900   GET-STORAGE-FOR-TSA.                                       00007120

00902   *    EXEC CICS
00903   *        GETMAIN
00904   *            SET    (TSA-POINTER)
00905   *            LENGTH (1340)
00906        END-EXEC.
00907        MOVE 1340 TO DFHEIV11 MOVE ' '       ' TO DFHEIVO CALL 'DFHE00007140
00908   -    'I1' USING DFHEIVO TSA-POINTER DFHEIV11.

00912   LOAD-DEPARTMENT-TABLE.                                     00007190

00914        SET DEPT-I     TO   ZEROES.                           00007210
00915        MOVE 'D'       TO   TWA-DEPT-TABLE-KEY-CODE.          00007220
00916        MOVE 1         TO   TWA-DEPT-TABLE-KEY-NUMBER.        00007230

00918   *    EXEC CICS
00919   *        HANDLE CONDITION
00920   *            ENDFILE (READ-DEPT-TABLE-EXIT)
00921        END-EXEC.
00922        MOVE ' '       ' TO DFHEIVO CALL 'DFHEI1' USING        00007250
00923        DFHEIVO GO TO READ-DEPT-TABLE-EXIT DEPENDING ON DFHEIGDI.
00924
00925
00926   *    EXEC CICS
```

Fig. 24.3. (Continued)

```
24     ORADO1A        18.38.45       07/27/80

         STARTBR DATASET ('DSXTABS')
    *            RIDFLD  (TWA-DEPT-TABLE-KEY)
    *            GTEQ                                                     00007290
    *
    *    END-EXEC.
         MOVE 'DSXTABS' TO DFHEIV3 MOVE '          ' TO DFHEIVO CALL
    -    'DFHEII' USING DFHEIVO DFHEIV3 DFHEIV99 DFHEIV98
         TWA-DEPT-TABLE-KEY.

    READ-DEPT-TABLE.                                                     00007340

    *    EXEC CICS
    *         READNEXT DATASET ('DSXTABS')
    *         SET      (TABLE-POINTER)
    *         RIDFLD   (TWA-DEPT-TABLE-KEY)
    *
    *    END-EXEC.
         MOVE 'DSXTABS' TO DFHEIV3 MOVE ' M        ' TO DFHEIVO CALL     00007360
    -    'DFHEII' USING DFHEIVO DFHEIV3 TABLE-POINTER DFHEIV98
         TWA-DEPT-TABLE-KEY DFHEIV98 DFHEIV98.

         IF DEPT-RECORD                                                  00007410
         THEN IF DEPT-NO EQUAL '999'                                     00007420
              GO TO READ-DEPT-TABLE-EXIT                                 00007430
              ELSE IF DEPT-DIVISION LESS THAN '85'                       00007440
                   SET DEPT-I UP BY 1                                    00007450
                   MOVE DEPT-NO TO TSA-DEPT-NO (DEPT-I).                 00007460

         GO TO READ-DEPT-TABLE.                                          00007480
    READ-DEPT-TABLE-EXIT. EXIT.                                          00007490

    CHECK-IF-TABLE-LOADED.                                               00007510

         IF DEPT-I EQUAL TO ZEROES                                      00007530
              GO TO TABLE-NOT-LOADED-ERROR                               00007540
         ELSE SET TSA-DEPT-CNT TO DEPT-I.                                00007550

    INITIALIZE-TSA.                                                      00007570

         MOVE CURRENT-DATE          TO TWA-CURRENT-DATE.                 00007590
         MOVE TWA-CURRENT-DATE-MONTH TO TSA-ORDER-ENTERED-MONTH.         00007600
         MOVE TWA-CURRENT-DATE-DAY  TO TSA-ORDER-ENTERED-DAY.           00007610
         MOVE TWA-CURRENT-DATE-YEAR TO TSA-ORDER-ENTERED-YEAR.          00007620
         MOVE OPERATOR-INITIAL      TO TSA-OPERATOR-INITIAL.             00007630
         MOVE 1340                  TO TSA-LENGTH.                       00007640

    *    EXEC CICS
    *         WRITEQ TS
    *         QUEUE  (TSA-QUEUE-ID)
    *         FROM   (TSA-AREA)
    *         LENGTH (TSA-LENGTH)
```

Fig. 24.3. (Continued)

```
25      ORAD01A        18.38.45       07/27/80

00978       END-EXEC.
00979   *   MOVE ' '      ' TO DFHEIVO CALL 'DFHEI1' USING DFHEIVO      00007660
00980       TSA-QUEUE-ID TSA-AREA TSA-LENGTH.
00981
00982
00983
00984   *   EXEC CICS
00985   *      FREEMAIN DATA (TSA-AREA)
00986   *   END-EXEC.
00987       MOVE ' '      ' TO DFHEIVO CALL 'DFHEI1' USING DFHEIVO      00007720
00988       TSA-AREA.
00989
00990
00991   *   EXEC CICS
00992   *      GETMAIN
00993   *         SET     (MAP1-POINTER)
00994   *         LENGTH  (958)
00995   *         INITIMG (HEX-ZEROES)
00996   *   END-EXEC.
00997   -   MOVE 958 TO DFHEIV11 MOVE ' '       ' TO DFHEIVO CALL 'DFHEI00007750
00998       '1' USING DFHEIVO MAP1-POINTER DFHEIV11 HEX-ZEROES.
00999
01000
01001
01002
01003       MOVE 'ENTER FIRST ORDER' TO MAP1-ERRORS (1).             00007810

01005   *   EXEC CICS
01006   *      SEND MAP ('ORADMO1')
01007   *         MAPSET ('ORADSO1')
01008   *         FROM   (MAP1-AREA)
01009   *         ERASE
01010   *   END-EXEC.
01011       MOVE 'ORADMO1' TO DFHEIV1 MOVE 'ORADSO1' TO DFHEIV2 MOVE '  00007830
01012   -   S ' TO DFHEIVO CALL 'DFHEI1' USING DFHEIVO
01013       DFHEIV1 MAP1-AREA DFHEIV98 DFHEIV2.
01014
01015
01016       MOVE '1' TO COMMAREA-PROCESS-SW.
01017
01019   *   EXEC CICS
01020   *      RETURN TRANSID ('ORAD')                               00007890
01021   *         COMMAREA (COMMUNICATION-AREA)
01022   *         LENGTH   (1)
01023   *   END-EXEC.
01024       MOVE 'ORAD' TO DFHEIV5 MOVE 1 TO DFHEIV11 MOVE '         00007910
01025       TO DFHEIVO CALL 'DFHEI1' USING DFHEIVO DFHEIV5
01026       COMMUNICATION-AREA DFHEIV11.
01027
01028
```

Fig. 24.3. (Continued)

```
26          ORADOIA      18.38.45      07/27/80

01030    *************************************************     00007970
01031    *                                                    00007980
01032    FINALIZATION SECTION.                                00007990
01033    *                                                    00008000
01034    *************************************************     00008010

01036    PREPARE-TERMINATION-MESSAGE.                         00008030
01037        MOVE JOB-NORMAL-END-MESSAGE TO TWA-OPERATOR-MESSAGE.   00008040

01039    JOB-TERMINATED.                                      00008060

01041    *    EXEC CICS
01042    *        SEND    FROM   (TWA-OPERATOR-MESSAGE)
01043    *                LENGTH (31)
01044    *                ERASE
01045    *    END-EXEC.
01046         MOVE 31 TO DFHEIV11 MOVE ' '     TO DFHEIVO CALL '00008080
01047    -    'DFHEI1' USING DFHEIVO DFHEIV99 DFHEIV98 TWA-OPERATOR-MESSAGE
01048         DFHEIV11.
01049
01050
01051    *    EXEC CICS
01052    *        HANDLE CONDITION
01053    *            QIDERR (END-OF-JOB)
01054    *    END-EXEC.
01055         MOVE ' '     TO DFHEIVO CALL 'DFHEI1' USING      00008130
01056         DFHEIVO GO TO END-OF-JOB DEPENDING ON DFHEIGDI.
01057

01058         MOVE EIBTRMID TO TSA-TERM-ID.                    00008170
01059         MOVE EIBTRNID TO TSA-TRANS-ID.                   00008180
01060

01062    *    EXEC CICS
01063    *        DELETEQ TS
01064    *            QUEUE (TSA-QUEUE-ID)
01065    *    END-EXEC.
01066         MOVE ' '     TO DFHEIVO CALL 'DFHEI1' USING DFHEIVO   00008200
01067         TSA-QUEUE-ID.
01068
01069

01071    END-OF-JOB.                                           00008250

01073    *    EXEC CICS
01074    *        RETURN
01075    *    END-EXEC.
01076         MOVE ' '     TO DFHEIVO CALL 'DFHEI1' USING DFHEIVO.   00008270
01077
01078
```

Fig. 24.3. (Continued)

```
27     ORAD01A     18.38.45     07/27/80

01080   ****************************************************************   00008310
01081   *                                                            *    00008320
01082   *  ABNORMAL-TERMINATION SECTION.                                  00008330
01083   *                                                            *    00008340
01084   ****************************************************************   00008350

01086   FILE-NOT-OPEN.                                                    00008370

01088   *    EXEC CICS
01089   *       XCTL PROGRAM ('TEL2OPEN')
01090   *    END-EXEC.
01091        MOVE 'TEL2OPEN' TO DFHEIV3 MOVE '    '  TO DFHEIVO CALL     00008390
01092   'DFHEI1' USING DFHEIVO DFHEIV3.
01093
01094   MAPFAIL-ERROR.                                                    00008420
01095        MOVE 'MAP FAILURE' TO MAJOR-ERROR-MSG.                       00008430
01096        GO TO PREPARE-ABORT-MESSAGE.                                 00008440

01098   PROCESS-SWITCH-ERROR.                                             00008460
01099        MOVE 'PROCESS ERROR' TO MAJOR-ERROR-MSG.                     00008470
01100        GO TO PREPARE-ABORT-MESSAGE.                                 00008480

01102   SIGN-ON-VIOLATION.                                                00008500
01103        MOVE 'SIGNON VIOLATION' TO MAJOR-ERROR-MSG.                  00008510
01104        GO TO PREPARE-ABORT-MESSAGE.                                 00008520

01106   TABLE-NOT-LOADED-ERROR.                                           00008540
01107        MOVE 'TABLE NOT LOADED' TO MAJOR-ERROR-MSG.                  00008550
01108        GO TO PREPARE-ABORT-MESSAGE.                                 00008560

01110   MAJOR-ERROR.                                                      00008580
01111        MOVE EIBFN     TO   OLD-EIBFN.                               00008590
01112        MOVE EIBRCODE  TO   OLD-EIBRCODE.                            00008600

01114   *    EXEC CICS
01115   *       DUMP DUMPCODE ('ERRS')
01116   *    END-EXEC.
01117        MOVE 'ERRS' TO DFHEIV5 MOVE '    '  TO DFHEIVO CALL 'DFH    00008620
01118   'EI1' USING DFHEIVO DFHEIV5.
01119   -
01120        MOVE 'MAJOR ERROR' TO MAJOR-ERROR-MSG.                       00008650
01121        GO TO PREPARE-ABORT-MESSAGE.                                 00008660

01123   PREPARE-ABORT-MESSAGE.                                            00008680
01124        MOVE JOB-ABORTED-MESSAGE TO TWA-OPERATOR-MESSAGE.            00008690
01125        GO TO JOB-TERMINATED.                                        00008700
```

Fig. 24.3. (Continued)

28   ORADO1A   18.38.45   07/27/80

INTRNL NAME	LVL	SOURCE NAME	BASE	DISPL	INTRNL NAME	DEFINITION	USAGE	R O Q M
DNM=3-000	01	COMMUNICATION-AREA	BL=1	000	DNM=3-000	DS 0CL1	GROUP	
DNM=3-031	02	COMMAREA-PROCESS-SW	BL=1	000	DNM=3-031	DS 1C	DISP	
DNM=3-060	01	AREA1	BL=1	008	DNM=3-060	DS 0CL99	GROUP	R
DNM=3-078	02	VALIDATION-ERROR-MESSAGE	BL=1	008	DNM=3-078	DS 0CL28	GROUP	
DNM=3-115	03	FILLER	BL=1	008	DNM=3-115	DS 5C	DISP	
DNM=3-131	03	VALIDATION-ERROR-LINE	BL=1	00D	DNM=3-131	DS 5C	DISP-NM	
DNM=3-162	03	FILLER	BL=1	00E	DNM=3-162	DS 3C	DISP	
DNM=3-181	03	VALIDATION-ERROR-MSG	BL=1	011	DNM=3-181	DS 19C	DISP	
DNM=3-211	02	JOB-NORMAL-END-MESSAGE	BL=1	024	DNM=3-211	DS 23C	DISP	
DNM=3-243	03	FILLER	BL=1	038	DNM=3-243	DS 0CL31	GROUP	
DNM=3-278	03	FILLER	BL=1	038	DNM=3-278	DS 15C	DISP	
DNM=3-297	02	MAJOR-ERROR-MSG	BL=1	04A	DNM=3-297	DS 16C	DISP	
DNM=3-322	02	HEXADECIMAL-ZEROES	BL=1	05A	DNM=3-322	DS 1H	COMP	
DNM=3-350	03	FILLER	BL=1	05A	DNM=3-350	DS 0CL2	GROUP	
DNM=3-372	03	FILLER	BL=1	05A	DNM=3-372	DS 1C	DISP	
DNM=3-391	03	HEX-ZEROES	BL=1	05B	DNM=3-391	DS 1C	DISP	
DNM=3-411	02	OLD-EIB-AREA	BL=1	05C	DNM=3-411	DS 0CL115	GROUP	
DNM=3-436	03	FILLER	BL=1	05C	DNM=3-436	DS 7C	DISP	
DNM=3-455	03	OLD-EIBFN	BL=1	063	DNM=3-455	DS 2C	DISP	
DNM=3-474	03	OLD-EIBRCODE	BL=1	065	DNM=3-474	DS 6C	DISP	
DNM=4-000	01	DFHEIVAR	BL=1	070	DNM=4-000	DS 0CL106	GROUP	
DNM=4-021	02	DFHEIV0	BL=1	070	DNM=4-021	DS 26C	DISP	
DNM=4-041	02	DFHEIV1	BL=1	08A	DNM=4-041	DS 8C	DISP	
DNM=4-058	02	DFHEIV2	BL=1	092	DNM=4-058	DS 8C	DISP	
DNM=4-075	02	DFHEIV3	BL=1	09A	DNM=4-075	DS 8C	DISP	
DNM=4-092	02	DFHEIV4	BL=1	0A2	DNM=4-092	DS 6C	DISP	
DNM=4-109	02	DFHEIV5	BL=1	0A8	DNM=4-109	DS 4C	DISP	
DNM=4-126	02	DFHEIV6	BL=1	0AC	DNM=4-126	DS 4C	DISP	
DNM=4-143	02	DFHEIV7	BL=1	0B0	DNM=4-143	DS 2C	DISP	
DNM=4-160	02	DFHEIV8	BL=1	0B2	DNM=4-160	DS 2C	DISP	
DNM=4-177	02	DFHEIV9	BL=1	0B4	DNM=4-177	DS 1C	DISP	
DNM=4-194	02	DFHEIV10	BL=1	0B5	DNM=4-194	DS 4P	COMP-3	
DNM=4-212	02	DFHEIV11	BL=1	0B9	DNM=4-212	DS 1H	COMP	
DNM=4-230	02	DFHEIV12	BL=1	0BB	DNM=4-230	DS 1H	COMP	
DNM=4-248	02	DFHEIV13	BL=1	0BD	DNM=4-248	DS 1H	COMP	
DNM=4-269	02	DFHEIV14	BL=1	0BF	DNM=4-269	DS 1H	COMP	
DNM=4-287	02	DFHEIV15	BL=1	0C1	DNM=4-287	DS 1H	COMP	
DNM=4-305	02	DFHEIV16	BL=1	0C3	DNM=4-305	DS 1F	COMP	
DNM=4-323	02	DFHEIV17	BL=1	0C7	DNM=4-323	DS 4C	DISP	
DNM=4-341	02	DFHEIV18	BL=1	0CB	DNM=4-341	DS 4C	DISP	
DNM=4-359	02	DFHEIV19	BL=1	0CF	DNM=4-359	DS 4C	DISP	
DNM=4-377	02	DFHEIV97	BL=1	0D3	DNM=4-377	DS 4P	COMP-3	
DNM=4-395	02	DFHEIV98	BL=1	0D7	DNM=4-395	DS 1H	COMP	
DNM=4-413	02	DFHEIV99	BL=1	0D9	DNM=4-413	DS 1C	DISP	
DNM=4-431	02	DFHEIBLK	BLL=2	000	DNM=4-431	DS 0CL51	GROUP	
DNM=4-452	02	EIBTIME	BLL=2	000	DNM=4-452	DS 4P	COMP-3	
DNM=4-469	02	EIBDATE	BLL=2	004	DNM=4-469	DS 4P	COMP-3	
DNM=4-486	02	EIBTRNID	BLL=2	008	DNM=4-486	DS 4P	DISP	
DNM=5-000	02	EIBTASKN	BLL=2	00C	DNM=5-000	DS 4P	COMP-3	
DNM=5-021	02	EIBTRMID	BLL=2	010	DNM=5-021	DS 4C	DISP	

Fig. 24.3.   (Continued)

29   ORADO1A   18.38.45   07/27/80

INTRNL NAME	LVL	SOURCE NAME	BASE	DISPL	INTRNL NAME	DEFINITION	USAGE	R	O	Q	M
DNM=5-039	02	DFHEIGDI	BLL=2	014	DNM=5-039	DS 1H	COMP				
DNM=5-057	02	EIBCPOSN	BLL=2	016	DNM=5-057	DS 1H	COMP				
DNM=5-075	02	EIBCALEN	BLL=2	018	DNM=5-075	DS 1H	COMP				
DNM=5-093	02	EIBAID	BLL=2	01A	DNM=5-093	DS 1C	DISP				
DNM=5-109	02	EIBFN	BLL=2	01B	DNM=5-109	DS 2C	DISP				
DNM=5-124	02	EIBRCODE	BLL=2	01D	DNM=5-124	DS 6C	DISP				
DNM=5-142	02	EIBDS	BLL=2	023	DNM=5-142	DS 8C	DISP				
DNM=5-157	02	EIBREQID	BLL=2	02B	DNM=5-157	DS 8C	DISP				
DNM=5-175	01	DFHCOMMAREA	BLL=3	000	DNM=5-175	DS 0CL4	GROUP				
DNM=5-202	02	PROCESS-SW	BLL=3	000	DNM=5-202	DS 1C	DISP				
DNM=5-225	88	INITIAL-ENTRY-TIME			DNM=5-225						
DNM=5-254	88	ORDER-VALIDATION-TIME			DNM=5-254						
DNM=5-286	02	OPERATOR-INITIAL	BLL=3	001	DNM=5-286	DS 3C	DISP				
DNM=5-312	01	LINKAGE-POINTERS	BLL=4	000	DNM=5-312	DS 0CL28	GROUP				
DNM=5-344	02	FILLER	BLL=4	000	DNM=5-344	DS 1F	COMP				
DNM=5-363	02	MAP1-POINTER	BLL=4	004	DNM=5-363	DS 1F	COMP				
DNM=5-385	02	PGM-POINTER	BLL=4	008	DNM=5-385	DS 1F	COMP				
DNM=5-409	02	TWA-POINTER	BLL=4	00C	DNM=5-409	DS 1F	COMP				
DNM=5-430	02	TSA-POINTER	BLL=4	010	DNM=5-430	DS 1F	COMP				
DNM=5-451	02	JOURNAL-POINTER	BLL=4	014	DNM=5-451	DS 1F	COMP				
DNM=5-476	02	TABLE-POINTER	BLL=4	018	DNM=5-476	DS 1F	COMP				
DNM=6-000	01	MAP1-AREA	BLL=5	000	DNM=6-000	DS 0CL950	GROUP				
DNM=6-022	02	FILLER	BLL=5	000	DNM=6-022	DS 12C	DISP				
DNM=6-041	02	MAP1-DUMMY-L	BLL=5	00C	DNM=6-041	DS 1H	COMP				
DNM=6-063	02	MAP1-DUMMY-A	BLL=5	00E	DNM=6-063	DS 1C	DISP				
DNM=6-085	02	MAP1-DUMMY	BLL=5	00F	DNM=6-085	DS 1H	COMP				
DNM=6-105	02	MAP1-ORDER-NUMBER-L	BLL=5	010	DNM=6-105	DS 1C	DISP				
DNM=6-134	02	MAP1-ORDER-NUMBER-A	BLL=5	012	DNM=6-134	DS 10C	DISP				
DNM=6-163	02	MAP1-ORDER-NUMBER	BLL=5	013	DNM=6-163	DS 10C	DISP				
DNM=6-190	02	MAP1-DOCUMENT-L	BLL=5	01D	DNM=6-190	DS 1H	COMP				
DNM=6-218	02	MAP1-DOCUMENT-A	BLL=5	01F	DNM=6-218	DS 1C	DISP				
DNM=6-243	02	MAP1-DOCUMENT	BLL=5	020	DNM=6-243	DS 8C	DISP				
DNM=6-266	02	MAP1-DEPARTMENT-L	BLL=5	028	DNM=6-266	DS 1H	COMP				
DNM=6-296	02	MAP1-DEPARTMENT-A	BLL=5	02A	DNM=6-296	DS 1C	DISP				
DNM=6-323	02	MAP1-DEPARTMENT	BLL=5	02B	DNM=6-323	DS 3C	DISP				
DNM=6-348	02	MAP1-ORDER-DATE-L	BLL=5	02E	DNM=6-348	DS 1H	COMP				
DNM=6-375	02	MAP1-ORDER-DATE-A	BLL=5	030	DNM=6-375	DS 1C	DISP				
DNM=6-405	02	MAP1-ORDER-DATE	BLL=5	031	DNM=6-405	DS 0CL6	GROUP				
DNM=6-433	03	MAP1-ORDER-DATE-MONTH	BLL=5	031	DNM=6-433	DS 2C	DISP				
DNM=6-464	03	MAP1-ORDER-DATE-DAY	BLL=5	033	DNM=6-464	DS 2C	DISP				
DNM=7-000	03	MAP1-ORDER-DATE-YEAR	BLL=5	035	DNM=7-000	DS 2C	DISP				
DNM=7-030	02	MAP1-LINE-I			DNM=7-030	DS 0CL83	GROUP	INDEX-NM		O	
DNM=7-048	03	MAP1-LINE-ITEM	BLL=5	037	DNM=7-048	DS 1H	COMP				
DNM=7-075	03	MAP1-ITEM-NUMBER-L	BLL=5	037	DNM=7-075	DS 1C	DISP				
DNM=7-106	03	MAP1-ITEM-NUMBER-A	BLL=5	039	DNM=7-106	DS 1C	DISP				
DNM=7-137	03	MAP1-ITEM-NUMBER	BLL=5	03A	DNM=7-137	DS 8C	DISP-NM				
DNM=7-166	03	MAP1-ITEM-DESCRIPTION-L	BLL=5	042	DNM=7-166	DS 1H	COMP				
DNM=7-202	03	MAP1-ITEM-DESCRIPTION-A	BLL=5	044	DNM=7-202	DS 1C	DISP				
DNM=7-238	03	MAP1-ITEM-DESCRIPTION	BLL=5	045	DNM=7-238	DS 19C	DISP				
DNM=7-272	03	MAP1-UNIT-L	BLL=5	058	DNM=7-272	DS 1H	COMP				

Fig. 24.3. (Continued)

30   ORAD01A   18.38.45   07/27/80

INTRNL NAME	LVL	SOURCE NAME	BASE	DISPL	INTRNL NAME	DEFINITION	USAGE	R	O	Q	M
DNM=7-296	03	MAP1-UNIT-A	BLL=5	05A	DNM=7-296	DS 1C	DISP				
DNM=7-320	03	MAP1-UNIT	BLL=5	058	DNM=7-320	DS 5C	DISP-NM				
DNM=7-342	03	MAP1-UNIT-COST-L	BLL=5	060	DNM=7-342	DS 1H	COMP				
DNM=7-371	03	MAP1-UNIT-COST-A	BLL=5	062	DNM=7-371	DS 1C	DISP				
DNM=7-403	03	MAP1-UNIT-COST	BLL=5	063	DNM=7-403	DS 7C	DISP-NM				
DNM=7-430	03	MAP1-COST-L	BLL=5	06A	DNM=7-430	DS 1H	COMP				
DNM=7-454	03	MAP1-COST-A	BLL=5	06C	DNM=7-454	DS 1C	DISP				
DNM=7-478	03	MAP1-COST	BLL=5	06D	DNM=7-478	DS 8C	DISP-NM				
DNM=8-000	03	MAP1-UNIT-PRICE-L	BLL=5	075	DNM=8-000	DS 1H	COMP				
DNM=8-033	03	MAP1-UNIT-PRICE-A	BLL=5	077	DNM=8-033	DS 1C	DISP				
DNM=8-063	03	MAP1-UNIT-PRICE	BLL=5	078	DNM=8-063	DS 7C	DISP-NM				
DNM=8-091	03	MAP1-PRICE-L	BLL=5	07F	DNM=8-091	DS 1H	COMP				
DNM=8-116	03	MAP1-PRICE-A	BLL=5	081	DNM=8-116	DS 1C	DISP				
DNM=8-141	03	MAP1-PRICE	BLL=5	082	DNM=8-141	DS 8C	DISP-NM				
DNM=8-164	02	MAP1-TOTAL-COST-L	BLL=5	322	DNM=8-164	DS 1H	COMP				
DNM=8-194	02	MAP1-TOTAL-COST-A	BLL=5	324	DNM=8-194	DS 1C	DISP				
DNM=8-221	02	MAP1-TOTAL-COST	BLL=5	325	DNM=8-221	DS 9C	DISP-NM				
DNM=8-249	02	MAP1-TOTAL-PRICE-L	BLL=5	32E	DNM=8-249	DS 1H	COMP				
DNM=8-277	02	MAP1-TOTAL-PRICE-A	BLL=5	330	DNM=8-277	DS 1C	DISP				
DNM=8-305	02	MAP1-TOTAL-PRICE	BLL=5	331	DNM=8-305	DS 9C	DISP-NM				
DNM=8-331	02	FILLER	BLL=5	33A	DNM=8-331	DS 0CL31	GROUP		O		U
DNM=8-345		ERROR-I			DNM=8-345		INDEX-NM				
DNM=8-367	03	MAP1-ERRORS-L	BLL=5	33A	DNM=8-367	DS 1H	COMP				
DNM=8-393	03	MAP1-ERRORS-A	BLL=5	33C	DNM=8-393	DS 1C	DISP				
DNM=8-419	03	MAP1-ERRORS	BLL=5	33D	DNM=8-419	DS 28C	DISP				
DNM=8-446	01	ORDER-MASTER-RECORD	BLL=6	000	DNM=8-446	DS VLC=2	GROUP				
DNM=8-478	02	ORDER-NUMBER	BLL=6	000	DNM=8-478	DS 10C	DISP				
DNM=9-000	02	ORDER-ALT-KEY	BLL=6	00A	DNM=9-000	DS 0CL9	GROUP				
DNM=9-026	03	ORDER-DEPARTMENT	BLL=6	00A	DNM=9-026	DS 3C	DISP				
DNM=9-052	03	ORDER-DATE	BLL=6	00D	DNM=9-052	DS 0CL6	GROUP				
DNM=9-078	04	ORDER-DATE-YEAR	BLL=6	00D	DNM=9-078	DS 2C	DISP				
DNM=9-103	04	ORDER-DATE-MONTH	BLL=6	00F	DNM=9-103	DS 2C	DISP				
DNM=9-132	04	ORDER-DATE-DAY	BLL=6	011	DNM=9-132	DS 2C	DISP				
DNM=9-159	02	ORDER-DATE-ENTERED	BLL=6	013	DNM=9-159	DS 0CL6	GROUP				
DNM=9-190	03	ORDER-DATE-ENTERED-MONTH	BLL=6	013	DNM=9-190	DS 2C	DISP				
DNM=9-224	03	ORDER-DATE-ENTERED-DAY	BLL=6	015	DNM=9-224	DS 2C	DISP				
DNM=9-259	03	ORDER-DATE-ENTERED-YEAR	BLL=6	017	DNM=9-259	DS 2C	DISP				
DNM=9-292	02	ORDER-TOTAL-COST	BLL=6	019	DNM=9-292	DS 5P	COMP-3				
DNM=9-318	02	ORDER-TOTAL-PRICE	BLL=6	01E	DNM=9-318	DS 5P	COMP-3				
DNM=9-348	02	ORDER-LINE-COUNT	BLL=6	023	DNM=9-348	DS 1H	COMP				
DNM=9-374	02	ORDER-ALL-LINES	BLL=6	025	DNM=9-374	DS VLC=1	GROUP		O	Q	U
DNM=9-402		ORDER-LINE-I			DNM=9-402		INDEX-NM				
DNM=9-421	03	ORDER-LINE-ITEM	BLL=6	025	DNM=9-421	DS 0CL44	GROUP				
DNM=9-452	04	ORDER-ITEM-NUMBER	BLL=6	025	DNM=9-452	DS 8C	DISP				
DNM=10-000	04	ORDER-ITEM-DESCRIPTION	BLL=6	02D	DNM=10-000	DS 19C	DISP				
DNM=10-035	04	ORDER-ITEM-DATE	BLL=6	040	DNM=10-035	DS 0CL6	GROUP				
DNM=10-069	05	ORDER-ITEM-DATE-MONTH	BLL=6	040	DNM=10-069	DS 2C	DISP				
DNM=10-106	05	ORDER-ITEM-DATE-DAY	BLL=6	042	DNM=10-106	DS 2C	DISP				
DNM=10-141	05	ORDER-ITEM-DATE-YEAR	BLL=6	044	DNM=10-141	DS 2C	DISP				
DNM=10-177	04	ORDER-UNIT	BLL=6	046	DNM=10-177	DS 3P	COMP-3				

Fig. 24.3.   (Continued)

```
31     ORAD01A          18.38.45          07/27/80
```

INTRNL NAME	LVL	SOURCE NAME	BASE	DISPL	INTRNL NAME	DEFINITION	USAGE	R	O	Q	M
DNM=10-200	04	ORDER-UNIT-COST	BLL=6	049	DNM=10-200	DS 4P	COMP-3				
DNM=10-228	04	ORDER-UNIT-PRICE	BLL=6	04D	DNM=10-228	DS 4P	COMP-3				
DNM=10-260	01	TWA-AREA	BLL=7	000	DNM=10-260	DS OCL215	GROUP				
DNM=10-284	02	TWA-LINE-ITEM-MAP	BLL=7	000	DNM=10-284	DS OCL83	GROUP				
DNM=10-314	03	TWA-ITEM-NUMBER-MAP-L	BLL=7	000	DNM=10-314	DS 1H	COMP				
DNM=10-345	03	TWA-ITEM-NUMBER-MAP-A	BLL=7	002	DNM=10-345	DS 1C	DISP				
DNM=10-379	03	TWA-ITEM-NUMBER-MAP	BLL=7	003	DNM=10-379	DS 8C	DISP				
DNM=10-408	03	TWA-ITEM-DESCRIPTION-MAP-L	BLL=7	00B	DNM=10-408	DS 1H	COMP				
DNM=10-447	03	TWA-ITEM-DESCRIPTION-MAP-A	BLL=7	00D	DNM=10-447	DS 1C	DISP				
DNM=11-000	03	TWA-ITEM-DESCRIPTION-MAP	BLL=7	00E	DNM=11-000	DS OCL19	GROUP				
DNM=11-037	04	TWA-DESCRIPTION-FIRST-MAP	BLL=7	00E	DNM=11-037	DS 1C	DISP				
DNM=11-075	04	FILLER	BLL=7	00F	DNM=11-075	DS 18C	DISP				
DNM=11-094	03	TWA-UNIT-MAP-L	BLL=7	021	DNM=11-094	DS 1H	COMP				
DNM=11-118	03	TWA-UNIT-MAP-A	BLL=7	023	DNM=11-118	DS 1C	DISP				
DNM=11-142	03	TWA-UNIT-MAP	BLL=7	024	DNM=11-142	DS 5C	DISP-NM				
DNM=11-164	03	TWA-UNIT-COST-MAP-L	BLL=7	029	DNM=11-164	DS 1H	COMP				
DNM=11-196	03	TWA-UNIT-COST-MAP-A	BLL=7	02B	DNM=11-196	DS 1C	DISP				
DNM=11-228	03	TWA-UNIT-COST-MAP	BLL=7	02C	DNM=11-228	DS 7C	DISP-NM				
DNM=11-255	03	TWA-COST-MAP-L	BLL=7	033	DNM=11-255	DS 1H	COMP				
DNM=11-279	03	TWA-COST-MAP-A	BLL=7	035	DNM=11-279	DS 1C	DISP				
DNM=11-303	03	TWA-COST-MAP	BLL=7	036	DNM=11-303	DS 8C	DISP-NM				
DNM=11-325	03	TWA-UNIT-PRICE-MAP-L	BLL=7	03E	DNM=11-325	DS 1H	COMP				
DNM=11-358	03	TWA-UNIT-PRICE-MAP-A	BLL=7	040	DNM=11-358	DS 1C	DISP				
DNM=11-391	03	TWA-UNIT-PRICE-MAP	BLL=7	041	DNM=11-391	DS 7C	DISP-NM				
DNM=11-419	03	TWA-PRICE-MAP-L	BLL=7	048	DNM=11-419	DS 1H	COMP				
DNM=11-447	03	TWA-PRICE-MAP-A	BLL=7	04A	DNM=11-447	DS 1C	DISP				
DNM=11-472	03	TWA-PRICE-MAP	BLL=7	04B	DNM=11-472	DS 8C	DISP-NM				
DNM=12-000	02	TWA-LINE-ITEM-ORDER	BLL=7	053	DNM=12-000	DS OCL44	GROUP				
DNM=12-032	03	TWA-ITEM-NUMBER-ORDER	BLL=7	053	DNM=12-032	DS 8C	DISP				
DNM=12-063	03	TWA-ITEM-DESCRIPTION-ORDER	BLL=7	05B	DNM=12-063	DS 19C	DISP				
DNM=12-099	03	TWA-ITEM-DATE-ORDER	BLL=7	06E	DNM=12-099	DS 6C	DISP				
DNM=12-128	03	TWA-UNIT-ORDER	BLL=7	074	DNM=12-128	DS 3P	COMP-3				
DNM=12-155	03	TWA-UNIT-COST-ORDER	BLL=7	077	DNM=12-155	DS 4P	COMP-3				
DNM=12-184	03	TWA-UNIT-PRICE-ORDER	BLL=7	07B	DNM=12-184	DS 4P	COMP-3				
DNM=12-214	02	TWA-TOTAL-COST	BLL=7	07F ⟵ (K)	DNM=12-214	DS 5P	COMP-3				
DNM=12-241	02	TWA-TOTAL-PRICE	BLL=7	084	DNM=12-241	DS 5P	COMP-3				
DNM=12-269	02	TWA-ORDER-RECORD-KEY	BLL=7	089	DNM=12-269	DS 10C	DISP				
DNM=12-302	02	TSA-QUEUE-ID	BLL=7	093	DNM=12-302	DS OCL8	GROUP				
DNM=12-327	03	TSA-TERM-ID	BLL=7	093	DNM=12-327	DS 4C	DISP				
DNM=12-351	03	TSA-TRANS-ID	BLL=7	097	DNM=12-351	DS 4C	DISP				
DNM=12-373	02	TWA-BINARY-FIELDS	BLL=7	09B	DNM=12-373	DS OCL16	GROUP				
DNM=12-403	03	TWA-LINE-DATA-CNT	BLL=7	09B	DNM=12-403	DS 1F	COMP				
DNM=12-433	03	TWA-JOURNAL-ID	BLL=7	09F	DNM=12-433	DS 1F	COMP				
DNM=12-457	03	TWA-POM-LENGTH	BLL=7	0A3	DNM=12-457	DS 1H	COMP				
DNM=12-481	03	TSA-LENGTH	BLL=7	0A5	DNM=12-481	DS 1H	COMP				
DNM=13-000	03	TSA-QUEUE-NO	BLL=7	0A7	DNM=13-000	DS 1H	COMP				
DNM=13-022	03	TWA-JOURNAL-LENGTH	BLL=7	0A9	DNM=13-022	DS 1H	COMP				
DNM=13-053	02	TWA-OPERATOR-MESSAGE	BLL=7	0AB	DNM=13-053	DS 31C	DISP				
DNM=13-083	02	TWA-CURRENT-DATE	BLL=7	0CA	DNM=13-083	DS OCL8	GROUP				
DNM=13-115	03	TWA-CURRENT-DATE-MONTH	BLL=7	0CA	DNM=13-115	DS 2C	DISP				

Fig. 24.3. (Continued)

32   GRAD01A   18.38.45   07/27/80

INTRNL NAME	LVL	SOURCE NAME	BASE	DISPL	INTRNL NAME	DEFINITION	USAGE	R	O	Q	M
DNM=13-150	03	FILLER	BLL=7	0CC	DNM=13-150	DS 1C	DISP				
DNM=13-169	03	TWA-CURRENT-DATE-DAY	BLL=7	0CD	DNM=13-169	DS 2C	DISP				
DNM=13-202	03	FILLER	BLL=7	0CF	DNM=13-202	DS 2C	DISP				
DNM=13-221	03	TWA-CURRENT-DATE-YEAR	BLL=7	0D0	DNM=13-221	DS 2C	DISP				
DNM=13-252	02	TWA-DEPT-TABLE-KEY	BLL=7	0D2	DNM=13-252	DS 0CL5	GROUP				
DNM=13-286	03	TWA-DEPT-TABLE-KEY-CODE	BLL=7	0D2	DNM=13-286	DS 1C	DISP			Q	
DNM=13-319	03	TWA-DEPT-TABLE-KEY-NUMBER	BLL=7	0D3	DNM=13-319	DS 4P	COMP-3				
DNM=13-357	01	TSA-AREA	BLL=8	000	DNM=13-357	DS VLC=3	GROUP				
DNM=13-378	02	TSA-POMAST-RECORD	BLL=8	000	DNM=13-378	DS 0CL433	GROUP				
DNM=13-411	03	TSA-ORDER-NUMBER	BLL=8	000	DNM=13-411	DS 10C	DISP				
DNM=13-437	03	TSA-DEPARTMENT	BLL=8	00A	DNM=13-437	DS 3C	DISP				
DNM=13-461	03	TSA-ORDER-DATE	BLL=8	00D	DNM=13-461	DS 0CL6	GROUP				
DNM=14-000	04	TSA-ORDER-DATE-YEAR	BLL=8	00D	DNM=14-000	DS 2C	DISP				
DNM=14-032	04	TSA-ORDER-DATE-MONTH	BLL=8	00F	DNM=14-032	DS 2C	DISP				
DNM=14-065	04	TSA-ORDER-DATE-DAY	BLL=8	011	DNM=14-065	DS 2C	DISP				
DNM=14-093	03	TSA-ORDER-ENTERED	BLL=8	013	DNM=14-093	DS 0CL6	GROUP				
DNM=14-123	04	TSA-ORDER-ENTERED-MONTH	BLL=8	013	DNM=14-123	DS 2C	DISP				
DNM=14-156	04	TSA-ORDER-ENTERED-DAY	BLL=8	015	DNM=14-156	DS 2C	DISP				
DNM=14-187	04	TSA-ORDER-ENTERED-YEAR	BLL=8	017	DNM=14-187	DS 2C	DISP				
DNM=14-222	03	TSA-TOTAL-COST	BLL=8	019	DNM=14-222	DS 5P	COMP-3				
DNM=14-249	03	TSA-TOTAL-PRICE	BLL=8	01E	DNM=14-249	DS 5P	COMP-3				
DNM=14-274	03	TSA-LINE-COUNT	BLL=8	023	DNM=14-274	DS 1H	COMP		O	Q	U
DNM=14-301	03	TSA-LINE-I			DNM=14-301		INDEX-NM				
DNM=14-318	03	TSA-LINE-ITEM	BLL=8	025	DNM=14-318	DS 0CL44	GROUP				
DNM=14-344	04	TSA-ITEM-NUMBER	BLL=8	025	DNM=14-344	DS 8C	DISP				
DNM=14-372	04	TSA-ITEM-DESCRIPTION	BLL=8	02D	DNM=14-372	DS 19C	DISP				
DNM=14-408	04	TSA-ITEM-DATE	BLL=8	040	DNM=14-408	DS 6C	DISP				
DNM=14-434	03	TSA-UNIT	BLL=8	046	DNM=14-434	DS 3P	COMP-3				
DNM=14-458	04	TSA-UNIT-COST	BLL=8	049	DNM=14-458	DS 4P	COMP-3				
DNM=15-000	04	TSA-UNIT-PRICE	BLL=8	04D	DNM=15-000	DS 4P	COMP-3				
DNM=15-030	02	TSA-OPERATOR-INITIAL	BLL=8	1B1	DNM=15-030	DS 3C	DISP				
DNM=15-063	02	TSA-DEPT-CNT	BLL=8	1B4	DNM=15-063	DS 1F	COMP		O	Q	U
DNM=15-085	02	DEPT-I			DNM=15-085		INDEX-NM				
DNM=15-101	02	TSA-DEPTS	BLL=8	1B8	DNM=15-101	DS 0CL3	GROUP				
DNM=15-123	03	TSA-DEPT-NO	BLL=8	1B8	DNM=15-123	DS 3C	DISP				
DNM=15-147	01	JOURNAL-RECORD	BLL=9	000	DNM=15-147	DS 0CL37	GROUP				
DNM=15-174	02	JOURNAL-OPERATOR-INITIAL	BLL=9	000	DNM=15-174	DS 3C	DISP				
DNM=15-208	02	JOURNAL-DATE-ENTERED	BLL=9	003	DNM=15-208	DS 6C	DISP				
DNM=15-238	02	JOURNAL-ORDER-NUMBER	BLL=9	009	DNM=15-238	DS 10C	DISP				
DNM=15-271	02	JOURNAL-DOCUMENT-NUMBER	BLL=9	013	DNM=15-271	DS 8C	DISP				
DNM=15-307	02	JOURNAL-TOTAL-COST	BLL=9	01B	DNM=15-307	DS 5P	COMP-3				
DNM=15-338	02	JOURNAL-TOTAL-PRICE	BLL=9	020	DNM=15-338	DS 5P	COMP-3				
DNM=15-370	01	DEPT-TABLE-RECORD	BLL=10	000	DNM=15-370	DS 0CL85	GROUP				
DNM=15-400	02	DEPT-TABLE-KEY	BLL=10	000	DNM=15-400	DS 0CL5	GROUP				
DNM=15-430	03	DEPT-TABLE-KEY-CODE	BLL=10	000	DNM=15-430	DS 1C	DISP				
DNM=15-465	88	DEPT-RECORD			DNM=15-465		GROUP				
DNM=16-000	03	DEPT-TABLE-KEY-NUMBER	BLL=10	001	DNM=16-000	DS 4P	COMP-3				
DNM=16-031	02	DEPT-NO	BLL=10	005	DNM=16-031	DS 3C	DISP				
DNM=16-048	02	FILLER	BLL=10	008	DNM=16-048	DS 30C	DISP				
DNM=16-067	02	DEPT-DIVISION	BLL=10	026	DNM=16-067	DS 2C	DISP				

Fig. 24.3.   (Continued)

37   ORADC1A   18.38.45   07/27/80

REG 6   BL =1

WORKING-STORAGE STARTS AT LOCATION 00100 FOR A LENGTH OF 000DC.

CONDENSED LISTING

Line	Verb	Address	Line	Verb	Address	Line	Verb	Address
373	ENTRY	009920	374	CALL	000938	385	MOVE	000940
385	CALL	009950	395	MOVE	000972	395	CALL	000982
396	GO	009998	407	MOVE	0009CC	407	CALL	0009DC
408	GO	0009F2	412	IF	000A22	413	IF	000A30
414	GO	000A3E	415	ELSE	000A44	415	IF	000A44
416	GO	000A52	417	ELSE	000A58	417	GO	000A58
419	IF	000A5E	420	GO	000A70	433	CALL	000A76
433	MOVE	000A80	433	MOVE	000A8A	434	MOVE	000A9A
438	MOVE	000AD4	439	MOVE	000AE2	448	MOVE	000AE8
448	MOVE	000AEE	448	CALL	000AFE	455	MOVE	000B44
459	SET	000B70	463	IF	000B78	464	MOVE	000B8C
465	ELSE	000B9A	465	SET	000BA0	466	MOVE	000BAC
467	MOVE	000BDC	469	IF	000BE6	471	ELSE	000C00
471	SET	000C00	472	MOVE	000C0C	473	IF	000C3C
474	MOVE	000C48	476	SEARCH ALL	000C52	478	GO	000C58
480	MOVE	000CAA	481	GO	000CB8	485	SET	000CC4
486	MOVE	000CD0	487	IF	000D00	488	MOVE	000D0C
492	IF	000D16	495	MOVE	000D5A	496	SET	000D68
497	MOVE	000D6E	498	ELSE	000D74	498	MOVE	000D7A
499	MOVE	000D86	500	IF	000D86	501	MOVE	000DC2
505	IF	000DCC	506	GO	000DDA	510	SET	000DE0
511	MOVE	000DE6	512	MOVE	000DF0	513	PERFORM	000DFA
517	GO	000E46	521	MOVE	000E4C	522	SET	000E56
523	MOVE	000E74	525	IF	000E92	526	IF	000EA0
527	MOVE	000EB0	528	ADD	000EB6	529	ELSE	000EC2
529	MOVE	000EC8	530	SET	000ECE	531	MOVE	000EDA
533	IF	000EF4	534	MOVE	000F00	535	ELSE	000F12
535	IF	000F18	536	GO	000F26	538	IF	000F2C
539	MOVE	000F3E	540	ELSE	000F48	540	IF	000F4E
541	MOVE	000F5C	543	SET	000F62	544	MOVE	000F6E
546	IF	000F88	547	MOVE	000F94	549	ELSE	000FA6
549	IF	000FAC	550	GO	000FBA	551	ELSE	000FC0
552	ELSE	000FC6	552	MOVE	000FC6	554	ADD	000FD0
556	IF	000FDC	557	IF	000FEE	558	MOVE	000FFE
559	ADD	001012	560	ELSE	00101E	560	MOVE	001024
561	MOVE	00102E	562	SET	00103E	563	MOVE	00104A
565	IF	001064	566	MOVE	001070	567	ELSE	001082
567	IF	001088	568	GO	001096	570	IF	00109C
571	IF	0010AE	572	MOVE	0010BE	573	ADD	0010D2
574	ELSE	0010DE	574	MOVE	0010E4	575	MOVE	0010EE
577	SET	0010FE	578	MOVE	00110A	580	IF	001124
581	MOVE	001130	582	ELSE	001142	582	IF	001148
583	GO	001156	585	IF	00115C	586	IF	00116E
589	ADD	00119C	590	ADD	0011A8	591	ELSE	0011B4
591	MOVE	0011BA	592	SET	0011CA	593	MOVE	0011D6
595	IF	0011F0	596	MOVE	0011FC	597	ELSE	00120E

Fig. 24.4.   The Procedure Division Condensed Listing.

38   DRAD01A   18.38.45   07/27/80

Line	Verb	Address
597	IF	001214
601	IF	00123A
604	ELSE	00126A
607	SET	001284
611	MOVE	0012B6
613	GO	0012DC
619	ADD	001322
621	MOVE	001340
625	IF	001376
627	IF	00139A
631	IF	0013CE
635	ELSE	00140E
638	ELSE	00142C
640	MOVE	001448
645	ELSE	001480
648	SET	00149A
654	GO	0014BA
659	MOVE	0014EC
662	ELSE	001532
665	IF	00154C
668	SET	00158A
671	MOVE	0015D2
673	GO	0015F3
678	ELSE	00162E
680	IF	001670
682	IF	00168C
688	IF	0016A0
695	IF	0016CC
698	ELSE	0016FC
699	SUBTRACT	001718
706	CALL	00173E
713	COMPUTE	0017A0
721	CALL	0017D2
732	CALL	001828
741	MOVE	00188C
749	CALL	0018CA
756	CALL	001908
759	MOVE	00191A
770	MOVE	001934
786	MOVE	001990
787	MOVE	0019B4
801	CALL	0019F4
815	MOVE	001A40
816	CALL	001A60
827	MOVE	001AD4
842	MOVE	001AE6
856	MOVE	001B3C
857	CALL	001B60
869	MOVE	001BA0
885	CALL	001BF2
890	MOVE	001C44
907	MOVE	001C78
914	SET	001CB8

Line	Verb	Address
598	GO	001224
602	MOVE	00124A
604	MOVE	001270
608	ELSE	0012C8
612	IF	0012E2
615	ADD	001350
620	SET	001382
622	MOVE	0013A8
626	GO	0013DC
628	SET	001414
632	ELSE	00142C
636	SET	001462
638	IF	001486
642	IF	0014C0
645	EXIT	00151C
649	IF	001538
656	IF	001576
660	IF	001596
662	MOVE	0015DC
667	MOVE	0015F6
669	ELSE	001634
672	IF	00167C
675	SET	00169A
678	MOVE	0016AE
681	GO	0016DA
683	GO	001702
689	IF	001728
696	SUBTRACT	001768
698	MOVE	0017B8
706	MOVE	0017E8
711	GO	001838
714	CALL	0018B4
722	MOVE	0018F4
732	MOVE	00190E
749	MOVE	001924
754	MOVE	00193A
757	MOVE	00199A
760	MOVE	0019EA
770	MOVE	001A4A
786	CALL	001ABA
794	MOVE	001ADA
801	CALL	001AF6
815	MOVE	001B46
822	CALL	001B96
828	GO	001C08
842	CALL	001C7E
856	MOVE	001CC0
862	MOVE	
869	CALL	
886	GO	
896	MOVE	
907	MOVE	
915	MOVE	

Line	Verb	Address
600	IF	001228
603	ADD	00125E
605	MOVE	00127A
610	IF	0012AA
612	IF	0012CE
616	ELSE	0012F4
621	MOVE	00133A
623	ELSE	00135C
627	IF	001394
630	MOVE	0013AE
633	IF	0013F0
636	IF	001414
639	MOVE	001438
643	MOVE	00146E
646	GO	001494
653	IF	0014E0
658	SET	001528
661	MOVE	001546
663	GO	001584
668	ELSE	0015C6
670	IF	0015E2
672	IF	001620
677	MOVE	001640
679	MOVE	001686
682	ELSE	0016A0
684	EXIT	001684
693	SET	0016EC
697	SUBTRACT	001712
699	ELSE	00172E
706	MOVE	00177C
712	MOVE	0017C2
721	MOVE	001818
732	MOVE	00187C
741	MOVE	0018BA
749	MOVE	001902
755	MOVE	001914
758	MOVE	00192E
770	MOVE	00194A
771	CALL	00199A
786	MOVE	0019A4
801	MOVE	0019EE
815	MOVE	001A36
826	MOVE	001A50
842	MOVE	001AC0
848	MOVE	001AE0
856	MOVE	001828
869	MOVE	00189A
885	MOVE	001B9A
889	CALL	001C36
896	CALL	001C5A
907	CALL	001C8E
916	MOVE	001CC8

Fig. 24.4.   (Continued)

39   ORAD01A   18.38.45   07/27/80

Line	Verb	Addr	Line	Verb	Addr	Line	Verb	Addr
922	MOVE	001CCE	922	CALL	001CDE	923	GO	001CF4
931	MOVE	001D22	931	MOVE	001D80	931	CALL	001D3C
943	MOVE	001D76	943	MOVE	001DEC	943	CALL	001D90
948	IF	001DDE	949	IF	001DFE	950	GO	001DF8
951	ELSE	001DFE	951	IF	001E38	952	SET	001E0E
953	MOVE	001E1A	955	GO	001E4C	956	EXIT	001E3E
960	IF	001E3E	961	GO	001E70	962	ELSE	001E52
962	SET	001E52	966	MOVE	001E94	967	ELSE	001E80
968	MOVE	001E8E	969	MOVE	001EAE	970	MOVE	001E9A
971	MOVE	001EA4	979	MOVE	001F0A	979	CALL	001EBE
988	MOVE	001EFA	988	CALL	001F48	997	MOVE	001F32
997	MOVE	001F38	997	MOVE	001F98	1003	MOVE	001F7A
1011	MOVE	001F8E	1011	MOVE	001FE8	1011	MOVE	001FA2
1012	CALL	001FB2	1017	MOVE	001FF8	1024	MOVE	001FEC
1024	MOVE	001FF2	1024	MOVE	00209A	1025	CALL	002008
1037	MOVE	002036	1046	MOVE	0020EE	1046	MOVE	002050
1046	CALL	002060	1055	CALL	002112	1055	CALL	0020AA
1056	GO	0020C0	1059	MOVE	002156	1060	MOVE	002130
1066	MOVE	002102	1066	MOVE	00218A	1076	MOVE	0020FC
1076	CALL	002140	1091	GO	0021B0	1091	MOVE	00215C
1092	CALL	00216C	1095	MOVE	0021C2	1096	GO	00219A
1099	MOVE	0021A0	1100	MOVE	0021D8	1103	GO	0021B6
1104	GO	0021BC	1107	CALL	0021F4	1108	MOVE	0021C8
1111	MOVE	0021CE	1112	MOVE	002228	1117	MOVE	0021DE
1117	MOVE	0021E4	1117	CALL		1120	MOVE	002212
1121	GO	002222	1124	MOVE		1125	GO	002232

STATISTICS   SOURCE RECORDS = 1125   DATA ITEMS = 248   PROC DIV SZ = 411   LIB
STATISTICS   PARTITION SIZE = 200584   LINE COUNT = 56   BUFFER SIZE = 19069   NOOPT
OPTIONS IN EFFECT PMAP RELOC ADR = NONE   SPACING = 1   FLOW   NOLVL
OPTIONS IN EFFECT NOLISTX   APOST   SYM   NOCATALR   LIST   NOXREF   STXIT
OPTIONS IN EFFECT CLIST   FLAGW   ZWB   SUPMAP   LINK   ERRS   SXREF
OPTIONS IN EFFECT NOSTATE   NOTRUNC   SEQ   NOSYMDMP   NODECK   VERB   CSYNTAX
OPTIONS IN EFFECT   NOCOUNT   NOVERBSUM   NOVERBREF
LISTER OPTIONS   NONE

Fig. 24.4. (Continued)

CUSTOMER INFORMATION CONTROL SYSTEM STORAGE DUMP   CODE=ASRA   TASK=ORAD   DATE=07/27/80   TIME=18 43 53   PAGE   1

PSW   (H)→ 071D0007 CC13D9C8

REGS 14-4   5011812A   0013D9DA   00000000   0013D9DA   0013EE90   00000006   00129157

REGS 5-11   5013E800   0012F00C   0012F2E3   0012F2E4   0013EAD0   0013C820   01100660

(A)

TASK CONTROL AREA (USER AREA) ADDRESS 12E8B8 TO 12EFBF   LENGTH 000708

000000	0012E800	00107234	01100660	00108EF0	0012EBC0	0011A746	88400100	003100A0	*..Y.........-...0........ ......*	12E8B8
000020	4011862A	0015F1A0	00000000	0015F1B0	00118804	80118BA0	0013F808	00117F70	* ....1........1.......8......*	12E8D8
000040	0012E800	48000058	0011A728	0012EC18	00118888	01100660	5011812A	0012F980	* ..Y..........................9.*	12E8F8
000060	6012IC38	00128800	AE120540	00000000	0000000A	00000540	00000000	0012D040	*-................ ....*	12E918
000080	FE00F988	D3F7F7F0	D6D9C1C4	C1E2D9C1	071D0007	C013D9C8	00000000	01F0F140	*..9.L770QRADASRA......RH.....01 *	12E938
0000A0	5011812A	0013D9DA	00000000	0013D9DA	0013EE90	00000006	00129157	5013E800	* .......R.......R............. .*	12E958
0000C0	0012F00C	0012F2E3	0012F2E4	0013EAD0	0013C820	01100660	0A040000	00010600	*..0...2T...2U......H....-......*	12E978
0000E0	00000000	00000000	24F40000	00000000	00000000	00000000	00000000	00000000	*.........4...................*	12E998
000100	000400F0	F0F0F0F8	F5F7F300	0900C3C8	C1C9D540	E2C1E640	40404040	40404040	*...00008573...CHAIN SAW *	12E9B8
000120	40000200	F0F0F0F2	F0000500	F0F0F1F0	F0F0F000	0600F0F0	F2F0F0F0	F0F00005	* .....00020...0010000...00200000..*	12E9D8
000140	00F0F0F2	F0F0F0F0	000600F0	F0F4F0F0	F0F0F0F0	F0F0F0F8	F5F7F3C3	C8C1C9D5	*.0020000...0040000000008573CHAIN*	12E9F8
000160	40E2C1E6	40404040	40404040	4040F1F0	F1F5F8F1	00020C00	10000C00	00000000	* SAW 101581 *	12EA18
000180	00000000	00000000	00000000	00000000	000000D3	F7F7F0D6	D9C1C400	00000F00	*.............L7700RAD.....*	12EA38
0001A0	00000000	00053C00	00000000	00000000	00000000	00000000	00000000	00000000	*........................*	12EA58
0001C0	00000000	00000000	00000000	00000000	00000000	00000000	00000000	00000000	*........................*	12EA78
0001E0	LINES TO 0002E0 SAME AS ABOVE									12EA98
000300	D3C9C6D6	E2E3D6D9	42000088	00000000	FF12EC48	B012192C	00121908	00000004	*LIFOSTOR...............Q....*	12EBB8
000320	0012F360	0012F07C	0012EA4B	0012F328	0012EA5D	00000014	00000004	0010C700	*..3-..0......3....)........G.*	12EBD8
000340	00121820	0012F0EC	0012F390	0012E8B8	001070F0	FE12EC48	F0000000	00000000	*.....0...3...Y....0....0......*	12EBF8
000360	8B000028	00000000	00000000	0011A728	00000000	00000000	00000000	00000000	*............................*	12EC18
000380	00000000	00000000	8B000028	00000000	48000068	0012EBC0	00000000	4011862A	*.........................*	12EC38
0003A0	0015F1A0	00000000	0015F1B0	00118804	80118BA0	0013F808	00117F70	0012E800	*..1........1.......8.......Y.*	12EC58
0003C0	48000058	0011A728	0012EC18	00118888	01100660	00000000	00000000	FE12EC80	*.........................*	12EC78
0003E0	F700E3E2	00121A64	89040000	D3F7F7F0	D6D9C1C4	00000000	00000000	00000000	*7.TS.......L7700RAD.........*	12EC98
000400	00000000	00000000	00000000	00000000	00000000	00000000	00000000	00000000	*........................*	12ECB8
000420	LINES TO 0006E0 SAME AS ABOVE									12ECD8
000700	8A0307B8	0012F980							*......9. *	12EFB8

TASK CONTROL AREA (SYSTEM AREA)ADDRESS 12E800 TO 12E8B7   LENGTH 000088

000000	8A0307B8	0012F980	00000000	00000000	8000008C	00117120	00129880	00000000	*......9................*	12E800
000020	00109138	00000000	00000000	00000000	00000000	FF11A6E4	00000000	0012F0EC	*......................U....0.*	12E820
000040	0012EFC0	0012EC18	00000000	0012F660	00000000	00000000	00000000	00000000	*................6-.........*	12E840
000060	00000000	00000000	00000000	C1E2D9C1	00000000	00000000	00000000	0012F390	*...........ASRA.........3.*	12E860
000080	FE12EC80	00000000	FE12EBB0	FE12EFB8	0013A28	0012EBC0	00000000	00000000	*......................*	12E880
0000A0	00100660	00000000	00000000	00000000	D6D9C1C4	00000000			*...-..........ORAD.... *	12E8A0

Fig. 24.5. The Transaction Dump.

CUSTOMER INFORMATION CONTROL SYSTEM STORAGE DUMP   CODE=ASRA   TASK=DRAD   DATE=07/27/80   TIME=18 43 53   PAGE 2

LIFO STACK ENTRY   ADDRESS 12EBC0   TO 12EC47   LENGTH 000088

```
000000  42000088 00000000 FF12EC48 B012192C   *.........0...3..0.*   12EBC0
000020  2012EA48 0012F328 0012EA5D 0012F07C   *....3...)....0..*     12EBE0
000040  0012F390 0012E888 001070F0 FE12EC48   *.3...Y...0....*       12EC00
000060  00000000 0011A728 F0000000 83000028   *......0....*          12EC20
000080  8B000028 00000000                      *.....*                12EC40
```

REGS 0 THRU 15   ADDRESS 155DCC   TO 155E0B   LENGTH 000040

```
000000  00000000 0013090A 0013EE90 00000006   *.....R.......*        155DCC
000020  0012F2E4 0013EAD0 0013C820 0013090A   *.2U.....H.....R..*    155DEC
```

COMMON SYSTEM AREA   ADDRESS 1070F0   TO 108EEF   LENGTH 001E00

```
000000  00000000 00000000 70155400 0013090A 0013EE90   *........R....R..*      1070F0
000020  00000006 00129157 5013EB00 0012F2E4 0013C820   *......0...2T...H.*     107110
000040  01100660 0012C088 0010023C 01298C0 17700000    *.......Y....*          107130
000060  0066E567 00465000 00002000 00100000 0018FFFF    *.V.........*           107150
000080  0010996F8 F0FFFFFF 0000001E 0015EBD8 00128520   *.80....Q.....D.F.*    107170
0000A0  00000000 00000000 00129840 00109138 1000FF00    *.......Q....*          107190
0000C0  000C0001 0091E00 00108EF0 00100A10 00100A10    *......0....*           1071B0
0000E0  401A0AC4 001150D0 00118804 0011F064 00121E4    *.D......Q...0....U*    1071D0
000100  00121908 00000000 001464A0 0110DBD0 00146490    *......Q....1...*      1071F0
000120  00117090 00119BF8 00100260 00122A28 00128400    *.......8....*          107210
000140  00000000 0015EE64 00100808 0122880 00000000     *......8...*            107230
000160  0014F1EA 00000000 00000000 01341C61 0014F4A0    *...1.....E../.4.*     107250
000180  00000000 00000000 00000000 00000000 FF1070A8    *......4M....*          107270
0001A0  07FE58F0 019C07FF 0134B035 000C0000 C1D9C5C1    *.0J....6.....WORKAREA*  107290
0001C0  0000000C 00C0000 03C003C 0008C000 0C000C00      *........*              1072B0
0001E0  1C001C00 00C0000 00C000C 00C000C 00C000C        *....*                  1072D0
000200  00000000 00000000 00000000 00000000 00000000    *....*                  1072F0
000220  LINES TO 0006C0 SAME AS ABOVE
0006E0  00000000 00000000 00000000 00000000 00000000    *....*                  107310
000700  LINES TO 0016A0 SAME AS ABOVE
0016C0  00000000 00000000 00000000 00000000 00000000    *.....*                 1077F0
0016E0  LINES TO 001DE0 SAME AS ABOVE
```

CSA OPTIONAL FEATURE LIST   ADDRESS 108EF0   TO 109077   LENGTH 000188

```
000000  00000000 00000000 00159BD0 0012532C 0015CC38 3015CC68   *......*          108EF0
000023  0014F122 0014EE10 00000000 0015C500 0015C500 00000000   *...X4...E.....*   108F10
000040  00000000 00000000 00149C98 00000000 00000000 00000000   *....*            108F30
000060  00000000 01F4D5D6 00C0FF00 00154D90 00000000 001070F0   *.4ND...(.....0*   108F50
000080  00109A28 00154B70 00153760 00150660 00000000 001F070F0  *....*            108F70
0000A0  001ADF0 00117F70 001C260 00108C60 00110E120 00122FC0    *...0....B...X..*  108F90
0000C0  00115020 00119510 0015E4F0 0010A020 0015D720 00124EC0   *......0....P...+*  108FB0
0000E0  001597C0 00154DE0 0015A7D0 00000000 0014FCA0 00000000   *...UD...(.....*  108FD0
000100  00000000 00000000 0010AF4 00141F0 00000000 00000000     *......4..0...*   108FF0
000120  00000000 001C000C 00C0001C 00C000C 00C000C 00C000C       *....*           109010
```

Fig. 24.5. (Continued)

```
                                                                                    109030
                                                                                    109050
                                                                                    109070

CUSTOMER INFORMATION CONTROL SYSTEM STORAGE DUMP    CODE=ASRA    TASK=ORAD    DATE=07/27/80    TIME=18 43 53    PAGE 3

CSA OPTIONAL FEATURE LIST        ADDRESS 108EF0    TO 109077    LENGTH 000188

000140   000C001C 000C000C 000C000C 001C000C                            *.........*
000160   001C000C 000C001C 000C000C 000C001C 000C000C 000C001C          *.........*
000180   000C000C 000C000C


TRACE TABLE             ADDRESS 1457F0    TO 14646F    LENGTH 000C80

TRACE HDR    00145920    001457F0   00146460   00146490

TRACE TABLE    ID REG14   REQD TASK   FIELD A    FIELD B     TRACE TYPE

145930   E1 132DFE   0004 0007   0012FA2C   0000060E   ........   EIP READNEXT ENTRY
145940   F5 11E9C8   B003 0007   C4E2E7E3   C1C2E240   DSXTABS    FCP GETNEXT
145950   F0 120476   4004 0007   20000000   00173058   ........   KCP WAIT DCI=DISP
145960   F5 120134   0015 0007   00000000   00000000   ........   FCP RESPONSE NORMAL
145970   E1 132DFE   00F4 0007   00000000   0000060E   ........   EIP READNEXT RESPONSE
145980   E1 132DFE   0004 0007   0012FA2C   0000060E   ........   EIP READNEXT ENTRY
145990   F5 11E9C8   B003 0007   C4E2E7E3   C1C2E240   DSXTABS    FCP GETNEXT
1459A0   F0 11B124   4004 0007   80000000   00173058   ........   KCP WAIT DCI=SINGLE
1459B0   F5 120134   0015 0007   00000000   00000000   ........   FCP RESPONSE NORMAL
1459C0   E1 132DFE   00F4 0007   00000000   0000060E   ........   EIP READNEXT RESPONSE
1459D0   E1 132DFE   0004 0007   0012FA2C   0000060E   ........   EIP READNEXT ENTRY
1459E0   F5 11E9C8   B003 0007   C4E2E7E3   C1C2E240   DSXTABS    FCP GETNEXT
1459F0   F0 120476   4004 0007   20000000   00173058   ........   KCP WAIT DCI=DISP
145A00   F5 120134   0015 0007   00000000   00000000   ........   FCP RESPONSE NORMAL
145A10   E1 132DFE   00F4 0007   00000000   0000060E   ........   EIP READNEXT RESPONSE
145A20   E1 132DFE   0C04 0007   0012FA2C   0000060E   ........   EIP READNEXT ENTRY
145A30   F5 11E9C8   B003 0007   C4E2E7E3   C1C2E240   DSXTABS    FCP GETNEXT
145A40   F0 120476   4004 0007   20000000   00173058   ........   KCP WAIT DCI=DISP
145A50   F5 120134   0015 0007   00000000   00000000   ........   FCP RESPONSE NORMAL
145A60   E1 132DFE   00F4 0007   00000000   0000060E   ........   EIP READNEXT RESPONSE
145A70   E1 132DFE   0004 0007   0012FA2C   0000060E   ........   EIP READNEXT ENTRY
145A80   F5 11E9C8   B003 0007   C4E2E7E3   C1C2E240   DSXTABS    FCP GETNEXT
145A90   F0 120476   4004 0007   20000000   00173058   ........   KCP WAIT DCI=DISP
145AA0   F0 10DBB8   4004 TC     44000000   00100TF8   .......8   KCP WAIT
145AB0   F5 120134   0015 0007   00000000   00000000   ........   FCP RESPONSE NORMAL
145AC0   E1 132DFE   00F4 0007   00000000   0000060E   ........   EIP READNEXT RESPONSE
145AD0   E1 132DFE   0004 0007   0012FA2C   0000060E   ........   EIP READNEXT ENTRY
145AE0   F5 11E9C8   B003 0007   C4E2E7E3   C1C2E240   DSXTABS    FCP GETNEXT
145AF0   F0 120476   4004 0007   20000000   00173058   ........   KCP WAIT DCI=DISP
145B00   F5 120134   0015 0007   00000000   00000000   ........   FCP RESPONSE NORMAL
145B10   E1 132DFE   00F4 0007   00000000   0000060E   ........   EIP READNEXT RESPONSE
145B20   E1 132DFE   0004 0007   0012FA2C   0000060E   ........   EIP READNEXT ENTRY
145B30   F5 11E9C8   B003 0007   C4E2E7E3   C1C2E240   DSXTABS    FCP GETNEXT
145B40   F0 120476   4004 0007   20000000   00173058   ........   KCP WAIT DCI=DISP
145B50   F5 120134   0015 0007   00000000   00000000   ........   FCP RESPONSE NORMAL
145B60   E1 132DFE   00F4 0007   00000000   0000060E   ........   EIP READNEXT RESPONSE
145B70   E1 132DFE   0C04 0007   0012FA2C   C000060E   ........   EIP READNEXT ENTRY
145B80   F5 11E9C8   B003 0007   C4E2E7E3   C1C2E240   DSXTABS    FCP GETNEXT
145B90   F0 120476   4004 0007   20000000   00173058   ........   KCP WAIT DCI=DISP
145BA0   F5 120134   0015 0007   00000000   00000000   ........   FCP RESPONSE NORMAL
```

Fig. 24.5. (Continued)

CUSTOMER INFORMATION CONTROL SYSTEM STORAGE DUMP   CODE=ASRA   TASK=DRAD   DATE=07/27/80   TIME=18 43 53   PAGE 4

TRACE TABLE	ID	REG14	REQD	TASK	FIELD A	FIELD B		TRACE TYPE
145B30	E1	132DFE	00F4	0007	00000000	0000060E	......	EIP READNEXT RESPONSE
145B40	E1	132DFE	0015	0007	0012FA2C	2C00060E	......	EIP READNEXT ENTRY
145B50	F5	11E9C8	B0C3	0007	C4E2E7E3	C1C2E240	DSXTABS	FCP GETNEXT
145B60	F0	120476	4004	0007	20000000	00173058	......	KCP WAIT DCI=DISP
145BF0	F5	120134	0015	0007	00000000	00000000	......	FCP RESPONSE NORMAL
145C00	E1	132DFE	00F4	0007	00000000	0000060E	......	EIP READNEXT RESPONSE
145C10	E1	132DFE	30C4	0307	0012FA2C	0000060E	......	EIP READNEXT ENTRY
145C20	F5	11E9C8	B003	0007	C4E2E7E3	C1C2E240	DSXTABS	FCP GETNEXT
145C30	F0	120476	4004	0007	20000000	00173058	......	KCP WAIT DCI=DISP
145C40	F5	120134	0015	0007	00000000	00000000	......	FCP RESPONSE NORMAL
145C50	E1	132DFE	00F4	0007	00000000	0000060E	......	EIP READNEXT RESPONSE
145C60	FD	00001C	0204	0007	0012FA2C	00000A02	TIME...	TIMING TRACE 18/42/53.4
145C70	E1	132F14	0004	0007	0012FA2C	00000A02	......	EIP WRITEQ-TS ENTRY
145C80	F1	12187A	8E04	0007	00120540	01100660	......	SCP GETMAIN
145C90	C8	115222	0004	0007	0012C7B0	8E120548	.G....	SCP ACQUIRED TEMPSTRG STORAGE
145CA0	F7	1218C6	4103	0007	D3FF7FF0	D609C1C4	L770DRAD	TSP PUTQ
145CB0	F1	12231A	F804	0007	00000038	01100660	......	SCP GETMAIN-COND-INIT
145CC0	C8	115222	0004	0007	00120000	98000040	......	SCP ACQUIRED TSTABLE STORAGE
145CD0	F1	121AEA	B704	0007	00120554	01100660	......	SCP GETMAIN-CONDITIONAL
145CE0	C8	115222	0004	0007	00120040	97120560	......	SCP ACQUIRED TSMAIN STORAGE
145CF0	F7	121FCC	0015	0307	00000000	00000000	......	TSP RESPONSE
145D00	F1	12183E	4004	0007	0012C7B0	01100660	.G....	SCP FREEMAIN
145D10	C9	11530C	0004	0007	0012C7B0	8E120548	.G....	SCP RELEASED TEMPSTRG STORAGE
145D20	E1	132F14	00F4	0007	00000000	00000A02	......	EIP WRITEQ-TS RESPONSE
145D30	E1	132F4C	0004	0007	0012FA2C	01100660	......	EIP FREEMAIN ENTRY
145D40	F1	11508A	4004	0007	0012C000	01100660	......	SCP FREEMAIN
145D50	C9	11530C	0004	0007	0012C000	8C120548	......	SCP RELEASED USER STORAGE
145D60	E1	132F4C	00F4	0007	00000000	C000C004	......	EIP FREEMAIN RESPONSE
145D70	E1	132F9A	0004	0007	0012FA2C	00000C02	......	EIP GETMAIN ENTRY
145D80	F1	115052	CC04	0007	0000003E	01100660	......	SCP GETMAIN-INIT
145D90	C8	115222	0004	0007	0012C600	8C0003C8	.H...H	SCP ACQUIRED USER STORAGE
145DA0	E1	132F9A	00F4	0007	0012FA2C	0000C002	......	EIP GETMAIN RESPONSE
145DB0	E1	133008	0004	0007	00000000	00001804	......	EIP SEND-MAP ENTRY
145DC0	FA	1247FE	0003	0007	000005E2	04000020	..S...	BMS OUT MAP MAPSET SAVE ERASE
145DD0	F2	1261AC	0804	0007	D609C1D7	E2F0F140	DRAPS01	PCP DELETE
145DE0	F2	126200	4004	0007	D609C1C4	E2F0F140	ORADS01	PCP LOAD
145DF0	F1	118572	8804	0007	00120095	01100660	......	SCP GETMAIN
145E00	C9	11530C	0004	0007	00138800	88002800	......	SCP RELEASED PGM STORAGE
145E10	C9	11530C	0004	0007	00136800	88002800	......	SCP RELEASED PGM STORAGE
145E20	C9	11530C	0004	0007	0013A000	88001800	......	SCP RELEASED PGM STORAGE
145E30	C9	11530C	0004	0007	0013F800	88000800	......	SCP RELEASED PGM STORAGE
145E40	C9	11530C	0004	0007	0013F800	88000800	.8....	SCP RELEASED PGM STORAGE
145E50	C9	11530C	0004	0007	0013D000	88001000	......	SCP RELEASED PGM STORAGE
145E60	C9	11530C	0004	0007	00133800	88001000	......	SCP RELEASED PGM STORAGE
145E70	C9	11530C	0004	0007	00135000	88001800	......	SCP RELEASED PGM STORAGE
145E80	C9	11530C	0004	0007	00134800	88000800	......	SCP RELEASED PGM STORAGE
145E90	C8	115222	0004	0007	00130800	88000800	......	SCP ACQUIRED PGM STORAGE
145EA0	F0	11862A	4004	0007	00000000	0011A746	......	KCP WAIT DCI=CICS
145EB0	F1	127F3A	9E04	0007	00130850	01100660	......	SCP GETMAIN
145EC0	C8	115222	0004	0007	0012D800	9E130858	..Q...	SCP ACQUIRED MAPCOPY STORAGE
145ED0	F1	124578	CC04	0007	000004E0	01100660	......	SCP GETMAIN-INIT

Fig. 24.5. (Continued)

CUSTOMER INFORMATION CONTROL SYSTEM STORAGE DUMP   CODE=ASRA   TASK=QRAD   DATE=07/27/80   TIME=18 43 53   PAGE 5

TRACE TABLE	ID	REG14	REQD	TASK	FIELD A	FIELD B		TRACE TYPE
145EE0	C8	115222	0004	0007	0012E060	8C0004E8	......Y	SCP ACQUIRED USER STORAGE
145EF0	F1	124846	8504	0007	001205D3	01100660	....L..	SCP GETMAIN
145F00	C8	115222	0004	0007	00129170	85120SE8	......Y	SCP ACQUIRED TERMINAL STORAGE
145F13	F1	124A00	4004	0007	0012E060	01100660	....	SCP FREEMAIN
145F20	C9	11530C	0004	0007	0012E060	8C0004E8	......Y	SCP RELEASED USER STORAGE
145F30	F1	124A00	4004	0007	0012D800	01100660	....	SCP FREEMAIN
145F40	C9	11530C	0004	0007	0012D800	9E130858	..Q....	SCP RELEASED MAPCOPY STORAGE
145F50	FC	126CA8	0103	0007	00810000	00100660	..Q....	ZCP ZARQ APPL REQ ERASE WRITE
145F60	FA	125EE6	0005	0007	00000000	00000000	....	BMS RESPONSE
145F70	E1	133008	00F4	0007	00000000	00001804	....	EIP SEND-MAP RESPONSE
145F83	E1	133056	0004	0007	0012FA2C	0000DE08	....	EIP RETURN ENTRY
145F90	F1	11970C	9304	0007	00120019	01100660	....	SCP GETMAIN
145FA0	C8	115222	0004	0007	0012D5A0	93120220	..N....	SCP ACQUIRED SHARED STORAGE
145F80	F2	119760	1004	0007	D609C1C4	F0FC140	QRAD01A	PCP RETURN
145FC0	F1	118A4A	4004	0007	0012F9E0	01100660	..9....H	SCP FREEMAIN
145F00	C9	11530C	0004	0007	0012F9E0	8C1303C8	..9....H	SCP RELEASED USER STORAGE
145FF0	F1	118B66	4004	0007	00131000	01100660	....	SCP FREEMAIN
146000	C9	11530C	0004	0007	00131000	88002800	....	SCP RELEASED PGM STORAGE
146010	F1	118B66	4004	0007	00130800	01100660	....	SCP FREEMAIN
146020	C9	11530C	0004	0007	00130800	88000800	....	SCP RELEASED PGM STORAGE
146030	F0	118992	8004	0007	00000000	0012C620	....	KCP DETACH
146040	D8	10AC20	0203	0007	02000000	00000000	..F....	SPP SYSTEM
146050	F5	10D7F0	0003	0007	0012C620	01100660	..F....	FCP DWE PROCESSOR
146060	F1	120D70	4004	0007	0012C620	90120038	..F....	SCP FREEMAIN DWE STORAGE
146370	C9	11530C	0004	0007	0012C660	01100660	..F....H	SCP RELEASED DWE STORAGE
146080	F1	120D70	4004	0007	0012C660	8F1200C8	..F....H	SCP FREEMAIN
146090	F5	120134	0015	0007	00000000	00000000	....	FCP RESPONSE NORMAL
1460A0	D8	10D95C	0015	0007	00000000	00000000	....	SPP RESPONSE
1460B0	F0	10AC2A	0304	0007	0011A746	00000000	....	KCP DEQALL
1460C0	F1	10ADA0	4A04	KC	0012E800	00000000	..Y....	SCP FREEMAIN
1460D0	C9	11530C	0004	KC	0012C800	8C0003C8	..H....H	SCP RELEASED USER STORAGE
1460E0	C9	11530C	0004	KC	0012C730	8F120078	..G....	SCP RELEASED FILE STORAGE
1460F0	C9	11530C	0004	KC	0012C5A0	8C000078	..E....	SCP RELEASED USER STORAGE
146100	C9	11530C	0004	KC	0012C550	8C000048	... . .	SCP RELEASED USER STORAGE
146110	C9	11530C	0004	KC	0012FF40	8C000048	....	SCP RELEASED USER STORAGE
146120	C9	11530C	0004	KC	0012FEF0	8C000078	..0....	SCP RELEASED USER STORAGE
146130	C9	11530C	0004	KC	0012FE70	8C000078	....	SCP RELEASED USER STORAGE
146140	C9	11530C	0004	KC	0012FE20	8C000048	....	SCP RELEASED USER STORAGE
146150	C9	11530C	0004	KC	0012FDB0	8C000068	....	SCP RELEASED USER STORAGE
146160	C9	11530C	0004	KC	0012FD80	8C120018	..9....	SCP RELEASED USER STORAGE
146170	C9	11530C	0004	KC	0012F930	8C000088	..9....	SCP RELEASED USER STORAGE
146180	C9	11530C	0004	KC	0012F6A0	8C000288	..6....	SCP RELEASED USER STORAGE
146190	C9	11530C	0004	KC	0012F290	8C000408	..2....	SCP RELEASED USER STORAGE
1461A0	C9	11530C	0004	KC	0012E800	8A030598	..Y....	SCP RELEASED TCA STORAGE
146180	F0	10DB88	4004	TC	44000000	001007F8	8	KCP WAIT
1461C0	F1	10EA54	4004	TC	00129170	80100660	....	SCP FREEMAIN
1461D0	C9	11530C	0004	TC	00129170	851205E8	......Y	SCP RELEASED TERMINAL STORAGE
1461E0	F1	10EAF8	6004	TC	00000000	80100660	....	SCP FREEMAIN ALL
1461F0	C9	11530C	00C4	TC	00129120	85000048	....	SCP RELEASED TERMINAL STORAGE
146200	F1	10E9F0	E404	TC	0000010F	80100660	....	SCP GETMAIN-COND-INIT

Fig. 24.5. (Continued)

CUSTOMER INFORMATION CONTROL SYSTEM STORAGE DUMP   CODE=ASRA   TASK=ORAD   DATE=07/27/80   TIME=18 43 53   PAGE 6

TRACE TABLE	ID	REG14	REQD	TASK	FIELD A	FIELD B		TRACE TYPE
146210	C8	115222	0004	TC	00129000	84000118	....	SCP ACQUIRED LINE STORAGE
146220	F0	10DBB8	4004	TC	44000000	001007F8	8	KCP WAIT
146230	FD	00002C	0104	TC	0066CDE0	0066E548	....V..	... REPEAT 00002 TIMES
146240	F0	113464	1104	TC	01100660	D6D9C1C4	....ORAD	KCP ATTACH-CONDITIONAL
146250	F1	10A91E	EAC4	TC	00080780	80100660		SCP GETMAIN-COND-INIT
146260	C8	115222	0004	TC	0012E800	8A0307B8	..Y.....	SCP ACQUIRED TCA STORAGE
146270	F0	10DBB8	4004	TC	44000000	001007F8	8	KCP WAIT
146280	F2	118804	0204	TC	D6D9C1C4	F0F1C140	ORAD01A	PCP XCTL
146290	F1	118572	8804	0008	000004F2	01100660	..2....	SCP GETMAIN
1462A0	C8	115222	8004	0008	0013C800	88002800	..H....	SCP ACQUIRED PGM STORAGE
1462B0	F0	11862A	4004	0008	88000000	0011A702		KCP WAIT DCI=CICS
1462C0	F1	1190FC	8C04	0008	0013D3BC	01100660		SCP GETMAIN
1462D0	C8	10C2A6	CC04	0008	00000128	01100660	......H	SCP ACQUIRED USER STORAGE
1462E0	C8	115222	0004	0008	0012F390	8C000138	..3....	SCP GETMAIN-INIT
1462F0	C8	115222	0004	0008	0012F00C	00000202	..0....	SCP ACQUIRED USER STORAGE
146300	E1	130192	0004	0008	0012F00C	00000202		EIP ADDRESS ENTRY
146310	E1	130192	00F4	0008	00000000	00000206		EIP ADDRESS RESPONSE
146320	E1	130188	0004	0008	0012F00C	00000206	..0....	EIP HANDLE-AID ENTRY
146330	F1	10BC96	CC04	0008	00000059	01100660		SCP GETMAIN-INIT
146340	C8	115222	0004	0008	0012F400	8C000068	..4....	SCP ACQUIRED USER STORAGE
146350	F1	10BD98	CC04	0008	00000040	01100660		SCP GETMAIN-INIT
146360	C8	115222	0004	0008	0012F540	8C000048	..5....	SCP ACQUIRED USER STORAGE
146370	E1	13D1B8	00F4	0008	00000000	00000206		EIP HANDLE-AID RESPONSE
146380	E1	13D212	0004	0008	0012F00C	00000204	..0....	EIP HANDLE-CONDITION ENTRY
146390	F1	10BC96	CC04	0008	00000070	01100660		SCP GETMAIN-INIT
1463A0	C8	115222	0004	0008	0012F590	8C000078	..5....	SCP ACQUIRED USER STORAGE
1463B0	F1	10BD98	CC04	0008	00000040	01100660		SCP GETMAIN-INIT
1463C0	C8	115222	0004	0008	0012F610	8C000048	..6....	SCP ACQUIRED USER STORAGE
1463D0	E1	13D212	00F4	0008	00000000	00000204		EIP HANDLE-CONDITION RESPONSE
1463E0	E1	13D2F4	0004	0008	0012F00C	00001802	..0....	EIP RECEIVE-MAP ENTRY
1463F0	FA	125080	0003	0008	00000505	00000020		BMS MAP MAPSET MAP IN
146400	F1	12537E	CC04	0008	00000274	01100660		SCP GETMAIN-INIT
146410	C8	115222	0004	0008	0012F660	8C000288	..6....	SCP ACQUIRED USER STORAGE
146420	F1	15AD78	CC04	0008	00000074	01100660		SCP GETMAIN-INIT
146430	C8	115222	0004	0008	0012F8F0	8C000088	..80...	SCP ACQUIRED USER STORAGE
146440	F2	126200	0404	0008	D6D9C1C4	E2F0F140	ORADS01	PCP LOAD
146450	F1	118572	8804	0008	00120095	01100660		SCP GETMAIN
146460	FD	00001C	0204	0008	E3C9D4C5	1843539F	TIME...	TIMING TRACE 18/43/53.9
1457F0	C8	115222	0004	0008	0013F800	88000800	..8....	SCP ACQUIRED PGM STORAGE
14580C	F0	11862A	4004	0008	88000000	0011A746		KCP WAIT DCI=CICS
145810	F0	10DBB8	4004	TC	44000000	001007F8	8	KCP WAIT
145820	F1	124AAC	C504	0008	000003B1	01100660		SCP GETMAIN-INIT
145830	C8	115222	0004	0008	00129120	850003C8	......H	SCP ACQUIRED TERMINAL STORAGE
145840	F1	124E88	4004	0008	00129000	01100660		SCP FREEMAIN
145850	C9	11530C	0004	0008	00129000	85000118		SCP RELEASED TERMINAL STORAGE
145860	FA	125EE6	0005	0008	00000000	00000000		BMS RESPONSE
145870	E1	13D2F4	00F4	0008	00000000	00001802		EIP RECEIVE-MAP RESPONSE
145880	E1	13D364	0004	0008	0012F00C	00000A04	..0....	EIP READQ-TS ENTRY
145890	F7	12192C	8903	0008	D3FF7FF0	D6D9C1C4	L77ORAD	TSP GETQ

Fig. 24.5. (Continued)

CUSTOMER INFORMATION CONTROL SYSTEM STORAGE DUMP   CODE=ASRA   TASK=ORAD   DATE=07/27/80   TIME=18 43 53   PAGE 7

```
1458A0    F1 121C38  AE04 0008  00120540  01100660  ........   SCP GETMAIN-CONDITIONAL
1458B0    C8 115222  0C04 0008  0012F980  8E120548  ...9....   SCP ACQUIRED TEMPSTRG STORAGE
1458C0    F7 121FCC  0015 0008  00000000  00000000  ........   TSP RESPONSE
1458D0    E1 130364  00F4 0008  00000A04  00000000  ........   EIP READQ-TS RESPONSE
1458E0    F2 14F3C8  6004 0008  00000000  00000000  ........   PCP ABEND
1458F0    F4 11812A  FEC4 0008  C1E2D9C1  00000000  ...ASRA    DCP TRANSACTION
145900    F0 155C58  4004 0008  80000000  00155E78  ........   KCP WAIT DCI=SINGLE
145910    F0 100B88  4004 TC    44000000  00107F8   .......8   KCP WAIT
145920    F0 155C58  4004 0008  8C000000  00155E78  ........   KCP WAIT DCI=SINGLE
```

TRANSACTION STORAGE-TS   ADDRESS 12F980   TO 12FECF   LENGTH 000550

```
000000  8E120548 0012F8F0  05400000  F0F0F0F0  F0F0F0F5  F0F0F0F0  F3F8F1F1  F0F1F5F0  *......80...0000000500003811015 0*  12F980
000320  F7F2F7F8 F0000000  00000000  00000000  00000000  00000000  00000000  00000000  *72780.........................*   12F9A0
000040  00000000 00000000  00000000  00000000  00000000  00000000  00000000  00000000  *...............................*  12F9C0
000060  LINES TO 000180    SAME AS ABOVE                                                                                      12F9E0
0000A0  00300000 00000000  00000003  00000000  00000000  00000000  00000000  0007C1D3  *...........................PAL*   12F820
0001C0  00000BE F0F0F3F0   F0F4F0F5  F0F0F8F0  F0F9F0F1  F0F0F1F2  F0F1F3F0  F0F1F3F0  *....00300400500700800901001201 30* 12F840
0001E0  F1F4F0F5 F5F0F1F6   F0F1F7F0  F1F8F0F0  F2F0F2F2  F2F3F0F2  F4F0F2F5  F3F6F0F3  *140150160170180190200202203204025* 12F860
000200  F0F2F6F0 F2F7F0F0   F2F8F0F2  F3F0F3F4  F3F0F3F5  F0F3F6F0  F3F6F0F3  F3F6F0F3  *026027028029030320330340350360 3*  12F880
000220  F7F0F3F8 F0F3F9F0   F4F0F0F4  F0F4F2F4  F4F0F4F3  F0F4F4F0  F4F4F0F4  F0F4F7F0  *703803904004104204304404504604 70* 12F8A0
000240  F4F8F0F4 F9F0F5F0   F0F5F1F0  F5F2F0F5  F3F0F5F4  F0F5F5F0  F5F6F0F5  F7F0F5F8  *480490500510520540550560570 580 59* 12F8C0
000260  F0F5F9F0 F6F1F0F6   F2F0F6F3  F0F6F4F0  F6F5F0F6  F5F0F6F7  F0F6F8F0  F6F9F0F7  *060610620630640650660670680690700 7* 12F8E0
000280  F1F0F7F2 F4F0F7F5   F0F7F6F0  F7F7F0F7  F8F0F7F9  F0F8F0F0  F8F1F0F8  F2F0F8F0  *107207407507607707807908008108020 *  12FC00
0002A0  F8F4F0F8 F5F0F8F6   F0F8F7F0  F8F8F0F9  F0F0F9F0  F1F0F9F2  F0F9F3F0  F9F5F0F9  *840850860870880900901092093 095096 *  12FC20
0002C0  F0F9F7F0 F9F8F0F9   F9F1F0F1  F0F2F1F0  F3F1F0F4  F1F0F5F1  F0F6F1F0  F7F1F0F7  *097098099101102103104105106107 0 *  12FC40
0002E0  F8F1F0F9 F1F1F1F1   F1F1F3F1  F1F4F1F1  F5F1F1F6  F1F1F7F1  F1F8F1F2  F1F2F1F2  *810911113114115116118121122123 1*   12FC60
000300  F2F4F1F2 F5F1F2F6   F1F2F7F1  F2F8F1F3  F1F3F1F3  F1F3F4F1  F3F5F1F3  F6F3F1F6  *241251261271281301311313134135136* 12FC80
000320  F1F3F7F1 F3F9F1F4   F0F1F4F2  F1F4F4F1  F4F6F1F4  F4F6F1F4  F7F1F4F8  F1F4F4    *137139140142143144145146147148141 *  12FCA0
000340  F9F1F5F1 F5F1F5F2   F1F5F4F1  F5F5F1F5  F6F1F5F7  F1F5F9F1  F6F0F1F6  F1F6F3F1  *915115215415515615715916016116631* 12FCC0
000360  F6F4F1F6 F5F1F6F6   F1F6F8F1  F6F9F1F7  F0F1F7F1  F1F7F2F1  F7F3F1F7  F4F3F1F7  *646516616716816917017117217317174*  12FCE0
000380  F1F7F5F1 F7F6F1F7   F7F1F7F8  F1F7F9F1  F8F0F1F8  F1F1F8F2  F1F8F3F1  F8F4F1F8  *175176177178179180181182183184 18*   12FD00
0003A0  F5F1F8F6 F1F8F7F1   F8F8F1F8  F9F1F9F0  F9F2F1F9  F3F1F9F4  F1F9F5F1  F9F4F5F1  *518618718818919019192193194195 1*   12FD20
0003C0  F9F7F1F9 F8F1F9F9   F2F0F0F2  F0F2F0F2  F0F4F2F0  F5F2F0F6  F2F0F7F2  F0F8F2F0  *971981992002020420520620720820 9*   12FD40
0003E0  F2F1F0F2 F1F5F2F1   F9F2F2F6  F2F2F9F2  F3F0F2F3  F4F2F4F1  F2F4F2F2  F4F7..    *210215219226229230234241242247..*  12FD60
000400  00000000 00000000   00000000  00000000  00000000  00000000  00000000  4F700000  *...............................*   12FD80
000420  LINES TO 000520    SAME AS ABOVE                                                                                      12FDA0
000540  00000000 00000000   8E120548  0012F8F0                                            *...............80           *       12FEC0
```

TRANSACTION STORAGE-USER   ADDRESS 12F8F0   TO 12F97F   LENGTH 000090

```
000000  8C000088 0012F660  D4D40000  00000001  00010001  00000000  00000000  00000000  *......6-MM.....................*   12F8F0
000320  0013F808 00000000  00000000  03000000  00000000  06D9C1C4  E2F0F140  00000000  *..8...........ORADS01.........*   12F910
000040  00000000 00000000  00000000  18500000  40000001  01015000  00000000  00000780  *.........8....................*   12F930
000060  00000000 01100660  0404000   00000000  00000000  01015000  FFFFFFFF  00000000  *......6-.......-...........-*     12F950
000080  00000000 00000088  8C000088  0012F660                                                                                 12F970
```

Fig. 24.5. (Continued)

```
CUSTOMER INFORMATION CONTROL SYSTEM STORAGE DUMP      CODE=ASRA      TASK=ORAD      DATE=07/27/80      TIME=18 43 53      PAGE   8

TRANSACTION STORAGE-USER      ADDRESS  12F660      TO  12F8EF      LENGTH  000290

000000   8C000288 0012F610 401256A6 0015A9C8   401258C0 001244CA 00000300 00000000   *......6.........H...............*   12F660
000020   00000000 00000000 00000000 00000000   00000000 00000000 00000000 00000000   *................................*   12F680
000040   00000000 0C000000 0C000505 C0000020   F0F1C140 00000000 D6D9C1C4 D4F0F140   *........................01A ....ORADM01 *   12F6A0
000060   D6D9C1C4 E2F0F140 000C0260 00000000   00000000 00000000 00000000 00000000   *ORADS01 ...B....80..80...........*   12F6C0
000080   00000000 00000003 00000000 00000000   0012F8F0 00000000 00000000 00000000   *.........80..80...........*   12F6E0
0000A0   00000000 00000000 00000000 00000000   1411A6E4 00000000 00000001 00000000   *.............U...................*   12F700
0000C0   00000000 00000000 00000000 00000000   00000000 03000000 00000000 00000000   *................................*   12F720
0000E0   00000000 00000000 00000000 0000001D   00000000 00000000 00000300 00000000   *................................*   12F740
000100   00000300 00000000 00000000 30000000   00000000 00000000 00000000 00000000   *................................*   12F760
000120   00000000 00000000 00000000 00000480   08129000 00000018 000000FF 0010066C   *................Q....Q...8.....%*   12F780
000140   00000000 40126200 00125208 0000048D   0012F660 0012F8F0 01100660 00000000   *.... ........8...6...6.-80..-...*   12F7A0
000160   0013F814 90125884 48000058 0110C700   0012F660 00000000 00000000 00000000   *..8.....d.....G...G.6-.--.-.....*   12F7E0
000180   00000000 00000000 00000000 00110000   00000000 00000000 00000000 00000000   *................................*   12F800
0001A0   00000000 00000000 C0000000 00000000   00000000 00000000 00000000 00000000   *................................*   12F820
0001C0   LINES TO 000260 SAME AS ABOVE
000280   00000000 00000000 8C000288 0012F610                                         *...........6.*   12F8E0

TRANSACTION STORAGE-USER      ADDRESS  12F610      TO  12F65F      LENGTH  000050

000000   8C000048 0012F590 5013D212 0010C5A0   0012F00C 0012F360 5013D1CA 0013CCA8   *.......5...K...E...0...3---J...*   12F610
000020   0012F420 5013EB00 0012F00C 0012F2E3   0012F2E4 0013EAD0 0013C820 0013C820   *...4...0...2T...2U......H...H.*   12F630
000040   0013CC98 0012F0EC 8C000048 0012F590                                         *...0.........5.*   12F650

TRANSACTION STORAGE-USER      ADDRESS  12F590      TO  12F60F      LENGTH  000080

000000   8C000078 0012F540 C012F5D7 00700302   00000000 00000000 00000000 00000000   *.......5 ..5P...................*   12F590
000020   00000000 00000000 00000000 00000001   00000100 00000000 00000000 00000000   *................................*   12F580
000040   00000000 00000000 00000000 00000000   12F61004 12F0EC02 12F61004 12F0EC00   *..........6.0...6.0...6.0.*   12F5D0
000060   00000000 00000000 00000000 00000000   00000000 000000FF 8C000078 0012F540   *...............5*   12F5F0

TRANSACTION STORAGE-USER      ADDRESS  12F540      TO  12F58F      LENGTH  000050

000000   8C000048 0012F4D0 5013D1B8 0010C5A0   0012F00C 0012F360 0013EB40 00118BA0   *.......4...J...E...0...3---  ...*   12F540
000020   0012F420 5013EB00 0012F0EC 0012F2E3   0012F2E4 0013EAD0 0013C820 0013C820   *...4...0...2T...2U......H...H.*   12F560
000040   0013CC98 0012F0EC 0012F4D0                                                  *...0.........4.*   12F580

TRANSACTION STORAGE-USER      ADDRESS  12F4D0      TO  12F53F      LENGTH  000070

000000   8C000068 0012F390 0012F500 C0590500   00040201 03000000 00000000 00000000   *.......3...5............3..5....*   12F4D0
000020   00000000 00000000 00000000 00000000   00000000 0112F540 0412F0EC 00000000   *.....0..5..0..5..0.*   12F4F0
000040   0212F540 0412F0EC 0312F540 0412F0EC   0412F540 0412F0EC 00000000 00000000   *.5..0..5..0..5..0.*   12F510
000060   FF000000 00000068 8C000068 0012F390                                         *...........3.*   12F530
```

Fig. 24.5. (Continued)

```
CUSTOMER INFORMATION CONTROL SYSTEM STORAGE DUMP   CODE=ASRA   TASK=DRAD   DATE=07/27/80   TIME=18 43 53   PAGE   9

TRANSACTION STORAGE-USER      ADDRESS 12F390   TO 12F4CF   LENGTH 000140

000000  8C000138 0012F488 0012FEC0 00000000  00000000 00000000 00000000 00000000  *................*  12F390
000020  00000000 00000000 8012F424 0012F610  00000000 0012F980 00000000 00000000  *............9...*  12F3B0
000040  0012F420 8012CA90 0013CA00 0012F610  00129120 00000000 0012F590 00000000  *....4...6......5.*  12F3D0
000060  00000000 00000000 00010000 00000000  00000000 0012F590 0012F4D0 00000000  *............5..4.*  12F3F0
000080  00000004 00000000 0012FOEC 0012FOEC  0012F488 80120588 0012D5B8 0012FO0C  *........4..N..O..O.*  12F410
0000A0  0012FOEC 00118DEC 4010C43E 00118BEC  40130822 00118DEC 0012F420 0013C8F0  *..O..D...H....4..HO*  12F430
0000C0  0012EFD0 0013C868 00118E68 00000000  0013C820 0010C260 0013D140 FF11A6E4  *.......Y..H..B--J..U*  12F450
0000E0  0012F390 0012E8B8 80000000 14000000  40C4C6C8 C5C9C240 0184353C 0080209F  *.3..Y....DFHEIB ...*  12F470
000100  D609C1C4 0000008C D3F7F7F0 00000369  0001700A 04000000 00000000 8C000138  *ORAD....L770....*  12F490
000120  00000000 00000000 00000000 00000000  00000000 00000000 8C000138 0012EFC0  *................*  12F4B0

TRANSACTION STORAGE-USER      ADDRESS 12EFC0   TO 12F38F   LENGTH 000300

000000  8C1303C8 0012E800 00000000 00000000  0013C920 5013EB18 0013E840 00118BA0  *..H..Y....I....Y.H.*  12EFC0
000020  0013DCCC 5013EB00 0013C920 0013CBF7  0013CBF8 0013EAD0 0013C820 0013C820  *.......I...7..8..H.H.*  12EFE0
000040  0013CC98 0013CA30 C0119CC6 00000000  00000000 D3C905C5 40F14060 40000000  *.......F...LINE 1 -*  12F000
000060  00000000 00000000 00000000 00000000  D1D6C240 D5D6D904 C1D3D3E8 40E3C5D9  *..........JOB NORMALLY TER*  12F020
000080  D4C9D5C1 E3C5C4D1 D6C240C1 C2D6D9E3  C5C44D60 60400000 00000000 00000000  **MINATEDJOB ABORTED)--*  12F040
0000A0  00000000 00000000 00000000 0603C440  60400000 00000000 00000000 0A04E800  *........OLD EIB.--...Y.*  12F060
0000C0  04010089 00404040 40404040 40404040  40406D9 C1C4D4F0 F14006D9 F14006D9  *........ORADNO1 OR*  12F080
0000E0  C1C4E2F0 F1400000 00000100 00000000  00000000 00000000 C1C4D4F0 C1D3D3E8  *ADS01........ORAD01 OR*  12F0A0
000100  00000000 00000000 00400000 00000000  00000000 00000000 5013D364 0010C5A0  *...........L..E.*  12F0C0
000120  0012F00C 0012F360 0013D264 00000001  0012F430 0012F420 5013EB00 0012F2E3  *....0--.K..4..4..2T*  12F0E0
000140  0012F2E4 0013EAD0 0013C820 00000000  0013CC98 20100048 00000048 00000000  *..2U...H..H...003.*  12F100
000160  0010C304 00000000 00000000 FFF0F0F3  00000000 00000002 00000001 00000003  *..C..............003.*  12F120
000180  01000000 00000000 00000000 00000000  00000000 00000000 00000000 00000000  *................*  12F140
0001A0  00000000 00000000 00000000 00000000  00000000 00000000 00000000 00000000  *................*  12F160
0001C0  00000000 00000000 00000000 00000000  00000000 00000000 00000000 00000000  *................*  12F180
0001E0  LINES TO 0002A0 SAME AS ABOVE                                               *................*  12F1A0
0002C0  00000000 00000000 00000000 00000000  00000000 D6D9C1C4 F0F1C140 0013C820  *..........ORAD01A ..H.*  12F280
0002E0  00000000 00000000 00000000 00000000  00000000 00000000 00000000 00000000  *................*  12F2A0
000300  00000000 00000000 00000000 00000000  0200000F 00000000 0000001C 3012F844  *................*  12F2C0
000320  0012F00C 00000000 0200000C 00000000  0012F488 80120588 0012F318 00129120  *....0...M..4..N..3.*  12F2E0
000340  00000BE 00130478 01000003 00000000  00000000 00000000 00000000 00129120  *........Z..9....*  12F300
000360  00000000 0012E988 0012F98C 00000000  00000000 00129157 0013DCCC 0013062A  *..........N..3...*  12F320
000380  03000000 FFFFFFE1 00000000 00000000  00000000 80129157 8012FOC5 00000000  *.........O.*  12F340
0003A0  0012F07C 0012EA48 0012F328 0012EA5D  0012FOE5 8012FOC5 00000000 00000000  *..3--.)..0V..0E.....*  12F360
0003C0  00000000 00000000 8C1303C8 00000000  00000000 00000000 00000000 00000000  *..H..Y.*  12F380

TERMINAL CONTROL TBL USER AREA ADDRESS 1007E8   TO 1007F7   LENGTH 000010

000000  00000000 00000000 00000000 00000000                                        *........*  1007E8
```

Fig. 24.5. (Continued)

```
CUSTOMER INFORMATION CONTROL SYSTEM STORAGE DUMP      CODE=ASRA   TASK=GRAD              DATE=07/27/80   TIME=18 43 53   PAGE   10

TERMINAL CONTROL TABLE          ADDRESS  100660  TO  100723        LENGTH  0000C4

000000   D3F7F7F0 99F20404 C0129120 00129120   0012E8B8 00003000 0D1007E8 10000000   *L770.2.............Y.....*   100660
000020   00000000 0C00C900 DD09C1C4 E2F0F140   03697D00 D6D9C1C4 E2F0F140 00000000   *......D6D9C1C4.....'.ORADS01...*   100680
000040   00000000 00000000 07801850 00000000   00000000 00C40000 00000000 00100548   *............D......*   1006A0
000060   0010C370E 00000000 0012D5A0 00000000   00000000 00000000 00840000 0003005C   *.......N..........*   1006C0
000080   00008C00 0C0005C 000C8100 00400000   40000000 00000000 00000000 00000000   *........*.....*   1006E0
0000A0   00000000 00000000 00000000 00001600   00000100 18500000 82000000 D40D0000   *..............MM...*   100700
0000C0   00000000                                                                     *....*                          100720

TERMINAL STORAGE               ADDRESS  129120  TO  1294EF         LENGTH  0003D0

000300   850003C8 00100664 03AA0000 000100F1   000300F0 F0F0F0F0 F0F0F5F0 F0000400   *...H..........1....0000000500...*   129120
000020   F0F0F0F0 F2F3F5F6 000100F0 F0F30006   00F1F0F1 F5F8F100 0400F0F0 F0F0F8F5   *0000.2356...003..101581...000085*   129140
000040   F7F30009 00C3C8C1 C9054D0E2 C1E64040   40404040 40040404 00020000 00020000   *73..CHAIN SAM.............00020.*   129160
000060   00D500F0 F0F1F0F0 F0F00006 00F00F00   F0F00500 F0000F0F0 F0F0F0F0 00000000   *.N.010000..00200000...0020000...*   129180
000080   0600F0F0 F4F0F0F0 F0F00000 00000000   00000000 00000000 00000000 00000000   *..00400000..................*   1291A0
0000A0   00000000 00000000 00000000 00000000   00000000 00000000 00000000 00000000   *....................*   1291C0
                   LINES TO  000300  SAME AS ABOVE                                                                    1291E0
000320   00000006 00F0F0F0 F2F0F0F3 F0F00000   00F0F0F0 F0F00000 00404040 40404040   *......000200000...000400000...*   129440
000340   40404040 40404040 40404040 40404040   40404040 40404040 40404040 40404040   *........*   129460
000360   40404040 40404040 40404040 40404040   40404040 40404040 40404040 40404040   *........*   129480
000380   40404040 40404040 40404040 40404040   40404040 40404040 40404040 40404040   *........*   1294A0
0003A0   40404040 40404040 40404040 40404040   40404040 40404040 40404040 40404040   *.....H....*   1294C0
0003C0   00000000 00000000 850003C8 00100664   40404040 40040000 00000000 00000000   *..................*   1294E0

PROGRAM STORAGE                ADDRESS  13C808  TO  13EF8F         LENGTH  002788

000000   C4C6C8C5 58F0F00C 0 7FF58F0 F00A07FF   00119186 0010C760 05F00700 900EF00A   *DFHE.00.......G--0....0.*   13C808
000020   47F0F082 00118DEC 0012F420 0013C8F0   0012EFD0 0013C868 00118E68 0012E800   *.00....4...H0......Y.*   13C828
000040   0013C820 0010C260 00130140 FF11A6E4   0012F390 0012E888 0012F430 4010C43E   *..H..8--J...U--3...Y--4..D.*   13C848
000060   0013C920 5013EB18 0013EB40 00118BA0   0013DCCC 5013EB00 0013C920 0013C8F7   *..I........7*   13C868
000080   0013CBF8 0013EAD0 9500E000 477F0FA2   0013CC98 0013CA00 00119C6C 58C0F0C6   *....8....H..H......OF*   13C888
0003A0   58E0C000 58D0F0CA 9500E000 477F0FA2   9610D048 92FFE000 47F0F0AC 98CEF03A   *.O....0-O..*   13C8A8
0000C0   90ED00DC 1850989F F0BA9110 0D480719   07FF0700 0013EAD0 0013C820 0013C820   *......0...H--H.*   13C8C8
0000E0   0013CC98 0012F0EC 0013D140 0013EAB6   C3D6C2C6 F2F5F5F1 D6D9C1C4 F0F1C140   *.....0--J...COBF2551ORAD01A*   13C8E8
000100   0013CC24 F0F761F2 F761F8F0 F1F848BF3   F848F4F5 00000000 00000000 00000000   *....0--J...07/27/8018-38-45..*   13C908
000120   03C 905C5 D5D6D9C1 C1D3D3E8 4DE3C5D9   E3C5C4C1 D6C240C1 C2D6D9E3 C5C4060   *LINE .....07/27/8018.38.45...JOB*   13C928
000140   D5D6D9C1 C1D3D3E8 40E3C5D9 D4C905C1   E3C5C4A1 D6C240C1 C2D6D9E3 C5C4060   *NORMALLY TERMINATEDJOB ABORTED -*   13C948
000160   60400000 00000000 00000000 00000000   00000000 0603C640 C5C9C200 00000000   *+-.......OLD EIB..*   13C968
000180   00000000 00000000 00000000 00000000   00000000 00000000 00000000 00000000   *........*   13C988
                   LINES TO  0001C0  SAME AS ABOVE                                                                    13C9A8
0001E0   00000000 00000000 00000000 00000C00   00400000 00000000 00000000 00118DEC   *........*   13C9E8
000200   00000000 00000000 00000000 00000000   00000000 00000000 00000000 00000000   *........*   13CA08
000220   00000000 00000000 00000000 00119C6   00000000 00000000 00000000 00000000   *........*   13CA28
000240   2010004B 00000000 00000000 00000000   00000000 00000000 00000000 00000000   *.....F......*   13CA48
000260   00000000 00000000 00000000 0013C920   00000000 00000000 00000000 00000000   *......I....*   13CA68
                   LINES TO  000380  SAME AS ABOVE                                                                    13CA88
0003A0   D6D9C1C4 F0F1C140 0013C820 00000000   00400000 00000000 00000000 00000000   *ORAD01A .H.......*   13CAA8
0003C0   00000000 00000000 00000000 0013C920   00000000 00000000 00000000 00000000   *.......I.......*   13CBC8
0003E0   00000000 00000000 00000000 0013C920   00000000 00000000 00000000 00000000   *........*   13CBE8
```

Fig. 24.5. (Continued)

```
CUSTOMER INFORMATION CONTROL SYSTEM STORAGE DUMP   CODE=ASRA   TASK=ORAD        DATE=07/27/80   TIME=18 43 53   PAGE  11

PROGRAM STORAGE                 ADDRESS  13C808  TO  13EF8F      LENGTH  002788

000400   00000000 00000000 00000000 00000000   00000000 00000000 00000000 00000000   *................................*   13CC08
000420   LINES TO 000440 SAME AS ABOVE                                                                                     13CC28
000460   00000000 00000000 0013DCCC 00000000   00000000 00000000 00000000 00000000   *................................*   13CC68
000480   00000000 00000000 00000000 00000000   0013EB40 0013C812 0013EE90 0013EB98   *..................  ..H.........*   13CC88
0004A0   0013C820 0013D296 0013D4E4 0013D536   0013D5EC 0013D600 0013D66C 0013DCC6   *..H...K...MU..N...N...O...O....F*   13CCA8
0004C0   0013DCCC 0013DEC0 0013DED4 0013E20A   0013E256 0013E2E0 0013E300 0013E402   *...........M..S...S...S...T...U.*   13CCC8
0004E0   0013E498 0013E596 0013E65E 0013E856   0013E86A 0013E950 0013E976 0013E9AA   *..U...V...W ..Y...Y...Z...Z...Z.*   13CCE8
000500   0013E9C0 0013E9D6 0013E9E2 0013E9EE   0013EA48 0013EA58 0013EA88 0013EAA6   *..Z...ZO..ZS..Z.................*   13CD08
000520   0013EAAE 0013D27E 0013D264 0013D278   0013D3C0 0013D406 0013D420 0013D472   *......K=..K...K...L...M...M...M.*   13CD28
000540   0013D4DE 0013D478 0013D47E 0013D59A   0013D62A 0013D65E 0013D74C 0013D6E8   *..M...M...M=..N...O...O ..P...OY*   13CD48
000560   0013D738 0013D76E 0013D7FC 0013D7E6   0013D7CC 0013D7E0 0013D8BC 0013D844   *..P...P...P...PW..P...P...Q...Q.*   13CD68
000580   0013D8A8 0013D97C 0013D904 0013D968   0013DA48 0013D9DA 0013DA34 0013DB02   *..Q...R...R...R.......R.........*   13CD88
0005A0   0013DA90 0013DAEE 0013DBCE 0013DB60   0013DBBA 0013DBEE 0013DC34 0013DC2E   *..............-.................*   13CDA8
0005C0   0013DCBA 0013DC4C 0013DCA6 0013DCE0   0013DD6C 0013DD58 0013DDAA 0013DE16   *................................*   13CDC8
0005E0   0013DE02 0013DE54 0013DEAC 0013DF38   0013DF22 0013DF48 0013E658 0013E61E   *..........................W...W.*   13CDE8
000600   0013E672 0013DCCC 00000100 FFE1FFFF   00030000 00630000 00000001 00020004   *..W.............................*   13CE08
000620   00000C00 00080000 000C0010 00200040   007D007F 00090181 002C0025 03BE053C   *.............  .'...............*   13CE28
000640   FFFD0000 001F0202 80000403 00000000   00000000 00000000 0206F000 04050406   *.........................O......*   13CE48
000660   03000000 0C000000 00000204 C0000424   01000000 00000000 00000000 D6D9C1C4   *............................ORAD*   13CE68
000680   D4F0F1D6 D9C1C4E2 F0F11802 D0000401   00000005 09000000 200A04E8 00040100   *M01ORADS01.................Y....*   13CE88
0006A0   8900C9D5 E5C1D3C9 C440D6D9 C4C5D940   D5E4D4C2 C5D9C9D5 E5C1D3C9 C440C4D6   *..INVALID ORDER NUMBERINVALID DO*   13CEA8
0006C0   C3E4D4C5 D5E340D5 E4D4C2C5 D9C9D5E5   C1D3C9C4 40C4C5D7 C1D9E3D4 C5D5E340   *CUMENT NUMBERINVALID DEPARTMENT *   13CEC8
0006E0   D5E4D4C2 C5D9F0F0 F1F3F2C9 D5E5C1D3   C9C440D6 D9C4C5D9 60C4C1E3 C5C9D5E5   *NUMBER00132INVALID ORDER-DATEINV*   13CEE8
000700   C1D3C9C4 40C9E3C5 D440D5E4 D4C2C5D9   C9D5E5C1 D3C9C440 C4C5E2C3 D9C9D7E3   *ALID ITEM NUMBERINVALID DESCRIPT*   13CF08
000720   C9D6D5C9 D5E5C1D3 C9C440E4 D5C9E340   C3D6E2E3 C9D5E5C1 D3C9C440 C3D6E2E3   *IONINVALID UNIT COSTINVALID COST*   13CF28
000740   C9D5E5C1 D3C9C440 E4D5C9E3 40D7D9C9   C3C5C9D5 E5C1D3C9 C440D7D9 C9C3C5C9   *INVALID UNIT PRICEINVALID PRICEI*   13CF48
000760   D5C3D6D4 D7D3C5E3 C540C4C1 E3C1D5D6   40D3C9D5 C540C9E3 C5D440C5 D5E3C5D9   *NCOMPLETE DATANO LINE ITEM ENTER*   13CF68
000780   C5C4C9D5 C3D6D9D9 C5C3E340 E3D6E3C1   D340C3D6 E2E3C9D5 C3D6D9D9 C5C3E340   *EDINCORRECT TOTAL COSTINCORRECT *   13CF88
0007A0   E3D6E3C1 D340D7D9 C9C3C5C0 02C00004   00008C00 0204C000 04130E00 00000000   *TOTAL PRICE.....................*   13CFA8
0007C0   00000000 0000D6D9 E3C5E2E3 0604F000   04280044 000C0480 00040000 4000D6F1   *......ORTEST..0............. .O1*   13CFC8
0007E0   1402F800 04000000 031804D0 00040000   00000562 04000020 0E08E000 0400001C   *...8............................*   13CFE8
000800   001804D1 00040000 00001520 04000020   C4E4D7D3 C9C3C1E3 C5406060 40D5D6E3   *...J..............DUPLICATE -- NOT*   13D008
000820   40C1C3C3 C5D7E3C5 C40C02E0 00040000   CC00D6D9 C4C5D940 C2E8D7C1 E2E2C5C4   * ACCEPTED.........ORDER BYPASSED*   13D028
000840   406040C3 D6D5E3C9 D5E4C518 04000004   00000000 05E20400 00200204 8000042C   * - CONTINUE...........S..........*   13D048
000860   00000000 00000000 00000000 0A068000   04000021 0C020480 00041400 00000000   *................................*   13D068
000880   00000000 000000C4 E2E7E3C1 C2E2060C   B0000400 20A00006 0ED40004 0100B000   *.......DSXTABS............M......*   13D088
0008A0   F9F9F9F8 F50A02E0 00040000 4100C5D5   E3C5D940 C6C9D9E2 E340D6D9 C4C5D904   *99985.........ENTER FIRST ORDER.*   13D0A8
0008C0   04300004 00000081 00004000 00000E08   00000400 001000E3 C5D3F2D6 D7C5D50E   *..........  ..............TEL2OPEN.*   13D0C8
0008E0   04800004 00000200 D4C1D740 C6C1C9D3   E4D9C5D7 D9D6C3C5 E2E240C5 D9D9D6D9   *.........MAP FAILUREPROCESS ERROR*   13D0E8
000900   E2C9C7D5 D6D540E5 C9D6D3C1 E3C9D6D5   E3C1C2D3 C540D5D6 E340D3D6 C1C4C5C4   *SIGNON VIOLATIONTABLE NOT LOADED*   13D108
000920   C5D9D9E2 1C028000 040000FE 00D4C1D1   D6D940C5 D9D9D6D9 5840D004 58404018   *ERRS..........MAJOR ERROR. ...   .*   13D128
000940   58104000 5010D224 58104004 5010D228   1B1158F0 C00405EF D2116070 C1B69240   *.. ...K... ...K....O....K.-.A.. *   13D148
000960   6082D206 60836082 41106070 5010D274   58E0D22C 4110E00C 5010D278 9680D278   *-.K.-.-...-...K...K.......K...K.*   13D168
000980   4110D274 58F0C004 05EFD211 6070C1C8   92406082 D2066083 60824110 60705010   *..K..O....K.-.AH. -.K.-.-...-...*   13D188
0009A0   D2749680 D2744110 D27458F0 C00405EF   58E0D224 4810E014 4130C010 4910C18E   *K...K...K..O......K...........A.*   13D1A8
0009C0   05204720 20228B10 000147C0 20224811   20188910 00025811 300007F1 0013000E   *...........................1....*   13D1C8
0009E0   000E000E D2116070 C1DA9240 6082D206   60836082 41106070 5010D274 9680D274   *....K.-.A.. -.K.-.-...-...K...K.*   13D1E8
000A00   4110D274 58F0C004 05EF58E0 D2244810   E0144130 C0104910 C18C0520 4720201E   *..K..O.......K..........A.......*   13D208
000A20   8B100001 47C0201E 48112018 89100002   58113000 07F10017 00184830 E0184930   *...................1...........*   13D228
000A40   C17858F0 C094078F 5820C098 58E0D228   95F1E000 07725810 C01407F1 5820C09C   *A..O...........K..1.........1....*   13D248
000A60   58E0D228 95F0E000 07725810 C04C07F1   5810C070 07F158E0 D2244830 E0184930   *..K..O.........1.....1..K.......*   13D268
```

Fig. 24.5. (Continued)

CUSTOMER INFORMATION CONTROL SYSTEM STORAGE DUMP   CODE=ASRA   TASK=DRAD   DATE=07/27/80   TIME=18 43 53   PAGE 12

ADDRESS 13C808   TO 13EF8F   LENGTH 002788

PROGRAM STORAGE

(hexadecimal storage dump listing)

Fig. 24.5. (Continued)

CUSTOMER INFORMATION CONTROL SYSTEM STORAGE DUMP   CODE=ASRA   TASK=QRAD   DATE=07/27/80   TIME=18 43 53   PAGE   13

PROGRAM STORAGE   ADDRESS 13C808   TO   13EF8F   LENGTH 002788

```
0010E0  D1FC94F0 E07A960C E07A4830 C1945A30    E09B5030 E09B5810 C0F407F1 C0F407F1  58E00238  13D8E8
0011O0  D203E077 C1960210 6011C277 92460622    D2006023 6022410O 001F5A00 D2585000  D2585000  13D908
001120  D2585B8E0 D2304140 E3305A40 D2585040    D2685B8E0 D268D21B E0006008 1B005900          1B005900  13D928
001140  D25859F0 C0FCC07F C0FCC07F 4140E060    5A400254 D2014000 C17E5810 C0F407F1          C0F407F1  13D948
001160  4100005D 59000258 58F0C0F4 077F5810    C02C07F1 58E00238 4830E033 4930C178          4930C178  13D968
001180  58F0C100 078F5820 C008D007 E0362000    5810C104 0771F873 D1F8E077 FC6201F9          FC6201F9  13D988
0011A0  E074F277 D200E036 F9460203 D1F958F0    C104077F F2770200 E036F4A4 E07FD203          E07FD203  13D9A8
0011C0  4830C19A 5A30E09B 5030E09B 5810C100    07F1D20B 601LC2A4 92406010 D205601E          D205601E  13D9C8
0011E0  601D4100 001F5A00 D2585000 D2585000    D2304140 E335A440 E3305A40 5A400254          5A400254  13D9E8
001200  D268D21B E0006008 1B005900 D2585B8E0    C1080777 58E00230 4140E06A 5A400254          5A400254  13DA08
001220  D2014000 C17E5810 C1000771 4100005D    59000258 58F0C100 077F5810 C02C07F1          C02C07F1  13DA28
001240  58E00238 4830E03E 4930C178 58F0C178    078F5820 C008D006 E0412000 5810C110          5810C110  13DA48
001260  0771F276 D200E041 F833E07B D2049A4F0    E07E960C E07E4830 C19C5A30 E09B5030          E09B5030  13DA68
001280  E09B5810 C10C07F1 58E00238 D203E07B    C1960211 601LC280 92406023 4100001F          4100001F  13DA88
0012A0  5A00D258 50000258 58E00238 4140E33D    5A400258 50400268 58E00268 D21B8E000          D21B8E000  13DAA8
0012C0  60081B00 59000258 58F0C114 077F5810    C02C07F1 5810C02C 077F158E0 4000C17E          4000C17E  13DAC8
0012E0  5810C10C C10C07F1 4100 00505900 D2585B8F0    C10C07F1 5810C02C C11C0771 D2384830          D2384830  13DAE8
001300  E0484930 C17858F0 C11807BF 5820C008    20005810 4830E048 C11C0771 F8730200          F8730200  13DB08
001320  E07BFC62 D201E074 F277D1F8 E04BF946    D1F8D201 077FF277 D206C011 C2C29240          C2C29240  13DB28
001340  FA44E084 D2034830 C19E5A30 E09B5030    E09B5810 C11807F1 D20C6011 4140E330          4140E330  13DB48
001360  601ED204 601F601E 4100001F 5A00D258    50000258 58E00230 4140E330 5A40D258          5A40D258  13DB68
001380  50400268 58E00268 D21B8E000 60081B00    59000258 58F0C120 077F58E0 D2304140          D2304140  13DB88
0013A0  E07F5A40 D254D201 4000C17E 5810C118    07F14100 00505900 D2585B8F0 C11807FF          C11807FF  13DBA8
0013C0  5810C02C 077F158E0 D2385830 E09B4930    C1A058F0 C124078F 5830E09B 4930C1A2          4930C1A2  13DBC8
0013E0  58F0C128 077F4800 C17C5900 D2585B8F0    C12C077F 5810C254 41200002C 1C024120          1C024120  13DBE8
001400  00531D02 50100260 5B8E00230 4140E025    5A400260 50400268 58E00268 58F00238          58F00238  13DC08
001420  D22BE000 F0533810 C13007F1 58E00238    5830E09B 4930C178 58F0C134 07F14100          07F14100  13DC28
001440  C13007F1 4100001F 5A00D258 50400268    58E00268 D21B8E000 60081B00 59000258          59000258  13DC48
001460  58E0D230 4140E33D 5A40D258 50400268    58E00268 D21B8E000 60081B00 077F14100          077F14100  13DC68
001480  58F0C138 077F58E0 D2304140 E0375A40    D254D201 4000C17E 5810C130 07F14100          07F14100  13DC88
0014A0  005D5900 D2585B8F0 C13007FF C1100777    00535A00 00535A00 D2545000 D2545810          D2545810  13DCA8
0014C0  D27007F1 41C0005D 59000258 58F0C13C    077F5810 C04007F1 41000053 59000254          59000254  13DCC8
0014E0  58F0C140 077F58E0 077F58E0 E09B4930    C17858F0 C140077F 41000O1F 5A00D258          5A00D258  13DCE8
001500  50000258 58E00230 4140E330 5A400268    50400268 58E00268 0213E000 C2DE58E0          C2DE58E0  13DD08
001520  D2689240 E01458E0 D26858F0 D2680206    E015F014 1B005900 59000258 58F0C140          58F0C140  13DD28
001540  58E0D230 D201E037 C17E5810 C14007F1    41000005D 59000258 58F0C140 077F5810          077F5810  13DD48
001560  C03407F1 5820C008 58E00230 D008E325    C148D771 F2780200 D206E015 E32558E0          E32558E0  13DD68
001580  D238F944 D203E07F 58F0C148 077F58E0    D23C58F0 D238F844 E01F907F 5810C14C          5810C14C  13DD88
0015A0  07F14100 001F5A00 D2585000 D2585B8E0    D2304140 E335A440 D2585040 D26858E0          D26858E0  13DDA8
0015C0  D268D213 E01C02F2 58E00268 9240E014    58E00268 58F00268 D206E015 F0141800          F0141800  13DDC8
0015E0  59000258 58F0C150 077F58E0 D2300201    E322C17E 5810C14C 07F14100 005D5900          005D5900  13DDE8
001600  D2585B8F0 C14C077F 5810C034 07F15820    C008 58E0 D2300D08 E3312000 5810C154          5810C154  13DE08
001620  0771F278 D200E031 58E00238 D25858B8F0    E08458F0 C154077F 58E00230 077F58F0 D268 58F0D238          58F0D238  13DE28
001640  F844E01E F0845810 C03407F1 4100001F    077F5810 C03407F1 4800C17C 4140E330          4140E330  13DE48
001660  5A40D258 50400268 58E00268 D214E000    C30658F0 D2689240 E01558E0 D26858F0          D26858F0  13DE68
001680  D268D205 E016F015 1B005900 D2585B8F0    C158077F 58E00230 D201E32E C17E5810          C17E5810  13DE88
0016A0  C03407F1 41000005D 59000258 58F0C034    077F5810 C03407F1 4800C17C 59000258          59000258  13DEA8
0016C0  58F0C038 077F58F0 C04007F1 1B005810    D2544120 00531D02 4A10C18A 4830E023 C178 58F0          C17858F0  13DEC8
0016E0  4010E023 4830E023 4930C1A4 58F0C15C    07DF58E0 D2385830 E09B4930 C17858F0          C17858F0  13DEE8
001700  C160077F 58E0D23C 4830E023 4830C18C    40300023 4830C18C 07F158E0 D23C4830          D23C4830  13DF08
001720  E0234B30 C18A4030 E0235810 C16407F1    58E0D23C 4830C18C 4030E023                    4030E023  13DF28
```

Fig. 24.5. (Continued)

```
CUSTOMER INFORMATION CONTROL SYSTEM STORAGE DUMP   CODE=ASRA   TASK=ORAD       DATE=07/27/80   TIME=18 43 53   PAGE  14

PROGRAM STORAGE              ADDRESS  13C808   TO  13EF8F        LENGTH  002788

001740  D20160B9 C1A6D208 6070C31B 92406079  D20F607A 60794110 60705010 D27458E0  *K.-.A.K.-.C.. -.K.- -...-...K...*  13DF48
001760  D22C4110 E0085010 D2784110 60B95010  D27C9680 D27C4110 D27458F0 C00405EF  *K.......K...-...K...K...K..O....*  13DF68
001780  58E0D234 58F0D23C D201E023 F0235820  C08C0522 58E0D234 4100E000 4810D24E  *..K..OK.K...O..........K.......K+*  13DF88
0017A0  58E0D23C 4120E000 413001B1 BF38C19F  0E025820 C08C0522 58E0D234 4830E023  *..K...........A...........K.....*  13DFA8
0017C0  4C30C1A8 4A30C1AA 58E0D238 4030E0A3  58F0D23C D209E089 F000D211 6070C324  *..A...A...K. ....OK.K...O.K.-.C.*  13DFC8
0017E0  92406082 D2066083 60824110 60705010  D2749680 D2744110 D27458F0 C00405EF  *. -.K.-.-...-...K...K...K..O....*  13DFE8
001800  58E0D224 4810E014 4130C010 4910C18C  05204720 201E8B10 000147C0 201E4811  *..K............A.................*  13E008
001820  20188910 00025811 300007F1 0016000D  D205609A C3369240 60A0D200 60A160A0  *............1....K.-.C.. -.K.-.-.*  13E028
001840  D2086070 C33C9240 6079D20F 607A6079  41106070 5010D274 4110609A 5010D278  *K.-.C.. -.K.- -...-...K...-...K.*  13E048
001860  58E0D234 4110E000 5010D27C 58E0D238  4110E0A3 5010D280 4110E089 5010D284  *..K........K...K.......K.......K.*  13E068
001880  9680D284 4110D274 58F0C004 05EF5820  C08C0522 D2086070 C3459240 6079D20F  *..K...K..O...........K.-.C.. -.K.*  13E088
0018A0  607A6079 41106070 5010D274 58E0D234  4110E000 5010D278 9680D278 4110D274  *- -...-...K...K.......K...K...K.*  13E0A8
0018C0  58F0C004 05EF5820 C08C0522 D20160B9  C1AAD208 6070C31B 92406079 D20F607A  *.O...........K.-.A.K.-.C.. -.K.- *  13E0C8
0018E0  60794110 60705010 D27458E0 D22C4110  E0145010 D2784110 60B95010 D27C9680  *-...-...K...K.........K...-...K...*  13E0E8
001900  D27C4110 D27458F0 C00405EF 58E0D240  58F0D23C D202E000 F1B1D205 E003F013  *K...K..O.......K .OK.K...1.K...O.*  13E108
001920  D209E009 F000F844 E01BF019 F844E020  F01E58F0 D230D207 E013F020 58E0D238  *K...O.8...O.8...O..OK.K...O...K.*  13E128
001940  D201E0A9 C1AAD201 60B9C18C D20160B0  C34ED208 607CC350 92406079 D20F607A  *K...A.K.-.A.K.-.C+K.-.C.. -.K.- *  13E148
001960  60794110 60705010 D2744110 60B95010  D2784110 E09F5010 D27C4110 60B05010  *-...-...K...-...K.........K...-...*  13E168
001980  D28058E0 D2404110 E0005010 D28458E0  D2384110 E0A95010 D2889680 D2884110  *K...K .......K...K..........K...K...*  13E188
0019A0  D27458F0 C00405EF D206608A C1EC9240  6091D206 6092C1F3 92406099 D20E607C  *K..O.....K.-.A.. -.K.-.A3. -.K.-.*  13E1A8
0019C0  C3599240 607FD209 6080607F 41106070  5010D274 4110608A 5010D278 411060D9  *C.. -.K.-.-...-...K...-...K...-R*  13E1C8
0019E0  5010D27C 411060D7 5010D280 41106092  5010D284 9680D284 4110D274 58F0C004  *..K...-P..K...-...K...K...K..O..*  13E1E8
001A00  05EF92F1 6000D201 60B9C179 D2086070  C3689240 6079D20F 607A6079 41106070  *...1-.K.-.A.K.-.C.. -.K.- -...-.*  13E208
001A20  5010D274 58E0D224 4110E008 5010D278  41106000 5010D27C 411060B9 5010D280  *..K...K.........K...-...K...-...K.*  13E228
001A40  9680D280 4110D274 58F0C004 05EFD206  608AC1EC 92406091 D2066092 C1F39240  *..K...K..O.....K.-.A.. -.K.-.A3. *  13E248
001A60  6099D201 60B9C17E D20E6070 C3719240  607FD209 6080607F 41106070 5010D274  *-.K.-.A=K.-.C.. -.K.-.-...-...K.*  13E268
001A80  4110608A 5010D278 58E0D230 4110E000  5010D27C 411060D7 5010D280 41106092  *..-...K...K.........K...-P..K...-.*  13E288
001AA0  5010D284 411060D9 5010D288 411060D9  5010D28C 411060D9 5010D290 411060B9  *..K...-R..K...-R..K...-R..K...-.*  13E2A8
001AC0  5010D294 9680D294 4110D274 58F0C004  05EF5810 C03C07F1 58E0D230 D218E33D  *..K...K...K..O............1..K.K.T.*  13E2C8
001AE0  C3809240 E356D201 E357E356 D201E010  C17E5810 C04007F1 D20160B9 C1ACD208  *C.. T.K.T.T.K...A=... .1K.-.A.K.*  13E2E8
001B00  6070C399 92406079 D20F607A 60794110  60705010 D27458E0 D22C4110 E0045010  *-.C.. -.K.- -...-...K...K.........*  13E308
001B20  D2784110 60B95010 D27C4110 605B5010  D2809680 D2804110 D27458F0 C00405EF  *K...-...K...-$..K...K...K..O.....*  13E328
001B40  58E0D230 D218E33D C3A29240 E356D201  E357E356 D206608A C1EC9240 6091D206  *..K.K.T.C.. T.K.T.T.K.-.A.. -.K.*  13E348
001B60  6092C1F3 92406099 D20E6070 C3B89240  607FD209 6080607F 41106070 5010D274  *-.A3. -.K.-.C.. -.K.-.-...-...K.*  13E368
001B80  4110608A 5010D278 4110E000 5010D27C  411060D7 5010D280 41106092 5010D284  *..-...K.........K...-P..K...-...K.*  13E388
001BA0  9680D284 4110D274 58F0C004 05EF92F1  6000D201 60B9C179 D2086070 C3689240  *..K...K..O......1-.K.-.A.K.-.C.. *  13E3A8
001BC0  6079D20F 607A6079 41106070 5010D274  58E0D224 4110E008 5010D278 41106000  *-.K.- -...-...K...K.........K...-.*  13E3C8
001BE0  5010D27C 411060B9 5010D280 9680D280  4110D274 58F0C004 05EFD211 6070C3CA  *..K...-...K...K...K..O.....K.-.C.*  13E3E8
001C00  92406082 D2066083 60824110 60705010  D2749680 D2744110 D27458F0 C00405EF  *. -.K.-.-...-...K...K...K..O....*  13E408
001C20  58E0D224 4810E014 4130C010 4910C18A  05204720 201C8B10 000147C0 201C4811  *..K............A.................*  13E428
001C40  20188910 00025811 300007F1 001058E0  D23858F0 D224D203 E093F010 D203E097  *............1....K..OK.K...O.K...*  13E448
001C60  C1ECD208 6070C3DC 92406079 D20F607A  60794110 60705010 D2744110 E0935010  *A.K.-.C.. -.K.- -...-...K........*  13E468
001C80  D2789680 D2784110 D27458F0 C00405EF  D20160B9 C1AED208 6070C31B 92406079  *K...K...K..O.....K.-.A.K.-.C.. -.*  13E488
001CA0  D20F607A 60794110 60705010 D27458E0  D22C4110 E0105010 D2784110 60B95010  *K.- -...-...K...K.........K...-...*  13E4A8
001CC0  D27C9680 D27C4110 D27458F0 C00405EF  4800C1B0 5000D264 58E0D238 92C4E0D2  *K...K...K..O........A...K...K..D.K*  13E4C8
001CE0  D203E0D3 C1B2D211 6070C3E5 92406082  D2066083 60824110 60705010 D2749680  *K..LA.K.-.CV. -.K.-.-...-...K...*  13E4E8
001D00  D2744110 D27458F0 C00405EF 58E0D224  4810E014 4130C010 4910C18A 05204720  *K...K..O........K..............A.....*  13E508
001D20  201C8B10 000147C0 201C4811 20188910  00025811 300007F1 0012D206 609AC3F7  *..........................1..K.-.C7*  13E528
001D40  924060A1 D2086070 C3FE9240 6079D20F  607A6079 41106070 5010D274 4110609A  *. -.K.-.C.. -.K.- -...-...K...-.*  13E548
001D60  5010D278 411060D9 5010D27C 411060D7  5010D280 58E0D238 4110E0D2 5010D284  *..K...-R..K...-P..K...K.....K..K.*  13E568
001D80  9680D284 4110D274 58F0C004 05EFD206  609AC3F7 924060A1 D2086070 C4079240  *..K...K..O....K.-.C7. -.K.-.D.. *  13E588
```

Fig. 24.5. (Continued)

CUSTOMER INFORMATION CONTROL SYSTEM STORAGE DUMP   ADDRESS 13C808   TO 13EF8F   CODE=ASRA   TASK=DRAD   LENGTH 002788   DATE=07/27/80   TIME=18 43 53   PAGE   15

```
PROGRAM STORAGE

001DA0   6079D20F  607A6079  41106070  50100274   4110609A  4110D278  58E0022C  4110E018    *-K.-....K.....K.....K....*   13E5A8
001DC0   50100227C  41106CD7  50100280  58E00238   4110ED02  50100284  41106D07  50100288    *..-..P..K......-.P..K...P*   13E5C8
001DE0   41106307  50100C28C  9680D28C  41100274   58F0C058  05EF5820  C16858E0  D24495C4    *..-.P-.A.-..D.......A..K.N*   13E5E8
001E00   E0300772  5820C16C  D502F005  C4100772   5810C058  07F15820  C16858E0  D2445040    *..-.A.N-D......l-A..K.N..*   13E608
001E20   E026C413  07824100  00035A00  D2645300   5813C054  07F14800  C1B05900  D26458F0    *.D.......-D.....l.A..K..0*   13E628
001E40   26858F0  D26858FC  D24D0202  E300F005   42200003  1D00  58100264   *A...K..K..0....A..K....*   13E648
001E60   CITDO77F  5810C078  07F11800  0A215BE0   42200003  1D00  58100264    *A..K..K.....A..K....*   13E668
001E80   E1B45820  C0900522  58100014  0A215BE0   23380207  E0CA1000  58E0023C  58F00238    *.K..K.K....-..0.K..K..K.*   13E688
001EA0   D201E013  F0CA02C1  E015FCCD  E015E017   F0D05B82  2228D202  E1B1F301  58E00238    *...0.K..0K..0..K..K..K.*   13E6A8
001EC0   D201E0A5  C1AED208  6070C415  07050010   D20F607A  60794110  60705010  2744110    *K..A.K..D-..K....K..K...*   13E6C8
001EE0   E093501C  027858E0  23C4110  E0005010   D27580E0  D2384110  E0A55010  2809680    *..K.....D..K....K..-.K.*   13E6E8
001F00   D2804110  027458F0  C0040EEF  D23C4110   05220208  6070C345  92406079  D20F607A    *K...K..0..-..K......-K-.*   13E708
001F20   60794110  60705010  027458F0  023C4110   E0005010  D2789680  D2784110  027458F0    *...-.K..0.K.....K..K...0*   13E728
001F40   C0040EEF  5820C090  05220201  06091AC   D2086070  C3999240  6079D20F  607A6079    *..-.A...K..-.......K-.-.*   13E748
001F60   41106070  50100274  58E0022C  41100E04   50100278  41106089  50100270  41136058    *..-.K..K....K...K..K..X*   13E768
001F80   D209E34F  E34ED206  608AC1EC  92406091   D2065092  C1F19240  6099020F  9240E34E    *..4N.4NK..A..@.K...A1@.-.T+*   13E788
001FA0   92406077  F2096080  607F4110  60705010   0274411C  608A5010  D2784110  607C03B8    *.@..-.-..K....-..K...-.C.*   13E7A8
001FC0   D27C4110  60D75010  02804110  60925010   2894960  2894110  D274S8F0  C00405EF    *K...P.K...-.K...K..K..0-*   13E7C8
001FE0   92F16000  D203600A8  C1ECD201  608C179   D2086070  C3689240  6079020F  607A6079    *A1-.....A.K..K.-.K....K-.-.*   13E7E8
002000   41106070  50100274  41106089  50100278   41106000  50100270C  41136089  50100280    *..-.K..K..K....K..K..K.*   13E808
002020   9680D280  41100274  58F0C004  50EF58E0   D2380207  E0A86029  9240E0C2  0206E0C3    *K...K..0.K..K....K..-.K.C*   13E828
002040   E0C202201  60B9C184  020F6070  C42F9240   607FD209  6080607F  41106070  50100274    *..-...A..-.C-@.-K..-.K..K.*   13E848
002060   41106009  50100278  41106007  50100270C   58E0D238  41100EAB  50100280  41106089    *..-.K..K..K...R.A..K..K.*   13E868
002080   50100284  9680D284  41100274  58F3C004   05EFD211  6070C3CA  92406082  D2066083    *K....K..-...K..-.K.-.K..*   13E888
0020A0   60824110  60705010  027449680  027441110   C00405EF  58E00224  481C0E014  00025811    *.-..-.K..0..-.A.K........*   13E8A8
0020C0   41300010  4910C18A  05204720  021C8810   0C147C0  20108910  20189910  00025811    *.-...A..-..K..0..........*   13E8C8
0020E0   30000F71  001558E0  023858F0  0224D203   E093601C  D203E097  F0080208  6070C30C    *...-..-..0.K.....K..K..C*   13E8E8
002100   92406079  D20F607A  60794110  60705010   D27441110  E0935010  02784110  0278411O    *.@..K-.-..K....K..K..K.*   13E908
002120   D2745BF0  C00405EF  02086070  C43E9240   6079020F  607A6079  41106070  50100274    *K..0.-...-.C>@.-K-.-..K.*   13E928
002140   96800274  41100274  58F0C004  05EF0207   609AC447  D2086070  C44F9240  6079020F    *K...K..0....-.D.K.-.DO@..*   13E948
002160   96800274  41106070  50100274  58F0C004   50100278  9680D278  41100274  5079020F    *K..-.K..0..K.K..K...*   13E968
002180   607A6079  41106070  50100274  4110609A   50100278  9680D278  41100274  58F0C004    *-.-..-.K..K.K..K..K..0*   13E988
0021A0   05EFD20A  604AC458  92406055  D2036056   E0300278  D20C604A  C4639240  6079020F    *..K.-.D.@.K..-..K.D.@..*   13E9A8
0021C0   60570201  6086057  5810C080  07F1020F   604C470   5810C080  07F1D20F  604C480    *-...-.K...l..-K-...l..*   13E9C8
0021E0   5810C080  07F158E0  02240201  6063E01B   D2056065  E01DD203  50A6C490  D2086070    *.K...-K...K..K...-K..D.K.-.*   13E9E8
00200   C4494940  6079020F  607A6079  41106070   50100274  41106070  50100278  9680D278    *D..@..-K-.-..-.K..K.-K.*   13EA08
00220   41100274  58F0C004  50EFD20A  604C49D   F2036056  F2036056  60551080  C08007F1    *..K..0.K.-.K..K....K.*   13EA28
00240   58E00238  D21EE0AB  603B5810  C6007F1   18004000  02440250  50150278  D24E58E0    *.K..-..K.-.K..-.K..*   13EA48
00260   D2344810  E0234C10  C1A84410  D24C4010   D24C4810  D24E4410  024C4010  D24E07F3    *.K..-.K.K..A..K.K..K.K.3*   13EA68
00280   41000188  40000250  58E0D23C  5810E184   4C10C180  4A10D25C  43100250  07F35830    *..K....K..-.K..-.K.2.K*   13EA88
0022A0   C0840533  05223830  C0880533  05250500   5008S050  D0045820  C0009500  20000779    *...2..................*   13EAA8
0022C0   92FF2000  96100048  50E00054  05F09120   D0487FEC  F0165800  B0489820  B0505BE0    *...O...O.............0*   13EAC8
0022E0   DO5437FE  96200048  41600048  41160004   4170C178  06700555  58401000  1E485040    *...K..........K..*   13EAE8
002300   10308716  50004180  D1F44170  D1F70510   58008000  1E085000  80008786  10000203    *.........J4.J7....K.*   13EB08
002320   D270C178  58600DF4  58E0D180  906D060   C3D60907  D74B40F1  FFF5FF4  F66003C2    *.K.J....5746-CB*   13EB28
002340   F140C3D6  D7EB09C9  C7C8E340  C9C2D440   C3D60907  4B40F1F9  F9F7F4F6  F4F66003    *.l COPYRIGHT IBM CORP. 1973*   13EB48
002360   D4F440C3  D6D7E8D9  C9C7C8E3  40C9C204   40C30609  D74B40F1  F9F7F3C6  C540F2F4    *M4 COPYRIGHT IBM CORP. 1973FE 24*   13EB68
002380   F6F3F5F6  C6C540F2  F4F6F3F5  90CF288   00C3C8C0  E2C3C8F0  F2F5F0  89800008    *6356FE 24657....OO.ILBDSCHO2500*   13EB88
0023A0   F1F261F2  F061F7F8  90CF288  1BB85841   00CC8840  0018182E  58820000  89000008    *12/20/78..2.........*   13EBA8
0023C0   88800318  1AB84122  00344640  F328412D   00604132  0001192FF  200018AB  1AA388A0    *......0.....2....*   13EBC8
0023E0   000289A0  00022680  50BA0004  44B0F28A   5850FC20  58410000  88400018  50400008    *......2..........*   13EBE8
```

Fig. 24.5. (Continued)

```
CUSTOMER INFORMATION CONTROL SYSTEM STORAGE DUMP   CODE=ASRA   TASK=ORAD        DATE=07/27/80   TIME=18 43 53   PAGE   16

PROGRAM STORAGE              ADDRESS  13C808  TO  13EF8F       LENGTH  002788

002400   9200A010 188E47F0 F0DC4640 F2724132   00015880 F2C058BA 000444B0 F27E9201   *.......00.. 2.......2.......2=..*   13EC08
002420   A01058C1 00005871 00041897 06704841   000E504A 000C1C64 1A7C1889 88800001   *...A............................*   13EC28
002440   89800001 15891807 4770F0BE 1B041A0C   88000001 584A0008 4480F28A 188E47F0   *..........0..............2....0*   13EC48
002460   F0D64188 00044858 00021A50 48980000   89900018 88900018 18690690 95888000   *00..............................*   13EC68
002480   4780F128 4720F110 95208000 4780F130   4720F214 95108000 4780F180 4740F19E   *..1...1.......1...2........1.. 1.*   13EC88
0024A0   95A08000 4780F1A6 4740F1FA 4490F290   97803000 47F0F21C 4490F290 47F0F21C   *......1.. 1...2.......02...2..02.*   13ECA8
0024C0   18B91AB5 9103B000 4740F15E 4490F2A2   18B94199 00018990 00041A9B 4490F29C   *......... 1 ..2...............2.*   13ECC8
0024E0   1AB341BB 000196FF B00047F0 F21C18B9   41990001 89900004 1A9B4490 F29696D0   *............02..............2...*   13ECE8
002500   30001AB3 41BB0001 96FFB000 47F0F21C   18B91AB5 9130B000 4740F128 4710F19E   *..............02.......... 1...1.*   13ED08
002520   4490F2A2 1A939730 900047F0 F21C4490   F2A247F0 F21C18B9 1AB59103 B0004740   *..2.........02...2..02.......... *   13ED28
002540   F1D418B9 41990001 89900004 1A9B4490   F29696F0 30001AB3 41BB0001 96FFB000   *1M...............2..0............*   13ED48
002560   47F0F21C 4490F2A2 18B94199 00018990   00041A9B 4490F29C 96203000 1AB341BB   *.02...2.....................2.......*   13ED68
002580   000196FF B00047F0 F21C18B9 1AB59130   B0004740 F19E4490 F2901A93 96F09000   *........02.......... 1...2....0..*   13ED88
0025A0   47F0F21C 4490F2A2 97803000 9101A010   4780F07A 4640F264 41320001 5890F2C0   *.02...2............0 . 2........2.*   13EDA8
0025C0   58BA0004 4480F284 4780F2A8 584A000C   4720F24C 1B041870 47F0F250 1A0418C0   *......2...2.........2.......02.....*   13EDC8
0025E0   15C74720 F26A1894 1A971B9C 1B881D84   47F0F0AA 1A3647F0 F0D258E1 000847F0   *.G..2...............00.....00K.....0*   13EDE8
002600   F2AC1A56 1A364188 000447F0 F0DCD200   80003000 D5009000 3000D200 30002000   *2...........00.K.....N.....K.....*   13EE08
002620   D2003000 5000F100 30005000 F1003000   3000D700 30005000 41E80004 58F0F2BC   *K.....1......1......P.......Y...02.*   13EE28
002640   981CF2C4 07FE0000 4013D4BC 0013EB98   0012F2F4 0012F2FC 0013EE90 00000001   *..2D.... .M.........24..2..........*   13EE48
002660   0012F420 5013EB00 0012F00C 0012F2E3   0012F2E4 0013EAD0 0013C820 0013C820   *..4........0...2T..2U.......H...H.*   13EE68
002680   0013CC98 00000000 01010101 01010101   01010101 01010101 01010101 01010101   *................................*   13EE88
0026A0   01010101 01010101 01010101 01010101   01010101 01010101 01010101 01010101   *................................*   13EEA8
0026C0   LINES TO 002740 SAME AS ABOVE                                                                                       13EEC8
002760   01010101 01010101 01010101 01010101   01010101 01010101 00000000 00000000   *................................*   13EF68
002780   00000101 01010101                                                         *........                        *   13EF88

PROGRAM STORAGE              ADDRESS  13F808  TO  13FCA7       LENGTH  0004A0

000000   D6D9C1C4 E2F0F140 00404040 00000000   00000000 D6D9C1C4 D4F0F140 048F04B0   *ORADS01 .     ........ORADM01 ....*   13F808
000020   03B105C6 C0C200CC 001850FF FE000000   00000000 00000000 0001037D 0000F100   *...F.B.......................'..1.*   13F828
000040   00001B02 F80018D7 E4D9C3C8 C1E2C540   D6D9C4C5 D9406060 6040C6C9 D3C540C1   *....8..PURCHASE ORDER --- FILE A*   13F848
000060   C4C40000 000D02F0 00BDD6D9 C4C5D940   D5E4D4C2 C5D97A00 00000A0D D800CB00   *DD.....0..ORDER NUMBER ......Q...*   13F868
000080   00000100 6000D600 00000802 F000DDC4   D6C340D5 D64B7A00 0000080D D800E600   *....-.0.......0..DOC NO.  .....Q.W.*   13F888
0000A0   00000100 6000EF00 00000B02 F0010FC4   C5D7C1D9 E3D4C5D5 E37A0000 00030DD8   *....-........0..DEPARTMENT .....Q*   13F8A8
0000C0   011B0000 000100F0 011F0000 000E02F0   015CC4C1 E3C540D6 C640D6D9 C4C5D97A   *.......0........0.*DATE OF ORDER *   13F8C8
0000E0   00000006 0DD8016B 00000001 00F00172   00000004 02F002D6 C9E3C5D4 0000000B   *.....Q.,......0........0.OITEM....*   13F8E8
000100   02F002E0 C4C5E2C3 D9C9D7E3 C9D6D500   00000402 F002F9E4 D5C9E300 00000502   *.0..DESCRIPTION......0.9UNIT.....*   13F908
000120   F002FFE4 C3D6E2E3 00000004 02F00308   C3D6E2E3 00000006 02F00310 E4D7D9C9   *0..UCOST.....0..COST......0...UPRI*   13F928
000140   C3C50000 000502F0 0319D7D9 C9C3C500   00000102 F00322F1 00000008 0DD80324   *CE.....0..PRICE.....0...1......Q..*   13F948
000160   00000013 01C8032D 00000001 00600341   00000005 0DD80348 00000007 0DD8034E   *.....H.......-.........Q........Q.+*   13F968
000180   00000008 0DD80356 00000007 0DD8035F   00000008 0DD80367 00000001 00600370   *.....Q........Q.........Q.......-..*   13F988
0001A0   00000001 02F00372 F2000000 080DD803   74000000 1301C803 7D000000 01006003   *.....0..2.....Q........H.'......-.*   13F9A8
0001C0   91000000 050DD803 98000000 070DD803   9E000000 080DD803 A6000000 070DD803   *......Q.........Q.........Q........Q.*   13F9C8
0001E0   AF000000 080DD803 B7000000 01006003   C0000000 0102F003 C2F30000 00080DD8   *......Q............-.........0.B3.....Q*   13F9E8
000200   03C40000 001301C8 03CD0000 00010060   03E10000 00050DD8 03E80000 00070DD8   *.D.....H.......-.........Q.Y......Q*   13FA08
000220   03EE0000 00080DD8 03F60000 00070DD8   03FF0000 00080DD8 04070000 00010060   *........Q.6.....Q.........Q........-*   13FA28
000240   04100000 000102F0 0412F400 0000080D   D8041400 00001301 C8041D00 00000100   *........0..4......Q.........H.........*   13FA48
000260   60043100 0000050D D8043800 0000070D   D8043E00 0000080D D8044600 0000070D   *-.........Q.........Q.........Q........*   13FA68
000280   D8044F00 00000800 D8045700 00000100   60046000 00000102 F00462F5 00000008   *Q.........Q.........-.-.......0..5.....*   13FA88
0002A0   0DD80464 00000013 01C8046D 00000001   00600481 00000005 0DD80488 00000007   *.Q.........H.........-.........Q.......*   13FAA8
```

Fig. 24.5. (Continued)

```
CUSTOMER INFORMATION CONTROL SYSTEM STORAGE DUMP   CODE=ASRA   TASK=ORAD    DATE=07/27/80   TIME=18 43 53   PAGE   17

PROGRAM STORAGE          ADDRESS 13F808     TO 13FCA7       LENGTH 0004A0

0002CC  0DD80 48E 00000008 0DD80496 00300007   0DD8049F 00000008 0DD804A7 00000001   *.Q......Q......Q......*   13FAC8
0002E0  00650 0480 02F004B2 F6000000           080DD804 84000000 1301C804 B0000000   *.-...Q..6....Q......H..*   13FAE8
000300  01006304 01000000 0500D804 D8000000    07000804 DE000000 080DD804 E6000000   *...-J...Q.Q......Q.W...*   13FB08
000320  070DD804 EF000000 080DD804 F7000000    01006005 00000000 0102F005 02F70000   *.Q......Q.7...... .0..7.*  13FB28
000340  00080DD8 05040000 001301C8 05000000    00010060 05210000 00050DD8 05280000   *..Q......H......-....Q.*   13FB48
000360  00070DD8 052E0000 00080DD8 05360000    00070DD8 053F0000 00080DD8 05470000   *...Q......Q......Q.....*   13FB68
000380  00010060 05500000 000102F0 0552F800    00000800 D8055400 00001301 C8055DD0   *..Q......0..8....Q.....*   13FB88
0003A0  00000100 60057100 0000050D D8057800    00000700 D8057E00 0000080D D8058600   *..-......Q......H.}....*   13FBA8
0003C0  00000700 D8058F00 0000080D D8059700    00000100 6005A000 00000102 F005A2F9   *..Q......0..9....Q.....*   13FBC8
0003E0  00000008 00D805A4 00000013 01C805AD    00000001 006C05C1 00000005 0DD805C8   *..Q......Q.=....-A...Q.H*  13FBE8
000400  00000007 0DD805CE 0000C008 0DD805D6    00000007 0DD805DF 00000008 0DD805E7   *...Q......0..Q..Q.....Q.X*  13FC08
000420  00000001 006C05F0 00000000 02F00666    E3D6E3C1 D3E24060 60606060 6E000000   *...0....0..TOTALS -----.*  13FC28
000443  090DD806 75000000 01006006 7F000000    090DD806 86000000 01006006 90000000   *.Q......-....Q.........*   13FC48
000460  1C03F806 E0D609C4 C5D940C1 C3C3C5D7    E3C5C440 606040C3 D6D5E3C9 D5E4C540   *.8..ORDER ACCEPTED -- CONTINUE *  13FC68
000480  40000000 1C01F807 07000000 1C01F807    30000000 1C01F807 5TFFFFFF FFFFFF00   *....8......8......8....*   13FC88

END OF CICS/VS STORAGE DUMP
```

Fig. 24.5. (Continued)

The Temporary Storage Area

Other main storage areas for the transaction are printed out after the regular trace table. Thus on page 510 are the blocks labeled "TRANSACTION STORAGE-XXX." You will notice a block labeled "TRANSACTION STORAGE-TS," which is the Temporary Storage Area. CICS/VS uses the first 12 bytes of this block, and thus the user area actually starts at B.

The Working-Storage Section

Other areas labeled "TRANSACTION STORAGE-USER" are those main storage areas secured for the task by CICS/VS or the application program. One of these is the WORKING-STORAGE section that CICS/VS secures for a program written with the command level feature to make the program automatically quasi-reentrant. This is C on page 512 and it is easy to locate from the literals ("JOB NORMALLY TERMINATED," etc.) and is one of the last blocks labeled "TRANSACTION STORAGE-USER." This is different from the working storage that is part of the program and which is shown as the first part of "PROGRAM STORAGE" on page 513.

The Symbolic Description Map Area

The symbolic description map area is labeled "TERMINAL STORAGE." This is D on page 513 and the first 12 bytes corresponds to the 12-byte FILLER of the symbolic description map.

The Program Load Address

A literal defines the starting point of the program and its value is always constant for an installation regardless whether this program is batch or on-line. It prints on the first line of the block labeled "PROGRAM STORAGE." In the case of a DOS/VS system, this literal is "05F00700900EF00A47F0F082." This is E on page 513 and the program address is thus 13C820 (13C808 + 18).

PROGRAM CHECK DEBUGGING

Of the several conditions that result in the abnormal termination of a task, only two are of importance to the application programmer. The first is a program check that happens on a logic error like the familiar data exception.* The second is an exceptional condition on a CICS/VS command.

CICS/VS automatically provides the programmer with a transaction dump that is used for debugging. For a program check, some additional information may also be read from the dump. Among these are:

1. The abend code.**   "ASRA" identifies the problem
                           as a program check. This is F on
                           page 504 (Fig. 24.5).

2. The transaction identifier   This is G.

3. The PSW.   This is H.

The first step in debugging this type of problem is to find the instruction that caused the abend. This is done by taking the last 3 bytes of the PSW, which is the address of the next instruction which would have executed had the abend not occurred, and subtracting from it the address where the program was loaded, E on page 513. Thus:

$$
\begin{array}{r}
13D9C8 \\
-\ \ \underline{13C820} \\
11A8
\end{array}
$$

From Fig. 24.4, page 501, noting the PROCEDURE DIVISION condensed listing, 11A8 corresponds exactly to statement 590. The

---

*Certain CICS/VS command "errors" result in a transaction abend where CICS/VS treats the problem (as far as generating the dump) like a program check. For instance, if a map specified in a command is not in the CICS/VS program library, an abend with an abend code ABMO results.

**The meaning of abend codes are found in the CICS/VS Messages And Codes Manual (Form SC33-0081-1).

instruction that actually executed when the abend occurred is the one before it and the corresponding statement is thus 589. This is I.

From Fig. 24.3, page 485, we see that statement 589(J) is an ADD statement. The operand 'TWA-COST-MAP' is definitely numeric from statement 586; thus it is the operand 'TWA-TOTAL-COST' that is the problem. From the DATA DIVISION map, page 499, we see that this field (K) is offset from the start of the Transaction Work Area by 07F. This field is L on Fig. 24.5, page 504, and is hexadecimal zeroes.

In fact, this field was not zeroed out in this program. If you refer back to the original File Add program example, Fig. 19.4, statements 00513 and 00514 were removed.

THE CICS/VS COMMAND EXCEPTIONAL CONDITION

The system default for most CICS/VS command exceptional conditions is a transaction dump with the task being aborted. The programmer may then determine the problem by checking the values of the EIBFN and EIBRCODE fields of the Execute Interface Block. However, to simplify the debugging of this type of problem, I suggest the following techniques:

1. Instead of allowing the system to generate the transaction dump, in which case the programmer will have to look for the Execute Interface Block, put the values of EIBFN and EIBRCODE in the WORKING-STORAGE section so they can be easily traced.

2. These are the 'OLD-EIBFN' and 'OLD-EIBRCODE' fields. They are preceded by a tracer* with value 'OLD-EIB' for easier tracing.

---

*A tracer is a FILLER in working storage with a distinct value; it is placed in front of important fields. Its only function is to help locate such fields in a dump.

3. The fields 'OLD-EIBFN' and 'OLD-EIBRCODE' are set to the corresponding values in the Execute Interface Block on a major exceptional condition that terminates the session. These are done at the MAJOR-ERROR paragraph in the ABNORMAL-TERMINATION section. Major exceptional conditions are those covered by the ERROR exceptional condition for unusual conditions not covered by a specific HANDLE CONDITION command.

4. Since the default generation of the transaction dump is replaced by the user routine, the programmer must issue the DUMP command at the same ABNORMAL-TERMINATION section to generate the dump.

The format of the DUMP command is:

> dump dumpcode (data value)
> *task*

The DUMPCODE operand specifies the literal (up to 4 bytes) that prints as the dump code in the listing to identify it. In the program examples, this literal is 'ERRS.' TASK is the default option and should be the one used to ensure that the dump is complete. Other options are not shown.

A transaction dump generated on a major CICS/VS exceptional condition, which will then cause the program to issue the DUMP command, is shown in Figure 24.6.

(A) → [ERRS]

```
CUSTOMER INFORMATION CONTROL SYSTEM STORAGE DUMP    CODE=ERRS    TASK=ORAD         DATE=07/27/80   TIME=19 01 28   PAGE   1

REGS 14-4    40159FFC   00000004   00000004   0012F360   0012F07C   8012F084   0012F420
REGS 5-11    5013E802   00000038   00000002   0010C700   00159TC0   0012F0EC   0012F390

TASK CONTROL AREA (USER AREA)   ADDRESS 12E888   TO 12EBBF   LENGTH 000708
000000  0012E830  30107234  11103660  00108EF0   0012EBC0  0017F040  80400100  00210000   *.Y......0.....0....*  12E888
000020  7011B124  0011B0E6  80609F4E  00183480   5011F096  00000001  00130400  406DABA4   *....M..-........0...*  12E8A8
000040  00000000  0011B818  4011B0E8  0011BAB0   44130170  001303C0  40159FFC  40103C0   *.......Y........Y...*  12E8C8
000060  40120070  40121CF4  C004C000  FE12EC48   5011F096  0012D096  0012E81C  00000000   *...4........Y.......*  12E8E8
000080  FE0000CA  D6D9E3C5  E2E34040  C5D9D9E2   00000000  00000000  0012EA41  5013E802   *.ORTEST  ERRS......*  12E938
0000A0  40159FFC  00000004  0012F360  0012F07C   8012F07C  0012F390  1C020000  00106D0   *........3...0...4..*  12E958
0000C0  00000038  00000002  0010C700  0012F0EC   0012F0EC  00000000  00000000  00000000   *..........G...0....*  12E978
0000E0  00000000  24F40000  00000000  00000000   00000000  00000000  00000000  00000000   *....4..............*  12E998
000100  00000000  00000000  00000000  00000000   00000000  00000000  00000000  00000000   *...................*  12E9B8
000120  00000000  00000000  00000000  00000000   000000F0  F0F0F0F8  F5F7F340  4040404040   *...........00008573*  12E9D8
000140  40404040  40404040  4040F0F1  4040F0F1   F2F0F8F2  0020C000  10000C00  20000C00   *.........0.012082..*  12E9F8
000160  0200000C  00040000  0CF0F0F0  F0F0F0F0   F2F1F503  F7F7F0D6  D9C1C400  00000000   *.........0000021SL770ORAD.*  12EA18
000180  00000000  51053C00  00000000  00000000   00000000  00000000  00000000  00000000   *...................*  12EA38
0001A0  00000000  00000000  00000000  00000000   00000000  00000000  00000000  00000000   *...................*  12EA58
0001C0  00000000  00000000  00000000  00000000                                            *........*            12EA78
                                                                                                                 12EA98
0001E0  LINES TO  0002E0 SAME AS ABOVE
000300  D3C9C6D6  E2E3D6D9  42000088  00000000   FF12EC48  5011EB20  8011EB82  9011EBDA   *LIFOSTOR.......b...*  12EAB8
000320  0012F360  0012F07C  0012F0A6  0012FF29   00000000  821303C0  0010C700  0010EBE3   *.3...0...0...........T.G*  12EAD8
000340  0011E770  0011BAB0  0012F390  00000000   FE12EC48  F0000000  00000000  20000C00   *..X......3.....Y....0.*  12EAF8
000360  88000028  00000000  0000C000  0011A728   00000000  00000000  00000000  70118124   *........X..+.....*  12EB18
000380  00000000  00000000  00000028  88000000   0012EBC0  00000000  00000000  00000000   *...................*  12EB38
0003A0  0011B0E6  80609F4E  00183480  5011F096   00130400  406DABA4  00000000  00000000   *...-.....0....Y.....*  12EB58
0003C0  0011B818  4011B0E8  0011BAB0  44130170   001303C0  00010600  00000000  FE12ECC0   *.......Y........5FC.....ORTEST*  12EB78
0003E0  F530C6C3  0011F180  10130C0  D6D9E3C5   E2E34040  00010600  00000000  0000000F   *5FC..1....ORTEST*     12EB98
000400  00000000  0012EA41  00000000  00000000   00000000  00000000  00000000  00000000   *...................*  12EBB8
000420  00000000  00000000  00000000  00000000   00000000  00000000  00000000  00000000   *...................*
000440  LINES TO  0006E0 SAME AS ABOVE
000700  8A3307B8  0013D0F0                                                                 *......0*

TASK CONTROL AREA (SYSTEM AREA)   ADDRESS 12E800   TO 12E8B7   LENGTH 000088
000000  8A3307B8  001300F0  00000000  00000000   8000008C  00117120  00129880  00000000   *......0...........0...*  12E800
000320  00109138  00000000  0012EC18  0012FF660   00000000  FF11A6E4  00000000  0012F0EC   *.............0....U....0*  12E820
000040  0012EFC0  0012EC18  0012F660  00000000   00000000  00000000  00000000  0012F390   *..........6...........3*  12E840
000060  00000000  00000000  00000000  FE12EB80   00109A28  0012EBC0  0012F390  00000000   *................0.....*  12E860
000080  0010C660  00000000  FE12EB80  00000000   D6D9C1C4  00000000                       *........ORAD....*     12E880
                                                                                                                 12E8A0

LIFO STACK ENTRY       ADDRESS 12EBC0   TO 12EC47   LENGTH 000088
000000  42000088  00000000  FF12EC48  5011EB20   8011EB82  9011EBDA  0010C700  0012F07C   *...........b........0*  12EBC0
000020  0012F0A6  0012FF29  00000000  821303C0   0011EBE3  0010C700  0011E770  0011BAB0   *.0...........T.G..X..*  12EBE0
000040  0012F390  0012E888  01070F0  FE12EC48   F0000000  00000000  88000028  00000000   *.3...........0....X..*  12EC00
000060  00000000  0011A728  00000000  00000000   00000000  00000000  00000000  00000000   *...+...............*  12EC20
```

Fig. 24.6. The Transaction Dump, CICS/VS Exceptional Condition.

```
CUSTOMER INFORMATION CONTROL SYSTEM STORAGE DUMP     CODE=ERRS    TASK=DRAD      DATE=07/27/80    TIME=19 01 28    PAGE  2

LIFO STACK ENTRY          ADDRESS  12EBC0      TO  12EC47     LENGTH  000088

000080   8BD00228 00000000                                                                              *........*                 12EC40

COMMON SYSTEM AREA        ADDRESS  1070F0      TO  108EEF     LENGTH  001E00

000000   00000030 00000000 30000000 70155400   00000004 00000004 0012F360 0012F07C   *....3--0.*          1070F0
000020   8012F0B4 0012F420 5013E802 00000038   80000002 001C6700 001597C0 0012F0EC   *.0..4...G.0.*       107110
000040   0012F390 0012C088 0010023C 0012E888   1901289F 001298C0 17700000 00000000   *.3....Y..*          107130
000060   0068B181 00465000 0008B000 00010810   00020300 00100000 0018FFFF 0080209F   *.....*              107150
000080   001096F8 F0FFFFFF 0000001E 0015EB08   00000002 00000000 00128520 C434C614   *..80...D.F.*        107170
0000A0   00000000 00000000 001298A0 00129840   00129880 001095A0 00109138 1000FF00   *..Q..*              107190
0000C0   000C0001 00091E00 00108EF0 00000000   00000000 00000000 00100A10 00000000   *..0...*             1071B0
0000E0   4010A0C4 00115DD0 00118804 0315D8F0   00155308 00100310 0011F964 00123IE4   *.D.....0.Q...U*     1071D0
000100   00121908 00000000 001464A0 0014F10C   00000000 00100054 0110DBD0 00146490   *......l......*      1071F0
000120   00117090 001198F8 00100260 0011B250   00122A28 0012848D 00128800 00000000   *......8-...*        107210
000140   00000000 00155E64 00100808 0011B090   00122880 00000000 00000000 00000000   *......*             107230
000160   0014F1EA 00000000 00000000 0015F404   0138F72C 00000000 00000000 0014F440   *..1.....7...4.*     107250
000180   00000000 00000000 00000000 0015F404   00000000 000C2030 E6D609D2 FF1070A8   *......M...*         107270
0001A0   07FE58F0 D19C07FF 01398485 0139CA88   00000000 00083C00 C1D9C5C1 C1D9C5C1   *.0.......DJ..WORKAREA*  107290
0001C0   0C000000 000C0000 003C003C 00008C00   00118C00 00083C00 0C000C00 0C000C00   *..*                 1072B0
0001E0   0C001C00 0C000C00 3C000C00 0C000C00   00000000 000C000C 0C000C00 00000000   **                  1072D0
000200   00000000 00000000 00000000 00000000   00000000 00000000 00000000 00000000   **                  1072F0
000220   LINES TO  000720  SAME AS ABOVE                                                                                           107310
0007A0   LINES TO  001700  SAME AS ABOVE                                                                                           107830
000760   LINES TO  001700  SAME AS ABOVE                                                                                           107850
021720   00000000 00000000 00000000 00000000   00000000 00000000 00000000 00000000   *......*             108810
001740   LINES TO  001DE0  SAME AS ABOVE                                                                                           108830

CSA OPTIONAL FEATURE LIST          ADDRESS  108EF0      TO  109077     LENGTH  000188

000000   00000000 00000000 30000000 00159BD0   0012532C 00000000 0015CC38 0015CC68   *.....*              108EF0
000020   0014F122 0014EE10 0014E7F4 00000000   00000000 0015C500 00000000 00000000   *..X...E..*          108F10
000040   00000000 00000000 00000000 000CFF00   0014EC98 00000000 00000000 001070F0   *..(....0*           108F30
000060   00000030 01F4D5D6 000000C0 00150660   0C154D90 00000000 00000000 001070F0   *.4ND..*             108F50
000080   0109A28 00154870 00153760 00150660   00000000 00000000 00000000 00121820   *..0...B...*         108F70
0000A0   0010ADF0 00117F70 0010C260 0010BC60   0010E120 0011E770 00124EC0 0014B6A0   *.0...B...X..*       108F90
0000C0   00115020 00119510 0015E4F0 0010A020   0015D720 0010D010 00124EC0 0014486A0  *...UO..P.+*         108FB0
0000E0   001597C0 001540E0 0015A7D0 00000000   00000000 0014FCA0 0014FCA0 00000000   *..l..*              108FD0
000100   00000000 00000000 00000000 00000000   0010DAF4 001141F0 00000000 00000000   *....4..0*           108FF0
000120   00000000 001C000C 000C000C 000C001C   000C000C 001C000C 000C000C 000C000C   *......*             109010
000140   000C001C 000C000C 000C000C 001C000C   000C000C 000C000C 000C001C            *....*               109030
000160   001C000C 000C000C 000C000C 000C000C   000C000C 000C000C 000C000C 000C001C   *....*               109050
000180   000C000C 000C000C                                                                                 *..*                109070
```

Fig. 24.6. (Continued)

CUSTOMER INFORMATION CONTROL SYSTEM STORAGE DUMP   CODE=ERRS   TASK=DRAD   DATE=07/27/80   TIME=19 01 28   PAGE 3

TRACE TABLE	ADDRESS	1457F0	TO	14646F			
	00145B40	00145F70		00146460	00146490		
TRACE HDR							LENGTH 000C80
TRACE TABLE							

	ID	REG14	REQD	TASK	FIELD A	FIELD B		TRACE TYPE
145B50	F5	120134	0015	0007	00000000	00000000	....	FCP RESPONSE NORMAL
145B60	E1	132E00	00F4	0007	00000000	0000060E	....	EIP READNEXT RESPONSE
145B70	E1	132E00	0004	0007	0012FA2C	0000060E	....	EIP READNEXT ENTRY
145B80	F5	11E9C8	B003	0007	C4E2E7E3	C1C2E240	DSXTABS	FCP GETNEXT
145B90	F0	120476	4004	0007	20000000	00173058	....	KCP WAIT DCI=DISP
145BA0	F5	120134	0015	0007	00000000	00000000	....	FCP RESPONSE NORMAL
145BB0	E1	132E00	00F4	0007	00000000	0000060E	....	EIP READNEXT RESPONSE
145BC0	E1	132E00	0004	0007	0012FA2C	0000060E	....	EIP READNEXT ENTRY
145BD0	F5	11E9C8	B003	0007	C4E2E7E3	C1C2E240	DSXTABS	FCP GETNEXT
145BE0	F0	120476	4004	0007	20000000	00173058	....	KCP WAIT DCI=DISP
145BF0	F0	10DB88	4004	TC	44000000	001007F8	8	KCP WAIT
145C00	F5	120134	0015	0007	00000000	00000000	....	FCP RESPONSE NORMAL
145C10	E1	132E00	00F4	0007	00000000	0000060E	....	EIP READNEXT RESPONSE
145C20	E1	132E00	0004	0007	0012FA2C	0000060E	....	EIP READNEXT ENTRY
145C30	F5	11E9C8	B003	0007	C4E2E7E3	C1C2E240	DSXTABS	FCP GETNEXT
145C40	F0	120476	4004	0007	20000000	00173058	....	KCP WAIT DCI=DISP
145C50	F5	120134	0015	0007	00000000	00000000	....	FCP RESPONSE NORMAL
145C60	FD	00001C	0204	0007	E3C904C5	1900337F	TIME....	TIMING TRACE 19/00/33-7
145C70	E1	132E00	00F4	0007	00000000	0000060E	....	EIP READNEXT RESPONSE
145C80	E1	132F16	0004	0007	0012FA2C	00000A02	....	EIP WRITEQ-TS ENTRY
145C90	F1	12187A	8E04	0007	00120540	01100660	....	SCP GETMAIN
145CA0	C8	115222	0004	0007	0012C780	8E120548	.G......	SCP ACQUIRED TEMPSTRG STORAGE
145CB0	F7	1218C6	4103	0007	D3F7F7F0	D609C1C4	L770DRAD	TSP PUTQ
145CC0	F1	12231A	F804	0007	00000038	01100660	....	SCP GETMAIN-COND-INIT
145CD0	C8	115222	00F4	0007	00120000	98000040	....	SCP ACQUIRED ISTABLE STORAGE
145CE0	F1	121AEA	B704	0007	00120554	01100660	....	SCP GETMAIN-CONDITIONAL
145CF0	C8	115222	0004	0007	00120040	97120560	....	SCP ACQUIRED TSMAIN STORAGE
145D00	F7	121FCC	0015	0007	00000000	01100660	....	TSP RESPONSE
145D10	F1	12183E	4004	0007	0012C780	01100660	.G......	SCP FREEMAIN
145D20	C9	11530C	0004	0007	0012C780	8E120548	.G......	SCP RELEASED TEMPSTRG STORAGE
145D30	E1	132F16	00F4	0007	00000000	00000A02	....	EIP WRITEQ-TS RESPONSE
145D40	E1	132F4E	0004	0007	0012FA2C	00000C04	....	EIP FREEMAIN ENTRY
145D50	F1	11508A	4004	0007	0012C000	01100660	....	SCP FREEMAIN
145D60	C9	11530C	0004	0007	0012C000	8C120548	.G......	SCP RELEASED USER STORAGE
145D70	E1	132F4E	00F4	0007	00000000	00000C04	....	EIP FREEMAIN RESPONSE
145D80	E1	132F9C	0004	0007	0012FA2C	00000C02	....	EIP GETMAIN ENTRY
145D90	F1	115052	CC04	0007	000003BE	01100660	....	SCP GETMAIN-INIT
145DA0	C8	115222	0004	0007	0012C800	8C0003C8	.H....H	SCP ACQUIRED USER STORAGE
145DB0	E1	132F9C	00F4	0007	0012C800	00000C02	....	EIP GETMAIN RESPONSE
145DC0	E1	13300A	0004	0007	0012FA2C	00001804	....	EIP SEND-MAP ENTRY
145DD0	FA	124F7E	0003	0007	000005E2	04000020	...S....	BMS OUT MAP MAPSET SAVE ERASE
145DE0	F2	1261AC	0804	0007	D609C1D7	E2F0F140	ORAPS01	PCP DELETE
145DF0	F2	126200	0404	0007	D609C1C4	E2F0F140	ORADS01	PCP LOAD
145E00	F1	118572	8804	0007	00120095	01100660	....	SCP GETMAIN
145E10	C9	11530C	0004	0007	00138000	88002800	....	SCP RELEASED PGM STORAGE
145E20	C9	11530C	0004	0007	00136800	88002800	....	SCP RELEASED PGM STORAGE
145E30	C9	11530C	0004	0007	0013A000	88001800	....	SCP RELEASED PGM STORAGE

Fig. 24.6. (Continued)

CUSTOMER INFORMATION CONTROL SYSTEM STORAGE DUMP   CODE=ERRS   TASK=DRAD   DATE=07/27/80   TIME=19 01 28   PAGE   4

TRACE TABLE	ID	REG14	PEOD	TASK	FIELD A	FIELD B		TRACE TYPE
145E40	C9	11530C	0004	0007	00139000	88001000	....	SCP RELEASED PGM STORAGE
145E50	C9	11530C	0CC4	0007	0013F800	88000800	..8....	SCP RELEASED PGM STORAGE
145E60	C9	11530C	3CC4	0007	0013E000	88001000	....	SCP RELEASED PGM STORAGE
145E70	C9	11530C	0004	0007	00133800	88001000	....	SCP RELEASED PGM STORAGE
145E80	C9	11530C	0CC4	0007	00135000	88001800	....	SCP RELEASED PGM STORAGE
145E90	C9	11530C	0004	0007	00134800	88000800	....	SCP RELEASED PGM STORAGE
145EA0	C8	115222	C0C4	0007	00130800	88000800	....	SCP ACQUIRED PGM STORAGE
145EB0	F0	11862A	4004	0007	88000000	0011A746	....	KCP WAIT DCI=CICS
145EC0	F1	127F3A	9E04	0007	00130850	01100660	....	SCP GETMAIN
145ED0	C8	115222	0CC4	0007	0012D800	9E130858	..Q....	SCP ACQUIRED MAPCOPY STORAGE
145EE0	F1	124578	CCC4	0007	00000E40	01100660	....	SCP GETMAIN-INIT
145EF0	C8	115222	0004	0007	0012E060	8C0004E8	......Y	SCP ACQUIRED USER STORAGE
145F00	F1	124846	8504	0007	0012D5D3	01100660	..L....	SCP GETMAIN
145F10	C8	115222	0004	0007	00129170	851205E8	......Y	SCP ACQUIRED TERMINAL STORAGE
145F20	F1	124A00	4004	0007	0012E060	01100660	....	SCP FREEMAIN
145F30	C9	11530C	0007	0007	0012E060	8C0004E8	......Y	SCP RELEASED USER STORAGE
145F40	F1	124A00	4CC4	0007	0012D800	01100660	..Q....	SCP FREEMAIN
145F50	C9	11530C	0CC4	0007	0012D800	9E130858	..Q....	SCP RELEASED MAPCOPY STORAGE
145F60	FC	126CA8	0103	0007	00810000	00100060	....	ZCP ZARQ APPL REQ ERASE WRITE
145F70	FA	125EE6	0005	0007	00000000	00001804	....	BMS RESPONSE
145F80	E1	13300A	00F4	0007	00000000	00001804	....	EIP SEND-MAP RESPONSE
145F90	E1	133058	0004	0007	0012FA2C	00000E08	....	EIP RETURN ENTRY
145FA0	F1	11970C	9304	0007	00120019	01100660	....	SCP GETMAIN
145FB0	C8	115222	0004	0007	0012D5A0	93120020	..N....	SCP ACQUIRED SHARED STORAGE
145FC0	F2	119760	1004	0007	0609C1C4	F0F1C140	DRAD01A	PCP RETURN
145FD0	F1	118A4A	4004	0007	0012F9E0	01100660	..9...H	SCP FREEMAIN
145FE0	C9	11530C	0004	0007	0012F9E0	8C1303C8	..9...H	SCP RELEASED USER STORAGE
145FF0	F1	118866	4004	0007	00131000	01100660	....	SCP FREEMAIN
146000	C9	11530C	0004	0007	00131000	88002800	....	SCP RELEASED PGM STORAGE
146010	F1	118866	4C04	0007	00130800	01100660	....	SCP FREEMAIN
146020	C9	11530C	0004	0007	00130800	88000800	....	SCP RELEASED PGM STORAGE
146030	F0	118992	8034	0007	00000000	00000000	....	KCP DETACH
146040	D8	10AC20	0203	0007	0012C620	0012C620	....	SPP SYSTEM
146050	F5	10D7F0	0003	0007	00000000	00000000	..F....	FCP DWE PROCESSOR
146060	F1	120D70	4CC4	0007	0012C620	01100660	..F....	SCP FREEMAIN
146070	C9	11530C	0004	0007	0012C620	9D120038	..F....	SCP RELEASED DWE STORAGE
146080	F1	120D70	4004	0007	0012C660	01100660	..F...H	SCP FREEMAIN
146090	C9	11530C	0CC4	0007	0012C660	8F1200C8	..E....	SCP RELEASED FILE STORAGE
1460A0	F5	120134	0015	0007	00000048	00000000	....	FCP RESPONSE NORMAL
1460B0	D8	10D95C	0015	0007	00000000	00000000	....	SPP RESPONSE
1460C0	F0	10AC2A	0304	0007	0011A746	00000000	....	KCP DEQALL
1460D0	F1	10ADA0	4A04	0007	0012E800	0000000J	..Y....	SCP FREEMAIN
1460E0	C9	11530C	0004	0007	0012C800	8C0003C8	..H...H	SCP RELEASED USER STORAGE
1460F0	C9	11530C	0004	0007	0012C5A0	8F120078	..G....	SCP RELEASED FILE STORAGE
146100	C9	11530C	0004	0007	0012C5A0	01100078	....	SCP RELEASED USER STORAGE
146110	C9	11530C	0004	0007	0012C550	8C000048	..E....	SCP RELEASED USER STORAGE
146120	C9	11530C	0004	0007	0012FEF0	8C000048	....	SCP RELEASED USER STORAGE
146130	C9	11530C	0004	0007	0012FEF0	8C000048	..O....	SCP RELEASED USER STORAGE
146140	C9	11530C	0004	0007	0012FF20	8C000078	....	SCP RELEASED USER STORAGE
146150	C9	11530C	0004	0007	0012FF20	8C000048	....	SCP RELEASED USER STORAGE
146160	C9	11530C	0004	0007	0012FFB0	8C000068	....	SCP RELEASED USER STORAGE

Fig. 24.6. (Continued)

CUSTOMER INFORMATION CONTROL SYSTEM STORAGE DUMP   CODE=ERRS   TASK=ORAD   DATE=07/27/80   TIME=19 01 28   PAGE 5

TRACE TABLE

ID	REGI4	REQD	TASK	FIELD A	FIELD B		TRACE TYPE
C9	11530C	00C4	KC	0012F9C0	8C120018	..9....	SCP RELEASED USER STORAGE
C9	11530C	0004	KC	0012F930	8C000088	..9....	SCP RELEASED USER STORAGE
C9	11530C	00C4	KC	0012F6A0	8C000288	..6....	SCP RELEASED USER STORAGE
C9	11530C	0004	KC	0012F290	8C000408	..2....	SCP RELEASED USER STORAGE
C9	11530C	00C4	KC	0012E800	8A030598	.V.....	SCP RELEASED TCA STORAGE
F0	10DB88	4004	KC	44000000	001007F8	8	KCP WAIT
F1	10EA54	4004	TC	00129170	80100660	....	SCP FREEMAIN
C9	11530C	0004	TC	00129170	851205E8	....Y	SCP RELEASED TERMINAL STORAGE
F1	10EAF8	6004	TC	00129120	80100660	....	SCP FREEMAIN ALL
C9	11530C	0004	TC	00129120	85000048	....	SCP RELEASED TERMINAL STORAGE
F1	10E9F0	E404	TC	0000010F	84000118	....	SCP GETMAIN-COND-INIT
C8	115222	00C4	TC	00129000	84000118	....	SCP ACQUIRED LINE STORAGE
F0	10DB88	4004	TC	44000000	001007F8	8	KCP WAIT
FD	00001C	0104	TC	00686C18	00686C18	...	REPEAT 00001 TIMES
F0	113464	1104	TC	01100660	D6D9C1C4	...ORAD	KCP ATTACH-CONDITIONAL
F1	10A91E	EA04	TC	00080780	80100660	.Y....	SCP GETMAIN-COND-INIT
C8	115222	0004	TC	0012E800	8A0307B8	.Y....	SCP ACQUIRED TCA STORAGE
F0	10DB88	4C04	TC	44000000	001007F8	8	KCP WAIT
F2	118804	0204	0008	0609C1C4	F0F1C140	ORAD01A	PCP XCTL
F1	118572	8804	0008	000004F2	01100660	..-2...	SCP GETMAIN
C8	115222	0004	0008	0013C8D0	88002800	..H....	SCP ACQUIRED PGM STORAGE
F0	11862A	4004	0008	88000000	0011A702	....	KCP WAIT DCI=CICS
F1	1190FC	8C04	0008	0013D3B0	01100660	....	SCP GETMAIN
C8	115222	0004	0008	0012EFC0	8C1303C8	.....H	SCP ACQUIRED USER STORAGE
F1	10C2A6	CC04	0008	00000128	01100660	..3...	SCP GETMAIN-INIT
C8	115222	0004	0008	0012F390	8C000138	..3....	SCP ACQUIRED USER STORAGE
E1	13D18C	00F4	0008	0012F00C	00000202	.0.....	EIP ADDRESS ENTRY
E1	13D18C	00F4	0008	0012F00C	00000202	....	EIP ADDRESS RESPONSE
E1	13D1B2	00F4	0008	0012F00C	00000206	.0.....	EIP HANDLE-AID ENTRY
C8	10BC96	CC04	0008	00000059	01100660	....	SCP GETMAIN-INIT
F1	10BC96	CC04	0008	0012F4D0	8C000068	..4....	SCP ACQUIRED USER STORAGE
C8	10BD98	CC04	0008	00000040	01100660	....	SCP GETMAIN-INIT
F1	115222	0004	0008	0012F540	8C000048	..5 ...	SCP ACQUIRED USER STORAGE
E1	13D1B2	00F4	0008	00000000	00000206	....	EIP HANDLE-AID RESPONSE
E1	13D1B2	00F4	0008	00000000	00000204	.0.....	EIP HANDLE-CONDITION ENTRY
F1	13D20C	0004	0008	0012F00C	01100660	....	SCP GETMAIN-INIT
C8	10BC96	CC04	0008	00000000	01100660	....	SCP ACQUIRED USER STORAGE
F1	10BC96	CC04	0008	0012F590	8C000078	..5....	SCP GETMAIN-INIT
C8	10BD98	CC04	0008	00000000	01100660	....	SCP ACQUIRED USER STORAGE
C8	115222	0004	0008	0012F610	8C000048	..6....	SCP ACQUIRED USER STORAGE
E1	13D20C	00F4	0008	0012F00C	00000202	.0.....	EIP HANDLE-CONDITION RESPONSE
E1	1302EE	0004	0008	0012F00C	00001802	....	EIP RECEIVE-MAP ENTRY
FA	125080	0003	0008	00000505	01100660	....	BMS MAP MAPSET MAP IN
F1	1253TE	CC04	0008	0012F660	8C000288	..6....	SCP GETMAIN-INIT
C8	115222	0004	0008	00000274	01100660	....	SCP ACQUIRED USER STORAGE
F1	15AD78	CC04	0008	0012F8F0	8C000088	..8....	SCP GETMAIN-INIT
C8	115222	0004	0008	0609C1C4	E2F0F140	ORADS01	SCP ACQUIRED USER STORAGE
F2	126200	0404	0008	0609C1C4	E2F0F140	ORADS01	PCP LOAD
F1	118572	8804	0008	00120095	01100660	....	SCP GETMAIN

Fig. 24.6. (Continued)

```
CUSTOMER INFORMATION CONTROL SYSTEM STORAGE DUMP    CODE=ERRS    TASK=DRAD          DATE=07/27/80    TIME=19 01 28    PAGE 6

1457F0  FD 00001C 0204 0008 E3C9D4C5 1901286F  TIME....  TIMING TRACE 19/01/28.6
145800  C8 115222 0004 0008 0013F800 88000800  ...8....  SCP ACQUIRED PGM STORAGE
14581C  F0 11862A 4004 TC   44000000 0011A746  ........  KCP WAIT DCI=CICS
145820  F0 10DB88 4004 TC   44000000 001007F8  ........8 KCP WAIT
145830  F1 124AAC C504 0008 00000381 01100660  ........  SCP GETMAIN-INIT
145840  C8 115222 0004 0008 00129120 850003C8  .......H  SCP ACQUIRED TERMINAL STORAGE
145850  F1 124E88 4004 0038 00129000 01100660  ........  SCP FREEMAIN
145860  C9 11530C 0004 0008 00129900 85000118  ........  SCP RELEASED TERMINAL STORAGE
145870  FA 125EE6 0005 0008 00000000 00001802  ........  BMS RESPONSE
145880  E1 13D2EE 0CF4 0008 0012F00C 0000A04.  ........  EIP RECEIVE-MAP RESPONSE
145890  E1 13D35E 0004 0008 0012F00C 01100660  ...0....  EIP READQ-TS ENTRY
1458A0  F7 12192C 8903 0008 D3F7FFF0 D6D9C1C4  L7700RAD  TSP GETQ
1458B0  F1 121C38 AE04 0008 01205540 01100660  ...9....  SCP GETMAIN-CONDITIONAL
1458C0  C8 115222 0004 0008 0012F980 8E120548  ........  SCP ACQUIRED TEMPSTRG STORAGE
1458D0  F7 121FCC 0015 0008 00000000 00000000  ........  TSP RESPONSE
1458E0  E1 13D35E 00F4 0008 0012F00C 00000A04  ...0....  EIP READ-TS RESPONSE
1458F0  E1 130F8C 0CF4 0008 0012FED0 0000C02.  ........  EIP GETMAIN ENTRY
145900  F1 115052 8C04 0008 00120181 01100660  ........  SCP GETMAIN-INIT
145910  C8 115222 0004 0008 0012FED0 8C1201C8  .......H  SCP ACQUIRED USER STORAGE
145920  E1 130F8C 00F4 0008 0000000C 0000C02.  ........  EIP GETMAIN RESPONSE
145930  E1 13E0OC 0004 0008 0012F00C 00000204  ...0....  EIP HANDLE-CONDITION ENTRY
145940  F1 10BD98 CC04 0008 00000A04 01100660  ........  SCP GETMAIN-INIT
145950  C8 115222 0004 0008 001300A0 8C000048  ........  SCP ACQUIRED USER STORAGE
145960  E1 13E0OC 00F4 0008 00000000 00000204  ...0....  EIP HANDLE-CONDITION RESPONSE   (C)
145970  F1 13E098 0004 0008 0012F00C 00000604  ...0....  EIP WRITE ENTRY
145980  C8 115222 CC04 0008 00130068 01100660  ...0....  SCP GETMAIN-INIT
145990  C8 115222 0004 0008 00130OF0 8C000078  ........  SCP ACQUIRED USER STORAGE
1459A0  F5 11E9C8 2803 0008 D609E3C5 E2E34040  ORTEST    FCP GETAREA   (E)
1459B0  F1 120BD8 CF04 0008 000001F1 01100663  ...I....  SCP GETMAIN-INIT
1459C0  C8 115222 0004 0008 00130170 8F000208  ........  SCP ACQUIRED FILE STORAGE
1459D0  F5 120134 0015 0008 00130170 00000000  ........  FCP RESPONSE NORMAL
1459E0  F5 11E9C8 4403 0008 D609E3C5 E2E34040  ORTEST    FCP PUT-NEW
1459F0  F1 120E62 9D04 0008 00130030 01100660  ........  SCP GETMAIN
145A00  C8 115222 0004 0008 00130380 90130038  ........  SCP ACQUIRED DWE STORAGE
145A10  C8 115222 8F04 0008 00130094 01100660  ........  SCP GETMAIN
145A20  F0 11B124 4004 0008 80000000 0017F040  ........0 SCP ACQUIRED FILE STORAGE
145A30  F1 120070 4004 0008 00130170 01100660  ........  KCP WAIT DCI=SINGLE
145A40  FD 00001C 0124 0008 00688180 00688180  ........  ...REPEAT 00001 TIMES
145A50  F1 120070 4004 0008 00130170 8F000208  ........  SCP FREEMAIN
145A60  C9 11530C 0004 0008 00130170 00000000  ........  FCP RELEASED FILE STORAGE
145A70  F5 120134 8215 0008 0013C3C0 00000000  ........  FCP RESPONSE
145A80  E1 11EB20 1003 0008 101303C0 00000000  ........  FCP RELEASE
145A90  F1 120070 4004 0008 00130380 01100660  ........  SCP FREEMAIN
145AA0  C9 11530C 0004 0008 00130380 90130038  ........  SCP RELEASED DWE STORAGE
145AB0  F1 120070 0004 0008 0013C3C0 01100660  ........  SCP FREEMAIN   (B)
145AC0  C9 11530C 0004 0008 001303C0 8F1300A8  ........  SCP RELEASED FILE STORAGE
145AD0  F5 120134 0015 0008 001303C0 00000000  ........  EIP WRITE RESPONSE   (D)
145AE0  E1 12F610 02F4 0008 82000000 00000604  ...0....  EIP DUMP ENTRY
145AF0  E1 13E434 FE04 0008 0012F00C C509D9E2  ..ERRS    DCP TRANSACTION
145B00  F4 1597FC 4004 0008 00000000 0015SE78  ........  KCP WAIT DCI=SINGLE
145B10  C9 155C58 0004 TC   44000000 001007F8  ........8 KCP WAIT
145B20  F0 10DB88 4004 0008 80000000 0015SE78  ........  KCP WAIT DCI=SINGLE
145B30  F0 155C58 4004 0008 80000000 0015SE78            KCP WAIT DCI=SINGLE
```

Fig. 24.6. (Continued)

```
CUSTOMER INFORMATION CONTROL SYSTEM STORAGE DUMP     CODE=ERRS   TASK=ORAD     DATE=07/27/80    TIME=19 01 28   PAGE   7

145B40        F0 10DBB8 4004 TC    44000000  001007F8   .......8 KCP WAIT


TRANSACTION STORAGE-USER    ADDRESS 1300F0        TO 13016F   LENGTH 000080
000000  8C000078 001300A0 D609E3C5 E2E34040   00000000 0811BAB0 00000000 00000000  *........ORTEST ..........*  1300F0
000020  00000000 00000000 00000000 00000000   00000000 00000000 00000000 00000000  *................*           130110
000040  00000000 00000000 00000000 00000000   00000000 00000000 00000000 00000000  *................*           130130
000060  00000000 00000000 00000000 FF000000   00000000 00000000 8C000078 001300A0  *................*           130150


TRANSACTION STORAGE-USER    ADDRESS 1300A0        TO 1300EF   LENGTH 000050
000000  8C000048 0012FED0 5013E00C 0010C5A0   00000025 0012F360 6013EAB0 00000051  *..........E....3...*        1300A0
000020  00129 1AA 5013EB02 0012F00C 0012F2E3   0012F2E4 0013EAD2 0013C820 0013C820  *..O...2T..2U...K..H...H..*  1300C0
000040  0013CC98 0012F0EC 8C000048 0012FED0                                         *..O.........*              1300E0


TRANSACTION STORAGE-USER    ADDRESS 12FED0        TO 13009F   LENGTH 0001D0
000000  8C1201C8 0012F980 F0F0F0F0 F0F0F0F2   F1F5F0F0 F5F8F2F0 F1F2F0F0 F7F2F7F8  *..H..9..000000215005820120007278*  12FED0
000020  F0000200 000C0004 00000C00 01F0F0F0   F0F8F5F7 F3C3C8C1 C9D540E2 C1E64040  *0.......00008573CHAIN SAM*          12FEF0
000040  40404040 40404040 F0F1F2F0 F8F20002   0C001000 00000000 00000000 00000000  *        012082..........*           12FF10
000060  00000000 00000000 00000000 00000000   00000000 00000000 00000000 00000000  *................*                   12FF30
000080  LINES TO 000100 SAME AS ABOVE
000120  00000000 00000130 00000000 00000000   00000800 00000000 00000000 00000000  *................*                   12FF70
000140  00000000 00000000 00000000 00000000   00000000 00000000 00000000 00000000  *................*                   130010
000160  LINES TO 0001A0 SAME AS ABOVE
0001C0  00000000 8C1201C8 0012F980                                                  *.....H..9.*                        130090


TRANSACTION STORAGE-TS      ADDRESS 12F980        TO 12FECF   LENGTH 000550
000000  8E120548 0012F8F0 05400000 F0F0F0F0   F0F0F0F2 F1F5F0F0 F5F8F2F0 F1F2F0F0  *......80..-.000000215005820120200*  12F980
000020  F7F2F7F8 F0000200 000C0004 00000C00   01F0F0F0 F0F8F5F7 F3C3C8C1 C90540E2  *72780.........00008573CHAIN S*      12F9A0
000040  C1E64040 40404040 40404040 F0F1F2F0   F8F20002 0C001000 0C002000 00000000  *AW............012082............*   12F9C0
000060  00000000 00000000 00000000 00000000   00000000 00000000 00000000 00000000  *................*                   12F9E0
000080  00000000 00000000 00000000 00000000   00000000 00000000 00000000 00000000  *................*                   12FA00
        LINES TO 000180 SAME AS ABOVE
0001A0  000000BE F0F0F3F0 F0F4F0F0 F5F0F0F7   00000000 00000000 00000000 0007C1D3  *.............PAL*                   12FB20
0001C0  F1F4F0F1 F5F0F1F6 F0F1F7F0 F1F8F0F1   F9F0F2F0 F2F2F0F2 F3F0F2F4 F0F2F5    *..00304005007008009010012013 0*    12FB40
0001E0  F0F2F6F0 F2F7F0F2 F8F0F2F9 F0F3F0F3   F2F0F3F3 F0F3F4F0 F3F5F0F3 F6F0F3    *140150160170180190200220230240025* 12FB60
000200  F7F0F3F8 F0F3F9F0 F4F0F0F4 F1F0F4F2   F0F4F3F0 F4F4F0F4 F5F0F4F6 F0F4F7    *026027028029030320330 34035036 03* 12FB80
000220  F4F8F0F4 F9F0F5F0 F0F5F1F0 F5F2F0F5   F3F0F5F4 F0F5F5F0 F5F6F0F5 F7F0F5    *703803904004104204304404504604 70* 12FBA0
000240  F6F5F0F6 F6F0F6F7 F0F6F8F0 F6F9F0F7   F0F0F7F1 F0F7F2F0 F7F3F0F7 F4F0F4    *480490500510520530540550560570580059* 12FBC0
000260  F0F7F6F0 F7F7F0F7 F8F0F7F9 F0F8F0F0   F8F1F0F8 F2F0F8F4 F0F8F5F0 F8F6F0F9  *06006106206306406506606706806907 007* 12FBE0
000280  F0F8F7F0 F8F8F0F8 F9F0F9F0 F0F9F1F0   F9F2F0F9 F3F0F9F5 F0F9F6F0 F9F7F0F7  *07020704075076077078079080081082 0*  12FC00
0002A0  F0F9F8F0 F9F9F0F9 F1F0F2F1 F0F3F1F0   F4F1F0F5 F1F0F6F1 F0F7F1F0 F1F0F4    *08408508608708808909009109209309509 6* 12FC20
0002C0  F0F9F7F0 F9F8F0F9 F9F0F9F1 F0F2F1F0   F3F1F0F4 F1F0F5F1 F0F6F1F0 F7F1F3    *09709809909102103104105106107010*   12FC40
0002E0  F8F1F0F9 F1F1F1F1 F3F1F1F4 F1F1F5F1   F1F6F1F1 F8F1F1F2 F1F2F1F2 F3F1F6    *810911111311411511611811211221 2231* 12FC60
000300  F2F4F1F2 F5F1F2F6 F1F2F7F1 F2F8F1F3   F3F4F1F3 F5F1F3F6 F0F3F1F3 F4F1F3    *24125126127128130131131331341351 36* 12FC80
000320  F1F3F7F1 F3F9F1F4 F0F1F4F2 F1F4F3F1   F4F4F1F4 F5F1F4F6 F1F4F7F1 F4F8F1F4  *137139140142143144145146147148144*  12FCA0
000340  F9F1F5F1 F1F5F2F1 F5F4F1F5 F5F1F5F6   F1F5F7F1 F5F9F1F6 F0F1F6F1 F1F6F3F1  *915115215415515615715916016116 31*  12FCC0
000360  F6F4F1F6 F5F1F6F6 F1F6F7F1 F6F8F1F6   F9F1F7F0 F1F7F1F7 F2F1F7F3 F1F7F4    *641651661671681691701711721731 74*  12FCE0
```

Fig. 24.6. (Continued)

CUSTOMER INFORMATION CONTROL SYSTEM STORAGE DUMP   CODE=ERRS   TASK=DRAD   DATE=07/27/80   TIME=19 01 28   PAGE   8

TRANSACTION STORAGE-TS   ADDRESS 12F980   TO 12FECF   LENGTH 000550

```
000383  F1F7F5F1 F7F6F1F7 F7F1F7F8 F1F7F9F1  F8F0F1F8 F1F1F8F2 F1F8F3F1 F8F4F1F8  *175176177178179180181182183184181*  12FD00
0003A0  F5F1F8F6 F1F8F1F8 F8F0F1F8 F9F0F1F8  F1F9F1F1 F9F2F1F9 F3F1F9F4 F1F9F5F1  *518618718818919019192193194195191*  12FD20
0003C0  F9F7F1F9 F8F1F8F9 F2F0F0F2 F0F3F2F0  F4F2F0F5 F2F0F6F2 F0F7F7F2F0 F8F2F0F9  *971981992002032042052062072082099*  12FD40
0003E0  F2F1F0F2 F1F5F2F1 F9F2F2F6 F2F2F9F2  F3F4F2F4F1 F2F4F2F4F7  F4F70000  *210215219226229230234241242247..*  12FD60
000420  00000000 00000000 0000C000 00000000  00000000 00000000 00000000 00000000  *................................*  12FD80
000540  LINES TO 000520 SAME AS ABOVE                                             *                                  *  12FDA0
000540  00000000 00000000 8E120548 0012F8F0                                       *..............80.                  *  12FEC0
```

TRANSACTION STORAGE-USER   ADDRESS 12F8F0   TO 12F97F   LENGTH 000090

```
000000  8C000088 0012F660 D4040000 00000001  00010001 00000000 00000000 00000000  *.......-6....MM....................*  12F8F0
000020  0013F808 00000000 00000000 00000000  00000000 00000000 D6D9C1C4 E2F0F140  *..8...............ORADS01*          12F910
000040  00000000 00000000 18500000 00000000  40000001 01015000 00000000 0000780  *.............................6--..*  12F930
000060  00000000 01100660 00404000 00000000  00000000 00000000 FFFFFFFF 00000000  *.................6--..*              12F950
000080  00000000 8C000088 0012F660                                                *                                  *  12F970
```

TRANSACTION STORAGE-USER   ADDRESS 12F660   TO 12F8EF   LENGTH 000290

```
000000  8C000288 0012F610 401256A6 0015A9C8  40125BC0 001244CA 00000000 00000000  *......6.......H...................*  12F660
000020  00000000 00000000 00000505 00000020  00000000 00000000 00000000 00000000  *...........................01A....*  12F680
000040  D6D9C1C4 E2F0F140 000C260 00000000  F0F1C140 0012F8F0 D6D9C1C4 D4F0F140  *.ORADS01...8-....01A....DRADM01*    12F6A0
000060  00000000 00000000 00000000 00000000  0012F8F0 0012F8F0 00000000 00000000  *..............80..80...............*  12F6C0
000080  00000000 00000000 00000000 00100660  0012F8F0 00000000 00000000 00000000  *..................................*  12F6E0
0000A0  00000000 00000000 00000000 00000000  1411A6E4 00000001 00000000 00000000  *..............U...................*  12F700
0000C0  00000000 00000000 00000000 00000010  00000000 00000000 00000000 00000000  *..................................*  12F720
0000E0  00000000 00000000 00000000 00000000  00000000 00000000 00000000 00000000  *..................................*  12F740
000100  00000000 00000000 00000000 00000000  08129000 000000FF 0010066C 00000000  *.................................Q*  12F760
000120  00000000 4D126200 00125208 000004B0  00000018 000000FF 00000000 00000000  *......G..6-..80.....6--..*           12F780
000140  0013F814 90125884 48000058 0010C700  0012F660 01100660 00000000 00000000  *..8.....G.....6--..*                12F7A0
000160  00000000 00000000 00000000 00110000  00000000 00000000 00000000 00000000  *..................................*  12F7C0
000180  00000000 00000000 00000000 00000000  00000000 00000000 00000000 00000000  *..................................*  12F7E0
0001A0  00000000 00000000 000260 SAME AS ABOVE                                    *..................6.*               12F800
000280  00000000 00000000 8C000288 0012F610                                       *                                  *  12F820
                                                                                                                       12F8E0
```

TRANSACTION STORAGE-USER   ADDRESS 12F610   TO 12F65F   LENGTH 000050

```
000000  8C000048 0012F590 5013D20C 0010C5A0  0012F00C 0012F360 5013D1C4 0013CCA8  *.....5...K...E...0...3...JD....*     12F610
000020  0012F420 5013EB02 0012F00C 0012F2E4  0013EAD2 0013C820 0013C820          *.4.....0...2T..2U...K..H...H..*      12F630
000040  0013CC98 8C000048 0012F590                                               *.0.....5.*                          12F650
```

TRANSACTION STORAGE-USER   ADDRESS 12F590   TO 12F60F   LENGTH 000080

```
000000  8C000078 0012F540 0012F5D7 00700402  00000000 00000000 00000000 00000000  *.5...5P...........................*  12F590
000020  00030000 00000000 00000100 00000000  12F61004 12F0EC02 12F61004 12F0EC01  *..........6...0...6...0.*            12F5B0
000040  00000000 00000000 00000000 00000001  12F61004 12F0EC02 8C000078 0012F540  *..............6...0.*               12F5D0
000060  1300A4D4 12F0EC00 00000000 00000000                                       *...0.....5 *                        12F5F0
```

Fig. 24.6. (Continued)

```
CUSTOMER INFORMATION CONTROL SYSTEM STORAGE DUMP        CODE=ERRS     TASK=QRAD        DATE=07/27/80    TIME=19 01 28    PAGE    9

TRANSACTION STORAGE-USER    ADDRESS 12F540    TO 12F58F    LENGTH 000050
000000   8C000048  0012F4D0  5013D1B2  C010C5A0   0012F00C  0012F360  0013EB40  00118BA0   *....4...J..E..O..3-...*      12F540
000020   0012F420  5013EB02  0012F00C  0012F2E3   0012F2E4  0013EAD2  0013C820  0013C820   *.4....O..2T..2U..K..H...H.*  12F560
000040   0013CC98  8C000048  0012F4D0                                                      *.....O....4.*               12F580

TRANSACTION STORAGE-USER    ADDRESS 12F4D0    TO 12F53F    LENGTH 000070
000000   8C000068  0012F390  0012F500  00590500   00040201  03000000  00000000  00000000   *....4...5.....*             12F4D0
000020   00000000  00000000  00000000  00000000   00118DEC  0112F540  0412F0EC  00000000   *.............5...0.*        12F4F0
000040   0212F540  0412F0EC  0312F540  0412F0EC   0000000   0412F0EC  00000000  00000000   *.5...0...5...0....*         12F510
000060   FF000000  00000000  8C000068                                                      *..........3.*               12F530

TRANSACTION STORAGE-USER    ADDRESS 12F390    TO 12F4CF    LENGTH 000140
000000   8C000138  0012EFC0  0012F488  00000000   00000000  00000000  00000000  00000000   *.........4........*         12F390
000020   00000000  00000000  00000000  00000000   00000000  00000000  00000000  00000000   *................*           12F3B0
000040   0012F420  8012F424  00130DA0  A011ECAA   00129120  00000000  0012F980  00000000   *.4...........9...*          12F3D0
000060   00000000  00000000  001300F8  001300F8   0012F590  0012F400  00000000  00000000   *........8...8...5...4...0.*  12F3F0
000080   01000004  00000000  00010000  00000000   0012F488  80120588  0012F0EC  0012F00C   *.........4.......0..*       12F410
0000A0   00000000  00118DEC  0012F0EC  4010C43E   4013C822  00118DEC  0012F0EC  0013C8F0   *.....0...D...H0...0...HO*   12F430
0000C0   0012EFD0  0013C868  00118E68  0012E800   0013C820  0010C260  00130D3A  FF11A6E4   *......H...Y..H..B-...U*     12F450
0000E0   0012F390  0012E888  80000000  010E0000   40C4C6C8  C56C9C240  01901D28C  0080209F   *.3...Y...H..DFHEIB.....*   12F470
000100   D6D9C1C4  0000008C  D3F7F7F0  000006BD   0017D01C  02000000  00000006  D9E3C5E2   *ORAD..L770.........ORTES*   12F490
000120   E3404000  00000000  00000000            8C000138  00000000                        *T........*                 12F4B0

TRANSACTION STORAGE-USER    ADDRESS 12EFC0    TO 12F38F    LENGTH 000300
(F)>
000000   8C1303C8  0012E800  00000000  00000000   0013C920  5013EB1A  0013EB40  00118BA0   *...H..Y......I......H.*     12EFC0
000020   0013C820  5013C820  0013CBF7  0013C8F7   5013C6F8  0013EAD2  0013C820  0013C820   *..H...H...7..H7..F8..K..H..H.*  12EFE0
000040   0013CC98  0013CA00  00119C6   00000000   D3C9D5C5  40F24000  40F24000  40000000   *...q...........LINE 2 -*    12F020
000060   00000000  00000000  00000000  00000000   D1D6C240  0506D9D4  C1D3D3E8  40E3C5D9   *..............JOB NORMALLY TER*  12F040
000080   D4C9D5C1  E3C5C4D1  D6C240C1  C2D6D9E3   C5C44060  40000000  00000000  00000000   *MINATEDJOB ABORTED --*     12F060
0000A0   00000000  00000000  04040404  04040D6D9   40E20000  00000000  1C028000  00000000   *............OLD EIB.......*  12F080
0000C0   040000FE  00000000  D6D3C440  C5C9C240   40404040  40D6D9C1  C4D4F0F1  40D6D9     *..........ORADM01 OR*      12F0A0
0000E0   C1C4E2F0  F140D6D9  E3C5E2E3  40400000   00000000  C5D9D9E2  40400000  00000000   *ADS01 ORTEST .....ERRS..*  12F0C0
000100   00000000  00018100  00400000   00000000  0012F430  00000000  5013EA34  0010C5A0   *...........4......E.*       12F0E0
000120   00000000  00400000  00000000   0012F420  5013EB02  0012F00C  00000000  00000000   *.....4....O..0....*        12F100
000140   0012F00C  0012F360  4013D21E   0013C820  0013CC98  20100048  00000000  00000000   *.0..3- .K..H...q.*         12F120
000160   0012F2E4  0013EAD2  0013C820   00000000  00000000  00000003  01000000  00000003   *.2U..K..H.....*            12F140
000180   0010C3D4  00000000  00000000   FFF0F0F5  00000000  00000001  00000003  00000000   *..CM.....005....*          12F160
0001A0   01000000  00000000  00000000   00000000  00000000  00000000  00000000  00000000   *................*          12F180
0001C0   00000000  00000000  SAME AS ABOVE                                                 *................*          12F1A0
0001E0   LINES TO 0002A0 SAME AS ABOVE                                                                                 12F1E0
0002C0   00000000  00000000  00000000   00000000  D6D9C1C4  F0F1C140  F0F1C140  0013C820   *.......ORADO1A ..H.*       12F280
0002E0   00000000  00000000  00000000   00000000  00000000  00000000  00000000  00000000   *.............*             12F2A0
000300   00000000  00000000  0400000F   00000000  0400000F  00000000  0000002C  0012FB44   *..............,...*        12F2C0
000320   0012F00C  00000000  0013D472   00000000  0012F488  8012D5B8  0012F318  02CC0051   *.0.....M....4...N..3...*   12F2E0
000340   0000008E  01000003  00000000   0012F488  0012F488  02CC0051  00129120  00000000   *........4...4....*         12F300
000360   0012FED8  0012E98C  00000000                                                      *..Q..Z..9......*           12F320
(G)
```

Fig. 24.6. (Continued)

```
CUSTOMER INFORMATION CONTROL SYSTEM STORAGE DUMP    CODE=ERRS    TASK=DRAD                DATE=07/27/80    TIME=19 01 28    PAGE 10

TRANSACTION STORAGE-USER     ADDRESS 12EFC0    TO 12F38F    LENGTH 0003D0
00038C  000000A6 FFFFFFE1 000C0000 C0000000   00000006 001291AA 0013DCD0 0013DCD0   *...0...0...Q..$.....0E......*  12F340
0003A0  0012F07C 8012FDB8 0012FED8 0012EA5B   8012EA41 8012FE0C5 00000000 00000000   *.................H.Y.*      12F360
0003C0  00000000 00030000 8C13D3C8 0012E800                                          *.................H.Y.*      12F380

TERMINAL CONTROL TBL USER AREA ADDRESS 1007E8    TO 1007F7    LENGTH 000010
000000  00000000 00000000 00000000 00000000                                          *..............*            1007E8

TERMINAL CONTROL TABLE        ADDRESS 100660    TO 100723    LENGTH 0000C4
003030  03F7F7F0 99F20404 00129120 00129120   0012E888 00000000 0010D7E8 10000000   *L770.2........Y......Y.....*  100660
000020  00000000 0C000000 0000B100 00000900   06807D00 06D9C1C4 E2F0F140 00000000   *.............DRADS01.....*   100680
000040  00000000 00000000 07801850 00000000   00000000 00C40000 00000000 0010C5A8   *...........N...........*     1006A0
000060  0010170E 00000000 0012D5A0 00000000   00000000 00840000 00000000 0000005C   *..........N........*         1006C0
000080  0000B8C0 0C0000SC 00C8100 00040000     00000000 00000000 00000000 0000005C   *..........*..............*   1006E0
0000A0  00000000 00000000 00000000 00001600   00000100 18500000 82000000 04040000   *.................MM.....*    100700
0000C0  00000000                                                                     *.....*                      100720

TERMINAL STORAGE              ADDRESS 129120    TO 1294EF    LENGTH 0003D0
000000  850003C8 00100664 03AA0000 00100F1    00300F0F F0F0F0F0 F3F0F2F1 F5000400   *...H.............1...0000000215...*  129120
000020  F0F0F0F0 F5F3F3F8 000100F0 F0F50006   00F0F1F2 F0F8F200 0400F0F0 F0F0F8F5   *00005328...005..012082...000085*    129140
000040  F7F30009 00C3C8C1 C9D540E2 C1E64040   40404040 40404040 00020F0 F0F0F2F0   *73...CHAIN SAM.........00020*       129160
000060  00050F0F F0F1F0F0 F0F00006 00F0F0F2   F0F0F0F0 F0F0F2F0 F0F0F000 00000000   *..010000...00200000...0020000...*  129180
000080  0600F0F0 F4F0F0F0 F0F00000 00000500   00000000 00000000 00000000 00000000   *..00400000..............*    1291A0
0000A0  00000000 00000000 00000000 00000000   00000000 00000000 00000000 00000000   *.........*                  1291C0
0000C0  00000000 LINES TO 000300 SAME AS ABOVE                                                                   1291E0
000300  00100006 00F0F0F0 F2F0F0F0 F0F00006   00F0F0F0 F4F4F0F0 F0F00000 00404040   *...000200000...000400000...*  129440
000320  40404040 40404040 40404040 40404040   40404040 40000000 00040400 40404040   *........................*    129460
000340  40404040 40404040 40404040 40404040   40404040 40000000 00040404 04040404   *........................*    129480
000360  40404040 40404040 40404040 40404040   40404040 40404040 04040404 04040404   *..........H......*           1294A0
000380  40404040 40404040 40404040 40404040   40404040 40400000 04040404 04040404   *........*                    1294C0
0003A0  40404040 00000000 850003C8 00100664                                          *....................*        1294E0

PROGRAM STORAGE               ADDRESS 13C808    TO 13EF8F    LENGTH 002788
000300  C4C6C8C5 58F0F00C 07FF58F0 F00A07FF   001191B6 001C760 05F00700 900EF00A   *DFHE.00....00........G..0...0.*  13C808
000020  47F0F082 00118DEC 0012F420 0013C8F0   0012EFD0 0013C868 00118E68 0012E800   *.00......4...H0......Y..*        13C828
000040  0013C820 001C260 0013D13A FF11A6E4     0012F390 0012E888 0012F430 4010C43E   *.H..B...J...U..3...Y..4..D.*    13C848
000060  0013C920 5013E81A 0013E840 00118BA0     0013C820 5013E802 0013C920 0013C8F7   *..I.......H......I..7*           13C868
000080  0013C8F8 0013EAD2 0013C820 00013C820    0013CC98 0013C4A00 00119DC6 58C0F0C6   *..8..K..H...H......F..0F*        13C888
0000A0  58E0C000 58D0F0CA 9500E0D0 47F0F0A2     9610D048 92FFE000 47F0F0AC 98CEF03A   *..........0...0..K..H..H*        13C8A8
0000C0  90EC000C 185D989F F08A911D 00480719     07FF0700 0013EAD2 0013C820 0013C820   *..........)...0.....K..H..H*     13C8C8
0000E0  0013CC98 012F0EC 0013D13A 0013EA88     C3D6C2C6 F2F5F5F1 D609C1C4 F0F1C140   *...J....0..J...COBF2551ORAD01A*  13C8E8
00010C  0013CC24 F0F761F2 F761F8F0 F1F84BF5     F64B8F5 00000000 00000000 D106C240   *.07/27/8018.56.35..........JOB*  13C908
000140  D5D609D4 C1D3D3E8 40E3C5D9 D4C905C1     E3C5C401 D6C240C1 C2D6D9E3 C5C44060   *NORMALLY TERMINATEDJOB ABORTED -*  13C948
```

Fig. 24.6. (Continued)

CUSTOMER INFORMATION CONTROL SYSTEM STORAGE DUMP   ADDRESS   13C808   TO 13EF8F   CODE=ERRS   TASK=ORAD   LENGTH   002788   DATE=07/27/80   TIME=19 01 28   PAGE   11

PROGRAM STORAGE

Fig. 24.6. (Continued)

```
CUSTOMER INFORMATION CONTROL SYSTEM STORAGE DUMP   CODE=ERRS    TASK=ORAD        DATE=07/27/80    TIME=19 01 28    PAGE   12

PROGRAM STORAGE                ADDRESS  13C808  TO  13EF8F     LENGTH  002788

000900   40E5C906 D3C1E3C9 D6D5E3C1 C2D3C540   D5D6E340 D3D6C1C4 C5C4C5D9 D9E21C02   * VIOLATIONTABLE NOT LOADEDERRS..*   13D108
000920   80000400 00FE00D4 C1D1D6D9 40C5D9D9   D6D95840 D0045840 40185810 40005010   *........MAJOR ERROR. ...  ... ...*   13D128
000940   D2245810 40045010 D2281B11 58F0C004   05EFD211 6070C1B0 92406082 D2066083   *K... ...K.....O.....K.-.A.. -.K.-.*   13D148
000960   60824110 60705010 D27458E0 D22C4110   E00C5010 D2789680 D2784110 D27458F0   *-...-...K...K.......K...K...K..O*   13D168
000980   C00405EF D2116070 C1C29240 6082D206   60836082 41106070 5010D274 9680D274   *....K.-.AB. -.K.-.-...-...K...K.*   13D188
0009A0   4110D274 58F0C004 05EF58E0 D2244810   E0144130 C0104910 C1900520 47202022   *..K..O......K............A.......*   13D1A8
0009C0   8B100001 47C02022 48112018 89100002   58113000 07F10012 000D000D 000DD211   *......................1........K.*   13D1C8
0009E0   6070C1D4 92406082 D2066083 60824110   60705010 D2749680 D2744110 D27458F0   *-.AM. -.K.-.-...-...K...K...K..O*   13D1E8
000A00   C00405EF 58E0D224 4810E014 4130C010   4910C18E 05204720 201E8B10 000147C0   *......K............A.............*   13D208
000A20   201E4811 20188910 00025811 300007F1   0016001A 4830E018 4930C178 58F0C090   *...............1...........A..O..*   13D228
000A40   078F5820 C09458E0 D22895F1 E0000772   5810C014 07F15820 C09858E0 D22895F0   *.........K..1...........1.......K..O*   13D248
000A60   E0000772 5810C048 07F15810 C06C07F1   58E0D224 4830E018 4930C178 58F0C014   *..........1.....1..K.........A..O..*   13D268
000A80   077F5810 C07007F1 D206608A C1E69240   6091D206 6092C1ED 92406099 D20E6070   *........1K.-.AW. -.K.-.A.. -.K.-.*   13D288
000AA0   C1F49240 607FD209 6080607F 41106070   5010D274 4110608A 5010D278 58E0D22C   *A4. -.K.-.-...-...K...-...K...K.*   13D2A8
000AC0   4110E004 5010D27C 411060D7 5010D280   41106092 5010D284 9680D284 4110D274   *.......K...-P..K...-...K...K...K.*   13D2C8
000AE0   58F0C004 05EF58E0 D23858F0 D2240203   E093F010 D203E097 F008D201 60B9C179   *.O.......K..OK.K...O.K...O.K.-.A.*   13D2E8
000B00   D2086070 C2039240 6079D20F 607A6079   41106070 5010D274 4110E093 5010D278   *K.-.B.. -.K.- -...-...K.......K.*   13D308
000B20   58E0D22C 4110E010 5010D27C 58E0D238   4110E0A5 5010D280 411060D9 5010D284   *..K........K...K........K...-R..K.*   13D328
000B40   41106089 5010D288 9680D288 4110D274   58F0C004 05EF58E0 D2309240 E33DD21A   *..-...K...K...K..O.......K.. T.K.*   13D348
000B60   E33EE33D 9240E35C D21AE35D E35C9240   E37BD21A E37CE37B 9240E39A D21AE39B   *T.T.. T*K.T)T*. T.K.T.T.. T.K.T.*   13D368
000B80   E39A4800 C17C5000 D2585820 C00858E0   D230DD09 E0132000 5810C09C 077158E0   *T...A...K........K.................*   13D388
000BA0   D23C58F0 D230D209 E000F013 5810C0A0   07F14100 001F5A00 D2585000 D25858E0   *K...OK.K...O........1........K...K...*   13D3A8
000BC0   D2304140 E33D5A40 D2585040 D26858E0   D268D213 E000C20C 58E0D268 9240E014   *K.. T.. K.. K...K.K...B...K.. ..*   13D3C8
000BE0   58E0D268 58F0D268 D206E015 F01458E0   D230D201 E010C17E 5820C008 58E0D230   *..K...OK.K...O...K.K...A=.......K.*   13D3E8
000C00   DD07E020 20005810 C0A40771 5810C0A8   07F14100 001F5A00 D2585000 D25858E0   *.................1.......K...K...*   13D408
000C20   D2304140 E33D5A40 D2585040 D26858E0   D268D216 E000C220 58E0D268 9240E017   *K.. T.. K.. K...K.K...B...K.. ..*   13D428
000C40   58E0D268 58F0D268 D203E018 F0171B00   5900D258 58F0C0A8 077F58E0 D230D201   *..K...OK.K...O......K..O.......K.K.*   13D448
000C60   E01DC17E 5810C0AC 07F15810 C01807F1   58E0D23C 4100E1B8 5000D210 5800E1B4   *..A=.....1.....1..K.........K......*   13D468
000C80   5000D214 D203D218 C0B0D201 D21EC180   58E0D230 D202D208 E02B9201 D21C4100   *..K.K.K...K.K.A...K.K.K......K...*   13D488
000CA0   D2084110 D21058F0 C00C05EF 88030000   58101000 1B015000 D26458E0 D23C58F0   *K...K..O....................K...K..O*   13D4A8
000CC0   D230D202 E00AF02B 5810C01C 07F15810   C0B407F1 4100001F 5A00D258 5000D258   *K.K...O.......1......1.......K...K.*   13D4C8
000CE0   58E0D230 4140E33D 5A40D258 5040D268   58E0D268 D218E000 C23758E0 D2689240   *..K.. T.. K.. K...K.K...B...K.. *   13D4E8
000D00   E01958E0 D26858F0 D268D201 E01AF019   1B005900 D25858F0 C01C077F 58E0D230   *....K..OK.K...O.......K..O.......K.*   13D508
000D20   D201E028 C17E5820 C0B858E0 D230D501   E031C250 07D25820 C0B8D501 E031C252   *K...A=.......K.N...B..K.....N...B.*   13D528
000D40   07B25820 C0B8D501 E033C250 07D25820   C0B8D501 E033C253 07B25820 C008DD01   *.......N...B..K.....N...B..........*   13D548
000D60   E0352000 5810C0B8 077158E0 D23C58F0   D230D201 E00FF031 D201E011 F033D201   *...............K..OK.K...O.K...O.K.*   13D568
000D80   E00DF035 5810C020 07F14100 001F5A00   D2585000 D25858E0 D2304140 E33D5A40   *..O.......1.......K...K...K.. T.. *   13D588
000DA0   D2585040 D26858E0 D268D211 E000C255   58E0D268 9240E012 58E0D268 58F0D268   *K.. K...K.K...B...K.. .....K..OK.*   13D5A8
000DC0   D208E013 F0121B00 5900D258 58F0C020   077F58E0 D230D201 E02EC17E 4100005D   *K...O......K..O........K.K...A=...)*   13D5C8
000DE0   5900D258 58F0C024 077F5810 C04007F1   1B005000 D25458E0 D238D203 E09BC182   *..K..O........ .1.....K...K.K...A.*   13D5E8
000E00   58F0D230 D205E06E F031D204 E07FC186   D204E084 C1865800 D2705000 D26C5800   *.OK.K...O.K...A.K...A...K...K...*   13D608
000E20   C0BC5000 D27058E0 D2385830 E09B4930   C17858F0 C0C0078F 4100005D 5900D258   *....K...K........A..O.........)..K.*   13D628
000E40   58F0C0C0 078F4100 02985900 D25458F0   C0C0074F 5810C028 07F15800 D26C5000   *.O............K..O............1..K...*   13D648
000E60   D2705810 C03007F1 58E0D238 D203E09B   C1861B00 5810D254 41200053 1D024A10   *K.......1..K.K...A......K..........*   13D668
000E80   C18C4E10 D208F307 600DD208 96F0600D   58E0D230 4140E037 5A40D254 5040D268   *A.+.K.3.-.K..O-...K.. ... K.. K.*   13D688
000EA0   58E0D238 58F0D268 D252E000 F0004830   E0004930 C17858F0 C0C4078F 5820C008   *..K..OK.K...O..........A..O.D.......*   13D6A8
000EC0   DD07E003 20005810 C0C80771 D207E053   E0034830 C18C5A30 E09B5030 E09B5810   *...........H..K..........A..............*   13D6C8
000EE0   C0C407F1 D2126011 C2674100 001F5A00   D2585000 D25858E0 D2304140 E33D5A40   *.D.1K.-.B.........K...K...K.. T.. *   13D6E8
000F00   D2585040 D26858E0 D268D21B E0006008   1B005900 D25858F0 C0CC077F 58E0D230   *K.. K...K.K...-......K..O.......K.*   13D708
000F20   4140E037 5A40D254 D2014000 C17E5810   C0C407F1 4100005D 5900D258 58F0C0C4   *. ... K.K. .A=...D.1...)..K..O.D*   13D728
000F40   077F5810 C02C07F1 58E0D238 4830E008   4930C178 58F0C0D0 077F9240 E05BD211   *........1..K.........A..O..... .$K.*   13D748
```

Fig. 24.6. (Continued)

PROGRAM STORAGE   ADDRESS   13C808   TO   13EF8F   LENGTH   002788

000F60	E05CE05B	5810C0D4	07F15820	C0D858E0	D2389540	E00E0772	D2126011	C27A4100	*.*.$...M.1...Q..K.. ....K.-.B ..*	13D768
000F80	001F5A00	D2585000	D25858E0	D2304140	E33D5A40	D2585040	D26858E0	D268D21B	*...K...K..K.. T.. K.. K...K.K.*	13D788
000FA0	E0006008	1B005900	D25858F0	C0DC077F	58E0D230	4140E042	5A40D254	D2014000	*..-....K..O.....K.. ... K.K..*	13D7A8
000FC0	C17E5810	C00407F1	4100005D	5900D258	07F5810	C02C07F1	5810C0D4		*A=...M.1...).K..O........l....M*	13D7C8
000FE0	07F158E0	D238D212	E05BE00E	4830C18E	5A30E09B	5030E09B	58E0D238	4830E021	*.1..K..K............K.........*	13D7E8
001000	4930C178	58F0C0E4	078F5820	C008DD04	E0242000	5810C0E8	0771F274	D1F8E024	*..A..O.U..............Y..J.8..*	13D808
001020	F822E074	D1FD94F0	E076960C	E0764830	C1905A30	E09B5030	E09B5810	C0E407F1	*8..J..O...........A............U.1*	13D828
001040	58E0D238	D202E074	C188D20B	6011C28D	9240601D	D205601E	60104100	001F5A00	*..K.K..A.K.-.B.. -.K-.-.-....*	13D848
001060	D2585000	D25858E0	D2304140	E33D5A40	D2585040	D26858E0	D268D21B	E0006008	*K..K...K.. T.. K.. K.K.K...-*	13D868
001080	1B005900	D25858F0	C0EC077F	58E0D230	4140E058	5A40D254	D2014000	C17E5810	*...K..O.....K.. ... K.K. .A=..*	13D888
0010A0	C0E407F1	4100005D	5900D258	58F0C0E4	077F5810	C02C07F1	58E0D238	4830E029	*.U.1...).K..O.U........l..K....*	13D8A8
0010C0	4930C178	58F0C0F0	078F5820	C008DD06	E02C2000	5810C0F4	0771F276	D1F8E02C	*..A..O.O..............4..2.J8..*	13D8C8
0010E0	F833E077	D1FC94F0	E07A960C	E07A4830	C1925830	E09B5030	E09B5810	C0F007F1	*8...J..O. ... .A...........O.1*	13D8E8
001100	58E0D238	D203E077	C187D210	6011C28D	92406022	D2006023	60224100	001F5A00	*..K.K..A.K.-.B.. -.K-.-..-....*	13D908
001120	D2585000	D25858E0	D2304140	E33D5A40	D2585040	D26858E0	D268D21B	E0006008	*K..K...K.. T.. K.. K.K.K...-*	13D928
001140	1B005900	D25858F0	C0F8077F	58E0D230	4140E060	5A40D254	D2014000	C17E5810	*...K..O.8...K.. .-. K.K. .A=..*	13D948
001160	C0F007F1	4100005D	5900D258	58F0C0F0	077F5810	C02C07F1	5810E033	4830E033	*.O.1...).K..O.O........l..K....*	13D968
001180	4930C178	58F0C0FC	078F5820	C008DD07	E0362000	5810C100	0771F873	D1F8E077	*..A..O.........K.........A..8.J8..*	13D988
0011A0	FC62D1F9	E074F277	D200E036	F946D203	D1F958F0	C100077F	F27D0200	E036FA44	*.J9..2.K...9.K.J9.OA...2.K.....*	13D9A8
0011C0	E07FD203	4830C194	5A30E09B	5030E09B	5810C0FC	07F1D20B	6011C29E	9240601D	*.K..-.A.........1K.-.8.. -.*	13D9C8
0011E0	D205601E	601D4100	001F5A00	D2585000	D25858E0	D2304140	E33D5A40	D2585040	*K.-.-..-...K...K.K.. T.. K..*	13D9E8
001200	D26858E0	D268D21B	E0006008	1B005900	D25858F0	C104077F	58E0D230	4140E06A	*K..K.K.....-...K...O.....K.. .*	13DA08
001220	5A40D254	D2014000	C17E5810	C0FCC07F1	4100005D	5900D258	58F0C0FC	077F5810	* K.K. .A=...1...).K..O......*	13DA28
001240	C02C07F1	58E0D238	4830E03E	4930C178	58F0C0FC	078F5820	C008DD06	E0412000	*.l..K......A.......O........OA.....*	13DA48
001260	5810C10C	0771F276	D200E041	F833E07B	D20494F0	E07E960C	E07E4830	C1965A30	*..A..2.K..8..K..O.=..-=.-.A..*	13DA68
001280	E09B5030	E09B5810	C10807F1	58E0D238	D203E07B	C187D211	6011C2AA	92406023	*........A.1.K.K..A.K.-.B.. -.*	13DA88
0012A0	4100001F	5A00D258	5000D268	58E0D230	4140E33D	5A40D268	58E0D268	D21BE000	*...K...K...K.. T.. K.. K...K*	13DAA8
0012C0	D21BE000	60081B00	5900D258	58F0C110	077F58E0	D2304140	E0755A40	D2540201	*K...-....K..OA....K.. K.K.*	13DAC8
0012E0	4000C17E	5810C108	07F14100	005D5900	58E0D230	5810C02C	07F158E0		* .A=..A..l...K.. .OA.......l..*	13DAE8
001300	D2384830	E0484930	C17858F0	C114078F	5820C008	DD07E04B	20005810	C1180771	*K.........OA.........K.....A.....*	13DB08
001320	F8730200	E07BFC62	D201E074	F277D1F8	E04BF946	D1FBD201	58F0C118	077FF277	*8.K......2.J8..9.J.K..OA...2.*	13DB28
001340	D200E048	FA44E084	D2034830	C1985A30	E09B5030	E09B5810	C11407F1	D20C6011	*K.......K...........1K.-.*	13DB48
001360	C2BC9240	601ED204	601F601E	4100001F	5A00D258	5000D258	58E0D230	4140E33D	*B.. -.K.-.-.....K...K...K.. T.*	13DB68
001380	5A40D258	5040D268	58E0D268	D21BE000	60081B00	5900D258	58F0C11C	077F58E0	* K.. K.. K...K.....-...K..OA......*	13DB88
0013A0	D2304140	E07F5A40	D254D201	4000C17E	5810C114	07F14100	005D5900	D25858F0	*K.. .. K.K. .A=..A..l...).K..O*	13DBA8
0013C0	C11407F1	5810C02C	07F158E0	D2385830	D25858F0	C128077F	5810D254	4120002C	*A........l...K......OA........K.K..*	13DBC8
0013E0	4930C19C	58F0C124	077F4800	C17C5900	D25858F0	C128077F	5810D254	4120002C	*..A..O.OA......l...K..OA........K..*	13DBE8
001400	1C024120	00531D02	50100260	58E0D23C	4140E025	5A40D268	50402268	D213E000	*.....K.-..K.. K-.K.. K-. K..K*	13DC08
001420	58F0D238	D22BE000	F0535810	C12C07F1	58E0D238	5830E09B	4930C178	58F0C130	*.OK.K..O...A.l.K.....A..OA..*	13DC28
001440	077F5810	C12C07F1	4100001F	5A00D258	5000D258	D20E6011	C2C99240	60200202	*...A..l.K....K...K.K.-.BI. -.K.*	13DC48
001460	60216020	58E02004	4140E33D	5A40D258	5040D268	58E0D268	D21BE000	60081B00	*-.-..K.. T.. K.. K.. K.K.-.-.*	13DC68
001480	5900D258	58F0C134	077F58E0	D2304140	E0375A40	D254D201	4000C17E	5810C12C	*..K..OA....K.. ... K.K. .A=..A..*	13DC88
0014A0	07F14100	005D5900	D25858F0	C12C077F	5810C02C	07F14100	005D5900	C12C077F	*.1..).K..OA........l.....K.*	13DCA8
0014C0	D2545810	D27007F1	4100005D	5900D258	58F0C138	077F5810	C04007F1	41000053	*K..l...).K..OA.......l.....1..*	13DCC8
0014E0	5900D254	58F0C13C	077F58E0	D2385830	E09B4930	C17858F0	C1C077F	4100001F	*..K.OA....K..OA..A..OA..*	13DCE8
001500	5A00D258	5000D258	58E0D230	4140E33D	5A40D258	5040D268	58E0D268	D213E000	*K...K...K.. T.. K.. K...K..K*	13DD08
001520	C20858E0	D2689240	E01458E0	D26858F0	D26BD206	E015F014	18005900	D25858F0	*BQ..K.. ...K..OK.K...O....K..O*	13DD28
001540	C14077F	58E0D230	D201E037	C17E5810	C13C07F1	4100005D	5900D258	58F0C13C	*A ....K.K..A=..A..l.....).K..OA..*	13DD48
001560	077F5810	C03407F1	5820C008	58E0D230	DD08E325	20005810	C1440771	F2780200	*...l.....K..........T......A....2.K..*	13DD68
001580	E32558E0	D238F944	D203E07F	58F0C144	077F58E0	D23C58F0	D238F844	E019F07F	*T...K.9.K...OA....K..OK.8...O.*	13DD88
0015A0	5810C148	07F14100	001F5A00	D2585000	D25858E0	D2304140	E33D5A40	D2585040	*..A..l...K...K...K..K.. T.. K.. *	13DDA8

Fig. 24.6. (Continued)

CUSTOMER INFORMATION CONTROL SYSTEM STORAGE DUMP   CODE=ERRS   TASK=ORAD   DATE=07/27/80   TIME=19 01 28   PAGE 14

PROGRAM STORAGE   ADDRESS 13C808   TO 13EF8F   LENGTH 002788

```
0015C0  D2685BE0 D268D213 E00DC2EC 58E0D268  9240E014 58E0D268 58F0D268 D206E015  *K...K..K....B...K...    ....K...OK.K...*  130DC8
0015E0  F0141800 59D0D258 58F0C14C 077F58E0  2300D201 E322C17E 5810C148 07F14100  *0.....K..OA........K..K.K.T.A=.A...l...*  130DE8
001600  00SD5900 D2585BFC C148D77F 5810C034  07F15820 C00858E0 D2300D08 E3312000  *.).K..OA........).K.K..K...*              130E08
001620  5810C150 0771F278 D200E331 58E0D238  F9440203 E0453BF0 C150077F 58E0D23C  *..A..2.K.T..K9.K....OA....K...*           130E28
001640  58F0D238 F844E01E F0845810 C03407F1  4100001F 5AD0D258 50D0D258 58E0D230  *.OK.8....O..K...l......K...K...K...*       130E48
001660  4140E33D 5A4DD258 50400268 58E0D268  D214E000 C30D58E0 D2689240 E01558E0  *.T.. K..P....K...K...C..K.K T.....K.*      130E68
001680  5B58B5F0 E016F015 18005900 59D0D258  D2585BE0 C154077F 58E0D230 D201E32E  *...0..0.......K..K..A......K...K.T.*       130E88
0016A0  C17E5810 C034D7F1 41000D50 59DD0258  58F0C034 07F7F810 C03407F1 4800C17C  *A=...l.)..K..  K..7.8....l..A.*           130EA8
0016C0  59D0D258 58F0C038 078F5810 C04007F1  1BD05810 D2544120 00531D02 4A10C18C  *.....OA......K...l...K.....A..*           130EC8
0016E0  58E0D23C 401DE023 4830E023 4930C19E  58F0C158 07DF58E0 D2385B30 E0984930  *K...A.....A...A.A..OA....K...l...*        130EE8
001700  58E0D23C C15C077F 58E0D23C 4830E023  58F0C158 07DF58E0 D2385B30 07F158E0  *K...A*..K...A...OA....K...l...*           130F08
001720  D23C4830 E0234830 C18C4030 E0235810  C16007F1 58E0D23C 4830E023 4830C18E  *K..A...A.A.....A..l.K...A...A.*           130F28
001740  40300023 D20160B9 C1AD0208 6070C315  92406079 D27C9680 D27C4110 60705010  *A...K...A.....K.K  K......K.O.K.l..*      130F48
001760  D27458E0 D22C4110 E0085010 0278A110  6089501D D27C9680 D27C4110 027458E0  *K...K.....K.....K.....K......K.O.K...*    130F68
001780  C00405EF 58FD0234 58F0D23C D201E023  F023S820 C0800522 C0880522 58E0D234  *....K..0.K..K.T..0.K..O...O...K.*         130F88
0017A0  4810D024 58E0D23C 4120E000 41300181  8F38C199 0ED25820 C0800522 58E0D234  *..K..O.A..A...K..A.........0.K.*          130FA8
0017C0  4830E023 4C30C1A2 4A30C1A4 58E0D238  4030E0A3 58F0D23C 0ED925820 E098C22C?  *..A.L.A..A..K...A.K..K.....*              130FC8
0017E0  607AC31E 92406082 D2066083 60824110  60705010 D274411D D27458E0 D27458F0  *.:C....K..K..K.l..K..K...K...K.0*        130FE8
001800  C00405EF 5BE0D224 4810E014 4130C010  05204720 01C8B10 00D147C0 ...         *....K.....K..A... ....H...*               130FC8
```
...

Fig. 24.6. (Continued)

```
CUSTOMER INFORMATION CONTROL SYSTEM STORAGE DUMP    ADDRESS 13C808    TO 13E8BF    CODE=ERRS    TASK=ORAD    LENGTH 002788    DATE=07/27/80    TIME=19 01 28    PAGE 15

PROGRAM STORAGE

001C20  05EF58E0 D2244810 E0144130 C0104910   C18C0520 4720201C 8B100001 47C0201C   *...K.........A.......K...OK.K...O-K.*  13E428
001C40  48112018 89100002 58113000 07F1000F   58E00238 58F00224 D203E093 F010D203   *....i..............1.....l....K.-O-K*  13E448
001C60  E097C1E6 02086070 C3D69240 6379920F   607A6079 41106070 02086070 C3159240   *..AW..-CD..-K..-..--.-K-.-..-CC.-K.-*  13E468
001C80  5010D278 96800278 41100274 58F0C004   05EFD201 6089C1A8 02086070 C3159240   *..K-..-...-..0..-K.--.AK..-..-CC.-K.*  13E488
001CA0  6079D20F 607A6079 41106070 5010D274   58E0D22C C1AA5000 5010D278 41106089   *..K.-..-.-K-...K-..K--A..-..-K-...-.*  13E4A8
001CC0  5010D27C 96800278 41100274 58F0C004   05EF4800 C1AA5000 026458E0 D23892C4   *..K--..-..-..0..-K...A..-...K.-KK.D*  13E4C8
001CE0  E02D0203 E0D3C1AC D2116070 C3D0F9240   60820206 58A0D288 41106070 5010D274   *...-..LA.K.-C...-...-A.-K..-.-K-...K*  13E4E8
001D00  96800274 41100274 58F0C004 05EF58E0   D2244810 E0144130 C0104910 C18C0520   *..-..-.0..-K...K.....A...........A..*  13E508
001D40  C3F19240 60A1D208 60700C3F8 92406070   D20F607A 58113000 07F10011 D206609A   *C1..-..K..-...K.-K.-..........-..-.*  13E548
001D60  609A5010 D2784110 60095010 027C4110   60D75010 D280598E0 02384110 E0025010   *..-K.-..-..-K...-K-..-.K...-...-K.*  13E568
001D80  028496806 D2844110 027458F0 C0040955F   D206609A C3F19240 60A1D208 6070C401   *..K-..K-..-K.0..-..-C1..-..K..-CD.-*  13E588
001DA0  92406079 D20F607A D20F6079 60794110   02744110 609A5010 D27858E0 D22C4110   *.-..K.-..K.--.-K.-.K-..-..K-.K-..*  13E5A8
001DC0  E0185010 D27C4110 60D75010 027458F0   D2384110 E0025010 D2844110 60705010   *.....-K-..-K...-K.0.K.....-K...-..-K*  13E5C8
001DE0  D2884110 60075010 028C9680 028C4110   D27458F0 C00405EF C054D7F1 C0540DFF1   *.K-..-.-K...-.K.-K.0..-.K..K.-.K.-.*  13E5E8
001E00  95C4E000 07725820 C1680502 E005C40A   07725810 C054D7F1 5820D164 58E0D244   *.D-.....A.........K-..K.-..-.A..-K.*  13E608
001E20  D53E1D026 C4DD0782 41000003 5E8E00023C   5000D264 58E0D23C 4140E188 5A400264   *N...D..A.-...K.-..K-...A.5A.K.*  13E628
001E40  5040D268 58E00268 58F0D244 D202E000   F0055810 C05007F1 4800C1AA 59000264   *.K-..K-..0.K..-..0..K...A....K.*  13E648
001E60  58F0C16C 077F5810 C07407F1 1B005810   58E00238 D207E0CA 100058E0 D23C58F0   *.0A.....K..-.1....-....K.-..-0*  13E668
001E80  5010E1B4 5820C08C 05225810 00140A21   E017F000 58F0D228 D202E1B1 F00158E0   *...-K.-....-..-.OK..0.K...-....0..-*  13E688
001EA0  D238D201 E013F0CA D201E015 F0C0D201   60790204 607A6079 41106070 5010D274   *.K-...0..K..-0..K-K.--.-.-K-...K*  13E6A8
001EC0  D238D201 E0A5C1A8 02086070 C40F9240   607920F 607A6079 60700C3F 58E0D23C   *.K-..AK..-..D.-..K.-.-..-.-..-K.*  13E6C8
001EE0  4110E093 5010D278 41106070 5010E000   5010D27C 58E00238 41100E0A5 58E0D23C   *...-.K-..-.-K-...-K--..-...-.A-K.*  13E6E8
001F00  96800280 41100274 58F0C004 05EF5820   C08C0522 D2016089 C33E9240 6079920F   *..-..-.0..-..-.K...-C3.-..-.*  13E708
001F20  607A6079 41106070 5010D274 58E0023C   5010D278 96800278 41100274 58F0C004   *..-.-K-...K-..K-..-..-.0..-*  13E728
001F40  58F0C004 05EF5820 C08C0522 D2016089   C1A6D208 6070C393 92460079 D20F607A   *0......-..-.K..-A.K.-C...-.K.--.*  13E748
001F60  60794110 60705010 D27458E0 D23C4110   E0045010 D2784110 6089D010 D27C4110   *.-K-..-K-.K-...-..K-..-..-K--.*  13E768
001F80  60585010 D280D9680 D2884110 6070C4010   C0040586 D2300210E330 C<1189240   *.-K-..-K.K-..-CD.$..K.-K.T-D-.-K-.*  13E788
001FA0  E34ED209 607FD209 E0D06000A CIE69240   60910206 6092C1ED 92406099 D20E6070   *T+K.T-K..AW-..-.K.-..AK.-..-K.-*  13E7A8
001FC0  C3B59240 607FD209 6080607F 41106070   5010D238 41106080A 5010D278 4110E000   *C..-..-K..-.-K-...-.K..-..-...*  13E7C8
001FE0  5010D27C 41106092 41106092 58E0C0040   D27858E0 9800D284 6074110 58F0C004   *..-...-...-0.K-.K--..K.-.0..-*  13E7E8
002000  05EF92F1 60000203 58E00238 D2016089   C179D208 6070C362 9240079 D20F607A   *...1...-...K-..-C.K.-C..-K.--.*  13E808
002020  58113000 07F10014 58E00238 58F0D224   D2784110 F010D203 E0D06093 89100002   *.........-.0.K.-K.-0-K.-...i..*  13E828
002040  28099680 D2804110 027458F0 C00405EF   58E00238 D216E0AB 60794240 E0C2D206   *..-..K-..-K.0..-..-.K...-.BK.*  13E848
002060  E0C3E0C2 D2016089 C1AED20E 6070C429   92406080 6079F410 E0A85010 5010D278   *..C...-A-K.-CD.-.-.K...K-..-K-*  13E868
002080  D2744110 60D95010 D27458F0 C00405EF   D27C58E0 02384110 E0A85010 02804110   *.K-..-K-.K.0..-K--..-.-K-..K-*  13E888
0020A0  60B95010 D2849680 41106070 5010D274   C004058E0 02116070 C3C49240 60820206   *.-K-..-..-.-K-...-...-CD.-.CD.-*  13E8A8
0020C0  60836082 41106070 5010D278 4720201C   8B100001 47C0201C 48112018 89100002   *.-A..-.-K-...K....K...i..*  13E8C8
0020E0  E0144130 C0104910 C18C0520 58F00238   D203E093 F010D203 E0D06093 89100002   *.....A...0..K.-0-K.-...i..*  13E8E8
002100  58113000 07F10014 58E00238 58F00224   4720201C 8B100001 47C0201C 48112018   *.....1...-..0...K....K...*  13E908
002120  C3D69240 6079920F 607A6079 41106070   D203E093 4110E093 5010D278 9680D278   *CD.-..K.--.-K-.-...-.K-..-.K-*  13E928
002140  41100274 58F0C004 05EFD208 C441D208   92406079 D20F607A 60794110 60705010   *..-..0..-.KD.K.-.K.--.-K-..-K*  13E948
002160  D2744680 D2744110 027458F0 C00405EF   D20769A C441D208 60700C449 92406079   *.K.D.K-..-K.0..-.-.CD.K.--K.--.*  13E968
002180  60D7F607A 60794110 60705010 D27458F0   609A5010 D2789680 D27458F0 C00405EF   *.-..-.-K-..-K.0..-K-..-K.0..-*  13E988
0021A0  C00405EF D20A6004A C4529240 60550D203   5810C07C 07F1D20C 604AC45D C4860086   *..-.K..KD.R.-.UK-..1K..-JCD.D..*  13E9A8
0021C0  92406057 02016058 60575810 C07C07F1   D20F604A C4A5810 C07C07F1 D20F604A   *.-.K-K..-K...1K.-JCA..K..1K.--*  13E9C8
0021E0  C47A5810 C07C07F1 58E00238 D2016063   E01BD205 6065E010 C48AD208 C7896680   *CK..K..1...-.K--D...-..CDK.C.i.*  13E9E8
002200  607DC48E 41100274 C00405EF D20A6004A   60705010 D2744110 6056D055 5810C07C   *.-D...-..-.K.-..-K.K-..UK..UK.-*  13EA08
002220  37F158E0 D23BD21E E0AB6D3B 5810C05C   C4979240 4000D24C 4000024C 41000025   *.1..-K...-K...-C..-.-K.-K....*  13EA28
002240  607C048E 058E00234 E0A86038 4C10C1A2   07F11B00 4000024C 4A10024E 4A10024E   *.-...-.-..L.A..1.-K.-K.-K.*  13EA48
002260  58E0D234 4810E023 4C10C1A2 4A10024C   4010D24E 4000024C 4A10024E 4010D24E   *...K..L.A.-K.-K.-K.-K.-K.*  13EA68
```

Fig. 24.6. (Continued)

```
CUSTOMER INFORMATION CONTROL SYSTEM STORAGE DUMP   CODE=ERRS   TASK=ORAD   DATE=07/27/80   TIME=19 01 28   PAGE 16

PROGRAM STORAGE        ADDRESS 13C808   TO 13EF8F   LENGTH 002788

002283  07F34100 01884000 025058E0 D23C5810 E1844C10 C1804A10 D2504010 D25007F3  *.3....K....K......A....K. .K..3*  13EA88
0022A3  5830C080 05330522 5830C084 05330522 50005008 50500004 5820C000 95002000  *.................0.........*     13EAA8
0022C3  077992FF 20009610 00485E0 0054059F0 91200048 47E0F016 58008048 10001E48  *.................-.........*     13EAC8
0022E3  58E00054 07FE9620 00484160 00044110 C0104170 C1780670 05505840 10001E48  *...............J4..J7......*     13EAE8
002303  50401000 8716500 4180D1F7 4170D1F7 05105800 80001E08 50008000 87861000  *K.K.A..J4..J......-.5746-C8*     13EB08
002323  D2030270 C1705860 D1F458E0 D1B09060 E0605E0  D05407FE FFF5F7F4 F660C3C2  *1 COPYRIGHT IBM CORP. 1973FE 2*  13EB28
002343  F140C3D6 D7E0D9C9 C7C8E340 C9C20440 C3D6D907 D74840F1 F9F7F3C6 F4F66D03  *M4 COPYRIGHT IBM CORP. 1973FE 2*  13EB48
002363  D4F440C3 D6D7E8D9 C9C7C8E3 40C9C204 40C3D609 D74840F1 F9F7F3C6 C54 0F2F4  *6356FE 246357....00-ILBDSCH02500*13EB68
002383  F6F3F5F6 C6C5540F2 F4F6F3F5 F7660001 47F0F018 C9D3C2C4 E2C3C8F0 F2F5F0F0  *12/20/78..2.........*            13EB88
0023A3  F1F261F2 F061F7F8 90ECF288 18885841 000C8840 0018182E 58820000 89800008  *.............0.....*             13EBA8
0023C3  88800018 1A884122 00044640 F0284120 00604132 000192FF 200018AB 1AA388A0  *..............2.......2....*     13EBC8
0023E3  000289A0 000206B0 508A0004 4480F28A 5850F2C0 58A1000C 88400018 50A40008  *.....00.. 2 .......2.....2.-*    13EBE8
002403  9200A010 188E47F0 F00C4640 F2724132 0001580  F2C058A A00044480 F27E9201  *.....A........2....2....0*      13EC08
002423  A0105BC1 00005871 00041897 06704841 000C504A 000C1C64 1A7C1889 88800001  *OO...............2.....1.*      13EC28
002443  89803001 15891807 4770F08E 18041A0C 88000001 584A0008 44B0F28A 188E47F0  *...-.-1....1..-2....-1..1.*      13EC48
002463  F0D64188 00044858 00021A50 48980000 89900018 88900018 18690690 95888000  *.............1..2....-02..-2..02.*13EC68
002483  4780F128 4720F110 95208000 4780F130 4720F214 95108000 47F0F21C 4780F180  *....1..-2....-2....2.*           13EC88
0024A3  95A08000 4780F1A6 4740F1FA 4490F290 97803000 47F0F21C 4490F290 4740F19E  *.02..-2....1..2....-02..-2..02.* 13ECA8
0024C3  18B91A85 91038000 4740F15E 4490F2A2 18B94199 00018990 0004 1A9B 4490F29C  *.02..-2....0 .-2.....2.*         13ECC8
0024E3  1AB341BB 00019F6FF B00047F0 F21C1889 41990001 89900004 1A984490 F29690D0  *.G..2....-02....-00K....*        13ECE8
002503  30001AB3 41B80001 96FFB000 47F0F21C F2A247F0 F21C1889 1A859103 B0004740  *.2......02.-02........1..1.*     13ED08
002523  4490F2A2 1A939730 89900004 1A984FF0 F29696F0 30001AB3 41B80001 96FFB000  *.2......02....-02...1..1.*       13ED28
002543  F1D41889 41990001 89900004 1A9B4490 F296F2F0 30001AB3 41B80001 96FFB000  *1M........2....0..K.....*        13ED48
002563  47F0F21C 4490F2A2 18B94199 00018990 0004 1A9B 4490F29C 96203000 1A83418B  *.02..2...2....1..2....-K..H.*    13ED68
002583  000196FF B00047F0 F21C1889 1A859130 B0004740 F19E4490 F2901A93 96F09000  *.02..........2....-K..H.*        13ED88
0025A3  47F0F21C 4490F2A2 97803000 9101A010 4780F07A 4640F264 41320001 5890F2C0  *.02....2....-02....0. .2..*      13EDA8
0025C3  588A0004 4480F284 4780F2A8 584A0000 4720F24C 18041870 4FF0F250 1A041BC0  *.02..2....2....-02....02.*       13EDC8
0025E3  15C74720 F26A1894 1A97189C 18881D84 47F0F0AA 1A3647F0 F0258E1 00000000  *.G..2....-02.......00K...-0*     13EDE8
002603  01CC98 00000000 00044FF0 F0DC0200 80003000 D5009000 30000200 30002000    *2........00-K....N....K....*     13EE08
002623  D2003000 5D00F100 30005000 F1003000 3000D700 30005000 4IE80004 58F0F28C  *.K..-1....P....Y...02..*         13EE28
002643  981CF2C4 07FE0000 40130484 0013E898 0012F2F4 0012F2FC 0013EE90 00000001  *.2D....M...24..2.......*         13EE48
002663  0012F420 5013E802 0012F00C 0012F2E3 0012F2E4 0013EA02 0013C820 0013C820  *.4.......2T..2U....K..H..*       13EE68
002683  001CC98 00000000 01010101 01010101 01010101 01010101 01010101 01010101    *........*                        13EE88
0026A3  01010101 01010101 01010101 01010101 01010101 01010101 01010101 01010101  **                               13EEA8
0026C3  LINES TO 0027A0 SAME AS ABOVE
002760  01010101 01010101 01010101 01010101 01010101 01010101 00000000 00000000  **                               13EF68
002780  00000101 01010101                                                         **                               13EF88


PROGRAM STORAGE        ADDRESS 13F808   TO 13FCA7   LENGTH 0004A0

000000  D609C1C4 E2F0F140 04040040 00000000 00000000 D609C1C4 D4F0F140 348F0480  *ORADS01 .    ........ORADMO1 ....1.*  13F808
000020  03810566 C0C200CC 001850FF FE000000 00000000 00000000 0001037D 000F100    *.F.8...........-F....1.*         13F828
000040  00001802 F8001807 E409C3C8 C4C5C540 D9406060 D9406060 6040C6C9 D3C540C1  *....8.PURCHASE ORDER ---- FILE A*13F848
000060  C4C40000 000D02F0 00000802 00000802 D5E4D462 C5D97A00 00000A00 0800C600  *DD....0.ORDER NUMBER .....Q..*    13F868
000080  00000100 60000600 00000802 F000D0C4 D6C34D05 D64B7A00 00000800 0800E600  *......-0....0.DOC NO. ....Q..*    13F888
0000A0  00000100 6000EF00 000006F00 01FF0000 C507C1D9 E3D4C5D5 E37A0000 00030008  *......-0..DEPARTMENT ....Q*       13F8A8
0000C0  01180000 000107F0 011F0000 000E02F0 015CC4C1 E3C54006 C640D6D9 C4C5097A  *.......0.0.*DATE OF ORDER *      13F8C8
0000E0  00000000 0008016B 00000001 00F00172 02F0020 6 C9E3C5D4 0000008  *.......0....0.OITEM....*          13F8E8
000100  02F002E0 C4C5E2C3 D9C9D7E3 C9D6D503 00000402 F002F9E4 D5C9E300 00000502  *.0..DESCRIPTION....0.9UNIT.....*  13F908
000120  F00 2FFE4 C306E2E3 00000004 02F00308 C306E2E3 00000006 02F00310 E40709C9  *0.UCOST......0.COST.....0.UPRI*   13F928
```

Fig. 24.6. (Continued)

```
CUSTOMER INFORMATION CONTROL SYSTEM STORAGE DUMP    CODE=ERRS    TASK=DRAD    DATE=07/27/80    TIME=19 01 28    PAGE   17

PROGRAM STORAGE        ADDRESS 13F808       TO 13FCA7       LENGTH 0004A0

000143  C3C50300 000502F0 03190TD9 C9C3C500  00000102 F00322F1 00000008 0DD80324  *CE.....0..PRICE.....0..1......Q..*  13F948
000160  00200013 01C8032D 00000001 00600341  00000005 0DD80348 00000007 0DD8034E  *....H..........0......Q....Q..+..*  13F968
000180  00000008 0DD80356 00000007 0DD8035F  00000008 0DD80367 00000001 00600370  *.................0.....0..Q......*  13F988
0001A0  00000001 02F00372 F2000000 080DD803  74000000 1301C803 7D000000 01006003  *.......0..2.....H.'...-..........*  13F9A8
0001C0  91203000 05000803 98000000 070DD803  9E000000 0800D803 A6000000 070DD803  *.............Q........0.B3...Q..*   13F9C8
0001E0  AF000000 080DD803 87000000 01006003  C0000000 0102F003 C2F30000 00080DD8  *............-..Q.........Q.......*  13F9E8
000200  03C40000 001301C8 03CD0000 00010060  03E10000 00050DD8 03E80000 00070DD8  *.D....H........Q.Y....Q..........*  13FA08
000220  03EE0000 000800D8 03F60000 070DD8  03FF0000 00080DD8 04070000 00010060  *.........0.4....Q.......H........*  13FA28
000240  04100000 000102F0 0412F400 00000800  D8041400 00001301 C8041D00 00000100  *...........0.6....Q....H.........*  13FA48
000260  60043100 03000500 08043000 00000700  60046000 00000102 F0046250 00000008  *Q.........0....5....Q...........*  13FA68
000280  08044F00 00000800 08045700 00000100  08046000 00000005 0DD80488 00000007  *.Q.....H...........Q...Q........*  13FA88
0002A0  0DD80498 00000001 01C80460 00000001  0DD8049F 00000008 0DD80488 0DD804A7  *.Q....0..6....Q.......Q.........*  13FAA8
0002C0  0DD8048E 00000013 02F00482 F6000000  08000804 84000000 1301C804 BD000000  *...0....7....H...................*  13FAC8
0002E0  00600480 00000001 01000000 D8000000  07000804 DE000000 0800D804 E6000000  *...J....Q........Q.W.............*  13FAE8
000300  01006004 01000000 080DD804 F7000000  01006005 00000000 0102F005 02F70000  *.............0..7.'..............*  13FB08
000320  070DD804 EF000000 00130108 05000000  00010060 05210000 00050DD8 05280000  *....Q...H...........0..5.........*  13FB28
000340  0008DD8 050A0000 00130108 05DD0000  00070DD8 053F0000 00080DD8 05470000  *...0......Q.......Q.....H.l......*  13FB48
000360  00070DD8 052E0000 00080DD8 05360000  00070DD8 053F0000 00080DD8 05470000  *....0..8......Q.......Q..........*  13FB68
000380  00010060 055000000 000102F0 0552F800  00000700 D8055400 00001301 C8055D00  *...-......0..8...Q...=...H.l.....*  13FB88
0003A0  00000100 60057100 00000500 08057800  00000700 D8057E00 00000800 D8058600  *.........0..9...................*  13FBA8
0003C0  00000700 08058F00 00000800 D8059700  00000100 6005AC00 00000102 F005A2F9  *......0.....H......A....Q.H......*  13FBC8
0003E0  00000008 0DD805A4 00000013 01C805AD  00000001 0DD805DF 00000008 0DD805E7  *.Q......Q...0.....0...Q..........*  13FBE8
000400  00000007 0DD805CE 00000008 0DD805D6  00000007 0DD805DF 00000008 0DD805E7  *...0...0..TOTALS ------....Q.X...*  13FC08
000420  00000001 006005F0 00000000 02F00666  E306E3C1 D3E24060 60606060 6E000000  *...Q.....0....-..0...-TOTALS.....*  13FC28
000440  09000806 75000000 01006006 7F000000  09000806 86000000 01006006 90000000  *...Q.....H.......A....Q.H........*  13FC48
000460  1C03F806 E0D6D9C4 C5D940C1 C3C3C5D7  E3C5C440 60604003 D6D5E3C9 D5E4C540  *..8..ORDER ACCEPTED -- CONTINUE *  13FC68
000480  40000000 1C01F807 07000000 1C01F807  30000000 1C01F807 57FFFFFF FFFFFF00  *..8.........8...................*  13FC88

END OF CICS/VS STORAGE DUMP
```

Fig. 24.6. (Continued)

A on page 525 is the literal 'ERRS,' which is the dump code. The command that caused the abend itself can be seen easily from the trace table. The same dump code 'ERRS' prints in the last entries of the trace table. This is B on page 530. The CICS/VS command that precedes this is the one that caused the problem, and it is the WRITE command. In between the Execute Interface Trace Entry at Issuance ("EIP WRITE ENTRY"), C, and the Execute Interface Trace Entry at Completion ("EIP WRITE RESPONSE"), D, the file is identified as "ORTEST," E. Therefore, the problem occurred on a write command to the ORTEST file.

To get a more accurate picture of the problem, the WORKING-STORAGE section will be investigated. From the 'TRANSACTION STORAGE-USER' data block at the bottom of page 533, we can see that:

1. EIBFN = X'0604'   F
2. EIBRCODE = X'820000000000'   G

The table of EIBFN codes are shown in Figure 24.7.

We can see that X'0604' is indeed the WRITE command (H).
The table of EIBRCODE values is shown in Figure 24.8.

You can see from I that if the first byte of EIBRCODE is X'82', and the first byte of EIBFN is X'06', the exceptional condition is DUPREC. This means that the CICS/VS error occurred because there was an attempt to write a new record and the key was a duplicate of the key of an existing record.

Code	Command
02 02	ADDRESS
02 04	HANDLE CONDITION
02 06	HANDLE AID
02 08	ASSIGN
04 02	RECEIVE
04 04	SEND
04 06	CONVERSE
04 08	ISSUE EODS
04 0A	ISSUE COPY
04 0C	WAIT TERMINAL
04 0E	ISSUE LOAD
04 10	WAIT SIGNAL
04 12	ISSUE RESET
04 14	ISSUE DISCONNECT
04 16	ISSUE ENDOUTPUT
04 18	ISSUE ERASEAUP
04 1A	ISSUE ENDFILE
04 1C	ISSUE PRINT
04 02	READ
06 04	WRITE	←(H)
06 06	REWRITE
06 08	DELETE
06 0A	UNLOCK
06 0C	STARTBR
06 0E	READNEXT
06 10	READPREV
06 12	ENDBR
06 14	RESETBR
08 02	WRITEQ TD
08 04	READQ TD
08 06	DELETEQ TD
0A 02	WRITEQ TS
0A 04	READQ TS
0A 06	DELETEQ TS
0C 02	GETMAIN
0C 04	FREEMAIN
0E 02	LINK
0E 04	XCTL
0E 06	LOAD
0E 08	RETURN
0E 0A	RELEASE
0E 0C	ABEND
0E 0E	HANDLE ABEND
10 02	ASKTIME
10 04	DELAY
10 06	POST
10 08	START
10 0A	RETRIEVE
10 0C	CANCEL

Fig. 24.7.   Table of EIBFN Codes.

```
,----------------------------------.
| Code |  Command                  |
|------|---------------------------|
| 12 02 | WAIT EVENT               |
| 12 04 | ENQ                      |
| 12 06 | DEQ                      |
| 12 08 | SUSPEND                  |
| 14 02 | JOURNAL                  |
| 14 04 | WAIT JOURNAL             |
| 16 02 | SYNCPOINT                |
| 18 02 | RECEIVE MAP              |
| 18 04 | SEND MAP                 |
| 18 06 | SEND TEXT                |
| 18 08 | SEND PAGE                |
| 18 0A | PURGE MESSAGE            |
| 18 0C | ROUTE                    |
| 1A 02 | TRACE ON/OFF             |
| 1A 04 | ENTER                    |
| 1C 02 | DUMP                     |
| 1E 02 | ISSUE ADD                |
| 1E 04 | ISSUE ERASE              |
| 1E 06 | ISSUE REPLACE            |
| 1E 08 | ISSUE ABORT              |
| 1E 0A | ISSUE QUERY              |
| 1E 0C | ISSUE END                |
| 1E 0E | ISSUE RECEIVE            |
| 1E 10 | ISSUE NOTE               |
| 1E 12 | ISSUE WAIT               |
| 20 02 | BIF DEEDIT               |
'----------------------------------'
```

Fig. 24.7. (Continued)

EIBFN Byte 0	EIBRCODE Byte	EIBRCODE Bit(s)	EIBRCODE Meaning
02	0	E0	INVREQ
04	0	04	EOF
04	0	10	EODS
04	0	C1	EOF
04	0	C2	ENDINPT
04	0	E1	LENGERR
04	0	E3	WRBRK
04	0	E4	RDATT
04	0	E5	SIGNAL
04	0	E6	TERMIDERR
04	0	E7	NOPASSBKRD
04	0	E8	NOPASSBKWR
04	1	20	EOC
04	1	40	INBFMH
04	3	F6	NOSTART
04	3	F7	NONVAL
06	0	01	DSIDERR
06	0	02	ILLOGIC[1]
06	0	04	SEGIDERR
06	0	08	INVREQ
06	0	0C	NOTOPEN
06	0	0F	ENDFILE
06	0	80	IOERR[1]
06	0	81	NOTFND
06	0	82	DUPREC
06	0	83	NOSPACE
06	0	84	DUPKEY
06	0	D0	SYSIDERR
06	0	D1	ISCINVREQ
06	0	E1	LENGERR
08	0	01	QZERO
08	0	02	QIDERR
08	0	04	IOERR
08	0	08	NOTOPEN
08	0	10	NOSPACE
08	0	C0	QBUSY
08	0	D0	SYSIDERR
08	0	D1	ISCINVREQ
08	0	E1	LENGERR
0A	0	01	ITEMERR
0A	0	02	QIDERR
0A	0	04	IOERR
0A	0	08	NOSPACE

[1] When this condition occurs during File Control operations, further information is provided in field EIBRCODE, as follows:
    bytes 1-4 = DAM response (OS/VS only)
    bytes 1 and 2 = ISAM response
    byte 1 = VSAM return code;
    byte 2 = VSAM error code

Fig. 24.8.   Table of EIBRCODE Codes.

EIBFN Byte 0	EIBRCODE Byte	EIBRCODE Bit(s)	EIBRCODE Meaning
0A	0	20	INVREQ
0A	0	D0	SYSIDERR
0A	0	D1	ISCINVREQ
0A	0	E1	LENGERR
0C	0	E2	NOSTG
0E	0	01	PGMIDERR
0E	0	E0	INVREQ
10	0	01	ENDDATA
10	0	04	IOERR
10	0	11	TRANSIDERR
10	0	12	TERMIDERR
10	0	14	INVTSREQ
10	0	20	EXPIRED
10	0	81	NOTFND
10	0	D0	SYSIDERR
10	0	D1	ISCINVREQ
10	0	E1	LENGERR
10	0	E9	ENVDEFERR
10	0	FF	INVREQ
12	0	32	ENQBUSY
14	0	01	JIDERR
14	0	02	INVREQ
14	0	05	NOTOPEN
14	0	06	LENGERR
14	0	07	IOERR
14	0	09	NOJBUFSP
18	0	01	INVREQ
18	0	02	RETPAGE
18	0	04	MAPFAIL
18	0	08	INVMPSZ[a]
18	0	20	INVERRTERM
18	0	40	RTESOME
18	0	80	RTEFAIL
18	0	E3	WRBRK
18	0	E4	RDATT
18	1	10	INVLDC
18	1	80	TSIOERR
18	2	01	OVERFLOW
1E	2	04	EODS
1E	2	08	EOC
1E	2	10	IGREQID
1E	0	04	DSSTAT
1E	0	08	FUNCERR
1E	0	0C	SELNERR
1E	0	10	UNEXPIN
1E	0	E1	LENGERR
1E	1	11	EODS
1E	2	20	EOC

[a] When this condition occurs during BMS operations, byte 3 of field EIBRCODE contains the terminal code. (See Figure 3.3-1)

Fig. 24.8. (Continued)

Index